Fourth Edition

Sociology in Everyday Life

David A. Karp
Boston College

William C. Yoels
University of Alabama, Birmingham

Barbara H. Vann
Loyola University Maryland

Michael Ian Borer
University of Nevada, Las Vegas

WAVELAND
PRESS, INC.
Long Grove, Illinois

For information about this book, contact:
Waveland Press, Inc.
4180 IL Route 83, Suite 101
Long Grove, IL 60047-9580
(847) 634-0081
info@waveland.com
www.waveland.com

For my parents,
Abraham and Rose, who taught love and respect
for learning through word and example.
—*David A. Karp*

In loving memory of my parents,
Harriet and Irving, for their lifelong support
and encouragement.
—*William C. Yoels*

For my parents,
William and Claradel Holcombe,
and my son Jesse, for always believing in me.
—*Barbara H. Vann*

To my father, Alan
and in loving memory of my mother, Stephanie,
who gifted me with curiosity and integrity.
—*Michael Ian Borer*

About the Authors

David A. Karp received his PhD in 1971 from New York University. He is Professor Emeritus of Sociology at Boston College. Professor Karp has coauthored the following books: *Sociology in Everyday Life* (1993, 1986); *Being Urban: A Sociology of City Life* (1991, 1977); *The Research Craft* (1982); *Experiencing the Life Cycle: A Social Psychology of Aging* (1993, 1982); *Symbols, Selves, and Society* (1979); *Speaking of Sadness* (1996); *The Burden of Sympathy* (2001); and *Is It Me or My Meds?* (2006). He has published work in *The Gerontologist, International Journal of Aging and Human Development, Qualitative Sociology, Symbolic Interaction,* and *The Journal of Contemporary Ethnography.*

William C. Yoels received his PhD in 1971 from the University of Minnesota. He retired in 2004 as Professor Emeritus of Sociology at the University of Alabama-Birmingham. Professor Yoels has coauthored the following books: *Sociology in Everyday Life* (1993, 1986); *Being Urban: A Sociology of City Life* (2015, 1991, 1977); *Experiencing the Life Cycle: A Social Psychology of Aging* (1993, 1982); and *Symbols, Selves, and Society* (1979). He has published work in *The American Journal of Sociology, Qualitative Sociology, The Sociological Quarterly, Sociology of Education,* and *Symbolic Interaction.*

Barbara H. Vann received her PhD from the University of Arizona in 1987. She is currently Associate Professor and Chair of Sociology at Loyola University Maryland. Professor Vann has coauthored *Sociology in Everyday Life* (2004). She has published work in *Communication Quarterly, Cultivating the Sociological Imagination: Concepts and Models for Service-Learning in Sociology, Czech Sociological Review, Disability & Society, Dreaming, Hawaiian Medical Journal, Journal of Sociology and Social Welfare,* and *Transformations.* She was the recipient of a Fulbright Fellowship (2014) during which she taught at Charles University, Prague, Czech Republic.

Michael Ian Borer received his PhD in 2005 from Boston University. He is currently Associate Professor of Sociology at the University of Nevada, Las Vegas. Professor Borer is the author of *Faithful to Fenway* (2008) and *The Intoxication of Craft* (forthcoming), the coauthor of *Sociology in Everyday Life* (2016) and *Urban People and Places* (2014), and the editor of *Varieties of Urban Experience* (2006). His work has been published in *City & Community, Journal of Popular Culture, Social Psychology Quarterly,* and *Symbolic Interaction,* among other journals and edited books.

Contents

PART TWO
ESTABLISHING SOCIAL ORDER   87

Preface

During the course of our teaching careers we have become increasingly dissatisfied with the focus of most introductory-level textbooks. Nearly exclusively, they are structured around macrosociological, institutional issues. If everyday interaction is treated at all, it is usually dealt with as a subheading in chapters on socialization, culture, or small-group study.

This is a serious omission for two reasons. First, the study of social interaction has always been a central concern of the sociological enterprise. Second, as we have come to learn very well, students taking introductory sociology courses are intent on learning something *immediately applicable to their everyday lives*. We have written *Sociology in Everyday Life* for those instructors who want to ground their treatment of traditional introductory topics in the stuff of daily life. This fourth edition is a completely revised and updated book. We think its title communicates the relevance of sociology for understanding our ongoing social experiences.

A key assumption underlying this book is that sociology's value lies in its ability to provide fresh insights into events and situations that students might ordinarily take for granted. In each chapter we show that there are underlying patterns to everyday life that affect who we are, who we want to be, and how others see us. These patterns become "obvious" only when we begin to look very hard at everyday phenomena and then apply sociological concepts to them. Although our focus is fundamentally on processes of interaction, we are careful to indicate the mutually transformative connections between social structures and everyday face-to-face encounters.

To accomplish our goals, the book is divided into three main parts. Part 1, consisting of three chapters, introduces key concepts in sociology (culture, socialization, roles, power, self, and the like) as well as the theoretical perspective that is maintained throughout the book. Most of our analysis of everyday life is derived from the symbolic interaction perspective, though the studies we refer to represent a variety of sociological viewpoints. The first three chapters, like all those in the book, are filled with examples that resonate with the daily experiences of college students. Part 2 centers on the construction and maintenance of order in social life. This part includes chapters on urban life and relations among strangers, the construction of intimacies, the distribution and use of power in daily life, everyday life within bureaucracies, and the experience of illness. Part 3 speaks to questions of disorder and change in everyday life. It includes chapters on deviance, aging, and contemporary social movements, including the search for self.

We have constructed the book so that the topics parallel those discussed in most introductory sociology courses. Instructors will find that it can be used flexibly—in conjunction with other core texts or as the central book in the introductory course, along with a number of shorter texts or one of the many excellent readers organized around microsociological principles.

Acknowledgments

Peter Hall of the University of Missouri, Jack Kamerman of Kean College, Del Samson of Montana State University, John Stimson of William Paterson College, and Louis Zurcher of the University of Texas carefully and most professionally reviewed earlier versions of the book. Their sophisticated knowledge of symbolic interaction and their sensitivity to the subtleties of everyday life helped us in expanding and clarifying our thoughts. Long association with the late Gregory P. Stone of the University of Minnesota also had an important influence on the development of the ideas in this book.

The third edition of *Sociology in Everyday Life* reflected the valuable contributions of students in the Self & Society course at Loyola University Maryland during the fall 2001 and 2002 semesters. It would not have been possible without the endeavors of Beth Barnyock and Marta Ziolo. The fourth edition was improved by important student discussions in Self & Society and Popular Culture at the University of Nevada, Las Vegas, during the 2013 and 2014 academic years. Special thanks to Laurie Prossnitz, Lori Meek Schuldt, and the team at Waveland.

David A. Karp
William C. Yoels
Barbara H. Vann
Michael Ian Borer

PART ONE

DEVELOPMENT OF
THE PERSPECTIVE

The focus of this book is on everyday life. Our work is based on the belief that a key measure of sociology's value and vitality is its ability to provide insight into the underlying structure of day-to-day life. Certainly, sociology should provide you with a way to understand how society as a whole is organized and ordered. At the same time, a sociological way of looking at things should be immediately applicable to your everyday life. We propose to show that there is an order and predictability to everyday life which becomes visible once you begin to look very hard at behaviors and situations you might otherwise take for granted. Sociological analysis has the power to let you see everyday behaviors and situations in a new way. Talking, using space, waiting, relating to members of the opposite sex, choosing clothing, presenting images of yourself to others, touching, behaving in classrooms, and meeting strangers are all behaviors that happen in culturally predictable ways.

The first part of this book, consisting of three chapters, is designed to accomplish three broad goals: (1) to introduce the study of everyday life as a legitimate concern in the study of sociology; (2) to provide you with knowledge of some of sociology's key concepts; and (3) to lay out the theoretical perspective that is most helpful in analyzing everyday events.

While close observation is required in order to comprehend how daily life is organized, you also need some tools to help you know what to do with your observations. Concepts and the theories built from them provide a blueprint for identifying underlying patterns in social life. In the first three chapters you will learn how such standard sociological concepts as culture, norms, values, roles, status, power, socialization, self, impression management, and interaction both direct the analysis of daily life and provide insight into its management.

1

In these chapters we also elaborate on a theoretical perspective in sociology called *symbolic interaction*. We will employ this theoretical view throughout the text as we investigate the various contexts of everyday life.

Chapter 1 presents a rationale for the study of everyday behavior. The notion that clear cultural expectations underlie daily activity is illustrated with examples of regularities in the use of time, space, and gesture. Beyond this, we emphasize how people's interpretations and definitions of social situations direct their behaviors. The questions of how individuals give meaning to various social situations are central to the perspective of symbolic interaction. An additional concern in chapter 1 is to show the significance of everyday behavior in studying how society itself is ordered. By the time you finish the first chapter you will possess several helpful ideas for looking at daily life in new ways.

Social life would be impossible without people's ability to define situations in shared ways. Chapter 2 elaborates on the important notion that human beings are symbol-using animals who collectively give meaning to the objects, events, and situations that make up their lives. We consider in detail the human capacity to symbolize, the socialization processes through which "selves" emerge, and the crucial importance of role-taking in human communications. The ability to engage in symbolic communication, we argue, not only makes social order possible, it also constitutes a continual source of nonconformity in social life. Chapter 2 can give you a deeper understanding of the symbolic interaction perspective and a better ability to use it yourself.

Chapter 3 shows how the assessment of meaning in interaction depends on information about others. Here we describe the kinds of information used to evaluate the people you physically encounter. We explain how such master attributes as gender, age, and race affect everyday relations and describe how people interpret each other's clothing, body type, and gestures. The chapter concludes by describing a view of interaction that stresses how individuals control information and foster impressions of self in everyday life. Chapter 3 builds on some of the key principles learned in earlier chapters.

1

Culture and the Organization of Everyday Life

A story is told about a man who became a fixture on the streets of Edinburgh, Scotland. He would stop people on Princes Street, a main thoroughfare, and ask them if they were sane. "If any replied Yes, he would retort— ah, but can you *prove* it? And, if they could not, he proceeded triumphantly to show them that *he* at any rate could prove his sanity, by producing his own certificate of discharge from a mental hospital" (Gellner, 1975:431). This little anecdote raises significant questions about how we show that we are sane and the criteria we use in deciding whether others are insane. Mental illness is a social construction. A pivotal issue seems to be whether a "competent authority" will state for the record that an individual is "sane" and normal or "insane" and abnormal (Curra, 2000). At the root of this difficulty is the fact that people's behaviors can be seen as appropriate or inappropriate only in terms of the societies and situations in which they take place. "Definitions of mental disorder are culture-bound; what is labeled crazy in one society or social context may be seen as perfectly normal in another—or possessed, extraordinary, saintly, inspired by the holy spirit" (Goode, 2001:381–82). Our interpretations of the world around us are context-dependent. Those interpretations, however, are neither static nor self-evident. They are products of our experiences and the labels passed down to us from those we trust or from those in power, or both.

In response to growing concern about cross-cultural misunderstandings, the American Psychiatric Association (APA) adopted guidelines in 1995 that explicitly recommend considering cultural and ethnic factors when diagnosing or treating patients. With the rise in immigration to the United States during the last several decades, doctors increasingly must diagnose and treat patients whose symptoms do not appear in Western textbooks (Goleman, 1995; Alegría et al., 2011). For example, whereas Americans sometimes fear that they will be embarrassed by their bodies, Japanese people sometimes experience disabling fears, known as "taijin kyofusho," that their bodies will embarrass *others*. Malaysian men may be stricken by "koro," the sudden and intense fear that their penises and testicles will recede into their bodies and kill them. Latin Americans can succumb to "bouffée délirante," sudden outbursts of excited, confused, violent, or agitated behavior (Weitz, 2001:193). Are these odd behaviors? Only within the context of U.S. cultural definitions of "normal" behavior (see box).

Female Circumcision? Or Female Genital Mutilation?

The topic of female circumcision, or female genital mutilation (FGM),* continues to be hotly debated among academics, governmental and nongovernmental organizations, and the popular press (Wade, 2009; 2012). Defenders of the practice (including some women) say it is a *cultural* issue and that the Western world simply does not understand or, put more strongly, Western critics are asserting a self-centered imperialism over their perceived inferiors (Nnaemeka, 2005). Western opposition to the practice has become part of United States policy on human rights that has attracted detractors claiming that such laws discriminate, rather than protect, immigrant communities. Isabelle Gunning (1999:51) argues that anti-FGM policies are less about women's well-being, but provide a means "for politicians to pretend to address race and gender issues."

Female circumcision has been performed since ancient times and continues to be practiced around the globe. Customary female genital surgery is far less familiar in the United States and other Western countries (though there are small pockets of immigrant groups that practice it). It is primarily practiced in many East and West African countries, among particular ethnic groups in other regions of Africa, and in some parts of Southeast Asia (for example, Malaysia) and the Middle East. In some African countries, the prevalence among women aged fifteen to forty-nine is very high (over 80 percent). These include estimates from Djibouti (93 percent), Egypt (91 percent), Eritrea (89 percent), Guinea (96 percent), Mali (85 percent), Sierra Leone (91 percent), Somalia (98 percent), and northern Sudan (89 percent) (Public Policy Advisory Network, 2012).

The primary purpose of female genital mutilation is to protect a girl from sexual temptations and thereby preserve her marriageability. There are firmly entrenched beliefs about the insatiable nature of female sexual desire in most practicing societies. The "uncut" are considered "dirty" and unmarriageable. Many parents say that if they fail to have their daughters cut, no respectable men will associate with the girls, who will end up "running wild like American women" (Dugger, 1996b; MacFarquar, 1996). In fact, many immigrants to the United States make tremendous sacrifices to save enough money to send their daughters back to their home country to have the operation performed (Dugger, 1996b). The practice was made illegal in the United States in 1997.

Westerners have difficulty understanding women's desire to continue this tradition. Critics of Western *ethnocentrism*—applying standards of our own culture to other cultures—point out that genital surgery increases women's status in societies where it is practiced. What might come as a surprise is the fact that clitoridectomies were not uncommon in the United States and Europe through the latter part of the 19th century. The practice was based on the belief that elimination of all sources of female sexual sensation would "cure" masturbation and prevent nymphomania—not to mention orgasm, which was considered an "ailment" that could be cured by removing the clitoris (Dreifus, 2000). Until the mid-1940s, clitoridectomies were routine for female patients in many mental hospitals. Views that women should be sexually "pure" are not limited to non-Western cultures.

Ethnocentrism notwithstanding, FGM is troubling. Women who have undergone FGM, often at a very young age, report that it is excruciatingly painful. FGM is seldom practiced under sterile conditions, with anesthesia and precise surgical instruments. The "surgery" is performed most frequently by untrained individuals who use sharp rocks, razor blades, kitchen knives, broken glass, or even their teeth. Short-term effects include excruciating pain, hemorrhage, tetanus, gangrene, and blood poisoning; long-term effects include sterility, increased difficulty in childbirth, permanent incontinence, painful intercourse, and lack of sexual pleasure.

(continued)

The practice of FGM is waning. Senegal, Togo, and at least five other African countries have banned clitoridectomy. Although some African women have been working to eliminate the practice in their own countries, there is considerable resistance from both women and men, who strongly object to having Western values imposed on them (Dugger, 1996a; MacFarquar, 1996; Wade, 2009; 2012). Waris Dirie, a Somali woman who underwent FGM at age 5 and later fled Somalia to escape an arranged marriage to a 60-year-old man, becoming a fashion model in London and United Nations special ambassador on FGM, says Westerners should not try to change African customs; changes must come from within countries themselves.

Will the practice continue? Probably. Though it will likely depend upon the way it is labelled, discussed, and, perhaps most importantly, performed. Misunderstandings persist all across the board. As Lisa Wade (2012:42) remarks:

> The heat in this debate is derived, then, from both sides erasing diversity in favor of stereotyping. Much in the same way that some scholars conflate "Africans" with "barbarism" and construct a thing called "female genital mutilation" out of a wide range of practices, some postcolonial critics (Western and non-Western alike) conflate "Western feminists" with "cultural imperialism" and construct a thing called "anti-FGM discourse" out of a diverse set of arguments.

As scholars, it is imperative that we retain a balanced view of today's cutting practices (including male circumcision) across non-Western and Western countries.

* Use of the term "circumcision" to describe the range of procedures performed on females is objectionable to some people on the grounds that it suggests a less severe procedure than occurs. Use of the term "genital mutilation" is offensive to others, particularly in instances in which no permanent alteration of the genitalia occurs (Williams and Sobieszczyk, 1997).

■ Cultural Expectations and Everyday Interactions

Like many around the world, as Americans we are born into an exceedingly complex **culture**. Its complexity derives from our increasingly pluralistic and diverse population made up of individuals with varying hopes, dreams, and desires. The term "culture" can be complex and elusive, which, in part, made it the 2014 "word of the year" because it was looked up more frequently than any other word (Steinmetz, 2014). At its most basic, *culture* means the collection of knowledge, beliefs, customs, and morals shared by members of a society or portion of a society. Our culture becomes so familiar to us at an early age that we tend to take it for granted. We normally do not question what we do and why we do it. Everyday life appears to be a reality that rarely requires explanation. It simply exists. The social world confronts us as an ordered and intelligible fact, regardless of whether we agree with that fact. We live our lives making moral judgments about what is right and what is wrong. We generally know which behaviors are proper and which would be improper in a given situation. Indeed, social life would be chaotic if we had to question at length the meaning of every behavior before we engaged in it. As Christian Smith contends, "to enact and sustain moral order is one of the central, fundamental motivations for human action" (Smith, 2003:11). When we pull up beside a car at a red light, we know we should not stare at the occupants. When we meet a person for the first time, we do not need to ask ourselves how long we ought to shake hands. We do not expect new acquaintances to reveal their life problems to us. We would likely fear a stranger who boarded a nearly empty bus or train and deliberately sat next to us. We expect students to shut off or at least mute their cell phones when they come to class (hint hint). There are, in short, an extraordinary number of **cultural expectations** we learn virtually from birth that lend order and organization to our daily interactions with others. Such "background expectancies" constitute the fundamental rules in accordance with which people normally act. These rules are often difficult to specify, though a quick Google search for "etiquette" will reveal that many book authors have tried. These rules, however, reflect our mutually held assumptions about proper and conventional behavior.

The central goal of this book is to analyze **everyday interactions** or communications from a sociological point of view. This first chapter provides a rationale for the study of routine social encounters in which everyone participates. The authors will also begin to outline the theoretical perspective we consider to be most valuable in exploring how transactions with others are accomplished. This is the **symbolic interactionist perspective** (see Fine, 1993; Hewitt and Shulman, 2010), which centers attention on how individuals interpret and give meanings to the daily interactions that make up their **social worlds**.

To begin our presentation of this perspective, we will first consider the numerous social conventions that serve as guides for human behaviors and the maintenance of social order. Beyond that, they also serve as the basis on which everyday interactions are analyzed and interpreted by individuals. They therefore have a bearing on both the power of society to influence individuals' behaviors and the power of individuals to change or manipulate society.

■ Social Conventions as Guides for Social Order

There are thousands of cultural expectations that guide the minute details of our everyday interactions with others. These expectations are expressed as social conventions, or **norms,** which make up the rules for acceptable behaviors. Several volumes would be needed to describe all the norms in American society, ranging from proper table manners to the enormously complex regularities of face-to-face and computer-mediated discourse. Together these norms make our daily encounters reasonably predictable, so we know what is expected of us and what to expect of others. Conventions such as those governing use of space, time, and posture or gesture also provide indications of the relative power, prestige, and status among the individuals taking part in interactions.

The authors of this book maintain that social life would be utterly unmanageable if there were no broadly shared consensus about how members of a society ought to conduct themselves in the myriad situations encountered in daily life. Social conventions or shared norms based on cultural expectations make everyday life possible and, by extension, constitute the basis for order in the society.

Spatial Conventions

The study of spatial conventions or norms regarding space between people in everyday behaviors has been labeled **proxemics.** Our **personal space,** "that piece of the universe you occupy and call your own" (Samovar and Porter, 2001), is contained within an invisible boundary surrounding the body. With few exceptions, we do not allow others to violate this personal territory. Cultures that stress individualism (for example, England, the United States, Germany, Australia) generally demand more space than do collective cultures. Many Africans, in contrast, "get physically close to complete strangers and stand even closer when conversing" (Richmond and Gestrin, 1998:95). This **territoriality** is evident in numerous types of daily encounters in American life. The next time you are waiting in an airline (or bus, or train) terminal, notice how people have arranged their luggage to create a zone surrounding them. On public transportation, notice how people go to great lengths to prevent someone from sitting in the seat next to them. Passengers often keep to themselves and purposefully disengage with others in order maintain a certain degree of stability during their trip among, and not with, others (Kim, 2012). Likewise, as many of you know, students in many classrooms soon develop a proprietary interest in their seats. They lay claim to a particular seat early in the term, which they thereafter feel they own for all practical purposes. And if someone is already in "your seat" when you get to class, you're likely to feel a shift in stability and order because your territory has been invaded and conquered by someone else's bottom.

Spatial conventions serve as an ordering device that sets rules and limits for most everyday interactions. In American society, normal conversational distance is about 2 feet, for example. We become increasingly uncomfortable when anyone comes closer. Imagine how you would react if a stranger came up to you and began to talk to you with his or her face only inches from yours. Such a person was depicted as "the close talker" in the *Seinfeld* episode "The Raincoat." In fact, much of Jerry Seinfeld's humor relies on the recognition and breaking of everyday conventions (Paolucci and Richardson, 2006).

The conventions about appropriate distance often work in conjunction with use of the eyes. In the elevator in a public building, for example, the occupants may avoid eye contact with one another by looking either at the floor or at the flashing numbers over the door. A plausible explanation is that eye contact is an invitation to verbal contact. The seminal interpretive sociologist Georg Simmel wrote that "the eye is destined for a completely unique sociological achievement: the connection and interaction of individuals that lies in the act of individuals looking at each other. This is perhaps the most direct and purest interaction that exists" (Simmel, [1907] 1997:111). As such, we tend to avoid making eye contact in order to avoid conversing with strangers in a situation where we think our personal space might be violated.

Four common distances used in interpersonal communication were distinguished by Edward Hall, an anthropologist who continues to have a considerable influence on analyses of everyday interactions across cultures. For his initial study, he used observations and interviews with middle-class adults, mainly in the northeastern United States, as a basis for categorizing the spatial conventions that govern the distances people maintain between themselves in their communications with one another.

The closest encounters, according to Hall, take place at 0 to 18 inches, or within **intimate distance.** They include activities such as lovemaking, wrestling, or whispering, which involve either actual body contact or very close proximity. At this distance, Hall says, "the presence of the other person is unmistakable and may at times be overwhelming because of the greatly stepped-up sensory inputs. Sight (often distorted), olfaction, heat from the other person's body, sound, smell, and feel of breath all combine to signal unmistakable involvement with another body" (Hall, 1969:116).

Encounters at 1.5 to 4 feet take place at **personal distance,** in Hall's terms. The space between individuals at this distance can be thought of as "a small protective sphere or bubble that an organism maintains between

itself and others" (p. 119). Most daily conversations take place within this range. Encounters that occur from 4 to 12 feet apart are said to take place at **social distance.** Interactions at casual social gatherings generally occur within this range. Encounters more than 12 feet apart are said to occur at **public distance,** "well outside the circle of personal involvement." In political addresses or theatrical performances, for example, "the voice is exaggerated and amplified, and much of the communication shifts to gestures and body stance" (p. 106).

In American society, conceptions of appropriate distance and personal space expand and contract, depending on the situation. How close to each other two people stand often is considered evidence of the degree of intimacy between them. Business conversations are carried out at one distance, talks between friends at another, and interactions between lovers at still another. The relative status or position of various people also can be inferred from the spatial distances they maintain. The distance between the teacher and the students in a classroom, for example, is a mark of the *differences* in their power and prestige. As the traditionally rigid status distinctions between teacher and student have been reduced in recent years, the way space is planned and used in classrooms also has changed. In many schools, raised platforms and fixed rows of seats have been replaced by movable chairs and circular arrangements, in hopes of facilitating more direct and informal interactions between students and teachers. "Flipping" the classroom by rearranging the space in unconventional ways has become a popular practice intended to more fully engage students and instructors alike (Tucker, 2012).

Hall and Hall's (1990) work details cultural variations in the use of and response to space. They show that perceptions of private territory, conversational distances, and public distances maintained by Americans, Germans, French, Japanese, and Arabs vary greatly. The arrangement of offices provides a good example of how culture affects use of space. In Germany, where privacy is stressed, office furniture is spread throughout the office. In Japan, on the other hand, where group participation is encouraged, desks may be arranged hierarchically in the center of a large, common room with no walls or partitions (McDaniel, 2000). Supervisors and managers are positioned nearest the windows. "This organization encourages exchange of information, facilitates multitask accomplishments, and promotes the Confucian concept of learning through silent observation" (Samovar and Porter, 2001:187). There has been a recent trend toward more "open space" floor plans. Today, more than 70% of U.S. employees work in an open office environment, and individual work spaces shrank from 225 square feet in 2010 to 190 square feet in 2013 (Cagnon et al., 2014.) Changing the places where people work, as the theory goes, will change *how* people work.

The way furniture is arranged in the home also communicates something about the culture. Visitors to the United States from France, Italy, and Mexico are often surprised at living rooms with furniture pointed toward the television. For them, conversation is important—facing seating toward a television hardly encourages people talking to one another (Samovar and Porter, 2001).

Spatial conventions constitute only one aspect of the cultural expectations that lend order and predictability to everyday interactions. Inferences about differences in power, prestige, and status among individuals based on their use of personal space must be confirmed or rejected by other aspects of their behavior, such as regard for time, facial expressions, posture, and verbalization.

Time Conventions

Seconds, minutes, and hours are not simply measures of time with a constant meaning. They assume different symbolic values in different contexts, under different circumstances, and in front of different audiences. The meanings we attach to time are specific to particular situations and may, like spatial conventions, attest to differences in power, prestige, and status among persons. Students place a greater subjective value on a professor's time than on their own, for example. Entering a professor's office, students often begin their conversations with the declaration "I know you're probably busy, but . . ." and during the conversation they look for cues to determine whether they are exceeding an "appropriate" time limit in the office.

While time is measured in such absolutely defined units as seconds, minutes, and hours, each interval is not experienced in an identical fashion. The time spent on an important job interview will carry a different meaning from the same amount of time spent on the tennis court, for example. Albert Einstein once commented on the relativity of time by saying that two minutes in an uncomfortable situation seems like two hours. Like all other features of any culture, time is experienced subjectively.

Time Concepts in Contemporary Societies.   There are clear understandings about most time conventions in American society. Imagine the reaction if you shook someone's hand for 60 seconds instead of the conventional 4 to 5 seconds, for example. Americans often plan their behavior to occur in a particular time sequence. As with other social conventions or norms, however, there is considerable variation in expectancies about time within the society, depending on circumstances and the individuals involved.

Temporal (time-related) conventions and perceptions are linked to a society's level of urbanization and industrialization. The more complex, rationalized, bureaucratized, urbanized, and industrialized a society is, the more rigorous, concrete, and linear its conception and treatment of time will be. In a highly developed urban-industrial society, precision of timing is of great importance (see chapter 11). In fact, there is a classic argument that an orientation to time, rather than to task or social activities, becomes the crucial characteristic of industrial capitalist societies (Thompson, 1967).

This argument is based on the classical writings of Karl Marx and Max Weber, two of the 19th-century thinkers who helped lay the groundwork for sociology. Marx believed that the regulation and exploitation of labor time is the central characteristic of capitalism; that is, the exchange of commodities is in effect the exchange of labor time. Capitalism entails the attempts by the **bourgeoisie** either to extend the working day or to work labor more intensively. Later writers have demonstrated just how much conflict in industrial capitalism is focused around time—capital's right to determine hours of work and labor's attempt to limit those hours (see, for example, Walsh and Zacharias-Walsh, 2001).

Weber demonstrated that the Protestant Ethic encouraged people to develop themselves as subjects oriented to saving time and maximizing activity: "Waste of time is thus the first and in principle the deadliest of sins. . . . Loss of time through sociability, idle talk, luxury, even more sleep than is necessary to health . . . is worthy of absolute moral condemnation" (Weber, [1904–5] 1930:158). As Benjamin Franklin said, "Time is money"— to waste time is to waste money (Weber, [1904–5] 1930:48).

Simmel, writing at the onset of the 20th century, described how life in the new "metropolis" required extensive use of clocks and watches in order for people's travel arrangements and appointments to occur efficiently. Efficient time management was part of the overly rationalized city. According to Simmel, "If all the watches in Berlin suddenly went wrong in different ways even only as much as an hour, its entire economic and commercial life would be derailed for some time" (Simmel, [1905] 1950:413).

Virtually all Americans, including many children, consider it essential to have a timekeeping device. In the late 20th century, it was typically a wristwatch. Today it is more likely to be some other type of handheld device, such as a cell phone, that displays the time. Americans often must know exactly what time it is. The city dweller's constant preoccupation with time and punctuality has been identified as a central characteristic of urban life. And the perceived acceleration of time has been noted as a key feature of late modern or postmodern times (Harvey, 1989; Flaherty, 2011). Conversely, attempts to combat the supposed need for instant gratification— express lanes and minute rice—have emerged in the form of such movements as "slow food" and "slow city" (Pink, 2008). Marked by an intentional effort to slow time down by respecting the daily rituals of eating and walking, these movements demonstrate the subjective nature of the ways that time is experienced.

Generalization about the connection between time perception and extent of urbanization notwithstanding, we should still be clear on the idea that the meaning of time varies from culture to culture. Differences in time orientation have a number of analogues in the way international business, for example, is handled and in the way people relate to one another. There is much more to business than just business in many parts of the world. Cultural distinctions in terms of protocol regarding appropriateness of jumping right into business discussions before a get-acquainted interlude can lead to problems. This cultural distinction is the greatest area of difference between American and Guatemalan styles of doing business, for example.

In Guatemala, a strong personal relationship precedes solid business opportunities, which is also the case for Latin America in general. According to an article in *Business America*, an inexperienced American visitor often tries to force a business relationship:

> The abrupt "always watching the clock" style rarely works in Guatemala. A better informed business executive would engage in small talk, indicate an interest in the families of his or her business associates, join them for lunch or dinner, and generally allow time for a personal relationship to develop. (*Business America*, 1994:8)

Think about the way Americans talk about time: "losing time," "saving time," "making time," "killing time," and so on. Life in industrialized society is so enmeshed with the clock that its inhabitants are often oblivious to how eccentric their temporal beliefs can appear to others (Levine, 1997). Robert Levine describes an exchange student from Burkina Faso in eastern Africa who found the concept of "wasting time" confusing because there is no such thing as wasting time in that country. What is truly wasteful, perhaps even sinful, is to not make sufficient time available for the people in your life (Levine, 1997). One of your authors has traveled to this country and observes that in this highly "relational" culture it would be seen as improper not to greet neighbors and have fairly lengthy conversations about their families. No one rushes, and the sort of frantic American relationship with time is nonexistent, at least in the villages.

As an exercise, you might pay attention over the next week or so to the way you think about and treat time. As you plan your study assignments, for example, do you devote one evening's study to your sociology, another evening for a second subject, and so on, or do you read in several subject areas each day? Which mode of studying do you find most comfortable and why? As you travel to your classes in the morning, do you leave extra time to ensure that you won't be late for class? If you happen to arrive late, how do you feel upon entering the room and what do you imagine is running through the mind of your professor? After class, as you are heading out to meet a friend for lunch, do you quickly excuse yourself from an unexpected conversation with a classmate or do you presume that the person waiting for you will understand if you are late? How late can you be without expecting your friend to be upset? Will he or she be angry if you are 30 seconds late, 2 minutes late, 5 minutes late, 10 minutes late, half an hour late? At what point do you call or send a text message? If you are the one waiting, how long will it be before you become angry with a tardy friend? It might even be interesting to do a small, informal poll with students you know from abroad. Do they think the way you do about these matters?

The Power to Make Others Wait. Bureaucracy, a predominant influence in modern society (see chapter 7), demands that much time be spent waiting for others or for goods and services. The study of delay in a mass-consumption society is a significant area of sociological inquiry because so much time must be spent waiting.

In the most immediate sense, delay may be caused by the relations between supply and demand for goods and services. Analysis of waiting, however, uncovers delay strategies used to exercise power and status in social interactions. The scarcity or monopolization of valued services creates situations that allow workers to exercise power over clients and customers, for example. Bureaucrats have notoriously abused their power to make people wait. They might not themselves possess anything of value, but in their work roles they control access to resources people need. We cannot even drive our automobiles without first acquiring licenses and registration papers from bureaucrats who, in fact, have low status within their organizations.

Others may keep us waiting because of the perceived importance of the services or knowledge they have to offer. Doctors usually have patients waiting for them, but a patient who fails to show up for an appointment will be charged for the unused time. Executives may regularly keep visitors waiting, "cooling their heels" in an outer office. Barry Schwartz observes, "In general the more powerful and important a person is, the more others' access to him must be regulated. Thus, the least powerful may always be approached at will; the most powerful are seen only by appointment" (Schwartz, 1974:847). In a similar fashion, welfare recipients are often forced to wait at welfare offices, which, in turn, reinforces their subordinate status to the state. "In those recurring encounters at the welfare office, poor people learn that, despite endless delays and random changes, they must comply with the requirements of agents and their machines" (Auyero, 2011:24). So while we recognize that time may be subjective, it is not untainted by other social conditions and forces.

Facial, Posture, and Gesture Conventions

Since the 1980s the study of **nonverbal communication** has become a major area of inquiry in the social sciences and has engaged the attention of researchers in the fields of sociology, psychology, anthropology, communications, linguistics, and neuroscience. Much of the research on facial expression, for example, is concentrated on the universal presentation of such emotions as interest, surprise, disgust, anger, fear, and sadness (Keltner, 1995). Findings from a study on the ability to interpret facial expression of emotion may be of particular interest to you (especially if you are trying to convince your parents that studying abroad is beneficial!). Using student populations from the United States, Germany, South Africa, and Japan, researchers found that those who had traveled outside their home country were better receivers of nonverbal cues than were others (Swenson and Casmir, 1998). And apparently reading literary fiction—the types of works you read in English or humanities-based classes rather than popular works like *Fifty Shades of Grey*—increases individuals' ability to empathize and read others' actions (Greenfeldboyce, 2013).

Research on nonverbal communication shows that meanings conveyed by people's gestures and postures vary from context to context (Carroll and

Russell, 1996) and cross-culturally (see box). **Kinesics,** the sociological study of body movement and gesture, is concerned with the shared cultural meanings attached to nonverbal behaviors. Consensus about the significance of postures, gestures, and expressions enhances our ability to explain and predict our own and others' behaviors in daily interactions.

Ray Birdwhistell (1952, 1970), a pioneer in this field, maintains that the majority of interactions utilize nonverbal communication. We give cues to our meanings by the way we stand, our facial expressions, and the position of our heads. We control most of these expressions and consciously use them to express a range of emotions from anger to disappointment to love. All communicative expressions are not easily controlled, however. We find it hard to control such physiological responses as a red face in an embar-

---

"V" is for Victory?

One of the arguments in this chapter, consistent with our social psychological viewpoint, is that behaviors carry quite different meanings in different settings. To be sure, assuming that certain nonverbal gestures carry the same meaning in other cultures can get you into a lot of trouble. Dane Archer, who is known for his use of video to explore cultural differences in gestures, states emphatically, "Gestures are definitely NOT a universal language, as people who have worked, lived, or studied abroad may have noticed" (Archer, 1997b:79). Travelers sometimes learn this the hard way, inadvertently committing offense by using the culturally "wrong" gesture. Archer urges travelers to practice "gestural humility"—that is, "the assumption that the gestures we know from home will not mean the same things abroad, and also that we cannot infer or intuit the meaning of any gestures we observe in other cultures" (p. 80). Even prominent political figures can blunder. President George H. W. Bush greeted a group of Australians with a gesture he understood as World War II British prime minister Winston Churchill's famous "V for victory" gesture. However, President Bush made the gesture *backward* (his palm facing his own face), effectively flashing the crowd with the British Commonwealth equivalent of the American "finger" (or "screw you") gesture. The Australians were more dumbfounded than insulted, not quite believing that a head of state would stoop to such an unpresidential act (Archer, 1997b:80). Bush wasn't the only one to get it wrong—Margaret Thatcher did the same thing when she was prime minister of the United Kingdom.

Archer has videotaped hundreds of hours of ESL (English as a Second Language) students demonstrating gestures, resulting in the documentary videos *A World of Gestures: Culture and Nonverbal Communication* (1991) and *A World of Difference: Understanding Cross-Cultural Communication* (1997a). These documentaries provide numerous examples of nonverbal communication with different cultural meanings. Perhaps the most famous is the American "OK" sign, which means "money" in Japan, "zero" in France, "homosexuality" in Ethiopia, and an obscenity in Latin America! Similarly, the American raised thumb gesture of "good luck" is a vulgar gesture meaning "sit on this" in Sardinia and "screw you" in Iran (Archer, 1997a). Other examples of nonverbal communication with different meanings in different cultures include holding hands, shrugging, silence, and use of eyes in interpersonal expressions (Singh et al., 1998). Bodily smells—whether natural or perfumed—have varying meanings across cultural and situational contexts (Waskul and Vannini, 2008; Borer, 2013).

If, however, you wish to avoid miscommunication, there is one gesture that carries virtually universal meaning. Most people will know that you mean to express appreciation when you smile.

rassing situation or involuntary hand tremors during high anxiety. Often we look for these expressions in others with whom we are interacting as a check on their emotions or attitudes.

An interesting example of the way our internal emotional states are reflected in outward appearance is the case of lying. Nonverbal behaviors that are significantly more frequent with lying include blinking and an increased number of what have been termed *adaptors*. These are nervous habits such as scratching or twiddling one's hair (Ford, 1996). Other physical cues believed to be associated with lying include an increased incidence of leaning forward, licking the lips, touching the nose, averting one's gaze, and handling objects (Henahan, 1999).

Raising the hand to the nose has been reported in many cultures as a movement associated with lying. This gesture may be related to the fact that the nose contains erectile tissues that engorge when a person is lying, sort of a "Pinocchio effect" (Henahan, 1999). Whether a lie is benign, such as a joke to make someone laugh, or malicious, to deceive someone and put him or her in harm's way, can often be determined by facial gestures. Consider, as Clifford Geertz (1973) did in his discussion of meaningful action, the distinction between blinks and winks. Blinks are involuntary. You've probably blinked a few dozen times while reading this chapter without even knowing it. Winks, on the other hand, are intentional. They are meaningful. A wink rather than a blink or a nose scratch can signal that a lie is meant for playful purposes or other nonthreatening intentions.

The simplest nonverbal gestures can communicate a great deal. Think of a skier or skater who falls and then exaggerates the effect by lying on the cold ground longer than necessary, with arms and legs flung out. Through such exaggeration the person may wish to communicate, "I know I look kind of silly, but understand that I am really a quite competent person and you should not take this momentary awkwardness very seriously." Sometimes gestures of this sort are used in conjunction with verbal utterances, as when a woman runs headlong to catch a bus or elevator before it leaves, only to have the doors close in her face. At this point she might stand, hands on hips, moving her head from side to side, muttering. Her comments are supposedly made to herself, but they also may be meant to be heard by anyone within earshot. They might be intended to communicate, "Understand that although this has happened, I remain fully in control of myself."

Avoiding Communication.   Nonverbal communication can be instrumental in avoiding communication. Moore (1998) observed "courtship rejection signals" by women attempting to discourage the attention of men in singles' bars. This is an interesting study, given that most research on courtship focuses on behaviors that individuals use to *attract* partners (see chapter 5). The women Moore observed used 17 behaviors to demonstrate disinterest or rejection, including facial expressions such as yawning, frowning, and sneering; gestures such as negative head shaking or putting hands in pockets; and posture patterns such as arm crossing or holding the torso rigidly. A number of signals involved the eyes—for example, *gaze avoidance*. This occurred when the woman did not make eye contact with the man, despite the fact that he was looking directly at her. She looked at other people or at another point in the room, or she made eye contact with someone else at the table. Other eye signals that functioned as rejection signals included *upward gaze*, when she looked at the ceiling, and *hair gaze*, when she drew her hair across her face and looked at the ends (Moore, 1998).

People often use props as an aid in such situations. We would be hard-pressed to explain why some people wear sunglasses on the subway, for example, unless we considered their use in shielding the "improper" use of eyes. Other props such as iPods or cell phones—Goffman (1963) would call these "involvement shields"—are also used to avoid any kind of contact with others who are physically present. Avoidance may itself be a form of social interaction—we must sometimes communicate to others that we do not wish to communicate. Particularly in urban interactions with strangers, we must systematically take one another into account in order to avoid unwanted encounters (see chapter 4). When such strategies don't work, however, we enter the sometimes dangerous world of the "peeping Tom" or the sexual predator. The unwanted gaze can be seen as infringement of the social norms of privacy in both private and public settings (Rosen, 2011).

Rules for Physical Contact

There also are clear conventions regulating actual physical contact between individuals (Henley, 1986). A commonplace behavior such as hand-holding is a highly regulated activity, for example. A few questions suggest the range of these regularities: Who can hold hands with whom? Is it more appropriate for women to hold hands in public than it is for men? Why? Is there an age-related factor influencing who can hold hands with whom? Would a female in her 20s feel uncomfortable holding her father's hand while walking down the street? Would a male of the same age feel self-conscious holding his mother's hand in a restaurant?

We share clear expectations about who may touch whom, on what part of the body, and in what context. Different meanings and symbolic significance are attached to different parts of the body. On the field, male athletes pat each other's bottoms after significant plays or outstanding personal efforts, but this same behavior elsewhere would hardly be interpreted as a display of male camaraderie. You might seek others' attention by lightly tapping them on the shoulder, but you would not grab them by the thigh. Sometimes it is considered appropriate for one person to touch another, but not vice versa. A teacher may, while explaining a point to a student, touch the student's shoulder. The student would hesitate to do the same to the teacher. Sometimes even the slightest touch (accidentally touching someone's foot under a dining table, for example) requires an immediate apology.

As with the other normative conventions detailed in this chapter, rules about touching vary considerably from culture to culture. Americans who normally do not touch other people unless they are on a fairly intimate basis will feel comfortable in Japan, England, Scandinavia, and Australia, where similar rules prevail. Americans who travel to Middle Eastern countries, Latin American countries, Italy, Greece, Spain, Portugal, or Russia may have to adjust to encounters, even among strangers, where people routinely touch each other. People from some Mediterranean cultures often hold the elbow of the person to whom they are speaking. For many Americans, this uninvited touching is nearly unbearable (Archer, 1997b).

A Blueprint for Everyday Life

This section has described only a small fraction of the types of rules and expectations that constitute a critical part of any culture. As the members of a society together acquire knowledge, beliefs, art, customs, morals, and other capabilities and habits, the culture evolves over time. A pattern of norms or conventions about what one can and cannot do in a given society emerges. A society is possible only because its members share these standards and cultural expectations.

Commonly held ideas about how one ought to behave provide members of the same culture with a blueprint for conducting their everyday lives. Knowledge of cultural rules and social conventions is not itself enough to ensure social order, however. Human beings constantly interpret and negotiate such rules.

■ Beyond Social Conventions:
The Interpretation of Everyday Life

The sociologist's job—to explain human behavior—would be quite simple if behaviors were the product only of the types of social conventions we have mentioned. Were that the case, we would only have to set about cataloging all of the rules to which people in American society normally conform. Alas, things are not quite so simple! It would be more accurate to say that these conventions or shared norms constitute the *boundaries* within which people interact. Alone they are not sufficient to explain how daily encounters are managed. Beyond knowledge of background rules, successful interaction requires engaging in a **process of interpretation** through which a situation is assessed and meanings are assigned to a person's own behaviors and those of others. Though our interpretations of people, places, and things may be different—since they depend upon such cultural factors as race, class, and gender identification, among others—the *necessary* act of interpretation in everyday life is at least one practice that all able-minded individuals have in common.

Assessing Meanings and Formulating Behaviors

It may very well be true that you know what to do when entering a new classroom for the first time because you have learned from an early age the general rules applicable to classroom behavior. You are unlikely to sit down in the chair behind the desk at the front of the room, for example. You have learned not to speak unless directed to do so by the teacher. If you want to talk, you would probably raise your hand and wait to be acknowledged by the teacher. And so on. Knowledge of these rules alone, however, will not allow you to predict fully the meanings and patterns of behavior that will become central in any particular classroom. That is, the rules that govern classroom behavior will be products of ongoing actions by the particular teacher and students involved, all of whom must constantly take the others' actions into account when formulating their own lines of action (Karp and Yoels, 1976).

As in any other setting, participants in the classroom will be engaged in an ongoing assessment of one another's actions. Students will soon define the situation as to whether in a particular class the teacher *really* wants discussion, whether it is safe to make one's opinion known, whether one ought to laugh at the teacher's jokes, and, if so, how raucously. Decisions of this sort cannot be anticipated or determined solely through knowledge of the general and learned conventions applicable to most classrooms.

Interpretation in the Acting Situation

Behavior is always produced via interpretation in the **acting situation.** The expectancies surrounding behavior in any situation always emerge from the interaction itself. They may be in a state of continual transformation. According to Herbert Blumer, "In the flow of group life there are innumerable points at which participants are redefining each other's acts" (1962:184). Interpretation is an ongoing process that is achieved through shared expectations. Though meanings are continuously negotiated, they are never negotiated totally anew as if new ideas are somehow created out of thin air without any relation to past encounters and situations.

Suppose someone approaches you and asks for a light for a cigarette. This is an apparently simple request, but, in fact, it is not immediately clear how you would respond. You probably would believe the other person's motives to be different under different circumstances, and in different time periods. Smoking was once a fairly ubiquitous behavior. Just watch a movie filmed before the 1990s. Or stream an episode of the television show *Mad Men*, which takes place in a New York advertising firm in the 1960s where everyone is lighting up, and often drinking liquor, at all times of the day in offices, restaurants, subways, and other public places. Situational factors or variables will influence the meaning you attach to the request for a light. Would the gender of the person make any difference in your interpretation? Would you possibly attribute different motives to a stranger and to a close friend making the same request? Would it make any difference where the request was made (at a friend's house, on campus, or outside a bar)? What role might such factors as the time of day, the age of the requester, or his or her dress, race, demeanor, and facial expression play in your interpretation of the request? How might you react if you recently quit smoking or knew someone who died of lung cancer? Even the most apparently simple human transactions may call forth quite different meanings, which we confer on them by piecing together bits of information in the situation.

Virtually all our behaviors depend on our ability to assess features of the situation in which we are acting and then define it. Some situations may require more extensive interpretation than others, however. In some situations we realize that we must be quite strategic in formulating our behaviors. In these situations we might engage in extensive mind work or mental gymnastics prior to acting. We might consciously try to manipulate those with whom we interact in order to control the **definition of the situation** they will come to have. These may be situations that we consider risky or in which we perceive obstacles to the realization of our goals.

■ The Individual–Society Relationship

The social conventions described in the preceding section lend support to a central idea in the symbolic interactionist approach to the study of sociology: *The capacity of humans to interact and communicate effectively with one another is a truly extraordinary ability and worthy of in-depth investigation.* The explanation of how social conventions reflect the social order and influence the interpretation of everyday events has brought out a number of general points. First, although we may not think much about it, there is a clear ordering to our everyday lives. There are underlying dimensions to everyday social life that can be discovered. Second, the coherence of everyday life depends on our possession of a truly remarkable range of knowledge. Third, our behaviors are a product of our ability to interpret social situations and confer meanings on them. Fourth, rather than being regarded as a given, social order should be considered a human accomplishment that requires explanation. Fifth, if we seek to understand how, in the broadest sense, a society is possible and how it operates as an ongoing concern, it is a good strategy to begin by exploring how we carry out our day-to-day interactions.

This approach also supports an even more general sociological theme: the relationship between the individual and the society. We live in a society that significantly influences our behaviors through numerous social conventions. At the same time, we exercise substantial freedom of action relative to those in the past and present living under highly restrictive control (for example, Hitler's Nazi Germany; South Africa under apartheid; the Khmer Rouge in Cambodia; Libya under Muammar Gaddafi's rule). The desire for freedom, which can come at a cost, is practically a universal human trait. It is a paradox of human existence that while societies influence human behaviors, humans sometimes also transform societies. We must entertain simultaneously the apparently contradictory thoughts that humans are social products and that society is a human product.

Understanding Freedom and Constraint in Social Life

The abiding theoretical questions of sociology flow from consideration of the connection between the individual and society: How do individuals become functioning members of a society? How and why do they become responsive to the demands of a society? Why do they conform to society's rules? How is it that some people refuse to do so? To what extent is behavior determined by **social structure?** Just how much can individuals change societies?

Nearly all the great classical social theorists were intrigued by these questions. On the whole, their theoretical work may be read as attempts to understand the nature of the **social bonds** existing between individuals and the bonding of individuals to the society (see box). Those who are considered the founding figures of sociology—Karl Marx (1818–1883), Émile Durkheim (1858–1917), Georg Simmel (1858–1918), Max Weber (1864–1920), Ferdinand Tönnies (1855–1936), and William Graham Sumner (1840–1910), among others—all broached questions of order and disorder, change and stability, deviance and conformity. These questions, of course, do not allow for single, definitive answers. They still are the guiding questions for

Émile Durkheim (1858–1917)

French sociologist Émile Durkheim was instrumental in establishing sociology as a social science, distinguishing "the scientific study of society and human behavior" from the field of philosophy and other social sciences. Central to Durkheim's work was the notion of society as a reality in its own right: Despite the variety of people within a society and the fact that some die and others are born, there is an order that exists above and beyond its specific components. Durkheim spoke of a "collective conscience;" the shared beliefs of members of a social unit. Perhaps most importantly, Durkheim showed that this order can be examined scientifically, through observations. These observations produce social statistics, or *social facts*, numbers that characterize a collectivity. For example, the birthrate of a society, although composed of thousands of individual births, is a statistic that exists at the level of society as a whole. Durkheim's emphasis on statistics reflected his personal concern to make sociology respectable to the ruling intellectual elites of the day. Then, as now, "science" was associated with numbers, with *quantitative* measurement. His classic work, *Suicide* ([1897] 1951), is based on a comparison of official statistics and historical records across groups.

Durkheim observed patterns in the data: Suicide rates in all the countries he examined tended to be higher among widowed, single, and divorced people than among married people; higher among people without children than among parents; and higher among Protestants than among Catholics. Rather than interpret this finding in terms of psychological states, Durkheim felt that the nature of *social* life was involved. He concluded that when group, family, or community ties are weak, people feel disconnected and alone. When these ties are strong, people have a supportive network that could protect to some extent against the individualism and alienation of life in modern society (see chapter 11).

Durkheim was a pivotal figure in the establishment of sociology in the French university system. His ideas not only had a profound impact in France but also played a major role in shaping American sociology.

sociological work, and sociologists collectively are still in the business of trying to understand just how societies and individuals influence one another. One thing seems clear, however. Comprehension of everyday life requires a conception of the individual–society relationship in which primacy is placed on neither the society nor the individual.

The authors of this book are convinced that any attempt to understand the operation of society that neglects the processes governing social interaction will be theoretically unsatisfying. Ultimately a society is composed of people interacting with one another. All explanations of human behavior must in some way account for individuals' intentions, motives, and subjective understanding of the situation in which they act. All human behavior is constructed from everyday **shared meaning structures.** We presume, in other words, that any effort to understand the operation of society as a whole must begin with and be built upon analysis of individuals' everyday lifeworlds. We agree with Peter Adler, Patricia Adler, and Andrea Fontana, who, in their review of critical works on the sociology of everyday life, comment, "Naturally occurring interaction is the foundation of all understanding of society. Describing and analyzing the character and implications of everyday life interaction should thus serve as both the beginning and end point of sociology" (1987:219). This is not to suggest that sociologists should give up the study of social structure in favor of the study of human interaction. Instead, we believe, along with a number of sociological theorists (see Maines, 2001; Fine, 2010; Harris, 2010) that the most fruitful sociological inquiries are based on an integration of the two levels of analysis, society and the individual. Simmel concluded one of his seminal essays on human interaction with the following mandate:

> One will no longer be able to consider as unworthy of attention the delicate, invisible threads that are spun from one person to another if one wishes to understand the web of society according to its productive, form-giving forces—this web of which sociology hitherto was largely concerned with describing the final finished pattern of its uppermost phenomenal stratum. ([1907] 1997:120)

These "delicate, invisible threads" are precisely the objects of inquiry that sociologists who recognize the foundational aspects of everyday life attempt to make visible. As the studies presented throughout this book suggest, we can detect these threads by focusing on the "form-giving forces" that individuals enact and rely upon to makes sense of their interactions, encounters, and experiences with others.

Too much sociology, we think, makes the mistake of accepting the **reification** of social structures by regarding them as having a life of their own independent of individuals. Much sociological work is based on the supposition that institutions are more than the sum of their parts and, once created, exert a force on individuals over which they have little control.

There is no question that institutions exert a strong force on individuals. Ample evidence of this can be found in the bureaucratic systems (see chapter 7) that provide a structure for the lives of college and university students. There are certain things you are required to do if you wish to remain within the system. You must show up for exams, you must pay your tuition, you must follow certain course registration procedures, and so forth. In that sense the structure is real, powerful, and has an obdurate quality that transcends the existence of any particular student. The university has an independent life in the sense that it existed as an institution before you were born and will, in all likelihood, continue to exist after you graduate and, hopefully, move on to greener pastures.

Does this mean that your behaviors are utterly controlled by the academic bureaucracy? Does it mean that sociologists need not be concerned with the interactions among individuals within the institution and the definitions and meanings they give to their lives in it? Of course not! It should not come as news that students manipulate academic institutions. Through interaction with others, you determine just how hard you will work in your courses. You make, consult, and access judgments about professors on RateMyProfessor.com. You and your fellow students could collectively choose to make life difficult for your instructors by such strategies as choosing not to participate in class discussion or conning them into letting you turn in late term papers.

We are committed to the idea that, in large measure, human beings act according to the *interpretations* they make of social life. Individuals are not merely puppets pushed around by forces over which they have no control. Substantially, they make their own worlds. Unlike atoms, molecules, or stable elements of the physical universe, they think, construct meanings, and respond creatively to their environments. Consequently, the social world is in a state of continual process, change, and production. Values and attitudes change. Behaviors once thought taboo become incorporated into the repertoire of conventional behaviors. New social forms are created to meet needs better, and unpredictable fads are devised.

Humans thus experience choice and discretion in their everyday lives. But it would be misleading to minimize the significance of the constraints within which they must act. The dramas of daily life occur within larger historical and institutional settings. Because people are born into a world that is itself a product of the actions of previous generations, many areas of social existence have already been staked out for them. There are understood limits on their behavior. Societies have moral as well as geographical boundaries. And every society has its caretakers (for example, police, judges, psychiatrists) who are entrusted with the responsibility for maintaining the integrity of those boundaries and the power to do so (see chapter 8).

The Dynamic Interplay of Expectations and Interpretations

In our view, therefore, human behavior must not be seen exclusively as either the product of the social structures enveloping people or a matter of individual will and choice. There is a dynamic interplay between society's expectations for individuals and their own responses in situations.

The nature of the relationship between individuals and social structures is beautifully captured in a statement by sociologist Wendell Bell. Some people, he says, rather than following along like rats in a maze, view the social structure as tentative and proceed by experimentally testing to learn what parts of it can be manipulated. In his words,

> At the extreme, such persons may decide that the social structure, the maze itself, is subject to some extent to their will and may decide to shape it, as best they can, to suit themselves. . . . Usually in cooperation with others, some people try to manipulate the real world to conform more closely to their images of the future; push out some walls, add some new openings, widen the passageways, create some new opportunities. (Bell, 1968:163)

While society sets the ground rules within which we act, we do not unthinkingly respond to society's expectations. Behavior is also partially the result of our personal, subjective interpretations of the situations we face. The most appropriate conception of daily life, therefore, requires that we understand human behavior as an ongoing interchange, or a *dialectic*, between freedom and constraint.

■ The Sociology of Everyday Life

The authors of this book advocate the study of everyday interactions as a central area of sociological study *in its own right*. We believe sociologists cannot afford to neglect the study of everyday life. On theoretical grounds, we maintain that the study of such interactions is necessary to understand social order and change in society. In a still broader sense, as we analyze various aspects of everyday lives in later chapters, we will be exploring the limits and potentialities of human beings' relations with each other. This is, by any standard, an important endeavor.

You may wonder that if the study of everyday interaction is as important as we believe it to be, why is it necessary to argue for its merits as an area of sociological investigation? The fact is that the processes governing everyday life and accounting for its order have been largely ignored by many sociologists who consider them as, at best, only the starting point for their own broader, more **macrosociological investigation** of large-scale processes and social structures. Much sociology, in this respect, leaves wholly unattended the grounds on which it is constructed. The sociologist Harold Garfinkel made this point some time ago when he said, "Although sociologists take socially structured scenes of everyday life as a point of departure they rarely see, as a task of sociological inquiry in its own right, the general questions of how any such commonsense world is possible" (1967:36). Garfinkel is arguing that efforts to understand society as a whole depend on the **microsociological investigation** of individuals' daily interactions (see box).

Garfinkel's Ethnomethodology

Harold Garfinkel developed *ethnomethodology* (literally, people or folk methods) as a technique for looking beneath the "taken-for-granted" surface of daily life. His goal is to understand how people produce meaning out of their experiences. First we must consider the "seen but unnoticed," expected background features of everyday scenes that members of a society use as a scheme of interpretation. People respond to background expectancies but are at a loss to say of what the expectancies consist. For these background expectancies to come into view, "one must either be a stranger to the 'life as usual' character of everyday scenes, or become estranged from them" (Garfinkel, 1967:37). He is most famous for his "demonstrations," designed to "produce reflections through which the strangeness of an obstinately familiar world can be detected" (p. 38). That is, by doing something that turns this world upside down, the unspoken reality is revealed.

Garfinkel sent his students out to expose this unspoken reality by "breaching" it. They entered elevators and stood facing the other occupants, rather than turning around to face the door. On visits home they acted as if they were strangers, asking permission to eat food, for example. In everyday conversations ("Hi, how are you?") they refused to respond in the expected manner ("What do you mean, 'how am I'? Physically? Emotionally?"). As you might expect, people's reactions were anything but positive, ranging from questioning the person's sanity to anger. The point was not to upset people but to upset the balance of everyday life, thus proving beyond doubt that certain taken-for-granted norms had been violated. According to Garfinkel, "there *is* order in the most ordinary activities of everyday life" (1996:7). The preoccupation in ethnomethodology's studies is "to find, collect, specify, and make . . . observable the . . . production and natural accountability of immortal familiar society's most ordinary organizational things in the world" (p. 6).

Why the Study of Interactions Has Been Neglected

A central reason why sociologists have failed to study everyday interactions systematically is their concern for conventional methods of scientific inquiry. Virtually since sociology's inception in the 19th century, sociologists have modeled their discipline after the natural sciences. They have been intent on using the same tools the natural scientist uses in their investigation of human behavior. We can call this "physics envy." This has led to a long-standing central concern with the establishment of causal laws about human society.

Moreover, social scientists have frequently embraced a version of scientific inquiry in which precise measurement of variables and the rigorous testing of propositions are the standard for judging scientific work. The notion that there is only one proper form of scientific inquiry is a somewhat naive conception of science, in our view. It immediately restricts the range of phenomena that may be investigated to those variables that are clearly quantifiable and hence measurable. Such a bias is reflected in the definition of a true behavioral *scientist* as a person who, when asked if he loves his mother, replies that he cannot answer until he has done an analysis of their correspondence.

We surely would not argue with attempts to measure accurately the variables of interest to social scientists. But the demand that social scientists be concerned only with observable, quantifiable, and measurable phenomena has directed attention away from basic processes of human communication, which often defy precise "measurement." Our idea of interaction is that people act in awareness of one another and mutually adjust their responses in light of the actions of others. We therefore want to consider such factors as their motives, their goals, the meanings they confer on the gestures of others, their identities, their self-concepts, and the processes through which they define social situations. These necessary elements for understanding social interaction are resistant to precise measurement. We must be concerned with what goes on in a person's head and how he or she interprets the information and sensory stimuli that make up social reality.

An appropriate metaphor might be the operation of a traditional clock. We cannot fully comprehend how such a clock works by looking only at the outside casing or examining only the regularity of the minute, hour, and second hands. Certainly it is easier to describe these visible outer mechanisms, just as it would be simpler only to document and measure actual behaviors. The study of interaction requires more: concern with the inner dialogue that people have with themselves both before they act and while they are acting.

A second reason sociologists have generally neglected the study of routine, everyday social encounters may be their long-standing preference for investigations of issues that have social policy implications. Sociologists have shown a preference for research areas that might persuade the public that sociologists have something to say about "important" issues. Understandably, they have concentrated their efforts on areas where they are likely to receive funding for their study. Funding agencies like definitive answers. Quantifiable measurements provide simple numerical answers to complex questions. Social problems such as juvenile delinquency, poverty, race relations, health delivery systems, aging, prostitution, drug addiction, environmental degradation, and gender and sex discrimination have always been and still are popular issues for sociological study. These areas provide much rich information on day-to-day interactions, but they have not typically been investigated with this goal in mind. As we will see in the following chapters, such is no longer the case.

What the Study of Interactions Should Accomplish

If the analysis of everyday interactions is to be accepted as a central area of sociological study, it must be able to accomplish specified goals. Our efforts ought to produce some type of new knowledge about human behavior. As Jack Katz (2001) suggests, we must be able to describe the "what," document the "how," and interpret and explain the "why" of social interactions and encounters.

Discovering Underlying Social Forms.   In some respects, the facts of everyday life are obvious and accessible to anyone who carefully observes.

For that reason, our goal is never simply description of everyday life. Certainly our analysis begins with careful description, but beyond that we seek to appreciate how the facts of everyday behavior reveal deeper, often hidden dimensions of social life. The trick of sociological analysis is to identify recurring patterns of social life reflected in a range of behaviors. If we are successful, our analyses will let us see a familiar set of facts from new angles, which will add new dimensions to our understanding. Another way to express the same thought is that our analyses should "penetrate" the obvious and thereby reveal underlying aspects of social life.

Ever since the first trees bore fruit, it has been apparent to everyone that apples fall from trees. Before Sir Isaac Newton purposely observed this event, however, no one had ever related the falling of apples to the motion of the planets. Newton's contribution was the conceptual breakthrough that revealed the laws of gravity. Once that underlying dimension of the physical world was uncovered, the fact that apples fall from trees became somewhat insignificant. Newton's law allowed scientists to understand the behavior of any falling body. The discovery of underlying dimensions that reveal commonalities in a whole class of events is the real task of scientific inquiry. Scientists are less concerned with the *content* of events than with the common forms taken by apparently dissimilar events.

The "obvious" empirical facts of social life are important in the same way. It is our job to make plain how the facts of everyday life reflect underlying social forms (Simmel, 1950) or dimensions. To illustrate the point, social scientists interested in a phenomenon such as "religious devotion" should not just investigate what goes on in churches. They would do well to study also such seemingly diverse phenomena as labor union meetings, behaviors on national holidays, football games, and punk rock concerts. These are all events that could profitably be understood as expressions of religious devotion. The same intensity and reverence associated with religious rituals and symbols underlie these phenomena. Clearly, contexts or situations that differ widely in content (the content of church services is quite unlike the content of football games) can nevertheless display common social forms.

A phenomenon such as embarrassment is interesting, but we do not suggest studying it only to describe embarrassing situations. Our broader intention is to use these descriptions as a starting point for thinking clearly about more general issues such as risk, identity, performances, and deviance in interaction (see chapter 9). To use an earlier example in this chapter, we might be interested in detailing conventions of "touching" behavior to gain insight into patterns of intimacy in society, elements of body image, and power relations (see chapter 6).

If we wish to investigate how people behave in stressful, anxiety-related, or uncomfortable situations, we could focus on contexts where we expect them to experience stress, anxiety, and discomfort. We might choose to observe students in dormitories before final exams, for example. It would be true that we were observing behaviors in a dormitory, but we would not be concerned with the context per se. We would be motivated to study dormitory life as a convenient context in which to develop an analysis of stress interaction. This analysis has significance far beyond the dormitory itself. In other words, sociological analysis must always carry us beyond the specific context we are investigating. The specific case of dormitory behavior becomes as incidental as apples falling from trees after we discover underlying elements of how humans behave under stress.

A danger faced by sociologists who study everyday life phenomena is the criticism that they are concerned with trivial events. We maintain, however, that sociological analysis of the routine events and worlds of everyday life often provides important insights and concepts that have a larger relevance for understanding social life. Throughout the following chapters we will be citing studies that provide a powerful explanation of human behavior. We can, however, mention here a few examples of the kinds of topics we have in mind. Gary Fine (1996) has studied the organizational culture and structure of restaurant kitchens. Arlie Russell Hochschild (1997) examines what happens "when work becomes home and home becomes work." Mitch Duneier and Harvey Molotch's (1999) study of urban street vendors uncovers the process of "interactional vandalism" in which street men are able to breach the norms of urban interaction. Yuki Kato (2011) found that suburban teenagers use the spatial metaphor of the "bubble" to both promote and criticize their middle-class identities and lifestyles. Colin Jerolmack (2013) explores the various ways that humans and animals—in his case, pigeons—interact in private and public places in order to uncover the differing meanings that individuals give to pigeons. A pigeon in New York, Berlin, and London, for example, is a bird of a different feather. Studies such as these affirm the necessity of looking at everyday life settings and interactions to understand the bases of social order and change in society at large.

Some of the most exciting and promising work is in the area of social inequality. Philippe Bourgois (1995) shows how the urban drug trade offers a path to status and economic success for young men who have no chance for industrial work nor the cultural capital to break into middle-class service jobs. Katheryn Edin and Laura Lein (1997) interviewed mothers on welfare to discover how they "make ends meet." Elijah Anderson (1999) shows how the desperate search for respect influences the everyday lives of young African Americans in the inner city. David Grazian (2007) uncovers how the masculine nightlife ritual of the "girl hunt" supports males' belief in the fantasy of the one-night stand as part of an ideology of male dominance and female passivity despite evidence to the contrary. And Patrick Grzanka and Justin Maher (2012) show how supposedly tongue-in-check websites such as Stuff White People Like reinforce white privilege by constructing a new and superficial kind of white "ethnicity."

Developing Sociological Skepticism. Unfortunately, there is no set of rules we can give that will allow you to discover the underlying forms of social life. What we can do in this book is let you see how social scientists think about everyday phenomena, the particular imagination or consciousness they bring to the study of everyday events, and the kinds of questions that guide their analyses. The production of good ideas is not a mechanical process, as Stanislav Andreski (1972:108) notes:

> The so-called methods of induction are in reality methods of verification; they tell us how to test hypotheses *but not how to arrive at them.* Indeed, the latter process is just as much a mystery as it was in the days of Socrates: all that is known is that, *in order to conceive fruitful original ideas, one must have talent, must immerse oneself in the available knowledge, and think very hard.* (emphasis added)

In the chapters that follow we will familiarize you with the ideas of those who have written about everyday behaviors and share the knowledge they provide. We also will continue to detail the elements of the theoretical perspective—symbolic interaction—that we consider most useful for analyzing everyday events. The central goal of this volume, however, is to compel you to think very hard about how your daily interactions are organized and made sociologically intelligible.

At the risk of sounding too dramatic, we want to develop in those who read this book a kind of sociological skepticism. Good sociology demands a degree of skepticism. It is the sociologist's obligation to question those features of reality that appear obvious. Sociologists must strive to become strangers to the events and phenomena in their daily lives that they most take for granted. As a sociologist, therefore, you must step outside your "normal" role as a member of the society and ask how your behaviors are structured and endowed with meaning. Good sociology requires you to be skeptical enough to believe that things are not always as simple as they appear to be. In his seminal "invitation" to think sociologically, Peter Berger wisely wrote:

> Sociology is justified by the belief that it is better to be conscious than unconscious and that consciousness is a condition of freedom. . . . We contend that it is part of a civilized mind in our age to have come in touch with the peculiarly modern, peculiarly timely form of critical thought we call sociology. Even those who do not find in this intellectual pursuit their own particular demon . . . will by this contact have become a little less stolid in their prejudices, a little more careful in their own commitments and a little more skeptical about the commitments of others—and perhaps a little more compassionate in their journeys through society. (Berger, 1963:175)

We presume, then, that those things "everybody already knows," those apparently obvious aspects of the society with which you have grown up from infancy and remain committed to, can be subjected to sociological analysis. It is, we will show, an analysis that provides insight into the way people produce and construct their everyday existences. In this respect, we take on the professional obligation of questioning aspects of social life that may seem obvious and unproblematic. Our subject matter does not have anything mysterious about it—we certainly grant that. The questions we ask about familiar life phenomena and the analyses deriving from these questions are intended to advance and deepen your understanding of the sociological topics to be discussed in the following pages.

The Everyday Self

From one day to the next, there are some beliefs, ideas, and feelings you bring with you. Of course we can all "wake up on the wrong side of the bed," as they say. But most days, we don't awaken wondering who we are, or at least not right away. Our early morning routines help remind us of who we are. Can you identify some of the material, temporal, and spatial "props" you use to help maintain your everyday self? Do you sit in the same seat at the dining table while you drink your coffee before you go to work or school in the morning? If not, in what other ways do you display or enact a core sense of self throughout your everyday activities?

■ Conclusion

The focus of this book is on the application of sociological principles, concepts, and ideas to your everyday life. It begins with the assumption that the value of sociology lies in its ability to provide fresh insight into events and situations that might ordinarily be taken for granted.

Space, time, gesture, and posture norms are examples of the underlying patterns in everyday life. These patterns become obvious only when we begin to look closely at everyday phenomena. Moreover, social order persists only because we share knowledge of an extraordinary range of cultural expectations. Beyond knowledge of the norms of social conventions based on these expectations, however, the meanings we attach to behaviors vary from context to context. Social norms only provide the boundaries for our encounters. We must, in addition, interpret the meanings our behaviors have in a particular setting.

While much of the analysis in this book concentrates on face-to-face interaction, we also point out that the dramas of daily life are played out within larger institutional and historical settings. As members of schools, families, churches or synagogues, and a multitude of other bureaucracies and institutions, we are obliged to behave in certain ways. Social structures diminish personal choice and discretion. At the same time, people manipulate social structures. Human behavior therefore is the product of neither the social structures enveloping individuals nor the individual's free will and choice. Rather, it is the result of a dynamic interplay between cultural expectations and people's interpretations of situations.

The notion that people must define and interpret the meanings of both their own and others' behaviors is basic to the perspective that guides our inquiry in this book—symbolic interaction. An important idea in this perspective is that individuals collectively shape, mold, and refashion their social worlds through the process of communicating with others and responding to their communications. Each chapter concludes with the mention of a specific type of "self" that is related to or emerges from the processes discussed in that chapter. This will help highlight the connections between individual selves and their social environments.

Because the analysis of interaction must be based on some clear set of ideas about human encounters and communication, our development of this perspective continues in the next chapter with consideration of the following issues:

1. What is the significance of interpretation in human interaction and communication?

2. How do objects take on meaning?

3. How do individuals come to evaluate the meaning of their own and others' acts?

4. What are the sources of innovation and unpredictability, and thus of nonconformity, in social life?

Definitions

acting situation: The immediate place or circumstances of an interaction (for example, a classroom) considered by individuals as they give meanings to their own and others' behaviors.

bourgeoisie: Karl Marx originally applied this term to the owners of the means of production in capitalist society who are concerned with minimizing costs and maximizing profits.

cultural expectations: Broad and widely shared cultural rules that reflect mutually held assumptions about proper and conventional behaviors in various social contexts.

culture: The complex whole that includes knowledge, beliefs, art, customs, morals, and any other capabilities and habits acquired and shared in common by the members of a society. A group's culture provides a blueprint for living, which is transmitted to subsequent generations.

definition of the situation: W. I. Thomas's concept, "What people believe to be real is real in its consequences" (Thomas and Thomas, 1928), which refers to an interactant's understanding of a particular setting.

everyday interactions: Those patterns of communication with others that regularly comprise our everyday lives.

intimate distance: The area around a person within which the most intimate encounters take place. In American society, intimate distance is between 0 and 18 inches.

kinesics: A field of inquiry in the social sciences in which people's communication through body gesture and posture is studied.

macrosociological investigation: Social science research that centers attention on the ways social structures function or society as a whole operates.

microsociological investigation: Social science research that centers attention on the ways in which people's daily, face-to-face communications are organized.

nonverbal communication: Any of the modes of communication (such as gesture or facial expression) other than verbal language.

norms: The range of rules, both written and unwritten, that dictate appropriate ways of acting in various social situations. Most social norms are unwritten and, once learned, are followed virtually automatically. *Laws* are norms of sufficient importance to society that they are written down. *Social conventions* are synonyms for shared norms in a society.

personal distance: The space maintained between a person and others during most routine interactions (such as conversations with friends). In American society, personal distance is between 1.5 and 4 feet.

personal space: The space that immediately surrounds a person's body. Others normally do not violate this space without permission. People's sense of personal space varies by culture and may expand or contract in particular social situations.

process of interpretation: The internal dialogues people have with themselves about the meanings of their own or others' behaviors in various acting situations.

proxemics: A field of inquiry in the social sciences in which the rules that govern people's use of space in their everyday relations are studied.

public distance: The space maintained between an individual and the audience for presentations such as public speeches. In American society, public distance is greater than 12 feet.

reification: The concept that social structures have a life of their own, independent of the individuals who ultimately create those structures.

shared meaning structures: The range of consensually held meanings about the world held by the members of a group or society. A shared meaning structure constitutes a group's view of reality.

social bonds: The connections of individuals to their societies that create feelings of loyalty, belonging, and integration.

social distance: The space maintained between a person and others during such casual gatherings as parties. In American society, social distance is between 4 and 12 feet.

social structure: The totality of social institutions such as government, the family, and religion that influences how individuals behave in a society.

social worlds: The totality of the various social locations that individuals occupy in society. Members of different classes and racial, religious, and ethnic groups inhabit different social worlds.

symbolic interactionist perspective: A theoretical perspective in sociology that focuses attention on the processes through which people interpret and give meanings to the objects, events, and situations that make up their social worlds.

territoriality: The space that individuals or groups believe they "own." Groups will take measures to protect their territory from "invaders." Studies of animal groups show that they too operate within territories, which they protect from outsiders.

Discussion Questions

1. Do you agree that there are no behaviors which are intrinsically deviant, that what we mean by deviance, mental illness, or insanity is a thoroughly cultural product?

2. What are some of the background expectancies concerning space, time, and gesture that operate in the classroom for this course?

3. Under what kinds of conditions do you believe people become most strategic in formulating their behaviors? What do they have to gain or lose in such situations?

4. In which aspects of your own life do you feel you have greatest freedom of choice, and in which areas do you feel most constrained by social structures? How much do you think people, individually or collectively, can change institutions such as universities?

5. What is your definition of *science*? What special problems does the social scientist studying human communication face?

6. Suppose your instructor asked you to observe behaviors in a local bar frequented by college students. What kinds of behaviors might it be important to record? What kinds of things might you be able to learn about interaction by observing behavior in a context like this? What general issues about human behavior could be examined by observing bar behavior? Where else might you investigate these same issues?

2

Socialization and the
Construction of Social Reality

CHAPTER OUTLINE

- ■ Symbolic Communication
- ■ Development of the Self through Interaction with Others
- ■ Social Reality and Nonconformity
- ■ Conclusion

In chapter 1 we stressed the idea that humans are not simply rule-following creatures. Norms or social conventions set the boundaries within which human interactions may occur, and situations are grounded in cultural expectations that the participants will interact in conventional ways. Through the process of interpretation, however, individuals may redefine situations while reinterpreting the behaviors expected of them. The symbolic interactionist perspective provides a picture of social life that neither reifies social systems nor sees individuals as perfectly free to fashion society (Hewitt and Shulman, 2010). Perceived meanings of behaviors are always liable to revision as individuals piece together information about themselves, others, and the arenas in which they interact. The social world cannot be seen as independent of people's definitions of it. Symbolic interactionists see meaning as variable and emergent. Meaning arises and is transformed as people define and act in situations. It is not merely dictated by culture. These points are cogently captured in Herbert Blumer's statement of the central premises of symbolic interaction (1969:2):

1. Human beings act toward things or situations on the basis of the meanings that the things or situations have for them.

2. These meanings are derived from or arise out of the social interactions individuals have with others.

3. These meanings are handled or modified through the interpretive process used by individuals in dealing with the things or situations they encounter.

These three premises (the first one in particular) call attention to the fact that things as such have no inherent meaning. Whatever meanings they have derive from the responses individuals make to them. And those responses are often learned behaviors and ideas. It is in this sense that humans live in a world of symbols and interact through **symbolic communication.**

The sociological study of everyday interactions analyzes how people through their communication with others socially construct and use the meanings that they then confer on things. The existence of shared meaning structures—that is to say, common definitions of **social reality**—must be assumed and taken for granted. But not all social groups construct identical versions of reality. Behaviors that deviate widely from what is expected become defined as **nonconformity** and can often come under attack by the majority, those in power, or both. In this chapter we will examine how symbols are used in the social construction of multiple social realities. Particular reference will be made to the process of *socialization*, which informs us about behaviors expected or considered "deviant" in our society.

■ Symbolic Communication

You may be sitting on a chair while reading this book. To know the "meaning" of a chair, you might reasonably rely on the definition of it as an object "on which you sit." That is what a chair is—something to sit on. An object's meaning, in other words, is defined in terms of how it is used. But there is nothing inherent in the object called a chair that dictates you must respond to it by sitting on it. Indeed, there are other uses; in movies set in the Wild West, for example, chairs are used as weapons in barroom brawls. And chairs come in all sorts of shapes and sizes and are made of a multitude of materials. Yet most people who understand the word "chair" will still point to these different objects to sit on and still call them each a "chair" because of their respective "chairness."

Our range of responses to an object is dependent on the social and cultural circles in which we live our daily lives. If strangers from a planet where chairs are nonexistent were to land on Earth, they would have difficulty figuring out that this object called a "chair" is something to sit on. We have to learn the meanings of things through symbolic communication with others.

The Difference between Symbols and Signs

Symbols are words, acts, and objects used intentionally to communicate and represent something. When we say that symbols represent something we are saying that they are, in Mead's terms, "meaningful" acts—they make sense to the person using them (Mead, 1934). This quality of symbols makes communication possibilities infinitely greater, complex ideas possible, and thinking (talking to oneself) a central characteristic of the symbol user (Charon, 2002).

Words are symbols; in fact, the only function of words is to be symbolic. Objects also can be made into symbols; for example, the U.S. flag symbolizes patriotism, a gold ring symbolizes marriage, a dove symbolizes peace. Acts also can be symbolic, such as shaking a fist at someone to indicate anger.

The physical characteristics of symbols can be irrelevant to their meaning. To Christians, a crucifix has meaning because it represents (or better, re-presents) a historical event, the Crucifixion of Jesus Christ, which they have designated as a divine event. Whether a crucifix is made of gold, iron, or wood is irrelevant to Christians, who define it as a holy object and respond to it reverently. As in the example of the chair, however, if strangers from another culture who hadn't heard of Christianity were to happen upon a crucifix, there is no way that the physical characteristics of the object would indicate to them what it represents. They would have to learn that meaning through communication with others. The crucifix also evokes a different response (that is, has a different meaning) for non-Christians, such as Jews, Muslims, or atheists.

Only humans assign meanings to things. Symbols mobilize our responses to the environment and help us bring together, or conceptualize, aspects of it. In contrast, animals live in a world of signs. A **sign** differs from a symbol in that its meanings remain constant. Its meaning is identified with its physical form and may be grasped through the senses (Becker, 1962:20). Animals, in short, can respond to their environments only in terms dictated by their physiology. Only humans, through symbolic behavior, are able to transcend the limits of their bodies through the development of such phenomena as technology and science. In so doing, we transform the environment through the meanings that we collectively, in communication with others, confer on it. As Ernest Becker put it, "Nature provides all life with H_2O, but only man could create a world in which 'holy' water generates a special stimulus" (1962:20).

The claim that human beings' capacity for symbolization distinguishes us from the lower animals is often disputed (see box). This is even truer in regard to animals higher up the evolutionary scale, such as chimpanzees and other primates.

Can Animals Communicate?

One of the most interesting and hardest-to-solve puzzles in the social sciences is whether primates are capable of any form of symbolic communication. As early as 1748, based on the notion that possession of language alone distinguished humans from other animals, Julien de La Mettrie proposed the experiment of teaching a young chimpanzee language through sign and vocal instruction. Although he published anonymously and his publisher, when hauled before the authorities, claimed not to know him, La Mettrie had to flee France and Holland (Leiber, 1995). It was not until the 20th century that systematic attempts to teach apes to speak were carried out. The question of whether apes can use language, however, remains unanswered.

In the 1960s, Beatrice and Allen Gardner, realizing that chimps in the wild appear to communicate mainly through gestures, began to teach American Sign Language to a chimp named Washoe. The Gardners never used verbal speech in Washoe's presence, only sign language. By the age of five Washoe had acquired a vocabulary of 160 signs and could put together "words" to form new "sentences" (Gardner and Gardner, 1969). Since then, many other chimpanzees have been taught sign language and to use other word symbols. A chimp named Lana at the Yerkes Primate Research Center in Atlanta learned to use various symbols on a computer keyboard to ask for food, companionship, and music. A bonobo named Kanzi, described as "the ape at the brink of the human mind" (Savage-Rumbaugh, 1998), learned his first words merely by watching his mother. Perhaps most famous is Koko, a gorilla who rhymes and jokes, makes up words when she does not know the name for an object ("finger bracelet" for ring), and clearly expresses emo-

There's No Such Thing as a Bad Dog

You may have had success teaching your dog to sit or to bark when it wants to go outside, but this does not mean you have an obedient pet. At the same time, a dog that ignores the command to sit or soils the carpet is not being disobedient. The reason is that the lower animals cannot be held responsible for either following rules or breaking them. Teachers often find it difficult to convince students that animals have no regard for rules. The following dialogue from one of our classes illustrates the rationale for the argument that animals react to the physical properties of objects (signs) without endowing them with the meanings attached to them (symbols).

Teacher: Let me try to illustrate this distinction between animal and human behavior by asking you this question: Can animals be deviant?

Student A: Sure, don't we punish animals for doing things we don't like? I have a dog that used to urinate in the house. After I gave the dog a few whacks with a rolled-up newspaper, he stopped doing it. Now all he's got to do is see the paper and he runs under the bed.

Teacher: But is the dog really responding to your commands in terms of symbols? Or is it merely responding to a particular physical stimulus without giving it any meaning? Let me try to make myself clear on this. You can get a dog to stop at a red light, a traffic light, by physically punishing it if it doesn't. But you must understand that that red light, like your rolled-up newspaper, can never be more than a sign to the dog. When we stop at a red light, on the other hand, we can think about the meaning behind the light. Why is it there? What would happen were it not there? You see, we understand the necessity for stopping at the red light. We recognize that people's safety depends on it. That's the essential difference.

Student B: I still don't understand why it's not possible for a dog to be deviant. The dog is breaking rules. Isn't that deviance?

Teacher: Deviance itself is a symbolic phenomenon. I mean, what is deviance? Is there any social act that is intrinsically deviant? Like anything else, it's human beings who confer the label *deviance* on a particular act. After all, people establish the social rules in the first place, and the departures get labeled as deviance. Can animals establish those rules?

Most students eventually acknowledge that animals neither make nor break the rules governing their conduct.

*For an in-depth ethnographic study of relationships between people and dogs, see *Understanding Dogs: Living and Working with Canine Companions* by Clinton Sanders (1999).

tions—you've probably heard about her love for kittens, and the sadness she experienced when her kitten "All Ball" (who was named by Koko) was killed.

In spite of such accomplishments, some researchers have questioned whether the apes had learned to use language the way humans do. Although they had clearly learned to use hand signs or symbols ("words") in appropriate situations, did they understand what the signs or symbols represented?

The PBS series *Nature* ran a miniseries called "Inside the Animal Mind" (2000), which explored the topics "Are Animals Intelligent?", "Do Animals Have Emotions?", and "Animal Consciousness." Some of the more intriguing findings included the following:

1. Honeybees deprived of their normal route between hive and nectar source complete their missions anyway, suggesting that they are able

to form pictures in their minds of the land surrounding the hive—a sort of mental map.

2. Ravens have the ability to solve difficult puzzles, such as untangling a knotted string to free up a treat or figuring out how to steal fish by hauling in an angler's untended line.

3. Chimps and elephants appear to be aware of death, grieving when family members die (as did Koko the gorilla when her kitten was killed).

4. Dolphins appear to recognize themselves in mirrors, and exhibit a keen awareness of the status and identity of other dolphins in their highly social groups.

Although examples of this sort are intriguing, they do not resolve the question of whether animals are self-aware in the way humans are. The debate is not whether animals can learn. The ongoing controversy is whether animals are capable of picturing the future, planning, improvising, and symbolically communicating with one another. There is no doubt that animals have managed to learn a code that includes some of the characteristic features of human communication. Nevertheless, there remains a gap between human language and communications of the sort demonstrated in research studies. Recent studies by sociologists have shown the important roles that animals play in the lives of humans as pets, companions, and interacting others (Jerolmack, 2009). Even though animals are essentially limited to the symbols they have been taught by humans, as Leslie Irvine (2008) argues, they can still develop something akin to what we think of as a "self." Humans, however, have the exceptional ability to continually create new, more complex verbal communications.

One way to frame this argument is to say that the major distinction between humans and nonhuman animals is that only human beings possess a culture, or collectively shared ideas, concepts, beliefs, and knowledge that can be transmitted to succeeding generations (see chapter 1). Lower animals may be said to operate within *social structures* in the sense that there is an order and predictability to their behaviors. This is a consequence of primarily biological instinct, however. Culture, in contrast, is a symbolic creation, and language has an important role in its construction.

In one of a series of early studies, Wolfgang Kohler (1927) placed a stack of bananas outside a chimpanzee's cage, just beyond its reach. He also placed a number of sticks inside the cage that could be fitted together to make a longer stick, thus enabling the animal to reach the fruit. Now it might be said that when, after much trial and error, the chimp fits the sticks together to reach the bananas, it has at that moment gained insight into a very abstract idea—the concept of addition. But—and this is the important point—without verbal language, the chimpanzee cannot transmit that abstract idea to others of its species. If a particular chimp has discovered the principle of addition, it remains, without language, forever its individual possession. It never becomes a collective, cultural possession that can be elaborated on to produce new mathematical principles and eventually such revolutionary discoveries as computers. In this respect, language reflects and is part of human culture. Language is also essential to the continuance of a culture and ongoing changes in it.

We are not suggesting that animals do not communicate. They do. For example, bees can, with great precision, communicate the location of food *via* physical movement, and sea animals (whales and dolphins) communicate danger warnings over long distances. Such communications are rooted in instinct, however. There is never any variation or elaboration of the available messages that can be transmitted. The content of the messages is genetically determined.

In contrast, it is the essence of human communication that there is no intrinsic or built-in meaning to the words constituting the language used. The same words can carry different meanings for different persons and groups, and certain words, used in particular contexts, can be considered either obscene or acceptable. The "N-word" is one of the most glaring examples. Randall Kennedy's popular and provocative book *Nigger: The Strange Career of a Troublesome Word* (2002) shows history and development of the changing social rules for those who are and who are not allowed to use the word. The meanings of words are constantly subject to change. Another good example is the word "gay," which now is more commonly construed as "homosexual" than "happy and excited," an earlier definition.

The Liberating Effects of Symbolic Communication

Symbolic communication (or symbolic behavior) also permits us to, in effect, liberate ourselves from the physical constraints of time and space. If we create a word, or verbal symbol, such as "house" to refer to the physical object called a house, we are free to talk about, think about, and refer to houses without the necessity of having a house in sight. It is possible to refer to houses that existed in the past as well as to conjure up houses that might exist in the future, not just in the United States, but elsewhere—even on other planets! The range of possible habitats for humans is limited only by our imaginations rather than by our physiology, as space trips to the moon and experiments in living under the oceans have demonstrated.

The use of symbols not only permits us to step outside the particular physical setting in which we find ourselves but, more important, it permits us to step outside ourselves. We can look at ourselves from the standpoint of others, put ourselves in their place, and anticipate how they are going to react to us. We can, in effect, look at ourselves as if we were objects and anticipate how others are going to respond to those objects. Verbal symbols (language) are critical in this situation, since the spoken word is heard simultaneously by both the speaker and those to whom it is addressed. The speaker can react to the word while monitoring the responses of others to what is being said.

George Herbert Mead, a major formulator of the symbolic interactionist perspective in the early 20th century, described symbolic communication as a "conversation of gestures," initiated by one individual giving a significant symbol—a gesture that arouses a similar response both in the one employing the gesture and in those who perceive it. Significant symbols may be behavioral, but humans rely for the most part on language. Humans produce responses in themselves and others by using words, and thus signaling their intentions or plans of action to one another. The key to this process is the fact that significant symbols arouse the same or a similar response in the one using the symbol and those who perceive it. Thus it is the significant symbol that is the basis for shared meanings in human life. For example, when you say to someone that you are sad, not only do you presumably arouse in that person an attitude of sympathy toward you, but you also stimulate yourself to feel sympathetic toward yourself. By thus arousing the same or a similar response in self and other, both see things in the same way (Hewitt and Shulman, 2010).

The ability to evaluate our own behaviors objectively, from the perspective of others, is necessary if we are to become "normal" functioning members of society. Once we acquire that ability, we possess what Mead calls **the self.** This conception of self relies on the premise that it arises from a process of learning through interaction.

■ Development of the Self through Interaction with Others

Just as symbolic communication requires an audience to which communications can be directed, so is the self formed and transformed through interaction with others. You were not born with a preformed self. Through the use of symbols you have learned to take on the attitudes, values, and moods appropriate to the particular social circles in which you participate. Through the reflected appraisals of others, you have come to define yourself as a certain kind of person.

More than a century ago, Charles Horton Cooley used the metaphor of a looking glass, or mirror, to characterize this process:

> A self idea . . . seems to have three principal elements: the imagination of our appearance to the other person; the imagination of his judgment of that appearance; and some sort of self-feeling, such as pride or mortification. (1902:152)

As people interact, based on their respective identities, they develop images of one another. People imagine their own appearance to others in terms of these images. That is, the person forms an image of the other, then imagines his or her appearance to the other from the standpoint of that image and feels good or bad accordingly. Cooley explained the **looking glass self** with the couplet: "Each to each a looking glass, reflects the other that doth pass" (Cooley, 1902).

Another way to think about it is as follows:

> I am not what I think I am.
> I am not what you think I am.
> Rather, **I am what I think you think I am.**

In fact, you have many identities that are established and validated (or invalidated) through the responses others make to you. The psychologist William James suggested in 1892 that humans have as many selves as they have memberships in various social groups. We belong to numerous social circles simultaneously—the family, a church or synagogue, friendship cliques—and adjust our behaviors to take into account the particular situation and the others with whom we are interacting. Others do the same with us. One does not act in a classroom, for example, as one does in a morgue—at least, we hope not! As Mead noted:

> We carry on a whole series of different relationships to different people. We are one thing to one man and another to another. We divide ourselves up into all sorts of different selves with reference to our acquaintances. We discuss politics with one and religion with another. There are all sorts of different selves answering to all sorts of different social reactions. (1934:142)

Role-Taking

The capacity to adjust one's behavior in response to particular social situations is termed **role-taking** by Mead. From the symbolic interaction perspective, the development of the self is inextricably bound up with the capacity to take the role of others (see box on the next page). Every act of role-taking simultaneously involves two dimensions: (1) people anticipating the responses that others are going to make toward them, and (2) people evaluating their *own behavior* in terms of the anticipated responses of others.

Such expressions as being proud of yourself or being ashamed of yourself illustrate the principle of role-taking. There is no way to experience such reactions as shame or guilt without introspectively evaluating and appraising our own behavior while taking into account the actions of others. It is in this sense that the self is both the subject and the object of our own acts. We engage in a behavior as an acting subject. We then introspectively evaluate the meaning of that behavior to ourself and to others based on the responses they have made to it—that is, we reflect back on our own behavior, viewing it much like an "object" to be studied and evaluated. Such internal evaluations then influence our future course of action. If, after thinking about our own behavior and how others have responded to it, we feel ashamed of something we did, for example, we will probably try to avoid acting that way again. We also can imagine how our doing something might appear to others—we might look foolish in their eyes, for example—before we actually engage in such actions. Based on our interpretations of how others might respond to that behavior, we can then modify our course of action to avoid possible embarrassment. The ability of people to both act and reflect on their actions from various perspectives lies at the root of what is distinctively human.

There is an important difference between role-taking and role-playing. Role-taking—the process of imaginatively putting yourself in another's

Put Up Your Hands! (Know What I Mean?)

For two people to interact or communicate, each must understand the point of view of the other. This may mean you have to mentally place yourself in some unlikely positions. If a robber tells you to put your hands in the air, for example, you have to think like the robber as well as the victim to behave as you are expected to. If you don't, you may save your wallet but not your skin.

Blumer (1969) suggests that a robbery can only occur if both the robber and the victim can put themselves in the place of the other person. Blumer imagines a scenario in which a man with a gun attempts to rob another man. The robber can only understand the logic of his own demand for the victim to put his hands in the air by being able to imagine what it means to face the barrel end of a gun. In fact, the robber could not even make the verbal demand ("Put your hands up in the air") unless he understood the meaning it would have for the victim. The victim, likewise, "has to be able to see the command from the standpoint of the robber who gives the command; he has to grasp the intention and forthcoming action of the robber" (p. 10). Interaction is always oriented to the future, to what the other person will do, and the only way to anticipate the future is through this kind of mutual role-taking.

A newspaper account told how robbers broke in on a party and demanded that everyone turn over their valuables. The guests, thinking it was a prank, refused to cooperate. They told the robbers to stop joking, while they continued to joke about it themselves. Faced with this totally unexpected reaction, the robbers were stymied in their efforts and finally fled the party empty-handed. They were arrested later trying to break into another house. Still confused, they told the police of their experience at the party.

Thus, even robbers must count on the mutual understanding of their victims if they are to make a success of their way of life. When the victim refuses to validate the robber's identity as a robber and defines him instead as a prankster, the robber must be willing to assume a new identity—even that of murderer—if the robbery is to succeed.

place and considering what they expect of you, or how they might respond to behaviors you are thinking of enacting—precedes role-playing. It is on the basis of role-taking that we fashion the roles we actually play and the role performances we undertake. We need to understand what is expected of us before we can play a role successfully. Note that our interpretations of others' perception and their actual perceptions of us may not always be aligned and can, of course, lead to misunderstandings, conflict, and the dreaded social faux pas.

The Socialization Process

The process through which individuals learn what others expect of them is called **socialization.** According to Mead, the development of the self occurs in childhood in two distinct phases of this process: the play stage and the game stage. Though Mead's early 20th-century writings on childhood play are probably the most important interactionist statement on self-development, we need to consider that "childhood" itself is a socially constructed category that can differ from one society to the next. For our purposes here, we can agree that childhood is at least a somewhat stable category of young persons who learn from adults and other children as they develop a self as well as strategies to engage with the world around them (Pugh, 2009; Corsaro, 2010).

The Play Stage.   The **play stage,** according to Mead, is the period in which children develop the ability to actually take on the characteristics associated with others in particular roles. They become able to look at themselves from the point of view of others. During this stage a girl, for example, learns to put herself in the role of a doctor, teacher, mother, athlete, or TV star. She is able to cast herself as a social object and then respond in the role of others to that object. In playing doctor, for example, she may talk to others as she interprets how a doctor might actually talk to her. During the play stage a girl or boy comes to realize that there is a direct linkage between a person's status (mother, father, police officer, and so on) and behavior. The importance of "child's play" in creating durable male and female roles, for better and for worse, has been noted by social scientists (Cahill, 1994; Blaise, 2012).

For Mead, the most important quality of children's role-playing during the play period is its unorganized character. During this period children pass from playing one role to another in an inconsistent, erratic fashion. They have proceeded beyond sheer imitation of others' behaviors, but they do not yet have any *unified* conception of themselves. In referring to the play stage, Mead notes:

> The child is one thing at one time and another at another, and what he is at one moment does not determine what he is at another. That is both the charm of childhood as well as its inadequacy. You cannot count on the child; you cannot assume that all the things he does are going to determine what he will do at any moment. He is not organized into a whole. The child has no definite character, no definite personality. (1934:159)

In the play stage children may be able to take the roles of particular others toward themselves, but as yet they fail to see how the behavior of others toward them represents the expectations of larger social groups. They are unable to view themselves from the point of view of the community or, even more abstractly, the society. They may understand, for example, what parents mean when they tell them to be good. They will learn later that it is not only their parents who expect them to be good, but others in the neighborhood, the school, and the larger society as well.

The Game Stage.   After children have mastered the ability to take the roles of particular others, they are presented more and more with the task of responding to the expectations of several persons simultaneously. According to Mead, it is participation in the **game stage** that equips the child for this task. Games are distinguished from play by the presence of an organized body of *rules* to which the participants must orient their responses. Rather than reacting to particular individuals, as in the case of play, children must now begin to see themselves in relation to *all* the roles played by the other participants.

To play baseball or fast-pitch softball, for example, a girl must know how her position (third base, let's say) relates to those of every other person on the team. When a ball is hit to her, she must realize that she should throw it to first base, not because she likes the person on first base but because that is what the rules of the game dictate in most circumstances. She must also conceptualize how her team stands in relation to the opposing team. She must throw to first base to put the batter out. That is what the game is all about.

In effect, then, for the game of baseball or softball to be played, all the participants must have a conception of how to act in relation to their own team and the opposing one. In doing so each player develops a conception of how a particular position is really part of a larger social organization called "the team." Mead observes that in the game stage, "a definite unity . . . is introduced into the organization of other selves!" In the play stage, by contrast, there is "a simple succession of one role after another" (1934:158–59).

If you think of the baseball or softball game as a metaphor for the organization of society in general, you can see that we are truly functioning members of a social order only when we know the basic "ground rules" and can organize our actions with reference to the whole group. Mead's terms for all of those countless others whose behaviors and expectations are considered and interpreted by individuals in formulating their own behaviors is the **generalized other.** The generalized other, it should be stressed, does not refer to any particular, concrete person. Rather, it is an abstract configuration of all the relevant *roles* and *rules* that we must take into account to function successfully in any social environment. In the case of the baseball or softball game, the team constitutes the most important generalized other to which the players must orient their actions.

The socialization process through which the child eventually comprehends societal expectations can be illustrated by an example from Peter

Berger and Thomas Luckmann's classic work, *The Social Construction of Reality* (1967). They note:

> There is a progression from "Mummy is angry with me now" to "Mummy is angry with me *whenever* I spill the soup." As additional significant others (father, grandfather, older sister, and so on) support the mother's negative attitude toward soup-spilling the generality of the norm is subjectively extended. The decisive step comes when the child recognizes that *everybody* is against soup-spilling, and the norm is generalized to "*One* does not spill soup"—"one" being himself as part of a generality that includes, in principle, all of society insofar as it is significant to the child. (1967:132–33; emphasis in original)

Components of the Self: The I and the Me

If we were to look at Mead's conception of the socialization process and the development of the self uncritically, we might be led to believe that all our behaviors are totally determined by others, leaving no room for us to do anything but conform completely to their expectations. This robotlike image does not align well with either our knowledge of people or our own life experiences, however. Although we are constrained by society, we do have some freedom of action. Mead takes this into account by introducing the idea that the self has two components—"the I" and "the me."

In chapter 1 we emphasized that everyday life must be analyzed in a way that takes into account both the expectations of society and the unique, individual interpretations of the world that people make. On the one hand, we formulate our behaviors in terms of our interpretations of the broad expectations of others in general, represented by the concept of the generalized other. Ultimately a society is possible only because the individuals in it carry around a picture of that society in their heads. People's behaviors constructed in terms of that picture of the generalized other reflect what Mead termed **the me.** The me represents the more conventional aspects of the self—those aspects that respond to social conventions. At the same time, because we are self-conscious, reflective beings, we can never completely predict what our own responses will be in any situation. **The I,** in contrast to the me, consists of those particular idiosyncratic, personal factors that enter into our communications with others.

In the previous example of the ball game, the third baseman, like every other player on the team, no doubt wants to play well. She wants her team to win. In that sense she organizes her own behaviors (the me) in terms of trying to follow the rules of the game and meet the expectations of fellow team members (the generalized other). But just how well she will play in a game cannot be predicted in advance. Her mind may wander, for example, and she may drop an easy pop-up. She might get angry enough at the umpire to show it and get thrown out of the game. The range of such unanticipated, novel, subjective responses reflects the operation of the I.

Development of the self is thus an ongoing process in which our actions are shaped by the continuous conversations we have with our "selves."

These conversations have two components. We ask ourselves: (1) What does society (the generalized other) want me to do in this situation? and (2) How do I personally feel about these expectations? Do I respond enthusiastically, angrily, halfheartedly? We are, in sum, only partially the product of the roles we learn from childhood onward. Our behaviors are affected not only by all our various learned social roles but also by our personal, subjective interpretations of the situations we face. This is the essence of *the self as process*. There is an impulse to act, imagined responses to such an act, imagined alternative actions, and some eventual resolution of the inner dialogue into some overt course of action. We can see this process in what takes place when, for example, we feel caught between what we want to do and what others want us to do. Suppose you have been invited to a party, but you would really rather spend a quiet evening at home. You might say to yourself, "If I go, I won't have a good time because I'm tired and don't feel like partying. But if I don't go, I'll hurt my friends' feelings. Maybe they'll understand if I explain that I'm tired. But what if they remember that I didn't go out with them last weekend? I guess I'll go but not stay long." You can hear the alternation between the I and the me in this internal conversation (Hewitt and Shulman, 2010).

Gender Identity.   Through taking the role of the generalized other, children learn the rules of public conduct and acquire skills in applying those rules in everyday interaction. A fundamental aspect of this process is the acquisition of **gender identity**.

In keeping with the premise that identity is socially anchored, interactionists reject the idea that gender identity is biologically determined. Rather, it is a product of social interaction.

> Gender identity is constructed as others reproduce sexually differentiated behavior by reinforcing interaction that is in keeping with gender ideals. The social construction of gender continues as children respond to others' expectations in a process of unwitting participation—a process that centers on children's active, but unaware, participation in fashioning gender. (Musolf, 1996:311)

To a great extent, children learn to become self-regulating participants in society. By displaying masculine and feminine behavior—that is, by claiming a gendered identity—individuals conform to the gender ideals of society. Thus, notions of gender not only are socially constructed but are reproduced. Gender-segregation behaviors are rehearsed in childhood and performed in adulthood (Cahill, 1994).

Assuming that the world as we know it is what we want to reproduce, gender ideals remain relatively static as conforming behavior is rewarded. To the extent that nonconformity (deviance) is no longer subject to punishment, gender ideals become more flexible and social change occurs. Each generation modifies gender ideals. Based on interviews with parents of preschool children, Emily Kane (2006) found that parents across racial and class backgrounds welcome what they perceive as gender nonconformity among their young daughters but tend to support the often rewarded ideals of masculinity for their sons. "Several [parents] noted that they make an effort to encourage their young daughters to aspire to traditionally male occupations and commented favorably on their daughters as 'tomboyish,' 'rough and tumble,' and 'competitive athletically'" (Kane, 2006:157). Boys, however, were expected to take on masculine traits at an early age, and parents reinforced these ideals by trying to thwart their desire to play with Barbie dolls. One father said that if his son "asked for a Barbie doll, I would probably say no, you don't want [that], girls play with [that], boys play with trucks" (p. 161). So while some norms of gender identities may change, others remain more static through the reinforcement of parents—which often begins before birth or adoption (Kane, 2009)—and society at large.

Socialization in general and gender socialization in particular vary across racial/ethnic lines and social/class boundaries. Earlier perspectives on race tend to be assimilationist, assuming that African Americans embrace and pass on to their children the gender norms of the dominant white society. An Afrocentric perspective challenges this view, maintaining that the unique historical experiences of blacks have worked to de-emphasize rigid gender distinctions and that relative gender neutrality exists in black families' child-rearing practices. Research by Shirley Hill and Joey Sprague (1999) supports this assertion. Whereas working-class whites in their study emphasize obedience and respect for boys, and lower-middle-class whites emphasize happiness and self-esteem for girls, blacks seem to make fewer gender distinctions overall. Other research on early childhood socialization suggests that Hispanic parents differ from parents of other ethnic groups in their child-rearing values and the interpersonal behavior they want their children to display at home and school (Zayas and Solari, 1994). And research on social class differences continues to find greater gender stereotyping among parents who are lower in social status, less educated, and full-time homemakers (Hoffman and Kloska, 1995). It seems clear that race and social class interact to shape the intergenerational construction of gender in families. Parents operate within their own specific economic and social constraints. In struggling within these constraints and with gendered expectations—both their own and the ones they read in others—they draw on the values they learned from their own families and communities, which are marked by race and class. "In parenting, and probably in the rest of life, race, class, and gender dynamics interact" (Hill and Sprague, 1999:497). Adopting an "intersectional" lens that recognizes such dynamics can be useful for understanding the ways that the socially constructed norms of race, class, and gender are reproduced and enacted (Denis, 2008).

The Interdependence of Self and Society. Mead's conception of the self refers, in the fullest sense, to the interdependence of the individual and the society. He locates the self in society. The creation of the self is an ongoing process that emerges from the person's interactions with others in society.

There is a point in the development of the self when people can view themselves from the perspective of others. At this point the person is able to treat the world as a symbolic entity—to endow the world with meaning and order. This capacity for symbolic behavior makes it possible for humans to coordinate their actions with those of others and thereby modify or even substantially transform society. The self is simultaneously a reflection of society as it exists and a source of change in it.

Our daily lives are describable in terms of these theoretical distinctions. Everyday behaviors represent a combination of conformity and novelty, of response to the expectations of others and more impulsive personal reactions to situations. In any situation, we cannot ourselves know exactly how we will act. Nothing is predetermined. We know the parameters within which we are expected to act, but such knowledge does not guarantee complete predictability of behavior. In a fundamental way, we really do not know how we are going to respond in any situation until we actually begin to act. We cannot, for example, fully anticipate feelings and expressions of anger, pleasure, relief, indifference, confusion, and the like as we move through even the most routine day-to-day situations.

Human behavior, in Mead's terms, is constructed through the interchange of the two aspects of the self—the I and the me. The me encourages conformity to societal expectations and reinforces existing social arrangements. By contrast, the I permits personal interpretations which allow for nonconformity, the construction of multiple social realities, and ultimately social change (see box).

■ Social Reality and Nonconformity

Social reality should not be thought of as a "thing" existing objectively "out there" in the world. Rather, reality is something that human beings continually negotiate, re-create, alter, and disagree on. Humans construct so much of the reality within which they live that it is difficult to identify one reality that exists for all people (Sarbin and Kitsuse, 1994). In a real sense reality is the product of a political process in which different individuals and groups vie to have their idea of reality become accepted as *the* reality for everyone (see chapter 6). The successful definition of alternate realities as inauthentic, pathological, or deviant reinforces the dominant view of reality and makes it appear more immutable and concrete than it actually is (Berger and Luckmann, 1967).

In our daily activities, we assume that we are responding to the same realities as others. Suppose, for example, that the clock radio awakens you with a news report. Simply in order to understand the news, you must assume that the words being used to describe the events mean roughly the same thing to the newscaster as they do to you. The newscaster makes the same assumption. In reporting some catastrophe such as an earthquake or tornado, for example, it is assumed that the listener knows what the phenomenon is. Rarely does a newscaster attempt to define such words as "tornado" or "earthquake."

In the Absence of Human Interaction

In November 1970, a nearly blind woman appeared at a Los Angeles welfare office with her 13½-year-old daughter. From about 20 months of age, "Genie" had been kept in a back room by her 70-year-old father (who later committed suicide), isolated from language (and significant human interaction), and frequently restrained on a potty chair. Genie was incontinent, could not chew solid food, spat indiscriminately, walked with a "bunny-like" gait, and could not speak. She was placed in the Children's Hospital of Los Angeles where she flourished amid the attention of psychiatrists and psychologists. She learned words, became more outgoing, and was able to communicate emotionally. Susan Curtiss, the linguist who worked with Genie, was particularly interested in testing the "critical period" theory of language acquisition, which is premised on the belief that if language is not learned by puberty, normal language development will not occur. Her book, *Genie: A Psycholinguistic Story of a Modern "Wild Child"* (1977), is a scientific account of Genie's development during the four years when federal grants provided support. Although Genie acquired many words and some grasp of syntax, she left out prepositions and articles and had difficulty using pronouns. One of the most interesting aspects of Genie's speech was her use of "I," "me," and "you" interchangeably. Compare this to Helen Keller:

> When I learned the meaning of "I" and "me" and found that I was something, I began to think. Then consciousness first existed for me. Thus it was not the sense of touch that brought me knowledge. It was the awakening of my soul that first rendered my senses their value, their cognizance of objects, names, qualities, and properties. Thought made me conscious of love, joy, and all the emotions. (Keller 1904/1908:117)

Keller's choice of "I" and "me" is significant, "for the pronouns form a system, a framework of consciousness and personhood; the words 'girl' and 'Helen' had come long before" (Leiber, 1997:336).

Genie never reached this point. After a period of flourishing, she reached a plateau and made little advance beyond, reinforcing the conclusion that there is a critical period for language acquisition. Unfortunately, Genie's story does not have a happy ending. After the four-year period during which federal grants provided support (when Genie was both nurtured and exposed to extensive language work and testing), Genie lived with her mother for a brief period. She was then placed in a succession of foster homes and later was permanently institutionalized, regressing to a point where she was distant and nonverbal. Though the stories of "feral children" have captured the imaginations of authors and publics alike—from Rudyard Kipling's Mowgli in *The Jungle Book* to the "pack" in Max Brooks's zombie apocalypse novel *World War Z*—situations like Genie's are heartbreaking, yet they're fortunately quite rare. Regardless, both factual and fictional tales point to the absolute necessity of socialization for childhood and adult human development.

Having been bombarded with the morning's scoreboard of human misery and happiness, you probably still have enough fortitude to leave your home and go out, entering the world of anonymous others. Consider the assumption of trust you must make to navigate your way through the day's activities. In going to your job or class, for example, you must assume that others share your understanding of the social conventions relating to personal safety. As a pedestrian, you assume that others know how to move their bodies or control their cars to avoid bumping into you (Whyte, 1988). Other pedestrians or drivers make the same assumption about you. If you are driving, you must assume that other drivers also know the meaning of green lights, stop signs, railroad crossings, and so forth. Think what driving in any metropolitan area would be like without such understandings.

While smooth daily functioning depends on the assumption of a commonly shared social reality, there is also an element of uncertainty in the construction of reality. You must anticipate that your own version may not be totally shared by others. You also cannot be completely sure how you and others will behave in an anticipated or ongoing interaction. In any social situation, allowances must be made for the unexpected behaviors of the participants.

Sources of Nonconformity

When behaviors seriously deviate from societal expectations, they are defined as deviance (see chapter 9) or nonconformity. In the interactionist perspective, nonconforming behaviors can be explained in terms of the human ability to symbolize and the existence of multiple social realities within the society. Generational differences also encourage the existence of deviant or nonconforming behaviors. Sometimes the more things change, the more they stay the same. Other times things just change, and that requires new interpretations and strategies of and for action (see Swidler, 1986).

The Ability to Symbolize.   Society does not just exist unto itself. It is formed through the symbolic communication occurring between two or more persons. Since, as we have noted, there is no inherent meaning in an object, it is always possible for individuals, through their symbolic activity, to redefine objects in ways that challenge existing definitions of reality. The transformation of the meaning of "Negro" to "black" in racial terms provides dramatic evidence of this. As a consequence of the 1960s civil rights movement, Americans of African descent began to think of the former term as something imposed on them by whites. The label "black" or "African American," carrying the meaning of racial pride and a rich cultural heritage, now is widely used. Similar changes have occurred in the definitions of "gender" (Epstein, 1997), "queer" (Gamson, 1995; Barker et al., 2009), and even "redneck" (Wray, 2006).

Symbolic behavior makes it possible to reject the symbols used by those in one's immediate physical surroundings and to identify with symbols used by others elsewhere. A person's **reference groups** (those groups providing standards for the person's behaviors) need not be confined to others who are physically present. In that sense, the ability to symbolize provides humans with a continual source of nonconformity. Ward Abbott illustrates how symbolic activity can lead to nonconformity in his statement about the relationship of the artist to the state:

> The artist is doubly subversive in that only a bullet can stop him. He feeds on changes as others shy away from them. Josip Brodsky, exiled in Siberia, infuriated officials by *enjoying his life there.* Unlike a banker, the artist carries his work in his mind. To express it, he needs only a stub of a pencil and a scrap of paper, or charcoal and any surface. One of the last acts of Gaudier-Brezka in the trenches of World War I, surrounded by

death and desolation, was to carve, out of a bit of blown-up rifle butt, a splendidly Brezkian sculpture. (Abbott, 1975:89; emphasis added)

The example of the subversive artist suggests that individuals are, to a substantial degree, responsible for determining their environments. The term *environment*, it is important to stress, encompasses *both* physical objects as well as our ideas about those objects. Like any symbolic construct, the meaning of an environment is something created and conferred on it by human beings acting through social communications with others. Even physical objects such as mountains and rivers can have vastly different meanings for members of different groups, based on how those groups intend to use such objects. For some Native Americans, for example, a mountain may symbolize a holy place where the spirits of one's ancestors reside. For modern recreationists, by contrast, the mountain may be a setting for sport and athletic activities such as mountain climbing and skiing. So physical objects, then, take on significance in people's lives as meanings are conferred on them, based on how those objects will be used.

There are, however, real limits to our capacity for totally determining what the nature of our immediate environments will be. However much the artists Brodsky and Gaudier-Brezka were able to redefine their lives in Siberia and the World War I trenches, they still had to cope with both the physical features of their wartime surroundings as well as the socially constructed decisions made by powerful "others"—such as politicians and military officers—who put them in those surroundings in the first place. Thus it can be argued that we both determine the environment and are determined by it.

Despite the physical and social constraints we face, the self-reflecting character of interactions makes nonconformity a continual possibility. To use the French philosopher Jean-Paul Sartre's term, it is "bad faith" to claim that we are utterly without choice in a particular situation. Even individuals being tortured decide when, or indeed whether, to give in to their tormentors. The choice in an extreme situation might be death, but it is an available choice.

The Existence of Multiple Social Realities. In highly diverse, stratified societies such as contemporary American society, several realities exist concurrently. People at different levels or locations in the society—possessing more or less power, prestige, and wealth—have differing images of the world. Definitions of reality adhered to by people are influenced by their position in the social structure, as Berger and Luckmann (1967) and, most notably, Karl Mannheim (1952) have suggested. Various racial, ethnic, and religious groups also engage in varied responses and therefore give differing meanings to their worlds. Moreover, individuals develop commitments to their distinctive values, attitudes, and lifestyles. They may even take action against those representing alternative or contrary versions of reality, particularly if the others' reality is perceived as threatening to their own (Scott, 1990).

Differences in power influence morality, values, and therefore the behaviors that are deemed socially acceptable. Everyone does not have an equal role in the development and maintenance of society's dominant or official versions of reality. In American society, for example, the medical profession's authoritative definitions of illness commonly prevail over those of Christian Scientists; psychiatrists' definitions of subjective experience prevail over those of patients; social service providers' definitions take precedence over clients' definitions of their own problems, and so on (Cahill, 1998). Psychiatrists, for example, have exercised substantial power in defining mental illness. Erving Goffman's (1961) classic piece on "the moral career of the mental patient" describes how mental institutions and their staffs convince patients to internalize the psychiatric view of reality and of themselves. In the "politics of reality" of the mental institution, patients are virtually powerless.

There are always some people who are unwilling to accept others' notions about proper behavior. If they seek one another out and agree to act collectively, they may decide to challenge the dominant version of reality. Sometimes these challenges are successful, and new expectations for behavior become institutionalized over time. The women's movement, for example, influenced legislation prohibiting gender-related discrimination in jobs and education, and it has altered in many ways the relations of men and women as colleagues, friends, and lovers. More often, however, challenges to established reality fail. Those with a strong investment in the status quo react quickly, vigorously, and sometimes violently to any threat to their reality. In every society, agencies (such as prisons and mental hospitals) and roles (such as shamans, psychiatrists, clergy, and police officers) are created to manage reality disrupters.

Goffman, in his numerous works (1959, 1961, 1963, 1971), describes the construction of social realities as a fluid affair. The maintenance of these realities is subject to the continual negotiation of the participants. If the term "subversion" were stripped of its political and negative connotations, it could be applied more broadly to everyday interactions. Individuals constantly bend or subvert established rules and expectations to their own purposes. They include students who turn in papers late and pedestrians who jaywalk, as well as drug users who steal to maintain their habit.

A continual source of nonconformity in society is the actions of people and groups seeking to have their versions of reality either accepted by others or translated into the accepted version of reality. Deviance and nonconformity arise from the variety of perspectives produced in different social worlds. We could say that when a person raised in one social world, equipped for travel on a particular symbolic highway, enters another world's symbolic thoroughfares, the result could be a multisymbol accident! Because we live in a pluralistic society defined by so many symbolic thoroughfares, individuals are often frustrated by the lack of clear-cut answers to the many paradoxes of their lives. For example, Christians who are fans of mixed martial arts have sought ways—often advice from others via online forums—to relieve the tension between their religious beliefs and their leisure activities because "'turning the other cheek' is clearly part of a different moral order than 'knock him out'" (Borer and Schafer, 2011:166). Symbolic conflicts do take place not only between persons but *within* them as well.

The Nature of Generational Differences.   Another source of nonconformity, in social terms, lies in the different viewpoints of the various generations in a society. Biologically, a generation may be thought of as a group of people who were born at about the same time. Sociologically, a **generation** should be regarded as people who have experienced similar *historical* events at similar points in their lives. Others who have not undergone such experiences at the same time in their own lives find it difficult to understand the meanings conferred on particular events by those who have. Depending on the nature of the historical situation, members of different generations may be thought of as inhabiting different social worlds and recognizing different social realities.

Generations establish collective memories based on their members' unique experiences of historical events occurring during adolescence and early adulthood. One study found that people's memories of World War II and the Vietnam War, for example, were strongly influenced by their age at the time of the event, with the memories being "strongest for those in their youth at the time of the event" (Schuman and Scott, 1989:366). While youth is no doubt a critical time period for all generations, the nature of the memories that each generation collectively retains will differ because young people in one generation experience different events from those who are young in other historical eras. The collective memories of the September 11, 2001, terrorist attacks have been, and continue to be, constructed and reconstructed through shared stories of and about the events (Polletta and Lee, 2006; Conner, 2012) and through digital Web-based archives such as WhereWereYou.org.

The development of generational experiences and styles provides evidence that the socialization process is not a completely repetitive one. New generations do not adopt the behaviors expected of them by their elders without question. Because they have not themselves had a hand in the creation of the reality they are expected to appropriate as their own, they are bound to experience it differently than do older generations. The older generations are confronted with the problem of legitimating their reality to the newer generations, and the newcomers may well challenge the assumption that they will accept it. Not being satisfied with the explanations of their elders, they may proceed to subvert that reality—through symbols of dress, music, language, and so on—in the course of their daily lives. At some point they may succeed in constructing a new reality, which they must then legitimate to their own children, and so on.

The concept of generation calls attention to a socially derived process related to the "rhythm" of social life. Because of its effects on the construction of social reality, it represents another continual source of nonconformity and change in society.

The Socialized Self

From the moment we're born, we necessarily rely on others. At first, it's simply for the basics of food and shelter. But as we grow older, we acquire language skills that allow us to have thoughts or conversations with ourselves. The conversations we have between our I and our me are informed by our social, cultural, and historical contexts. Can you imagine how different you might be if you grew up in another time period? Another country? With other parents? With other friends? Is there anything about you that you think would remain the same despite such drastic changes to your socialized self? If so, what? And, perhaps more importantly, how?

■ Conclusion

Our concerns in this chapter have been primarily theoretical, and the discussion has been somewhat abstract. To conclude that there is no relationship between the issues discussed and your everyday life would be to miss an important point, however. You cannot begin to understand how associations with others are ordered and made predictable and sensible unless you have some theoretical understanding of human relations.

As we noted in chapter 1, sociological analysis, particularly the analysis of everyday events, requires more than simple description. To get beyond description and discover underlying forms of social interaction, sociologists adopt various theoretical perspectives. The authors of this book have adopted the perspective of symbolic interaction. In this chapter we have introduced the central concepts in the interactionist perspective: symbolic communication, the emergence and development of the self through interaction, the process of role-taking, the existence of multiple social realities, and the sources of nonconformity in social life. We believe that these ideas provide a foundation for an understanding of human interaction and communication, and we will refer to them throughout this volume.

Symbolic communication provides a means of predictable interactions in a world where things and situations have no fixed meanings. Symbols mobilize our reactions to the world and help us coordinate our actions with the actions of others through socially shared meanings. They help us conceptualize the social world in which we live. By conferring meanings, we can transform our environment in concert with others.

The symbolic interactionist perspective stresses the interconnections between people and society. As originally conceived by George Herbert Mead, it provides a picture of social life in which individuals make their own interpretations of the situations in which they are involved, while simultaneously taking societal expectations into account. Analytically, this idea is expressed in Mead's description of the relationships between the generalized other, the I, and the me. The components of the self operate together to maintain a balance between conventional behavior and nonconformity. The social self thus both reflects society as it exists and provides a means of changing it.

Any social encounter requires role-taking, or understanding the positions of other people. To role-take successfully, we must continually assess available information about others. We cannot engage in meaningful communication with others without first identifying who they are. Knowledge of others' social attributes, such as their age, sex, and occupation, strongly affects our judgments about the type of people they are. In the next chapter we will examine the central role of information in role-taking efforts.

Definitions

game stage: The stage of the socialization process during which children become able to understand the morality of their own behaviors. The game stage is distinguished from the play stage in that children orient themselves to a body of rules that spell out proper behavior.

gender identity: A sense of self in terms of femininity or masculinity; that is, as feminine or masculine.

generalized other: An abstract configuration of all the relevant rules and roles that we must take into account to function successfully in any social environment. In the most abstract sense, the generalized other is society as a whole.

generation: A group of people who have experienced similar historical events at similar points in their lives. Members of different generations inhabit different social worlds and recognize different social realities.

looking glass self: Cooley's notion that our self is based on our interpretation of others' appraisals of us. That is, others are like a mirror in which we see ourselves reflected. However, that reflection is what we *imagine* others think of us, not necessarily what they might really think.

nonconformity: Behaviors that deviate from generally held cultural expectations or social norms.

play stage: The stage of the socialization process during which children learn certain roles by playing at them, as when they play doctor, nurse, police officer, and so on.

reference groups: Any social group used by an individual as a standard for evaluating his or her behavior. One need not officially belong to a group to have it as a reference group.

role-taking: The process through which individuals imaginatively put themselves in the positions of other people to evaluate how others see them and their behaviors. Individuals ordinarily modify their behaviors on the basis of their role-taking efforts.

sign: An object to which a fixed, unchanging response is made. In contrast to a symbol, a sign is characterized by the fact that its meaning is identified with its physical form. Animals generally respond to objects as signs, not as symbols.

social reality: The totality of meanings about the world on which the members of a group or society agree. It is possible that diverse individuals and groups will hold distinct pictures of reality. In any complex society there are multiple realities.

socialization: The process through which people learn the behaviors required by their cultures. It is also the process through which culture is transmitted from one generation to the next. Without the process of socialization, society could not exist.

symbol: An object to which any meaning can be assigned. The meanings assigned to symbols can be arbitrary and are not determined by the physical characteristics of objects or the sensory experiences they may cause.

symbolic communication: Communication that involves people's ongoing interpretations of one another's actions.

the I: One of two aspects of the human self, it is the spontaneous, creative, unpredict-able part of the self. The I consists of subjective, idiosyncratic, and unanticipated factors that enter into our communications with others.

the me: One of two aspects of the human self, it is the part of the self that is conven-tional; the conforming, rule-following part.

the self: The view of oneself derived from the ability to evaluate one's behaviors from the point of view of others, ultimately from the point of the standards of soci-ety as a whole. The self is capable of both acting (as a subject) and then, through an ongoing internal conversation, reflecting on its actions (as an object).

Discussion Questions

1. Do you think that human beings are uniquely different from other ani-mals because of their symbol-using capacity? What does it imply about the distinctiveness of human communication that we can discuss this and other questions in class?

2. Can anything you do (or think, for that matter) have any meaning apart from your assessment of how some other people are likely to evaluate your behaviors?

3. Reflect on your activities during a typical day. To what extent do your behaviors represent a combination of conformity and novelty, of your responses to the expectations of others and more impulsive reactions to situations? In which kinds of situations is it hardest for you to anticipate just how you will behave? In which situations is it easiest?

4. Think of a time when you did not conform to some person's or group's expec-tations. Now think of a situation in which you did not want to conform to the expectations of others but did so anyway. What distinguished the two situa-tions? In what way were your behaviors constructed in response to symbols?

5. What is the relationship between the kinds of games people play as chil-dren and the kinds of roles they later perform in adult life?

6. The authors suggested that every generation is confronted with the prob-lem of legitimating its view of reality to the next generation. In what areas do you feel that your own conception of reality is fundamentally different from that held by your parents? Describe some of the symbols that reflect the different generational realities.

Suggested Audiovisuals

PBS. 1994. *Secret of a Wild Child.*
PBS. 2000. *Nature: Inside the Animal Mind.*
PBS. 2011. *How Smart Are Animals?*
The Gorilla Foundation. *A Conversation with Koko.*

Sociology on the Web

You might enjoy checking out http://www.koko.org, the website for The Gorilla Foundation/Koko.org, P.O. Box 620530, Woodside, CA 94062.

3

Understanding Interaction

Living in a modern society and engaging in everyday activities involve virtually constant interactions in a variety of settings and with a multitude of people, each of whom may demand a different posture. A person's attempts to get along with others or to get his or her own way with them in these various social arenas can require an astounding amount of practical and social knowledge. There also must be reasonable agreement among the people involved on their view of social reality. Otherwise human communication—and society itself—would be impossible.

■ The Need for Communication in Role-Taking

The process through which we act in awareness of others and continually adjust our own behaviors in accordance with the way others are acting depends on our distinctively human ability to role-take, as we noted in chapter 2. To infer correctly the intentions, motives, and goals of others, and therefore to predict their future behaviors, we must put ourselves in their place and attempt to view the situation as they do. We cannot gauge the meanings of others' acts and then respond appropriately unless we achieve some understanding of the way others are interpreting and making sense of the situation. Such role-taking is, of course, mutual. All people in any particular interaction are simultaneously formulating their behaviors in accordance with their assessments of the perceptions and expectations of others.

Failed Communications

This does not mean that the capacity for role-taking necessarily ensures that all interactions occur smoothly and without difficulty. In many everyday encounters, role-taking leads to incorrect inferences about others. We frequently find it difficult to understand why others act as they do. There is the possibility that our attempts at role-taking will lead us to formulate a definition of the situation that varies from the definition held by those with whom we are communicating. When this happens, a **failed communication** can result.

The college classroom is a setting that offers numerous possibilities for failed communications. Teachers often proceed under one set of assumptions about "intellectual work" while students operate under another.

Teachers tend to value critical thinking. They may respond critically to comments made by students and push students to defend their own points of view. The teacher's goal—to help students think more analytically—may be misperceived by the students, however. They may consider teachers to be flaunting their superior knowledge or, worse still, to be putting the students down. The authors have identified this situation as the beginning of a vicious circle of sorts. The more that teachers try to instill in students a critical attitude toward their own ideas, the more students come to see faculty members as condescending (Karp and Yoels, 1976). In the classroom, as elsewhere, a host of misunderstandings may arise when people define the situation differently.

The greatest difficulty in assessing the meanings of another's actions ordinarily arises in those situations where we know very little about the other person. Differences in experiences, biographies, and cultural backgrounds increase the likelihood that two people will not understand one another. Those who have traveled in foreign countries should recognize the difficulty of role-taking with cultural strangers. In our own country, we tend to regard with caution the members of ethnic, class, or racial groups whose patterns of speech, grooming, dress, and demeanor vary from our own. The French historian Fernand Braudel (1981) argued that the most visible cultural differences between the elite, or ruling classes, and the masses have always involved speech, etiquette, protocol, and even body language. Poor people who manage to achieve high rank may still find it difficult to overcome cultural barriers that exclude them from full membership in higher social circles. They may not immediately know how to talk, walk, and generally act "correctly."

Several studies on the subjective experience of social mobility illustrate this. David Karp's (1986) study of professionals who came from working-class circumstances suggests that our original class position is a status requiring negotiation throughout our life. People do not shake off their original class position, as a snake sheds its skin, but continue to feel the lingering effects of their inherited class membership. Despite having risen into the ranks of professional workers, respondents in Karp's study reported continued feelings of marginality, discomfort, and inauthenticity. In a study of working-class students in elite law schools, Robert Granfield (1991) found that although these students entered law school with class pride, it began to diminish fairly quickly. The students came to define themselves as different from non-working-class students and began to view their class backgrounds as a burden, leading them to experience a "crisis in competency." Granfield describes this as a "hidden injury of class" (Sennett and Cobb, 1973), a psychological burden that working-class students experienced as they came to acquire the "identity beliefs" associated with middle-class society. Working-class students dealt with class stigma by managing information about their backgrounds using such strategies as adopting the dress code of higher-class students and developing different interpersonal skills. As one author explains, "Working-class people do not have the quiet hands or the neutral faces of the privileged classes" (Zandy, 1995:5). The "getting into college game" may even be "rigged" by or for high-status individuals, according to Michael Schwalbe. For those who go to the best colleges and have access to the best jobs after graduation, it "isn't about raw intelligence. It's about growing up with books, living in a safe neighborhood, having enough to eat, and not having a family life disrupted by economic emergencies" (Schwalbe, 2008:76). The so-called winners of the game are also those who create the rules on how to play it. Learning those rules is easier to do for students who grow up adhering to them. For others, it's easy to get left behind because, as the popular *Hunger Games* books and movie series attest, the odds are never in their favor.

Academics are not exempt from experiencing the pains of social mobility (Hurst, 2010). Diane Reay (1997), who has written about working-class women who become academics, suggests that these women are unlikely ever to feel at home in academia. In her own case, she vacillates between getting angry about middle-class privilege and feeling guilty because she is now implicated in it. According to Reay, her own experience of growing up working-class has left vivid memories of the heritage and history of her social origins imprinted on her consciousness. However, "that consciousness, rooted in working-class affiliation, appears increasingly to be a misfit; a sense of self both out of place and out of time" (p. 79).

We can never experience exactly what another person is experiencing because we cannot be that person. We can only approximate through imagination what it must be like to be a given person in a given situation. Moreover, everyone is not equally able or willing to see the world as others do. In some cases the people involved are simply insensitive. In other situations they make little effort to take others' roles. In chapter 6 we will elaborate on the difference in role-taking between those in more powerful and less powerful positions.

The Importance of Information

In theoretical terms, role-taking requires us to distinguish between identification *with* and identification *of* others (Stone, 1962). In role-taking, one person tries to identify *with* another person or group and tries to imagine how others are seeing and conceiving a given situation. Before such identification with others can be made, however, it is necessary to place, categorize, or define them. Knowledge or identification *of* others' social class, gender, age, race, and the like is a requisite of the role-taking process. In other words, successful role-taking is heavily dependent on the *information* we pick up about others during the course of our interactions with them.

The building up of information is essential to the continuance of interactions. If we incorrectly assess both the information we possess about others and the amount and nature of the information they possess about us, the communication is likely to fail; that is, both persons in an interaction may incorrectly judge how much information of the other they actually possess.

Further, the information they believe they have may be wrong. In either case, the result could be a "fractured interaction" as individuals act either out of ignorance or on the basis of incorrect information. Such interactions may result in embarrassment (see chapter 9) or, in the extreme case, the alienation of people from one another.

This chapter explores more deeply the relationships among information, role-taking, and the attribution of meanings in interactions. We will consider in detail the categories of information employed in assessing others, the manner in which information is processed, and the ways in which these assessments of others affect daily interactions. We will also consider how information is controlled to create favorable definitions of self in various situations.

■ Gathering and Processing Information about Others

When we confront others, particularly those about whom we have little biographical information, we form a total picture of them—a kind of gestalt—by considering simultaneously and fitting together a number of highly visible cues or clues about them. The specific meanings we attach to any attribute of a person may be modified as we assess it in conjunction with the person's other attributes. Our assessment depends on a mix of cognitive rationality and embodied emotionality. As Randall Collins (2004) argues, individuals' previous encounters affect their current ones by helping individuals align their "emotional energy" with those with whom they're interacting in order to create a sense of solidarity. The psychological, emotional, and existential need for social bonds is so strong that individuals necessarily become adept at reading others to conform to and with their behaviors and emotions. In most situations, we identify or form a more or less definite picture of others by taking into account their social attributes, such as age, gender, and race; their physical attributes, such as attractiveness, posture, facial expressions, and body type; their clothing; and their discourse, or what they say.

Information Provided by Social Attributes

Meaningful social interaction is rooted in the definitions of ongoing situations arrived at by the people involved in them. Participants in any encounter must be mutually oriented to the social expectations concerning the setting, to the purpose of their communications, and to any available information about others. Certain **social attributes** have informational significance because they help define the identities of self and others.

Individuals bring with them to all social encounters their own expectations about what to anticipate from other people with certain attributes. As a result of the socialization process Americans have experienced, for example, we have learned the significance in our society of being male or female, black or white, young or old. We have learned how to deal with these categories of people and, on occasion, how to manipulate them. Our interactions depend on our images or categorical conceptions of persons possessing such social attributes. For better or worse, we begin our interactions with culturally given conceptions of the ways that women or men; blacks, whites, Hispanics (etc.); Jews, Christians, Muslims (etc.); and teenagers or the elderly, to name a few categories, are likely to behave.

A large number of attributes may define a person socially or indicate a person's **social status.** A woman might, for example, simultaneously occupy the statuses of Phi Beta Kappa, Republican, member of the Better Business Bureau, CEO, and mother. Sociologists make a useful distinction in discussing the properties of social attributes by differentiating between ascribed and achieved statuses. **Ascribed statuses** are those which are acquired at birth (such as sex and race), and **achieved statuses** are acquired during the course of a person's life (such as educational, organizational, and occupational statuses). This distinction alone, however, does not indicate the relative importance of the many statuses a person may occupy. And while the distinction is analytically useful, an attribute such as "gender" exists somewhere in between an ascribed and achieved status because masculinity and femininity are not natural or essential categories but are, rather, socially constructed and performed during interactions (West and Zimmerman, 1987).

The Master Attributes.   Some statuses are substantially more central than others, both to the way individuals view themselves and to the way others view them. Such highly visible, essentially unalterable attributes as race, gender, and age sharply define a person in any situation. Because these attributes are so powerful, tending to supersede any other definitions of self that an individual might present to others, they are referred to as **master attributes.** Recent news reports recount numerous examples of ill treatment experienced by middle-class blacks in restaurants, banks, and other public settings that illustrate the primacy of race over class. Even individuals of high status are not exempt from such treatment, as in the case of black movie star and comedian Chris Rock, who has begun taking "selfies" every time police pull him over while driving. In March 2015, he posted a picture online when he was stopped for the third time in less than seven weeks. The picture was accompanied by the following text: "Stopped by the cops again wish me luck." Clearly his ascribed racial status took precedence over his achieved class status. In an incident that resulted in considerable media attention, black secret service agents sued Denny's restaurants because of their treatment at a Denny's in Annapolis, Maryland. They alleged that they were kept waiting nearly an hour to be seated while white agents and other white patrons were seated promptly.

One strategy used by African Americans in all income classes to cope with racism is to put on a defensive "shield." Joe R. Feagin and Melvin P. Sikes (1994) describe a conversation with a retired music teacher in her 70s who is black. She contrasts her life with that of a white woman, who, like her, bathes, dresses, and puts on cosmetics before leaving the house each morning. Unlike the white woman, however, this black woman must also put on her "shield" just before she leaves the house; that is, she has to be pre-pared psychologically and to steel herself in advance for racist insults and acts, and she has to be prepared every day even if nothing adverse happens on a particular day.

The information provided by such master attributes as gender, age, and race is so familiar that we can easily lose sight of its importance for the con-duct of our everyday affairs. We may recognize just how dependent we are on such knowledge only when we are confronted by a situation where it is not available. Our interactions with others would be considerably compli-cated if their gender suddenly became unclear, for example. Our role-taking ability depends heavily on our ability to assess others' genders, and we would become disoriented in the absence of this information.

The overwhelming significance of gender as a strategic piece of infor-mation in guiding interactions is illustrated by transsexuals. These are indi-viduals whose biological sex does not match their self-identification in terms of gender—"a girl brain in a boy body" or vice versa (Mason-Schrock, 1996). Presentation of self becomes the determining factor in being able to fully "pass" in society as a member of the opposite sex; that is, the transsex-ual individual must be able to cue "correct" gender identity. Transsexuals must learn to dress as a member of the opposite sex, walk, talk, use ges-tures, and so on. Much time, attention, and effort is given to learning the ways of presenting oneself differently from the gender identity in which one was socialized as a child. It is on the basis of this presentation of self that others respond to the individual.

Much early socialization is directed toward recognizing the significance of gender and the appropriate behaviors associated with sexual differences. Conceptions of manhood and womanhood are cultural products acquired through interaction with others. Gender is one attribute that is ordinarily considered fixed and unchangeable. This piece of identity information per-vades our lives in countless ways. Though it is often questioned only in the case of those who seek to alter that status (see box on the following page), arguments against the traditionally heteronormative gender binary (i.e., male/female) have become common among sociologists and within commu-nities fighting for gender equality (see Schilt and Westbrook, 2009).

Names are also a central feature of a person's identity. Like gender, name is a piece of information that grounds the person's identity in the eyes of society. Both gender and name are "identity pegs" that become part of a person's official, documented identity.

Kate Bornstein's (2013) experience as a transgendered individual illus-trates the extent to which gender and name "anchor" biographies and social identities:

> Changing my name from Al to Kate was no big deal in Pennsylvania. It was a simple matter of filing a form with the court and publishing the name change in some unobtrusive "notices" column of a court-approved newspaper. Bingo—done. The problems came with changing all my docu-ments. The driver's license was particularly interesting. Prior to my full

gender change, I'd been pulled over once already dressed as a woman, yet holding my male driver's license—it wasn't something I cared to repeat. (p. 28)

"I Don't Know How I'm Supposed to Refer to You"

Alice Myers was a "tomboy" growing up who dreamed of playing goalie for the U.S. Olympic hockey team. Her hair was so short and spiky that a sixth-grade teacher told Alice's parents, "Your son is doing well in my class." By the summer after her junior year in high school, Alice had realized that she was transgendered. When senior year began, Alice had become Alex, who wore a coat and tie to class. According to Myers, it confused his teachers, who were unable to control the class at times. He reported that one teacher took him aside and said, "I don't know how I'm supposed to refer to you." When Myers applied to Harvard, his college interview ended abruptly when the interviewer noticed the name Alice on a form while Alex, in coat and tie, sat before him. (Alex explained his change of gender.) A week later, Myers was called in for another interview because the alumnus who interviewed him had been unable to give a fair opinion.

Myers legally changed his name during the summer of 1996 when he turned 18. He managed to keep his biological sex (female) secret for his first two months at Harvard, but the presence of so many of his former classmates made anonymity impossible. According to Myers, "For the first few weeks people were treating me as a nerdy, sort of conservative white guy." In November, he came out to other dorm residents. Although there was no open hostility, according to one of his dormmates, "some of the guys here don't know what to make of him."

At Harvard, Myers sparked a campus-wide argument that reflects a larger debate in American society, and in the medical community, about the boundaries of gender and sex. And there has been some success. Myers successfully lobbied Harvard's student government to add protections for transgendered undergraduates to its constitution and appealed to the administration to change its discrimination policy to protect transgendered individuals. At the same time, the Cambridge city council voted unanimously to include protections for "gender expressions" in the city's Human Rights Ordinance.

Myers describes himself as a living, breathing example of the notion that gender and sex don't naturally go together, that gender is a construct. "Man and woman—those are societal molds," says Myers. "I think it's a big trap. I believe gender and sex are two different things. They are not complementary forces. . . . And I'm hardly the first person to feel this way" (Mathews, 1997:1E).

The way medical teams manage the gender assignment of intersexed infants (hermaphrodites who are born with ambiguous genitals) illustrates the idea that gender is as much a social as it is a biological reality. Kessler (1996) has criticized physicians who rush to surgically "correct" genital ambiguity, pointing out that their decisions are influenced as much by cultural factors as by medical ones: medical technology is used to convert the non-normative (intersexuality) into the normative (either male or female). According to Kessler, this "correction" is not done because it is threatening to the infant's life but because it is threatening to the infant's culture. By preserving gender "normalcy," other people won't have to deal with those whose gender does not neatly fit into one of two categories. Such preemptive procedures can prove to be socially damaging to the child through adolescence and adulthood (G. Davis, 2013). The growing visibility of the transgender movement indicates that there is a significant segment of the population that feels recognition of a "third gender" (intersexual) is more important than people's discomfort in interactions with those who "don't fit the model" (Coventry, 1998).[*]

[*] For more information, see the website of the Intersex Society of North America (ISNA), http://www.isna.org.

She goes on to describe the reactions at the DMV. The first officer she encountered, not noticing that the name on the license is a male one, assumes the reason for her name change is marriage or divorce. He flirts with her and calls her "honey." When another officer notices that the name on the license is a male one and points this out to the first officer, he is, according to Bornstein, "crestfallen."

The issue of names and gender identity reached a fever pitch in April 2015 when famed Olympic champion and, for younger generations, reality television star Bruce Jenner sat down with ABC's Diane Sawyer to reveal his "real" gender identity. Though he was male—anatomically and hormonally—Bruce declared that he always felt female and had been going through the process of becoming a woman on and off since the 1980s. A few months later, the June cover of *Vanity Fair* magazine featured an elegantly coiffed Jenner dressed in a cream-colored bustier. Three simple words ran across the image: "Call me Caitlyn." The public reaction to Jenner's transition varied widely from triumphant support to critical claims about privilege to downright nasty bigotry. Regardless, the name change was clearly as important as both the emotional and physical changes that Jenner had endured. The name change was a public declaration that forever changed the way he, now *she*, will be addressed.

Processing Master Attributes. The identity difficulties of transsexual and transgendered individuals illuminate the extraordinary importance of gender as part of our self-definitions, the definitions that others have of us, and the implications these normally mutual definitions have for the way we order our encounters. Much the same case can be made with regard to the other master attributes of age and race. Like gender, they are aspects of others upon which we rely in making judgments about the kinds of people they are, the kinds of behaviors we might expect of them, and the attitudes and values they are likely to hold. Therefore, they help us judge the kinds of behaviors in which we might properly engage in our encounters with others.

The manner in which we use the information revealed by these attributes to formulate our behaviors is somewhat complicated. It is not simply a matter of attributing significance to these attributes *one at a time*. We do not consider them singly and in isolation from each other. Instead, we formulate a conception of people based on a **configuration of attributes,** or the statuses they simultaneously occupy. People are not just male or female, they are *young* males, *old* males; *young* females, *old* females; *young, black* males, *young, white* females; and so forth. Because these statuses are possessed in combination, the number of categorical conceptions we must store in our minds is large.

Our conceptions of age, for example, are more specific than just young or old. If we only add the frequently used category of middle-aged, the number of combinations of age along with race and gender increases. The issue is further complicated because age is a continuous variable with year values that can range from 0 to more than 100 in a series of steps. Our assessment of someone's age is therefore quite sophisticated. A matter of even a few years can influence our judgments about what a person can and cannot or should and should not do (see chapter 10).

There are also many racial distinctions within the black-white dichotomy. Distinctions are made between light- and dark-skinned blacks in the United States, for example, and in countries such as South Africa even finer distinctions constitute the basis for racial oppression. Studies suggest that in the United States, employers view darker African American men as violent, uncooperative, dishonest, and unstable (Kirschenman and Neckerman, 1998), thus excluding them from employment and blocking their access to rewards and resources (Thompson and Keith, 2001). Researchers have reported similar findings about Latinas and Latinos and the relationship between skin color and intragroup job sites where workers are of the same ethnicity (Morales, 2009). Black women of all ages have shown a tendency to prefer lighter skin and believe that lighter hues are perceived as most attractive by black males (Chambers et al., 1994; Robinson and Ward, 1995). Since, like age, race is also a continuous variable, the number of possible combinations of the attributes of gender, age, and race is huge.

The Ongoing Search for Information.   We can quickly make inferences about people who possess different configurations of these master attributes. In the presence of other people for the first time, we assess virtually instantaneously their age, gender, and race, and on this basis we form some preliminary judgment about them. Our evaluation of these attributes sensitizes us to what we can generally expect from such people. The judgments we make after picking up this **face information** cannot be final, however. Our preliminary conceptions of others may prove incorrect as the interaction proceeds, and we must be prepared to make continuous revisions in light of their actual behaviors.

The search for salient or conspicuous information about other people does not begin and end with assessment of the master attributes. Once we make a preliminary judgment about others based on these attributes, we begin to search out additional information to help us confirm, reject, or modify these early judgments. In most encounters, other central sources of information are available from which we can make inferences about these people. The information provided by social attributes is complemented by information from such attributes as physical appearance and clothing, which are easily observed and therefore serve as important cues for role-taking.

Information Provided by Physical Attributes

Advertising attests to the enormous emphasis placed on physical appearance in American society. If our teeth are not white enough, our haircut is not in the latest style, our bodies do not have an agreeable odor, we weigh too much or too little, or our complexion is not clear, we are told that we are unattractive and our interactions with others will suffer. We may be convinced that if our appearance is unattractive or incorrect, we will be denied opportunity for intimacy with others.

Physical appearance—encompassing height, weight, facial characteristics, posture, mannerisms, and grooming—certainly plays a large part in nearly all social interactions. These features of self provide cues as to what we can expect from others and they from us. Like age, race, and gender, **physical attributes** also serve as a basis for judging the kinds of people others are or appear to be.

The importance of physical attributes in our assessments of self and others emphasizes the significance of symbols in the person-perception process. In chapter 2 the distinction between signs and symbols was described in terms of a crucial difference between fixed and socially conferred meanings. We do not respond to the attributes of others merely as signs. It is not, for example, the physical characteristics of clothing as such that we respond to but the meanings given to certain types of clothing. In the same way, no intrinsic meaning is attached to shortness, tallness, thinness, or fatness. The meanings conferred on these physical attributes are culturally and historically established, and there are wide variations in the values attached to them.

Appearance and Attraction. Body image and physical appearance affect our perceptions of ourself and others, as well as our interactions with one another (see box on the next page). Our awareness of the influence that our physical appearance has on others' perceptions of us is illustrated in the care and preparation involved in the way we present ourselves in public. When in a public setting, as Goffman (1963a) pointed out, individuals are

What Is Beautiful Is Good—Still True?

In a landmark study, Dion, Bersheid, and Walster (1972) showed participants photographs of attractive and unattractive individuals and asked them to rate these people on a series of personality traits. They found that attractive individuals were perceived as more sensitive, kind, sociable, interesting, outgoing, strong, poised, and exciting than unattractive people. These findings stimulated more than 25 years of research into the physical attractiveness stereotype. The attractiveness stereotype has become so pervasive in frequency and strength that Dion and colleagues' (1972) suggestion that "what is beautiful is good" has become axiomatic (Perlini et al., 1999). In addition, perceptions of physically attractive individuals are often influenced by "halo effects"—that is, others judge them as having other, actually unrelated, positive characteristics, such as social skills (Ashmore and Longo, 1995). Physical attractiveness affects individual prospects in social institutions such as work, education, and marriage. The perception of beauty translates into social rewards. Organizations may communicate in either implicit or explicit ways cultural ideals about beauty. The popular clothing outlet Abercrombie & Fitch was sued in the early 2000s because of the company's desire to hire employees who embody the "A & F Look." Employees who did not fit the desired image were either fired or transferred to less visible positions.

Physical attractiveness affects our perceptions of ourselves and others, as well as the quality of our social relationships. And there are real consequences regarding perceived physical attractiveness in the realms of the workplace (like hiring and promotion), in court cases, in everyday life interactions, and for individuals' psychological and emotional well-being (Frevert and Walker, 2014). The following findings are typical:

1. Women in U.S. society are held to certain beauty standards; physical appearance continues to play a large part in how women's worth is assessed (Wood and Fixmer-Oraiz, 2014); in many contexts, physical attractiveness is valued more in women than in men (Buss and Kenrick, 1998; Kwan and Trautner, 2009).

2. Women who undergo cosmetic surgery imagine they are being perceived more favorably than they were prior to the operation, and they begin to behave in a manner that they believe appropriate for "attractive" women (Gimlin, 2000).

3. In personal ads, men continue to seek young, attractive partners; women are more likely to seek financial security (Lance, 1998).

4. There is a negative bias toward unattractive women in hiring decisions (Marlowe et al., 1996).

5. Girls have a greater likelihood of being negatively affected by the feminine ideal of physical attractiveness than boys have of being negatively affected by the masculine ideal (Franzoi, 1995). In fact, for many women, physical attractiveness may be detrimental to both hiring and promotion (Johnson et al., 2010).

6. More attractive persons are perceived to have more achievement-related traits and greater initiative (Chia et al., 1998).

7. Women of color are especially disadvantaged by the dominant culture's beauty norms, for a central component of idealized beauty is whiteness. Nonwhite women go to great lengths to more closely resemble the idealized image of white beauty (Rooks, 1996; Glenn, 2008). Creams for lightening skin and chemical treatments to straighten hair are two common techniques used by black women; Asian women are turning to cosmetic surgery to "Caucasianize" their eyelids (Kaw, 1994; Karupiah, 2013).

expected to have their "faculties in readiness for any face-to-face interaction that might come his [or her] way in the situation" (p. 24). One of the most evident means by which individuals express such readiness is "through the disciplined management of personal appearance or 'personal front,' that is, the complex of clothing, make-up, hairdo, and other surface decorations" that they carry about on their person (p. 25). In a classic study of "the interaction order of public bathrooms," Spencer Cahill and colleagues (1985) observed that individuals often enter public bathrooms with no apparent purpose other than the management of their personal front. Most public restrooms are equipped for this purpose, offering coin-operated dispensers of a variety of "personal care products," and almost all have at least one mirror to aid individuals in reconstructing their personal front in what Lofland (1972) termed a "readiness check."

We respond to mirrors as if they represent an unseen audience. The reflected appraisals of ourselves we get from mirrors allow us to anticipate the responses others may make to us. In terms of the discussion in chapter 2 of the self as both the subject and the object of our actions, we present ourselves to the mirror and then stand outside this presented object, trying to view it from the perspective of others.

The extent to which people worry about their physical appearance is, to some degree, a function of the situation. In some contexts physical appearance affects the nature of interactions more than in others. This is evident in the case of physical disability. The image of a person with a disability as one who is weak and disempowered is a potent image, one from which individuals with disabilities may choose to distance themselves. One individual, who thinks of herself as "just a person with an impairment" and who "feels normal" in that her self-awareness is not premised on who people think she is but on what she feels herself to be (Watson, 2002:516), describes her frustration when nondisabled people fail to see this: "That really gets my goat. You know, when you are trying to live a normal life and every time you achieve something they sort of pat you on your head and say 'Ain't that good?' and you don't need that."

For some individuals with disabilities, the biggest challenge is "living in a system in which people with an impairment are subordinated through relations that are contradictory to their own views of their self" (Watson, 2002:521). Rather than accepting this subordination, however, they challenge it by refusing to define themselves as "other."

Appearance and Character Assessment. Not only do we discriminate or rank people in terms of their physical attributes, we also make inferences about the "kinds" of people who display particular physical attributes. That is, we make inferences about others' personalities and even their moral characteristics as we assess them physically. This assessment includes people's smell or, in some cases, odor—the distinction between the two terms is culturally determined and context dependent (Waskul and Vannini, 2008). Warranted or not, we form preliminary conceptions of others as confident, strong-willed, prudish, sentimental, withdrawn, happy, jolly, evil, tough, honest, sincere, dangerous, intellectual, stupid, and the like.

Our evaluation of others' facial expressions is especially crucial in our "reading" of their attitudes and emotions (Eckman, 1992). Our assessment of others' faces is central to the view we come to have of them. In most interactions we spend a good deal of time looking directly at faces. Facial expressions, purposely or unwittingly, express an enormous variety of attitudes and emotions (Carroll and Russell, 1996). For example, research shows that people's different expectancies for emotions according to gender are used to interpret facial expressions. E. Ashby Plant and coauthors (2000) found that women and men posing the same negative ambiguous facial expression were attributed "feminine" and "masculine" emotions, respectively. That is, women were thought to be expressing sadness, whereas men were thought to be expressing anger.

Other physical characteristics such as posture and gesture are also used as a basis for inferences about others' emotions, attitudes, and character. People are viewed as being more or less open, accessible, aloof, rigid, and so forth depending upon their gestures and stance.

Erving Goffman's classic study of stigma (1963b) provides the underpinnings for much of the research on physical appearance. His work focused on the negative social consequences of visible disabilities and other socially devalued attributes. Individuals with visible physical differences are at greater risk of being perceived as unattractive and viewing themselves as unattractive.

Obesity is a stigmatized characteristic in American society (Kwan, 2009). Natalie Allon's classic work on obesity (1971) describes it as "a central target for human vindictiveness and puritanical zeal." According to Allon, "The public condemns and scorns the overweight, who are viewed as handicaps to themselves" (p. 217). A number of studies on public reaction to obesity support the idea that obese persons are held in low esteem, criticized, and stigmatized precisely because they are considered responsible for their own condition. Overweight is viewed as a voluntary condition because such people are thought to have control over the condition of their own bodies.

Despite his potentially good intentions about weight and public health—though we know the expression about the path that good intentions can pave—U.S. surgeon general Richard Carmona characterized obesity as the "terror within," that "unless we do something about it, the magnitude of the dilemma will dwarf 9-11 or any other terrorist attempt" (Associated Press, 2006). What happens when the view of an overweight person is conflated with a terrorist? The stigmatization of obese individuals comes full circle when they accept the legitimacy of others' negative definitions of them. Overweight people are in a peculiarly disadvantaged position because (1) they are discriminated against, (2) they are made to feel that they deserve such discrimination, and (3) they may come to accept their treatment as just (Cooper, 2010).

Overweight individuals come to view themselves as fat by internalizing societal conceptions about weight that lead to the recognition of one's body as something other than "normal." These individuals are forced to appropriate a "fat" identity and deal with the difficult interactions that often result (Degher and Hughes, 1999). Nonacceptance of personal responsibility for overweight may be self-protective. A study of children ages 9 to 11 found that children who attributed their overweight to an external factor had more positive self-esteem. This was also true of children who believed their weight did not influence social interaction outcomes (Pierce and Wardle, 1997).

People use various strategies to cope with the negative character of obesity, including avoidance, compliance, rejection of societal definitions, compensation, and accounts to explain their obesity (Degher and Hughes, 1999). **Accounts** in the form of excuses or justifications are given by people when social interaction is disturbed by rule violations (Scott and Lyman, 1968). Sometimes response to the stigmatization of obesity is in the form of rejection or resistance, such as verbal assertion, physical aggression, self-acceptance, activism, enlightenment, and even flamboyance (Joanisse and Synnott, 1999).

The stigma attached to obesity in American society makes it abundantly clear that assessments of others' morality and general worth are made on the basis of their appearance. The growth of dieting workshops, plans, and organizations, as well as low-calorie food industries on which Americans yearly spend billions of dollars, is persuasive evidence of the general concern with weight. A rigid cultural value is placed on thinness, and those who are noticeably overweight are evaluated negatively. Children develop negative attitudes about overweight as young as six years old and may exclude fat children from play. They already associate obesity with a variety of negative characteristics such as laziness and sloppiness (Dietz, 1998), and these strong negative stereotypes about obesity are difficult to change (Anesbury and Tiggemann, 2000). Discrimination against overweight children begins early in childhood and becomes progressively institutionalized. This finding is particularly significant given that obesity is now the most prevalent nutritional disease of children and adolescents in the United States (Dietz, 1998; Paradis, 2011).

There is some evidence of subcultural variation. White women appear to engage in a greater degree of negative stereotyping of large women, especially large white women, rating them lower on attractiveness, intelligence, job success, relationship success, happiness, and popularity than average or thin women. Interestingly, black women do not show the same denigration of large women, especially large black women (Hebl and Heatherton, 1998).

Obese individuals experience weight-related difficulties with their families, in romantic relationships, and at school or work. Feelings of loneliness and isolation stemming from discrimination by employers, health practitioners, and the general public are common patterns (Joanisse and Synnott, 1999) and often lead to further negative self-perceptions and decreased mental and physical well-being (Schafer and Ferraro, 2011). Obese individuals must not only cope with the stigma of being fat and the interactional difficulties that occur because of this but also face employment discrimination (Paul and Townsend, 1995). Women in particular pay a penalty for being obese (Pagan and Davila, 1997), suffering lower pay in entry-level managerial positions and lower occupational status (Haskins and Ransford, 1999). Dalton Conley and Rebecca Glauber (2005) report that increases in women's body mass result in a decrease in family income and later occupational prestige. Based on our discussion thus far, it should not be surprising that cultural standards of beauty are more critical criteria for evaluating the worth of women in American society than for evaluating men. Cultural messages about the rewards of thinness and the punishment of obesity are everywhere. Most women accept society's standards of beauty as "the way things are," even though these standards may undermine self-image, self-esteem, or physical well-being (Kwan and Trautner, 2009). Because women believe that their bodies fail the beauty test, American industry benefits enormously, continually nurturing feminine insecurities. Images of the culturally desirable female body are presented through the media, and these images are everywhere—television, movies, billboards, online, in print. Women's magazines, with their glossy pages of advertising and beauty advice, hold up an especially devious mirror, offering "help" to women while at the same time presenting a standard nearly impossible to attain (Hesse-Biber, 1996; Roy, 2008).

Given the pervasiveness of the message that their self-worth is tied to "looking good" coupled with a nearly fetishistic "cult of thinness" in American society, women, more than men, are dissatisfied with their bodies. In fact, a meta-analysis of gender differences in attractiveness and body image based on 222 studies over a 50-year span showed dramatic increases in the number of women who have poor body image (Feingold and Mazella, 1998). Numerous studies have concluded that eating disorders have steadily increased, primarily among women (Muth and Cash, 1997; Easter, 2012), and that this increase is a result of the erosion of body image (body satisfaction) engendered by heightened societal pressures on women to be thin and attractive (Garner and Kearney-Cooke, 1996). Young white women, for example, are likely to want to achieve an appearance portrayed in the media, even when they regard such images as unrealistic and largely artificial (Milkie, 1999). Despite powerful media images, research has consistently shown that African American women worry less than women of other races about weight, dieting, or being thin (B. Molloy and Herzberger, 1998).

The cultural emphasis on thinness as an ideal for women carries another danger. When females are encouraged to focus so intensely on their bodies, they may give less attention to more important aspects of identity. Joan Brumberg claims that for many young women in the United States, the body has become an all-consuming project, one that takes precedence over all others (1997).

Effects of Clothing on Appearance. The way people dress also provides information about them. Sociologists have focused on the status differentiation functions of fashion from the early days of the discipline—Thorsten Veblen's (1899) conspicuous consumption; Georg Simmel's (1904) insights into the social psychology of fashion—continuing to the more recent work of Pierre Bourdieu (1984) on cultural capital and Fred Davis (1992) on ambivalence in the meaning of clothing. We make assessments of the ethnicity, social class, occupations, social values, moods, emotions, and even political ideologies of those we encounter on the basis of their clothing. The ways others are dressed provide cues we can use in formulating our behaviors toward them. Clothing also is a prop that helps us project the images of ourselves that we choose to present. It provides a way to manipulate the images we publicly present of ourselves and project the identity that the wearer wants to express. This is simpler than is the case with other physical and social attributes. Gender and race, for example, are extremely difficult to modify.

Racism and the other subtle badges of symbolic power are expressed through wardrobes and body language. Phillipe Bourgois (1995) discovered that appearance and clothing were a significant barrier to middle-class employment for the inner-city youth he studied. It was not just that they did not have the money for clothes, but they had no idea what clothes to choose. They did not know when their clothes would elicit ridicule or anger. One individual was hurt when his supervisor accused him of "looking like a hoodlum" on the days when he thought he was actually dressing well. Another dropped out of an employment-training program because of the humiliation of having an inappropriate wardrobe. He feared he might appear to be "a buffoon on parade" on the days when he was trying to dress up. He admitted that the precipitating factor in his decision not to go back to the job-training program was when he overheard someone accusing one of his female friends of "looking tacky" after she proudly wore her new clothes at the first class. "As a matter of fact, Primo had thought she had looked elegant in her skintight, yellow jumpsuit when she came over to his apartment to display her new outfit proudly to him and his mother before going to class" (p. 162).

Information Provided by Discourse

The necessary information for role-taking in interactions is not acquired solely by observing others' social (or master) and physical attributes. Interactions are accomplished through both appearance and discourse, which is the actual "text" of the communication or conversation. Seminal interactionist Gregory P. Stone suggests that appearance and discourse have at least equal significance in any theory of human communication:

> Appearance and discourse are in fact dialectic processes whenever people converse or correspond. They work back and forth on one another, at times shifting, at other times maintaining the direction of the transaction. . . . In all cases, however, discourse is impossible without appearance which permits the requisite identifications with one another by the discussants. (1962:91)

The information on others provided by social and physical attributes sets the stage for verbal encounters. Before we can talk to people with different attributes, we use the information we have to decide what we can expect from them, which lends some predictability to our encounters. We make reasonable guesses about others' future behaviors. However, as you have no doubt learned through your own interactions, we cannot rely solely on such guesses. We must be prepared to modify our images of others as the interaction proceeds.

Much of the information considered important for predicting others' behaviors must be ferreted out during verbal discourse. The search for relevant information and the corresponding role-taking occur throughout the interaction process. Such aspects of others' identities as their occupation, social class affiliation, ethnicity, marital status, educational level, religion, prejudices, and political beliefs cannot be fully determined through observation alone. Verbal discourse furthers the search for such aspects of others' identities.

Many of our inquiries about others are designed to elicit this information. Consider the information-seeking intentions that lie behind the following types of verbal probes, which are often heard in the course of conversation:

Question Asked	Possible Information Sought
Does your spouse work?	Are you married?
Did you belong to a college fraternity?	What is your education?
Where do you live?	What is your social class?
Did your kids learn about that in church?	Do you have children? What is your religion?
Do you find enough time away from your job to do that?	What is your occupation?
What do you think about politician X's position on that issue?	What are your political attitudes?

We not only seek out information about others, we also frequently find it useful to provide selective information about ourselves. We deliberately present certain images of ourselves by the way we stand, our dress, and our general demeanor—what Goffman referred to as "sign vehicles" (Goffman, 1959). We also provide selective information about ourselves in our verbal communications. Jill Nelson (1994) describes the internal struggle she experienced during an interview with the *Washington Post* as she realizes that she—a black woman—is being stereotyped by her interviewer—a white man—rather than being seen for who she really is. She finally lets it drop that she spent three years at prep school and that her parents have a home in Martha's Vineyard. His response: "He grins. It's as if he's suddenly recognized that the slightly threatening black guy asking for a hand-out on the street is actually a Harvard classmate fallen on hard times. The bond of the Vineyard makes me safe, a person like him" (p. 6). She realizes that the job is hers. "Simply by evoking residence on Martha's Vineyard, I have separated wheat from chaff, belongers from aspirers, rebellious chip-on-the-shoulder Negroes from middle-class, responsible ones" (p. 6).

Goffman (1959) makes the distinction between **expressions given** (verbal symbols or their substitutes, which one uses admittedly to convey information) and **expressions given off** (nonverbal, presumably unintentional conveyance of information). To illustrate, Goffman cites an incident from a novel in which an Englishman named Preedy who is vacationing in Spain makes his first appearance on the beach:

> But in any case he took care to avoid catching anyone's eye. First of all, he had to make it clear to those potential companions of his holiday that they were of no concern to him whatsoever. He stared through them, round them, over them—eyes lost in space. . . . If by chance a ball was thrown his way, he looked surprised; then let a smile of amusement lighten his face (Kindly Preedy), looked around dazed to see that there *were* people on the beach, tossed it back with a smile to himself and not a smile *at* the people, and then resumed carelessly his nonchalant survey of space. (Sansom, 1956:230, in Goffman, 1959:4–5)

This example suggests an important point about the interaction process: *Human beings are capable of manipulating the information they provide to others in order to present certain self-images.* We conceal, control, and give off certain bits of information about ourselves to realize certain desired ends in our transactions with others. Since we carefully monitor the information we provide others, we must presume that those with whom we interact are doing the same. This knowledge certainly complicates our interactions, as we must sometimes question whether and to what extent others are presenting authentic or deceptive images of themselves.

■ Controlling Information and Managing Impressions

The communication and interaction process we have been describing in this chapter takes the following form. Two people come into each other's presence and immediately begin to assess each other. Each begins to pick up as much information as possible about the other's physical and social attributes. This information is important if each person is to have some degree of control over the interaction and to elicit a response from the other person that can be considered favorable. As the encounter proceeds, however, the participants do more than rely on the cues gleaned from each other. Beyond that, they begin to put on a performance and try to project certain identities of themselves. This part of the process is called **impression management.**

The idea that individuals systematically control the information they provide to others about themselves in order to manage the impressions they are presenting is basic to a view of human interaction called the **dramaturgical view.** This view of interaction is most closely associated with the writings of Erving Goffman (1959, 1963a, 1963b, 1967), who was sympathetic to the idea we have presented that individuals must be capable of assigning meanings to their own and others' behaviors in order to communicate. Goffman's work falls within a symbolic interaction frame of reference because he agreed that individuals must learn to interpret, through role-taking, their transactions with others and to formulate the meanings of their encounters. However, in Goffman's work, certain aspects of this process are emphasized. The dramaturgical view of interaction sees individuals not simply as *role-takers* but equally as **role-makers**. People do not merely interpret meanings, they also purposely create and manipulate meanings.

In the analogy suggested by the dramaturgical view of interaction, the essential reality of life is a series of fabricated roles, and society is a theater in which everyone is an actor engaged in a perpetual play. Goffman's view of human behavior indicates that he took seriously Shakespeare's claim (through the character of melancholy Jacques in *As You Like It*) that "all the world's a stage, And all the men and women merely players" (act 2, scene 7). Goffman's writings have had a profound effect on the way that social scientists think about the character of social interaction and have generated a body of literature around his ideas. These works include interpretations of Goffman's writings (Burns, 1992; Manning, 1992; Shalin, 2014), research elaborating theoretically on the dramaturgical metaphor of behavior as performance (Kivisto and Pittman, 2001; Edgley, 2013), applications of the impression-management notion to specific settings (Copp, 1998), and the connections between impression management and sensory stimuli (Waskul and Vannini, 2008). For a thorough introduction, examination, and collection of Goffman's work, see Charles Lemert and Ann Branaman's *The Goffman Reader* (1997). The general significance of Goffman's thinking for the sociology of everyday life is well stated by Spencer Cahill in Joel Charon's (2001) text on symbolic interaction theory:

> To Goffman . . . human beings act on a stage; they perform for others; they impress and they are impressed. They are both actors and audiences. And they often form a cooperative performance team that works to present a unified front to others. We know we do this; others know we do this; we know that others know we do this. Life is drama, and to understand interaction, self, or society we must consider this fact. (p. 191)

Presenting the Right Impression

In the dramaturgical view, individuals construct their **presentations of self** in a calculated and often contrived way. They do so not only to give a favorable impression of themselves but also to establish specific definitions of the acting situation.

> When an individual appears before others his [or her] action will influence the definition of the situation which they will come to have. Sometimes the individual will act in a thoroughly calculating manner, expressing himself [or herself] in a given way solely in order to give the kind of impression to others that is likely to invoke from them a specific response he [or she] is concerned to obtain. (Goffman, 1959:6)

Although this may sound as if Goffman is reading a Machiavellian kind of manipulation into human interactions, he did not see contrivance and chicanery everywhere. According to Cahill, Goffman emphasizes the intrinsically cooperative and moral character of human interaction:

> He shows us that mutual performance creates the mutually acceptable rules that form the basis of orderly social interaction. I perform for you and present myself in a way I choose. You perform for me and present yourself in a way you choose. Some of this performance is honest, some dishonest. Yet, if there is no clear evidence of deception, we agree to respect each other's performance and treat each other accordingly. Out of this agreement arises the morality that guides our acts and allows for the continuation of our interaction. (Charon, 2001:192)

By fabricating impressions, we try to control the definition of the acting situation that others come to have, and in so doing we set the future course of the interaction.

The dramaturgical view also assumes that humans are approval-seeking animals. We wish to be applauded by others for the self-images we present. We are eager to receive approval for our behaviors, opinions, and attitudes. We want to be seen as worthwhile, social, proper people, so we try to present our "best face" to others. To accomplish this end, we seek out information about others and systematically control information about ourselves. We particularly strive to exclude information we perceive as damaging to ourselves.

Sometimes we go to extremes to conceal biographical information about ourselves, as when we believe the hidden information would somehow taint our identities. Given the tendency to map each other into racial and ethnic categories that trigger associated racial or ethnic meanings, which in turn influence interaction (Kang, 2000), some people seek to disavow their ethnic or racial statuses. Jerry Kang, an Asian American law professor, describes several occasions when interactants' lack of knowledge of his racial status facilitated interaction. He has bought cars through a buying agent, mostly because he is too busy to negotiate with car dealers but also because he worries that he may receive worse offers than a similarly situated white male. Shielding his status effectively removes racialized negotiations from the car-buying ritual. Another example comes from his finding housing for a college summer job over the telephone. He arranged to live with a graduate student, who agreed to pick him up at the airport:

> I told him my height, what kind of jacket I had, and that I wore glasses. He told me that he had red hair, which would make him easy to spot. I later learned that neither he nor my immediate supervisor knew that I was Asian American until we met face to face. My phone voice, grammar, and accent did not prompt them to flip out of the default assumption: white. As for my name, they somehow heard "Jerry *King*." (Kang, 2000:1133)

The telephone inadvertently cloaked his race until the face-to-face meeting with his roommate: "If he were uncomfortable or particularly elated about living with an Asian, neither discomfort nor joy would have been triggered until we met at the airport," Kang noted (p. 1134).

Other kinds of information may also be concealed. To present an integrated, consistent, and proper impression of ourselves in everyday situations, we carefully monitor our actual behaviors. We make use of various devices to conceal our participation in improper or unconventional activities. Goffman described the "involvement shields" people use to give the impression of being properly involved, though they are not strictly conforming to the obligations of a social setting. They might use their hands to cover their eyes if they cannot keep them open when attention is demanded, or use a portable shield such as a newspaper to stifle a yawn. They may use their hands to cup a cigarette in places where smoking is not allowed or frowned upon. They sometimes sustain a pose of deep interest when they are, in fact, uninterested in a conversation. You no doubt have, at one time or another, nodded agreement to something you did not hear or understand (in class, perhaps?).

Contrary to a number of psychological models of the human being, Goffman did not view people as having one identity. Rather, he asserted, individuals have **multiple identities,** a repertoire of identities, and can choose from among these available identities the one that they judge best suits the expectations of a given audience. Goffman described humans as persons of *appearance.* It matters little what we actually are, therefore. What most matters is *what we appear to be.* And this is inevitably true because it is on the basis of our appearance—on the basis of the images, identities, impressions, and information we provide to others about ourselves—that others will formulate their conceptions of us.

Mutual Protection.   While we conceal certain aspects of ourselves so others will think of us as proper, there is another way in which information control is related to the appearance of propriety. The preservation of orderly interaction depends on the mutual protection of the individuals involved. The ultimate display of social morality is a person's attempt to protect the social images of others. Life, therefore, should not be viewed as an endlessly competitive struggle in which individuals aggressively protect only their own interests.

A basic feature of social interaction is that individuals tend to conduct themselves in encounters in such a way that both their own image and the images of the other participants are protected. Both the construction of a favorable personal impression and the protection of others' fabricated impressions involve information control. In Goffman's terms, individuals "show respect and politeness, making sure to extend to others any ceremonial treatment that might be their due. They employ discretion; they leave unstated facts that might implicitly or explicitly contradict or embarrass the positive claims made by others" (1967:16).

Conformity.   In the usual sociological view of conformity, when individuals internalize social norms, their behaviors conform to societal expectations. Society, in effect, gets inside their heads. The price of nonconformity, under the condition of internalization, is not simply the scorn of one's fellow human beings but, more important, scorn for oneself. Individuals conform because not to do so engenders guilt. From this perspective, norms are not merely guidelines. They assume a moral force.

Goffman provided an alternative view of conformity, at least implicitly. The dramaturgical analyst sees most human behavior as highly stylized and ritualized. It is performed in accordance with the rules, but not necessarily motivated by a *belief* in the rules. As individuals move from one setting or situation to another, they may simply adopt the interactional posture most appropriate for that situation.

Cynicism and Sincerity in Role-Taking

If we do not believe in the rules but conform merely because we are expected to do so in the situation, the honesty and sincerity of our behaviors may be suspect. In the dramaturgical view, society is viewed as a stage on which the actors, with premeditation, manipulate and withhold information about themselves and sometimes offer false information. The question is to what extent the role-players or performers are being consistent with their own image of self. Indeed, the dramaturgical model raises the question of just where to locate the person's "real" self or even whether there is a real self. When you act one way in front of your same-sex friends and an entirely different way in the company of the opposite sex, which of the two behaviors reflects your true self more accurately? When you display thoroughly proper table manners at a formal affair and the next day at dinner gruffly demand that your roommate "pass the goddamn butter," which of the two performances best reflects the kind of person you really are? Or are you both kinds of persons, simply alternating in a chameleonlike way from one situation to the next?

Everyday interaction is characterized by not only an expressive order but an emotional order as well. Since the 1970s, sociologists have studied and written about the social shaping and consequences of human emotions. In particular, Arlie Russell Hochschild proposed that human emotions are shaped by learned but implicit "feeling rules." According to her, individuals manage not only their outward expression of emotions but also their very feelings in order to conform to such rules. That is, they not only express but also attempt to feel what they think they should be feeling. In a book titled *The Managed Heart* (1983), Hochschild notes that in postindustrial society more and more jobs are requiring workers to manage their feelings. Occupations such as flight attendant require constant smiles and cordial behavior, even when customers become nasty or abusive. Hochschild warns that the "emotional labor" required in the growing number of service occupations will take a heavy psychological toll from workers who are required to put on cynical role performances as a matter of course.

A number of investigators have found this idea useful in examining emotion management in various contexts: Brents, Jackson, and Hausbeck

(2010) with sex workers in legal brothels; Copp (1998) with instructors at a sheltered workshop for people with developmental disabilities; George (2008) with personal trainers; Hansen (1996) with temporary workers; Kolb (2014) with victim advocates and counselors; Konradi (1999) with rape survivors in a courtroom setting; Leidner (1993) with fast-food workers; Pierce (1996) in law firms; Smith (2008) with "dramatic" professional wrestlers; Staske (1998) between close relational partners; Yoels and Clair (1994, 1995) with medical residents in an outpatient clinic, and others.

It would be a mistake to assume that everyone is always being cynical in the performance of their roles, however. The issue is not, we think, whether a person puts on performances, plays roles, or manipulates others. We all do that. The question of sincerity or cynicism in role-taking turns rather on whether performers *believe in their own performances*. We may think of role performances as sincere when individuals present themselves to others as they really believe themselves to be. Only when they rationally set out to deceive others by presenting false information about themselves can it be called a cynical role performance.

An observer of another's behavior cannot always determine whether the performance is cynical or sincere. Only the person producing the act knows whether he or she is being dishonest. Two people could put on concretely identical performances, one of which would be sincere and the other cynical. As an example, in a program that provided shelter, food, and drug and alcohol rehabilitation to homeless men, the requirement to show a commitment to recovery in order to participate led to cynical as well as sincere role performances (Weinberg, 1996). Weinberg observed that it was widely assumed among program participants that many of their peers merely *pretended* commitment to remain sheltered, "feigning a desire for sobriety in order to enjoy the benefits of 'three hots and a cot' (three meals a day and a bed), to satisfy court orders or to escape the myriad other adversities of skid row street life" (p. 141). As a result, the enactment and appraisal of authentic commitment to recovery became a central organizing feature of the program and a source of interactional tension between clients. Although there was always the possibility that one was being hustled by a potential malefactor, the possibility that one was being offered a genuine self-expression by someone trustworthy and authentically committed to recovery was also there. Individuals dedicated to their own recovery had to develop techniques to protect themselves from betrayal by others in the program, as well as techniques to determine who was and was not worthy of emotional investment. If they were to be trusted by others in the program, they also had to develop techniques for convincing others that they themselves were authentically committed to recovery and worthy of trust.

The only time a cynical performance can be uncovered as such is when it fails—when it falls through, and the person's true intentions are therefore made plain. In Weinberg's study, if a client who professed commitment was discovered with alcohol or drugs, his cynical performance had failed.

A person may eventually come to believe in a performance that was originally cynical. For example, young people may act intellectually to gain the status associated with being considered intellectuals in some situation. At the outset they may sustain this performance even though they do not believe themselves to be intellectuals. If they are accorded the status of an intellectual by others and recognized for their intellectual performance, however, at some point they might come to believe in their own originally cynical performance. The music they once listened to, the books they once read, and the museums they once attended only to provide props for this particular performance become over time true sources of pleasure. Their image as intellectuals has been incorporated into their conception of self.

Modifying the Situational View of Self

The concept of self appears throughout this book. In chapter 2 we described George Herbert Mead's conception of self as a process in which people objectively evaluate their behaviors from the perspective of the generalized other. This implies that a person presents different selves in different situations. To employ Mead's term, a person has not one *me* but a number of *me*s, each corresponding to a situationally proper role.

Goffman also offered a highly situational view of the self: as people move from one acting situation to another, their self-presentations change, often dramatically. In this interactionist view, individuals construct and perform roles in terms of both the norms governing particular situations and the specific responses they want to invoke from others. According to dramaturgical theorists, individuals remain detached from the roles they perform, changing presentations of self each time they enter a new situation.

Critics have charged that the dramaturgical metaphor is committed to an overly fluid, changeable notion of the self. They have questioned whether the self is always discrete, called forth only by the situation and the audience. These critics suggest that there are order and stability in the self, as well as some consistency in presentations of self, which transcend particular settings. Some organizing attribute or unifying principle in the self keeps a person from being only a bundle of situationally constructed roles.

Personality theorists such as the psychologists Sigmund Freud, Abraham Maslow, Harry Stack Sullivan, and Erik Erikson argued for the development of a personality structure that controls or coordinates situational presentations of self. Although they frequently stressed different themes and processes, all understood human beings as developing a distinct, bounded, identifiable conception of themselves (a personal identity, if you will) that has continuity through time.

Through interaction with others, we appear to develop early in childhood a conception of ourselves—perhaps as intelligent, shy, confident, physically attractive, or clumsy. If people do develop an overriding, independent, and relatively stable view of themselves, we must somewhat amend or revise the situationalist stance of the dramaturgical model. We need not reject Goffman's emphasis on the performance features of interaction. We simply have to acknowledge that basic and pervasive elements of self-conception may lie behind and motivate the particular performances individuals choose, the images they project, and the manipulations they attempt. A complete explanation of behavior must incorporate both the immediate character and requirements of social situations and the unique, subjective conception of self that individuals bring to every situation.

The Interacting Self

The New Testament's prescriptive warning "Judge not, lest you be judged" is a popular saying that most Americans hear one way or another. This "holy" edict, however, does not conform to reality that we negotiate through our interactions with others. For better and for worse, we live in a judgmental world. The interacting self belongs to anyone who is judged by others or judges others, both of which are regular occurrences in everyday life and, for the most part, psychologically and emotionally necessary. Making judgments does not mean that you are a bad or unethical person. "Reading" others is necessary for both positive and negative encounters with friends and strangers. In what types of situations do you feel you are being judged by others and, whether implicitly or explicitly, engage in impression management? In which situations do you judge others and, whether implicitly or explicitly, they engage in impression management?

■ Conclusion

In the first three chapters we have been asking: How do individuals organize, interpret, and give meaning to their own and others' behaviors? To answer this question, we have analyzed how individuals form a conception of others to make judgments about their interests, motives, values, attitudes, and character. They also try to manage the impressions of themselves that they present in order to control social situations and appear proper.

Information gathering is an important part of the person-perception process and the basis for the theoretical idea that *identification of* others precedes *identification with* them. From the interactionist perspective, information is critical to role-taking and so to meaningful human communication and interaction. The master attributes—gender, age, and race—are especially significant in the definitions that individuals come to have of others. The absence of these key pieces of information can create confusion and uncertainty in daily interactions.

Preliminary evaluations of others based only on these attributes may be incorrect, however. Individuals, therefore, continue to seek out information to refine their conceptions of others before and during their interactions. Elements of physical appearance such as height, weight, facial characteristics, posture, grooming, and clothing, as well as discourse, are noticed carefully. Beyond such information, which is immediately observable, verbal communications can provide knowledge of others' attitudes and values by seeking out information on their educational levels, occupations, and religions.

The dramaturgical model of interaction stresses the manner in which information is controlled to create definitions of situations. The idea that people present manufactured selves to each other, striving to appear proper in each other's eyes, rings true as a general statement about interaction. But presentations of self vary with particular settings. Some situations in everyday life require more extensive interpretation, calculation, and "self-work" than others do. There are some contexts in which individuals become especially concerned with the effects of their performances on others. In the following chapters we will examine how our relations with strangers and intimates involve us in different configurations of self, meaning, and informational analysis.

Definitions

accounts: Excuses or justifications given by individuals when social interaction is disturbed by rule violations.

achieved statuses: Those social statuses that are acquired during the course of individuals' lives and over which they may exert some control (for example, occupational level, educational attainment, or marriage into a higher social position).

ascribed statuses: Those social statuses possessed by individuals over which they have no control (for example, race, gender, age, and circumstances of birth).

configuration of attributes: The whole range of attributes about others that we take into account as we try to assess the kinds of people they are and the behaviors we might expect from them.

dramaturgical view: A perspective that uses theatrical metaphors to describe and analyze social interaction. The basic idea is that individuals present themselves to others in a manner analogous to a stage actor's presentation of a role to an audience.

expressions given: Verbal symbols or their substitutes, which one uses admittedly to convey information.

expressions given off: A wide range of actions performed for reasons other than the information conveyed, presumably unintentionally, but which nevertheless convey information.

face information: Information about aspects of a person's identity that can be gleaned simply by observing him or her. Race, gender, demeanor, and clothing, for example, are normally visible as soon as we encounter another person. It is on the basis of face information that we make preliminary judgments about the likely behaviors of others.

failed communication: An instance in which those interacting respond to each other on the basis of fundamentally different definitions of the situation.

impression management: The process through which individuals consciously try to foster particular images of themselves to gain control of a situation or the approval of others.

master attributes: Those statuses that are most central to both the way people view themselves and the way others view them. Race, gender, and age are three attributes that sharply define a person in any situation and tend to supersede other definitions of self that an individual might present to others.

multiple identities: Several identities from which individuals may choose in staging a particular performance, according to the dramaturgical view of interaction. From the repertoire of identities at their disposal, people ordinarily choose to present the identity that in their opinion best suits the expectations of a given audience.

physical attributes: Those aspects of self that define an individual's physical appearance and provide cues to the expected behaviors of others. Physical attributes include height, weight, expression, posture, and gesture.

presentations of self: The ways in which individuals present themselves to others in order to evoke a favorable impression and control definitions of situations.

role-makers: Human beings who create and manipulate meanings through the roles they choose to perform. All human beings are role-makers to the extent that they do not unthinkingly act out socially prescribed roles.

social attributes: Those aspects of self that define an individual's location in society. Among social attributes are race, gender, ethnicity, occupation, and religion. We build up a picture of others based on our knowledge of their various social attributes.

social status: An individual's position in society based on social attributes, including the ascribed statuses of race, gender, and age as well as achieved statuses such as wealth, education, and occupation. Status indicates the degree of prestige, esteem, and power conferred on individuals because of these attributes.

Discussion Questions

1. Think of a time when your attempts to role-take with another did not succeed. What happened to the interaction? How did it proceed? Why did you have difficulty role-taking? In what kinds of situations generally do people have the most difficulty assessing each other's meanings?

2. Which of your social attributes or statuses do you consider as most centrally defining your identity? Describe how you think those attributes affect the way others respond to you.

3. Describe some of the ways in which you feel that individuals' physical attractiveness influences their own behaviors and the behaviors of others toward them. Do you think that physical appearance affects the lives of men and women differently in American society? If so, how do you account for this difference?

4. Devise some simple experiments to demonstrate for yourself the significance of the clothes you wear in determining how others treat you in a variety of settings. Would you be treated differently by clerks in department, specialty, or discount stores, depending on your clothing, for example? What kind of experiment would you construct? Where would you conduct it? How would you alter the type of clothing worn by the experimenters? Which reactions would you particularly want to record?

5. Do you agree or disagree with Erving Goffman's picture of humans as strategic, manipulative, sometimes insincere managers of impressions? In what ways might contrived performances be necessary for maintaining social order?

6. Is there such a thing as a "real" self, or are we only a bundle of situationally constructed roles? What do you think is the linkage between someone's "stable" personality attributes and the particular self he or she presents in a given situation?

PART TWO

ESTABLISHING SOCIAL ORDER

Part two demonstrates how the elements of face-to-face communication can be employed to analyze aspects of everyday life. Our concern centers on the ways in which people establish predictable, meaningful patterns of behavior in a wide variety of daily settings. The four contexts discussed in this part are contacts between strangers, or urban public encounters; contacts between intimates; relationships in the world of work in bureaucracies; and the institutions that shape our experience of health and illness. We also consider the definitions of the situations people create through their participation in various social arrangements, and we examine how power and status differences affect face-to-face encounters. The chapters in part two will help you understand that the meanings of any human relationship are socially constructed; that is to say, people establish meanings through their daily communications with one another.

Chapter 4 is concerned with how people perceive and interact with others in anonymous public places. Our analysis proceeds from the observation that people in public places are strangers to one another. They employ various adaptations to cope with the huge volume of stranger contacts experienced in cities and may adopt strategies to avoid direct communication. The consideration of stranger relations in chapter 4 describes the connections among information, trust, and risk in *any* interaction.

The substance of chapter 5 is intimate relations. This chapter begins with the argument that intimacy is a socially constructed, symbolic phenomenon. The meanings of intimacy vary both historically and in terms of individuals' personal attributes. The building of relationships is an ongoing process, and strangers go through typical stages in their transformation into intimates. The last sections of chapter 5, which look at the literature on living together, staying single, and divorce, give you some idea of recent changes in the meanings given to intimacy, sexuality, and commitment.

In our analyses of relations among strangers and intimates, we touch on questions of power only briefly. Chapter 6 provides an important addition to our treatment of social interaction by stressing the differences in access to decision-making processes for various individuals and groups. As a result of these differences, some individuals are in more strategic positions than others to have their definitions of the situation translated into actuality. There is also a relationship between role-taking ability and the power accorded the positions occupied in society. You will see that such daily behaviors as staring, pointing, crowding, touching, and interrupting others' conversations are all functions of power differentials between people.

Chapter 7 expands on the importance of the positions a person occupies in the social order by focusing more specifically on everyday life in bureaucratic organizations. Contacts between people in modern societies are increasingly mediated by the intervention of third-party agencies such as insurance companies, government bureaus, and the courts. Our treatment of bureaucratic life emphasizes the concepts of multiple realities, the processes of negotiation, and the symbolic foundations of social structures. You will be shown how people's locations in the organizational hierarchy of a work organization shape their conceptions of their jobs. You will also learn how workers strive to achieve some degree of autonomy in their work lives.

The last chapter in part two examines the meanings attached to health and illness in America. Here, as throughout this book, we demonstrate that every human experience must be viewed from the subjective perspectives of the individuals going through it. Illness would seem at first glance to be thoroughly an objective fact. Either one is sick or one is well. Rather, health and illness are in large measure the product of ethnic, class, and cultural differences, as well as an outcome of the negotiations between "patients" and the health care system. In the second part of chapter 8 we present a case study of one "illness"—depression—which exemplifies the notion that the experience of illness, like everything else, is a product of meanings arising out of human communication.

4

Everyday Urban Relations
Contacts among Strangers

When we were children, we were taught to avoid strangers and even fear them, for our own protection. Who knew what a stranger might really want who stopped you on the street asking for directions, approached to sell you something, or chose a seat next to you on a bus? Because we cannot know for sure what the motives of strangers are, we learn to regard them with suspicion.

Strangers are strange precisely because we know little or nothing about them. Their lives may be guided by symbol systems different from our own, and they may not share our concept of social reality. In such a case the essential meanings they give to objects, events, and situations will be different from our own. This difference is what makes communication and interaction with strangers so difficult. These types of encounters, however, have become the norm as urbanization has become a worldwide phenomenon, with the majority of people living in or near cities (Monti et al., 2014). As the frequency of interactions with strangers in our everyday lives has become more common and important, so has the need to study and understand these interactions and the geographic, demographic, and spatial conditions that foster and support them.

■ Sociological Definitions of the Stranger

The stranger has always intrigued sociological theorists. Georg Simmel, for example, was concerned not with one-to-one relationships between strangers but with new relationships between an individual and a larger social system (a group, an institution, a community). Simmel conceived of the special quality of the stranger as the person who "comes today and stays tomorrow" (1950b:13). The stranger's status always remains peripheral or marginal to groups with which interactions are being sought. The best example is the successful trader or merchant who has direct dealings with a number of groups but does not seek assimilation into any of them. The stranger's distinctive position is to be near to and distant from a group at the same time.

In American sociology, the stranger as a social type has often been equated with what the early 20th-century sociologist Robert Park referred to as **marginal man,** or what we today would call *marginal person.* He applied the idea to immigrant racial and ethnic groups in the city who remain marginal members of urban society because they are in the process of giving up their old cultures without having fully assimilated the culture of the new. The marginal person stands between the two cultures as "one who lives in two worlds, in both of which he is more or less a stranger" (Park, 1928:892). The "wandering Jew," historically without a homeland, was the best example of the stranger or marginal person by Park's definition.

Alfred Schutz (1960) also described the stranger in terms of an individual's relationship to organized group life. His analysis focuses on the definition of the stranger as one who is not knowledgeable about the cultural pattern of the group to which admission is sought. For a stranger approaching a group, the relevancies of everyday life are not the same as for the group's members. The stranger therefore is not sure how to interpret social situations, events, and behaviors. The stranger, puzzled by the apparent incoherence and inconsistency of the group's cultural pattern, is likely to question elements of group life that full-fledged members take for granted. In Schutz's words, "The cultural pattern of the approached group is to the stranger not a shelter but a field of adventure, not a matter of course but a questionable topic of investigation, not an instrument for disentangling problematic situations but a problematic situation itself and one hard to master" (1960:104).

For Peter Berger and Hansfried Kellner (1970), an essential element of the concept of strangeness is the fact that unacquainted individuals come from different face-to-face contexts and **areas of conversation,** with different biographies and life experiences. Their pasts have a similar structure, but because they do not have a shared past, they are likely to define situations in different ways.

Sociologists have defined the stranger concept in specialized ways. We will adopt a more conventional use of the term *stranger* and differentiate between those who are **biographical strangers,** because we have never before met them and have no information about their pasts, and those who are **cultural strangers,** because they occupy symbolic worlds different from our own. We are cautious in the presence of both those whom we have never met before and those who do not share our values, attitudes, or lifestyles.

Much of a person's time is spent in front of an audience of strangers. Public thoroughfares are crowded with people who are biographical and often cultural strangers to one another. Each time you enter a subway, stand in a line, go jogging in a city park, attend a concert, or shop in a discount store, you are in effect performing in front of an audience of people you have never seen before and whom, in all likelihood, you will never see again.

When biographical or cultural strangers confront one another, they typically put on a performance that reflects the uncertainties in such encounters. In this chapter we will explore the uncertainties that accompany relations with strangers and the strategies which can be employed to take them into account. Patterned and predictable presentations of self are necessary if individuals are to manage and make sense of their daily lives in public places.

■ The Paradox of Doubt and Trust

Social life could not proceed in an orderly fashion if a **norm of trust** did not underlie our behaviors with others (Semmes, 1991; Seligman, 2000). By and large, we trust that others' spoken words and actions really represent the kinds of individuals they are. Each day we face situations that demand such trust. For example, in dealing with store clerks or restaurant servers, there is a moment when we hand them our money or our credit or debit card and must trust them to complete the transaction honestly by returning with the proper change or running the charge correctly. Normally we must, in order to get through the day, trust that others mean us no harm, that we are not being purposely misled in our encounters with them. Social life would be intolerably complicated if we had to routinely suspend the norm of trust.

While trust is essential in order to maintain an ordered social life, there is always some measure of doubt about the true motives, goals, and intentions of others. This is because role-taking efforts can never be perfect; we can never identify absolutely with others. All social interactions, even those between intimates, therefore involve some measure of doubt or risk. Our inability to suspend doubt fully in our social interactions presents the paradox that we must doubt and trust others at the same time. It is true that ordered interaction proceeds on the general assumption of trust, *but we can never be certain that such an assumption is perfectly safe.* A comment by a Greenwich Village resident interviewed by Mitch Duneier in his study of life on city sidewalks reflects the conflict surrounding the issue of trust: "That's what cities are about. . . . You want to be able to trust in the kindness of everyone around you . . . [but] you can't ever look anyone in the eyes, you have to be really guarded and it actually ends up being sort of rude" (1999:199).

Trust is an aspect of everyday life with which we must cope all the time. However, it is one of those "taken-for-granted" aspects that we seldom analyze. Sometimes we are sharply aware of our distrust of others and the reasons for this distrust. At other times we may be only vaguely aware that we are uneasy and distrustful in the presence of certain people.

We are most likely to distrust others, as a general rule, when they obviously have different social attributes than we do. An unshaven, slovenly man approaching a woman who does not know him on a dark city street could be assumed to be a mugger, for example. Those who try to initiate encounters when there are discrepancies in their attributes are likely to find their motives misinterpreted. We depend heavily on immediate observation of others to determine whether we can trust them and whether interaction with them is therefore permissible. We carry around pretty clear expectations about the appropriateness of interactions between people with particular attributes.

Race, for example, may particularly affect interaction between people who do not know one another. Elijah Anderson (1999) described the importance of race in determining people's reactions to black males in public encounters in his study of a racially mixed neighborhood in Philadelphia. Although the white residents do not think that the black people they ordinarily see on the streets are bound to rob them, Anderson said, the fact that there have been several incidents of black people robbing a bank and committing other crimes in the area gives "a peculiar edge to race relations between blacks and whites" (p. 17). Both blacks and whites are aware that young black males are disproportionately involved in crime. "A black male walking into the stores, especially a jewelry store, can see this phenomenon. The sales personnel pay particular attention to people until they feel they have passed inspection, and black males are almost always given extra scrutiny" (p. 17).

Jerry Kang, an Asian American lawyer, described his own reactions:

> After a long conference, I am walking in a strange downtown, late at night, looking for a taxi. I see two people approaching me. From a distance, I ascertain their rough size. From their clothing and body shape, I guess that they are male. As they walk closer, I see that they are Black. For reasons I cannot explain, my heartbeat quickens, and I become anxious, glancing around for other people. I begin taking a few steps to cross to the other side of the street but decide against it. Instead, I grip my briefcase more tightly, closer to my body, then walk at a faster pace. As I pass the Black men, I peek over my shoulder just to make sure that they have walked on by. (Kang, 2000:1140)

Encounters with strangers pose special trust problems because we have no information about them, other than face information, or that which is obtainable through immediate observation. Sometimes a person's general appearance or location can tell us a good deal about him or her. In the presence of strangers, however, information of this sort is usually incomplete and possibly unreliable. To judge with assurance the genuineness of others' performances and the meaning of their behaviors, we must know about their "areas of conversation." The more we know about others' biographies and life experiences, the better we are able to role-take with them. To illustrate the point, knowing that a woman is diabetic helps us interpret what she is doing by injecting some substance into her arm with a hypodermic needle. If we have knowledge of her biography as a diabetic, the interpretation "maintaining her health" is a far more credible explanation of her behavior than "maintaining her habit." Sometimes people may deliberately attempt to create an atmosphere that affirms trust when surface signs might indicate otherwise. Brent Staples (1992) described the measures he has adopted in his nighttime walks through New York streets to thwart perceptions of those who may fear he is a "dangerous black man"—he whistles classical music!

How Cabdrivers Size Up Strangers.   The relationship between face information and trust is especially crucial in some interactions with strangers. City cabdrivers, for example, who must be in continual contact with strangers, adopt certain strategies to assess which ones to accept as passengers. James Henslin documented the informal criteria cabdrivers use in sizing up the trustworthiness of passengers. He conceptualizes trust in dramaturgical terms: "Trust consists of an actor offering a definition of himself and an audience being willing to interact with the actor on the basis of that definition" (2007:180). Like everyone else, cabdrivers must determine the conditions under which they have reason to question the performances put on by others. In deciding whether a passenger is to be trusted, they consider: (1) the setting in which the person is picked up, (2) the characteristics of the person as judged by his or her appearance, and (3) the individual's behavior. In other words, cabdrivers simultaneously consider the characteristics of the *person* they pick up, the *places* where they pick them up, and the *poses* adopted by their passengers.

Cabdrivers ordinarily accept a person's self-definition as a passenger who wishes to be taken to a particular destination. Sometimes, however, they have reason to distrust a person's performance as a legitimate passenger. Each time a passenger approaches, the driver must decide if it is safe to make the trip. The driver's trust judgments are made on the basis of the individual's age, race, gender, general demeanor, and social class; the neighborhood and the time of the day of the pickup; and the announced destination of the passenger. When the configuration of these factors indicates the need for distrust, the prudent driver usually decides to pass up the potential passenger.

Like people in general, when deciding whether to trust or distrust a stranger, cabdrivers rely heavily on commonly accepted stereotypes about social classes and groups in American society. The results of Henslin's study indicated that drivers expect comparatively less trouble from passengers in upper- and middle-class areas, females, whites, and the very young or very old.

The Case for Being Uncertain about Strangers in Public Places. Mutual strangeness puts limits on people's role-taking capacity and therefore on the ways they can and will relate to each other. The following propositions sum up the reasons why interactions between strangers have a large element of uncertainty in them.

1. There is a measure of uncertainty attached to *any* interaction since we can never be completely certain of another's motives.

2. The uncertainty of risk decreases as we acquire more information about others, since the accuracy of our role-taking increases.

3. Strangers in public places possess no biographical information about each other.

4. It follows that public relations between strangers carry particularly great uncertainties.

It should be noted, however, that even while images of tensions based on race, class, gender, and other attributes of "strangeness" (that is, whatever is different from us) still feed our images of cities and the way various kinds of people fill them, sociologists have observed ways that people can be different and alike at the same time and in the same place (Borer, 2008; Deener, 2012; Monti, 2012). In Elijah Anderson's more recent work (2011), he observed how some minority persons in Philadelphia had found civility and in some cases even friendship in unaccustomed places. His characterization of the "cosmopolitan canopy" details the kinds of opportunities that arise for diverse city dwellers to enjoy one another's company. In his study of central Philadelphia, Anderson finds spaces separate from the street where the diversity of the people there is part of the attraction. These are places like the Reading Terminal, food courts, sports arenas, certain shopping areas, and parks, where diversity is expected and people can let down the guard they frequently maintain in other urban public spaces. These cosmopolitan canopies encourage civility and mutual curiosity. Diverse people may develop the kinds of social competencies and sophistication that allow them to get along.

■ The Structure of Everyday Public Behaviors

Public behaviors seldom require more than a passing acquaintance, and strangers typically confront each other in highly anonymous situations. While the ability to remain anonymous increases the potential for individual freedom of action, it does not decrease the constraints imposed on individual behaviors by society. In fact, anonymity must be created and maintained through *social relationships*, and this is itself a social effort. Rather than being a state which is *independent* of social relationships, therefore, anonymity must be produced by people interacting with one another. The structure of public behaviors between strangers is reinforced by efforts to maintain the **norm of anonymity.**

Efforts to Remain Anonymous

The creation of anonymity through interaction can be seen in the efforts people make to avoid unnecessary encounters with unfamiliar others. As in many other public contexts, individuals engage in what Erving Goffman (1963) described as **civil inattention** when they are forced to recognize others' presence while trying to minimize the possibility of a "focused" interaction with them. In other words, they try to minimize the interactional claims that others might make on them. Lyn Lofland has argued that civil inattention may be viewed as the necessity of city life in that it "makes possible co-presence without co-mingling, awareness without engrossment, courtesy without conversation" (1998:30). But as Lofland notes, this is not because of the "stimulus overload" that concerned Simmel, or the psychological shutdown thought to result in the "typical" urban attitudes of emotional coldness and unconcern. "Civil inattention suggests that when humans in the public realm appear to ignore one another, they do so *not* out of psychological distress but out of a ritual regard, and their response is *not* the asocial one of 'shut down' but the fully social one of politeness" (1998:30; emphasis in the original). Candace West (1999) provides a great example:

> I notice a supreme test of civil inattention just outside the window of the shop. A man is walking down the street with black grease paint on his face, a hat with Viking horns on his head, and a huge spear, which he is carrying upright in his fist. . . . As he moves toward other pedestrians, they do their best to seem urbane—catching sight of him from about 8 feet away and averting their eyes as they near him—but whipping their heads around to stare at him, just after he passes by. (p. 8)

This interactional effort is, of course, reciprocal. Many individuals in the situation are doing the same thing, though today a good number of folks would be recording the modern-day Viking with their smartphones and posting pictures and videos to various social media sites.

Passengers on subways or buses tend to choose seats that maximize their distance from fellow travelers. They limit their visual attention to props they may have with them (cell phones, books, magazines, newspapers) or to advertising over the windows; they take great pains to avoid physical contact once the subway car or bus begins to get crowded. These regulations, shared and known about by all participants, are designed to limit the accessibility of unacquainted individuals to one another. By utilizing knowledge of these regulations—or, as Lofland calls them, *principles*—along with a general understanding of what's expected in public behavior, "strangers are able to communicate to one another messages such as: 'I want my privacy and am not available to be spoken to or encountered in any way;' 'I know you are present and you know I am present but we are, of course, each invisible to the other;' or 'I am not intruding and will not intrude into your personal space; in fact, I am going out of my way to avoid doing so'" (Lofland, 1998:34–35).

There are, of course, circumstances when it is acceptable for civil inattention to be breached. Carol Gardner (1995) found in her observations that "stranger etiquette" permits someone with a dog or a child to be "approached at will" (p. 93). Duneier and Molotch (1999) observed that in Greenwich Village (as elsewhere), strangers pet one another's animals or ask about a toddler's identity ("Oh, is this your grandson?"). According to these authors, "Perhaps to the advantage of both parties, the dog or child serves to modulate intimacy, permitting, in effect, indirect communication via the dependent creature" (p. 1279). However, dogs (and children) can also induce and sustain unwanted interaction, as in the case of Keith, a homeless African American street vendor, who calls to a dog being walked by a white woman:

> Keith: "Come here, Dottie." . . . Pulling on the leash, the dog tugs her owner over to Keith who begins playing with Dottie. Keith: "Sit down." The dog sits as Laura, the dog's owner, stands by looking distracted, pulling on the leash. (Duneier and Molotch, 1999:1281)

The interaction continues for a few minutes, with Keith primarily talk-ing to the dog but attempting to engage its owner in conversation. "The woman has the dog by the leash, which means that when Keith gains access to the dog, he has the woman by the leash. Developing rapport with a dog who does not recognize class or race distinctions helps Keith entangle a woman who does" (p. 1282).

Efforts to Ensure Public Privacy

The order of public life is clearly demonstrated in situations where a person's moral identity is called into question. Think of the places where you might go where others might question your values. Adult stores and sex toy shops? Anarchist bookstores? A KKK rally? David Karp (1973) studied the behaviors of customers of pornographic bookstores and movie theaters in Times Square. Karp observed a number of strategies employed in these settings to ensure a kind of **public privacy**. In the bookstore, shoppers main-tain a strict impersonality toward one another. Under no circumstances do they make physical or verbal contact, and the clerks quickly eject anyone who interferes with the privacy of other customers. The normative structure appears to demand silence and careful avoidance of any focused interaction. Customers adopt techniques that allow them to complete their purchases as quickly and unobtrusively as possible. They are more likely to make a pur-chase if left alone. Customers strive to appear as uninterested as possible.

Similarly, efforts to maintain public privacy can be observed in a ciga-rette shop: "Now, the only store in town that allows smoking on its premises" (West, 1999). West describes the discomfort involved in this experience:

> Arriving at the doorway of this shop, I am aware of other pedestrians who studiously avert their eyes from me as I enter. Buying cigarettes these days feels like buying tampons did when I was 13—making an acutely stigmatizing purchase that you hope nobody notices. . . . Not only do non-smokers look away from smokers as the latter enter this shop but also smokers themselves avoid looking at one another as they pull cartons from the shelves. Skulking out with my plain unmarked bag. . . . (p. 8)

Such settings encourage a highly structured social situation in which privacy norms are standardized and readily understood. The system works so that each person's bid for privacy is complemented by the behaviors of others. Even in anonymous public places such as Times Square, people are very much constrained in the production of their behaviors. Despite the impersonality and anonymity of daily life, and despite the fact that actions in the public domain are overwhelmingly performed in front of strangers—and sometimes even recorded by them on smartphones—it is necessary to constantly engage in impression management. When it comes to maintain-ing a proper image of ourselves, everyone counts, both intimates and strangers. Impression management strategies used by customers in strip clubs, for example, seem to indicate that "more than relying on dress or body adornment, they depended on conversation, gesture, and facial expressions to try and convey whatever image they wanted to the strippers, or friends, or to other customers" (Wood, 2000:21–22). Customers seem to guard their expressions to keep other customers or the strippers from thinking they are enjoying it too much. According to one club dancer, "If they're even that much more attracted to you, that makes them kind of squirm and look around like 'someone's going to think I'm enjoying this too much,' you know, like 'I'm not supposed to be watching her like this'" (p. 21).

An example illustrating the sometimes elaborate strategies adopted by strangers to maintain a distinctive public privacy can be found in Laud Humphreys's classic *Tearoom Trade: Impersonal Sex in Public Places* (1970). Humphreys analyzed the behaviors of homosexual men meeting in public restrooms (known as "tearooms"). He describes these settings as well-organized places where the participants strictly abide by the rules. The activities of approaching the room, positioning oneself inside it, signaling one's availability, contracting for the nature of the sexual exchange, completing the sexual act, coping with intrusions, and finally leaving the situation are carefully patterned. Nearly all these negotiations occur without any verbal interaction between the participants.

The importance of Humphreys's study goes far beyond description of the particular behaviors he documented. The fact that these kinds of behaviors can be accomplished at all serves as a broader commentary on the orderliness of everyday public activities. In Humphreys's words:

> Analysis of the highly structured patterns that arise in this particular situation increases our understanding of the more general rules of interaction by which people in routine encounters of all kinds manage their identities, create impressions, move towards their goals, and control information about themselves, minimizing the costs and risks in concerted action with others. (1970:ix)

Although Humphreys's book won a prestigious sociological award, it also gave rise to controversy, raising serious questions about ethics in sociological research.

New technology has the potential to change social relations in public places. Cell phones, for example, raise interesting questions about public privacy: "Is it, for example, proper to talk about private matters on a mobile phone in public places?" (Persson, 2001). Perhaps more to the point: Why do people, who normally keep their private lives to themselves, sometimes reveal the most intimate details to strangers around them when speaking on cell phones in public places? The cell phone seems to make us feel as if we are alone, even in public places where we are surrounded by many other people. This suggests that the phones, in the same way as newspapers or books when one is dining alone in public, serve as "involvement shields" (Goffman, 1963); that is, objects used to make oneself seem inaccessible to others (Persson, 2001). Those within earshot engage in civil inattention, not showing that they hear what may be intimate details about the caller's life. It is no surprise, then, that modern etiquette books have a paragraph on cell phone etiquette.

With technological innovation comes the need for new rules regarding civil inattention and public privacy. The use of smartphones to make video recordings of people may sometimes cross lines of propriety. Individuals who are recorded without their knowledge or consent may feel that their privacy has been invaded. Such feelings can result when the behavior of the smartphone user violates or appears to violate the established social norm for visual behavior. This norm, as Goffman (1963) long ago observed but which still applies today, holds that it is customary for people who are present in a public setting but are not interacting to engage in civil inattention. This ritual consists of a glance of acknowledgment that the other person is present, followed by restraint of further visual attention. Visual attention after the acknowledgment can be construed as a breach of etiquette or, more seriously, as an invasion of privacy (Crabb, 1996; Kim, 2012).

Impression Management with Strangers

The patterns of behavior followed in the situations described in the previous section not only maintain the norm of anonymity and assure public privacy but also are designed to protect personal identities, minimize social risk, and give the appearance of propriety. Thus, they are examples of the impression management techniques people use to foster particular images of themselves in their interactions with others (see chapter 3). They also are examples of the **self-management techniques** people use to control the identities they present to others and to protect themselves when in the presence of strangers.

Lofland used an interactionist perspective to study the self-management techniques used by strangers in their everyday interactions. Her work was based on the following assertion: "If a person is to exist as a social being, as an organism with a self, there must be some minimal guarantees that in interaction with others he [or she] will receive the affirmation and confirmation of himself [or herself] as 'right'" (1971:95). The risk for the self in confronting strangers in public places is that they may be unable to provide this confirmation. An encounter with a stranger may even *disconfirm* the other person's "rightness."

The State of Involved Indifference

In their efforts to maintain anonymity and protect public privacy, strangers in public places adopt elaborate strategies to avoid one another. This does not mean that they are entirely uninvolved with one another, however. Strangers in public places also adopt mechanisms to produce ordered relationships. Even the **avoidance behaviors** engaged in by strangers are highly coordinated social activities demanding some degree of cooperation. To suggest that humans are like atoms anonymously floating around one another at random is not a very insightful description of the public relationships of strangers. It fails to account for the means by which public life is managed and ordered. While strangers rarely talk with one another or

exchange information of a private nature, it is nevertheless clear that public life is *ordered* rather than chaotic (see box).

Lofland (1998) has suggested that we think in terms of people carrying around and consulting (symbolically) guidebooks to help them define the situation and direct their own conduct. Some of her titles are: *Grammars of Motility*, which recommends rules of social and physical movement in the public realm; for example, how to make one's way through crowded streets and intersections, choose a seat in a crowded bar or restaurant or bus, escape unwanted attention, and so on; *Urban Visual Aids: Rules for Coding Space, Appearance, and Behavior*, "a book devoted to detailing the 'interpretation principles' by which urbanites make sense of the raw data emanating from their physical and social environment and thus define the situations in which they find themselves" (p. 28); *Verbal Sociability Customs*, "a volume that assists them in determining when, with whom, and how they may or may not try to engage their fellow urbanites in direct conversation" (p. 28).

Although this tells us much about interaction in the public realm, she suggests that what we know of the normative system of the public realm is probably more easily grasped if we conceive of it in terms of "overarching principles" rather than in terms of a plethora of narrowly focused rules (see box on p. 102).

The authors of this book suggest that there is a fragile balance between noninvolvement and cooperation in the structure of public relationships. Strangers try to avoid involvement with others to protect themselves from unwanted and risky encounters. At the same time, they orient their behaviors toward others and cooperate enough to ensure some degree of order and sense in their everyday lives. Like the pedestrians on the sidewalk, they

Going with the Flow

What strikes researchers with the discipline and patience necessary for careful observation of public behavior is the orderliness and patternedness with which city denizens seem to conduct even their most fleeting and ostensibly "trivial" encounters (Lofland, 1998). "For order to be possible, people must behave like competent pedestrians and must expect copresent others to act accordingly" (Wolfinger, 1995:323). Clearly there are social conventions that order this commonplace behavior in an anonymous situation. Yamori (1998) describes the "banded structure" shown by a collectivity of pedestrians on a large crosswalk in Osaka, Japan:

> . . . flows of pedestrians pass by each other, forming in orderly fashion into a few bands or lanes. Each band contains either one or the other of the two groups of pedestrians walking in opposite directions from each other. It achieves a smooth traffic flow of pedestrians without which they would bump and jumble into each other in a disorganized mass. (p. 530)

Once the structure is created at a macro level, it constrains individual behavior in a crowd. For example, after the banded structure has been established in a crosswalk, late-coming pedestrians are not likely to walk against or across the established stream of people. Instead, they are forced to follow preexisting traffic patterns even if for some reason they do not want to (Yamori, 1998:541).

It appears that pedestrian order depends essentially on two social rules: (1) people must behave like competent pedestrians, and (2) people must trust copresent others to behave like competent pedestrians. But why do people believe that other users of public places will indeed behave like competent pedestrians? Nicholas Wolfinger (1995) decided to find out by exploring a particular case in which pedestrian interactions may become problematic: roller-skating. Roller-skating presents many challenges to the normal order of public space interaction. For example, the characteristic weaving motion of a skater makes him or her seem out of control, and skaters move quickly, which may surprise pedestrians. Collisions are potentially more consequential. Wolfinger surmised that the challenges roller-skating poses to pedestrians should allow special insight into the organization of public interaction.

Wolfinger engaged in first-person observation as he roller-skated approximately six miles several times a week commuting to and from the University of California, Los Angeles. He was able to create many situations where normal pedestrian order broke down (following Garfinkel, 1963), which provided diverse opportunities to examine the social dynamics of trust in public space.

Wolfinger observed that people usually looked uncomfortable in situations in which their trust was threatened (e.g., when caught by surprise because they hadn't seen him coming, or when he skated behind someone for a period of time without passing), indicating that people rely on safe passages as a matter of course. Troublesome situations test the trust that people generally take for granted. Pedestrian interaction is inherently social because it depends on the ritualized production of trust between copresent users of public space. When order is threatened, pedestrians often respond with specific remedial behaviors, such as apologies. When pedestrians apologize, they acknowledge an infraction of trust and reaffirm their commitment to the bargain.

It is the ritualization of remedial measures that enables continued order in public places (à la Goffman, 1971). In this respect, pedestrian life is but a microcosm of social order. And public spaces are characterized to a great extent by order. The considerable attention paid to the disorderliness of public spaces in the United States "overlooks our day-to-day experiences; the great majority of our interactions with strangers in public places proceed comfortably and smoothly. We implicitly place confidence in scores of strangers every day, and they almost invariably oblige. Certainly, our streets are not devoid of hazards, but in sheer numbers they pale in comparison to the countless acts of trust we each experience every day" (Wolfinger, 1995:338).

Lofland's Principles of Public Face-to-Face Interaction

1. **Cooperative motility.** "Most of us get through doors without incident, most pedestrians don't collide with other pedestrians, most buses and cars do not flatten human beings, and most people do not get body parts crushed by closing elevator doors. Most of the time our movement through the public realm is simply *uneventful*, and it is so because humans are *cooperating* with one another to make it so" (Lofland, 1998:29).

2. **Civil inattention.** According to Goffman (1963): "What seems to be involved is that one gives to another enough visual notice to demonstrate that one appreciates that the other is present (and that one admits openly to having seen him), while at the next moment withdrawing one's attention from him so as to express that he does not constitute a target of special curiosity or design" (pp. 83–84). "It is practiced on buses, in restaurants, on park benches, in airplanes, in hotel lobbies, even on that stereotyped symbol of urban alienation, the subway" (Lofland, 1998:30).

3. **Audience role prominence.** "Humans often quite enthusiastically assume the audience role in the face of what are very serious problems, even catastrophes" (Lofland, 1998:32).

4. **Restrained helpfulness.** "Specifically targeted and clearly limited requests for mundane assistance and a response of restrained helpfulness . . . are a constant feature of life in the public realm. 'Could you tell me the time?' is answered by 'it's 5:12'" (Lofland, 1998:32).

5. **Civility toward diversity.** "In face-to-face exchanges, confronted with what may be personally offensive visible variations in physical abilities, beauty, skin color and hair texture, dress style, demeanor, income, sexual preference, and so forth, the urbanite will act in a civil manner, that is, will act 'decently' vis-à-vis diversity" (Lofland, 1998:32).

From Lofland, L. 1998. *The Public Realm: Exploring the City's Quintessential Social Territory.* New York: Aldine de Gruyter.

---

systematically take each other into account in public places to avoid unwanted encounters. In sum, we are offering a "mini-max" description of public encounters. Strangers are obliged both to *minimize involvement* and to *maximize order*. They must take each other into account while simultaneously protecting their own and others' privacy: "What is everybody's business in the country is nobody's business in the city where people must see everything while averting their eyes" (Erickson, 2001:34).

The idea of **involved indifference** as a basis for interactions with strangers may seem contradictory. We use this term to communicate that although strangers may not engage in direct verbal interactions, they nevertheless produce their behaviors from a careful assessment of those around them. Everyday public life "works" because of the subtle blending of involvement, indifference, and cooperation.

■ The City as a World of Strangers

The volume of contacts between strangers is greatest in anonymous city places. According to Lofland, "the city provides, on a permanent basis, an environment composed importantly of persons who are personally unknown to one another—composed importantly of strangers" (1998:xi). The connecting possibilities in the city make it a liberating place for many people: "The sheer mass of people allows for personal autonomy and creativity that is often chased out of less dense environments" (Erickson, 2001:34).

The Volume of Interactions in Cities

By definition, cities are places where large numbers of individuals with varied backgrounds live crowded together in a limited space. Urban areas are no longer limited to cities, however. They include the surrounding towns and suburbs in metropolitan areas and megalopolises, in which several adjacent cities are merged. Along the East Coast, for example, an unbroken metropolitan area with more than 100 people per square mile stretches from Kittery, Maine, to Quantico, Virginia. This megalopolis of more than 40 million people, popularly known as Boswash, includes the cities of Boston, New York, Philadelphia, Baltimore, and Washington, DC.

American society has become predominantly urban. In 2010, some 230 million people—accounting for 80 percent of the American population—lived in metropolitan areas. Almost one-third of Americans (30 percent) lived in metropolitan areas of at least 5 million people. With modern transportation and communication, very few small towns are still considered rural. In large cities, however, the density of the urban population greatly increases the number of possible contacts between people. The population of New York City, for example, was more than 8 million in 2010 (U.S. Census Bureau, 2010). In midtown Manhattan you probably would not know intimately any of the thousands of people who would pass you by. Such a phenomenon constitutes an essential distinguishing feature of urban life, according to Lofland, who refers to the "public realm" as "made up of those spaces in a city which tend to be inhabited by persons who are strangers to one another or who 'know' one another only in terms of occupational or other nonpersonal identity categories (for example, bus driver–customer)" (1998:9).

Social scientists have constructed explanations of everyday interactions based on the volume of potential interactions in anonymous urban settings. Georg Simmel argued that because urban dwellers are bombarded with far more stimuli than they can possibly manage, they must maintain superficial, impersonal relationships with fellow urbanites. He contrasts urban and rural life in this respect:

> With each crossing of the street, with the tempo and multiplicity of economic, occupational and social life, the city sets up a deep contrast with small town and rural life with reference to the sensory foundation of psychic life. The metropolis exacts from [a human being] as a discriminating creature a different amount of consciousness than does rural life. Here [in rural life] the rhythm of life and sensory mental imagery flows more slowly, more habitually and more evenly. . . . The sophisticated character of metropolitan psychic life becomes more understandable as

over against small town life which rests upon deeply felt and emotional relationships. (1950a:410)

For Simmel, a central difference between the resident of the metropolis and the resident of the small town is the former's more rational response to the world. In his classic essay "The Metropolis and Mental Life," he describes the urban person as reacting "with his head instead of his heart." To cope with the shower of highly varied stimuli characterizing urban life, individuals must be selective in terms of the stimuli to which they will respond. As the social psychologist Stanley Milgram (1970) put it, urban people, facing **stimulus overload,** must develop clear **norms of noninvolvement**.

Behaviors in Urban Settings: Selectivity and Noninvolvement

Because of stimulus overload and the constant presence of biographical strangers in urban public places, urbanites must learn to set priorities for the events and people to which they will pay attention. Certain situations, in fact, become effectively invisible. Few people passing through an inner-city area pay much attention to the homeless persons on the street. They cannot, because if they stopped to help every such person, they could accomplish little else.

The contexts of everyday life often carry different meanings for men than for women. One useful way to think about variation in urban experience is in terms of the question, "Who can be where, when, and doing what?" We propose that urban places and times are not equally accessible to men and women. Any well-socialized urbanite knows that it is dangerous for women to be in certain city areas, especially at night. To the extent that men and women have different access to activities, places, and times, they have different subjective experiences of urban life. Moreover, while everyone is constrained to abide by norms of noninvolvement in public places, women are especially vulnerable to unwanted attentions by men and so must be more vigilant about protecting their privacy.

Goffman (1963) referred to women (also pets and children) as "open persons" who can be addressed without conventional opening devices (p. 63). This is clear in Duneier and Molotch's (1999) description of women's experiences with street men in Greenwich Village. They found that a common genre of street talk involves men calling out to women who do not respond. For example, as a woman passes by, one street man calls out, "I love you baby." Her response: "She crosses her arms and quickens her walk, ignoring the comment" (p. 1273). Carol Brooks Gardner (1995) has called attention to these types of interaction as something women frequently experience as abusive (one particular example—not being able to pass by a construction site without being yelled at). She suggests that these interactions perhaps signal the oft-claimed fact of male privilege in public spaces, which is enforced at the extreme through women's physical vulnerability and the omnipresent threat of rape. The streets are areas in which gender, race, and class dominance are acted out.

The process of objectifying women is heightened when accompanied by racist and xenophobic remarks such as those experienced by the Latina teenagers interviewed by Esther Madriz (1997). Not only does objectification serve to dehumanize, which is always a first step toward domination and violence, but it also provokes feelings of powerlessness and alienation (Madriz, 1997). The particular strategies women must adopt in public places to minimize being sexually harassed by men are reflective of power differences between men and women (see chapter 6). That is, men feel the right to stare (and often to make comments) at women passing on the street while women must carefully avert their eyes lest they be mistakenly seen as inviting the attention of men. Gardner comments:

> Women in public have their respectability to preserve. They may be in public but they are not supposed to be part of public life, not supposed to be out to strike up an acquaintance. If acquaintance happens, it must be under circumstances that do nothing to suggest that the woman has initiated it. . . . It is important to appreciate that avoiding the appearance of accessibility is routinely important to women in public places, not only to women attempting to prevent crime. (1988:387–88)

One of the Latina teens interviewed by Madriz told her:

> I try to be careful, that's all. [What do you mean by being careful?] I just dress conservative . . . no gold, no tight pants or sweaters. I wear my skirts all the way to my knees. . . . I also avoid going out at night by myself, avoid the wrong people. (1997:46)

On the other hand, a group of poor Puerto Rican teenage girls expressed the way they think a woman should dress:

> I dress the way I want . . . I even wear my gold. I love big earrings and gold chains. We should be able to dress the way we want . . . that is nobody's business. . . . If they think we look too sexy, that's their . . . problem, not mine. . . . Why is it that men can dress the way they want and women cannot? (Madriz, 1997:46)

However, Madriz reports that despite their belief that women have the right to dress the way they want, some are aware that if something happens to them, they are going to be blamed for their own victimization.

"Streetwise" middle-class people, women and men alike and across racial categories, develop skills—what Anderson has called "the art of avoidance"—to deal with their feelings of vulnerability to violence and crime (1990:209).

Urbanites also use mechanisms in their homes to block off or filter out certain encounters with strangers before they have a chance to occur. Living in an apartment house with a uniformed attendant to monitor who goes into and out of the building or in a gated community with a security guard accomplishes this screening. Phone calls also may be monitored by having an unlisted phone number and/or using "caller ID" to restrict others' telephone access.

The mechanisms of selectivity and noninvolvement adopted by city dwellers in their daily interactions in a world of strangers are sometimes used as an explanation for their alleged detachment in public relationships. The popular stereotype of urbanites is that they are cold, indifferent, brusque, and generally uncaring. We question whether people who live in the city really have colder personalities than those who live in the country, however. The often-cited failure of people in the city to offer help to someone in trouble has been found to be due less to their indifference than to the **diffusion of responsibility** that results when there are many bystanders who might intervene (see box).

Somebody Ought to Do Something

An incident that took place more than 50 years ago has been widely publicized as an example of the apathy and indifference of city people and their failure to get involved when help is needed. Kitty Genovese, returning to her home in Queens, New York, shortly after 3:00 A.M., was attacked by an assailant with a knife. In response to her screams, "Oh my God, he stabbed me! Please help me!" lights went on in a number of apartments and people peered out. One man called out, "Let that girl alone!" But no one called the police, though 38 people later testified that they had heard her screams. The attacker was scared off but returned twice to finish the murder.

The assumption that these bystanders had failed to intervene because of their alienation or apathy to urban life was challenged by two social psychologists, John Darley and Bibb Latane. They conducted laboratory experiments in which the participants were led to believe that someone was being victimized or in trouble, and then their offers to help—or failure to offer it—were observed. Darley and Latane's results were summarized in a book entitled *The Unresponsive Bystander: Why Doesn't He Help?* (1970).

In one of Darley and Latane's ingeniously conceived studies, participants were placed in separate rooms and allowed to communicate only by microphone. In this way they could hear other study volunteers but could not see them. At some point the investigators played a recorded, staged tape of a person experiencing an epileptic seizure. The study participants believed the person heard on the tape was another volunteer. In one experimental variation each person was led to believe that she or he alone had heard the seizure. In other cases everyone was made to believe that a number of other people also heard the individual in trouble. The findings confirmed that subjects were far more likely to help when they thought no one else had heard the incident. Indeed, the greater the number of people who were thought to have heard it, the less likely each individual was to help.

These and similar studies by Darley and Latane offer strong support for the proposition that the *more* bystanders there are in an emergency, the *less* likely any one bystander is to intervene to provide aid. Each person, aware that others are witnessing the event, assumes that one or more of these others will take the responsibility to intervene. The result of this "pluralistic ignorance" is that no one steps forward. Darley and Latane suggest that this is how Kitty Genovese could have been murdered while others listened and looked on. It also helps explain how smashing windows of women motorists and grabbing their purses in full view of a crowd of onlookers, or extorting grade-schoolers' lunch money on a busy playground, can become everyday interactions for would-be thieves.

Darley and Latane's work has generated a considerable body of research examining a large number of situational variables: ambiguity of the situation, severity of the victim's distress, victim's level of dependency, style of the request for help, degree of threat in the situation, and the physical attractiveness of the victim, among other factors (Laner et al., 2001; O'Brien, 2010; Cohen, 2013). With regard to bystanders, a large number of studies have found no differences between women and men in rates of helping; however, a few have found differences, perhaps due to the nature of help required in the situation. "Active, doing, spontaneous, and anonymous acts are more likely to be carried out by men than by women. Women are more likely to help than men (as a small number of studies have found) when helping is more planned, formal, personal, and less likely to involve direct intervention" (Laner et al., 2001:27).

Characteristics of the victim seem to make a difference in decisions to help strangers. Laner and associates (2001) included a dog, a child, and a woman as victims of violence in their study, assuming that the dog would have the least support for intervention because of the greater value placed on human life. Respondents were given vignettes portraying violence in a public setting, varying the victim, and were asked how likely they were to intervene on behalf of the victim. Although the findings were as expected (children had the highest likelihood for intervention, then women, then dogs), the authors were surprised by the closeness of the means and lack of significance for the differences. They surmised that perhaps intent to intervene has more to do with the bystander than the victim; that is, in a situation in which a person or a dog is being attacked, people who have the appropriate capacity and beliefs will report an intention to intervene, regardless of the victim. Another interpretation is that the norms regarding intervention are similar across victims (Laner et al., 2001).

This study did find that gender of the bystander interacts with the type of victim in predictions of whether a person will intervene. Men and women were equally likely to report an intention to intervene, but women were most likely to indicate they would help children, while men were most likely to indicate they would help women.

Other findings were that perceptions of self as strong and aggressive predicted intent to intervene, whereas actual physical size did not. Experience breaking up fights was found to be an important predictor of intent to intervene, and people who rated themselves as more sympathetic than others were also significantly more likely to say that they would intervene on behalf of a victim (Laner et al., 2001).

What do you think you would do?

Interactionists, in fact, question the existence of unique rural and urban personality types as an explanation of behavior. They believe instead that people everywhere respond more coolly and with greater distrust to others they do not know. Any observed differences in the public behaviors of urban and rural residents can be understood in relation to the fact that urbanites are confronted much more often by strangers. As Milgram said, "Contrast between city and rural behavior probably reflects the responses of similar people to very different situations rather than intrinsic differences in the personalities of rural and city dwellers. The city is a situation to which persons respond adaptively" (1970:1465).

Although there is a situational basis for public behaviors, in most situations urbanites abide by the norms of noninvolvement. They rarely implicate themselves in one another's public lives. Strangers in public places appear, by and large, to avoid one another. In most public settings in American society, we close ourselves off from interaction with others. We typically avoid excessive eye contact because we do not want to encourage others to talk to us. We make use of portable props ("involvement shields") such as newspapers and cell phones to insulate ourselves from those around us. We try to maximize our personal space as we travel on buses, sit in waiting rooms or theaters, stand in lines, or simply walk along the street. As an editorial in the *New York Times* describes:

> So people wear sunglasses in the rain. They carry their eyes fixed in their skulls, immobile, unreflective. They let you see that they are purposely not looking. On the subways they bury their heads in books, in romances that turn on the erotic, expressive power of interlocking eyes, or they read the rum ads over and over again. (Klinkenborg, 2000:A26)

Most of our interactions are brief and highly impersonal—"fleeting" relationships that occur between or among persons who are personally unknown to one another and are of brief duration. "Characteristically, although not necessarily, fleeting relationships involve no spoken exchanges and when such exchanges do occur, they are, by definition, brief and likely to be in the form of inquiry/reply" (Lofland, 1998:53); an accidental bump and an "I'm sorry," or, "Can you tell me the time?" and the reply, "It's just noon." These are, we might say, interactions without a "career." They have no past and virtually no possibility of future. In terms of sheer volume, fleeting relationships are the most representative of urban life. We can understand these as patterns of avoidance resulting from the need for city dwellers to protect themselves from stimulus overload and the uncertainties of interactions with strangers.

Tolerance for Alternative Lifestyles

The city not only provides the most opportunities for contacts with biographical strangers. It also is the context in which individuals are likely to have the most contact with cultural strangers, or members of groups that do not share their beliefs, attitudes, ideologies, or values. An urban society supports a great diversity of class, ethnic, racial, and **alternative lifestyle groups,** such as homeless individuals. In managing their involvements with one another, members of culturally different groups must take into account the uncertainties and intolerance that arise when information about others is biased or incomplete.

Identification with individuals perceived as cultural strangers is more difficult than identification with those with whom we believe we share similar backgrounds. For example, the preexisting stereotypes of poor and homeless individuals held by many people often serve to cast these individuals as cultural strangers (Vann, 1999). This can lead to interactional difficulties, as when upper- and middle-class pedestrians are confronted by panhandlers (Duneier and Molotch, 1999), or when college students experience fear and perhaps even disgust prior to a community service experience with homeless individuals (Vann, 1999). It may also result in instances of "everyday" intolerance such as children on a school bus throwing pennies—and insults—at homeless men waiting outside the Salvation Army for dinner (Snow and Anderson, 1993). It can even lead to what we might call legally enacted intolerance—for example, antipanhandling statutes such as those passed by New York City, Seattle, Atlanta, Cincinnati, Dallas, the District of Columbia, San Francisco, Santa Barbara, Long Beach, Philadelphia, New Haven, Raleigh, and Baltimore, among other places, in response to claims that, along with such things as unsanitary streets, crime, and graffiti, interactions between street people and pedestrians were eroding the city's "quality of life" (Duneier and Molotch, 1999).

Political groups quarrel, residents write angry letters to newspapers or post inflammatory comments online, and racial conflicts flare up (see box on the following page). Around certain issues, whether in rural or urban areas, it is difficult for groups to sustain a tolerant attitude toward other groups they have defined as adversaries.

Anderson's (1999) work illuminates the inner-city conflict between those who live by the "code of the streets"—a set of informal rules governing interpersonal public behavior, including violence—and those who identify more with mainstream values. This code is largely a cultural adaptation to a profound lack of faith in the police, who are viewed as representing the dominant white society and not caring to protect non-white inner-city residents, and the judicial system. The code requires that people must—at least—give the impression that they are able to take care of themselves. This is accomplished by "going for bad"; that is, a presentation of self through facial expressions, gait, and verbal expressions that indicates a predisposition to violence. "Their manner conveys the message that nothing intimidates them" (p. 79). The object of the exercise is to prevent others from "messing with" them. "For those who are invested in the code, the clear object of their demeanor is to discourage strangers from even thinking about testing their manhood" (p. 77). Although most people in inner-city communities are not totally invested in the code, a street-oriented demeanor is sometimes a necessity. The "decents" are trying hard to be part of mainstream culture, but the racism, real and perceived, that they encounter helps legitimate the oppositional culture of the streets, and so on occasion they adopt street behavior. The problem, according to Anderson, is that

> a vicious cycle has thus been formed. The hopelessness and alienation many young inner-city black men and women feel, largely as a result of endemic joblessness and persistent racism, fuels the violence they engage in. This violence serves to confirm the negative feelings many whites and some middle-class blacks harbor toward the ghetto poor, further legitimating the oppositional culture and the code of the streets in the eyes of many poor young blacks. Unless this cycle is broken, attitudes on both sides will become increasingly entrenched, and the violence, which claims victims black and white, poor and affluent, will only escalate. (p. 325)

Spatial and Racial (Dis)order

Race and space are intricately connected across most American cities. Though rioting does not occur often enough to say it happens frequently, it has become a common response to racial tensions fueled by perceived and acknowledged acts of injustice. And it often happens in response to acts of injustice committed by those in power, like the police, against marginalized and non-white persons and communities. The riots that took place in the streets of Baltimore—a city that has an enduring tradition of poor inter-race relations and race-based residential segregation (Rosenblatt and DeLuca, 2012)—after a still-unexplained preventable death-by-beating of an African American 25-year-old man were not atypical. The young man, Freddie Gray, was arrested by the Baltimore Police Department for possessing what the police alleged was an illegal switchblade. Gray fell into a coma while being transported in a police van and was subsequently taken to a trauma center where he died a few days later on April 19, 2015. People took to the streets to protest the persistent practices of unacceptable police brutality against African Americans, a topic that has historical precedents in both the somewhat distant past (from the 1960s civil right movement to the infamously video-taped beating of Rodney King) and the recent past (the deaths of Eric Garner in New York and Michael Brown in Ferguson, MO, among other incidents).

While rioting was not atypical, neither was the reaction by "mainstream" (read: white) Americans who haven't had to stare down the barrel of a police officer's revolver at a "routine" stop. In his article following both the violent and peaceful protests in Baltimore, journalist Matt Taibbi (2015) wrote:

> America responded the way it usually does in a race crisis: it changed the subject. Instead of using the incident to talk about a campaign of hundreds of thousands, if not millions, of illegal searches and arrests across decades of discriminatory policing policies, the debate revolved around whether or not the teenagers who set fire to two West Baltimore CVS stores after Gray's death were "thugs," or merely wrongheaded criminals. (p. 40)

Such a cavalier, off-handed response ignores the larger, more sociologically significant issues that lurk behind the tragic deaths of Gray and others. The daily abuses at the hands of the police in Baltimore, and elsewhere, have sustained a general sense of unrest and anxiety in many low-income minority-dominated neighborhoods.

Based on his visit to post-uprising Baltimore, Taibbi called attention to the everyday interactions that are fueled by and continue to fuel racial tensions.

> Go to any predominantly minority neighborhood in any major American city and you'll hear the same stories: decades of being sworn at, thrown against walls, kicked, searched without cause, stripped naked on busy city streets, threatened with visits from child protective services, chased by dogs, and arrested and jailed not merely on false pretenses, but for reasons that often don't even rise to the level of being stupid. (2015:42)

Looking across the main area of the protests and riots, a longtime Baltimore resident told Taibbi: "I can guarantee if you look up here and look down there, it might be five people who ain't been fucked over by the police. . . . It's small shit—they get taken advantage of" (p. 42). And it's the "small shit" that is sustained by keeping marginalized persons in marginalized neighborhoods, further limiting potentially positive encounters between strangers and eliminating chances to create an overarching urban culture based on inclusivity rather than exclusivity (Monti, 2012).

Bourgois (1995) presents a similar picture of social marginalization in a neighborhood in East Harlem, "El Barrio," in his study of individuals involved in the underground crack economy. By embroiling themselves in the underground economy and proudly embracing street culture, these individuals are seeking an alternative to their social marginalization. Isolating themselves in inner-city street culture serves as a way to remove any danger of having to face the humiliations inevitably confronting them on venturing out of their social circle to seek legal employment.

Intolerance is especially likely when the members of a group perceive, correctly or incorrectly, that their economic interests are threatened. Such a perception is a dominant factor in the animosity between the ethnic and racial groups that abound in the city. When working-class whites see increasing numbers of immigrants who are people of color, they may fear that they will be displaced in jobs and put at a disadvantage in the competition for scarce resources. As Lillian Rubin's (1994) analysis of working-class white ethnics demonstrates, when faced with the prospect that the in-migration of people of color could threaten their own hard-won advances, her respondents expressed clear anti-immigration and racist beliefs, perhaps best summed up by a remark made by one respondent: "Is this a white country, or what?" (Rubin, 1994:172).

The city also fosters tolerance for differences in behavior and group lifestyles, however. According to the pioneering urban sociologist Louis Wirth (1938), cities have historically been the melting-pot of races, peoples, and cultures, not only tolerating but rewarding difference.

Urban people are comparatively more sophisticated about lifestyle diversity. As we have noted elsewhere, it would seem that the basis of the difference between cities and towns, and between large, complex environments and small, relatively closed social circles becomes clearer insofar as such differences are manifested in a social psychological way. In the small town one may easily lose one's individuality in relationship with others, whereas in the large city one establishes one's individuality *through* social relationships with others (Karp et al., 1991).

Social Contracts among Groups. It appears that urban tolerance is based on a specific type of interaction between members of diverse groups, what Howard S. Becker and Irving Louis Horowitz (1972) referred to as a kind of *social contract*—a silent, unwritten bargain that minority group members will moderate their behavior to make them acceptable to other groups around them. Mary Pattillo's (1998) study of a particular middle-class black neighborhood in Chicago that, although middle-class, is home to one of the top gang leaders and drug dealers in Chicago offers support for this idea. Despite the fact that young people in the neighborhood are as easily introduced to the gangs and their drug business as they are to the neighborhood political organization, the two coexist and maintain what residents refer to as a "quiet neighborhood." Pattillo concludes: "There exists a system of interlocking networks of responsible and deviant residents that sometimes paradoxically, and always precariously, keeps the peace" (p. 747). Other authors agree, concluding that regardless of the social class and racial composition of a neighborhood, most people share a "common goal of living in an area relatively free from the threat of crime" (Bursik and Grasmick, 1993:15; Monti et al., 2014).

Lofland (1998) distinguishes between negative and positive tolerance. Negative tolerance is defined as "the capacity to 'put up with' another's difference from self because the different other is simply not perceived and/or because self and other do not intersect" (p. 238); in other words: out of sight, out of mind. As long as a meal program or transitional housing for homeless individuals is "not in my backyard" (NIMBY), I have no objection to feeding or housing the homeless. Positive tolerance, on the other hand, is "the capacity to 'put up with' another's *fully recognized* differences from self even under conditions of intersection and, perhaps, sometimes, to do so with a mild appreciation for our enjoyment of those differences" (p. 238). An excellent example of this is Laurie Stone's (1993) wonderful description of her interactions—and feelings about those interactions—with three homeless individuals she regularly encountered:

> I try to sort out how I feel. I started out meaning to save her [a homeless woman who is being beaten] from Jerry, but now I see that she is dealing with him herself. So what do I want with this trio? Not to reform or rescue them—or, if I do, I don't want to want those things. I feel an affinity. They tolerate my voyeurism. I allow for their self-destructiveness. And we all love the street. (p. 294)

Becker and Horowitz apparently have only a *positive* notion of tolerance, however. They imply that tolerance exists in cities because the various groups involved consciously value it and agree to ensure it. While this is undeniably often so, it may equally be the case that tolerance in cities is a by-product of avoidance; that is, city people may develop social procedures that minimize the probability that they will come into intimate contact with those with whom they do not agree.

The Spatial Ordering of City Activities.   Social ecologists provide a picture of the city in which diverse groups are segregated and have little contact with one another. There are clear territorial groupings composed of people with similar characteristics or various national backgrounds who restrict their activities to well-defined areas.

In this view there is a **spatial ordering** to city activities and corresponding places where those activities happen (Harvey, 1989; Borer, 2006). Properly socialized urbanites know that certain types of people will be found in specific areas of the city. People can choose to be in areas of the city where they will come into contact with people engaging in certain behaviors or practicing different lifestyles, or they can choose to avoid such contact. They have, in other words, **controlled contact** with various lifestyles or marginal groups. If, for example, they want to avoid contact with prostitutes or those selling pornography, they can simply avoid areas of the city where such people are likely to be found. Tolerance is contingent on this controlled contact. The spatial segregation of groups and activities provides a comforting predictability in encounters with cultural strangers. It follows that tolerance is likely to break down when the conditions for controlled contact are not met. A public clamor is likely when members of certain groups begin to appear in areas where they "don't belong"; for example, when prostitutes appear in suburban commercial strips.

Of course, we do not always wish to avoid those whom we perceive as having unusual lifestyles. We may welcome the opportunity to observe the behaviors of cultural strangers or to participate in ethnic or neighborhood festivals. Every city has certain public parks or areas where representatives of a range of lifestyles and social types can come into contact and become familiar with one another. Perhaps one of the best examples of such an area is Manhattan's Greenwich Village, "a place of contemporary extremes of wealth as well as marked ethnic and racial difference" (Duneier and Molotch, 1999:1264). The Village's cultural tradition is well known across the world as arty, bohemian, and freethinking. It is a visitor destination for people coming from other parts of the world, as well as other neighborhoods of the city, and a prime location for "people watching." Though contact with strangers can serve as a means for dispensing and sharing cultural knowledge, it can also reaffirm stereotypes when ethnic neighborhoods become mere cartoons or inauthentic representations of what they once were or, for that matter, never were. Jerome Krase has shown how some ethnic enclaves can be manipulated and commodified by city officials to promote tourism rather than cross-cultural exchange (also see Gotham, 2005, on "urban spectacles" and tourism). According to Krase (2012):

> In the spectacle of the ethnic theme park the social value of the ethnic neighborhood, produced by the immigrant, is transformed by its capacity to produce festivals, restaurants, and other amusements for outsiders. In essence the place and its inhabitants are sold. Some less-known examples of this phenomenon are the Danish-themed quaint shops and windmills in Solvang, California and the imitative Eastern European commercial architecture of Cleveland, Ohio's Slavic Village that lies beside the less exotic, but more authentic, United States Registered Historic District of Warszawa. (p. 18)

The "theming" of urban enclaves is often manifested through changing how places look. The visual aspects of the built environment influence the experience of urban places by giving cues and clues about what types of interactions take place there and between whom.

William H. Whyte's (1988) study of urban space indicated how important public spaces are to the quality of urban life. He noted how people themselves determine the number that is right for a place, and they do it well. "People need not worry that they might make a place too attractive, too overrun by people. It is the reverse that they should be worrying about. The carrying capacity of most urban spaces is far above the use that is made of them" (p. 172).

The spatial ordering of activities in cities allows urbanites to maintain a limited level of intimacy with cultural strangers. By being able to control the place and timing of contacts with others and by knowing what kinds of behaviors to expect of people in certain city areas, urbanites can monitor the extent of their involvement with cultural strangers, which in turn can have varying effects on residents' perceptions of neighborhood social order and satisfaction (Dassopoulos et al., 2012).

Middle-class society increasingly has been able to disassociate itself from the ethnically distinct, urban-based working poor and unemployed who inhabit the inner city. Budget cuts and fiscal austerity have accelerated the trend toward public sector breakdown in impoverished urban neighborhoods, while services improve, or at least stay the same, in Anglo-dominated, wealthy suburban communities. As Bourgois (1995) describes:

> The concentration of poverty, substance abuse, and criminality within inner-city enclaves such as East Harlem is the product of state policy and free market forces that have inscribed spatially the rising levels of social inequality. . . . More subtly, this urban decay expresses itself in the growing polarization around street culture in North America, giving rise to what some observers call a "crisis in U.S. race relations." (p. 241)

According to Bourgois, it is the institutionalized expression of racism—the de facto apartheid and inner-city public sector breakdown in the United States—that government policy and private sector philanthropy need to address if anything is ever to change significantly in the long run.

According to Douglas Massey and Nancy Denton (1993), most Americans vaguely realize that urban America is still a residentially segregated society, but few appreciate the depth of black segregation or the degree to which it is maintained by ongoing institutional arrangements and contemporary individual actions. In their book *American Apartheid*, these authors describe the relationship between spatial ordering and poverty:

> Segregation concentrates poverty to build a set of mutually reinforcing and self-feeding spirals of decline into black neighborhoods. When economic dislocations deprive a segregated group of employment and increase its rate of poverty, socioeconomic deprivation inevitably becomes more concentrated in neighborhoods where that group lives. The damaging social consequences that follow from increased poverty are spatially concentrated as well, creating uniquely disadvantaged environments that become progressively isolated—geographically, socially, and economically—from the rest of society. (p. 2)

Isolating poverty-stricken urban "ghettos" puts them out of sight and out of mind. Unfortunately, these areas, whether consisting of high-rise public housing or diamond-in-the-rough brownstones, are often noticed only when wealthy developers, real estate speculators, and affluent buyers take over and, almost inevitably, push longtime residents out through the process of "gentrification" (see Brown-Saracino, 2013).

■ Establishing Relationships with Strangers

While the city provides a setting in which strangers can protect themselves from the intrusion of others, too much emphasis can be placed on their lack of direct interaction with one another. There are occasions when strangers come together and freely interact. There are situations in which people can begin to dissolve the strangeness between them. The usual conception of risk and uncertainty in interactions with strangers can be reduced in certain circumstances. A paradox of modern-day life is that although information and interaction have been dislodged from physical location to a great extent due to electronic communication, there are unprecedented opportunities for connection. However, connection is not synonymous with community.

> Spontaneous and unprogrammed public life is perceived as risk laden. Public activity has moved into quasi-private physical public places such as shopping malls, gated communities, health clubs, and play zones. An attribute of such "public places" is surveillance, monitoring, and control, the very things decried in demands for privacy. In an age of increasing demands for protection of a right for privacy, Americans willingly give up privacy in exchange for safety, retreating into private worlds devoid of duty but filled with controlled contact. (Gumpert and Drucker, 1998:422)

Effects of Social Settings and Situations

As casual observation indicates, strangers are more likely to meet and begin relationships in some settings or situations than in others. In some settings, such as cocktail parties, such meetings are likely, and in others, such as bus stops, they are unlikely. Between these extremes there is a range of contexts where the likelihood of strangers meeting is greater or less (classrooms, ball games, plays, laundromats, and so forth). Why is it easier for strangers at a baseball game to strike up conversations than those in, say, an elevator? To answer this question we will briefly consider the effects of settings, contexts, and situations on interactions with strangers.

Settings cannot be defined only in physical terms. A toy store is a place with a lot of toys, salespeople, cash registers, and so forth, but such a description would not capture the distinction between a store selling children's toys and a store selling adult sex toys. Even if someone were to describe the colors of the toys, we would not fully appreciate how the two places differ. A more accurate way to define these places would be in terms of the social conventions governing the nature of the interactions that occur in them.

Definitions of Behaviors. We cannot understand the meaning of another's behavior without considering the setting in which it occurs. For example, to assign a meaning to the behavior of one person striking another with a fist, we would have to know whether it happens in a neighborhood bar, the middle of Times Square, or a boxing ring in Madison Square Garden. The same behavior can assume different meanings in different places. In a nutshell, place matters (Borer, 2006).

We tend to excuse others for acting improperly with the explanation that they have never been in the situation before. In essence we are saying, "She should be excused because she does not know the rules here. She does not know the meaning her behavior carries in this setting." More directly still, "He thinks he knows the meaning of his behavior, and he is correct that it is the meaning of his behavior somewhere else, but he does not know that the same behavior carries a different meaning here." We use the phrase "acting out of place" to describe such improprieties.

Extraordinary events can change the character of settings. When the normal character of a setting becomes abnormal, or an ordinary setting becomes somehow extraordinary, and all involved recognize that fact, definitions of behavior change. It may be perfectly appropriate to begin conversations where ordinarily to do so would be considered improper. Conversations between strangers become allowable in stalled subway trains or elevators or when motorists are stuck in traffic, for example. Goffman notes:

> During occasions of recognized natural disaster, when individuals suddenly find themselves in a clearly similar predicament and suddenly become mutually dependent for information and help, ordinary communication constraints can break down. . . . What is occurring in the situation guarantees that encounters aren't being initiated for what can be improperly gained by them. And to the extent that this is assured, contact prohibitions can break down. (1963:36)

Information about Others.   The context of a situation not only provides information that helps define the meaning of behavior. It also may indicate certain aspects of individuals' identities or details of their biographies, which can make it easier to initiate interactions. Sometimes a person's mere presence in a setting gives out a good deal of information about that person. When you encounter a group of strangers in a university classroom, you can safely assume a good deal about them, such as their social class and values. Seeing a crowd of people standing on a street corner waiting for a red light to change would tell you little about such strangers, however.

The difference that the social setting or context makes in an interaction is related to the amount of information it provides about the individuals taking part (see chapter 3). Some contexts provide more information about those in them than others do. In fact, an anonymous place can be thought of as one that provides little or no information about the people in it. *The likelihood of strangers meeting and beginning interactions is greatest in those settings that provide the most information.* The more information we possess about another, the more easily and correctly we can assess whether those with whom we begin a transaction will reciprocate in an acceptable fashion. Some settings give off enough information about the individuals in them to substantially reduce the uncertainties normally accompanying interactions with strangers.

A city's social well-being often depends upon the presence and accessibility of informal gathering places. Ray Oldenburg (1989) called such settings "third places" because they exist outside or beyond the realms of home (our first place) and work (our second place). They provide an escape from the monotony of the home-to-work-to-home cycle by bringing people together for playful conversation, leisure, and stranger interaction. Third places can range from small neighborhood hangouts such as coffee shops or pubs (Milligan, 1998; 2003) or can be larger and more well-known places such as ballparks or historic sites (Borer, 2008).

How Strangers Meet

Once people decide to begin an interaction, they must find some way to initiate it. In the usual case, talk is preceded by a series of nonverbal gestures indicating the individuals' openness to interaction. This preparatory stage preceding verbal interaction is in effect a risk-reducing mechanism. Without directly committing themselves to an interaction, people use nonverbal communications to obtain a reading of others' willingness to respond. At this stage the level of their involvement is slight, and if their own gestures are not positively responded to, they may gracefully disengage from their invitational efforts.

People who want to engage in interaction can let their interest be known with various types of nonverbal gestures. In full view of those around them and in a deliberate fashion, they may make a point of removing territorial markers (clothes, books, and so forth) from areas close to them to indicate that their personal space will not be violated should someone choose to approach them. They may engage others in eye contact and smile, or make a show of not being involved in any activity that demands their attention.

On occasion, people go beyond these purely nonverbal gestures by making statements aloud, ostensibly to themselves but clearly directed to those around them. The following occurrence in a laundromat, reported in a student term paper, is a typical example:

> One girl sat down next to me and started biting her nails. A few minutes later she opened a textbook of New Testament something or other and flipped through it. She put the book down, as if really bored with it, and she got up and read notices on the wall. Then she blurted out to no one in particular, "They [the machines] take forever."

Another laundromat conversation began this way:

> I sat down next to a guy who was reading something and I began reading an essay in *Time* magazine. Every once in a while this fellow would start to laugh out loud to himself.
>
> At one point he started to laugh very hard.
>
> "All right now, what's so funny? What are you reading?"
>
> "*Finnegan's Wake*. It's so full of puns . . ."

According to the norm of noninvolvement, the usual procedure for strangers in public places is to communicate systematically that they do not wish to become involved in an interaction. These kinds of nonverbal and verbal initiatives, however, which are also based on the commonly understood rules of noninvolvement, are designed to communicate just the opposite. They communicate to others an openness for interaction. When these moves for opening up interaction succeed, they do so precisely because the procedures for closing oneself off from interaction are so widely used and understood.

When conversations are begun, ordinary issues such as weather, work, traffic, or the price of food are typical opening topics. No one can pretend ignorance of such things. People are normally constrained to respond when such issues have been raised, and just mentioning them is taken as an indication of openness for interaction. These openings are specifically used and understood as ritualized throwaway lines whose only purpose is to initiate conversation. Such topics also serve as vehicles for probing the willingness of others to engage in conversation. Should they decline, their reluctance can be communicated without personally discrediting or embarrassing those making the probe.

One strategy for those who wish to begin an encounter is to make things go wrong purposely. People may pretend to be lost when they are not; they may show puzzlement about what is happening around them; or they may purposely bump into another person, so some kind of remedial interaction is necessary. These strategies are used to create a situation where the ordinary becomes extraordinary and interaction is more acceptable.

As noted earlier in the chapter, pets and small children figure into interaction with strangers. Studies have found that being accompanied by a dog increases the frequency of social interactions, especially with strangers (Robins et al., 1991; McNicholas and Collis, 2000; Wood et al., 2005; Tissot, 2011). It is a particular type of interaction, however, that does not violate Goffman's notion of civil inattention (West, 1999). Of course, as Duneier and Molotch (1999) note, dogs (and children) can also induce (and sustain) unwanted interaction, as when a male street person addresses remarks to a dog to force interaction with its female owner. According to these authors, this is what might be called "interactional vandalism" in that a subordinate person breaks the tacit basis of everyday interaction that is of value to the more powerful. In this case, the street person is depriving the woman of something crucial—"the ability to assume in others the practices behind the social bond" (p. 1290).

> Much more is going on than the breaking of conventional "rules of etiquette." . . . Through the pacing and timing of their utterances, the men offer evidence they do not respond to cues that orderly interaction requires. . . . That another cannot be presumed to, *of course*, socially collaborate . . . undermines trust. . . . Without it, the individual teeters on social vertigo. (Duneier and Molotch 1999:1290)

The Geographical Self

Either by Buddha, Buckaroo Bonzai, or your local barista, it's been said that "wherever you go, there you are." Perhaps. Though maybe your "self" and your identity are always connected to the places you go or come from. Because all our social encounters are *emplaced*—that is, they happen somewhere—we can easily recognize that places influence how and with whom we interact. Our behaviors at home differ from those at work and from those in "third places." It seems reasonable, then, to say that our "selves," or at least some parts of our "selves," change from one place to the next. How does place affect the way you see your "self" and how you think others see you? What types of interaction techniques do you use to protect your private "self" in public places?

■ Conclusion

The manner in which people manage their public encounters is determined by the fact that public places are almost exclusively populated by people who are strangers to one another. They are biographical strangers who know nothing of one another's pasts, cultural strangers because they live in different social worlds, or both. Relationships between strangers pose special role-taking problems that make them uniquely risky and uncertain.

Every interaction carries a measure of uncertainty and risk. There is the chance that the images a person presents to others will be found unacceptable or that events will cast an unfavorable light on the individual. It also is never possible to be absolutely sure of others' attitudes, goals, and motives. The probability of doubt is greater in public encounters since strangers, as they try to role-take, must rely solely on information they can acquire through observation. Sometimes this face information is sufficient to persuade individuals that they can or cannot, should or should not, try to communicate directly with others. More typically, though, it is recognized as an incomplete basis for making these decisions.

City dwellers are confronted with public situations in which the number of potential encounters with strangers is enormous. They adapt to the volume of possible contacts and the role-taking problems inherent in urban relationships by structuring their public lives in ways designed to minimize the chances of unpleasant or unwanted encounters. More important, they adopt norms of noninvolvement that insulate them from unnecessary contact with strangers.

People in anonymous public settings adopt certain strategies to communicate their desire to maintain public privacy. Avoidance behaviors do not fully explain the complexity of ordered public life, however. People also are constrained to follow the norm of anonymity. They mutually orient their behaviors to construct a situation in which others' actions are intelligible, their own self-images are protected, and risky contacts are reduced. In public life, people seek to maximize order while minimizing involvement with others. They create a delicate balance between indifference and cooperation in their public transactions.

Unacquainted people may also adopt strategies to open up interactions. In some contexts, people relax their noninvolvement stance, enjoy communicating with others, and begin to establish long-lasting relationships. Situations vary in their capacity to support relationships among strangers.

Strangers comprise only one part of our social worlds, however. Relationships with strangers stand at one end of an interaction continuum, with intimate relationships characterized by deep commitment and trust at the other end. As Stanford Lyman and Marvin Scott have observed, a relationship is not established completely until the individuals involved "reciprocally regard one another as persons whom they know fully and for whom they have sincere affection, deep trust, and broad commitment" (1970:48). In the next chapter we will explore the processes involved in the transformation of strangeness to intimacy.

Definitions

alternative lifestyle groups: Groups whose members exhibit a lifestyle that differs in significant ways from that adopted in mainstream, conventional society.

areas of conversation: Topics of mutual interest to both participants in a conversation. The participants also share a common understanding of the meaning of such topics.

avoidance behaviors: The ways in which strangers seek to avoid involving themselves in the affairs of others.

biographical strangers: People who have no knowledge of one another's life histories.

civil inattention: The act of appearing to be uninvolved in the affairs of others. Individuals engage in this behavior when they are forced to recognize the presence of others but want to avoid interaction with them.

controlled contact: The manner in which members of one group regulate the contact they have with members of other groups.

cultural strangers: People who have no shared frameworks for interpreting social reality. They occupy different symbolic worlds.

diffusion of responsibility: A phenomenon of behavior whereby no member of a group is regarded as clearly responsible for taking action in a situation that seems to demand it.

involved indifference: A way of taking others' presence into account while avoiding intrusion in their affairs. Strangers are obliged to minimize involvement while they maximize public order.

marginal man: A person who participates in the social activities of two different social groups without identifying completely with either group. A marginal person in a society is a stranger.

norm of anonymity: A shared expectation that individuals will not intrude on one another's privacy.

norm of noninvolvement: A shared expectation that strangers will not intrude on the activities of one another.

norm of trust: A shared expectation that others will act in the ways we expect them to.

public privacy: A situation in which strangers in public places try to maintain a strict impersonality in their interactions with one another.

self-management techniques: The range of self-conscious strategies people use to ensure that they will project a positive image of self in front of any audience.

spatial ordering: The ways in which various groups are associated with particular geographic areas. In the city, certain types of people and activities can be found in certain neighborhoods.

stimulus overload: Bombardment with more stimuli than people can possibly respond to. Urbanites must develop clear norms of noninvolvement to deal with the excess of stimuli they encounter.

Discussion Questions

1. How do you interpret the authors' claim that we must simultaneously doubt and trust others as we interact with them? Would social life be impossible if it were not rooted in a general norm of trust? Under what conditions do you become most distrustful of others?

2. Suppose you are asked to try to establish a relationship with a stranger. In what settings would you find it easiest to do so? In what kinds of settings would you be unwilling to try to meet someone? Why? What characteristics or attributes of another person would make a difference in your willingness to approach him or her? Why? What would you consider the biggest risks in carrying out such an assignment?

3. Do you think there is such a thing as a distinctive urban personality?

4. Describe some of the techniques you use to protect your privacy in public places. To what extent do you take others into account in formulating your own behaviors, even though you have no direct verbal communication with them?

5. Do you believe that cities provide greater freedom to practice unusual lifestyles than small towns do? If so, what is it about cities that fosters greater tolerance for unconventional lifestyles? When is such tolerance most likely to break down?

6. What behaviors can you think of that would constitute transgressions of noninvolvement norms in anonymous settings? How do you imagine people would react to such rule infractions?

5

Family, Friendship, and Love
Contacts among Intimates

The need for intimate relationships is so strong that it has given rise to an industry devoted to helping compatible singles connect with one another. There are singles' bars, apartment complexes, and cruises, as well as dating services and other operations designed to bring people together. Newspapers regularly run ads for singles events, such as "Celebrating single: Caribbean cooking demonstration and free wine tasting." Make no mistake, it is big business. The online dating site industry is worth more than $1 billion (VanderMey, 2013). That's a lot of money, and a lot of people looking for love, companionship, and intimacy.

Operation Match, the first computer dating business in the United States, was organized by a Harvard sophomore and launched in 1965 (Mathews, 1965). The response was overwhelming, and thousands of college students happily spent $3 each (about $22.50 in 2015 dollars; U.S. Bureau of Labor Statistics, 2014) on the chance that they would meet others whom they would find attractive and who would be attracted to them. The process has become more sophisticated and more costly as the intimacy industry has become more firmly established. The Internet revolutionized the singles industry. Online dating services blossomed—by 2012 there were an estimated 2,500 online dating sites in the United States, though fewer than 25 of these are considered "major" (Online Dating Magazine, 2012). According to a 34-year-old female New Yorker, online dating is more convenient and comfortable than scouring dreary Manhattan bars and haranguing friends to set her up. "As you get older you know fewer and fewer people who aren't married, but go online and there are hundreds of people who are single. It makes you feel a lot less alone" (*Newsweek*, 2001:46) (see box).

People of all ages devote considerable time to thinking about, worrying about, analyzing, developing, or trying to end intimate relationships. The advice columns of daily newspapers, blogs, television programming, films, and popular fiction all indicate the extent to which the quality of our relations with family, friends, and lovers occupies our time and thoughts.

It may not be an exaggeration to say that love has become a *social problem* of sorts in the United States. As a popular song once put it, many people may be "looking for love in all the wrong places." The urgency of the search

Finding Love on the Web

Technology is changing the way we do romance. Computer-knowledgeable singles are turning to the World Wide Web in increasing numbers for personal ads. One of the pioneers of online dating is U.S.-based Match.com. It launched in 1995 and by 2013 claimed 1.9 million "paid core subscribers" and "sites in 25 different countries, in eight different languages spanning five continents" (Match.com, 2013). According to Match.com's "vice president of romance," "The Internet addresses the problem that professional, single people face today. It's fast, affordable and convenient" (quoted in Choat, 2000:49). Silverstein and Lasky's *Online Dating for Dummies*, available in condensed form in checkout lines at grocery stores or as a digital download for e-readers, notes, "Any activity that has at least 20 million participants must be a mainstream activity if not a social movement, right?" (2011:87).

People feel comfortable with the level of anonymity provided by websites. On a website you can hide behind a user name and an e-mail address, giving out your phone number—or photo—only when you choose to (Sprout, 1997). The anonymity lessens the immediate risk of meeting another person, but it comes with other risks, especially when moving a relationship from online to in person. According to the director of Cyberangels.org, an Internet safety watchdog group, "It's like going to a bar blindfolded and then going home with someone" (quoted in Anderson, 2001). At the time Anderson's article was published, the Cyberangels were handling about 600 cases of cyberstalking a day, and about 10 rape reports in a month. According to the director, "It all happens because of a disconnect that makes people feel like they know a stranger intimately" (p. 38). Some services recognize these dangers and advise their users to proceed with caution. eHarmony claims to eliminate 20 percent of its applicants due to their questionable emotional stability (Anderson, 2001). Popular magazines including *GQ*, *Elle*, and even *The Atlantic*, as well as a host of "self-help" books, have published rules for online dating, such as "practice common sense," "be honest," "take your time," and "pay attention to the signs" (Starling, 2000).

Another downside is that the seemingly perfect match on-screen may not live up to expectations when the individuals meet. One problem appears to be false advertising. Experienced online daters urge honesty, but many confess to small exaggerations. Skeptics argue that the Internet doesn't convey the overall gestalt of a person, that impalpable physical essence. Without any information besides text, readers project their own fantasies onto other people. Worse still, users can carefully edit their e-mails and present themselves in the most flattering way (*Newsweek*, 2001). Research has shown that many online daters regularly and even habitually present themselves in the brightest light possible. Catalina L. Toma and Jeffrey T. Hancock (2010) found that self-perceptions of physical attractiveness are related to how daters decide to present themselves. Conventionally unattractive daters, and particularly women, often compensate for their lack of attractiveness by enhancing their photographs and descriptors of physical appearance. This strategy—one that embraces exaggeration and deception—is more the norm than the exception (Whitty, 2008). For some individuals, online romance erases the awkwardness of first meetings and makes communication easy. People with disabilities, for example, prefer to use the Internet in looking for dates and potential partners. According to one user, it is a way to weed out people who are uncomfortable with disabilities. She says, "I am an attractive woman, I think men are just afraid to approach me [in person]. People are afraid of what they don't know. In my [online] ad, I try to make it clear I am a lot more than my disability. I want the reader to know although I am disabled my life is very enriched and I lead an active life" (quoted in Lynch, 1999).

(continued)

Though Internet dating might seem like a way to disrupt or challenge social distinctions, there are dating sites for everyone and every taste, it seems. A limited sampling includes:

- for African Americans, Blacksingles.com and blackplanet.com
- for black professionals, LoveNubianStyle.com
- for Jewish singles, JDate.com and supertova.com
- for Catholics, CatholicSingles.com and CatholicSoulmates.com
- for Protestants, BigChurch.com
- for Hindus, Jeevansathi.com
- for Ivy League graduates, GoodGenes.com
- for international travelers, AnastasiaDate.com
- for gay men, gay.com and the online company Gaydar, which also has its own Internet radio station
- for lesbians, PinkSofa.com and PinkCupid.com
- for tall people of all sexual orientations, TallFriends.com
- for those with an interest in rural life, countrysingles.com and FarmersOnly.com
- for individuals over 50, ourtime.com and silversingles.com
- for those who have or desire facial hair, StachePassions.com
- for zombie enthusiasts, ZombieHarmony.com
- for fans of the sitcom *Seinfeld*, FestivusPassions.com
- for marijuana smokers, 420dating.com
- and there's the offbeat TheSpark.com, which asks the sign-up question, "Which would you rather kill, Puppy or Kitten?"

For those with smartphones, there's even a phone dating app (*New York Times*, 2015).

What does it all mean? According to one source, this is courtship as it once was, before the advent of the singles bar:

> There is plenty of conversation but no touching. With the computer serving as a chaperone, guaranteeing that no one gets too close, tastes are compared, as are family backgrounds, hopes and dreams. Much as sites such as Priceline and eBay encourage old-fashioned economic behavior—one bids, one negotiates, one doesn't pay retail—the dating sites serve as nineteenth-century parlors where couples sit in chairs and chat. Even the word *chat* is slightly antique, recalling porch swings and glasses of iced tea. (*Time*, 2000:73)

is evidenced by a trip to any local bookstore, where the shelves in the self-help section are routinely filled with titles promising the formulas for the right ways and places to find love.

■ Intimate Relationships in Contemporary Society

The idea that human beings require identity-sustaining relationships with intimate others is not new. The **need for affiliation** is a theme that has always been present in social science literature (Schacter, 1959). In 19th-century sociological theory, concern was expressed that industrialization and urbanization were destroying intimate bonds between individuals. Theorists such as Ferdinand Tönnies and Émile Durkheim sought to explain the effects of the transformation of social life from small preurban or peasant communities to large cities. Alexis de Tocqueville's *Democracy in America*, published in 1835, warned that some aspects of the American character—what he was one of the first to call "individualism"—might eventually isolate Americans from one another and thereby undermine freedom. Although the theoretical conceptions of these writers vary, their ideas generally reflect agreement on the following four points:

1. Modern society is characterized by increased rationality and individuality.

2. People are less well integrated into modern society than they were in preurban communities.

3. Relationships between people in modern society become more contractual, artificial, and contrived.

4. Ties to primary groups (family, neighborhood, and friendship groups) are weaker in modern society.

Although some of these propositions have been questioned (c.f., Karp et al., 1991; Monti et al., 2014), there can be no doubt that contemporary society does impose a variety of unique pressures on human relationships. Both social science literature and the popular media discussed the changing character of human relations in the 20th century. Rapid social change, the urge toward achievement and social mobility, and the weakening of community associations were said to have produced a pervasive rootlessness in modern people (see also Bellah et al., [1985] 1996). The failure to sustain intimate relationships is often cited as a serious shortcoming in urban-industrial society (see box on the next page).

Intimacy not only dominates our everyday consciousness but also serves as a yardstick against which we can evaluate the quality of our everyday lives. The level of intimacy we perceive in any encounter affects our presentations of self, impression management, and the kinds of information about ourselves we reveal to others. In general, the configuration of expectations, obligations, and reciprocities governing any relationship is bound up with the degree of intimacy between the people involved. How we allocate our time and the social circles we enter and leave cannot be understood apart from the networks of intimate relationships we sustain. Inquiry into the structure and operation of everyday life therefore demands serious consideration of the manner in which we define, interpret, and give meaning to relations of intimacy.

Alone in the Lonely Crowd

Intimacy plays a critical role in psychological growth and well-being, and a lack of intimate interactions has been associated with loneliness (Prager and Buhrmester, 1998; Reis and Shaver, 1997). According to a legion of columnists, therapists, and pastors, Americans have become starved for intimacy (Duin, 1999).

In 1950, David Riesman described Americans as living lonely lives in the midst of a crowd of lonely people. In a classic book titled *The Lonely Crowd*, he proposed that the American character changed from the *inner-directed* personality of the 19th century, motivated by an internalized set of achievement goals, to the *other-directed* personality of the 20th century, motivated by a desire for the approval of peers and associates. The modern personality is sensitive to cultural expectations and responds to the cues others give about the behaviors they expect. Such modern people find it difficult to establish lasting intimate relationships with others because they have no firm values to base them on. Riesman describes the other-directed person as "at home everywhere and nowhere, capable of a rapid if sometimes superficial intimacy with and response to everyone" (1950:25).

Fifty years later, Robert Putnam's *Bowling Alone* (2000) echoed that theme. Putnam used bowling as a symbol for the decline of American associational life; that is, between 1980 and 1993, the total number of bowlers in the United States increased by 10 percent, while league bowling decreased by 40 percent. Putnam expressed concern that Americans were in danger of becoming a nation of strangers to one another without adequate social bonds to tie them together. In a section of the book titled "So What?" Putnam described the importance of connection: "People who have active and trusting connections to others—whether family members, friends, or fellow bowlers—develop or maintain character traits that are good for the rest of society" (p. 288). The effect of disengagement on our personal lives is particularly sobering; among adult Americans, life satisfaction declined steadily during the second half of the 20th century, at least partly due to social connectedness. "Young and middle-aged adults today are simply less likely to have friends over, attend church, or go to club meetings than were earlier generations," Putnam said (2000:335). Research on Americans' use of time in the late 20th century showed that they watched more TV and socialized less (Robinson and Godbey, 1997). The percentage of people driving to work alone rose from 76 percent to nearly 85 percent between 1980 and 1990; carpoolers dropped from 24 percent to 15 percent of commuters over the same period.

At the turn of the millennium, Laura Pappano wrote about the new loneliness of people who are overcommitting and underconnecting in *The Connection Gap: Why Americans Feel So Alone* (2001). This aloneness is played out in the way we eat (single-serving frozen meals), watch TV (with earphones), work (telecommuting), play (bowling), fall in love (personal ads), marry (or don't), socialize (e-mail), and shop (online).

Today, in the 21st century, more people are single, either by choice or by chance, than at any other time in history. In his book *Going Solo: The Extraordinary Rise and Surprising Appeal of Living Alone* (2012), Eric Klinenberg claims that in big cities such as New York, about half of all households are one-person households. He argues that people who live alone tend to spend more time socializing with friends and neighbors than people who are married do. Paradoxically, living alone is not an entirely solitary experience because it may, in turn, foster pro-social behavior.

■ The Interactionist Perspective on Intimacy

Students often resist sociological analyses of personal relationships. When asked to describe some of the social factors that might account for the way intimate relationships are conducted in American society today, students in the courses taught by the authors of this book have argued that it is impossible to generalize about intimacy. Among other things they say: "It depends upon the individual." "No two people relate to one another the same way." "You can't define what love is."

To some degree the students are correct: No two relationships are the same, even when the social characteristics of the participants are very similar. Each relationship emerges out of the unique context in which the individuals encounter each other. They also are correct that any attempt to provide an absolute, clear, permanent definition of intimacy, love, or friendship would be fruitless. We agree that a relationship is intimate only when the participants in the relationship define it that way. At the same time, we maintain that the criteria used in arriving at such a definition are *social* in origin.

Intimacy as a Social Construction

As we noted in chapter 2, social life would be impossible if there were no general consensus concerning the meanings people give to objects, events, and situations in their lives—if people were not generally agreed on the meaning of symbols. The definitions given to intimacy depend on both the general values of the society in which individuals live and the more specific values of the groups to which they belong or with which they identify (see Jamieson, 2012).

These roots in socially shared definitions are what allow us to carry our analysis of intimacy beyond the assertion that each human relationship is unique. Relationships of love and friendship can only be understood as symbolic or **social constructions,** which by themselves have no intrinsic meaning. For example, feelings of romantic love and passion surely have a physiological component to them. Scientists have discovered that oxytocin, a brain chemical known to stimulate lactation and mother-child bonding, may be partly responsible for romantic love as well (Brownlee, 1997). Anthony Walsh, the author of *The Science of Love: Understanding Love and Its Effects on Mind and Body,* describes love as a natural high, similar to being "hopped up on coke" (1996:35). The rush is fueled by elevated levels of *neurotransmitters,* brain chemicals such as dopamine, norepinephrine, and phenylethylamine (Price, 1999). Because these bodily responses can be found across cultures, we can be secure in the fact that there are some biological universals. As Jonathan Turner and Jan Stets argue,

> There can be no doubt, of course, that social structure, culture, and socialization experiences have enormous effects on how particular emotions are expressed, just as humans' innate capacities for language are conditioned by culture, but this does not mean that the capacity for the

emotions is purely the product of an emotion culture and socialization into this culture. (2006:46)

The distinctions among such emotions as love, jealousy, anger, and anxiety, however, are not based on our body reactions alone, but rather on the way we interpret and label our experiences (Thoits, 1989). Our definitions of our emotions, as well as others' emotions, can have profound effects on how and with whom we interact in intimate ways.

Consider what you might feel on "some enchanted evening." Your eyes meet the stranger's across a crowded room, you smile warmly at each other, and as you approach each other, oblivious to others in the room, you experience increased heart and respiratory rates, flushing of the face, dryness of the mouth, and slight body tremors. Aware of these physiological responses, you may decide that you are experiencing love at first sight. You have learned from your peers, from television and movies, from books and magazines, and from the Internet that such feelings can be interpreted as love. The feelings we have described do not *have to be* interpreted as love, however. If we did not know the context in which the feeling occurred and simply knew that an individual had experienced higher heart and respiration rates, flushing, dry mouth, and body tremors, we could make a variety of interpretations concerning what was happening. It could be that the individual was high on drugs, suffering from the flu, or experiencing any one of a number of diverse emotions—fear, anger, anxiety, jealousy, or embarrassment, not necessarily love. Our emotional states are symbolic states. As such, they require interpretation and labeling to establish their meaning.

Much the same point can be made concerning the meanings attached to sexuality. The ways in which individuals pursue and engage in sexual relationships reflect the social attitudes of both society as a whole and the groups with which the individuals are affiliated. Our capacity for intimate sexuality is in part a function of biological maturity, but we become sexual through a learning process. What turns us off or on reflects culturally defined and learned ideas about sexuality. There is evidence to suggest that culture profoundly affects how people perceive love, how susceptible they are to falling in love and with whom, and why they feel sexual desire. There are wide variations in the kinds of sexual behaviors that are forbidden, tolerated, or encouraged in various cultures, including clear differences between sexual practices in smaller, preliterate societies and the larger, more complex societies of developed countries (Kelly, 2001). For example, societies vary in terms of the type and appropriateness of foreplay, ranging from those in which men might fondle a woman's breasts only immediately prior to intercourse to those in which foreplay might last for hours. It might surprise you to learn that there are societies where kissing is thought to be disgusting. Oral sex is a routine practice in some societies and taboo in others. And cultures vary in terms of coital positions that are thought both desirable and permissible (see Hyde and DeLamater, 2013). In Sweden, for example, premarital sex is accepted, people are expected to be sexually knowledgeable and experienced, and Swedes are likely to associate sex with pleasure—what we might refer to as a "sex positive" society. In Ireland, however, Roman Catholics are supposed to heed the church's strict prohibitions against sex outside of marriage, birth control, and the expression of lust. The experience of sexuality in these two countries is different because the *rules* are different (Schwartz and Rutter, 1998). Even within a particular region or culture, various political, economic, and social changes can also affect people's sexual attitudes and behaviors (Hatfield and Rapson, 1996).

Another indication that social influences play a larger role in shaping sexuality than biology does is the changing notions of male and female differences in desire through history. The norms governing sexuality are so powerful that it is impossible to imagine the absence of such norms. In fact, most examples of "liberated" sexuality involve breaking a social norm—for example, having sex in public rather than in private. The social norm is always the reference point. Because people are influenced from birth by the social context of sexuality, their desires are shaped by these norms (Schwartz and Rutter, 1998). Some norms are explicit, such as laws against adult sexual activity with minors. Others are implicit, such as norms of fidelity and parental responsibility. In a changing, complex society such as the United States, the rules may be in flux or indistinct at any given time. Perhaps this ambiguity is what makes some issues of sexuality so controversial today. And the continued ambiguity over labels of sexual preference and orientation have been at the center of many public debates ranging from marriage equality and civil unions to employment and "don't ask, don't tell" policies in the military.

Throughout this book we have been sustaining the idea that the meanings of objects, events, and situations reside in our responses to them. The meanings attached to the body itself are illustrative of this point. As pointed out in chapter 3, standards of beauty are clearly culture bound. While contemporary American women evaluate themselves in terms of a "cult of thinness," the paintings of Peter Paul Rubens and others indicate that historically there is nothing universal about this standard; indeed, many societies view larger women as more attractive. It is also the case that in different societies different parts of the body, especially the female body, are eroticized. Whereas female breasts are a focus of erotic attention in the United States, other societies may place greater erotic emphasis on the neck, arms, or ankles.

It is worth pointing out that a great deal more is known about the way that heterosexual men respond to female bodies than vice versa. As some feminists suggest, the fact that specific body parts of women can be isolated as erotic objects may be related to the general objectification of women intrinsic to male-dominated societies. Those who hold such a view feel particularly outraged about the image of women in materials ranging from magazine advertisements to *Playboy* to hard-core pornography.

Although researchers have not been able to conclusively establish a direct causal link between viewing pornography and violence against women, there is substantial evidence that pornography, especially violent pornography, is a factor that contributes to violence against women. Research with men, including sex offenders, shows that pornography helps shape a male-dominant view of sexuality, contributes to a user's difficulty in distinguishing between fantasy and reality, and is often used to initiate victims and break down their resistance to particular types of sexual activity. According to one author (Jensen, in Dines, Jensen, and Russo, 1998), pornography provides "a training manual for abusers" (p. 119; see also Jensen, 1995). To be sure, not all pornography is violent, but often the objective of pornography is the objectification and control of women—male dominance of the female body for the purpose of sexually arousing the male consumer—and often violence is one of the ways pornography accomplishes this (Dines et al., 1998). To be clear, debates about the pros and cons of pornography abound and serve as evidence for the multiple meaning of socially constructed objects and practices (C. Smith and Attwood, 2014).

Perhaps more dubious because of the ways they implicitly objectify the female body, everyday media also affect sexual attitudes and beliefs. In a study in which men and women were shown advertisements depicting female models as sex objects, or ads with female models competently performing various nontraditional roles, the men who saw the sexist advertisements increased their tendency to gender stereotype and also scored higher than other research participants on a scale measuring attitudes supportive of rape and sexual aggression (Lanis and Covell, 1995). In an experimental study of young adult males' exposure to female centerfold images, past exposure to objectifying media was positively correlated with all five "centerfold syndrome" beliefs: voyeurism, sexual reductionism, masculinity validation, trophyism, and nonrelational sex. Recent exposure to centerfolds interacted with past exposure to predict three of the five centerfold syndrome beliefs (Wright and Tokunaga, 2015).

Our general point that the meanings attached to sexuality are social in origin is reflected in the vocabulary we use to describe people in terms of sexual behaviors, particularly the differential evaluation according to gender. The association of sex with female immorality starts in childhood, as is made clear by Orenstein's (1994) interviews with middle-school students, which found the sexual double standard alive and well. According to the girls Orenstein interviewed:

> At Weston, girls may be "sluts," but boys are "players." Girls are "whores"; boys are "studs." Sex "ruins" girls; it enhances boys. In their youth, they may be snips and snails and puppy dogs' tails, but by adolescence, boys learn that they are "made of" nothing but desire. . . . Girls are, in fact, supposed to provide the moral inertia that (temporarily) slows that force. . . . The Weston girls themselves participate in this dynamic, shunning sexually active girls, but excusing male behavior by saying, "Boys only think with their dicks." (Orenstein, 1994:57)

Despite the norm of "true love" currently accepted in American culture, personal choice and indiscriminate sexuality have often been construed as socially disruptive. Disruptions to the social order include liaisons between poor and rich; between people of different races, ethnicities, or faiths; and between members of the same sex (Schwartz and Rutter, 1998). "Forbidden relationships," like those between single women and married men, can sometimes reinforce and intensify social norms and expectations because participants rely on a good deal of secrecy to avoid shaming (Richardson, 1988). Schwartz and Rutter note that traditional norms of marriage and sexuality have maintained social order by keeping people in familiar and "appropriate" categories, with offenders punished by ostracism or curtailed civil rights and conformists rewarded with social approval and material advantages. They remind us that although it hardly seems possible today, mixed-race marriage was against the law in the United States until 1967. And until the Supreme Court's ruling in June 2015 stating that states must recognize same-sex marriages, committed same-sex couples were routinely denied legal marriages, income tax breaks, and health insurance benefits; heterosexual couples take these social benefits for granted.

Our discussion and various examples affirm that definitions of intimacy vary because they are social constructions with no fixed meaning. They have their roots in both general societal values and more specific values of the groups and people with whom an individual frequently communicates. The meanings also vary historically and according to the social attributes of the participants. Society's interest in controlling sexuality is expressed in the debates regarding sex education. Debates about sex education in elementary, middle, and high school illustrate the importance to society of both the control of desire and its social construction (Schwartz and Rutter, 1998) (see box).

To Educate or Not? The Controversy over Sex Education

The question at the core of the debate over sex education is, "Does formal learning about sex increase or deter early sexual experimentation?" Those who favor sex education hold that children benefit from early, comprehensive information about sex. Providing young people with an appropriate vocabulary and accurate information both discourages early sexual activity and encourages safe sexual practices for those teens who will not be deterred from sexual activity (Sexuality Information and Education Council of the United States [SIECUS], 1995). On the other hand, opponents of sex education are intensely committed to the belief that information about sex changes teenagers' reactions and values and leads to early, and what they believe are inappropriate, sexual behaviors (Whitehead, 1994). Conservative groups hold that sex education, if it occurs at all, should emphasize abstinence ("Just say no!") rather than practical information.

What does the scientific research say? In June 2001, U.S. surgeon general David Satcher issued a report that provoked an immediate strong reaction from the White House of President George W. Bush. The report, *The Surgeon General's Call to Action to Promote Sexual Health and Responsible Sexual Behavior*, was based on scientific review papers by experts and recommendations from national conferences. The report cited a number of sexually related public health problems, including the following:

(continued)

- the infection of 12 million Americans each year with sexually transmitted diseases (STDs)
- 800,000 to 900,000 Americans living with HIV, with one-third of them unaware that they are even infected
- unintended pregnancies accounting for nearly one-half of all pregnancies in the United States
- an estimated 1.36 million abortions in 1996
- an estimated 104,000 children becoming victims of sexual abuse each year
- reports that 22 percent of American women and 2 percent of American men have been victims of rape (Satcher, 2001)

The report called for strategies focusing on increased awareness, implementation and strengthening of interventions, and expanding the research base relating to sexual health matters. A key strategy for increasing awareness is the availability of school sexuality education that not only encourages abstinence from sex but also provides reliable information about birth control. Evaluation evidence indicates that programs that include both strategies either have no effect on initiation of sexual activity or, in some cases, delay the initiation of sexual activity (Kirby, 1999; 2001). Although a majority of Americans favor some form of sexuality education in the public schools and also believe that some sort of birth control information should be available to adolescents (T. Smith, 2000), "abstinence only" programs, which bar any talk of contraception, are the only ones supported by conservatives. President Bush and conservative allies were not happy with the report's finding that there is simply no evidence that teaching abstinence from sex works (nor with the lack of evidence to support the religious right's assertion that gay individuals can become straight).

According to Satcher, the primary purpose of the *Call to Action* is to initiate a mature national dialogue on issues of sexuality, sexual health, and responsible sexual behavior. He quotes an Institute of Medicine (IOM) report, *No Time to Lose* (Institute of Medicine, 2000):

> Society's reluctance to openly confront issues regarding sexuality results in a number of untoward effects. This social inhibition impedes the development and implementation of effective sexual health and HIV/STD education programs, and it stands in the way of communication between parents and children and between sex partners. It perpetuates misperceptions about individual risk and ignorance about the consequences of sexual activities and may encourage high-risk sexual practices. It also impacts the level of counseling training given to health care providers to assess sexual histories, as well as providers' comfort levels in conducting risk-behavior discussions with clients. In addition, the "code of silence" has resulted in missed opportunities to use the mass media (e.g., television, radio, printed media, and the Internet) to encourage healthy sexual behaviors. (Satcher, 2001:17–18)

According to Satcher, we must all share the responsibility for initiating a national dialogue, working at every level of society to promote sexual health and responsible sexual behavior.

Historical Changes in the Meaning of Intimacy

The social conventions concerning intimacy in a society have been different in various historical periods. In *Gone with the Wind*, Rhett Butler sweeps the protesting Scarlett O'Hara off her feet and carries her to an upstairs bedroom. According to Civil War–era definitions of appropriate male-female relationships, Butler's behavior would be interpreted as intense passion. Men could plausibly disregard women's attempts to rebuff their sexual advances because men were expected to be aggressive in such situations and women were expected to protest. With the exception of black males, who could be lynched for improprieties as slight as looking the "wrong" way at a white woman, it would have been unthinkable to define behaviors like Rhett's as rape. Today there are quite different interpretations of such male-female interactions. In the context of present values, raised consciousness, and changed legal standards, it is unlikely that Rhett Butler's behavior would be interpreted today as mad passion or romantic devotion. However, changes in attitudes and conventions often happen gradually. Today too many men still do not comprehend that having sex after a woman says no or when she is incapable of giving consent is, in fact, rape.

Rape is legally defined as sexual intercourse (vaginal, oral, or anal) that occurs by means of force or threat of force. Rape, however, need not involve physical force and legally applies to those situations in which the victim—by reason of unconsciousness, mental illness, intellectual disability, or intoxication—is incapable of giving consent to sexual relations.

Although this is a fairly straightforward definition, the crime of rape is still viewed in American society in terms of a collection of myths about rapists and rape victims, including the notions that some women enjoy "being taken" by force; that women initially say no to men's sexual advances to appear "respectable" and must be "persuaded" to give in; that many women provoke men by teasing them and therefore get what they deserve.

Recent research has revealed that a sizable amount of violent crime, including rape, involves people known to one another. A rape case involving a victim who knows or is familiar with her assailant is known as *acquaintance rape*. Between 2005 and 2010, 78 percent of sexual violence against women involved an offender who was a family member, intimate partner, friend, or acquaintance. During that same period, more than 50 percent of rapes occurred at or in the victim's home and the vast majority (83 percent) of offenders did not use a weapon (U.S. Department of Justice, 2013). One form of sexual assault that almost always occurs in the victim's home is *marital rape*, the sexual assault of a woman by her husband. It was not until 1977 that the Oregon state legislature repealed the marital exemption to its rape statute, and two years later the first marital rape conviction occurred. Marital rape is now a crime in all 50 U.S. states, although in some states rape by a husband is defined more narrowly than rape by a stranger (Bergen, 1998). Research indicates that marital rape often accompanies other forms of family violence, and it occurs in 9 to 14 percent of all U.S. marriages (Bergen, 1996). This is not a situation in which one spouse wishes to have sex and the other does not but gives in out of love or to please. Marital rape is a brutal physical assault that may have a graver impact on a victim than stranger rape, given that the assailant is a person whom the victim knows and, at least at one time, loved and trusted (Bergen, 1996).

Acquaintance rapes are especially common on college campuses. Despite claims by some (such as Roiphe, 1993) that the term *date rape* is being misapplied to cases involving boyfriends verbally coercing their girl-friends to have sex, or to intercourse that occurs because the woman is intoxicated and becomes "sexually confused," empirical research indicates that the incidence of acquaintance or date rape on college campuses is a serious problem. Sadly, sexual assaults and date rapes, or at least those that are reported, are on the rise. The number of "forcible rapes" that were reported at four-year colleges increased 49 percent between 2008 and 2012 (U.S. Department of Education, 2014).

Acquaintance rape remains a controversial topic because of confusion around the definition of the term *consent*. In an attempt to clarify this definition, Antioch College in Ohio adopted in 1994 what has become "an infamous policy delineating consensual sexual behavior" (Curtis, 1997). According to the policy, the definition of *consent* is based on continuous verbal communication during intimacy—the person initiating the contact must take responsibility for obtaining the other participant's verbal consent as the level of sexual intimacy increases. Even if you have had a particular level of sexual intimacy before with someone, you must still ask each and every time (see *The Antioch College Sexual Offense Policy*, in L. Francis, 1996). Although the policy was ridiculed and lampooned by many people, based on the criticism that it reduced the spontaneity of sexual intimacy to what seemed like an artificial contractual agreement, this attempt to remove ambiguity from the interpretation of consent was hailed by some as the closest thing yet to an ideal of "communicative sexuality" (Curtis, 1997).

Studies of college students have found that many young men and women believe that under some circumstances it is all right for a man to force a woman to have sex (Schwartz and DeKeseredy, 1997). These authors and others (Benedict, 1997; Sanday, 1990, 1996) have found that among all-male social networks, especially those such as fraternities and athletic teams where heavy drinking is the norm, certain women, particularly those who are intoxicated, are considered "legitimate sexual targets." Some men believe that even when a woman says no to sex, it is still acceptable to continue their sexual advances. Peggy Sanday's (1990) study of a college fraternity detailed how male definitions of consenting sexuality can become so stretched that instances of several men having sex with a nearly unconsciously drunk woman were considered legitimate (the men termed such events "pulling train" or "gang banging"). Their definition was that women who became drunk and acted flirtatiously were "asking for it," and that plying a woman with alcohol was one of several appropriate strategies used in "working a yes out" when a woman initially showed no interest in sex or explicitly said no.

Boswell and Spade (1996) found differences between fraternities that were characterized by women students as "high risk" or "low risk" in terms of likelihood of being raped. "High-risk" fraternities were characterized by members who treated women as subordinates and kept them at a distance, active discouragement of ongoing relationships with women, routine degradation of women, and more participation in the "hook-up" scene, thus increasing the probability that women would become faceless victims. "Hooking up," a phenomenon that Boswell and Spade found seemed to have replaced dating on most college campuses, was defined by men in this study as something that happens "when you are really drunk and meet up with a woman you sort of know, or possibly don't know at all, and don't care about. You go home with her with the intention of getting as much sexual, physical pleasure as she'll give you, which can range anywhere from kissing to intercourse, without any strings attached" (1996:139). Women's version of hooking up differed. Women said they hooked up only with men they cared about and described hooking up as kissing and petting but not sexual intercourse. Many women said that hooking up was disappointing because they wanted longer-term relationships.

The views expressed in Boswell and Spade's 1996 study, however, may not be the case anymore as sexual mores have shifted. In her book *Hooking Up: Sex, Dating, and Relationships on Campus* (2008), Kathleen Bogle proposed that, like dating, hooking up is a specific type of socialization tool used to find romantic partnerships. She noted that from the beginning of the 20th century until the early 21st century, "there have been three distinct scripts guiding young men and women's intimate lives" (2008:12). These scripts (i.e., cultural norms and expectations) have changed from "calling" to "dating" to "hooking up." According to the college students and alumni she interviewed, hooking up is about more than just sex, though that is often the immediate goal. Rather, the long-term goal to find a partner is still very much a part of the hooking-up script.

The Parent-Child Relationship. A clear example of historical change in the quality and nature of intimate relations involves the norms governing the relationships between parents and children. Here we can refer back to a theme raised in chapter 1 in which we argued that the meanings of everyday life must be understood within the broad frames of history and social structure. Even such a commonsense idea as what it means to be a child varies at different times and particularly as the economic structure of society changes. The place and meaning of childhood is different in an agrarian economy than in an industrial economy. In agricultural societies married couples had a large number of children because they needed the help to run their farms. In industrial societies fertility rates drop dramatically, and too many children may be seen as a hindrance to one's own mobility in society. In his pioneering work *Centuries of Childhood* (1962), the French social historian Philippe Aries demonstrated that the meanings of children as a social category and of childhood as a life-cycle period are shaped by particular historical circumstances.

Aries argued that childhood was "discovered" as a separate life stage during the 16th and 17th centuries in Europe. He demonstrated that childhood carried a fundamentally different meaning in the Middle Ages (from about the 400s through the 1400s) than in the contemporary world. In the Middle Ages, children were considered to be small adults. The equality of their relationship with adults was reflected in numerous customs. Parents and children wore similar clothing, participated in identical work and play activities, and even exchanged sexual jokes. As the dominant form of the family institution changed from the **extended family,** which included several generations of a kinship network, to the **nuclear family,** which was composed only of a father, a mother, and their children, the father assumed absolute control over both mother and children. The extent of such domination is reflected in the laws of the period. In 17th-century Massachusetts, children over the age of 16 were subject to the death penalty for cursing or striking their parents or for refusing to obey their orders.

During the early period of industrialization in Europe and the United States, children came to be seen as an economic resource, valued in large measure by the contribution they could make to the family's well-being. In this period there were no child labor laws, and it was common for even young children to work 14 or more hours per day in the expanding factories of the industrial world. The meaning of childhood shifted yet again with the emergence of American cities, taking root first among the middle class in the early 19th century and spreading to encompass working-class children by the early 20th century. "Not surprisingly, middle-class children were redefined as vulnerable innocents in need of full-time care and devoted attention in the same era as their mothers were being redefined as the guardians of virtue and morality, the ideal keepers of the domestic sphere" (Farrell, 1999:22). Despite class differences, which sharpened as the United States industrialized during the 19th century and produced clear distinctions in the life experiences of children, "the middle-class model of the vulnerable and defenseless child who required a mother's full-time care" gained dominance as the cultural norm, if not the behavioral reality, by the middle of the century (p. 23). Between the 1870s and the 1930s, working-class as well as middle-class children began to be sentimentalized and reinterpreted as innocent and vulnerable, a process that involved a significant cultural shift from a belief in the economic usefulness of children to one in which children were understood as economically useless but morally and emotionally priceless (Zelizer, 1985). According to one author, by the start of the 20th century, "American children were beginning to serve more the psychological than the economic needs of adults" (Cross, 1997:85).

Although expectations about parent-child relationships continue to vary with the ethnic, religious, and social class characteristics of families, most 21st-century parents seek to be friends with their children and try to foster mutual respect for all family members' behaviors and opinions. The family circle typically resembles a democracy in which the children have the right to participate in the decision-making process. It is, however, an imperfect democracy. Because parents have full responsibility for their offspring, they have authority over them and are expected to exert strong control over their lives.

Social Status and the Meaning of Intimacy

The meanings attached to family, friendship, and love relationships also vary with a person's social status (see chapter 3). At various levels of the social structure of American society, there are variations in the definitions and meanings assigned to these relationships.

Friendships, for example, are distinguished from family relationships by their voluntary character. The saying, "You can pick your friends but you can't choose your relatives" contains much truth and has significant sociological implications. First, we expect friendships to be less binding than family relations. Indeed, one way we describe "close" friendships is to invest them with a familial status. A woman might affirm the closeness of her friendship with another woman by saying, "She is like a sister to me." "Kindred spirits," a quaint phrase in Victorian literature, carries the same sentiment as the more current phase "going for brothers" used by black men to describe friendships based on trust and mutual responsibility. Friendships, of course, vary in intensity. A range of terms is used to describe gradations of nonkin intimacy, from *acquaintance* to *friend, close friend,* and *best friend* (with its cyberspace variant BFF—*best friends forever*).

The meanings we give to friendship and other intimate relationships reflect a person's social attributes, including the ascribed statuses of age, race, and gender, as well as achieved statuses such as occupation, education, and social class (see chapter 3). We will consider how two of these attributes, gender differences and social class, affect the maintenance of intimate relationships among friends and in the family.

Gender Differences. The voluminous social science literature on **gender roles** adds up to the conclusion that perhaps even more than class or age, gender, along with race or ethnicity, defines one's identity, opportunities, and constraints. Social definitions of friendship and intimacy reflect traditional stereotypes of men's and women's roles (Wood and Fixmer-Oraiz, 2014). Both women and men perceive women as more attentive, caring, and responsive, and a majority of both sexes report that friendships with women are more close and satisfying than those with men (Werking, 1997). One need only take a walk to a local grade school at recess time to note differences in the way that young children play and form friendship groups. From a very early age boys and girls form sex-segregated friendship groups, which differ in size and content of activities. Girls tend to engage in more cooperative play in which a major activity is talk and the expression of feeling, whereas boys tend to interact in more instrumental ways forming into larger, more amorphous groups and engaging in competitive games (Leaper, 1996; Hardin and Greer, 2009).

The fact that women use talk as a primary way to develop relationships and men generally do not underlies several gender-linked patterns in friendship. First, communication is central to women friends, whereas activities are the primary focus of men's friendships. Second, talk between women friends tends to be expressive and disclosive, focusing on details of personal lives, people, relationships, and feelings; talk in men's friendships generally revolves around less personal topics such as sports, events, money, music, and politics. Third, in general, men assume a friendship's value and seldom discuss it, whereas women are likely to talk about the dynamics of their relationship. Finally, women's friendships generally appear to be broader in scope than those of men; that is, women tend not to restrict their disclosures to specific areas but to invite each other into many aspects of their lives (Wood and Fixmer-Oraiz, 2014).

Traditional gender stereotypes suggest that men tend to disclose less than women due to sociocultural prohibitions against intimacy between men (Floyd, 1997) and because men are socialized to hide their emotions in order to avoid appearing weak or homosexual (Monroe et al., 1997). Although not all studies have found gender differences in self-disclosure, some studies have shown differences in men's and women's perceptions of and experiences with intimacy (Hendrick, 1997), same-sex friendships (Parks and Floyd, 1996), and self-disclosure (Dolgin and Minowa, 1997). These studies suggest that women generally tend to self-disclose more frequently than men. A study by Wagner-Raphael, Seal, and Ehrhardt (2001) found that in relationships with women, men divulge personal feelings and express emotion, whereas men's same-sex relationships involve sharing personally relevant facts and shared activities. The reported ability of men to be emotionally expressive with women may reflect the impact of recent changes in gender roles on intimate cross-sex relationships.

The centering of attention on human relations learned by girls from a very early age sets the stage for the nature of male and female friendships and continues into adulthood. Married or single, employed or not, women make 10 to 20 percent more long-distance calls to family and friends than men, are responsible for nearly three times as many greeting cards and gifts, and write two to four times as many personal letters as men. Women spend more time visiting with friends, though full-time work blurs this gender difference by trimming friendship time for both sexes. "Keeping up with friends and relatives continues to be socially defined as women's work" (Putnam, 2000:95), or what Di Leonardo (1987) referred to as "kin work." Even in adolescence women are more likely to express a sense of concern and responsibility for the welfare of others. And although American boys and girls in the 1990s used computers almost equally, boys were more likely to use them to play games, while girls were more likely to use them for e-mail (Putnam, 2000, Hardin and Greer, 2009).

You might test the notion of kin work against your personal experiences. Who sends the birthday and holiday greetings in your home? Who cooks the holiday dinners and invites the relatives? If your family is at all typical of contemporary American families, the odds are that it is probably a woman (or women) doing these things. In most American families, women still consider it their duty to worry about family members and to take care of their everyday needs.

The gender patterns of activity established on kindergarten playgrounds sustain themselves throughout the life courses of men and women as such patterns are reinforced by cultural standards and structural arrangements. Together these factors result in women possessing more than men the social skills that foster greater intimacy within friendships. We might also presume that the differences we have been describing in this section help us understand some of the communication difficulties men and women may have in their own intimate relationships (Newman et al., 2008). Women usually have to encourage men to talk about their deepest feelings, something they find difficult to do. "Can we talk about us?" is the opening of innumerable conversations that end in misunderstanding and hurt (Wood and Fixmer-Oraiz, 2014). For most women, communication is a primary way to establish and maintain relationships with others. They engage in conversation to share themselves and to learn about others (Johnson, 1996). For women, talk *is* the essence of relationships, and women's speech tends to display identifiable features that foster connection, support, closeness, and understanding (Wood and Fixmer-Oraiz, 2014). Men, on the other hand, use communication to do things and solve problems. In general, men are inclined to think a relationship is going fine as long as there is no need to talk about it. They are interested in discussing the relationship only if there are particular problems to be addressed. These underlying assumptions held by women and men about what constitutes communication explain why "lack of communication" is the most common complaint of women about their marriages, whereas men in the same marriages do not typically mention communication as a problem. A recent study about the ways that teenagers communicate through text messages found significant gender differences in both what and how much was written (Ling et al., 2014). It noted that teenage boys thought that their female counterparts sent texts that were overly long, prying, and containing unneeded elements.

Gender roles have been changing, however, as women have entered the labor force in increasing numbers since the mid-20th century. In 1960, the rate for married women's labor force participation was about half that for single women, with 31.9 percent of married women and 58.6 percent of single women in the paid labor force. In 1980, the rate for married women was 77 percent that of single women, with 49.8 percent of married women and 64.4 percent of single women in the paid labor force. By 2010, the rates had almost converged, with 61.0 percent of married women in the paid labor force, compared to 63.3 percent of single women (U.S. Census Bureau, 2012). Dual-earner couples have become the norm. The rates for mothers are even more striking. By 2009, 61.6 percent of married women with children under age 6 were in the paid labor force, compared to 67.8 percent of single women with children under age 6 and 55.9 percent of married women with no children under age 18 (U.S. Census Bureau, 2012). Despite the dramatic increase in women's labor force participation, gender inequity in the labor force continues (see chapter 6).

The growing social science literature focusing on the intersection of work and family (Hochschild and Machung, 1989, 1997; Jacobs and Gerson, 2009; Bianchi and Milkie, 2010), as well as the regular appearance of articles in women's magazines, websites, and blogs, testify to the importance of the issue of balancing the competing and often overwhelming demands of paid work and family commitments. In fact, this is perhaps the most central challenge in women's lives in the 21st century. Much scholarship has concentrated on the experiences and consequences of the "second shift" (Hochschild and Machung, 1989) put in by employed women and the balancing act between work and family roles (Milkie and Peltola, 1999). When both marriage partners work outside the home, critical questions are raised about how to divide the everyday household tasks. These kinds of questions can lead to intense feelings of resentment on the part of the wife, who, despite the increased popularity of the image of an involved family man and societal espousal of egalitarian values, continues to shoulder most of the burden of household labor. Even more recent studies reveal only slight changes from previous patterns of housework allocation. Gender segregation of tasks continues, with wives performing the "core," traditionally female, tasks to a large degree and men concentrating their household labor on other, more episodic or discretionary tasks (Bianchi et al., 2000; Hook, 2010).

Intimate relations within the home are bound to be affected by wives' efforts to negotiate an equitable distribution of household chores, as well as their desire to be recognized as equal partners in the rights and responsibilities of the marriage. Wives' perceptions of unfairness have a tremendous impact on the marriage, resulting in negative associations such as depression, thoughts of divorce, and actual breakups (Greenstein, 1996; Rogers and Amato, 2000). This finding holds true across racial and ethnic groups (Stohs, 2000; Hook, 2010). When Joanne Stohs asked the African American, Asian American, Hispanic American, and Middle Eastern Americans in her sample about reasons for marital conflict, the issue of "unfair share" was cited more frequently than any other. Another study that included middle-class and working-class dual-earner couples found that for middle-class wives, perceptions of equity had the strongest effect on marital conflict (Perry-Jenkins and Folk, 1994).

Effects of Social Class.   Social class position also influences the meanings attached to friendship. There is, for example, a strong relationship between **social mobility** and the maintenance of friendship ties. Some people maintain strong allegiances to the same friends throughout their lives, while for others friendships are much more transitory and entail few obligations. Position in the occupational structure has a lot to do with the processes of friendship choice and development, the social contexts in which friends are made, the influence of social mobility on friendship ties, and the significance of the workplace for friendship development.

Sociological studies have found that for lower- and working-class men, friendships require substantial commitments and the fulfillment of an extensive set of mutual obligations. Indeed, the requirements of friendships in these classes are said to be so extensive and morally binding that they can stand in the way of occupational and educational achievement.

In his classic study of a Boston slum community, *Street-Corner Society: The Social Structure of an Italian Slum* (1955), William Foote Whyte explained how the friendship loyalties of a group of "corner boys" (actually men in their 20s and 30s, mostly second-generation immigrants) restricted their social mobility. He described them as so tied to their group through a network of reciprocal obligations and so unwilling to sacrifice their friendships that they failed to get ahead. For example, friends were expected to share whatever money they had. Such a friendship norm prevented these young men from adopting the middle-class values of thrift, savings, and investment, and made the eventual financing of a college education or business career impossible. A leader of the corner gang—a man named Doc— expressed his feelings about his friends when he told Whyte:

> I suppose my boys have kept me from getting ahead. . . . But if I were to start over again—If God said to me, "Look here, Doc, you're going to start over again and you can pick out your friends in advance," still I would make sure that my boys were among them—even if I could pick Rockefeller and Carnegie. . . . Many times people . . . have said to me, "Why do you hang around these fellows?" I would tell them, "Why not, they're my friends." (1955:180)

This group distinguished levels of friendship, ranging from an inner circle of individuals to others who remained at the periphery of a network of personal relationships. To be among the inner circle of another person required trusting that person like kin, with the usual claims, obligations, expectations, and loyalties that such a status implies. The result was a contradiction between the requirements of friendship and the desire to get ahead. More recent interviews with working-class members suggest that this contradiction still exists and can be a source of acute strain or tension.

The friendship model of lower- and working-class men contrasts with the ways upper-middle-class men in managerial occupations construct and define their friendships. In another famous book, *The Organization Man* (1956), William H. Whyte described the friendships of career-oriented, rising young executives as short-lived and largely utilitarian. Friends were frequently *cultivated* for their potential value in career advancement. Such friendships were often dissolved or forgotten when the aspiring executive moved up the corporate ladder or left the area. Breaking off friendship ties when they posed an obstacle to mobility did not create moral dilemmas for these men. They clearly recognized the need for an extensive network of the "right" friends, and who these friends were could change at each point in their career development.

■ From Strangers to Intimates:
The Construction of Love Relationships

Despite the variability in the ways individuals construct, maintain, and change the quality of their relationships with family members, friends, and lovers, it is possible to identify an **intimacy process** with certain common elements. This section is concerned with one part of that process: the construction and development of love relationships. It explores the steps through which two strangers typically become intimates—meeting, dating, becoming committed to each other, falling in love, and often marrying. While the specifics of the process through which strangers are transformed into lovers may vary widely, the socially prescribed benchmarks or stages of these relationships are much alike.

We share certain expectations about the appropriateness of intimate relationships. We expect to fall in love, have sex, and get married within well-recognized time frames. Adults typically define teenagers' first attempts at establishing intimate relationships as infatuation or "puppy love"; they are considered too young to experience the real thing. At the other extreme, people who remain unmarried into their thirties may be considered "problems" by parents, relatives, and friends—the stigma associated with singlehood has declined but has not disappeared, particularly for women (Chasteen, 1994; Klinenberg, 2012). Similarly, sexual relationships between teenagers could be considered improper if not immoral, but status as a virgin after the middle to late twenties could be a source of embarrassment.

In American society, the completion of formal education seems to be a key point in intimacy time conceptions. High-school students who do not go on to college are more likely to marry soon after graduation. For others the college years are thought to be an appropriate time to fall in love. Indeed, because college students constitute a readily accessible sample of participants for research studies, most of the generalizations concerning the process through which individuals fall in love come from studies of college students. To understand this process, we must first appreciate the conception of love that guides the construction of our intimate relations.

The Romantic Love Ideal

Some years ago a Korean graduate student who was becoming visibly distressed as she neared the completion of her master's degree work confided she had been receiving letters from her parents indicating that she would be married upon her return to South Korea. Throughout her education in the United States she had known that she would eventually be expected to marry the person her parents chose for her. Now, however, she did not want to return to South Korea, and she certainly did not want to marry someone she had never met. She knew it would be a breach of cultural tradition to refuse her parents' wishes, but she had adopted American values that consider love to be the sole basis for marriage. The standards of her society, we note, are more typical of what young men and women experience around the world than is the Western notion that love should be the basis for marriage. Here, as elsewhere, we should place cultural values in historical context.

The **romantic love ideal,** formulated in France and Germany during the 12th century, filtered down from the nobility to the lower classes over the centuries. In its pure form the ideal of romantic love involves the notion that each of us has one person in all the world that we are meant to love: Although "love is blind," we will recognize our "true love" at first sight. The role of *fate* in this process is a strong feature of the romantic ideal. We are expected to "fall in love" and to believe that "you were meant for me!" From adolescence on, we wait for that moment when "that old black magic has me in its spell" (see box).

Love Makes the World Go Round: The Code of Romance

It is often asked whether art imitates life or vice versa. Although it is difficult to answer this question, one thing is certain. The romantic ideal is celebrated in music, art, cinema, and literature. One particularly thriving industry caters to the apparently unquenchable thirst for romance stories. Romance fiction is an extremely lucrative business, holding the largest share of the U.S. consumer print book market in 2012 at 16.7 percent and generating about $1.4 billion in both print and e-book sales in 2013 (Romance Writers of America, 2014). Harlequin, the number one romance publishing house, publishes the work of about 1,300 authors and churns out 110 titles a month in 34 languages and sells them in more than 100 countries. Harlequin was bought in 2014 by Robert Murdoch's News Corp. for about $415 million. Murdoch was interested in Harlequin in large part because of the publisher's presence in stores such as Walmart as well as its international reach (James, 2014).

Despite the popularity of romance fiction, it remains stigmatized as "trashy novels." Readers often find it necessary to employ face-saving strategies in social situations, such as concealing the reading and criticizing the books to other readers (Brackett, 2000).

So what exactly is romance fiction? Today the genre encompasses a wide range of books from contemporary to historical, racy to gentle, realistic to paranormal (Saricks, 1999). According to one author, a romance is defined as "a love story in which the central focus is on the development and satisfactory resolution of the love relationship between the two main characters, written in such a way as to provide the reader with some degree of vicarious emotional participation in the courtship process" (Kristin Ramsdell, quoted in Saricks, 1999).

Characters fall into easily identifiable categories. Men are handsome, strong, and elusive; women are strong, bright, and independent. Moral and social issues are often significant themes (alcoholism, the role of women in society, post-traumatic stress disorder). The women are not always beautiful, but they are—without fail—bright, independent, interesting, and articulate (Saricks, 1999). Many of the female characters are now either much more sexually driven than in days gone by or not even present at all. Formerly taboo sexual topics and combinations are more present than ever as romance novels have pushed further into the sensuous world of erotica. "GLBT romance, including male/male and ménage stories, continues to become more popular as our society begins to embrace the idea that love is love and that a good romance story isn't bound by gender," says one publisher who specializes in nontraditional romance e-books. "Readers are asking our authors to step out of their comfort zones and provide stories about bi characters, multiple partners, and many other combinations of sexualities" (Naughton, 2012).

Publishers, authors, and readers attribute the changes to many factors, but one stands out above the rest. We can call it the "Fifty Shades Phenomenon." Within six weeks of the books' publication, more than 10 million copies of E. L. James's *Fifty Shades* trilogy, an erotic romance series about the sexual exploits of a domineering billionaire and an inexperienced coed, had been sold in the United States. In two years, 100 million copies—including those in English and 51 other

(continued)

languages—have been purchased by readers wanting a relatively sanitized look into the world of bondage and sadomasochism, or BDSM (Kellogg, 2014). These numbers, however, do not account for countless individuals who have borrowed the books from a friend or a library. "The explosion of *Fifty Shades of Grey* on the scene marks the first time one of these erotic romances has gone mainstream in such a big way," says St. Martin's Press editor Rose Hilliard. "Many readers discovered for the first time that they enjoy erotic romance, and now they're buying more of it. We've seen this happen with our own erotic romance author Sara Fawkes, whose previously self-published, e-serial BDSM novel, *Anything He Wants*, sold 100,000 e-books in five weeks" (quoted in Naughton, 2012).

The effects of the "Fifty Shades Phenomenon" go beyond the publishing industry. The popularity of these sort-of-racy-but-not-*too*-racy books has supposedly increased sales and home uses of handcuffs, rope, and lingerie. "Adult" retailer Lovehoney produced and sold an official *Fifty Shades* range of merchandise including leather masks and paddles. The record company EMI even released *Fifty Shades of Grey: The Classical Album*. The original set of novels has also spawned a cottage industry of spoof books, both in e-book and paperback formats (such as *Fifty Shades of Beige, Fifty Shades of Bacon,* and *Fifty Shames of Earl Grey*), as well as a few off-off-Broadway musical parodies such as *Cuff Me* and *Spank!*

Although love ought to be the sole basis for marriage according to the romantic ideal, most of us recognize the discrepancy between ideal and real. We may generally subscribe to the romantic ideal, but we also know that life rarely corresponds to ideals, that people do not and ought not to marry *only* because they are in love. Most young people are socialized to believe that love is necessary for marriage, but it is not always a sufficient reason to marry. We have a negative view of anyone who would marry *exclusively* for money, status, prestige, or security. But we also consider anyone foolish who would marry a poor person rather than a wealthy one, other factors being more or less equal.

In an early well-known study, Willard Waller (1938) analyzed the dating patterns among young people (particularly college students) and found that, contrary to popular belief, men were more likely than women to hold to the romantic ideal. In other words, women were *less* romantic than men. Because of women's traditional dependence on men, in Waller's view, the process of mate selection was of much greater consequence to them. Women, therefore, had been comparatively less idealistic and more rational and cautious in love relationships.

If only the romantic ideal were operating in mate selection, we should expect that Cupid's arrow would strike only where there was romantic electricity between two people. Were this the case, we should expect that marriages would easily cut across class, racial, ethnic, and religious lines. However, even a casual glance at the marriage announcements in the Sunday newspaper illustrates that the vast majority of people marry within strict social channels. Although we are theoretically free to marry anyone who catches our eye, selection is generally limited to those we meet and can confidently introduce to relatives and friends. These considerations automatically reduce the "pool of eligibles" to those who are not all that different from ourselves. The tendency to pick a partner who shares our ascribed characteristics—race, religion, ethnicity, social class—is called **homogamy**. Young people today are able to travel a lot farther from home, at an earlier age, and more frequently than in the past, so their chances of meeting someone different from themselves have increased. As a consequence, in terms of ethnicity and religion especially, an increasing number of marriages are *heterogamous*—that is, between people who differ in one or more of the ascribed characteristics.

Although religion and ethnicity have diminished in prominence, race remains a powerful factor in real-world choices of marriage partners. For example, marriages between blacks and whites comprised only 3 of every 1,000 marriages in 1980 and only 6 out of 1,000 in 1998—a 100 percent increase, but still a small percentage of the population. Even after the 2008 election of the biracial Barak Obama as president—which some observers claimed ushered in a "postracial" era in the United States—only 7.9 percent of all interethnic or interracial marriages in 2010 were between blacks and whites; 25 percent of Asian American women and 12 percent of Asian American men were married to a person not of Asian descent; and 28 percent of all married Hispanics had a non-Hispanic spouse. Nevertheless, **endogamy**—the principle that people should marry within a certain group— is still the social norm in the United States (U.S. Census Bureau, 2012).

The Process of Falling in Love

You probably have known people who claim to have fallen in love at first sight—perhaps you have yourself. For most people, however, the development of a love relationship is a gradual process. Although social scientists have offered more recent models of what the falling-in-love process is like (e.g., Sternberg, 1988), we still find most useful Ira Reiss's (1960) description of the **wheel theory of love** in which the four stages of a love relationship—rapport, self-revelation, mutual dependency, and need fulfillment— are represented by the spokes of a wheel (see figure 5.1 on the following page). According to Reiss, we proceed through these stages one at a time and in order. Before we are willing to reveal significant identity information about ourselves to another person, we must first have achieved a certain level of rapport with that person. Self-revelation then sets the stage for a sense of mutual dependency. The final stage in this process is the belief that the other person fulfills our basic needs.

Research conducted on various aspects of mate selection and marriage suggests that there is indeed considerable regularity and rationality to the process. Using Reiss's wheel theory as a general guide, we can analyze the movement from rapport to self-revelation to commitment and marriage, as well as the factors that sometimes hinder such movement.

Rapport and Self-Revelation: "You Think You Know Me, but You Don't." Meeting a stranger—at a party, through the introduction of mutual friends,

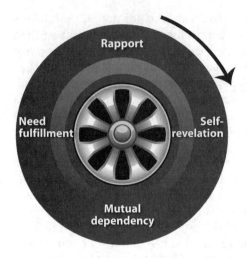

Figure 5.1   The Wheel Theory of the Development of Love

Source: Adapted from Ira Reiss, "Toward a Sociology of the Heterosexual Love Relationship," *Marriage and Family Living* 22 (May 1960):143. National Council on Family Relations.

in a class or church group—usually starts with casual conversation and the exchange of superficial biographical information. College students meeting at a party engage in fairly ritualistic conversation: "What year are you in? What is your major? Where are you from?" If one of the participants has no desire to continue the conversation, this incipient relationship is easily ended. If the individuals wish to pursue the relationship, the conversation becomes progressively less superficial and more far-reaching, as each person seeks to learn more about the other. The desire to continue a relationship, however, may be more related to assessments of physical attractiveness than to social or personality attributes, at least for men (Kwan and Trautner, 2009).

There are factors other than appearance that influence whether two people will embark on a romantic relationship, such as similarities in lifestyle, psychological traits, and beliefs about sexuality and marriage (Houts and Robins, 1996; Lamm et al., 1998, Uecker, 2008).

The Impression Management Stage.   After two people have begun to interact, their primary goals typically are to determine the issues on which they agree and disagree and to assess the significance of their similarities and differences. While the **manifest function** of dating is to teach partners how to negotiate differences (e.g., which movie to rent or where to go to eat), the **latent function** is to prepare them for the skills necessary to maintain long-term relationships.

Complicating the information assessment during the initial stages of a relationship is the deliberate impression management engaged in by both parties. Individuals may be so intent on establishing a relationship that they systematically present attitudes and values they believe will be acceptable. Each will be careful to feel out the other person before expressing an opinion that might be disliked enough to bring an end to the relationship. Identity information is manipulated to present the proper first impression.

Courtship is, then, a unique period in the love relationship in which each person typically offers an idealized image of herself or himself and is willing—even eager—to accept the idealized image the other person presents. When the couple learns more about each other, it may nonetheless come as a surprise if the original presentation of self turns out to have been deliberately manipulated to create a favorable impression. In fact, relationships may end when one or both persons are forced eventually to conclude, "I thought I knew her [or him], but I didn't."

As we noted in chapter 3, people manage impressions of themselves by systematically concealing information they consider potentially damaging in the encounter while at the same time seeking out information about the other person. It is relatively easy to manipulate information about attitudes and values. Other items of identity information, however, are difficult to hide or conceal, such as the ascribed attributes of ethnicity, race, religion, and social class. These social class attributes also serve as a **relationship filter.** If people discover that others' ethnic, religious, or class affiliations are too different from their own to be acceptable, they are likely to end the relationship at an early stage. The ability to garner resources may initially serve as a relationship filter (Ganong et al., 1996).

Premarital romantic relationships consist primarily of the joint pursuit of leisure, and, to the extent that people "date" with the idea of selecting a mate, partners are likely to evaluate how congruent their ideas are about who will be responsible for what after marriage. This led one group of researchers to focus on couples' similarity in leisure interests and role preferences. They hypothesized that similar couples might be expected to fall more deeply in love, be less ambivalent about the relationship, experience less conflict, and escalate their commitment to marriage more rapidly (Houts and Robins, 1996). Their findings supported the idea that compatibility affects the developmental course of premarital relationships, especially for men. The more compatible couples were in their leisure preferences, the more men reported they loved their partner during courtship and engaged in communication designed to increase satisfaction. The more couples agreed on role performance preferences (food preparation and financial tasks), the less conflict or negativity was reportedly experienced by both men and women and the less ambivalence was reported by women.

Supplied with the information the participants have provided about themselves and the symbols defining their social worlds, the couple must then decide whether the worlds they respectively inhabit are close enough that they will eventually be able to produce and sustain a common reality. Social science studies have found that if two people have highly dissimilar biographies, they will be unlikely to produce such a reality. It is the obvious disparity in biographies that forms the substance of such legends as Cinderella, for example. Cinderella is a fairy tale precisely because it relates the story of a successful love relationship despite vast differences in the individuals' biographies.

When a relationship endures beyond the point of self-disclosure and the participants are dating each other "seriously," they begin to try to interpret their level of commitment to the relationship. And to guarantee that their relationship will continue, they must make a commitment to each other.

Mutual Dependency and Commitment: "All I Ever Need Is You."   If the love relationship continues, eventually it reaches the point where the participants' everyday lives are much intertwined. At the stage of mutual dependency, the couple's relationship has ceased to be their private affair. The individuals have probably been publicly defined as a couple. When this **public definition** has been applied, their relationship becomes more exclusive, and they are bound in a complex web of expectations. Not only do the participants have new expectations of each other, so do their friends and family. The couple is issued joint invitations; one is expected to accompany the other to social gatherings; and when they are apart, each partner is expected to be able to account for the other's ideas, attitudes, and whereabouts. The partners signal the seriousness of their relationship to each other, family, and friends by engaging in a variety of activities generally understood to indicate a growing level of commitment. Such symbolic gestures may include spending time together every day rather than just on weekends, introducing the partner to relatives, bringing the other person to such important family events as weddings and annual gatherings, purchasing expensive gifts for each other, and making it "Facebook official" (i.e., changing one's Facebook status to "in a relationship" (Papp et al., 2012).

The point of mutual dependency is a time when the relationship may undergo severe tensions and stresses. These difficulties are often related to the growing intensity of commitment demanded in the relationship. Their own and others' expectations for the couple may cause one or another to feel smothered by the pressure to make a permanent commitment. In the past, there often were gender differences in the meanings attached to commitment. Traditionally, males have been socialized to view the acceptance of a long-term relationship as a surrender of their freedom and independence, while females have been socialized to seek the security of a permanent commitment. Now women also are becoming wary of losing their identity in a relationship. Many women refuse to subordinate their interests to those of their male partners and would not hesitate to dissolve a relationship where they are treated as only an appendage to the man. In a study of late-adolescent romantic relationships at the turn of the millennium, males and females did not report significantly different levels of commitment as measured by a "Commitment to Relationship Scale" and "Feelings of Entrapment Scale" (Galliher et al., 1999). In fact, in approximately half of the couples, girlfriends reported more commitment than boyfriends, while the opposite pattern emerged in the other half.

For some couples, graduation from college precipitates a **commitment crisis**:

> Everyone's asking when you're going to get married/move in/have that baby/buy a house. One of you is stalling because you're not entirely convinced you want to move the relationship onto a deeper level of intimacy and commitment. Sometimes, a nudge from others can make us push through silly fears and take the leap. But . . . outright pressure and nosy interference can send us in the opposite direction—flying over the edge to freedom. (Cox, 2000:324)

One frequent cause of breakups at this stage is that parents or friends dislike or disapprove of the dating partner. Your friends, for example, may demand to know what you see in your companion. In college, as in high school, students place a great deal of weight on the evaluations of their peers. Many students also form friendships with slightly older persons, such as seniors, graduate students, or young faculty members, who can offer guidance in the place of their parents. Conflicts with parents can easily threaten a developing relationship. If parents who have dreamed of sending their son or daughter to medical school perceive an intimate relationship as a potential threat to this plan, for example, they may demand: "Stop seeing this person or we will stop paying for your education." Parents' control over students' financial welfare can easily extend to control over their love lives.

In years past it was not unusual for a woman to subordinate her own career plans to those of a man in order to sustain a relationship. Today female and male college students do not differ in their desire for success or expectations to achieve. Women in the United States today are more likely to endorse egalitarian gender role attitudes than they were in past centuries and decades (Harris and Firestone, 1998; Wilcox and Nock, 2006), including college women's marriage role expectations (Botkin et al., 2000). If college men do not share these attitudes, relationships may founder at this point unless arrangements can be made for both individuals to pursue their own career goals.

There is some evidence that college students—black and white, male and female—are generally egalitarian in their attitudes. Students believe, for the most part, that male and female romantic partners should be equivalent in education and occupational status, or that men should be superior to their partners in these areas. One difference between females and males that has the potential to strain relationships is the expectation on the part of men that they will do less parenting than their partners. The women expect equality in parenting (Ganong et al., 1996; Shirani et al., 2012).

The popular stereotype of a love relationship that ends before marriage features poor pitiful Pearl pining away for a lost love. Such endings actually are harder on men, however, according to a classic study of breakups before marriage by Charles Hill, Zick Rubin, and Letitia Peplau (1977). This study distinguished between "his breakup" and "her breakup." His breakups are more devastating because men find it more difficult to believe that they are no longer loved. The difference might be explained by women's greater practicality in love relationships. As one of the female respondents in the survey for this study noted, "I don't think I ever felt romantic about David— I felt practical. I had the feeling that I'd better make the most of it." The partners in a lasting relationship are likely to share equal commitments to it, according to these researchers. Their data indicate that only 23 percent of equally involved couples broke up, compared to 54 percent of those in relationships where one person was more committed than the other.

Because the couples studied were college students, Hill, Rubin, and Peplau found that relationships tended to break up at clear demarcations in the school year: May–June, September, December–January. Understandably, the person interested in terminating the relationship found it easier to suggest just before vacation, "It might not be a bad idea for us to date others while we are apart." Also, as might be expected, each partner's conception of the terminated relationship differed according to whether he or she had acted in the role of "breaker-upper" or "broken-up-with." There is a tendency for each partner to claim to have initiated the breakup. It is obviously preferable to define a situation as one in which you have exercised power and controlled another person's behavior rather than the other way around.

Wanting to end a relationship is not unusual. Individuals may discover through frequent interaction that they no longer wish to be involved. In one study of 415 university students, 89 percent of males and 88 percent of females reported that they had been involved in at least one previously broken relationship (Laner, 1995). Many relationships end in the face of pressures, but many partners also develop a commitment to a relationship just because it has continued for a long time. Intimate relationships often develop a momentum of their own as a result of sheer endurance. Investing time and energy in their own relationship while forgoing them with others commits people; often they remain in the relationship even when it becomes a painful one.

Whatever the dynamics of a relationship are that lead two people to declare their commitment to each other, the next step in their intimacy normally is plans for marriage. Today, however, it is not uncommon for individuals to decide to live together without marriage or to remain single. For some, living together represents a satisfactory alternative to marriage; for others, it is viewed as an additional opportunity to test out their relationship. To be sure, people have been marrying much later in life than in earlier decades, and the numbers of men and women in their late 20s and early 30s who have never married more than doubled between 1970 and 2010 (U.S. Census Bureau, 2012). Because of the magnitude of these changes, the meanings of commitment, intimacy, sexuality, and marriage have changed accordingly.

■ Alternatives to Marriage

In recent years there has been much discussion in both the popular press and academic literature about the perception that a sexual-moral revolution has occurred. Sociologists agree that there have been significant changes in sexual norms and behavior, but they disagree on the specific nature of these changes, just when they began, or whether they are tapering off. However, studies offer general support for the idea that a "sexual revolution" began during the turmoil of the 1960s. The same cultural atmosphere in which hippies and young political activists were challenging conventional standards about race relations, political authority, and structure of work was extended to changing norms about sexuality. The result was a striking increase in premarital sexuality that appeared to peak in the early 1980s.

According to Kinsey and his associates (1953), only about one-fifth of 19-year-old women had premarital intercourse during the 1940s and early 1950s. By the early 1980s the corresponding figure was between two-thirds and three-fourths (Hofferth et al., 1987). For men, in the 1940s and 1950s about 45 percent of 19-year-olds had experienced heterosexual intercourse. By the late 1970s the figure was about 80 percent (Gebhard, 1980). In the first decade of the 21st century, data accumulated in a national survey indicated that although the gap in premarital sexual experience between young men and young women has closed, the percentages were lower than those reported in earlier decades. According to the CDC's Center for Health Statistics, 43 percent of never-married teenaged females and 42 percent of never-married teenaged males had experienced sexual intercourse at least once (Centers for Disease Control, 2011). Despite the liberalization of attitudes toward premarital sex, teenagers today are *less* likely to actually engage in the act than previous generations. We can see this as an example that sex, sexual relations, and partnerships are not static categories and that their meanings and practices can change over time, sometime in unexpected or unpredictable ways.

Living Together

The steady increase in the number of men and woman living together led to a new census category for the 1980 count of Americans. The category was "Persons of the Opposite Sex Sharing Living Quarters," or POSSLQ for short. By 1988, the number of POSSLQs stood at 2.6 million couples, four times the estimated number in 1970 (U.S. Census Bureau, 1989). The Census Bureau now uses the term "unmarried partners," defined as two unrelated people sharing living quarters and a "close personal relationship." They are distinguished from roommates who share space simply to save money. The number of unmarried partners was up almost 72 percent during the 1990s, from 3.2 million in 1990 to 5.5 million by 2000 (Roylance, 2001a), and then increased to 6.8 million by 2010 (U.S. Census Bureau, 2012). Although one tends to think of cohabitants as being college-aged, most are over age 25 and have only a high school education. It has been estimated that close to half of all American children will spend some part of their childhood living with one parent and her or his live-in partner (Smock, 2000) and that most cohabitants will eventually marry (about 55 percent); however, 40 percent will end the relationship within five years of the beginning of the **cohabitation** (Bumpass and Lu, 2000).

Although common sense suggests that premarital cohabitation should provide the opportunity for couples to learn about each other, strengthen their bonds, and increase their chances for a successful marriage, the evidence suggests just the opposite. Premarital cohabitation tends to be associated with lower marital quality and increased risk of divorce (Smock, 2000). Numerous studies have attempted to explain this; two explanations have received empirical support. The first, termed the *selection* explanation, refers to the idea that people who cohabit before marriage differ in important ways from those who do not, and these differences increase the likelihood of marital instability. The second explanation is that there is something about the *experience* of cohabitation that increases the likelihood of marital disruption (Smock, 2000; Stanley et al., 2006).

Steven L. Nock (1995), for example, described cohabitation as an *incomplete institution*, "not yet governed by strong consensual norms or formal laws" (p. 74). The absence of these institutional norms is a plausible explanation for much of the poorer quality of cohabiting relationships. Nock compared national data on 499 cohabiting couples and 2,493 married couples and identified three major differences:

1. *Less commitment.* Cohabitants were more likely than married couples to report that ending their relationship would have fewer negative consequences. This finding is supported by the research of Renata Forste and Koray Tanfer (1996), who found that cohabitants were also less willing to be sexually monogamous than married partners were.

2. *Poorer intergenerational relationships.* Cohabitants were more likely than marrieds to report poorer relationships with both mothers and fathers, indicating a lack of emotional and financial support.

3. *Lower relationship happiness.* Cohabitants reported that they were slightly less happy than spouses reported being. (See also Newport, 1996)

Perhaps cohabitants have lower-quality relationships, lower institutional commitment, and less hope for the future of their relationships because cohabitation draws people who are not ready to commit to each other or to the institution of marriage. Some research has found that men and women lacking economic stability are likely to cohabit, suggesting that cohabitation may provide an attractive alternative for those lacking the economic stability required for marriage (Clarkberg, 1999; Halliday Hardie and Lucas, 2010). Moving in together appears to be perceived more as an ambiguous commitment rather than a "trial marriage" (Lindsay, 2000). Perhaps most serious is the finding that domestic violence rates are higher in cohabitation relationships (Waite, 1999–2000).

As we noted earlier, during courtship individuals tend to selectively present their best self, emphasizing or exaggerating positive qualities and behaviors and minimizing or concealing negative ones. This tendency also applies to cohabiting couples who eventually marry. Cohabitants assume that because they are living with their partner, this is the way the partner is and will behave in marriage. This is not necessarily true. After marriage, a new self may emerge and perhaps shock the partner.

Despite research showing a higher dissolution rate for marriages of couples who lived together prior to the marriage than those of noncohabitants (Smock, 2000; Waite, 1999–2000), many couples who live together contend that cohabitation leads to better marriages. Single people living together report satisfaction with some aspects of the situation and problems with other features, and they generally recommend cohabitation. It can provide couples with the emotional security of an intimate relationship but at the same time allow them to maintain independence in many areas. Cohabitants enjoy the spontaneity of a relationship based on love, not law.

Cohabitation often encourages people to establish a meaningful relationship instead of playing superficial dating games. Long periods of intimate contact afford an opportunity for self-disclosure and may foster emotional growth and maturity. Living with someone can be annoying at times, but cohabitants may gain a deeper understanding of their partner's needs, expectations, and weaknesses.

Domestic Partnerships. In the 2000 census, officials routinely recorded same-sex "spouses" as "unmarried partners" as a result, according to a census official, of "a much more cognizant awareness on our part of changes in the living arrangements of people in the 1990s" (Roylance, 2001b). Increasingly, businesses, local governments, and academic institutions started recognizing the rights of **domestic partners** (people who live together in a committed relationship) to be covered by the same benefits as married employees. However, in 1996, when it appeared that the Supreme Court of Hawaii might sanction same-sex unions, a majority of other state legislatures proposed laws to bar homosexual marriages and deny recognition to those performed in other states. Congress passed the Defense of Marriage Act of 1996 that releases states and other territories of the United States from an obligation to recognize same-sex marriages under the laws of another state (see Nock, 1999). This was voided, however, on June 26, 2015 when the U.S. Supreme Court, in a 5 to 4 decision, declared that states cannot keep same-sex couples from marrying and must recognize their unions. The Supreme Court said that the right to marry is fundamental. Stating the majority's opinion, Justice Anthony Kennedy wrote that under the 14th Amendment's protections, "couples of the same-sex may not be deprived of that right and that liberty." The court's landmark decision will certainly have social, economic, and political ramifications that will play out in untold ways in years to come.

Staying Single

Recent years have seen a sharp increase in the number of unmarried adults (never married, divorced, widowed) in American society. "Singlehood," not marriage, is now the most common lifestyle among people in their early 20s. The unmarried population in the United States constitutes a diverse group of singles. More than a quarter of all households in the United States (accounting for more than 26 million people) are single-member households (U.S. Census Bureau, 2012). As reported earlier in the chapter, these numbers partially result from the fact that, compared to earlier decades, people are delaying marriage until later in life. Many people are pursuing college educations, preparing for jobs or careers, and spending more time pursuing recreational or other activities before "settling down." Many people are living together, at least for a while, rather than getting married. The median ages for first marriage—nearly 27 for men and 25 for women—are the oldest ever recorded by the Census Bureau (in the case of the men, exceeding what it had been in 1890—26.1). Nevertheless, marriage is still the norm—nearly 95 percent of all Americans eventually marry (U.S. Census Bureau, 2012).

The decision to marry (and its timing) differs for women and men. Many women perceive that career advancement is slowed by marriage and the chances of one's future occupational success are improved by postponing marriage. Deferring marriage is not, however, useful for men's career advancement, so men lack that motivation for remaining single.

While there are many benefits in marriage, there are usually parallel incentives for being single, particularly independence and autonomy. One goal of marriage is companionship, or avoidance of being alone. According to a *Time* magazine/CNN poll at the turn of the millennium (Edwards, 2000), 75 percent of women said that companionship was what they missed most because of being single; only 4 percent said sex. Although companionship and having someone to talk to is important, one of the biggest advantages of remaining single is independence. Single adult women in the United States are more self-confident and selective than they have ever been, assuming many of the social, economic, and sexual freedoms previously reserved for single men (Edwards, 2000). Only 34 percent of single women said they would settle for less than a perfect mate if they couldn't find one, compared with 41 percent of men (Edwards, 2000).

Less social stigma is attached to remaining single today, with single people less likely to be perceived as socially inadequate. Nevertheless, some unmarried people still encounter stereotypes. Never-married heterosexual men may be suspected of being gay; single women may worry that they are being perceived as promiscuous. Single adults of both sexes must contend with the inaccurate view that they are lonely, workaholics, and immature. These stereotypes help support the traditional assumption in American society that to be truly happy and fulfilled, a person must get married and raise a family. To help counter these societal expectations, singles have formed numerous support groups, such as the Alternative to Marriage Project (http://www.unmarried.org). Although being single is more socially acceptable than it used to be, many people still get married because it is expected of them.

Married people experience a consistently higher level of well-being across a number of dimensions, including financial well-being, happiness, health, and family/job satisfaction. Cohabitants fall between married and unmarried on the happiness scale (Waite, 2000; Waite and Gallagher, 2000). Married men and women feel that their lives have more meaning and purpose than unmarried individuals do, and it is this sense of meaning and purpose that seems to be responsible for the better psychological health of husbands and wives (Burton, 1998). Single individuals have higher levels of loneliness compared to married individuals. Marriage lowers loneliness to a greater degree in men than in women (Stack, 1998). According to one well-known family sociologist, "Most social scientists who have studied the data believe that marriage itself accounts for a great deal of the difference in average well-being between married and unmarried persons. Indeed, loneliness is probably the negative feeling most likely to be alleviated simply by being married" (Glenn, 1997:11).

Single-Parent Families

Single-parent families, in which there is only one parent present to care for the children, can hardly be viewed as a rarity in the United States. In 1998, a single parent headed about 19 percent of white families with children under 18, 34 percent of Hispanic families with children, and 54 percent of African-American families with children (U.S. Census Bureau, 1999). Though the percentage of single-parent households in the United States increased from 11 percent in 1970 to 18 percent in 2012, the realities are heavily skewed toward minorities. African American children (55 percent) and Hispanic children (31 percent) are considerably more likely to live with one parent than non-Hispanic white children (21 percent) or Asian children (13 percent) (U.S. Census Bureau, 2013). However, census data obscures the extent to which there may be a cohabiting adult in the household; it is estimated that 40 percent of children born to unmarried mothers are raised in homes with two adults, at least for part of the time (Bumpass and Lu, 2000).

■ Divorce

The media frequently report that one out of every two marriages ends in divorce. However, much that has been written about the American divorce rate is not accurate. The divorce rate has not risen since the early 1980s. There was a sharp upturn in the late 1940s, most likely due to hasty wartime marriages or marriages that could not survive a long separation. Then came two decades of low divorce rates. The upward trend resumed in the late 1960s, continued through the 1970s, and peaked in 1981. After briefly leveling off, the divorce rate started dropping in the 1990s and continued to decline through the first decade of the 21st century (U.S. Census Bureau, 2012). The census report partly attributed the small declines in divorce to a recent jump in couples cohabitating as well as rising median ages before marriage. People are waiting longer before making long-term commitments.

In an average year there are about 1 million divorces in the United States, a rate of more than 9 divorces per 1,000 existing marriages (U.S.

The Symbolic Dimension of Divorce

The profound value attached to marriage engenders an important problem of meaning when couples go through divorce. That is, because most people get married with the belief that marriage is forever, they face a difficult interpretive problem in explaining why theirs is ending. To resolve the problem, they *undo* the previous meaning of their marriage.

Joseph Hopper was a participant and observer in an extensive four-year fieldwork and interview study focused on the experiences of divorcing people. Among those he interviewed, there was an important, socially meaningful way in which divorce was literally an *undoing* of marriage. As Hopper explains:

> In other words, it was not merely a transition from one kind of relationship to another or the end of one phase and the beginning of another; it was far more than the separation of two intimately related people. It was a retroactive nullification—a substantive and thoroughgoing reinterpretation—of what once existed. (2001:432)

For most of those interviewed, marriage was considered a sacred bond that was presumed to last forever. The ideal of marriage pervaded the reality of their daily lives; they knew divorce was common, but most said they had eliminated thoughts of divorce as a possibility for themselves: "I thought we'd stay together forever."

Dissolving marriage (even a "bad" marriage), then, involves substantial symbolic work, because it is essentially a process of "profaning the sacred."* To dissolve the sacred, in the words of the foundational sociologist Émile Durkheim, requires transformation "*totius substantiae*—of the whole being" such that the old object would "cease to exist, and . . . another [was] instantly substituted for it" (Durkheim, [1915]1965:54). The divorcing people Hopper interviewed were involved in "constructing deeply rooted and fundamental reinterpretations of their marriages that went to the core of what had constituted those marriages" (p. 435).

Hopper found that the distinction between *initiator* and *noninitiator* was important because even though each had to explain the same circumstance of marriage being dissolved, "the interpretive burden was shaped differently depending on whether one had to justify the decision or respond to it; and this . . . set the stage for the intense conflict that followed" (p. 435).

Initiators of divorce come to see their marriage as not having been a true marriage from the start, so efforts to preserve it seem absurd. "With a negative chronology that went back to the beginnings of their marriages, most initiators subsequently argued that there was something fundamentally wrong with their marriages, something irrevocably flawed" (p. 436). This solved the interpretive problem they faced: "The sacred was not really violated, for there was nothing sacred to begin with" (p. 437).

The emerging interpretations of their marriages as false were not happily received by the noninitiating partners. "They were, in fact, being told that their marriages were phony, pretend, and untrue" (p. 440). As Hopper explains, "The fact that noninitiating partners did not conceptualize their marriages as irretrievably and fundamentally bad only exacerbated the interpretive difficulty they faced" (p. 440). The solution for noninitiators appeared to be a sense that "they and their marriages were evidently victims of initiators' deceit" (p. 440). Some noninitiators came to believe that their partners were out-and-out liars; Hopper frequently heard the word "manipulative" used to describe initiating spouses.

"The Big Lie, then, emerged as the interpretive counterpart to The Marriage That Never Was," Hopper says (p. 442). Although these interpretations may help individuals explain why their marriage is ending, they put partners dramatically at odds with each other. Hopper explains:

> Initiators saw their marriages as irrevocably, even originally, broken, a frame of reference that made noninitiators' reluctance to agree seem crazy and vengeful. Noninitiators reasserted a frame in which marriage was sacred and in which initiators' ending them seemed to be yet another maneuver in a nonobvious pattern of deceit. Some noninitiators reacted with threats, violence, or suicide attempts. This, of course, only confirmed the idea that they were dangerous and crazy. (p. 442)

Hopper concludes:

> Thus, initial hypotheses conjured to resolve certain dilemmas became self-fulfilling prophecies, and new problems and realities emerged. . . . Each partner provoked the other and confirmed negative images of themselves; a cycle of preemptory and protective moves—a dynamic of conflict through which most divorces subsequently unfolded—was begun. (p. 442)

Hopper has shown that the symbolic structure and logic of how divorce narratives get constructed can generate the conflict that typically characterizes divorce. His findings suggest that family researchers should look closely at "the symbolic dimension of family life to understand how interpretive processes may themselves be a source of important phenomena in families" (p. 443).

*Durkheim ([1915]1965) made a sharp distinction between the sacred and the profane. Marriages were sacred in the sense that the social collectivity brought them into being—they represent and embody the power, sentiments, and beliefs of society. Nearly every divorced person with whom Hopper spoke evidenced some conviction in the sacredness of marriage, "A sacredness or inviolability that set marriage apart from other kinds of relationships" (2001:433).

Census Bureau, 2012). The American divorce rate is somewhat higher than that for other modern societies, but so too is our marriage rate—the two tend to move together. Because divorces usually take place early in a marriage (within the first ten years), most men and women will remarry, men sooner and at a higher rate than women. The older and better educated the divorced woman, the lower her chances of remarriage because the pool of eligible prospects—divorced, widowed, or never-married educated men—is small. Men seeking to remarry tend to dip into a larger pool, filled with younger and less-educated women.

Although the social stigma has largely disappeared, the economic consequences of divorce for women remain strongly negative (Smock et al., 1999; Jansen et al., 2009). There also are negative outcomes of divorce for children, particularly loss of economic security and potentially stunted cognitive development (Kim, 2011). In terms of noneconomic consequences, women appear to fare better emotionally after separation and divorce than men do (Arendell, 1995). This finding is attributed to the fact that women are more likely than men not only to have a stronger network of supportive relationships but also to benefit from divorce by developing a new sense of self-esteem and confidence since they are thrust into a more independent role. On the other hand, men are more likely to have been dependent on their wives for domestic and emotional support and have a weaker external emotional support system. As a result, divorced men are more likely than divorced women to date more partners sooner and to become remarried more quickly (Arendell, 1995).

Divorce often constitutes a dramatic transformation of a close, personal, and usually harmonious relationship into one that is deeply antagonistic and bitter. It is clearly a *process* rather than a single event, affected by the larger structure of meanings that define marriage in our culture, along with the interpretive logic that people use to make sense of their own experiences (Hopper, 2001; A. Francis, 2012).

The Intimate Self

Everything is relative, including your relatives. We don't get a chance to pick our families but, in modern democratic societies, we can choose our friends and lovers. Wait. Do we? How much freedom do we have when it comes to our intimate relations with others? From soul brothers to soul mates, even our most personal and cherished desires are connected to larger social forces that influence platonic and sexual attraction. How free is your intimate self's ability to choose whom you befriend or ask out on a date?

■ Conclusion

This chapter began with the somewhat circular conception of intimate relationships as those which the participants define as intimate. Our goal has been to extend this idea by analyzing how people come to define their relationships as intimate. Relations of love and friendship are without intrinsic meaning and must be understood as symbolic constructions deeply rooted in social life. Individuals soon learn the values of the society and their immediate reference groups concerning the meanings of love, friendship, and family relationships.

Like any symbol whose meaning by definition is not fixed, the concept of intimacy is subject to substantial historical and contemporary variation in meanings. The meanings of sexual relations and relations of parents and children have changed over time, for example. The meanings given to love and friendship also vary with such social attributes as age, occupation, race, ethnicity, gender, and social class. The substantial differences in the definitions given friendships by males and females and by people in different social classes are particularly apparent in the connection between social mobility and the nature of friendships ties.

Intimate relationships are continually being interpreted and reevaluated by the participants in a regular, patterned process. The wheel theory of love describes the process through which strangers are transformed into intimates. The typical movement of such a relationship is from achievement of rapport to self-revelation to mutual commitment. The next step normally would be plans for marriage. In recent years, however, many young people have chosen to live together without marriage or to remain single. These efforts to refashion social ties have brought changes in the meanings given to intimacy and commitment.

Our treatment of intimate relations has been based on the assumption that individuals are joint participants in the construction of their social relationships. In most relationships, however, they are not equal participants. Some individuals have restricted choices about how they can respond to others and about the meanings conferred on objects, events, and situations. In the next chapter we will focus on the important issue of the distribution and application of power in everyday life.

Definitions

cohabitation: A situation in which unmarried couples live together and share the same household.

commitment crisis: A situation in which a person must make a decision about how important a relationship is to him or her.

domestic partners: Two unrelated adults who reside together; agree to be jointly responsible for their dependents, basic living expenses, and other common necessities; and share a mutually caring relationship.

endogamy: The principle that people should marry within a certain group.

extended family: A household made up of a married couple plus other relatives, often including several generations. The extended family includes a kinship network of people related by birth or by marriage.

gender roles: Societal and cultural expectations that regulate feminine and masculine behaviors.

homogamy: The tendency to pick a partner who shares our ascribed characteristics—race, religion, ethnicity, social class.

intimacy process: The ways individuals establish a relationship of emotional closeness with one another.

latent functions: The unintended consequences of the ways in which an organization or institution actually operates.

manifest functions: The explicit, or stated, purposes of an organization or institution.

need for affiliation: The perceived need or desire for meaningful relationships with others.

nuclear family: Traditionally defined, a family consisting only of a husband, a wife, and their children.

public definition: The ways in which others in an immediate social circle define an individual. Two individuals who have been publicly defined as a couple become bound in a web of societal expectations.

relationship filter: Subtle devices by which individuals determine if they have anything in common with one another.

romantic love ideal: The notion that the love of two people for each other is the only basis for marriage.

social construction: Meanings of things and situations that are created by people through their interactions with one another.

social mobility: The process by which people make changes in their occupation or social class.

wheel theory of love: A metaphor used by Ira Reiss to describe the circular process by which two people pass through phases of increasing intimacy with each other.

Discussion Questions

1. Do you agree with the authors' point of view that intimacy is a social construction—that relationships of love and friendship are symbolic productions and have no intrinsic meaning? Why or why not?

2. How would you describe the distinguishing characteristics of a love relationship? What are the distinctive obligations and expectations defining love relationships? How do such obligations and expectations differ from those defining friendship relationships?

3. Describe a relationship that you have had with a boyfriend or girlfriend. Did the relationship pass through discernible stages as it developed? Do these stages conform to those named in the chapter? Are there similar stages to the breakup process?

4. How would you characterize the attitudes of your friends toward premarital sex? How has knowledge about the existence of sexually transmitted diseases (STDs) influenced the behaviors of college students?

5. Would you interpret the increase in the number of unmarried people choosing to live together as signaling basic shifts in the meanings people are giving to intimacy and commitment? Why or why not?

6. What do you think are the positive and the negative aspects of being single?

6

Power and Stratification

The Politics of Interaction

CHAPTER OUTLINE

■ Power Relations in the Macro and Micro Worlds
■ The Relationship of Power to Role-Taking
■ The Subtle Faces of Power in Everyday Interactions
■ Conclusion

Karl Marx, a noted observer of human affairs, remarked long ago: "Human beings make history, but not under conditions of their own choosing." While symbolic interactionists would agree, they would put it that individuals jointly construct reality, both socially and symbolically (see chapter 2). However, everyone in a society does not participate equally in the construction of social worlds. People with various ascribed and achieved attributes and members of various social classes have varying opportunities to gain access to the decision-making processes in a society. These differences are reflected in the prevailing systems of social stratification.

We are born into a social world whose symbols have been prefabricated by the activities of previous generations (Schuman and Scott, 1989). Their actions have resulted in the construction of social realities whose existence we, as newcomers, must acknowledge if we are to operate as "sane" and "normal" members of society. We see here evidence of the social dialectic between freedom and constraint discussed in chapter 1. We are free to make choices and decisions in our everyday lives, but the range of alternatives from which we choose is the result of historical and institutional factors beyond our control.

For many social scientists, **social stratification** is simply a ranking of the people in a society from upper class to lower class, according to such measures as their income, education, or occupation. Symbolic interactionists believe it more appropriate to think of social stratification as a **power** phenomenon; that is, in discussing stratification, we are really talking about how opportunities, or **life chances**, are distributed in a certain society. People's access to such valued goals as well-paying jobs; positions of prestige and status; opportunities for a long, comfortable life; and even adequate health care are determined to a large extent by their *position* in the stratification system. It is in terms of these life chances that the importance of history, as Marx suggested, becomes evident.

Americans generally believe that rewards should be distributed on the basis of personal merit and one's contributions to the social good. This belief legitimates the economic and class system of the United States. When an idea is legitimated, it is taken for granted and becomes part of the cultural fabric of daily life. The deep, unconscious agreements that make up the structure of legitimacy can be expressed in the concept of *hegemonic culture*, the dominant culture.

The concept of **hegemony** is associated with the Italian sociologist Antonio Gramsci (1928–1971). According to Gramsci, the process of domination is a pervasive and enduring part of our entire experience—at home, at school, at work, in church, at leisure, as well as in politics and government. Ideas and practices become legitimate as the result of powerful groups' success in institutionalizing their definitions. Unfortunately, most Americans do not recognize that the economy and its class system are the historical creation of power groups. The work of sociologist C. Wright Mills in the 1950s and 1960s elaborated the concept of a hegemonic U.S. culture by pointing to economic concentration at the top of the stratification structure in the hands of a small **power elite**—what in the 21st century came to be known as "the 1 percent"—and the control of the masses through ideology, fear, and consumerism.

Interactionists have focused their attention on understanding the ways in which social position affects individuals differently. Social position can have profound effects on self-development, for example. Regardless of what one thinks of oneself, certain characteristics denoting social status affect interaction in certain predictable ways, and these interactions affect one's sense of self.

The distinction between ascribed and achieved statuses is particularly important in this regard. As described in greater detail in chapter 3, ascribed statuses are those society confers on us at birth, such as gender and race, while achieved statuses are those attained during the course of our lives, such as our organizational and occupational statuses. In contemporary American society, despite a great deal of official rhetoric to the contrary, our ascribed-status characteristics have much to do with the nature of our life chances. One lesson of social science, alas, is that one must choose one's parents with great care!

Symbolic interaction is interested in the *processes* that produce and reproduce inequality. To study these processes, both **quantitative methods** and **qualitative methods** are used. Quantitative analyses provide information about how resources such as wealth, power, and prestige are distributed (*who* has *how much* of *what?*). Qualitative research can examine these processes directly; for example, what happens in face-to-face interaction so that a form of inequality is the result, or, how are symbols and meanings created and used to sustain the patterns of interaction that lead to inequality (Schwalbe et al., 2000)? A number of qualitative studies have looked at the reproduction of inequality (for extensive reviews, see Horowitz, 1997; Harris, 2006).

■ Power Relations in the Macro and Micro Worlds

Those who have comparatively greater access to scarce and highly valued resources such as jobs and money have a power advantage in everyday, face-to-face relations. Interactions between men and women, husbands and wives, even children and parents are inextricably bound up with the issue of power between **superiors** and subordinates. The process by which a dominant group defines into existence a subordinate group has been referred to as *othering* (Fine, 1994). This process entails the invention of categories and ideas about what marks people as belonging to these categories; for example, skin color as the basis for a racial group, African Americans (or blacks), that historically has been treated with prejudice and discrimination in the United States.

Face-to-face relations between members of different social classes, racial and ethnic groups, and genders must be seen within the broader context of power relations. In this sense everyday interactions are political acts, and they can be studied within the frame of the *politics of interaction*, thereby taking into account these power differentials.

This interface between individuals' daily lives and the social organization of the society also shows clearly the manner in which personal biographies intersect with the larger arenas of history and social structure. As Peter and Brigitte Berger put it, we simultaneously inhabit two worlds, the **micro world** and the **macro world**:

> First of all, crucially and continuously, we inhabit the micro world of our immediate experience with others in face-to-face relations. Beyond that, with varying degrees of significance and continuity, we inhabit a macro world consisting of much larger structures and involving us in relations with others that are mostly abstract, anonymous and remote. Both worlds are essential to our experience of society, and . . . each world depends upon the other for its meaning to us. (1975:8)

The Bergers suggest that any analysis of face-to-face behavior must consider it within the context of broader institutional arrangements. Similarly, any analysis of an institution, such as religion or education, must take into account its origin in the daily communications among its members. To use the terms introduced in chapter 1, both macrosociological and microsociological investigation are necessary for the analysis of behavior.

The Broad Contours of Power: Money and Jobs

In contemporary American society, access to the means for the production and distribution of wealth is a crucial factor in one's ability to establish a dominant position in the stratification system. To begin our analysis, we will sketch the broad outlines of how certain resources are distributed in American society.

Family Income and Wealth.   Table 6.1 presents data on the distribution of family income in the United States in the period 1950–2012, during which the concentration of income fluctuated slightly but remained virtually unchanged. The fifth of the population with the highest income, which accounted for 42.7 percent of the nation's total income in 1950, accounted for an even larger percentage (48.9 percent)—in fact, almost half of total income—in 2012, a trend that seems to be growing, with potentially trouble-

Table 6.1   Distribution of Family Income, United States, 1950–2012

Year	Lowest fifth	Second fifth	Middle fifth	Fourth fifth	Highest fifth
1950	4.5%	12.0%	17.4%	23.4%	42.7%
1960	4.8	12.2	17.8	24.0	41.3
1970	5.4	12.2	17.6	23.8	40.9
1980	5.1	11.6	17.5	24.3	41.6
1989	4.6	10.6	16.5	23.7	44.6
1999	4.3	9.9	15.6	23.0	47.2
2012	3.8	9.2	15.1	23.0	48.9

Source: U.S. Census Bureau, 2013, *Historical Income Tables—Families*, Table F-2.

some repercussions. Though the percentage of income held by the lowest fifth changed hardly at all, from 4.5 to 3.8 percent during this period, the downward trend is disturbing—an overall trend reflected in the middle three fifths as well. Only those families in the highest fifth experienced an upward trend: they increased their percentage by more than 5 points while everyone else lost ground.

The gap in income between the bottom fifth and top fifth is large, indicating significant income inequality. This differential becomes even more striking when we look at the top 5 percent, who held 21.3 percent of total income in 2012. In effect, then, this 5 percent of families accounts for a larger share of total family income in the United States than that of the total income of the bottom two quintiles—40 percent of all families.

Membership in the upper class, at the top of the stratification system, is determined by *wealth*, or total assets, rather than just family income or earnings. Whereas income is monetary gain, wealth includes stocks, bonds, real estate, business equity, and other investments and is most often measured in terms of "net worth." In fact, wealth produces income in the form of dividends on investments or profits from business assets. More than income, wealth contributes to the perpetuation of the class hierarchy because wealth can be passed down from generation to generation. This enables the rich to stay rich, and it does not lead to significant change in the distribution of wealth. Entrance into the ranks of the wealthy occurs mainly through inheritance or, for a few, the ability to amass a fortune through extraordinary business success or achievement in professional sports or entertainment.

Wealth is even more unevenly distributed than income in the United States. Although there was a decline in the maldistribution of wealth (and income) from the mid-1960s through the 1970s, the trend reversed itself sharply in the 1980s. By 1998, the wealthiest 10 percent of the population owned more than 70 percent of all wealth (Mishel et al., 2001).

Between 1900 and 1980, there was little change in the 20 to 25 percent of wealth owned by the top 1 percent of the U.S. population (Domhoff, 1983). It is this 1 percent at the top of the stratification system that may be considered the "upper class." The gap between the very wealthy and everyone else has grown enormously since the late 20th century. In 1965 the richest 1 percent of Americans held 37 percent of the nation's wealth; by 1979 their share had dropped to 22 percent. After 1979, however, it rose sharply. By 1998, the top 1 percent—referred to as the "Super Rich" by economist Edward Wolff (1995)—owned almost 40 percent of total wealth. The 1 percent are executives, doctors, lawyers, and politicians, among other things. Within this group of people is an even smaller and wealthier subset of people, 1 percent of the top, or .01 percent of the entire nation. In 2012, those people had incomes of over $27 million, or roughly 540 times the national average income. Altogether, the top 1 percent control 43 percent of the wealth in the nation. Even more shocking, it is projected that the world's wealthiest 1 percent is likely to control well over 50 percent of global wealth by 2020 (Hardoon, 2015).

For the latter third of the 20th century, political sociologist G. William Domhoff studied the upper class. In his classic work *The Higher Circles* (1970), Domhoff documented the exclusiveness and impermeability of upper-class social worlds. He also noted the gender distinctions in management of this wealth:

> The American upper class is based upon large corporate wealth that is looked after by the male members of the intermarrying families that are its basis . . . [while upper-class women] participate in a great many activities which sustain the upper class as a social class and help to maintain the stability of the social system as a whole. (p. 56)

It is the men who "look after" the wealth, however.

Social changes, particularly the feminist movement, have affected the socialization of wealthy young women since Domhoff first wrote about this group. Many private schools are coeducational, and women graduates are encouraged to go to major four-year colleges rather than finishing schools. Women of the upper class are more likely to have careers—there are examples of women who have risen to the top of their family's business. Women are also more likely to serve on corporate boards. Despite these changes, Domhoff suggested that there may be even less gender equality in the upper class than there is in the professional stratum, and it is not clear how much more equality will be attained (1998).

Domhoff concluded that the upper class is essentially a ruling class (1970, 1983, 1998). He posited that there is a readily apparent relationship between those who own or control a disproportionate share of society's wealth, those who exercise control over major corporations, and those who greatly influence the governmental elite. He emphasized the social nature of the dominant corporate ownership and managerial class. The cohesiveness of this ruling group is largely a product of their common upper-class ties, Domhoff concluded:

> They belong to the same exclusive social clubs, frequent the same summer and winter resorts, and send their children to a relative handful of

private schools. Members of the corporate community thereby become a *corporate rich* who create a nationwide *social upper class* through their social interaction. (1998:2)

Although sociologists and other social commentators had been documenting the increasing power of the upper class for decades, the rest of the world took notice in 2008 when the American financial system experienced its most serious crisis since the Great Depression. Because of the global nature of markets in the 21st-century economy, what happened in the United States in 2008 generated ripple effects throughout the world. There are many accounts of how and why this financial crisis happened. The notion that the *extremely* wealthy were in charge, and were corrupt, and were ruining it for the rest of us was effectively framed by the Occupy Wall Street movement. Movement organizers famously claimed to speak for "the 99%" in contrast to, and against, "the 1%." Wall Street came to represent the wealthy and purportedly corrupt 1 percent in the upper class. Framing the issue as the "haves" versus the "have nots" brought more general issues of economic inequality into focus.

Effects of Ascribed-Status Characteristics. To a dramatic extent, ascribed-status characteristics such as gender and race are embedded in the institutions of American society. Differential access to positions of power and prestige is built into the organization of society, or the macro world. This macro world sets the stage for the daily dramas of the micro world as people engage in face-to-face contacts.

Women's occupational opportunities. Women's access to better-paying jobs has been consistently restricted, though the earnings of women relative to those of men have increased slightly in recent years. The median wage for female workers with full-time jobs was 62.2 percent of that of full-time male workers in 1970, 63.3 percent in 1980, 73.2 percent in 1998, 76 percent in 2000, and 81.2 percent in 2010 (see table 6.2). The earnings difference between women and men varies by demographic group. Among African Americans and Hispanics, for example, women's earnings were more than 90 percent of men's; for whites, women's earnings were about 80 percent of men's. Young women and men (16 to 24 years old) had fairly similar earnings. For example, women 20 to 24 years old earned 93.8. percent as much as did men of the same age. Middle-aged and older female workers did not

Table 6.2   The Male–Female Earnings Gap, United States, 1970–2010

Year	Women's median earnings as percent of men's (full-time positions)
1970	62.2%
1975	61.9
1980	63.3
1989*	68.9
1998	73.2
2000	76.0
2010	81.2

* The U.S. Census Bureau changed its processing procedures in 1987; as a result, the 1989 figures are not directly comparable to those of prior years.

Sources: U.S. Census Bureau, *Statistical Abstract of the United States,* 1999, 2000; U.S. Department of Labor, Bureau of Labor Statistics, 2001 and 2012.

fare as well: among workers 55 to 64 years old, the women's-to-men's earnings ratio was the lowest of all age cohorts at just 75.1 percent (U.S. Department of Labor, 2012).

The male-female gap is wider in some occupations than in others. Census data indicate that in 2009, while women professionals overall earned 80.2 percent of male professionals' earnings, women managers earned 72.4 percent of male managers' earnings, and women in sales earned 66.2 percent of male counterparts' earnings. Women's employment in occupations with high earnings has grown. In 2009, 51.7 percent of full-time wage and salary workers in executive, administrative, and managerial occupations were women, up from 34.2 percent in 1983. Over the same period, women's employment in professional specialty occupations rose from 46.8 percent to 57.5 percent (U.S. Department of Labor, 2012).

Despite increased representation in the higher-paying managerial and professional occupations, women remain a relatively small proportion of other high-paying occupations, such as protective service and precision production, craft, and repair. In both managerial and professional occupational categories, women and men tend to work in different specific occupations. In professional specialty occupations, where women earn the most, they are much less likely than men to be employed in some of the highest-paying occupations, such as engineering and mathematical and computer science. Women are more likely to work in relatively lower-paying professional occupations, such as teaching and nursing (U.S. Department of Labor, 2012). Most female professionals are employed in traditional occupations such as elementary and secondary teaching and nursing. Women are not well represented in such professions as college teaching, medicine, and law. Indeed, the greater the prestige of a profession, the smaller the proportion of women in it. In 2010, for example, women held 83 percent of the teaching positions in American elementary schools, 57 percent of high school positions, but only 38.5 percent of the teaching positions in colleges and universities. Although women are making increasing inroads into professional fields, currently they constitute only 10.5 percent of all engineers, 31 percent of all physicians, and 29 percent of lawyers and judges. The male-female earnings gap ranges from 71.0 percent for physicians to 80.4 percent for engineers and architects (U.S. Department of Labor, 2012).

Racial/ethnic income differences.   There also are racial and ethnic differences in access to occupations, which largely determines family incomes. Table 6.3 compares median family income in the United States for whites, blacks, Hispanics, and Asian/Pacific Islanders between 1970 and 2013. During this period the gap between black and white median incomes remained fairly consistent and has remained very large indeed. Interestingly, since 1990, median family income of Asians and Pacific Islanders has consistently surpassed that of white families.

The lingering economic gap between whites and blacks (and, to some extent, between whites and Hispanics) has prompted debate among sociolo-

Table 6.3   Median Family Income by Race and Hispanic Origin, 1970–2013*

Year	All Families**	White	Black	Hispanic	Asian/ Pacific Islander
1970	$52,825	$54,800	$33,616	NA	NA
1980	56,585	58,956	34,113	39,609	NA
1990	61,082	63,781	37,014	40,484	72,992
2000	68,626	71,733	45,554	46,590	84,703
2010	64,356	67,217	41,234	41,988	80,361
2013	63,815	67,255	41,588	42,269	76,755

* In 2013 dollars.
** Includes other racial categories not shown separately.

Source: U.S. Census Bureau, 2013, *Historical Income Tables-Families,* Table F-5.

gists over whether this gap is attributable to lingering racism, to something unique about the African American experience that contributes to the group's continued economic disparity, or to deeper structural forces that impede the attainment of economic equality (Marger, 2002). The black population is by no means homogeneous in terms of economic status. In fact, some scholars have suggested that there are really "two black Americas"— one that has established itself solidly within the middle and working classes, and one that is isolated and not fully part of the mainstream workforce (Gates, 1998). But this doesn't mean that life is easy for the former. Studies of upwardly mobile African Americans have shown the existence and reproduction of continued tensions of race and class. Recent studies of middle- and working-class African Americans living in the suburbs demonstrate the difficulties connected to the ascribed status of race, even for those who are supposedly "making it" (Pattillo, 2000; Lacy, 2007; Murphy, 2010).

The aggregate difference in socioeconomic status between African Americans and Americans of European ancestry is readily apparent. African Americans experience lower incomes and much higher rates of poverty and unemployment. African Americans are also underrepresented in jobs at the top of the occupational hierarchy and overrepresented at the bottom.

The percentage of blacks below the poverty line remains three times greater than the percentage of whites. The substantially greater percentage of blacks below the poverty line accounts in large measure for the general differences between income patterns for blacks and whites. Another contributing factor is the increasing number of female-headed, single-parent families, who earn considerably less than two-parent families.

The low income and high poverty rates of Latinos, particularly Mexicans and Puerto Ricans, reflect their generally lower occupational levels. Except for Cubans, Latinos are underrepresented in the higher-status occupational categories and overrepresented in the lower ones. Hispanics also experience high unemployment rates. More than 20 percent of all Hispanic families fall below the poverty line, which is nearly three times the percent-

Table 6.4   Persons in Poverty, High School and College Graduates by Race/Ethnicity, 2013

	White	Black	Hispanic	Asian/ Pacific Islander	Total population
Persons in poverty	9.3%	27.2%	23.5%	10.5%	14.5%
High school graduates	90.1%	81.8%	63.0%	84.7%	85.2%
College graduates	35.2%	21.8%	15.0%	53.2%	31.7%

Source: U.S. Census Bureau, 2013, *People in Poverty by Selected Characteristics: 2012 and 2013*, Table 3; Educational Attainment in the United States: 2013.

age for white families. Table 6.4 correlates percent in poverty with educational attainment, by race or ethnicity.

One of the most striking features of tables 6.3 and 6.4 is the high ranking of Asian Americans compared to the other ethnic categories. That is, Asian Americans rank higher than most ethnic groups in family income, occupational prestige, and educational attainment. Some sociologists and psychologists point to cultural factors, such as values that emphasize the importance of education, as an explanation. Another possible explanation has to do with the fit between the opportunity structure of contemporary American society and the class background of the new Asian immigrants. A disproportionate number of highly skilled and educated individuals comprise the Asian immigrant population. The success of Asian Americans has, however, brought racially and ethnically motivated criticism and disparagement. Often hailed as the "Model Minority," Asian Americans are still subject to stereotyping and racial framing that continue to marginalize this large and deceptively heterogeneous population (Chou and Feagin, 2008; Zhang, 2010).

Social Class, Power, and Self-Concept

Perhaps no aspect of social position has a more fateful hand in individuals' control over their own lives than their membership in a particular **social class**. Social classes are largely distinguished from one another in terms of the resources and power their members possess. Social identities provide status and enhance (or diminish) self-esteem. The process of attaining a positive social identity is a challenge for members of stigmatized, negatively valued groups (Howard, 2000; Mustillo et al., 2012). Studies of working-class and lower-class members, for example, have demonstrated the effects of powerlessness on one's self-concept.

Men and Work. Sociologists have analyzed the connection between the dominant values of American society and the specific values of lower- and working-class males. In one well-known study of black "street-corner men" in Washington, DC, Eliot Liebow (1967) contended that their behaviors can be understood in terms of a social class position that renders them powerless and virtually ensures their failure to succeed by middle-class standards.

To protect themselves from the assaults on their self-conceptions created by repeated failures in work and family settings, these men constructed what Liebow called a "shadow system of values." He maintained that they actually subscribe to middle-class achievement values but are unable to realize them because of the constraints imposed by their ascribed class position. They therefore develop an alternative value system. Unable to sustain the breadwinner role, for example, the men respond by depreciating the value of family life. Reluctant to face unemployment or a demeaning job every day, they demean the value of work. Without the resources to raise their children as they would like, they limit their intimacy with them. In short, the street-corner man's behavior "appears not so much as a way of realizing the distinctive goals and values of his own subculture, or of conforming to its models, but rather as his way of trying to achieve many of the goals and values of the larger society, of failing to do this, and concealing his failure from others and from himself as best he can" (Liebow, 1967:222).

Liebow showed how the daily, face-to-face relationships of men with their wives, lovers, friends, and children related to the broader configurations of power in the society. He also illustrated how the "hurts" of a powerless class position influenced individuals' self-conceptions and their patterns of adaptive behavior.

In another book with much the same theme, *The Hidden Injuries of Class* (1973), Richard Sennett and Jonathon Cobb presented interviews that described how working-class men created their own interpretations of dominant American social values. The emphasis in American society on

achievement is continually reaffirmed in education and the mass media. Americans are socialized to measure a person's worth, honor, and respect in terms of individual achievement. It follows that those who fail to achieve in the work world suffer from feelings of self-doubt and shame.

Working-class men, near the bottom of the occupational scale, must somehow adapt to a society that measures their value in terms of occupational achievement. There is a sort of "Catch-22" operating in this situation. Those who are born into a powerless, dependent, and subordinate social class position come to feel bad about themselves because they lack autonomy. A social sleight of hand occurs whereby the victims of a system of institutionalized inequality are socialized to blame themselves for that state of affairs. According to Sennett and Cobb, these men "know they are supposed to work hard, and do the best they can. They see that a few do 'make it,' but not, as far as can be seen, because of anything different about them. To keep going in the face of this riddle, a defense . . . is needed" (p. 201).

A respondent in Lillian Rubin's (1994) study of working-class families articulates the experience of many working-class individuals in the wake of changes in the economy:

> Used to be you worked hard, you figured you got someplace. Not any-more. . . . We did everything we were supposed to do—worked hard, saved some money, tried to raise our kids to be decent law-abiding peo-ple—and what do we get? . . . The #@*& company goes belly-up and look at me now. (p. 126)

According to Rubin, the hope that sustained working-class individuals through bad times in the mid-20th century—the belief that if they worked hard and played by the rules, they would eventually grab a piece of the American dream—has been shattered.

Changes in the macro-structural context of work (Wilson, 1987, 1996; Kasarda, 1989, 1995; Small and Newman, 2001; Sennett, 2006; MacLeod, 2009; Brenner et al., 2012) have powerfully altered the living conditions of working- and lower-class males, especially inner-city minority residents. Jobs that once served to secure the lives and identities of many working-class people are swiftly becoming a thing of the past. In the span of a few decades since the mid-20th century, foreign investment, corporate flight, downsizing, and automation left members of the working class without a steady family wage, which, compounded with the dissipation of labor unions, left many white working-class men feeling emasculated and angry (Weis et al., 2004). In fact, the working-class white men interviewed by Lois Weis and her colleagues said that they felt under siege in their jobs, their neighborhoods, their homes, and their schools, no longer holding the position of privilege that they sensed was rightfully theirs.

The stagnation of wages in the late 20th century among the working class and part of the lower middle class created a growing fissure between this group and the upper middle class. Although the latter may also depend on their salaries for income, they are ordinarily able to supplement them with interest, dividends, capital gains, and other nonwage sources (Kacapyr, 1996) that are not necessarily available to working-class individuals. Some of the gap between high- and low-wage workers is explained by education. Workers at the high end of the occupational hierarchy, whose jobs require higher education, increased their income at the same time that those with only a high-school diploma or less suffered a sharp decline in wages (Levy, 1998). By 1998, male college graduates were earning 68 percent more than those with only high-school diplomas (Danziger and Reed, 1999).

The sharp decline in inner-city employment rates was an instrumental factor in the creation of female-headed (i.e., male-absent) families. William Wilson's (1996) research in Chicago found that only one-quarter of the black families whose children lived with them in inner-city neighborhoods in Chicago were husband-wife families, compared with three-quarters of the inner-city Mexican families, more than one-half of the white families, and nearly one-half of the Puerto Rican families. In census tracts with poverty rates of at least 40 percent, only 16.5 percent of the black families with children were husband-wife families. Marriage rates dropped much more sharply among jobless black fathers than among employed black fathers, although this drop applied only to younger men in the 18-to-31 age range (Testa and Krough, 1995). Wilson concluded:

> In the inner-city ghetto community, not only have the norms in support of husband-wife families and against out-of-wedlock births become weaker as a result of the general trend in society, they have also gradually disintegrated because of worsening economic conditions in the inner city, including the sharp rise in joblessness and declining real incomes. . . . The decreasing marriage rates among inner-city black parents is a function not simply of increased economic marginality or of changing attitudes toward sex and marriage, but of, as Testa (1991) emphasizes, "the interaction between material and cultural constraints." (Wilson, 1996:97)

One reason for concern about the sharp decline in the marriage rate is that children living in one-parent families in the United States suffer from many more disadvantages than those in married parent families. As shown in table 6.5 on the next page, in 2013 the poverty rate for single female–headed households of all racial categories with children under age 18 (45.5 percent) was much higher than for married couple households with children under age 18 (9.5 percent), and it was higher for blacks (54.0 percent) and Hispanics (52.3 percent) than for whites (33.6 percent) and Asians or Pacific Islanders (22.7 percent).

The position of inner-city black women in the labor market is also challenging. Their high degree of social isolation in impoverished neighborhoods reduces their employment prospects. Although they may be considered by some employers as more acceptable as workers than the inner-city black men, their social isolation is likely to provide few supports for moving into white-collar employment (Wilson, 1996; Lichter et al., 2012).

Table 6.5   Persons in Poverty by Household Type with Children under 18, by Race and Hispanic Origin, 2013

Household type	White	Black	Hispanic	Asian/ Pacific Islander	All racial categories*
Married couple	4.9%	16.8%	13.9%	7.5%	9.5%
Male householder, no wife present	16.1%	32.3%	24.2%	19.7%	22.7%
Female householder, no husband present	33.6%	54.0%	52.3%	22.7%	45.5%

*Includes other racial categories not shown separately.

Source: U.S. Census Bureau, 2014, *CPS 2014 Annual Social and Economic Supplement.*

Women, Work, and Family Politics.   Working-class women also suffer from the "hidden injuries of class." Like working-class men, they also feel trapped and demeaned by jobs that have little social worth and prestige in American society. Stuck in boring, routine jobs as clerical workers, sales personnel, or factory workers, it is not unusual to experience hidden injuries that are work-related. Thomas Gorman (2000) related the following comments from a secretary: "One boss used to belittle us. He was a pig. He said, 'I only hired you because you graduated from high school—it doesn't take a brain surgeon to work in a job like this.' I was ashamed that all I had was my associate's degree" (p. 105).

Gorman noted that the injuries experienced at work may be carried over to other situations. Although the feelings of injury are hidden, they constantly shape daily interactions among members of different social classes. Among Gorman's working-class respondents, these interactions at times had the effect of increasing their contempt for the middle class. Three things in particular emerged as sources of anger for the working-class respondents: middle-class language, middle-class clothing, and middle-class attitudes. Working-class individuals expressed resentment at attempts by middle-class college graduates to showcase their language skills, they referred to middle-class people as "suits," and they complained about the attitudes that college-educated, white-collar workers have toward those without a college education. According to Gorman, members of the working class struggle to find dignity in a society that is quick to judge one's worth on the basis of income, educational credentials, and occupational prestige. "There was a feeling among many working-class respondents that college-educated, white-collar workers look down on them or think they are better than them" (2000:102–3). Many of the working-class respondents said they considered middle-class college graduates "perpetual students; they waste time and money in college just to get a piece of paper that does not guarantee a job" (p. 103).

As we noted in chapter 5, there has been a vast increase in the numbers of women in the labor force. The home itself often becomes a forum for family politics in which wives seek an equitable trade-off for the work they do outside the home. Questions of power become critical in such situations. Among working-class couples, the wife's decision to look for paid full-time work may be experienced by the husband as a threat to his masculinity and a challenge to his ability to perform in the role of family breadwinner. As one working-class male in Rubin's (1994) study of working-class families so eloquently put it:

> I know my wife works all day, just like I do . . . but it's not the same. She doesn't *have* to do it. I mean, she *has* to because we need the money, but it's different. It's not really her job to have to be working; it's mine. . . . Know what I mean? I'm not saying it right; I mean, it's the man who's supposed to support his family, so I've got to be responsible for that, not her. And that makes one damn big difference. (p. 85)

The white, working-class male respondents in Weis and colleagues' 2004 study of working-class men echoed this sentiment; they were well aware that they could no longer support a family on their own but needed their wives' income. Nevertheless, they continued to believe that the meaning of maleness is to go out, earn a living, support a family.

Despite the increase of women working outside of the home and the rise of dual-earner families across most social classes, a significant gender gap in housework persists due to reinforced beliefs about gender roles and power dynamics. For men, their identities are often connected to breadwinning (Kimmel, 2006) rather than housework, leaving traditional household responsibilities to their wives (Mannino and Deutsch, 2007) and thereby maintaining a traditional gender power structure (Risman and Davis, 2013). And during crises like the economic recession that began in 2008, which led to the loss of jobs by many men and women, the situation at home still remained the same, except more tense and strained (Legerski and Cornwall, 2010).

The macrolevel industrial changes noted in the previous section have clearly altered the power arrangements in those working-class families in which previously only the husband worked full time. The 1980s and 1990s marked a time when jobs for working-class men became scarce, unions became weak, and the relatively privileged position of white working-class men was threatened. The women with whom working-class men associated became independent, and equal rights and affirmative action were seen as threats. Traditional bases of white male power—head of the family, productive worker, and access to "good" public sector and/or unionized jobs— eroded rapidly (Fine et al., 1997). According to Weis and associates (2004), because of the loss of real material space inside working-class culture (due to what these men perceived as privileging of racial/ethnic minorities— affirmative action), white working-class men turned to the family in an attempt to assert or reassert dominance in that realm. While this may have always been the case, as Rubin's earlier work (1976) suggests, the move to sustain dominance in the white working-class home is particularly important during times of economic distress.

■ The Relationship of Power to Role-Taking

If you think of the world in dramaturgical terms (see chapter 3) as a Shakespearean stage on which everyone is a player of roles, then in real life, as in any play, some roles evoke much more respectful attention and applause than others. Some people are able to elicit far more consideration and respect for their wants, desires, and needs than are others. Indeed, in daily encounters with others, this is the most basic face that power presents. The powerful *demand* attention and interest. They do it overtly through the resources at their disposal to punish people who ignore them. And they do it covertly through the way people are socialized by society's institutions— family, school, church, and so on—to respect those whom society deems most worthy.

Role-taking has been described as the basic process by which people develop their selves (see chapter 2). By putting themselves in the role (i.e., the "place") of others, individuals are able to view themselves from the perspective of others, while anticipating how others are going to respond to them. This is certainly accurate as a general statement about interaction, but something is missing. That missing ingredient, we suggest, is the acquisition and use of power.

Many learned treatises have been presented on the nature of power, but for our purposes it is sufficient to conceive of *power* as the English scholar R. H. Tawney defined it years ago:

> Power may be defined as the capacity of an individual, or group of individuals, to modify the conduct of other individuals or groups in the manner which he desires, and to prevent his own conduct being modified in the manner in which he does not. (1931:229)

This definition indirectly acknowledges the necessity of taking the role of others in order to communicate with them meaningfully. But some people face much less pressure to engage in role-taking than do others. Their power allows them to demonstrate insensitivity, callousness, or indifference to the desires of others. Others must respond sensitively and, above all, accurately to the wishes of the powerful.

In the process of role-taking, the requirements for accuracy vary with the power of the position occupied by the role-taker. In Erving Goffman's terms (see chapter 3), some individuals "make" the roles and others are constrained to "take" them; that is, some people's symbols evoke a more deferential response than do others'. As an example of how the more powerful make the roles that the less powerful must take, consider the situation of women in the corporate world. Women who manage to rise above the glass ceiling emphasize the need to develop similarities with male peers to be successful. They use strategies such as altering appearance to fit the proper business attire (a suit) and changing speech and behaviors to conform to situations with other (male) elites *because they know that this is the way male elites expect them to look and behave* (Davies-Netzley, 1998; emphasis added).

The Less the Power, the Better the Role-Taking

Studies of the relationships between power and role-taking ability have generated an interesting body of findings. Generally, role-taking ability varies inversely with the degree of power ascribed to social positions. The possession of power, and especially authority, to some extent lessens the need to role-take with accuracy (Hewitt and Shulman, 2010). Individuals in lesser positions of power are required to have more accurate perceptions of their superiors' behaviors than vice versa. Abused women, for example, develop keen role-taking abilities to anticipate, prevent, and minimize their partner's physical violence (Forte et al., 1996). Batterers, on the other hand, demonstrate less role-taking ability (Goodrum et al., 2001); in fact, batterers' levels of empathy (a form of role-taking) appear to be inversely related to their levels of violence (Holtzworth-Munroe and Stuart, 1994; Kolb, 2014).

In the study of batterers conducted by Goodrum and colleagues (2001), almost 60 percent of the batterers expressed either no empathy or limited empathy when they described their partners' emotional pain following an abusive incident. Some of those with limited empathy seemed to exhibit simultaneous ability and inability to take the role of the other. For example, one subject explained that although he felt bad about an episode in which he pushed his partner to the ground, he "needed" to use violence to get his message across. Goodrum and colleagues explain this in terms of *emotional* versus *viewpoint* role-taking; that is, the batterer role-takes his partner's emotions but not her viewpoint. The difference is that emotional role-taking is less likely to challenge one's position in an argument (and perhaps a relationship) than viewpoint role-taking. Male batterers, more than nonviolent men, feel threatened by challenges to their authority and views, and they often react to such threats with violence (Goodrum et al., 2001). This finding echoes Diana Scully's (1990) earlier finding that convicted rapists were deficient in their ability to take the role of the other (i.e., their victims). She argues that people in power are not pressed to understand the "other" because their place of power in society allows them to set the terms of their interactions with others.

These findings suggest that the inability to see oneself from the perspectives of others makes it difficult for the person to experience emotions such as guilt, shame, or embarrassment—emotions which have the effect of making us control our own behaviors in light of the anticipated negative responses of others. So we see here how both self-control and social control are part of a mutually reinforcing network of self–other communications. Rapists and batterers often lack either the willingness or the ability to imagine the responses of others—the victim and the community—to their acts of physical aggression. The batterers in the Goodrum study, however, did express more tolerance for the views of important others (such as children or police) of themselves than they did for their intimate others' views. The authors surmise that perhaps these parties represent less of a threat to the batterer's place in his intimate relationship and therefore may be able to exercise power over the batterer that his partner cannot.

The position the person occupies, not just within some organization but within society as a whole, is an important factor. The question of power is not simply a matter of individuals' personality characteristics. This is another demonstration of the importance of seeing the larger institutional order as the setting within which daily life occurs. One of the less obvious ways people exercise power in everyday life is through their control of the physical setting in which interaction occurs:

> Role-making and role-taking do not occur in a vacuum, but in the midst of props, physical objects, machines, locations, buildings, and habitats that have human meaning and usually are human creations. People do not merely interact in social spaces provided by roles, but in banks, stores, homes, physicians' offices, schools, parks, automobiles, beaches, factories, halls, and myriad other places, each with its objects, colors, sounds, and other physical attributes. . . . It follows that whoever has the power to control the physical elements of a situation also has considerable power to control how people in that situation will act. (Hewitt and Shulman, 2010:176–77)

The next time you are in a doctor's office (or a professor's!), notice how the setting influences the interaction. How are the seats arranged? Is there a desk in between you and the doctor (medical or academic)? What do you think might happen if you started rearranging the office space? How far do you think you would get until you were told to stop or received some form of punishment?

The use of physical settings to display power and control the behavior of others is something many of us encounter early in our lives. In his study of American middle-class high schools, Murray Milner (2004) uncovered the ways that teenagers use space and territory as a means for exerting or conforming to power relations. Space is segregated along lines of status groups from, and often by, the "cool kids" for the rest of us. According to one student, "At lunch, 'cool' kids sat at the front of the cafeteria. This allowed for all the 'cool' people to sit [in] one place . . . and be seen" (p. 54). Spatial segregation and social boundaries, as discussed in chapter 4, are not unique to teenagers. They affect where we live and with whom we interact. Sometimes everyday life takes on many of the characteristics of a high school cafeteria.

Studies such as those just described have raised a number of interesting questions about how differences in ascribed status affect role-taking ability. If, as they demonstrate, power and the ability to role-take are inversely related, we can hypothesize that women generally take the roles of men more accurately than men take the roles of women because women continue to have less power than men in both the micro world of the family and the macro world of the society. Studies of nonverbal interaction lend support to this and similar propositions (see box).

Role-taking ability also varies among racial groups—certainly an area in which there are substantial power differentials. Despite many whites' declarations that they are "colorblind" and "don't see race" (Bonilla-Silva, 2006), they function with a high degree of privileged power to make such claims. That is, the ability to take the role of being "colorblind" is in itself a

Gender and Nonverbal Communication: The Role of Power

Research generally has found consistent gender differences in nonverbal communication. Women and men do different things with their eyes, faces, voices, and bodies. Women tend to be more expressive of emotions than men, which may be the result of socialization that encourages females to be sensitive to others. Women not only tend to display feelings more clearly but also seem to be more skilled than men at interpreting others' emotions. A recurring question is whether this well-documented gender difference in nonverbal sensitivity is best understood as stemming from deep-seated differences between the sexes or whether it is due to structures that create power inequities between women and men (LaFrance and Henley, 1994).

Women's decoding skills probably result from a combination of socialization that emphasizes nurturing and pleasing, as well as the way power is distributed in society. Women are expected to respond expressively to others. Smiling sends the message that one is approachable, interested, friendly—part of the cultural definition of femininity. Gender socialization is so ingrained that women find it difficult not to smile, even when they deliberately try to refrain (Wood and Fixmer-Oraiz, 2014). However, the findings on gender and smiling are mixed. Although women may smile more than men overall, it may be that gender-related behavior depends on the nature of the context. Hecht and LaFrance (1998), for example, found a sex difference in smiling when women and men were in equal-power positions but no sex differences between high-power women and men or low-power women and men.

The idea that women's nonverbal skills are linked to gender-differentiated power within our society was first suggested by Helen Hacker (1951) and was greatly expanded in the 1970s by work that documented other inequalities in the small stuff of everyday life. This research produced a considerable body of evidence in support of the idea that those who are oppressed learn to interpret others in order to survive. For example, classic research by Nancy Henley ([1977] 1986) found consistent patterns in nonverbal behavior for minorities, women, and individuals in subservient roles.

The basic thesis of the unequal power explanation of women's greater ability to decode nonverbal behaviors of others is that it falls to people of lower power to be able to read the cues of someone possessing higher power because their ability to respond appropriately, if not their very survival, may depend upon it (LaFrance and Henley, 1994). As in the case of women who have been battered by men, being able to anticipate and avoid the men's rage is important to survival (Tatum, 2000). However, a meta-analysis of studies examining "subordination" and nonverbal sensitivity found little overall support for the subordination hypothesis (Hall et al., 1997), leading these authors to conclude that nonverbal sensitivity may wax and wane as a function of particular roles and situations.

Gender differences in use of nonverbal behaviors to supplement verbal communication are found consistently. Since masculine socialization emphasizes self-assertion and dominance, we would expect men to use more nonverbal behaviors than women to complement, repeat, and highlight their verbal messages. This highlighting has the effect of increasing the visibility and force of male speech. Feminine socialization highlights relationships, deference, and expressiveness, so women learn to specialize in nonverbal functions such as complementing and highlighting that add emphasis and feeling to their communication (Wood and Fixmer-Oraiz, 2014).

Another aspect of nonverbal communication used differently by men and women is eye contact. Whereas women frequently use nonverbal signals to invite others into conversation, men more frequently use them to sustain control of interaction. For example, women signal interest and involvement with others by sustaining eye contact, whereas men generally do not hold eye contact (Wood and Fixmer-Oraiz, 2014). This has an effect on the relationship messages commu-

(continued)

nicated by nonverbal means, such as responsiveness (conveying interest and involvement). In one study, females showed responsiveness by maintaining more eye contact and direct body orientation, whereas males displayed responsiveness by leaning forward and adopting postures congruent with the person speaking (Guerrero, 1997).

And then there's the matter of perception of "nonverbal courtship signals" (Moore, 2002). Monica Moore's research on nonverbal courtship and rejection behaviors finds that not only do men rate invitational behaviors (licking lips, leaning forward, flipping hair) more positively than women, but men also see signals of rejection (looking at the ceiling, yawning, looking away) as sending a less potent message than that perceived by women.

form of power not available to others, particularly racial and ethnic minorities. A classic work by Judith Rollins (1985) explored the relationship between white elite women and the women of color who worked for them as domestics. The domestics engaged in acts of deference toward their employees: addressing the employer as "ma'am," accepting often useless gifts such as used clothing and acting grateful, and always appearing to be inferior to their employer. These women knew that if they appeared to be in a better position (i.e., more educated) than their employer expected them to be, they ran the risk of threatening the employer's belief in the innate inferiority of blacks. The domestics' stronger consciousness of the "other" functioned to both help them survive in the occupation and maintain their self. It was clear from Rollins's interviews that the domestics did not view themselves as inferior to their employers.

Collective identities generally provide social and emotional compensations for subordinate statuses that sustain systems of inequality. Charlotte Wolf (1994) theorized that people in subordinate social positions attempt through a reality-construction process to translate coercive relationships into dependency relationships, to maneuver oppressors into accepting obligations toward them. Her theory was based on analysis of responses of Japanese Americans during their World War II relocation to internment camps, of African American slaves, and of 19th-century American women of European descent.

Conning Strategies of the Powerless

Erving Goffman defined **deference** as a type of ceremonial activity "which functions as a symbolic means by which appreciation is regularly conveyed to a recipient," "something a subordinate owes to his superordinate" (1956). The inferior other must recognize the superior as such and must exhibit confirming behaviors or suffer consequences. When the powerless are denied the opportunity to engage in overt confrontations with their superiors, they must resort to more subtle means to avoid the damaging effects of the power of others over themselves (Kemper, 2011).

Studies of race and ethnic relations have demonstrated that when members of the dominant group and members of subordinate groups engage in face-to-face relations, the latter often must resort to indirect **conning strategies** to maintain their self-esteem. As the book *Roots* by Alex Haley (1976) poignantly demonstrates, the **frontstage** performance of the slaves shuffling along and saying "Yes, sir, massa," was a role brutally forced on them by the slaveholders. Behind the scenes, in what Goffman (1959) called the **backstage** region, they could let their guard down and indicate their awareness of the roles they had been coerced into performing. Wolf (1994) described black slaves who, "coolly calculating the situation, sometimes said they were 'puttin' ole massa on'"—clearly an attempt to shape interaction into channels less threatening and more advantageous to the slaves. She described Jermain Loguen, a black slave who, "returning to his master after an absence of several months, wrote that he played his part of being so happy to see him with a calculated charade of feigned deference: '[I went] through the ceremony of servile bows and counterfeit smiles . . . and other false expressions of gladness'" (Loguen, 1859:226, as quoted in Wolf, 1994:376).

Qualitative studies of oppressive situations often highlight the strategies people use to cope with the deprivations of subordinate status. Some of the strategies may have positive consequences; others resist inequality or seek to abolish it. The modal adaptation to inequality is acquiescence: accepting one's place within existing hierarchies of status, power, and wealth, while trying to make that place reasonably comfortable. Other possibilities, however, include trading power for patronage, forming alternative subcultures, dropping out, and "hustling"—economic activity that is officially considered illegal or dishonest. Qualitative research shows, however, that most strategies of adaptation have dual consequences, challenging some inequalities while reproducing others (Schwalbe et al., 2000). For example, female strippers are able to enhance their earnings by performing in ways that feed men's sexual fantasies—a conning strategy—but while this strategy may pay off for individual strippers, the larger consequence is reproduction of the sexist imagery that helps sustain the subordination of women in general (Frank, 1998).

Adaptation to subordinate status can be collective, in effect creating alternative subcultures. For example, Bourgois (1995) showed how the urban drug trade offered a path to status and economic success for young men who had no chance for industrial work, nor the **cultural capital** to break into middle-class service jobs.

■ The Subtle Faces of Power in Everyday Interactions

Power does not simply exist outside of our "selves" as an objective or external force. Instead, *"actual* bodies live with and through power" (Westhaver, 2006, p. 616, emphasis in the original). The pervasiveness of power in our daily affairs can be demonstrated by numerous examples of verbal and nonverbal interactions. Deference behaviors, for example, are varied in character: they may be linguistic, gestural, spatial, task-embedded, or part of the communication structure involving who initiates speech, speaks more frequently, and receives more attention (Goffman, 1956). Individuals who talk a great deal, interrupt others, and maintain high levels of eye contact while speaking are often believed to possess higher status, regardless of what they are actually talking about (Hall et al., 2005). These nonverbal cues are performances of power. A variety of nonverbal "gestures of dominance and submission," as the social psychologist Nancy Henley (1986) put it, mark the behavioral responses that acknowledge the power of others. These behaviors include staring, touching, interrupting, and crowding another's space, as well as the gestures of frowning, looking stern, and pointing.

Power Talks: The Names People Use

The ways in which we address one another may on the surface appear to be merely forms of etiquette. On a deeper level, however, they can be viewed as inextricably bound up with questions of power. Forms of address are powerful verbal symbols for affirming and reaffirming distinctions among people.

Have you ever, for example, called your boss by her or his first name without asking permission to do so? And has your boss ever asked your permission to use your first name? Probably you address your boss in some titular fashion such as Mr., Ms., Doctor, or Professor, while the boss calls you by your first name. You call your parents Mom and Dad or Mother and Father, while they address you with your first name or some endearment. You might say, what else should we call them and they us? But why is that so "natural"? We suggest that there is a power dimension to such common forms of address.

As creatures in a symbolic world, we use terms to refer to ourselves and others that convey a great deal about who and what we are. Our very conception of self is intimately related to the names we use to describe ourselves. Does a man refer to himself, for example, as Robert or Bob? Does a woman want others to call her Katherine or Katie? We self-consciously fashion our names, within limits, to achieve some agreement with our beliefs about who we are and hope to be.

The use of first names rather than titles like Mr. or Ms. in relations with others represents a particular form of association. The exchange of first names is a way of quickly establishing intimate relationships. We must be careful here, however, since the use of first names is frequently decided by those who have the most power in a relationship. They have the prerogative of intruding into the intimate details of others' lives, though the others are denied similar access to details of theirs. Superiors easily become personal and familiar with subordinates, but the latter are not permitted to get personal. In public settings, boundaries of inclusion may be constructed through ploys such as recognizing by first name certain individuals. In a study of city commission proceedings (Futrell, 1999), commissioners were observed to manage interaction by recognizing by first name administrators, their assistants, and other participants linked to the commission. These expressions of familiarity served to assign an added degree of legitimacy and significance to these individuals during the meeting. On the other hand, commissioners' use of first names was sometimes used toward members or groups most likely to present argument. In this case, inclusion was used in an attempt to mollify these individuals (Futrell, 1999).

Staring

In American society, one of the privileges of power is the ability to intrude upon another's personal space by prolonged staring without suffering the consequences. Should those of lower status engage in similar behavior, they might be asked to explain their insubordination or lack of respect for their superior's position. The term *insubordination* means precisely failure to acknowledge one's subordinate status in the presence of a superior.

A large body of research on gaze indicates that, other factors being equal, men show more visual dominance in mixed-sex interactions than women do (Aitchison, 2013). Visual dominance is a pattern of looking at the other more while speaking than while listening, and it is associated with perceived competence and influence (Ridgeway and Smith-Lovin, 1999). The relevance of gender to the setting affects gaze as well. Dovidio and colleagues (1998) found that when mixed-sex dyads turned from a "gender-neutral" task to a "masculine" task, men's greater visual dominance and rate of gesturing became exaggerated. When the dyad shifted to discuss a "feminine" task, however, women displayed more visual dominance and gestured more than men. These shifts in gaze and gesture patterns reflect changes in the behavioral power and prestige orders of the dyads (Ridgeway and Smith-Lovin, 1999).

Touching

You have probably been in situations where a superior—a boss or teacher, for example—has approached and put his or her arm around you, perhaps to compliment you on something you had done. It is hard to imagine the positions reversed, however, with you putting an arm around a boss or teacher. The right to invade another's personal space through touching is another privilege of power and status. There is empirical evidence, for example, that men are more likely to invade others' spaces and to use touch to assert power, even when their interest is unwelcome. Women's training to "be nice" to others may make them reluctant to speak forcefully to a boss or coworker whose touches are unwanted. Socialization practices and the gendered identities they foster shed light on sexual harassment in workplaces and educational institutions (Wood and Fixmer-Oraiz, 2014).

Qualitative studies, along with quantitative analyses (McLaughlin et al., 2012), suggest that responses to sexual harassment are grounded in the organization of power relations at work (Lopez et al., 2009). The deferential behavior of temporary clerical workers, stemming from the feminized and powerless status of their job, increases workers' vulnerability and potential for experiencing sexual harassment. Female *and male* temporary workers have little recourse but to tolerate or ignore harassment (Rogers and Henson, 1997). Service workers are another powerless group of workers with little recourse. Subjected to constant sexual comments, leering, and touching from customers, these workers may be reluctant to complain about these behaviors to managers (Williams et al., 1999). In one case study (Adkins, 1995), it was clear that reporting such behavior would not result in a complaint of sexual harassment, but more likely in loss of the job and even further psychological and emotional distress (Berdahl, 2007).

Interrupting

Interrupting others' conversations is another behavior that has to do with the exercise of power in everyday affairs. Think about your own experiences in talking with someone of higher status than yourself. Who would be more likely to interrupt, you or the other person? One of the most widely contested areas of gender and language is whether men interrupt their conversation partners more often than do women. Although some investigations have replicated Don Zimmerman and Candace West's (1975) often-cited finding that men tend to interrupt more often than women do, there have also been contradictory results indicating either an absence of gender difference or even that women interrupted more than men (Aries, 1996). To address this discrepancy in findings, one study conducted a meta-analysis of 43 published studies comparing adult women's and men's interruptions during conversations (Anderson and Leaper, 1998). Because men have more often been associated with dominance in conversational interruptions, the study's authors hypothesized that men would be found to make more *intrusive interruptions* than women. (*Intrusive interruptions* were defined as those which suggest a dominating motivation on the part of the interrupter, as when the interrupting speaker successfully takes over the conversational floor.) Although the findings indicated that men were more likely than women to initiate interruptions, the magnitude of gender difference was not large.

These authors noted that the *type* of interruption made a difference. As Deborah Tannen (1994) has noted, some interruptions, which she described as "overlaps," occur when a second speaker begins speaking at what could be a transitional place such as the end of a clause. According to Tannen, women and members of cultural communities she describes as "high involvement" often overlap with one another in speech as a way of demonstrating cooperation and enthusiasm. She proposed that cooperative overlapping is "supportive rather than obstructive, evidence not of domination but of participation, not power but . . . solidarity" (p. 62). She argued that by assuming that interruption is a monolithic conversational device, "we are forced into a position that claims that high-involvement speakers, such as blacks and Jews and, in many circumstances, women, are pushy, aggressive, or inconsiderate or foolishly noisy" (p. 73). When interpreting interruption as a form of domineering behavior, the type Anderson and Leaper refer to as intrusive interruptions may be the most relevant. Intrusive interruptions function to usurp the speaker's turn at talk with the intent of demonstrating dominance. In contrast, interruptions that include back-channel listening responses (a conversational form such as uttering "uh-huh," which communicates the listener's support for and encouragement of the speaker) or affiliative overlaps may demonstrate enthusiasm, agreement, or rapport.

Anderson and Leaper (1998) concluded that any tendency for gender differences in conversational interruptions may be more likely to be detected when the more narrowly defined intrusive interruption category is used. When they analyzed these interruptions separately, the effect size was larger. They found that men interrupted more than did women, particularly in groups of three or more persons (versus dyads), suggesting that if interrupting is a demonstration of dominance, the need to display dominance is greater in a more public situation with witnesses than in one-to-one interactions in which pressure to act more stereotyped may be lessened.

Crowding Another's Space

One of the prerogatives of privilege and power is the freedom to restrict others' access to one's property and to circumvent the activities of inferiors. Most suburban communities in the United States have enacted housing standards and zoning ordinances that make it difficult for low-income people to live in such communities, for example. These restrictions by local governments prohibit the construction of low-cost housing and the location of apartment houses and businesses in residential areas. The introduction of zoning ordinances was related to the desire of the emerging middle class, beginning in the 19th century, to establish barriers between itself and those considered inferior. By the 1920s, building restrictions and zoning ordinances bolstered divisions within metropolitan areas of the United States:

> During the 1920s developers added to the list of protective restrictions in the deeds to subdivision lots, and among these restrictions were covenants forbidding sale or rental of the property to blacks, Jews, or others who might destroy the ethnic homogeneity of the suburban enclave. By 1923 there were 183 communities, containing 40 percent of the nation's urban population, that had enacted zoning ordinances, and the number of zoned municipalities was to increase rapidly during the remainder of the decade. (Teaford, 1986:70–71)

Places reflect and reinforce hierarchy by extending or denying life chances to groups located in detrimental spots. Segregated urban neighborhoods with physical, social, and cultural deterioration (whether due to the exodus of middle-class minorities or to racist real estate practices) have made it difficult for residents to better their conditions (Massey and Denton, 1993; Wilson, 1996; Seligman, 2005; Oliver and Shapiro, 2006).

Gendered segregation via the geography and architecture of places contributes to the subordination and spatialized social control of women, either by denying access to knowledge and activities crucial for the reproduction of power and privilege or by limiting mobility more generally within places defined as unsafe, physically threatening, or inappropriate (Davidson and Bondi, 2004; McDowell, 1999; Spain, 1992; Valentine, 1989). Gender-differentiated use of space is another indication of the asymmetry between females and males. From the playground to the boardroom, males are more likely to have space for themselves.

Places have their own power, apart from the powerful people or organizations that occupy them. The capacity to dominate and control people or things comes through the geographic location, built-form, and symbolic meanings of a place (Gieryn, 2000; Borer, 2006). Police squad cars in Los Angeles maintain order in part by patrolling boundaries and restricting access—using place as a means to decide who and what properly belongs where (Herbert, 1997). As noted in chapter 4, on-the-street harassment of women or racial minorities is one way to keep disadvantaged groups "in their place" (Duneier and Molotch, 1999; Gardner, 1995).

In 1969 Edward T. Hall coined the word *proxemics* to refer to space and our use of it (see chapter 1). Proxemics offers insight into the relative power and status accorded to various groups in society. Space is a primary means by which a culture designates who is important, who has privilege. Consider who gets space in our society (executives with big corner offices, wealthy families with large houses). Who gets space and how much space they get indicate power. Usage of private space illustrates the interplay between the organization of the institutional, macro world and the dynamics of face-to-face encounters in the micro world.

Henley (1986) noted:

> Our world is set up so that powerful humans own more territory, move through common areas and others' territory more freely, and take up more space with their bodies, possessions, and symbols. We yield space to them and they grab it from us, either openly or covertly as the occasion (and our acquiescence) allow. Even that corner of the world we call our own . . . will not gain us the resources, privileges, the pleasures, even the survival possibilities that come with the space of the powerful. This is what "position" means in life. (p. 42)

Frowning, Looking Stern, Pointing

Power and status give superiors license to express their anger, outrage, and displeasure with subordinates. Think of how you might have to handle your own anger if you were particularly upset with something your boss did. Could you tell your boss right out how angry *you* are? Probably not. More likely, you would have to express your real feelings more diplomatically to avoid provoking the boss's wrath. If you were in your boss's place, it would be much easier to express your resentment, disappointment, or other negative feelings. The gesture of pointing at another person may also be seen as a power play. Children may be told by adults that pointing, like staring, is not polite. But you never hear an adult admonish another adult not to point at children for the same reason. People in power can point at others and order them forward, backward, and, if need be, even sideways with a simple movement of their fingers. The classic example would be that of the traffic officer in the middle of the intersection, directing traffic by gesturing or pointing in various directions. Needless to say, we usually obey such pointers. In a broader sense, as William H. Whyte (1988) suggested, we must orient our actions to avoid continually colliding and bumping into others, both figuratively and literally. Society provides us with authority figures, analogous to traffic officers, who have the license to "point" us in the "proper" directions.

The Coerced Self

The idea of personal freedom and autonomy is so powerful in American culture that it is often taken for granted. It is important to remember that this cherished value is an *idea*, that it is more like a goal rather than an actual empirical fact. As such, we can explore situations where some people are able to act more freely than others. We can explore situations whereby individuals' ideas about freedom are influenced by their social position. And we can explore the ways that freedom and power are practiced in everyday life. During the course of your day, in what situation do you feel the most free? In what situations do you feel the most constrained or coerced? What social factors do you contribute to these feelings?

■ Conclusion

The idea that social life represents a balancing of freedom and constraint, which is an integral part of the interactionist perspective, is related to human beings' capacity for acting upon their surroundings, exercising choice, injecting new meanings into social life, and changing the world through the process of interaction. In this chapter we have elaborated on the constraint side of the life equation. We have tried to show that opportunities for personal choice are not equally distributed throughout the social system. The plain fact is that some people are "freer" than others to control their personal destinies.

Whole categories of people can be distinguished in terms of the relative power they possess. Wealth is highly concentrated in the hands of a tiny segment of the population, for example. Comparisons of men with women and whites with nonwhites along any power dimension reveal a patterned, institutionalized, culturally rigid system of superiors and subordinates. In each case, those with little power must show deference to those with the resources to affect them directly. Studies illustrating the relationship between power and role-taking consistently have found that powerless people must be more accurate role-takers than the powerful.

The most comprehensive social groupings involving varying levels of power are called social classes. People who are born into social classes at the lower end of the stratification system have little opportunity for occupational success and then are devalued because they do not succeed. We briefly traced some of the adaptations that lower- and working-class women and men make to this situation, pointing out that the poses such people adopt in their relationships with family and friends are a direct consequence of their social positions.

Power makes its presence felt throughout our daily lives. The way we look at people, what we call them, and where we travel all are instances in which we must be cognizant of our proper place in the social order. Staring, touching, interrupting, crowding another's space, frowning, and smiling are often political acts. Through such routine behaviors, power differences are expressed and maintained. Should we step out of line or forget our roles, the powerful will quickly respond. The politics of interaction operate in both the macro world of social structures and the micro world of face-to-face relations.

The general point made in this chapter is that people's daily interactions reflect the constraints of their particular social positions. It is possible to conceive of social positions in an even broader sense, however. We can consider a person's place in the organizations that characterize modern urban-industrial societies. In the following chapter we will examine the nature of life in bureaucracies, the organizational setting which most characterizes American society.

Definitions

backstage: Private areas of social life that are off-limits to those who are not members of a group.

conning strategies: The subtle, indirect ways in which the powerless try to manipulate the powerful.

cultural capital: The knowledge, skills, habits, values, and tastes that are acquired in the course of socialization and which can be turned to one's advantage in particular social settings. (Bourdieu, 1977)

deference: Behavior that functions as a symbolic means by which appreciation is regularly conveyed to a recipient; something a subordinate owes to his or her superordinate.

frontstage: Public areas of social life in which those who are not group members can participate and affect the behavior of group members.

hegemony: A term coined by sociologist Antonio Gramsci to refer to the power derived from controlling the construction of dominant ideologies in a society.

life chances: The ways in which people's opportunities in life are related to their place in society. Examples include the likelihood of living a long life, staying healthy as opposed to being sick, and attaining a high-paying job.

macro world: The broader institutional and historical setting in which people's daily lives take place. Relations with others in this world are more abstract, anonymous, and remote. (Berger and Berger, 1975)

micro world: The world of everyday, direct face-to-face relations between individuals.

power: The ability to get others to do what one wants, while preventing them from changing one's own behaviors.

power elite: Sociologist C. Wright Mills's term for the small group of power-holders at the top of the stratification structure consisting of members of the corporate world, the executive branch of the federal government, and the military.

qualitative methods: Research methods in which objects, behavior, or relationships are evaluated in words rather than numbers.

quantitative methods: Research methods in which objects, behavior, or relationships are evaluated in numbers rather than words.

social class: Groupings of people based on their common standing on rankings of education, occupational prestige, and income.

social stratification: The hierarchical ordering of a society in terms of the income, education, or occupation of people in it.

subordinates: Those who have a lesser status than others.

superiors: Those whose status gives them power over others.

Discussion Questions

1. Which of your ascribed attributes do you think have been or possibly will be important in determining your life chances positively or negatively? From among those you name, which seem most influential?
   What do your answers to these questions suggest about the ideology that the United States is a land of equal opportunity?

2. Think about an occasion when you felt powerless and oppressed. In that situation, who do you feel was doing the most accurate role-taking, you or the more powerful person? Which of your own or the other person's behaviors illustrate this differential role-taking sensitivity? What strategies did you employ to cope with your powerlessness?

3. How would you elaborate on the idea that such behaviors as staring, touching, interrupting, crowding someone's space, and frowning are often *political* acts?

4. How would you respond to the arguments that lower-class individuals who are unemployed are simply lazy and do not want to work, or that such people just do not hold middle-class achievement values?

7

Social Organization
Life in Bureaucracies

The power that individuals can exercise is not simply a matter of personality characteristics. Rather, as we argued in chapter 6, it is dependent on the positions people occupy in society, as determined by their achieved and ascribed statuses. In this chapter we will extend this argument to include people's positions in bureaucratic organizations, such as those in the institutions of education and work, which exert a large influence on daily interactions.

In calling attention to the organizational nature of social life, we are focusing on one of the central dimensions of modern existence, the extent to which behaviors are shaped by **bureaucracy** and the bureaucratic form of organization. You were probably born in a bureaucratically organized medical setting called a hospital, for example. Your parents paid for your arrival into the world through such bureaucracies as an insurance company or health maintenance organization (HMO). As a child, you probably entered society through bureaucratic institutions such as the public schools, which grouped you into grades composed of children of a similar age. You moved through this organization in steps, passing from the lowest grades up to the final year of high school. Because you have chosen to continue your schooling in a college or university, you again are experiencing the progression from new student to senior.

▪ The Pervasive Effects of Bureaucracy

For most American adults, even the smallest daily experiences are shaped by large-scale bureaucratic organizations. Waking up in the morning, we may turn on the radio or television and listen to the news presented by a local station owned by a national corporation. The network gets its information from a worldwide news source such as the Associated Press. More important, the national corporation has a great deal of control in deciding what local affiliates present—at the turn of the millennium, the leading corporations controlled about 90 percent of all technology, including what goes into the mass media, information systems, and popular culture (Boggs, 2000). Even if we decide to skip the TV and instead turn to our smartphone, the news feed that streams to us from cyberspace is provided through our Internet browser, which is most likely maintained by a corporation.

Our breakfast foods are provided by multinational corporations. Then we get into our mass-produced cars and drive to work, with a state-issued license, on highways built and maintained with funds allocated by state and federal agencies. We are likely to work for a bureaucratically organized firm, which employs large numbers of people with officially designated job titles. We encounter bureaucracies when we pay taxes, seek medical services at a hospital or clinic, have a question about a cell phone bill, try to make a change in a utility service, or engage in numerous other everyday activities.

Arriving home at the end of the day, we read our mail, which has been delivered by another government bureaucracy, the U.S. Postal Service. Although many corporations urge us to "go green" and sign up for paperless billing, the mail may still include computerized bills from utility companies, banks, credit card agencies, and department stores—organizations that maintain a keen interest in our prospects and locations as long as we occupy a numbered niche in their computer systems. Corporate organizations dominate the state apparatus, own and control the mass media, profoundly shape education and medicine, and penetrate into even the most intimate realms of social life (Boggs, 2000).

In modern American society, people are continually confronted with problems that cannot be resolved informally and must be referred to government agencies, business organizations, insurance companies, or the courts. Because our society is composed of hundreds of millions of people of diverse backgrounds, it is almost impossible to establish policies that would be sensitive to all the subtle meanings of individual behaviors. The bureaucratic solution is to set standardized procedures and rely on elaborate systems of rules and regulations for interactions between individuals in specific situations. Society seems to have reached a point where individual behaviors are increasingly controlled and directed by the policies of large-scale public and private organizations.

There are costs to this system. According to Robert Bellah and colleagues (1996), "We spend much of our time navigating through immense bureaucratic structures—multiuniversities, corporations, government agencies—manipulating and being manipulated by others" (p. 150). Individualism has been transformed into a "bureaucratic individualism" where "freedom to make private decisions is bought at the cost of turning over most public decisions to bureaucratic managers and experts" (Bellah et al., 1996:150).

Charles Edgley and Dennis Brissett have written a book decrying the fact that we have become *A Nation of Meddlers* (1999):

> Meddling in the lives of others is now the republic's most visible obsession. Examples are everywhere—from national crusades against bad habits such as drinking, smoking, and gambling to the efforts . . . to create a "fragrance-free" work environment. . . . In Phoenix, Arizona, the city council passes a law requiring that the installation of a swimming pool be accompanied by the child-proofing of any access from the house to the pool, even if no children reside in the house. (p. 1)

The list goes on and on. Edgley and Brissett are particularly critical of the "meddling" done by workers and bureaucrats in the helping professions, although this meddling is described in euphemistic terms: "Social workers, for instance, never meddle; they engage in 'professional intervention strategies'" (p. 3).

■ The Bureaucratization of Modern Life

Noted sociologists such as Émile Durkheim ([1895] 2014) and Max Weber ([1922] 1946) traced the origins of modern society to the processes of urbanization and industrialization that began in the late 18th century. The rise of the industrial city was accompanied by such developments as the capitalist economy, technological advances, and new social categories such as the working class (or **proletariat**, to use Karl Marx's term), which arose to meet the factory system's demand for workers.

From Mass Society to Organizational Society

The development of industrial technology and the factory system of production attracted newcomers of varied social origins to the cities. Peasants prevented from farming by agricultural reforms or "enclosure acts" were forced to seek their livelihoods in the urban factories. The most dramatic effect of these processes on social life was the separation of work from the home, however. As Peter Laslett put it, the result was a **mass society**:

> The factory won its victory by out-producing the working family, taking away the market for products of hand-labour and cutting prices to the point where the craftsman had either to starve or take a job under factory discipline himself. . . . We can say that the removal of the economic functions from the patriarchal family at the point of industrialization created a mass society. It turned the people who worked into a mass of undifferentiated equals, working in a factory or scattered between the factories and mines, bereft forever of the feeling that work was a family affair, done within the family. (1971:18–19)

The factory system brought the introduction of labor for wages and mechanized methods of production marked by repetition and standardization. During the early phases of industrialization in both Europe and the United States, some women—especially unmarried women, women from the lower classes, and minority women—worked in the factories. A sex-based division of labor developed, with women working with smaller equipment and machinery on average, concentrated in jobs in the textile industry. The jobs women performed paid lower wages than those performed by men, who were viewed as the primary breadwinners. Women employed in factories continued to be responsible for domestic work at home, creating for the first time a "double shift" or "second shift" for women consisting of eight or more hours of paid work followed by another shift of work at home (Dunn, 1997; Bianchi et al., 2012; Hochschild, 2012). The effects of industrialization on the lives of workers led to various reform movements, often headed by women, which attempted to improve working conditions. The union activist Mary Harris "Mother" Jones reported the horrendous plight of women and children in industry, "condemned to slave daily in the washroom (of breweries) in wet shoes and wet clothes . . . in the vile smell of sour beer, lifting cases . . . weighing from 100 to 150 pounds" (Woloch, 1994:238).

Efforts to make human workers as efficient as machines led in the early 20th century to the development of administrative techniques called **scientific management**. An industrial engineer, Frederick Taylor ([1911] 2014), developed ideas for a factory workplace in which the division of labor was highly specialized and individual work tasks were minutely scrutinized and reduced to their most basic elements. Managers sought to take over control of the production process from the hands of the workers, in line with a distinctive characteristic of bureaucratic functioning—**control from the top down**.

Between the period of rapid westward expansion and industrial growth that followed the Civil War (1861–1865) and the 1917 entry of the United States onto the world scene in World War I, American society passed through the most rapid and profound transformation in its history. New technologies, particularly in transport, communications, and manufacturing, pulled the many semiautonomous local societies into a vast national market. The new economically integrated society emerging at the turn of the 20th century developed its own forms of social organization, political control, and culture. The new social form, capable of extending the control of a group of investors over vast resources, huge numbers of employees, and often great distances, was the business corporation (Bellah et al., 1996). Beginning about 1875, social, economic, and political trends in the United States prepared the way for what Robert Presthus (1978) called the **organizational society**, characterized by large-scale bureaucratic institutions in virtually every area of social life. And as bureaucratic organization influences the various domains of everyday life, it becomes more difficult to make both grand and small-scale changes. The bureaucratic structure reinforces a high degree of organizational rigidity (Smith and Wiest, 2012).

The Rise of the Service Economy

According to Bellah and coauthors (1996), the most distinctive aspect of 20th-century American society was the division of life into a number of separate functional sectors: home and workplace, work and leisure, white-collar and blue-collar, public and private. This division suited the needs of the bureaucratic industrial corporations. One of the most significant changes has been in the types of work done by the majority of adults in American society. The data in table 7.1 on the next page on major occupational groups in the United States show a substantial increase in the proportion of the workforce in **white-collar occupations**, which includes clerical and sales positions, from 18 percent in 1900 to 59 percent in 1989, but then almost no change between 1989 and 2013. The percentage of workers employed in all **blue-collar** occu-

Table 7.1   Percentage of Labor Force in Types of Occupations, United States, 1900–2013

Type of occupation	Years							
	1900	1920	1940	1970	1982	1989	2000	2013
White-collar occupations	18%	25%	32%	48%	55%	59%*	60%	61%
Professional and technical	4	5	8	14	17		19	
Managers, officials, and proprietors	6	7	7	11	12		15	
Clerical	3	8	10	17	19		14	
Sales	5	5	7	6	7		12	
Blue-collar occupations	37%	41%	39%	36%	30%	27%	25%	20.5%
Craft and kindred workers	11	13	12	13	12		11	
Operatives	13	16	18	18	13		10	
Nonfarm laborers	13	12	9	5	5		4	
Service occupations	10%	8%	12%	12%	14%	12%	14%	18%
Service workers, except private households	4	5	7				11	
Farm occupations	38%	27%	17%	4%	3%	3%	2.5%	0.6%
Farmers and farm managers	20	15	10					
Farm workers	18	12	7					

*Total percentage of workers in the category.

Source: U.S. Department of Labor, Bureau of Labor Statistics, 2014, *Household Data Annual Averages*, Table 9: Employed persons by occupation, sex, and age.

pations declined through much of the 20th century and into the 21st century, dropping from 37.0 percent in 1900 to 27.0 percent in 1989 to 20.5 percent in 2013. Employment in farm occupations experienced a huge drop between 1900 (38 percent) and 1970 (4 percent), then remained fairly constant for the rest of the 20th century—ranging between 2 and 4 percent—but dipped below 1 percent in the 21st century, to a mere 0.6 percent in 2013.

Skilled blue-collar craft workers and operatives, who make up the membership of the large national labor unions such as the United Automobile Workers and United Steelworkers, more or less held their share of the labor force throughout the 20th century until the early 1980s recession. The years since then, however, have witnessed a steady decline in the percentage of workers in the labor force who are unionized, falling from 20.0 percent in 1983 to 11 percent in 2013 (U.S. Bureau of Labor Statistics, 2015). As of 2013, government workers had a substantially higher unionization rate (38.7 percent) than workers in the private sector (7.5 percent). Blacks continued to have higher unionization rates (15.0 percent) than whites (12.2 percent) and Hispanics (10.3 percent). Union members' median weekly earnings were higher than those of workers not represented by unions, although this disparity reflects a variety of influences in addition to coverage by a collective bargaining agreement.

One author (Troy, 2001) referred to the situation of unionism in the private sector as the "twilight of organized labor," meaning that he did not expect it to recover either the membership or the market share it had in the recent or historical past. The United States is not unique in the decline of private sector unions; the International Labour Office in its *World Labour Report* stated that "in a large number of countries around the globe, trade unions have experienced a considerable drop in membership over the past decade" (International Labour Office, 1997:2). The United States led the way, however, and its descent has been deeper than in other countries (Troy, 2001). To put this in historical context, about 35 percent of the U.S. labor force was unionized in 1955. Almost sixty years later, that percentage shrunk to about 11 percent (U.S. Bureau of Labor Statistics, 2015).

One of the most notable transformations in the U.S. labor market since World War II has been the rising share of employment in the services industry and the declining share in manufacturing. Despite some slowing during the economic downturn in 2008, the services industry continues to expand (Henderson, 2012). This industry is part of a larger category called *service-producing industries* and has the largest share of employees in the service-producing group. Included in this category are a broad variety of **service occupations**, such as health care, advertising, computer and data processing services, personnel supply, private education, social services, and legal services (Meisenheimer, 1998). There is a wide variety of average hourly earnings among these jobs. Some have earnings below the average for retail trade, the lowest-paying major industry group. These include child day care; detective and armored car services; automotive services (except repair); services to buildings; and laundry, cleaning, and garment services. Other service industries have average hourly earnings above the average for mining, the highest-paying major industry; for example, information technology (IT), legal services, and engineering and management services. Most service industries pay somewhere in between. In health services, the largest services industry, average hourly earnings are about a dollar higher than the average for all services (Meisenheimer, 1998).

The shift of employment away from manufacturing and toward services has caused considerable consternation among some labor market observers, policy makers, business leaders, and workers. Because average wages are higher in manufacturing than in services, some observers view the employment shifts as generally representing a shift from "good" to "bad" jobs. However, because of the diversity of job quality in the services industry—many industries within services equal or exceed manufacturing and other industries on measures of job quality—employment shifts away from manufacturing and toward services do not necessarily signal a deterioration in overall job quality in the United States (Meisenheimer, 1998). More than just average pay must be examined when assessing the quality of jobs in each industry. "The quality of services industry jobs is especially diverse, encompassing many of the 'best' jobs in the economy and a substantial share of the 'worst'" (Meisenheimer, 1998:45).

By 1970, white-collar workers were employed in large-scale organizations where the conditions of work included standardization, impersonality, specialization, a hierarchy of authority, and dependence. Such organizations, moreover, could provide the research and management skills that intensified these conditions. The growth of white-collar work was the force behind the emergence of a new social category: the **new middle class** of corporate managers, salaried white-collar professionals, salespeople, and office workers. By contrast, the old middle class that had dominated American society was composed of farmers, self-employed businessmen, and independent professionals (Mills, 1956).

■ Thinking about Bureaucracy

Nineteenth-century social scientists, living through the monumental social changes that accompanied industrialization and urbanization, sought to comprehend their effects on both individual behaviors and society. Max Weber ([1922] 1946) was among the first to identify the characteristics of bureaucratic organizations, which he considered to be the most efficient means of managing or controlling large groups of people. Numerous social scientists have advanced ideas on the nature and consequences of this organizational form and have debated the issue of its dehumanizing effects. The symbolic interaction perspective is that bureaucratic organizations are not separate entities with a life of their own but are created and sustained by the daily interactions of their members (see Strauss, 1978; McGinty, 2014). Even when they seem far outside the control of humans, bureaucracies, like any other type of organization, are "inhabited institutions" (Hallett and Ventresca, 2006) comprised of and dependent upon interacting individuals and groups.

Weber's Model of Bureaucratic Organizations

A bureaucracy, according to Weber, has certain readily identifiable characteristics, such as a clear-cut and specialized **division of labor**, a **hierarchy of authority**, and an elaborate system of rules and regulations. Bureaucracies are organized in a pyramidal fashion, with power concentrated in the hands of a few officials in the higher positions. Employees at one level are responsible to those immediately above them and exercise authority over those immediately below them. The division of labor is carefully specified by formal descriptions of job content and the range of authority entailed in the various positions. In the name of efficiency and to eliminate needless motion and time from the production process, tasks are divided into their most basic operations. In working situations, however, as many observers have pointed out, bureaucracies can generate a good deal of excess paperwork and encourage buck-passing and other procedures that actually are counterproductive. In the words of one author:

> Bureaucratic organizations live by, maintain, and modify an autonomous world of their own creation. This world deserves to be called

papereality, not because it may misrepresent reality but because it functions as a binding representation. As soon as something (e.g., a word, a document, or a bill) is allowed to stand for something else (e.g., agreements, decisions, or purchase power), then, as every thief and counterfeiter knows, the representation becomes as valuable as the thing represented. (Dery, 1998:686)

Think about the last time you needed an "official" transcript!

In most bureaucracies employees are listed by job title in a personnel department, which has an administrative staff to perform the necessary specialized record keeping. The emphasis on files and record keeping is not simply an internal personnel matter but rather reflects a much deeper quality of organizational life—the tendency to reduce relationships with customers and clients to definable categories of behavior. Individuals are dealt with in terms of the category into which they fall. Universities, to choose an example close to home, have separate files for students in good standing, students on probation, students who lack the necessary courses for admission, and so on.

Weber's model of bureaucracy emphasizes the **meritocracy** inherent in such organizations. Employees are supposed to be hired on the basis of their personal merit or individual abilities, independent of political considerations, family ties, or personal favoritism. Career movements within the organizations also are supposed to reflect meritocratic principles, with the most competent employees rising to the highest positions. In practice, however, the system often fails to work this way. The well-known *Peter Principle* describes the idea that employees in a hierarchy tend to rise to their individual levels of incompetence—and remain there. It suggests that individuals who are doing their work competently are singled out for promotion until they are given a job in which their incompetence becomes apparent. Then the promotions stop and the employees remain in their highest positions, where they continue to perform incompetently. Scott Adams, creator of the popular comic strip *Dilbert*, has developed a typology of "boss types" that includes the categories "incompetent-harmless" and "incompetent-evil" (Adams, 1998). The popularity of *Dilbert* highlights the cynicism felt by many employees about the effectiveness of management (Feldman, 2000).

For Weber, bureaucratic organizations exemplified a principle that he termed **rationalization**: the systematic and logical application of formal rules and procedures to every aspect of modern life. In his writings, Weber demonstrated how this principle came to permeate all spheres of life, ranging from economic activities to even art and classical music. In the final analysis, Weber remained deeply pessimistic about the prospects for a fully human life in a world in which bureaucratic policies continually reduce people to files in anonymous record-keeping systems. An example of the extremes such policies can produce can be seen in the experiences of the character Joseph K. in Franz Kafka's haunting novel, *The Trial*.

The "McDonaldization" of Society

George Ritzer builds on Weber's idea of rationalization with his theory of the "McDonaldization" of society, which he defines as "the process by which the principles of the fast-food restaurant are coming to dominate more and more sectors of American society as well as the rest of the world" (2000:1). Ritzer's work is premised on the idea that whereas the processes of rationalization and bureaucratization described by Weber have continued, if not accelerated, the bureaucracy has been supplanted by the fast-food restaurant as the best exemplification of this process. That is, the characteristics Weber identified as being advantages of bureaucracy—efficiency, predictability, quantification, control over people through the replacement of human judgment with the dictates of rules, regulations, and structures—exemplify the fast-food industry as well as many other modern organizations. McDonaldization affects education, work, health care, travel, leisure, dieting, politics, the family, and virtually every other aspect of society. Just think about the many fast-food businesses that have adopted the McDonald's model: Burger King, Wendy's, Dunkin' Donuts, Pizza Hut, Kentucky Fried Chicken, Taco Bell, and Subway. It should come as no surprise that the model (which is extremely successful) has been extended to "casual dining"—more upscale, higher-priced restaurants with fuller menus, for example, Applebee's, Outback Steakhouse, Chili's, Olive Garden, and Red Lobster. According to a *New York Times* article about one such chain: "Despite the fawning service and the huge wine list, a meal at [a] Morton's [steak house] conforms to the same dictates of uniformity, cost control and portion regulation that have enabled American fast-food chains to rule the world" (Collins, 1996). And then, of course, there's Starbucks and, consequently, "Starbucksization" (Ritzer, 2010). Other types of business are increasingly adapting the principles of the fast-food industry to their needs: Toys "R" Us, Kidsports Fun and Fitness Club, Jiffy Lube, AAMCO Transmissions, Midas Muffler & Brake Shops, Hair Plus, H&R Block, Pearle Vision Centers, Kampgrounds of America (KOA), KinderCare, Jenny Craig, Home Depot, Barnes & Noble, PetSmart, and Walmart (Ritzer, 2000:3).

Moreover, the rational principles that underlie the fast-food restaurant not only are spreading throughout American society, but through the rest of the world as well. Just about half of McDonald's restaurants are outside the United States (compared to 25 percent in the mid-1980s). Other nations have developed their own variants, such as Canada's chain of coffee shops called Tim Hortons (which, along with Burger King, is owned by Restaurant Brands International); Paris has a large number of fast-food croissanteries; India has a chain of fast-food restaurants that sells mutton burgers; and so on. According to Ritzer, "McDonaldization has shown every sign of being an inexorable process, sweeping through seemingly impervious institutions and regions of the world" (2000:2).

One of the hallmarks of McDonaldization is the incorporation of scientific management, leading Ritzer to write about "McJobs"—jobs specifically connected to the McDonaldization of society. He noted that it is not just that these are "simply the deskilled jobs of our industrial past in new settings"; rather, McJobs have a number of new characteristics, including "many distinctive aspects of the control of these workers" (1998:63). These jobs not only reach new depths in **deskilling**, but they also entail control of the self through **emotional labor**. That is, a number of service organizations insist that workers exhibit cheerfulness and friendliness toward customers as part of the service encounter. Perhaps the best example of this is exemplified in the Disney theme parks (see box).

The Disneyization of Society

Alan Bryman proposes that a case similar to McDonaldization can be made for what he calls "Disneyization"—"the process by which the principles of the Disney theme parks are coming to dominate more and more sectors of American society as well as the rest of the world" (1999:26). Bryman identifies four dimensions of Disneyization that are discernible in and have implications for (late) modernity: (1) theming, (2) dedifferentiation of consumption,* (3) merchandising, and (4) emotional labor. It is emotional labor that is at issue here.

The behavior of Disney theme park employees is controlled through scripted interactions, and encouraging emotional labor is one of the key elements (Bryman, 2004). The ever-smiling Disney employee has become a stereotype of modern culture. These employees' demeanor is designed, among other things, to convey the impression that the employees are having fun too and therefore not engaging in real work. However, it was not quite that way at the beginning. In Disneyland's early days, Walt Disney was appalled by the behavior of some of the park's staff toward visitors. They lacked training and were gruff and unhelpful. The only employees who exhibited the kind of behavior Walt wanted were the attraction operators who had been trained by the company itself. The Disney University was created precisely to inculcate the necessary training, and it introduced a new vocabulary of "friendly phrases" (France, 1991:22). Since then, Disney has developed seminars that introduce executives from all types of organizations to this distinctive approach to human resource management (Eisman, 1993). A number of management texts have emphasized this ingredient in the success of Disney theme parks (Connellan, 1996).

Sometimes the emotional requirements of the job ("Smile!") are resented by Disney employees (Project on Disney, 1995). This is a reflection of the demands of emotional labor, just as it was for the flight attendants studied by Hochschild (1983). Most Disney staff, however, accept the emotional requirements of the job. Even among some former Disney employees who had adverse employment experiences, there seems to be a certain ambivalence that combines a degree of admiration with a recognition that the job was not for them (Zibart, 1997).

Bryman ties Disneyization into theories of consumerism. The emotional labor of Disney employees "serves to convey a sense that the employee is not engaged in work, so that the consumer is not reminded of the world of work and can get on with the happy task of buying, eating, gambling and so on. The smiling, helpful demeanor may also encourage spending in its own right" (Bryman, 1999:43). It's a small world, after all!

*This term refers to the general trend where forms of consumption associated with distinct institutional spheres become interlocked with each other and increasingly difficult to distinguish; e.g., shopping at theme parks. Walt Disney realized early on that Disneyland had great potential as a vehicle for selling food and various goods (Bryman, 1999, 2004).

Weber's "Iron Cage"

Although Weber recognized bureaucracy's fundamental rationality, he had serious reservations about it. Believing that bureaucracy's influence on every aspect of life could erode individual freedom and responsibility, and that its structuring of behavior could suppress human feelings and values, Weber referred to bureaucracy as an "iron cage" ([1922] 1946).

Analysts of bureaucratic life have suggested a number of changes in Weber's model that would allow a less jaundiced view of such organizations. Jay Klagge (1997), for example, reconstructs the bars of the iron cage into a playground structure. That is, as Klagge revisualizes it, the bureaucratic structure of organizations is similar to the jungle gyms found on the typical playground. Rather than being imprisoning, Klagge argues,

> these structures, although rigid, cold, and sterile, provide the framework upon which and within which organization members act, reflect, imagine, and create. In this metaphor, work is recognized as the creative playground of adults. Life is given to the lifeless structure through the creativity and energy of those who engage it. Organizational life is played out in daily dramas as members give meaning, life, and ethics to the sterile structure. In sum, the iron cage of bureaucracy, being a neutral structure, calls for the creative, ethical, energetic play of adults that most of us know by the name of "work." (Klagge, 1997:67)

Viewing bureaucracy as a playground structure offers a more positive view than Weber's iron cage. In Klagge's view, bureaucracy is a neutral apparatus upon which either positive or negative acts may occur. The outcome depends on how the apparatus is used. Klagge explains:

> Softening the rigidity of the iron bars, warming the coldness of the cage, and breathing life into the sterile structure can result in positive outcomes. Our childhood memories of the iron cage ought to be the most powerful, positive, and important referents provided by this metaphor . . . [in that] everyone has a rich childhood playground experience base from which to draw. Granted this experience base provides positive and negative memories, friendly and unfriendly encounters, and exciting and boring scenes, but these experiences that require energy, imagination, creativity, and commitment also correspond to life in a public bureaucracy. (1997:76)

Klagge's rosy view is that playful action on the iron cage can become a daily experience.

H. George Frederickson takes another approach, arguing that bureaucracy is a form of beauty and that organization and the work of organizations, including what is described as administration or management, can be beautiful (2000). Although hierarchy is still the norm, modern-day hierarchy "hardly resembles the rigid boxes and lines associated with the early era of scientific management" (p. 49). According to Frederickson,

> when hierarchy is out of balance, often in the direction of too great an emphasis on order, it becomes static and out of touch with its changing

context. When hierarchy is in balance—combining enough order to engender trust and predictability, enough fairness to include workers in important decisions and to give them the required security to ensure their loyalty, enough fixing of responsibility to satisfy political leaders, and enough leadership to imagine the future—could it not be said that all of those who are part of that hierarchy have created something beautiful? (p. 52)

He continues:

Because beauty is subjective, one has at least some choice of the occupation or organization that holds the prospects for beauty. When there is extensive self-identity with an organization, it can be said that these positive human feelings approximate beauty. And when there is alienation—negative human feelings—between individuals and their organizations, it is the opposite of beauty. Beauty in the organizational sense, then, is based on experience. (p. 53)

This idea certainly fits with the symbolic interactionist perspective on bureaucracy, which we explore further in the next section.

The Symbolic Interaction Perspective on Organizations

The symbolic interaction perspective stresses that organizations are humanly created phenomena. They owe their origin, maintenance, and eventual change to the daily interactions and communications taking place among their members. According to this view, people transform their social organizations as well as themselves through their interactions with one another. Organizational life, therefore, is not preordained but is shaped by fluid processes. Humans live in a world of socially constructed meanings, which can always be changed through dialogues like those in which the civil rights activists of the 1960s engaged to redefine the meaning of the word *black* (McAdam, 1989). In the face of life's uncertainties, individuals create social organizations such as bureaucracies to serve both as tools to achieve various goals and, in the broadest sense, as avenues to make the world meaningful and thereby manageable. By imposing some sense of social structure, organizations make the terrors occasioned by life's imponderable mysteries more bearable and predictable.

We live in a world of increasing complexity, characterized by the growing influence of multinational corporations whose business operations cut across the boundaries of individual nation-states. The deep structural impacts of a highly globalized and interconnected market system still need to be fully demarcated. As Benjamin Barber has beautifully put it:

McWorld is a product above all of all of popular culture driven by expansionist commerce. Its template is American, its form is style, its goods are images. It is a new world of global franchises where, in place of the old cry, "Workers of the world unite! You have nothing to lose but your chains!" is heard the new cry, *"Consumers of the world unite! We have everything you need in our chains!"* (1996:78; emphasis added)

While bureaucracies embody the formal characteristics Weber identified, such as a hierarchy of authority and the division of labor, there is also a great deal of leeway in any organizational environment. To use Karl Weick's (1976) felicitous phrase, in all organizations there are enough "loose couplings," or situations marked by uncertainty or ambiguity, so that individuals must supply their own definitions of reality.

The way an organization is structured, how its set of occupations is organized, and the way it connects with the outside world affect the specific behaviors and cultures in the workplace (Fine, 1996). As organizational members respond to and redefine the formal rules of bureaucratic settings, they construct **informal subcultures** within the organization, which play important roles. In his study of restaurant kitchens, Gary Fine (1996) found that each restaurant he observed had cultural traditions known by the kitchen staff, which they used as points of reference. For example, nicknames were common, argot (slang) developed, and often this culture was connected to humor. In particular, horseplay, teasing, and pranks served to provide interpersonal closeness and create shared memories among the restaurant workers he studied. Much of the horseplay was centered on food (playing catch with a steak or a cauliflower) and tools (dueling with knives), sometimes transforming "work space into a playground" and "generating satisfaction within a structure that does not have worker satisfaction as an explicit goal" (p. 120). Teasing—a marker of community in that its existence shows that there is enough looseness in relationships that one person can make a joke at another's expense without the belief that those sentiments are real—was used to bring new workers into the group. Pranks also are central to the establishment of interpersonal closeness in restaurant kitchens. Although major pranks (as opposed to minor ones) were rare, they were vividly described in interviews. As Fine explains, "Memories and reports of memory are shared by workers; this sharing connects them in a powerful web. They have a humor culture" (p. 123).

Fine concludes: "All workplaces, but small workplaces in particular, have cultures that emerge from the doing of work and cannot easily be constructed by management. The culture becomes a reality for all those who are a party to it" (p. 137).

Subcultures provide different experiences to organizational members, according to their positions in the hierarchy. In effect, organizations are thickly populated by multiple realities (see chapter 2). The meanings that constitute these realities define what the organization is in terms of human behaviors.

The interactionist approach to the study of bureaucracy emphasizes the ongoing, interpretive communication process by which members construct their own organizational realities (Hallett et al., 2009; McGinty, 2014). It suggests that organizations should be viewed as the result of a process of **negotiated order** rather than as fixed in granite or completely regulated by an organizational chart of official positions. Researchers such as Anselm Strauss (1978, 1993) argue that the social order reflects ongoing negotiations between participants as they deal with each other to get things done. In this view, negotiation is not just a specific human activity or process that appears in particular relationships such as diplomacy and labor relations. Rather, it is "of such major importance in human affairs that its study brings us to the heart of studying social orders. . . . A given social order, even the most repressive, would be inconceivable without some forms of negotiation" (Strauss, 1978:234–35).

In thinking about bureaucracies, the interactionist perspective is principally concerned with how people respond to formal rules and procedures. New meanings are created by those at the top and the bottom of the hierarchy, despite official patterns of authority and control. Efforts at spontaneity and innovation continually occur, even though the "higher-ups" attempt to mold the behaviors of the "lower-downs" into highly predictable forms. Life in a bureaucracy, then, is determined more by the informal interactions of individuals than by the formal rules and procedures of the organization.

■ Work in Bureaucracies

From the interactionist view that bureaucracies have no life of their own but are constructed by the interactions of their members, it follows that the way to study life in bureaucracies is to examine the experiences of the members. In contemporary American society, the need or desire to work leads most adults to become involved in corporate organizations.

Social scientists have studied the conditions of corporate life by identifying a new social ethic and examining leadership in relation to the employee's position in the organizational hierarchy. They have explored the multiple realities of corporate life, including the psychological isolation of top-level executives, the frustrating status of secretaries, and the routine, predictable, powerless jobs of unskilled blue-collar workers.

The Protestant Ethic (Work) versus the Social Ethic (Managing)

William H. Whyte's controversial mid-20th-century study *The Organization Man* (1956) called attention to a fundamental change in the nature of American society: the transformation of the **Protestant Ethic** into the **social ethic**. Earlier generations of Americans had believed that work is service to God and respectability goes hand in hand with the accumulation of wealth through hard work, competition, and individual effort. In the 1950s, Whyte argued, a new ethic oriented toward cooperation and managing others' work was emerging. This social ethic was ideally suited for life in a world of large, bureaucratically administered corporations.

The social ethic was based on three major premises: "A belief in the group as the source of creativity; a belief in 'belongingness' as the ultimate need of the individual; and a belief in the application of science [to human relations] to achieve the belongingness" (Whyte, 1956:7). Such beliefs encouraged loyalty and total commitment to the organization. A person's private life and innermost desires were considered secondary to smooth organizational functioning.

Whyte concluded his study with a plea for the accommodation of individualism within the corporate social ethic. He was not pining for a nostalgic return to the wide-open frontier of the 19th century or the rugged individualism of such "robber barons" as John D. Rockefeller and Andrew Carnegie. Rather, he was urging corporate leaders to act more flexibly in the creation of job tasks and to pay more respect to the unique differences in individuals' skills and talents. In short, he was arguing that "the individual is more creative than the group" (p. 445) and that corporate policies should not obscure this fact by their unquestioning standardization and compartmentalization of behaviors.

The title of his study, *The Organization Man*, reflected a corporate ideology which regarded man (literally; women were only peripherally involved in the corporate world) as existing as a unit of society: "Of himself, he is isolated, meaningless; only as he collaborates with others does he become worthwhile, for by sublimating himself in the group, he helps produce a whole that is greater than the sum of its parts" (pp. 7–8).

Organization Man Meets Organization Woman

Under the original auspices of *The Organization Man*, gender was not an issue (Coates, 1997). However, it has become crucial to understanding contemporary corporate culture. The traditional image (one gaining resurgence now with employers) was that employees put in extra effort beyond the paid cycle. "Organization Man" as described by Coates was a workaholic; this trait, however, is not compatible with the other responsibilities in women's lives (see chapter 5). There is a need to make a distinction between women and men concerning their perceptions of their organizations and their roles within.

Grant Coates (1997) set out to uncover the similarities between men and women in relation to those aspects of corporate culture that are prominent in the literature: training, commitment, and values. Coates surveyed 220 managers in the United Kingdom; 60 men and women from the original survey were interviewed about their experience of work. The study sought to uncover the motives and meanings individuals have in relation to work and organizations and whether women and men are interpreting the messages of corporate culture similarly. One important point is that while women represented one-third of overall managers in the study, they represented only 4.3 percent of executive positions compared to 9.9 percent of men. By far the largest single group overall was middle managers (47 percent), and even in this case only 35 percent of the women had attained this level. The vast majority (60 percent) of women were junior managers.

Corporate success for women in the study meant learning male-type behaviors and male emotional expression. According to one of Coates's interviewees, "It's like a man wearing a skirt to work and expecting to be taken seriously. I have to look like a woman and act like a man. I guess it's what schizophrenics must feel like" (1997:11).

Coates explains: "Organizations thus assert in subtle ways what employees feel and how they can express those feelings" (1997:11). Subtle sexual stereotyping defines who has control of the presentation of self and the images to which individuals must perform (Coates, 1994).

Interviewees were asked if they felt themselves to be "team players." Women interviewees overwhelmingly answered that they were. Women also expressed levels of commitment to their organization similar to those of male interviewees. If women were not committed, it was due to the bureaucratic management style of their organization. Many women interviewees indicated that they shared the values of their organization. However, this was not generally reflected in the particular position of women. While many women felt committed to their organization, they also felt their job did not give them self-respect/esteem within the organization. This was also true for status. Women continued to be marginalized from the organizational benefits that men apparently received. Coates concludes:

> In gender terms the data illustrated that women were as likely to be drawn under the umbrella of organizational ethos; that they were as

> likely and more so to feel committed to the organization. This in general supports the claim that the OM (Organization Man) analysis could not be applied to contemporary organizations as they now encompass women much more fully. Under CC [Corporate Culture] women express themselves in similar terms to men. This has not necessarily been the wholesale eradication of female attributes, but a meeting of paths, on women's part. For example, men now see the family as increasingly important in their career decisions, whereas women do so less. However, women now compare favorably with men in terms of commitment, loyalty and trust, and are, in some cases, better bets for long term future employees, as they are less likely to leave for other jobs or self-employment. They are also as likely to relocate to wherever the organization decides. This however, has encompassed a loss of femininity. (Coates, 1997:21–22)

Corporate culture has yet to figure out how to deal adequately with gender (women) in the organizational setting. Coates's analysis suggests that Organization Man has met Organization Woman; OW has adopted OM's masculine attributes and thus lost some degree of femininity; however, OW continues to be marginalized. Though many companies have adopted workplace diversity initiatives ranging from equal opportunity employment advertising to "affinity" or diversity mentoring programs for women and racial and ethnic minorities, the success and consequences vary greatly. The culture and demographic composition of the organization determine much of the outcomes of such attempts to help underrepresented workers gain positions, legitimacy, and authority (Dobbin et al., 2011).

"The End of Employment as We Knew It."   This subheading is the title of a chapter in Robert Reich's *The Future of Success: Working and Living in the New Economy* (2002). Reich's premise is the following:

> Organizations used to be recognizable: they were shaped like pyramids, with top executives, layers of middle-level managers and staff, and a large number of people doing relatively simple and repetitive tasks at the bottom. . . . Now bureaucratic controls are no longer necessary for coordinating large numbers of people. People can coordinate themselves through the Internet. . . . In a few years, a "company" will be best defined by who has access to what data, and gets what portion of a particular stream of revenues, over what period of time. (p. 84)

Reich described how the logic of the new economy—which is founded on quick innovations and on surges in demand—is changing the employment relationship. Fewer working people are "employees," as the term traditionally has been used, a situation that Reich expected to continue into the future. Reich explained: "You won't be an utterly free agent selling your individual services in the open market to the highest bidder, nor will you be an 'organization' man or woman. . . . Even if you're *called* a full-time employee, you're becoming less of an employee of an organization than you are a seller of your services to particular customers and clients, under the organization's brand name" (p. 89).

Steady work (a predictable level of pay from year to year) has disappeared for all but a handful of working people—although as Reich noted, tenured professors who write about employment are among the rare holdouts! There is a new precariousness, as it is almost impossible for any organization to guarantee a consistent stream of income to its workers. Many organizations are dependent on "soft money," in that earnings vary with contracts, grants, or sales. "Much has been said about the rising tide of temporary workers, part-timers, freelancers, e-lancers, independent contractors, and free agents," Reich commented (p. 98).

In the old economy, people got ahead by being well liked. The successful Organization Man was accepted by all. David Reisman's (1950) "other-directed" personality sought above all else to be approved of by his peers. According to Reich, in the new economy you get ahead not by being well liked but by being well marketed: "The goal is no longer to fit in or to gain the approval of one's peers. It's to stand out among one's peers, to dazzle and inspire potential customers, or people who will connect you to them" (2002:154). Personal worthiness is measured by one's net worth, Reich continued: "By making your personality into a marketable commodity and selling it successfully, you can increase your worth and thus gain worthiness in the divine eyes of the market" (p. 154).

The sale of the self makes relentless demands on one's life and encroaches on one's personal relationships, in that all relationships turn into potential business deals. Unlike Reisman's "other-directed man" who wished only to be liked, Reich's "new market-directed man or woman wants only to make a deal. Yet when friends, relatives, and casual acquaintances become vehicles for selling oneself, all relationships can become tainted with ulterior motive" (p. 156). Reich's analysis is disquieting:

> Reisman's other-directed person of mid-century America was in danger of losing his identity to the group. The market-directed person at the start of the new century is in danger of selling it. Which is the greater danger? Once, the worst thing that could be said of someone was that he had sold out. Now the worst thing that can be said is that he's not selling. (p. 157)

The necessity of selling one's self to the corporation was one of the most lamentable aspects of white-collar work for post–World War II sociologists, who decried the rise of the "personality market" in which people are required to sell themselves by marketing attractive images of themselves. **Alienation** from the products of one's labor was far less alarming than the alienation of the laborer from himself or herself (Jurca, 1999). In today's image-conscious society, the demands of running a successful organization make what people do with their emotions a central issue for employer direction and control. Because of the shift from the industrial production of goods to the post-industrial production of services, for many, job success depends on one's ability to produce speech, action, and emotion that symbolize a willingness to "do for" the customer or client (Bulan et al., 1997; see also Hill and Bradley, 2010).

Although interactive work usually is characterized by formal affective requirements, it also can include the informal mastery of "people skills" that workers require of themselves and which may affect all work-related interactions, not just those involving customers or clients. For example, paralegals interviewed by Lively (2001) created a set of norms for professional behavior—appear competent, maintain a credible front—which they employed not only at work but also in their presentation of themselves to the community. "Whether in or out of the firm, with coworkers, clients, or employers, these paralegals linked their ability to monitor and control any of their behaviors that might be construed as unprofessional or interfering with their ability to be, or appear, competent" (p. 355).

Bulan and colleagues (1997) conceptualized these formal and informal expectations as a set of *affective requirements* that potentially govern all workplace interactions. They used the term *affective* because they assume that workers must be able to manage their emotional self-presentations to support the emotional culture of the workplace and to fulfill the emotional expectations of other interactants. They distinguished these affective requirements from Hochschild's (1983) concepts of emotional labor and feeling rules: "While emotional labor refers to the actual 'management of feeling' to create the appropriate facial and bodily display, 'affective requirements' refers to the *organizationally imposed rules* requiring such facial and bodily display" (Bulan et al., 1997:237). Recall the box on Disney earlier in the chapter.

Women in the New Economy.   Although women have made progress in entering the world of executives, they continue to face difficulties in trying to pierce the seemingly impenetrable "glass ceiling"—the set of subtle barriers that seem to inhibit women and minorities from reaching the upper echelons of corporations, government, and academia in the United States (Blau et al., 2002). There remains, however, an extremely low representation of women in the senior ranks of management. According to a report on S & P 500 companies (Catalyst, 2015), even though women make up 45.5 percent of the corporate labor force, only 4.6 percent of CEOs (Chief Operating Officers) are women. Women also were sparsely represented on corporate boards of directors in these firms, holding 19.2 percent of board seats, up from 11.2 percent in 1993 (Catalyst, 2015).

The reality for most women is that they are not at the top in the bureaucratic workplace. In her classic *Men and Women of the Corporation* (1977), Rosabeth Kanter described what life is like at the bottom of the bureaucratic white-collar world by examining the secretary-boss relationship. A subsequent study by Lynda Ames (1996) provided a good illustration of the symbolic interaction perspective on bureaucracy. Ames conducted a participant observation of secretaries in a large, public bureaucracy. For a year, she worked as one of seven secretaries in a regional office of a state department of social services. As a result, she was part of some of the situations and events she observed. Although subject to *compartmentalization* (workers separated by department, which may have the effect of isolating them), the women's day-to-day working habits resisted its negative effects. The women reduced the effects of status distinctions among themselves by sharing and helping arrangements that circumvented the formal organizational status hierarchy and compartmentalization.

Although the activities Ames observed still exhibited much attention to the formal hierarchy, she described them as being essentially nonbureaucratic, even antibureaucratic (1996:44). Ames called such responses "contrarieties" in that "the contrary character of their actions was clear in their attempt to determine *themselves* how to do their work rather than execute predefined tasks. Thus isolation was reduced and the support staff could operate with a somewhat greater degree of autonomy than bureaucratic structure normally allowed" (p. 45). Given the lack of power and autonomy and lack of reward in terms of respect and wages, it was not surprising to Ames that workers exhibited resistance to the demeaned character and to the demeaning treatment such work received from other workers, such as the professionals in the organization. Workers' day-to-day activities, in response to those conditions, could be both accommodating *and* contrary to those conditions.

The work experiences of secretaries reflected both gender domination and bureaucratic domination (Ames, 1996). Ames found that the structures of domination were seen and resisted by the secretaries, yet taken for granted and consented to—even constructed—by them. The social realities that the more powerful members constructed—in this case the professionals in the organization—differed from the realities perceived by the secretaries. Within their own subculture, secretaries developed negotiating skills to reconcile their realities with those of the bosses and to accommodate to the rules and regulations of the organization, both formal and informal. Their **autonomy**, or ability to control the bureaucratic world in which they work, depended upon their ability to negotiate within an arena where the rules were set by those who had official power and authority.

Glenn and Feldberg (1989) called attention to the deskilling of clerical workers, where both the *variety* of skills required in a job and the skill *levels* required for the job were reduced. The combined effect of these aspects was to place further limits on the already limited levels of autonomy experienced by clerical workers. Kovacik's (2001) study of female restaurant servers and clerical workers described how some workers were able to experience a degree of autonomy through their "poetic resistance" to the confining gender scripts of "pink-collar" work. This type of work, with its depressed wages (tips excluded) and relatively low status, requires "performing some caricature of femininity on the job" (p. 22). The poetry written by these workers "resists such scripts by offering counter-performances, alternative rhetorics, in which secretaries and waitresses emphatically call attention to their presence as individuals and as members of a collective" (p. 23). For example, a secretary-poet imagined working-class women in control of the technology that currently controls them; a waitress-poet showed the disdain that servers often feel for customers:

> We write down on a pad
> what it is they want,
> but we don't let them see it.
> They think we remember,
> So we let them.
> They watch what moves
> under the black swing of skirt,
> how the candles underlight
> the faces that lean to clear
> their plates. (Balliro, 1995)

The poet observes the patrons sexualizing the waitresses, romanticizing them as they do their job. But instead of feeling demeaned, the waitresses engage in subtle power plays of their own (Kovacik, 2001:30).

Autonomy and Job Satisfaction

The issue of autonomy in the workplace also is central to the lives of blue-collar workers, whose daily activities are likely to be as unchallenging and unrewarding as those of female white-collar workers. Many working-class males experience drudgery or heavy exertion (or both) in their work, compounded by the knowledge that they have little chance of improving their economic status (Rossides, 1997). Industrial plants in the United States are typically still organized in terms of ideas formulated in the early 1900s by Frederick Taylor. Work tasks are bureaucratized and structured to provide management with maximum control over workers' jobs. By the process of deskilling, the skilled components of production jobs are replaced by tasks that require repetitive actions rather than talents developed on the job by experienced craftworkers. Workers, in general, are more satisfied with jobs that allow variety rather than repetition (Lambert et al., 2001). Unskilled blue-collar workers can exert little control over their work, so it comes as no surprise that assembly-line work is associated with low levels of **job satisfaction**. Craftworkers, however, show the highest levels of job satisfaction and pride (Hodson, 1996) due, in part, to the positive connections between creativity, embodiment, and emotional rewards (Thurnell-Reed, 2014.)

The relationship between income and job satisfaction is not straightforward. That is, we cannot assume that high pay automatically equally job satisfaction. According to a survey conducted by The Society for Human Research Management (2015), financial compensation and pay was ranked fourth—slightly ahead of job security—on the list of important factors contributing to overall employee job satisfaction. It was preceded, in rank order, by "respectful treatment of all employees at all levels" at the top spot, "trust between employees and senior management" in second, and "overall benefits" as the third most important contributor to job satisfaction.

Jobs lower down in the prestige pecking order require different kinds of extrinsic motivations to sustain worker interest. Research in the service sector has found that service-based employees who understand the standards for service in their organization and who feel that management supports these standards are more satisfied with their jobs (Susskind et al., 2000). In service-based organizations, employee feedback about job performance—sometimes immediately from the customer, or through weekly meetings with team members and supervisors—leads to increased job satisfaction (Andrews and Kacmar, 2001). In a survey of bank and hospital workers, positive feelings about work were higher for both women and men when they felt effective in their work with people, spent more time interacting with employees, had greater control over work, and had higher levels of job involvement. In addition, positive feelings about work were associated with being older and having a higher income (Bulan et al., 1997).

Getting around Top-Down Control. Since the working conditions of unskilled workers are largely dictated by management, they face the constant problem of trying to achieve some degree of control over their own jobs without being reprimanded, laid off, or fired by management. Workers develop strategies for protecting and maximizing their dignity in the workplace, which Hodson (1996) described as "attempts to defend or regain dignity in the face of work organizations that violate workers' interests, limit their prerogatives, or otherwise undermine their autonomy" (p. 722). Studying workers' autonomous strategies for defending and maximizing their dignity on the job poses some difficult challenges because these "strategies are subtle and at times cloaked in duplicity" (p. 723).

The lower one's position in the organization, the more one's behavior is channeled in the service of goals established by the decision-making activities of higher management. Those whose positions are relatively less powerful cannot bargain to influence agency outcomes in any substantial way. They can, however, engage in what Brower and Abolafia (1997) called "politics from below," defined as "actions or intentional inaction that defies, opposes, or sidesteps the rules, roles, or routines of the organization. . . . It is not merely an annoyance or anomaly; it is a frequent and purposeful everyday mode of organizational activity" (p. 308). "Lower participants" invariably socially construct "local rationalities" (Abolafia, 1996) from which they make sense of their everyday routines and make decisions for resolving dilemmas.

For an organization to function efficiently and to reduce alienation in its workers, participants must feel that they belong. One effective strategy of connecting workers to work is for management to put forth the metaphor that the organization is a family, "a primary group providing personal self-image, community, and local culture" (Fine, 1996:113). The metaphor may be claimed explicitly by the organization in a "self-serving or sincere attempt to increase worker loyalty; on other occasions workers will make this point themselves" (p. 113). A quotation from an interview with a restaurant employee illustrates Fine's point: "I like the closeness that you have in the kitchen. I love people in kitchens. . . . It's like a family" (p. 113).

Given their opposite positions in the corporation's hierarchy of authority, it is not at all surprising that workers at the bottom and managers at the top have different conceptions of the reality of the work situation. In fact, multiple realities exist within an organizational setting. Donald Roy's ([1959] 1982) classic study of machine operators found that the workers divided their workday with break times that they heavily invested with their own meanings. While management saw the workday as composed of distinct units of clock time marked by check-in, lunch, and checkout, the workers created intermediate periods, which they referred to with such terms as "coffee time," "peach time," "banana time," and "fish time." Other planned interruptions were called "window time" and "pickup time," and the staggered hours of two coworkers were called "quitting time for Sammy and Ike." The workers in Roy's study endowed these interruptions with a variety of meanings that made a boring day endurable and, at times, enjoyable for them. The breaks were events that stood out from the rest of the day and could be looked forward to as times when joking, socializing, and good-humored heckling might reaffirm the humanity and personal identity of the workers. In banana time, for example, Ike would "steal" a banana from Sammy's lunch box every day, while crying out "Banana time!" In response, Sammy would appear to make a fuss. All the actors played their parts in this little scenario with such skill and verve that it became an event that all eagerly awaited. These created "times" had the effect of stimulating group interactions that "not only marked off the time . . . but gave it content and hurried it along" (p. 246).

The 21st-century version of "banana time" may lie in the Internet, which "has supplied new dimensions to workplace recreation. It infuses opportunities for diversion into everyday work contexts—although the individuals with whom one enjoys banana time can be many miles distant" (Oravec, 2002). Although concern has been voiced about the potential for abuse, constructive use of online recreation may perhaps ultimately make workers more productive (see box). In fact, employers of "knowledge workers" or "knowledge intensive workers" (e.g., information technology professionals) have seen the value of play for bolstering creativity and a supposed "play ethic" at work. "Playing together, instead of working together, may be a saner, more fruitful way for highly capable 'knowledge employees' to find a liveable life within companies and institutions" (Kane, 2004:257). Some scholars argue that it is important for the employees to stop thinking about work only and to let their minds wander, be it for fun or to rest, as the nature of the job is intrinsically complex (Alvesson, 2004). Doing so helps blur the traditionally stringent lines between formal work and informal, though potentially formalized, play. A recent article from within the world of management argues that putting physical whimsical or playful objects around an employee's desk or workspace can blur that line and help make work more fun, which will allegedly be beneficial to the company and the employee: "Bring humor into the workplace with you. Bring small toys or objects for your pockets or desk—and take time out to play with them," and take part in such actions as "having fun, laughing, telling jokes, engaging in banter" (Mann, 2009:37).

Though bringing more play into the work life has been a popular trend and remains attractive to younger generations, it is not without its critics (Kunda and Ailon-Souday, 2005; Fleming and Sturdy, 2009; Dale, 2012). When employees are encouraged to be themselves rather than some sort of "cheerful robot" (as C. Wright Mills called it) conforming to an externally engineered and predefined organizationally based identity, they are in effect asked to bring their nonwork self into the workplace. In this way, one's private life can become exposed and potentially exploited under what is called "neo-normative control" (Fleming and Sturdy, 2009). "Neo-norma-

Playing at Work

Workplace realities have changed in a tightening economy. For many employees, the social and recreational activities they need to function at their best have to be obtained during breaks and unoccupied moments in the workplace rather than after work. Online recreation helps make long, demanding working hours more tolerable. According to Jo Ann Oravec, associate professor in the College of Business and Economics at the University of Wisconsin at Whitewater, allowing for reasonable amounts of online recreation can have considerable advantages, both for the individuals involved and the organization as a whole (2002). Not only can it serve to open blocked creative channels, but it may provide stress relief as well.

Oravec points out that managers have often used organizationally sanctioned recreation as a perquisite—a bonus for acceptable conduct—and although softball and bowling leagues, picnics, and celebrations may be viewed in cynical terms, they can help provide "part of the glue that holds the at-work community together" (2002:62). As employees telecommute or put in long and irregular hours, the adhesive that binds organizations has been increasingly conveyed through electronic channels. "Whether organization-approved fantasy football, discussion group and collaborative filtering forums, joke-of-the-day contests, or other recreations are ultimately successful will depend on how they fit into everyday working experiences" (p. 62).

Although the importance of recreation and play is widely recognized for children, it is only slowly being understood in adult terms. Author and musician Pat Kane has proposed that a "play ethic" be fostered, which accommodates the adult requirement for play (Kane, 2014). Oravec suggests that a "work/play ethic" is more appropriate, "fostering a balance between effort that is immediately productive and other forms of human expression" (2002:63).

And it probably does make for more contented workers. According to the president of a market research firm for businesses that surveyed workers on Internet usage in the workplace, it's just an electronic extension of flexible work policies to meet employees' general needs:

> When companies allow employees to spend a few moments online each day to handle personal issues, such as making dinner reservations, planning a trip or selecting a last-minute gift, these employees are able to better balance the demands of their work and home lives.... When employees feel their employers are supportive of a balanced work and home life, they tend to become more productive, loyal, and committed to their company. (quoted in Rabbit, 2000)

Forms of online diversion are already becoming an integral part of everyday workplace life. With effort on everyone's part—managers become more flexible and employees learn self-discipline and skills of balancing work and play—constructive use of recreation can help the entire organization work harder and play harder. Anyone up for a quick game of Words with Friends?

tive control involves the selective enlistment of the private dimensions of employee selves through a process of "existential empowerment," Fleming and Sturdy explained. "Control is achieved when what was once protected from the organization via cynicism and psychological distancing is appropriated as a corporate resource to enhance output" (2009:571). If the self is entirely exposed to the organization, especially in the name of work-based fun and frivolity, then what resources do individuals have to draw on to resist new forms of top-down control? And what does it mean to "be yourself" when you are told to do so . . . by your boss?!

Negotiating a More Satisfactory Order. Interactionists note that the relationship between management and labor is not fixed. In fact, it is always negotiated in practice. "The precise amount of time workers have off, their opportunities for conversation, their personal autonomy results from local situational conditions" (Fine, 1997:186). Organizational interaction is embedded within a complex set of structural and cultural relations (Fine, 1996). The structure of the organization is mediated by interactional relations and cultural images. Fine's analysis of restaurant kitchens suggests that the decisions and social organization in an organization (in his case, the kitchen) are channeled by the needs of actors to create pleasant and smooth workdays, and equally by the needs of the organizations to operate in a highly competitive market environment. The relations of power and authority that operate within organizations have real consequences if these relationships are breached; they do not stand apart from interaction systems. Both actors and external forces set constraints in which interaction is played out (Fine, 1996).

The symbolic interactionist perspective underlines the centrality of the interactional domain for accomplishing work. The workplace becomes a staging area in which meanings are generated, often through talk, which have effects on relationships and on patterns of action. According to Fine, "Talk and action come to constitute the workplace" (1996:222). The way that an organization has been structured, with its set of occupations, the way that an organization connects with clients and suppliers, and the way that an occupation organizes itself in its domain of expertise affects the specific behaviors and cultures in the workplace (p. 111). Fine continues:

> The effects of organization on interaction patterns are equally real. . . . Interaction patterns are altered by forces over which individual actors have little control. For instance, the pace of work, which generates patterns of interaction, is constrained by forces derived from management or externally imposed: the availability of resources provided by management (material and personnel), the work assignments . . . and the customer flow. (p. 222–23)

Fine's point is that in restaurants, as in other organizational environments, interaction is not an autonomous realm but is contingent on structural forces.

The Institutionalized Self

Unless you live way off the grid, encounters with bureaucratic institutions and organizations occur regularly. Whether you're in line at the Starbucks drive-through or online buying books through Amazon.com, the principles of predictability and efficiency are at play. What happens to the self, *your* self, when either buying something from or working for a bureaucratic institution? Are you simply a "carrier" or a cog in the machine of the institution? Or can you express your "self" through humor, poetry, or other means in order to assert at least a minimal amount of autonomy? If so, does your doing so give the institution more or less power over who you are or want to become?

■ Conclusion

The emergence of large-scale bureaucratic organizations can be linked to the process of urbanization, industrialization, and the development of capitalism and technology. Factories and corporations were organized to ensure maximum managerial control over workers' activities. Bureaucracies also were organized to control government functions. Now bureaucracy is shaping a wide variety of everyday behaviors. Contacts between intimates and strangers are mediated by the intervention of third-party agencies such as insurance companies, government bureaus, and the courts.

Scholars, beginning with Max Weber in the early 20th century, have used various approaches in thinking about bureaucracy. Interactionists view organizations as created, maintained, and changed through the daily interactions of their members, using the process of negotiated order. Complex organizations therefore include multiple realities, which people experience in varying ways depending on their position in the organization's hierarchy of authority. Informal subcultures define the organization in terms of human behaviors rather than rules and regulations.

In the world of work, people's locations in the hierarchy—executives, secretaries, and blue-collar workers, for example—shape their conceptions of the job and the organization. Workers with little autonomy in their jobs strive to achieve some degree of control over their work lives through collective arrangements with their peers in similar situations.

In the following chapter we will explore another sphere of life—that of health and illness—where people often find themselves dealing with bureaucratic rules and regulations concerning eligibility for treatment, as well as encountering medical personnel in settings having bureaucratic features.

Definitions

alienation: The sense of being cut off from one's labor. People create the world through their labors but then become constrained by the very things they have created.

autonomy: The ability to control one's own daily activities. Autonomy is particularly sought in the workplace.

blue-collar occupations: Work in which people use their hands as well as their minds to make a product or supply a service.

bureaucracy: A principle of organization characterized by a hierarchical structure of authority, the clear specification of work tasks, and an elaborate system of rules and regulations. The goal of a bureaucratic organization is to maximize efficiency.

control from the top down: A system of authority that is characteristic of bureaucracies. The orders are issued by upper management, and those lower down in the hierarchy of authority are expected to comply without resistance.

deskilling: The process by which the skilled components of production jobs are replaced by tasks requiring little skill or talent.

division of labor: The assignment of specific functions as tasks in the workplace to accomplish a group goal.

emotional labor: Effort required of workers to produce, suppress, or alter their feelings to display the appropriate emotion. (Hochschild, 1983)

hierarchy of authority: The chain of command in an organization, which specifies who can issue orders to whom.

informal subcultures: The unique ways of doing things developed by members of various subgroups in an organization. These subcultures, which often have no formal structure, form an *informal organization* that sets the norms for behaviors within the formal organization.

job satisfaction: The extent to which people find their work enjoyable and meaningful.

mass society: A large-scale society in which the status distinctions between various groups have been blurred.

meritocracy: A principle of organizational functioning that would allocate rewards on the basis of the quality of a person's performance. Hiring and promotion are supposed to be done solely on the basis of personal merit or ability.

negotiated order: The process by which members construct organizations. Negotiation by individuals also is the process by which social order is constructed.

new middle class: A social category composed of corporate managers, salaried white-collar professionals, salespeople, and office workers.

organizational society: An urban-industrial society characterized by the presence of large-scale bureaucratic organizations.

proletariat: The working class. Karl Marx applied the term to industrial workers who were prevented from owning the means of production—that is, the factories where they worked.

Protestant Ethic: The notion that the ultimate value and meaning of life are to be found in hard work and industrious labor. Work is regarded as service to God and a mark of respectability.

rationalization: The systematic and logical application of formal rules and procedures to every aspect of modern life. According to Max Weber ([1922] 1946), bureaucracy exemplifies this principle.

scientific management: An effort to organize work, particularly in the factory, in terms of the principles of scientific efficiency. The idea was developed by Frederick Taylor ([1911] 2014) to promote task specialization and control of workers' activities by management.

service occupations: Work in which people perform various services for others rather than producing a product.

social ethic: The notion that the ultimate value and meaning in life are to be found in one's acceptance by others.

white-collar occupations: Work that is primarily mental in character and salaried. White-collar workers provide the support services needed for industrial production.

Discussion Questions

1. Have you ever had a dispute concerning a bill with a bureaucratic organization—a credit union, hospital, insurance company, or cell phone provider, for example? What kinds of frustrations, if any, did you experience in trying to rectify the situation?

2. How have your experiences in college supported the notion of the university as a bureaucratic organization? What strategies have you developed to "get around" the official bureaucratic rules? Which ones have been the most successful?

3. Fifty years ago your grandmother probably would never have imagined suing her neighbor because she fell on ice in front of the neighbor's house. Nowadays such actions are commonplace. What kinds of situations do you think might be brought into the courts in the future as bases for suing another person?

4. Think of an incident in which you had an argument or disagreement with a stranger. Is there anything about that incident that led you to think about going to court to settle the issue? What does such an incident reveal about everyday life in a bureaucratic society?

5. In the past workers formed labor unions as a collective response to the alienating conditions in bureaucratic factory settings. Do you think white-collar workers will form organizations to make their jobs more meaningful in the face of increasing bureaucratization? What kinds of organizations would these be?

6. If you have ever worked in a bureaucratic setting—an office or factory, for example—how did your place in the organization's hierarchy influence your view of how the organization functioned? How do you think your boss and colleagues viewed the organization?

7. Numerous critics have noted how bureaucracies make individuals "faceless" by reducing them to particles in a mass of particles, which allows individuals to blend into the mass and not have to take personal responsibility for their actions. What might be the political consequences of this process?

8

Health and Illness

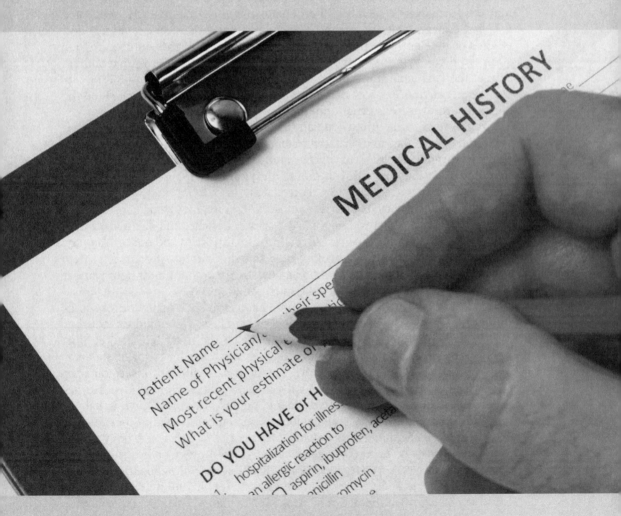

CHAPTER OUTLINE

- Health as a Cultural Construction
- Health Care Access
- When Doctors and Patients Meet
- The Social Construction of Illness Identities
- Conclusion

It would be impossible to reflect on contemporary American society without being continually reminded of our concern with and preoccupation about matters pertaining to "health." Perhaps today you woke up early to be sure you had enough time for a run before class (need those endorphins!) and slipped on an electronic bracelet to measure your heart rate and count your steps. In today's mail you received a special offer on a one-year membership at the local health club, and this month's fitness magazine had the latest "expert advice" on how many minutes of aerobic activity are needed for optimal cardiovascular functioning.

You agreed to try a new restaurant in the evening, and the first thing you did on perusing the menu was to engage in a mental calculation of saturated fat grams, cholesterol, carbs, and sodium contained in the various food items—or maybe you even pulled out your smartphone and looked for some estimates online. Having figured out the "costs" and "benefits" to your health of the various choices, you settled in to enjoy your chosen meal. Maybe you splurged a little on a hard-to-resist dessert, and so an after-dinner walk was in order to burn off the extra calories. At the end of the day, when you updated your Facebook page with a description of your activities, a friend told you about a blog post on a new diet plan that might help you get rid of those excess pounds you've been trying to lose.

Of course, the extent to which people engage in such behaviors is something that will vary by age, gender, and social class. We would expect that middle-aged, middle-class Americans would be the most likely to exhibit health concerns, although the research on eating disorders presents alarming and disturbing statistics on how the American cultural obsession with beauty and thinness seriously disadvantages young women (see Hesse-Biber, 1996). Socially constructed "ideal" bodies affect the ways that both men and women, as well as transgendered persons, understand their bodies and the bodies of others (Lorber and Moore, 2007). Gendered body ideals are underscored by a fundamentally ageist view of older bodies in the face of strong social pressures to maintain bodies that are young looking in order to retain their social currency (Calasanti and Slevin, 2001). The Protestant Ethic so powerfully enunciated by Max Weber many years ago (see chapter 7) may find its new focus in the body as something to be worked at with the same kind of discipline and diligence formerly reserved for one's job. The body—and the image it projects—is molded and shaped with the concerned attention one used to pay to the product one was manufacturing. In short, the body and its healthful functioning have become a project for huge numbers of Americans.

In the broadest sense, we want to argue in this chapter that the term *health*, like any other concept created by human beings, is fundamentally *symbolic* in character; that is to say, it has no inherent or intrinsic *meaning*. Whatever meanings it has derive from those conferred on it by people acting in concert, through communication with other human beings. Recalling the central propositions of symbolic interaction discussed earlier, we must seriously consider that (1) the term *health*, like any other symbol, submits to a multiplicity of meanings; (2) those meanings attached to health emerge out of our interactions with others; (3) the meanings of health are likely to be modified and reinterpreted, depending on the definitions of the situations in which we act; and (4) the meanings of health will vary *cross-culturally*.

In the sections to follow we will briefly explore how health can be seen as a **cultural construction**. After discussing such issues, we will then focus on what happens when patients bring a health problem to a doctor. We will conclude the chapter with a discussion of how patients make sense of and learn to live with a pervasive contemporary problem—clinical depression.

■ Health as a Cultural Construction

From a purely commonsensical point of view, health seems to be a pretty clear-cut issue; either you are sick or you aren't. Sickness, we tend to think, is a category comprised of physically based phenomena. When the body exhibits certain *symptoms*, we "know" that we are ill or that we ought to see a doctor for a diagnosis. Once we begin to see *health* and *illness*, however, as terms whose meanings vary across societies, we can begin to appreciate how the interpretive process involves socially based judgments about the human body and its functioning. Dennis Waskul and Phillip Vannini note,

> From a general interactionist perspective, the body is always more than a tangible, physical, corporeal object—infinitely more than "a mere skeleton wrapped in muscles and stuffed with organs"—the body is also an enormous vessel of meaning of utmost significance to both personhood and society. (2012:3)

The body is a social object that is the physical and empirical connection between us and others. As such, the ways that others think about our constantly changing bodies—as healthy, as sick, as beautiful, as ugly—are influenced by the cultural norms of particular groups or societies.

In a classic article written in the mid-20th century, the medical historian Erwin H. Ackerknecht (1947) eloquently argued against the view that disease was a strictly physical phenomenon by noting the important role that social factors play in the definition and treatment of what is considered a disease. According to Ackerknecht, "Medicine's practical goal is not primarily a biological one, but that of *social adjustment* in a given society . . . even the notion of disease depends rather on the *decisions of society* than on objective facts" (1947:142–43; emphasis added). As the following examples illustrate, societies differ dramatically in their response to the *same* bodily, physical symptoms:

> Pinto (*dyschromic spirochetosis*), a skin disease, is so common among many South American tribes that the few *healthy* men that *are not* suffering from pinto are regarded as *pathological* to the point of being excluded from marriage. . . . Intestinal worms among the African Thongas are not at all regarded as pathological. They are thought to be necessary for digestion. (Ackerknecht, 1947:143; emphasis added)

Not only is the definition of what constitutes an illness or pathological condition subject to cultural variations, but in an even more far-reaching sense, one's *experience* of bodily symptoms is shaped by social processes and expectations as well. In one of the earliest social science treatments of this issue, Mark Zborowski (1953) illustrated how responses to pain for hospitalized males in a Veterans Administration hospital varied by the respondent's ethnicity. White Protestant patients tended to respond optimistically toward their prospects for recovery while viewing doctors as experts to whom one went when needing "mending," much like bringing a car to an auto mechanic for repairs. Jewish patients, for example, evidenced a great deal of philosophical concern and anxiety about their condition while displaying a pessimistic orientation toward the future course of their illness. Predominantly Roman Catholic Italian American respondents, by contrast, were more interested in getting the pain stopped immediately; unlike the Jewish respondents, Italian Americans had little concern about the larger "meanings" of the pain. Although Zborowski's work has been criticized for its limited sample, broad and overly stereotypic generalizations about ethnic groups, and the fact that subjects were studied only in a medical setting, it pointed the way to understanding cultural variations in the expression and possibly also the experience of pain (Freund and McGuire, 1999).

Pain researchers are increasingly exploring the effects of demographic and cultural factors on pain. The *biopsychosocial* model of pain maintains that the experience of pain is sculpted by interactions among biological, psychological, and social factors. To date, pain researchers have mainly focused on documenting racial and ethnic differences in pain (Edwards et al., 2001), as well as gender differences (see box).

Another illustration of cultural differences in the health arena can be seen in the different effects of *collectivism* and *individualism* on patient–physician interaction. Individualists tend to be more concerned about the consequences of their own behavior and their own needs, interests, and goals, whereas collectivists tend to focus on the impact that their behavior has on others and are more willing to sacrifice personal interests to save face and maintain harmony (Young and Storm Klingle, 1996). Although people in every culture have both collectivist and individualist tendencies, there is an emphasis on individualism in the West (particularly in the United States) and collectivism in the East. Collectivist societies are more likely to practice holistic medicine (e.g., traditional Chinese medicine), whereas individualistic societies tend to use a **biomedical model**. The individualistic–collectivistic distinction, including the distinction between focus on the self versus the

The Influence of Social Processes and Expectations on the Experience of Pain— Gender Matters

Pain is a multidimensional experience involving biological, psychological, and social processes. Pain is unique as a medical phenomenon because its measurement relies on individuals' accounts of what they are feeling as well as doctors' observations of pain-related behavior. Pain generally involves more than simply a physical sensation, because it is imbued with meaning. Pain expression—how a person shows and behaviorally responds to pain—is clearly influenced by sociocultural factors. The ability to control the social presentation of pain even under conditions that inflict a great deal of pain may be interpreted as a sign of one's moral status. The expression "big boys don't cry," for example, reveals a 20th-century U.S. cultural expectation that males should repress the expression of pain (Freund and McGuire, 1999).

Are there differences in the prevalence of specific common pain conditions for men and women? If differences exist, what might be the reasons for them? Most of the epidemiologic data collected in the 20th century on sex differences in chronic pain are in the form of prevalence differences. Women reported more temporary and persistent pains, more severe pain, more frequent pain, and pain of longer duration than did men (Unruh, 1996). The most common chronic pain conditions in women included migraine headaches; oral facial pain, including temporomandibular disorders (TMD); musculoskeletal pain; abdominal pain; and a variety of pelvic pains, including endometrial pain, menstrual pain, postpartum pain, and pelvic floor disorders (Meisler et al., 1999).

What is it about being female or male that can influence these differences in prevalence? Perhaps there are anatomic or physiologic or genetic differences between women and men that affect transmission of pain signals. Or, differences may exist in the ways men and women perceive pain, or in the ways people think about pain. That is, perhaps there are differences in people's emotional experiences in relation to pain and how they cope with it. For example, willingness to report pain is an important issue, one that is probably influenced by differential socialization of women and men. A number of 20th-century authors have suggested various social learning influences on sex differences in pain behavior. Koutanji, Pearce, and Oakley (1998) posited that social roles for women are more supportive of pain expression and pain awareness, making them more cognizant of their own and others' pain. Klonoff, Landrine, and Brown (1993) found that males were less likely to disclose pain to others and associated feelings of embarrassment with having to admit pain.

Generalizations about certain groups' responses to pain must be used cautiously and not become the basis of stereotyping. Although we may have typical ways of expressing ourselves, social situational factors can affect how we will express ourselves. *Expressing* pain is not the same as *feeling* pain; for example, acting stoic does not mean that one feels no pain. Even if people from various social categories (social classes, gender, or cultures) do present pain differently, social and cultural factors also influence how observers interpret their pain expressions (Freund and McGuire, 1999).

other, has implications for beliefs about health and illness, expectations for the relationship between the health care provider and the patient, and health communication preferences (Armstrong and Swartzman, 2001; Logan and Hunt, 2014). Specifically, the Asian value on harmonious relationships results in an indirect, unassertive communication style (Kim and Wilson, 1994). This value suggests that Asian Americans would have a difficult time asserting themselves with physicians and that this might cause them to shy away from patient participation and collaborative medical decision making. For example, in a study in Hawaii of mainland American and Asian American patients (Young and Storm Klingle, 1996), Asian American patients perceived themselves as participating less in the medical interview than did patients from mainland American culture, possibly due to cultural differences in beliefs about the appropriateness of patient participation. This finding has important implications in that patient participation increases patient commitment to medical decisions and patient satisfaction and decreases misunderstandings and unrealistic expectations associated with prescribed treatments.

> Thus, patients who participate are more likely to choose treatments that they are able to follow. Throughout the decision-making process, patients have a chance to clarify information and weigh the advantages against the disadvantages. At the end of this process, the patient should have picked the "best" option. (Young and Storm Klingle, 1996:34)

As we have seen, cultural definitions and expectations play a crucial role in what comes to be seen as sickness and how that sickness will be experienced. In the United States, access to health care is perhaps the most critical determinant of how sickness and health are experienced. Let us turn to this issue.

■ Health Care Access

Who Goes to the Doctor?

Access to health care is important for prevention and for prompt treatment of illness and injuries. Use of preventive health services helps reduce **morbidity** and **mortality** from disease. While use of some preventive services has been increasing, disparities continue in use of preventive health care by race and ethnicity and by family income.

Coverage by health insurance, either private or public (e.g., Medicare or Medicaid), is a key indicator of access to medical care. According to data from the 2012 National Health Interview Survey (NHIS), 45.5 million Americans (14.7 percent) were without health insurance (National Center for Health Statistics, 2012). Especially among men, Hispanics and blacks are less likely to have health insurance than non-Hispanic whites. Health insurance is highly correlated with income, however, and the difference in insurance coverage between white and black men can be explained almost entirely by differences in income.

The U.S. health care system has changed from a *fee-for-service* system, where doctors set the fee and patients pay only for what is done on each visit, to one dominated by **health maintenance organizations** (HMOs) and other forms of **managed care**. As physician fees and the costs of hospital stays escalated in the late 20th century, many people with private health insurance could no longer afford the premiums. Employers began to cut back on what they could offer. The combination of high costs and shrinking coverage created a "health care crisis" that was met in part by the emergence of HMOs and other managed care. Enrollment in HMOs, the dominant form of managed care, increased from 9 million in 1980 to almost 77 million in 1998 (National Center for Health Statistics, 2000). The majority of insured workers are in some form of managed care; however, not all workers are insured. Despite the passing of the Affordable Care Act in 2010, which certainly reduced the numbers of uninsured U.S. citizens, sizable numbers of working-class and middle-class people possess insurance that is inadequate for handling major medical problems (Sanger-Katz, 2014). We can see, then, that the decision to present an illness to a doctor is the result of an interpretive process taking place within the **structural constraints** of the distribution of available medical services.

Minorities and Health Care

How individuals experience the health care system differs according to social factors. Given what we have learned about the gender-, race-, and class-based organization of society, it should come as no surprise that these play a significant role in health and health care.

Members of minority groups—for example, African Americans, Hispanics, gays, lesbians, bisexuals, HIV-infected individuals, and the mentally ill—experience difficulties in accessing adequate medical care (Light, 2012). Individuals who belong to more than one of these groups may experience difficulties exponentially greater than those faced by members of only one group (Wainberg, 1999). Health care providers are not immune to labeling, preconceptions, fears, and beliefs that may interfere with provision of adequate health care. Cultural barriers may make it difficult for doctors to gain patients' cooperation or to understand patients' beliefs or wishes (Olafsdottir and Pescosolido, 2009).

A review of more than 100 studies by the Institute of Medicine found that racial minorities in the United States received worse health care than whites, even when the minorities had the same income and health insurance as whites. Racial stereotyping by doctors under increasing time pressure to see as many patients as possible may have contributed to the inferior treatment of minorities, according to the report. Some minorities have a mistrust of doctors that can worsen the problem. Among the study's findings:

- Whites are nearly four times more likely than blacks to receive coronary bypass surgery when they need it.
- Nearly twice as many black prostate cancer patients as whites received no treatment for the disease.

- Black and Hispanic patients with HIV or AIDS were 24 percent less likely than whites to receive protease inhibitors.

- Among people who sought care in an urban emergency room, blacks were more likely to be denied authorization by managed-care providers.

Among the solutions suggested are cultural education programs for health care providers, increased awareness of bias, better education for patients, and more federal money for the civil rights office of the U.S. Department of Health and Human Services. In addition, there is a need for more minority physicians. There has been little progress made in opening the medical field to blacks and Hispanics since 1968, when 3.5 percent of physicians in the United States were minorities: in the early 21st century, 3.9 percent of physicians were minorities (Pelton, 2002).

Gays, lesbians, and bisexuals may receive inadequate care because of homophobia. The HIV/AIDS epidemic of the late 20th century in particular reflected the issues of access and allocation of health care. Fear of contagion may hinder the care of HIV-positive individuals. Unfortunately, already stigmatized minorities are affected to the greatest extent by HIV.

Gender and Health Care

According to a report released by the National Women's Law Center, the Oregon Health and Science University, and the University of Pennsylvania School of Medicine entitled *Making the Grade on Women's Health: A National and State Report Card* (2010), women are second-class citizens when it comes to health care in the United States. Nearly one in five women ages 18 to 64 lacks health insurance; for those with insurance coverage, it is often inadequate to meet women's needs. Because women are often excluded from medical research, doctors know less about how to recognize and treat diseases among women. There are substantial disparities in women's health care by state and by race, ethnicity, socioeconomic status, and other factors (National Women's Law Center, 2010).

There were improvements compared to previous years, such as increased efforts to screen for life-threatening illnesses such as cervical and colorectal cancer. There was little progress in reducing the number of uninsured women, however. Only five states and the District of Columbia improved Medicaid coverage for pregnant women. Only four states improved Medicaid coverage for single parents. "Poverty, unhealthy life-styles, poor mental health, violence, lack of education, and low income continue to interfere with women's ability to achieve good health in every part of the country" (National Women's Law Center, 2010).

There are significant gaps not only in health research relating to conditions that primarily affect women but also regarding racial, ethnic, and socioeconomic disparities in disease prevalence and treatment. We know now, for example, that African-American women are disproportionately at risk of dying from heart disease.

The 2010 *Report Card* gives the United States a failing *F* grade in 13 of the 26 graded indicators. The most disturbing trends have been a marked increase in the proportion of women who report binge drinking and a considerable decline in the percentage of women who get a regular Pap test, the primary test to detect cervical cancer.

■ When Doctors and Patients Meet

Interaction between physicians and patients does not always follow a preset course in which all parties work together under the same set of mutual understandings. There is potential for misunderstanding, uncertainty, even noncompliance. Various social factors affect doctor–patient interaction.

Presenting an Illness

The patient presents an **illness**—*that is,* a lived experience of discomfort, disease, or response to pain—to the physician. That lived, subjective experience is transformed by the doctor using a biomedical explanatory model into a less ambiguous, more controllable entity called a **disease**, which is amenable to medical monitoring. Illness, then, is a *social construction.* That is, it does not exist in the world as an objective condition; rather, it exists *because we have defined it as existing* (Weitz, 2009).

In presenting an illness experience to a physician, what does a typical patient want from the doctor? Such a question calls our attention to the importance of the ongoing interpretive process in which all human beings engage as we continually assess and reassess our life experiences. As such, sociologists have sought to reveal and "unpack" the fundamentally collaborative and contingent nature of "doctor-patient" medical encounters (Heritage and Maynard, 2006).

What Patients Want and Get

According to participants in one study in which subjects were asked to describe their "ideal doctor," 60 percent mentioned the doctor's personality, with the majority saying that doctors should be easy to talk to, friendly, and sympathetic (Finlay and Jones, 1998). Participants in another study described a "bad doctor" as "someone who treats patients as if they were on a 'production line,' who 'doesn't spend time with you,' who hurries and does not listen to the patient's concerns or questions" (Lupton, 1996:160).

Patient satisfaction is recognized by many health care providers as a legitimate measure of health care quality and safety. The major determinants of patient satisfaction are the physician's interest in patient **psychosocial concerns** and the quality of communication between physician and patient. Patients' conceptions of the types of clinician behavior that lead to trust and communication include terms like "listening," "friendly," "respectful," "nonjudgmental," "eye contact," "reassuring" (Mechanic and

Meyer, 2000). Many of the behaviors referred to are skills that can be taught. Despite the fact that contemporary health researchers increasingly advocate a patient-centered, holistic approach encompassing the patient's lifeworld and subjective experiences as essential aspects of medical practice, this is not the focus of most medical school training. According to one group of authors:

> Through classroom, laboratory, and ward experiences students quickly learn that "real" medicine applies a biomedical model to physically based diseases while ignoring the extraneous psychosocial "wrapping" in which the diseased body presents itself. (Baker, Yoels, and Clair, 1996:174)

By the time U.S. medical students have graduated and completed residencies, they will have been exposed to almost seven years of socialization that powerfully communicates to them that "listening to patients' stories may be a nice thing to do, but is really an 'extra,' to be indulged in only after the real work of medicine is accomplished" (Baker et al., 1996:178).

Despite some physicians' reluctance to delve into such areas, patients want these matters discussed and are more satisfied with the care received when they are (Schauffler et al., 1996). High levels of socioemotional behavior of physicians increase patient self-disclosure, trust, satisfaction, and likelihood of recommending the physician (Roberts and Aruguete, 1999). Patients who trust their providers are more likely to cooperate in treatment in ways that facilitate outcomes (Kao et al., 1998; Mechanic, 1998). Patients who are more dissatisfied with physicians' socioemotional behavior are more likely to change physicians (Gandhi et al., 1997; Kaplan et al., 1996).

Part of the reluctance of physicians to engage in "patient-centered" visits, particularly visits in which psychosocial concerns are addressed, is the perception that these visits are more time-consuming than biomedical exchanges and more likely to overwhelm a tight schedule. However, in a study examining physicians' communication patterns, this was not found to be the case (Roter et al., 1997). In fact, psychosocial visits averaged only a few minutes longer (22.9 minutes) than the narrowly biomedical visits (20.5 minutes). Patients gave the highest satisfaction ratings to visits marked by a psychosocial pattern of communication, particularly regarding a sense of partnership and support. However, the frequency of these visits was quite low (less than 10 percent). The narrowly biomedical pattern was associated with the lowest levels of both patient and physician satisfaction; 66 percent of these visits were characterized as physician-dominated and narrowly focused on biomedical concerns (Roter et al., 1997).

We should note that visits in the Roter study are longer than those in many managed care organizations, where face-to-face time is reduced to 10 to 12 minutes. Managed care is having a tremendous impact on patient-physician relationships. Modern managed care is:

> more than ever before characterized by contractual relationships specifying services . . . to which an enrollee is entitled. . . . Thus, as with the purchase of other commodities and services, managed care may be char-

acterized by the old buyer-beware approach used in the general marketplace rather than by the more trusting, respectful relationship of the
doctor and patient in the past. (Kronenfeld, 2001:301)

Patients are aware of physicians' new roles and responsibilities, as well
as restrictions imposed by HMOs and other managed care organizations. In
this environment, patients experience a loss of individualized and personalized care, partly due to restrictions on whom a patient can see and how the
patient must move through the health care delivery system, resulting in a
barrage of criticism. Americans give choice a high priority and are not
accustomed to some of the restrictions on access and choice of specialists.
In response, managed care organizations are placing growing importance
on both physician and patient satisfaction studies (Kronenfeld, 2001;
Groene, 2011). Though opportunities for patients to share feedback and
inform health-care providers have increased and are increasingly wel-
comed, the concept of "patient satisfaction" remains poorly defined, making
it difficult to measure. Surveys conducted by for-profit agencies often blend
health-care quality and patient satisfaction, which could lead patients to
request and ultimately receive treatments that are medically unnecessary
(Junewicz and Youngner, 2015).

Although a great deal of the discussion of the importance of patient satisfaction deals with its importance for private-sector managed care, it also
has relevance for assessing the delivery of care in systems for low-income
individuals. Although a variety of public and private programs provide care
for low-income individuals, little is known about patient satisfaction (see
box on the following page).

Managed care plans cannot afford to ignore physician satisfaction—it
affects both quality of care and patient satisfaction. Under managed care,
physicians' clinical autonomy may be compromised, as they often must
obtain approval before beginning care, prescribe only authorized drugs, or
follow specified treatment plans for given ailments. In addition, managed
care has pressed physicians to abandon entrepreneurial solo practices and
their own fee-for-service schedules and to accept working in ever-larger
group practices and receiving payment via capitation, salary, or third parties' fee schedules. Another impact of managed care is that physicians have
considerably less control over their patient pool, as patients enter and leave
practices based on their employers' contracts with managed care firms. All
of these factors have the potential to contribute to physician dissatisfaction.
However, participation in managed care does not have to lead to physician
dissatisfaction (Schultz et al., 1997). A study by Warren, Weitz, and Kulis
(1998) found that "whereas physicians 20 years ago may have been horrified
at the prospect of managed care, physicians now accept it as the rules of the
game . . . and recognize that the price of refusing to play by those rules is
bankruptcy" (p. 364). It is not clear from this study, however, whether
changes in patient/physician relationships have had much effect on physician satisfaction because physicians have learned to manage such patients
without spending much time or giving up clinical autonomy or because phy-

Patient Satisfaction and Income: Insurance Matters

The University of Kentucky Survey Research Center conducted a statewide telephone survey to examine patient satisfaction across a variety of health insurance programs (Mainous et al., 1999). The sample consisted of three groups: (1) individuals with private insurance; (2) individuals with Medicaid, public insurance for the low-income and underserved; and (3) individuals served by a charity program for uninsured indigents (below 100 percent of Federal Poverty income, ineligible for Medicaid). In general, private insurance individuals were more educated, had higher incomes, better health status, and were less likely to be minority. The low-income groups are relatively similar except that Medicaid recipients are more likely to be female and younger.

Satisfaction was measured by the patient's assessment of his or her most recent outpatient visit in the past 12 months and included questions about satisfaction with the personal manner of the person seen, length of time spent waiting at the office, time spent with the person seen, explanation of what was done.

Those with private insurance were significantly more satisfied than individuals in the low-income programs. There was no difference in satisfaction among the low-income individuals, regardless of health financing program. The authors conclude that these results seem to indicate the importance of patient socioeconomic status in patient satisfaction with care. That is, regardless of insurance, the lower the patient's income, the less satisfied the patient is with the care received. This suggests the possibility of a system of care where private insurance patients receive one type of care and low-income individuals receive another.

Although the study did not assess the interaction between patient and physician except through the patient's perspective, the authors suggest that a possible explanation for the difference in patient satisfaction may stem from differences in physician attitudes toward their patients and their problems. Personal interactions have been shown to be particularly important in patient satisfaction. Particularly significant is the respect shown by the physician to the patient in this interaction. Individuals in the low-income groups in this study had significantly lower ratings than their private insurance counterparts on the item assessing satisfaction with the personal manner (courtesy, respect, sensitivity, friendliness) of the caregiver they saw.

sicians have concluded that educated patients are easier to work with and have better outcomes. Moreover, a push toward more "patient-centered" training has yielded mixed results regarding actual health outcomes and benefits due, in part, to the persistence of asymmetrical power dynamic between doctors and patients (Pilnick and Dingwall, 2011).

Alternative Medicine

A countertrend, perhaps, to the rise of managed care is alternative medicine, which involves use of a wide variety of practices outside the clinical mainstream to promote health and potentially cure diseases. Alternative interventions include acupuncture, use of traditional herbs as medicine, massage, meditation, and other practices. Alternative medicine is attractive because it is "relatively inexpensive, incorporates a high degree of choice, involves accessible practitioners of lower status than physicians, and produces few negative side effects" (Vandenburgh, 2001:287). Although measurable health outcomes from alternative medicine are not always established, patients often choose it because it provides a degree of control they feel they lack with conventional health care.

Interest in alternative therapies has grown rapidly in the United States among those with chronic or acute illnesses as well as healthy people interested in avoiding illness. Millions of people use alternative health care providers. The most widely cited data on use of alternative therapies come from two national, random surveys conducted in 1990 and again in 1997 (Eisenberg et al., 1998). This research looked at use of 16 alternative therapies, including chiropractic, acupuncture, megavitamins, "folk" remedies, and biofeedback. According to these surveys, 42 percent of American adults used some form of alternative care in 1997, compared with 34 percent in 1990. Respondents made more visits in 1997 to alternative health care providers than to general and family practitioners combined. The trend has steadily increased since then in United States and across Europe (Baarts and Pedersen, 2009).

Women are more likely than men to use alternative therapies, especially those who are upper-income, middle-aged, college-educated, not African American, and suffering from chronic health problems (Astin, 1998; Eisenberg et al., 1998; Fairfield et al., 1998; Krauss et al., 1998). Alternative therapies are generally used to complement rather than replace traditional medicine. Many HMOs have begun to include coverage for some alternative practices.

Some authors argue that the rise of alternative healing reflects dissatisfaction with the mismatch between doctors' concerns and patients' concerns (Schneirov and Geczik, 1996). That is, doctors typically are concerned with diagnosis and treatment, whereas patients are primarily concerned with the impact of illness on their lives (Mechanic, 1995). Patients can be left feeling like depersonalized objects, dissatisfied with the care they receive. Matthew Schneirov and Jonathan David Geczik argue that alternative healing offers patients the opportunity to work as collaborators with health care providers. Their research indicated that alternative health care users shared several beliefs, including the belief that modern medicine focuses too much on surgery and medication to treat symptoms rather than lifestyle changes to prevent illness. They conclude:

> The alternative health movement may be seen as part of a larger wave of discontent with the bureaucratic-administrative state, its reliance on expert systems, and the way it coordinates people's health care practices "behind their backs"—without their knowledge and participation. (1996:642)

In a similar vein, when health is conceptualized as "well-being," alternative health practices often challenge the dominant biomedical domain. Eeva Sointu (2006) notes that alternative health often frames patients' experiences as returning to a state of well-being perceived in terms of harmony, fulfilment, and a "natural contentment" (2006:335). In this sense, well-being is seen as potentially available even to the terminally ill. Sointu emphasizes that the term *well-being* is open to personal definition and subjective assessment, pertaining in particular to how the individual feels about himself or herself (2006:336), which is consistent with both a desire for personalized care and a transformation in our ideas of how health is achieved.

The Internet as a Source of Health Care Information

The Internet is another factor with the potential to affect interaction between patients and health care providers (Kivits, 2013). At the turn of the millennium, Jeff Goldsmith (2000) suggested that use of the Internet to obtain health information "will enable patients to begin their dialogue with physicians at a much higher level and provide them with leverage to influence the health care process" (p. 151). Traditionally, physicians have been the purveyors and integrators of health care information. Increased access to this information via the Internet means that the doctor is no longer necessarily the "distributor, interpreter, and filter of information in the health care setting," resulting in a "shifting paradigm of practitioners as information provider to information broker" (Bischoff and Kelley, 1999:42).

Although the Internet provides vast amounts of information to guide people in their health care decision-making processes, one cannot ignore the fact that there is a significant division in American society between those who use and have access to the Internet and those who do not (Cotten, 2001). Income is the strongest predictor of online access, and there is a racial gap in Internet access (Zach et al., 2012). The utility of the Internet to improve medical care remains poorly characterized, especially for those living in economically depressed urban areas (Robinson et al., 1999). There is evidence to suggest that individuals who have preventable health problems and lack health insurance coverage are less likely to have access to and use Internet-related technologies (Eng et al., 1998; Zach et al., 2012). Inequitable distribution of Internet technology may widen social disparities already existent in health care and health outcomes (Mandl et al., 1998; Rains, 2008).

On the positive side, the Internet may be a potential alternative health care resource. Some research suggests that individuals who use the Internet frequently are more likely than infrequent users to take action that affects their diagnosis and treatment. Based on her study of personal Web pages of women with breast cancer, Victoria Pitts (2004) found that gaining medical knowledge from the Internet is "used as a way to level the hierarchal relationships that exist between patient, doctor, and the medical industries" (p. 43). Patients can also use the Internet as a medium to write about their experiences and how to navigate the health care system and "decode" medical language, which can, in some cases, lead to better doctor–patient dialogue.

Online support programs may lead to reduced economic costs associated with particular health problems. Moreover, access to support groups through the Internet, particularly for individuals who are physically challenged or who are not mobile, may be key to decreasing loneliness, anxiety, and depression (Cotten, 2001). Participating in and helping define the social norms of the online support group may also help sufferers gain a sense of authority over their condition (Armstrong et al., 2012).

The Health Care Crisis

We have seen that the rise of managed care has raised concerns about the quality of health care now available in the United States. A more serious problem is that the increased cost of health care and the resulting decrease in access to it challenges the very basis of the U.S. health care system. Given the number of both uninsured and underinsured people in the United States, access to health care services will remain one of the nation's major political issues for the foreseeable future, despite the enactment in 2010 of the Patient Protection and Affordable Care Act (informally known as "Obamacare" after the president who signed it into law).

The final issue we want to discuss in this section concerns the phenomenon of illness and the self.

Illness and the Self

When someone becomes ill, not only are finances, mobility, and independence lost but also the familiar sense of self (Frank, 2000). "The self is disrupted; the community through which one knows oneself disappears" (Richardson, 2000:333). What Arthur Frank refers to as the "illness story" begins when life suffers a *disruption* (Becker, 1997) that renders its previous "point" either forgotten or no longer viable. Not only are one's plans disrupted but also the basis of the interactionist notion of the self—a self grounded in the need for others' recognition. The ill and disabled are typically denied this recognition. For example, a woman named "Sarah" (described in Rosenfeld and Faircloth, 2004) had severe disabilities from lupus and resultant crippling osteoarthritis. She refused to wear her prescribed neck brace in public because it caused her discomfort and constrained her movements and, perhaps more important, because she thought others saw her as "a walking zombie" when she wore it. Even though the brace was intended to assuage the physical pain, she implied that the pain of losing her self and being seen by others as less than fully human was worse.

Frank uses Ritzer's (2000) notion of "McDonaldization" (see chapter 7) to show how medicine alienates one from one's self "because commodified medicine incarnates a person as a blip on a monitor, numbers on a chart, specimens in a tube, computerized printouts, research data, money" (Richardson, 2000:334).

When Americans enter typical U.S. hospitals, for example, they are usually required to don a standardized hospital gown of some sort; there is little space in their room for placing large numbers of personal mementos. They often will encounter medical specialists of various kinds for the first time while in the hospital—doctors with whom they have had no prior contact. Various kinds of hospital **identity markers**, such as wristbands, are usually worn, and one begins to be treated by others—doctors, nurses, and other patients—

as a "patient." The hospital and its routines are organized in such a way as to continually remind the patient that one's identity as a *body in need of repair* is far more salient than one's personal life history and subjective experiences. The ultimate effect of such processes is to make the person feel less like an "individual" and more like a member of an undifferentiated aggregate called *patients.* It appears, then, that being ill in an American hospital is to be in a place where one's sense of oneself as a unique person is sadly diminished.

This is a reflection of the shift in American medicine that occurred during the 20th century, from "the more intimate setting of the hearth and bedside to the more impersonal, bureaucratic world of clinics, large-scale hospitals, and health maintenance organizations" (Baker et al., 1996:191). What was an "often home-based, person-centered, emotionally laden form of practice" became transformed into "a technical, procedurally driven activity; an activity in which only such procedures (not time spent talking to patients) are paid for by health care insurers" (p. 192).

The typically brief actual doctor–patient encounter launches the patient toward experiencing herself or himself as simply a body. According to one author, an essential feature of 20th-century medical practice was "the dislocation of the case from the patient's bedside and indeed from the patient's physical presence" (Atkinson, 1995:149). Patients resent doctors who do not treat them as "real people" with feelings. Patients want to be viewed as individuals rather than "part of a mass of anonymous patients" (Lupton, 1996:161).

Interestingly, humor can play a central role in allowing both doctors and patients "to navigate the ambiguous boundaries of *body and self* intrinsic to medical encounters, while simultaneously maintaining the traditional doctor/patient status order" (Baker et al., 1997:181). That is, "When examining patients, doctors may subtly invoke their power to cross at will from the physical into the social by joking with patients while raising possibly intrusive questions about personal lifestyle matters such as smoking, drinking, and sexual practices" (pp. 181–82). Patients, by responding in a "nervously humorous" manner to such medically legitimate intrusions by doctors, "tacitly acknowledge physicians' control over the agenda, while also distancing and protecting the self 'in' the body" (p. 182). Such probing, however, also puts physicians in the role of **moral entrepreneurs** who are "custodians and enforcers of mainstream societal moralities" (Baker et al., 1996:192). Patients (especially lower-income minority patients) may experience the "powerful medical gaze of high-status professionals as morally judgmental as well as therapeutically curative" (p. 193).

We need much more research on what patients are experiencing and the meanings they are constructing in response to the different encounters taking place in the broader medical setting. In the last decades of the 20th century, medicine underwent extensive scientific and technological rationalization. According to one prominent medical sociologist:

> Nevertheless, the treatment of disease remains substantially a humanistic endeavor that must take account of the fact that the ills of patients are in important ways a product of the larger environment, the socio-cultural

context, and the ways people live their lives. Medical care has deep significance for those who are sick and their loved ones and it is inevitably
tied to the values and meanings that shape their actions and associations.
(Mechanic, 2002)

The ultimate question, of course, is how such experiences play out in terms
of patient health outcomes and the quality of medical care.

In the 21st century, increased attention is being paid to the connection
between patients' illnesses and the larger context of their lives. Some hospitals have recognized that even changes in the physical environment—such
as the inclusion of artwork in patient rooms and public areas—can improve
the quality of health care ("Art in Health Care Facilities," 2009). There is a
growing body of literature that supports the notion that the physical environment of hospitals and other care facilities has an effect on the healing
process and the well-being of patients and staff. The way a "healing environment" is built can improve patient privacy and comfort and also contribute to reducing errors such as falls and infections (Huisman et al., 2012).

Having examined a broad range of issues pertaining to the diagnosis of
an illness, we now want to focus on how people deal with a pervasive current life problem—clinical depression.

■ The Social Construction of Illness Identities*

As your authors have argued throughout this book, we human beings
are constantly in the business of **negotiating social reality**. Yet although
negotiating the reality of social life is, therefore, an inevitable and generic
human task, some statuses and social conditions create an unusual degree
of uncertainty or ambiguity and thereby require more intensive efforts at
sense-making. In fact, according to one of your authors, "Social reality is a
very messy thing" (Karp, 1996:20). Ambiguous situations are especially
useful for analysis because they illustrate in high relief how people cope
with situations demanding particularly extensive interpretive work.
Depression is a particularly good example, not only because of the large
number of people who are affected by it but also because it provides a case
study for considering how individuals arrive at illness definitions and then
reconstruct their identities accordingly.

To study how people deal with such conditions, David Karp interviewed
50 people "officially" diagnosed as depressed. In his book *Speaking of Sadness* (1996), people described how their lives, feelings, attitudes, and perspectives have been influenced by depression. This approach differs from
much of the research on depression (and there is a lot of it), which generally
focuses on causation and treatment, presented from the vantage point of
"experts." Although these studies are valuable, what is missing is the point
of view of the people experiencing it. In Karp's words, "Research about a

---

*This section borrows from David Karp, *Speaking of Sadness: Depression, Disconnection, and
the Meanings of Illness* (New York: Oxford University Press, 1996).

feeling disorder that does not get at people's feelings seems, to put it kindly, incomplete" (p. 12).

Karp found it remarkable how candidly most of those interviewed spoke about their experiences, which provided a depth of insight not generally attainable through clinical studies. In particular, the acquisition of an identity as a "depressed person" is "often the product of a long journey aimed at discovering the kind of self one is" (Karp, 1996:48). Given that depression is a health problem that dominates lives and often seems fundamentally intractable, how, we might ask, do depressed individuals create explanations, understandings, agreements, and common **illness ideologies** to impose some order onto such a hazy and ill-understood life condition?

Depressed individuals face a number of interpretive tasks as they endeavor to make sense of their situation. They go through a process of defining what is wrong with them and attaching a label to their experience; that is, a process of **achieving a diagnosis**. When a label has been attached to moods and behaviors, everyone seeks to understand the causes of their condition. Efforts to appreciate whether depression is explained by biology (nature) or environment (nurture) are an ongoing puzzle.

The experiences of Karp's respondents suggest regularities in the depression experience. A depression consciousness arises in an extraordinarily patterned way, making it possible to analyze the depression experience as a "career" sequence characterized by distinctive identity transformations, or "turning points" in identity. That is, each juncture in the career requires a redefinition of self. Although there was considerable variation in the timing of events, all the respondents in Karp's study described a process of moving through particular identity turning points in their view of themselves and their problem with depression:

1. A period of *inchoate feelings* during which they lacked the vocabulary to label their experience of depression;

2. a phase during which they conclude that *something is really wrong with me*;

3. a *crisis stage* that thrusts them into a world of therapeutic experts; and

4. a stage of *coming to grips with an illness identity* during which they theorize about the cause(s) of their difficulty and evaluate the prospects for getting beyond depression (Karp, 1996:57).

The Career Path of Depression

All of Karp's respondents described a period during which they had no vocabulary for naming their problem, sometimes going back to ages as young as three or four. Respondents typically went for long periods feeling different, uncomfortable, marginal, ill at ease, scared, and in pain without labeling this as depression. In the words of one respondent:

> Well, I knew I was different from other children. I should say that from a very early age it felt like I had this darkness about me. Sort of shadow of

myself. And I always had the sense that it wasn't going to go away so eas-
ily. And it was like my battle. And so, from a very early age I felt, okay,
"There's something going on here, [but] don't ask me for a word [for it]."
It hurts me. I feel sad. (Karp, 1996:57)

Even when ill feelings did not emerge until later in life, individuals initially ascribed their difficulty to immediate life circumstances—such as a
failed relationship or job problems—and believed that as soon as the situation changed, their discomfort would disappear. However, when circumstances change and mood problems persist, the explanation for what is
wrong must be redefined. A major cognitive shift occurs when people come
to see that the problem may be internal, not situational. That is, something is
wrong with *them*. The rejection of situational theories for bad feelings is a
critical identity turning point. Full acceptance that one has a damaged self
requires acknowledgement that "I am not the same as I was, as I used to be"
(Karp, 1996:62). So the second phase of the illness career involved the recognition that they possessed a self that was working poorly in every situation.

At some point, everyone interviewed experienced a crisis of some sort—
in particular, hospitalization. At this point they could not prevent their situation from becoming public knowledge. And whether they were hospitalized
or not, everyone reached a point where they had to rely on psychiatric
experts. After individuals received an "official" diagnosis of depression and

consequent treatment with medication, the need to redefine their past, present, and future in illness terms was greatly accelerated.

Achieving a Diagnosis

At the point of crisis, people fully enter a therapeutic world of hospitals, mental health experts, and medications, and for many, this occurs simultaneously with first receiving the "official" diagnosis of depression. Official diagnoses and labeling are critically important in the illness career. Knowing that you "have" something that doctors regard as a specific illness imposes definitional boundaries onto an array of behaviors and feelings that previously had no name. Being diagnosed suggests the possibility that the condition can be treated. As one respondent describes:

> It [getting a diagnosis] was a great relief. I said, "You mean there is something wrong with me. It's not some sort of weird complex mental thing." I was like tying myself up in knots trying to figure out what strange mechanism in my mind was producing unhappiness from this set of circumstances. . . . It's like, "No, you're sick!" (sigh) There was an enormous relief. (Karp, 1996:66)

Achieving a diagnosis is a critical stage in helping people identify and interpret the meaning of their experiences. The good news associated with achieving a diagnosis is that one finally has a name and category to attach to a whole history of troubles, and thereby a partial explanation for those troubles. The bad news, however, is that the diagnosis puts one into the devalued category of those with a "mental illness." The **interpretive dilemma** for individuals is to highlight the positive features of the diagnosis while avoiding those that are potentially stigmatizing or personally unacceptable. The response of one of Karp's respondents to being asked if she thought of herself as having a disease reflects the ambivalence and confusion heard in the answers of many others:

> I think of it less as an illness and more something that society defines. That's part of it, but then, it *is* physical. Doesn't that make it an illness? That's a question I ask myself a lot. Depression is a special case because everyone gets depressed. . . . I think that I define it as not an illness. It's a condition. When I hear the term illness I think of sickness . . . [but] the term mental illness seems to me to be very negative, maybe because I connect it with hospitalization. . . . I connect it with how people define people who have been hospitalized. . . . It's something that I can deal with. It's something that I can live with. I don't have to define it as a problem. But the thing about mental illness is that it lasts. . . . Once a diagnosis always a diagnosis. (Karp, 1996:53)

However, having a diagnosis still leaves unanswered the ultimate causes(s) of one's problem. Achieving a diagnosis, in other words, is the starting point for further interpretive work about causation and personal responsibility.

Anyone who has taken a basic course in sociology or psychology learns about the **nature/nurture debate**. For most people the debate remains at an abstract level, removed from the stuff of daily life. For those suffering from depression, however, efforts to appreciate whether their condition is explained by biology or environment is an ongoing puzzle. Although a few respondents were willing to define their condition as a mental illness, most wanted simultaneously to embrace the definition of their problem as biochemical in nature while rejecting the notion that they suffer from a "mental" illness.

> If you say illness, that means there's something wrong with you . . . especially a psychiatric label. That means I'm defective. If you told me I was diabetic I wouldn't think of it as bad. (Karp, 1996:73)

Adopting the view that one has a biochemically sick self constitutes a comfortable *account* for a history of difficulties and failures and absolves one of responsibility. The interpretive dilemma for Karp's respondents was to navigate between rhetorics of biochemical determinism and a sense of personal efficacy.

> There was a sense of relief when I started finding out that the medication was helpful, because then I could say it was a chemical problem and that I'm not looney tunes and that, you know, it's not a mental illness which sounds real bad to me. . . . So, in a sense it was very comforting to be able to use the word chemical imbalance as opposed to mental illness. (Karp, 1996:73)

Because all the individuals included in Karp's study had at some point been diagnosed and treated for depression by doctors, there is a built-in bias in the sample toward acceptance of a medical definition of depression's cause and the proper response to it.

Looking for Dr. Right

As several cultural observers (e.g., Edgley and Brissett, 1999) have noted, the behaviors of people in today's society are dominated by "experts." Experts advise us on virtually every aspect of our lives; they follow us through the life course. They are there when we are born and follow us each step along the way, eventually to our graves. Many people have come to feel reliant on experts to tell them how to maintain their health, how to become educated, and how to raise their children. Most critical to the present discussion, however, is the fact that medical experts now tell us when our bodies and our "selves" need repair and the proper procedures for doing it. The medical profession has played a key role in the rise of what might be termed a **therapeutic culture** (Rieff, 1966; Polsky, 1991; Wright, 2008), with its focus on finding a "cure" for whatever ails you. In fact, the term *therapeutic* suggests a life focused on the need for cure (Bellah et al., 1996). Medical control over more and more areas of life is legitimated, typically by asserting and establishing the primacy of a medical interpretation of that area. This process has been referred to as **medicalization** (see Conrad and Schneider, 1992). According to some critics, especially of psychiatry, the medical model is used to support an essentially political reality. These writers point out that the term *healthy*, as used in the medical model, can be replaced by the word *conforming* and that in societies where it predominates, the medical model is often used in lieu of the law or religious sanctions to legislate behavior. According to Peter Berger and Thomas Luckmann (1967), teachers, judges, physicians, and other health professionals constitute a coalition of **universe maintenance specialists** who set norms defining proper and improper behavior, deviant and conforming behavior, sick and healthy behavior. Specifically considering the social-control role of psychotherapy, Berger and Luckmann state:

> Therapy entails the application of conceptual machinery to ensure the actual or potential deviants stay within the institutionalized definitions of reality. . . . Since therapy must concern itself with deviation from the "official" definition of reality, it must develop a conceptual machinery to account for such deviations and to maintain the realities thus challenged. This requires a body of knowledge that includes a theory of deviance, a diagnostic apparatus, and a conceptual system for the "cure of souls." (1967:112)

Those who have long histories as patients are uncertain about the proper role of psychiatrists in defining reality and the adequacy of their conceptual knowledge for curing the soul. On the one hand, these individuals see psychiatrists as the professional experts who hold out the possibility of helping them. However, for every person who talks of having found a warm, sensitive, and sensible psychiatrist, there are those who tell psychiatric horror stories involving, as they see it, insensitivity and incompetence. Karp was surprised at the virulence of the animosity expressed toward psychiatrists by those he interviewed. Although many of those interviewed eventually found psychiatrists whom they trusted and from whom they benefited, early in their treatment individuals saw psychiatrists as "oppressively evangelistic 'true believers' in biochemical causes of depression," a view that they did not at that time hold (Karp, 1996:89). This negative evaluation can be seen in the frequency and regularity with which respondents angrily labeled their doctors "pill pushers." As one respondent put it:

> This particular doctor was such an asshole. He sounded like a used car salesman for antidepressants. He was just like so gung-ho. "Oh yeah, you're the typical depressed [person], here's the drug that will cure you. Let me know if you go home and just want to kill yourself or something. We'll try something different for you." And I hated him. I just really hated him. (Karp, 1996:89–90)

Karp surmises that perhaps the relationship between extremely depressed, vulnerable patients and powerful psychiatrists intrinsically generates friction, discomfort, and anger. Because the gap between the expectations that patients bring to psychiatric professionals and what their doctors can actually deliver may be great, disillusionment may be inevitable. That is, perhaps patients and doctors have very different versions of therapy's "reality." Where patients want warmth, understanding, even love, they encounter detached professionals who often do not even inquire about their feelings, only their symptoms. This mutual misunderstanding can be heard in the way that patients talk about searching for the "right" doctor:

> It is really hard with depression. It's like you've got to get to the right doctor who's going to understand it. (Karp, 1996:117)

> The woman who became my analyst completely misunderstood the problems. She kept criticizing me. I mean, it turns out that [it] was just wrong. She wasn't right for me anyway. (p. 117)

> I was seeing one therapist for awhile, and that didn't work out, and I started seeing another one. . . . I think he's the best doctor I've ever had. He just knows what the hell I'm talking about. He's empathetic but he's not, you know, coddling. (p. 117)

Repetition of the theme of finding the therapist who is "right for you" reminded Karp of stories about soured romances. The respondents' accounts parallel comments often heard in everyday conversation about falling in and out of love. People's relations with a series of therapists might be seen as similar to a pattern of "serial monogamy": finding someone you believe is right for you, becoming dependent on that person for meeting certain needs, making a commitment, eventually realizing that you may have made the wrong choice, leaving the relationship, and searching once more for the person who is *really* right for you.

Although some people seem to have found the right psychiatrist for themselves, the more typical pattern appears to be one of disillusionment about the efficacy of psychiatry. And if some are disillusioned with psychiatrists, others are downright angry. Predictably, the most profound expressions of anger toward psychiatrists that Karp heard were reserved for those who exercised complete control over respondents in hospitals when they had little choice about their treatment. For example:

> I remember I saw this doctor who looked like a frog. I hated him. No, he looked like a pig. I didn't like his personality and he kept asking me questions about sex and stuff. It made me uncomfortable and I just didn't like him as a person. He was a shrink. And then comes that whole power thing. Psychiatrists and mental health workers, but particularly psychiatrists, have the power to decide when you are going to leave, if you are going to leave, if you can go out on a pass, when you can go out on a pass, if you're good, if you're not good, that sort of thing. (Karp, 1996:120)*

> This guy was just a supercilious, superior, arrogant prick. . . . I had the feeling that he was just looking down on me as a semi-vegetable, and did me absolutely no good at all. (p. 120)

> The doctor I had [in the hospital] was an idiot. (p. 120)

---

*A film that illustrates this well is *Girl, Interrupted* released in 1999 and based on Susanna Kaysen's 1993 book of the same title, which was based on her experiences in a mental institution.

In the end, the biggest disappointment for patients may be the eventual realization that doctors can't easily fix them. Despite the magic of Prozac (see box) and other drugs that are part of the new generation of antidepressants that certainly help those with depression feel measurably better, a "cure" remains elusive. Among the 50 people in Karp's study, there were a *few* who said that as a result of medical treatment (primarily drug treatment), their depression had vanished. For the others, depression comes and goes, with medication only modestly alleviating problems (or doing nothing at all). "Belief that this treatment, this new therapist, this new form of therapy, or this drug that you haven't tried yet might be the thing to finally cure you generates for many a frustrating cycle of high hope followed by varying degrees of disillusionment" (p. 123).

Despite physicians' best efforts, most of the patients with whom Karp talked came to realize that their therapists will not clear away their confusion about depression. "In a more fundamentally existential way, many con-

Prozac and the Self

Since its introduction in 1987, more than 35 million people worldwide have taken the antidepressant Prozac. Almost as soon as it hit the market, it was hailed as a miracle drug. By 1990 Prozac had become the top-selling antidepressant in the world (Zuckoff, 2000). In Peter Kramer's influential book, *Listening to Prozac* ([1993] 1997), he put forth the view that Prozac transforms the self. Perhaps most controversial was the claim (based on patients' experiences) that the new selves created were the "real" selves. The so-called "Prozac debates" have frequently been cast in terms of a search for the foundations of the "modern self" and whether these are located in chemical or in sociopsychological phenomena (Lyon, 1996). Kramer described his patients as feeling "better than well" on Prozac, reporting noticeable improvement in their popularity, business sense, self-image, energy, and sexual appeal. He argued that Prozac can (and perhaps should) also be used to remove aspects of our personality we find objectionable, likening the use of Prozac to overcome undesirable psychological traits to the use of cosmetic surgery in overcoming undesirable physical ones (Kramer, [1993] 1997).

But if Prozac does make people "better than well," how might its popularity affect social life? Critics fear that Prozac (like other drugs that may modify character) is aimed not so much at "sick patients" as at people who already function at a high level and want enriched memory, enhanced intelligence, heightened concentration, and a transformation of bad moods into good ones (Begley, 1994). In the fast-paced, achievement-oriented American society of the 21st century, motivations for gaining a competitive edge are obvious. Those who earn higher grades, sell more cars, or come across as more charming and attractive can reap enormous financial and social benefits (Newman, 2002). This idea is also evidenced by the increasing use of such prescription drugs as Ritalin and Adderall by students for optimizing educational goals and ideals (Davis-Berman and Pestello, 2005; Loe and Cuttino, 2008.) But what about those who do not use the drug, either for reasons of principle or because they can't afford it? Do they risk losing out and becoming the less rewarded and less valuable members of the community (Rothman, 1994)?

The technological possibilities of Prozac raise important issues about the role of medicine in defining deviance, controlling behavior, constructing personality, and ultimately determining social life and the culture that guides it (Newman, 2002).

clude that their depression is likely never to be fixed once and for all" (1996:123). As one respondent so eloquently put it:

> I have a feeling of unpredictability and lack of control over something that has a life of its own [and] that contradicts my feeling of mastery. And I know that now. I've had this experience for so long that I'm going to be up and that I'm going to be down and I suppose it makes it a little bit easier. (Karp, 1996:124)

Recognition that the pain of depression is unlikely to disappear eventually provokes a redefinition of its meaning, of its place in one's life. As we have seen over and over again in this text, human beings confer meaning onto *everything* in their worlds. In the case of depression, the meaning of its pain can be refashioned. Most of Karp's respondents were not stumped when he asked, "Is there anything *good* about having depression?" Several felt that they had a deeper and more accurate picture of human nature and social life than happy people, even expressing disdain toward family and friends whose happiness they saw as built on a distortion of what the world is "really" like. Others viewed depression as the price paid for insights that were inaccessible to others (Sylvia Plath comes to mind). The word "sensitivity" came up most frequently when the values of depression were cited, with people indicating that depression had given them a more profound appreciation for others' difficulties. In the words of one respondent:

> I think depression has made me a stronger person somehow. I mean in learning to handle this kind of thing. I think that I've had to develop skills and abilities that I wouldn't otherwise. And sensitivities too. I think it's made me more compassionate. I think, because of it, I know what it's like to go through something like that and I'm more curious about other people and what they're going through. [I'm also] more intent in trying to make some meaning out of the whole thing [life]. . . . (Karp, 1996:130)

Along with the problems associated with managing their daily lives, individuals with affective disorders must cope with a "mental illness" status. They must deal with the fact that to suffer from depression is not only debilitating but also casts one into a deviant, disvalued, and sometimes stigmatized status. Beginning with Goffman's (1963) groundbreaking formulation of the problem of **stigma**, social scientists have studied how groups as diverse as overweight individuals, wheelchair users, and people with HIV/AIDS manage information and adopt behavioral strategies that serve to protect tainted identities (as will be discussed further in chapter 9). Despite the increased awareness of depression, those diagnosed as depressed know they have a condition that is conventionally defined as a mental illness. That is, they fall into a category with a range of "others" who have what Goffman terms "blemishes of individual character." It is not surprising, then, that depressed people may adopt "passing" strategies similar to others whose stigmatized conditions are not immediately visible. Self-management may simply take the form of keeping one's unacceptable identity secret.

> Of course, you could never tell anybody, because [of] the stigma. . . .

> Depression is a mental illness, Sssssh! Don't talk. Don't tell anybody. . . . Nobody talked because of the stigma attached, depression being a mental illness.

> All I know is that I could never run for political office.

> I'm still afraid of people. I feel if I don't tell them [about my depression] I can never really become close to them. . . . I can't even make just fun friends because I need so much to talk to people and let everyone know about it, but I can't because it's just too damaging. (Karp, 1996:46)

Sociological literature contains many examples of how stigmatized individuals attempt to foster more positive definitions of their situation. Subcultures, for example, not only provide support for alternative, nonstigmatizing definitions of a common circumstance but also may have a larger agenda of responding to negative definitions with the aim of changing them. Although those with a range of mental illnesses have begun to enter the arena of "identity politics," depression is a unique case because the most critical assaults on the self come from within. Although those with depression may want a greater public understanding of their "illness," when they are in the middle of an episode of depression, they feel a self-hatred far greater than could possibly be expressed by others toward them. As people cycle through depression, "the dialectical intersection of self and society" can be plainly seen. In Karp's words:

> The process begins with a range of bad feelings. Chief among them is that one possesses a deeply problematic self, a self that feels socially uncomfortable. At a point, it becomes a self deemed wholly unworthy of public presentation. Such feelings lead, as we have seen, to social withdrawal. Withdrawal, in turn, makes the performance of social functions difficult and sometimes impossible. The inability to meet social obligations expands the disdain and hatred people feel toward themselves, thus sustaining and extending the felt need to withdraw. In this way, depression is characterized by an ongoing and mutually reinforcing double stigmatization—by self and society. (1996:47)

Individuals with depression learn to navigate between rhetorics of "victimization" and "positive thinking" in a way that accounts for their situation while empowering them to do something about it. Also, since those with diagnosed affective disorders are thrust into a world of therapeutic experts, much discussion is designed to affirm that, despite their dependence on physicians, they are the ultimate experts on the value of therapeutic interventions. Such a posture also helps them realize a sense of competence in a situation where their competence is dangerously undermined. In this regard, while the individuals discussed in this section have a distinctive life problem with which to contend, they are quite like every human being. At one time or another we all face life circumstances that are difficult to fathom and where our competence is actually or potentially called into

The Embodied Self

As we move through our everyday lives, sometimes we can get lost in either our screens or just the "flow" of routine behaviors, which can easily push us into the Cartesian trap of separating the mind and the body. But even when we're sending e-mails or engaging in virtual worlds, our bodies are still somewhere doing something. And these bodies are susceptible to germs, bacteria, viruses, and other contaminants. As much as we think of our selves as mental or psychological constructs, they are intricately connected to our bodies, bodies that feel the pleasures and pains of the physical worlds we live in and through. How much does your body play into the way you see your self and how others see you? Does your sense of self change when you're sick with a cold or are diagnosed with something more lasting and severe?

question. How we rely on one another to negotiate such situations in ways allowing us to preserve a positive self-image is, therefore, a problem of general sociological interest.

■ Conclusion

This chapter has examined several issues pertaining to definitions of health. We have seen that the term *health*, like any other symbolic construct, displays considerable variation in meanings across cultures. Based on such definitions, people's experiences of illness will differ as well. For example, how a person responds to pain is influenced by sociocultural factors, such as gender expectations. How individuals experience the health care system also differs according to social factors, in particular income and race or ethnicity. Having health insurance coverage is a key indicator of access to medical care. The rates of uninsured and underinsured people pose a concern in health care. Since interactions between patients and doctors constitute a prime arena in which health definitions are established, we devoted considerable attention to what happens when doctors and patients meet. We called attention to several features of medical practice, such as the briefness of typical office visits and the emphasis on biomedical rather than psychosocial issues—factors which play a role in the diagnostic process. Managed care is having a tremendous impact on patient–physician relationships, and the increasing use of alternative medicine may reflect a countertrend to the rise of managed care. The Internet is another factor with the potential to affect interaction between patients and health care providers.

We are particularly interested in the effect of illness on the self. In the last part of the chapter we examined the social construction of illness identities, focusing on clinical depression. The ambiguous nature of this ailment—its lack of clear "location" in either the body or the mind—makes the question of its meaning especially problematic. As we have argued throughout this book, people construct the meanings of their lives through ongoing conversations with others; in this sense, then, individuals experiencing depression are illustrating as well some of the generic features of how meanings are created.

In the final part of this book, we will devote our attention to the larger social contexts in which meanings are created. In the last three chapters we will deal with the themes of deviance, personal change, and social change. We will consider how everyday deviances upset the fragile order of everyday life. In addition, our treatment of the humanly constructed life cycle and the ongoing transformations of personal identity will locate changing social selves within the broad sweep of history.

Definitions

achieving a diagnosis: A process, often taking many years, during which people seek to acquire a clear definition of the illness from which they suffer. Being given an "official" diagnosis by medical experts is a critical benchmark in the process of defining oneself in terms of a particular illness.

biomedical model: The dominant therapeutic orientation in the United States, essentially disease-oriented or illness-oriented rather than patient-oriented. The key to effective medical care is believed to be correct diagnosis of some physiological aberration followed by proper application of the curative agent.

cultural construction: Social meanings created by people, which vary from one culture to another.

disease: A biological problem within an organism.

health maintenance organizations (HMOs): A form of managed care based on prepayment for health care by patients who agree to use member physicians and hospitals.

identity markers: Symbolic creations that serve to represent one's identity to others.

illness: The lived experience and social consequences of having a disease, discomfort, or pain.

illness ideologies: Explanatory schemes used to interpret and justify a particular diagnosis of what is "causing" an illness.

interpretive dilemma: A problem of meaning posed when a situation, such as illness, is intrinsically unclear. All life situations require human interpretation to endow them with meaning, and thus an interpretive dilemma is problematic.

managed care: A medical system in which physicians and hospitals contract with employers to cover the health care needs of employees for a fee agreed upon in advance.

medicalization: The process of legitimating medical control over an area of life, typically by asserting and establishing the primacy of a medical interpretation of that area.

moral entrepreneurs: People who are constantly on crusades to establish rules, implement them, and then label those who do not follow them as offenders.

morbidity: The amount of disease, impairment, and accident in a population.

mortality: The number of deaths in a population.

nature/nurture debate: A fundamental debate regarding explanation of virtually all human behaviors. The debate is whether human behavior is a product of *nature* (biology and genetic structure) or the result of *nurture* (cultural learning). The relative influences of nature and nurture in explaining psychiatric disorders are especially difficult to decipher.

negotiating social reality: The social process by which people communicate to one another a sense of what is "real."

psychosocial concerns: Problems of daily living, issues regarding social relations, feelings, and emotions.

stigma: An attribute that has a deeply discrediting effect on the individual who possesses it, reducing the individual from a whole, usual person to a tainted, discounted one. Erving Goffman (1963) identifies three types: abominations of the body—the various physical deformities; blemishes of individual character; and "tribal" stigmas of race, nation, and religion.

structural constraints: The ways in which the social organizational features of a setting or environment constrain and set limits on possible modes of behavior.

therapeutic culture: American society's disposition to think of an increasing range of human behaviors as expressing underlying psychological pathologies that should be treated by growing numbers of psychiatric experts. The term was first used by Philip Rieff (1966).

universe maintenance specialists: Those societal roles which allow the occupants to set norms defining what is to be considered proper, normal, and "healthy," as opposed to deviant, immoral, or "sick."

Discussion Questions

1. Do you think Americans are more, or less, concerned about their health than Europeans, for example, are? How would go about studying such an issue? What kinds of data sources would you look for?

2. What seems to be the key determinant of access to health care? Who is most likely to lack adequate access to health care?

3. Have you ever been hospitalized? If so, how were you treated and how did it make you feel? Specifically, what impact did it have on your *self*?

4. When being examined by a doctor, have you ever felt that there were communication problems during the examination? How did you address such problems? Are there things you would have liked to have said or done that you didn't do for some reason or another?

5. If you could design the "ideal" medical system in which patients would get the best health care possible, what would such a system look like?

6. Everyone feels "blue" from time to time. What, in your view, distinguishes those who simply feel bad because of some situation in their life and those who suffer from clinical depression? Have you ever felt bad enough to seek out the help of a psychiatric expert? If you did, how did that experience shape your definition of self? If you have never seen a psychiatrist or psychologist, do you have an image of people who are regularly involved in therapy, and if so, what sort of image?

PART THREE

DISORDER AND CHANGE
IN EVERYDAY LIFE

Perhaps the most fundamental sociological question is how order is possible in society. How society hangs together is an ongoing concern. So far in this book, we have focused on those features of social life that give it stability, predictability, and order. We would be theoretically shortsighted if we neglected the study of change and disorder in social life, however. While we have stressed the idea that human beings are symbolic animals who collectively give meaning to their worlds, it is also true that everyone does not abide by the same set of social rules or share the same significant symbols and social realities. Moreover, human beings and society are constantly changing. In part three it will become clear to you that the symbols and meanings which make a life coherent in certain circumstances may not "work" in others.

One source of disorder in social life is the fact that people break rules. Individuals who accidentally fail to follow social norms may experience embarrassment as the structure of social interaction is momentarily threatened, and their identities are called into question. As a result, they are likely to experience discomfort, dis-ease, and personal dis-order. In chapter 9 we will analyze how social encounters sometimes go awry and how people try to fix such fractured interactions.

Transgressions of cultural expectations also can have more serious consequences for individuals and society. Some people so consistently break the conventional rules of society that they are labeled as criminals or mentally ill, for example, and may seem to threaten social order to the extent that they are removed from society altogether. Chapter 9 will give you an understanding of how both everyday deviances and those that envelop a person's whole life can threaten the social order.

The social order is also continually subject to change, which is characteristic of the entire life cycle from birth to death. Each significant point in the life cycle, such as childhood, adolescence, middle age, and old age, requires the adoption of new roles, statuses, and identities. Chapter 10 will explore the meanings people confer on the process of aging throughout the course of their lives.

In the analysis of aging, we will examine processes of change at two levels. Not only do people change as they move from one age status to another, but aging must also be understood within the context of broader cultural, structural, and historical changes. For example, the meanings given to different age categories (such as middle or old age) certainly are not the same now as they were at the turn of the twentieth century. Purely from a statistical point of view, the significance attached to age categories varies with such demographic factors as the number of people falling into each age category and changes in life expectancy. Structural changes such as these result in changing interpretations of specific phases of the life cycle. The theoretical perspective of symbolic interaction also emphasizes how people occupying different locations in society experience aging differently. Chapter 10 will help you see, for example, how occupational careers structure the way people think about aging, and how the power positions of women compared to men influence the social process of aging.

Discussions of both deviance and aging should lead you to think about how individuals deal with disorder and change in their lives. Both involve the analysis of identity change. The most powerful kind of personal dislocation, however, results when people become uncertain of their identities, when they have trouble answering the question—Who am I?

Questions of personal identity are linked to broad historical changes in society. In simpler preurban societies, the question of identity raised no problems. People had little difficulty knowing who they were, and battalions of psychiatric experts and talk-show hosts did not exist to help them "find themselves." Numerous social scientists have observed that one of the most dramatic consequences of industrialization has been the rapid, widespread increase in geographical and social mobility for large segments of the population. The sense of rootlessness which often accompanies industrialization has led to enormous concern with questions of identity, self-worth, alienation, and the larger significance of life. In the final chapter of this book, you will learn how the issue of personal identity has been brought to the forefront of contemporary consciousness in the Western world.

9

Deviance

Imagine that you have made an appointment with your sociology professor to discuss a term paper. Because your meeting extends through the lunch hour, the professor takes out a brown-bag lunch and, shortly after, a smear of ketchup adorns the professor's cheek. Now you have a bit of a problem on your hands. How should you deal with this situation? A little thought suggests that all of the choices open to you pose difficulties. You could immediately interrupt the conversation and inform the professor of the smear, but such communications are typically reserved for intimates, such as a wife or husband. Your second alternative is to pretend that there is nothing wrong about the situation and hope that the professor will wipe off the smear in the normal course of things. This strategy also involves some risk, however. The situation might be punctured by the appearance of a colleague who would immediately remark on the professor's social blunder. Then the professor would realize that you had known about it for some time and had pretended not to see it. The professor's discovery of the smear under this circumstance could heighten the discomfort felt by everyone in the room.

Social life abounds with similar situations in which people's behaviors or presentations of self somehow harm or compromise the identities they are trying to present. These situations may make them appear to be wrong, incorrect, improper, or possibly even immoral, and they may feel awkward, uneasy, or embarrassed as a result. In some situations a person's presented self or identity becomes so compromised or tainted that the result is a fractured interaction. The social situation may even completely break down. In this sense everyday life is risky because of the ever-present possibility that events will make a person "look bad." Even in the most routine encounters we may be defined by others as improper, nonsocial, or deviant.

■ Everyday Deviances and Deviant Careers

In this chapter we are departing momentarily from conventional discussions of deviance, which typically address such issues as various kinds of criminal behavior, delinquency, drug use, prostitution, and mental illness. These are broad, **lifestyle deviances** that effectively involve people in lifelong deviant careers. The causes and solutions of many of these types of behavior, the extent of the harm they do, and what can be done about them are controversial (Curra, 2000). Individuals who behave in these ways are considered deviant when they are labeled as such by those in positions of power in the society. In the second part of this chapter we will consider how and why people become involved in deviant subcultures. Before that, however, we will analyze the **everyday deviances**—the occasional improprieties that temporarily mark certain individuals as somehow nonconforming, awkward, or improper.

The interactionist perspective on deviance differs from the traditional sociological definition of deviance as violation of the social order, in that the focus is on the *meaning* of an act as deviant or not—that is, deviance is a matter of *negotiation* and social definition, not something inherent in a particular act or behavior. Circumstances clearly affect the meanings of various acts in the eyes of those involved, both offenders and observers. A classic definition by Edwin Schur illustrates that deviance is a matter of degree, not an all-or-none classification. Behavior is deviant to the extent that it comes to be viewed as involving a personally discreditable departure from a group's normative expectations, and it elicits interpersonal or collective reactions that serve to "isolate," "treat," "correct," or "punish" individuals engaged in such behavior (1971:24).

The interactionist perspective on deviance is based on the premise that the meaning of an act as deviant or not is contained in the social response it produces rather than merely in the act itself. This reflects the symbolic interactionist view we have used throughout the book that objects take on meaning according to how people act toward them. Deviance remains a vital and relevant subject of study because, as Patricia and Peter Adler (2006) claim, we now live in a "deviant society":

> Deviance is all around us. It is ubiquitous. Now, more than ever, we see a barrage of case studies that stretch our imaginations of how far deviance can go, how far beyond the evolving limits of human (in)capacity this technologically advanced, warp speed society can take us. . . . Whether it be tattoos, cigarettes, new drugs, creative forms of sex, or multibillion dollar fraud widely perpetrated, people incorporate these new forms of behavior into their repertoire and accept (or reject) the creativity of the human soul for expanding the boundaries of normative behavior. As Frank Zappa, a cultural icon from the '60s used to say, "Without deviation from the norm, progress is not possible." This is heady stuff, and speaks to the heart of the sociological enterprise. Deviance is not marginal, it is central to what we do. (2006:131–32)

Whenever people make judgments about others' behaviors or identities, deviance is relevant. When certain acts are labeled as "deviant," such deviant acts often reflect negatively on the identities of those who engage in them. The response of others to an individual's perceived deviance often has tremendous impact on how these individuals see themselves. Responses set the "deviant" individual apart from others and subject him or her to differential treatment, often negative. This social treatment establishes and sometimes controls the identities of those who are labeled deviant (Hewitt and Shulman, 2010:245).

The principal characteristic of most everyday deviances is that they may be unsettling or embarrassing, but they mar a person's identity only momentarily. Embarrassment may cause only limited discomfort, or it can be so intense that it disrupts an interaction. Much of the intensity level depends on the context and the social actors within it. Later in the chapter we will discuss the process of labeling and deviant careers.

Everyday deviances are far less dramatic than those that envelop a person's whole life. After all, we are not thrown in jail for embarrassing ourselves. Nevertheless, it is important to study everyday deviances to understand how society hangs together. While in a statistical sense few people are involved in lifelong deviant careers, everyone must continually create, sustain, and repair the social interactions that comprise everyday life. A key assumption of this book is that any theoretical conception of how a society operates must begin with an understanding of how the everyday, face-to-face encounters of its members are ordered.

Our interactions are inherently fragile things, easily disrupted by inappropriate remarks, improper displays of emotionalism, lack of bodily control, and the like. Further, there is a deep morality in everyday life, which requires efforts to protect both our own and others' identities in our interactions. In those instances where our selves—and thus our social situations—are somehow tarnished, we are charged with the responsibility of setting things right. People who have been properly socialized know how to improve situations when there is the perception that they have done something embarrassing or somehow wrong. To shed some light on how and why encounters sometimes go awry and how people try to fix fractured interactions, we will consider the nature of embarrassment and its relation to roles, identities, and social organization.

■ Embarrassment and Social Organization

If a social scientist wants to know what normally keeps a social system in balance—that is, in **social equilibrium**—it is a good strategy to examine what happens when that equilibrium is disturbed. **Embarrassment**, one such disturbance, arises out of individuals' knowledge that others are evaluating them negatively. This knowledge can produce feelings of social discomfort great enough to impede a person's thought, speech, and action, making it difficult or impossible to continue an interaction. By showing what happens in these circumstances, studies of embarrassment can reveal a good deal about the social order and the basic requirements of successful role performance.

While we all know from experience what constitutes an embarrassing situation, those social scientists who have written on the subject recognize that there is a cluster of emotions and experiences that overlap each other. When you think deeply about the meaning of embarrassment, it becomes necessary to consider just how embarrassment is to be distinguished from shyness, shame, or generalized social anxiety, for example. Analysis of each of these social and emotional states is not simply an exercise in semantics but is necessary as part of the process of thinking through just what precipitates each of them and how people remedy the problems each creates.

It seems immediately clear that the distinguishing characteristic of embarrassment in contrast to shyness, for example, is that the latter characterizes a person whereas the former is the product of social interaction (Crozier, 1990). People are shy; awkward social situations create embarrassment. Shyness is most closely associated with a lack of social self-confidence, expressed in low self-esteem in social situations and concern about lack of social skills. "Shy people lack confidence about their ability to know what to say to people or how to manage a social situation. This is much more important for their shyness than fear of being negatively evaluated by others" (Crozier, 2001:175). Lack of self-confidence, or self-competence, was a key finding in Susie Scott's (2005) analysis of self-defined shy persons. Her research participants "indicated that shyness involved feeling that they were less socially skilled and poised for interaction than those around them: they felt unable to grasp the script that other people seemed to be using" (p. 93). They felt that others were more equipped than they were to deal with social encounters, which lead many of them to seek isolation rather than interaction in their daily lives.

A common observation in almost all shyness research is that the consequences of shyness are deeply troubling (see box on the next page). Shy individuals don't take advantage of social situations, they date less, they are less expressive verbally and nonverbally, and they experience more loneliness than do nonshy people. Extreme shyness that continues into later years can result in chronic social isolation that leads to increasingly severe loneliness and related psychopathology, even to chronic illness and a shorter life span (Henderson et al., 1999).

The linkage between embarrassment and shame seems somewhat closer in that both states eventuate from an individual's recognition that he or she has visibly broken social rules that cast doubt on the adequacy of his or her identity. Until the late 20th century, the view was that embarrassment is a less intense degradation of self than shame (embarrassment as a mild form of shame). According to this view, embarrassment normally involves relatively trivial breaches of social rules and the person breaking the rules is not seen as having done it on purpose. Shame results when the rules broken are seen as more serious and when the actor is viewed as having had control over the rule-breaking behavior. (We are thought less personally responsible for dropping a bowl of soup in our lap than for having knowingly cheated on a college examination.) There is intuitive appeal to the idea that embarrassment is weak, whereas shame is strong; however, more recent data suggest, contrary to the traditional view, that shame and embarrassment are distinct emotions (see box on p. 261), and do not differ simply in intensity (Keltner and Buswell, 1997; Tangney et al., 1996).

The Shyness Institute

The Shyness Institute is a nonprofit research corporation founded in 1994 and dedicated to research on shyness, social phobia, and related anxiety disorders. Its codirectors are Lynne Henderson and Philip Zimbardo, the latter perhaps best known for the infamous Stanford prison experiment (Zimbardo, 1986). Designed to examine the effects of social roles on the person, the mock-prison study revealed sadistic behavior on the part of the "guards," while "prisoners" relinquished basic human rights and demonstrated anxiety, depression, and sleep disturbances (Henderson, 1999). In Zimbardo's words, "good boys" were transformed into "evil guards" and "healthy boys into pathological prisoners" (Zimbardo, 1999). One of Zimbardo's students noted the similarity between these dynamics and those experienced by the problematically shy; that is, the problematically shy person submits to critical and authoritarian aspects of the self and others, and he or she becomes unduly compliant or avoidant (Henderson, 1999).

This finding led Zimbardo to conduct research on shyness, a topic he continues to pursue into the 21st century. In the late 20th century he focused on explaining the apparent increase in shyness. His research at a half dozen colleges in the 1990s found that more than 50 percent of individuals were willing to label themselves as shy, compared to 40 percent a decade earlier. Zimbardo attributed this increase to two factors: (1) the negative impact of all the then-new technology on social behavior (yes, the Internet), and (2) changes in the social structure of families, in part influenced by the undermining of family life by the intrusion of work into private time. In terms of technology, Zimbardo stated:

> As technology insidiously invades every aspect of our lives, it makes us passive reactors to virtual reality, eliminating human face-to-face reality wherever possible. Technology and the affluence associated with it generally isolates people from other people.... It replaces service personnel with computer chips that are cheaper and more efficient.... It replaces shopping in book stores and retail stores with web buying. It replaces playing in the streets with friends with watching kids play on TV or with video game characters or with chat room conversations. It replaces conversations and schmoozing with friends and colleagues with efficient information exchanges via e-mail.... There is the illusion of interaction with electronic mail exchanges, but it is an illusion. (1999:15–16)

Zimbardo argued that the increasing amount of time spent in social isolation engaging in technological activities decreases social opportunities, taking time away from human contact. As a result, young people are not doing the things necessary to learn the basic and complex skills involved in social interaction. The lack of these basic social skills promotes feelings of shyness. Older people who may not have been shy are now beginning to feel awkward in face-to-face conversations because they are becoming acclimated to the ease and comfort of electronic communication. (Admit it—don't you sometimes prefer e-mail and text messaging to talking with an actual person?)

In addition, smaller families, single-parent families, dual-earner families, mobile families, lack of nearby extended family, taking work home, working longer hours, commuting longer distances, fear of crime in the streets—all these factors combine to reduce opportunities to practice being a social animal, for both kids and grown-ups. Perhaps that's why Zimbardo came to regard shyness as an index of social pathology; that is, the extent of shyness in society may be an index of the degree to which there is a disruption in the bonds that form the human connection. Zimbardo expressed the following concern:

> If shyness has increased by 10 percent in the last decade so that at least half of our population are willing to label themselves as shy, that is cause for alarm. It is an epidemic in the making, a silent one, which makes it all the more terrifying to me. The social forces and technological takeover of our lives will grow greater in the coming years. What does that tell us about the spread of shyness and the loss of the human connection? (1999:17)

You can visit the Shyness Institute's website at http://www.shyness.com.

In general, Tangney and colleagues' (1996) findings were that embarrassing events were lighthearted, things at which the participants wanted to laugh and at which they thought others would laugh. Shameful events differed in that participants expected no one to laugh at those events. Shamed individuals felt more responsibility and regret, more anger and disgust with themselves, and believed that others, too, felt anger toward them. Keltner and Buswell (1997) concluded that although embarrassment and shame are similar in important ways, they differ in that embarrassment follows from violations of conventions, whereas shame follows from the violation of moral rules. However, a study designed to test these ideas did not find support for the moral-conventional distinction (Sabini et al., 2001). Rather, those authors suggested that embarrassment involves an *apparent flaw of character*—of the self—rather than a mild, real flaw. Slipping on an icy side-

Embarrassed? Or Ashamed?

People do not seem to have much difficulty recalling events that caused them to experience shame and embarrassment. In a study in which participants were asked to produce events that made them feel shame, embarrassment, or guilt, the 51 participants came up with 757 events (Keltner and Buswell, 1997). Social life is very precarious! The most common triggers of embarrassment were: (1) physical pratfalls, e.g., slipping on ice, (2) cognitive shortcomings, e.g., forgetting someone's name, (3) loss of control over the body, e.g., burping out loud, (4) shortcomings in physical appearance, e.g., walking around with toilet paper stuck to one's shoe, and (5) failure at privacy regulation, e.g., accidentally walking in on others having sex. Shame, on the other hand, was most commonly caused by (1) poor performance, (2) hurting others emotionally, (3) failing to meet others' expectations, (4) disappointment in oneself, and (5) role-inappropriate behavior. It seems that people are able to distinguish between the two emotions, and the appraisals involved in embarrassment and shame are of different kinds of failings.

In other studies (e.g., Sabini et al., 2001), students were asked to imagine scenarios and indicate whether they would feel shame or embarrassment (and to what degree). Try some of these yourself:

1. You are attending a formal party at your boss's house. Everyone present is prominent in your workplace as well as your community. After getting a cup of punch, you head for the patio. As you stride toward the group outside, you slam into the sliding glass door that you thought was open, spilling the drink all over you. You hear the muted laughter, and a few people ask you if you are all right.

2. Your professor has agreed to give the class a take-home essay exam, provided you won't discuss the exam with anyone. Your roommate is in the same class and has already written the test by Sunday afternoon. You start Sunday evening and cannot come up with anything intelligent to say. You glance over at your roommate's desk and see the completed paper. Because you are suffering from a block, you look at the answers and copy some of them, rewording them as best you can. You hand in the exam the next day. A few days later, the professor calls you into his/her office and tells you that he/she knows you have cheated and that you may be expelled.

Think about the most recent event in your life when you experienced shame or embarrassment. When it happened, you probably didn't analyze it in these terms, but think about it now—did you feel shame, or was it embarrassment?

walk, for example, is not a violation of convention but a failure of a different sort, of motor control. In fact, these sorts of events are often funny in retrospect in part because they typically do not reveal serious flaws of the self. The implications of the event depend not on the behavior per se but on what the behavior says, or seems to say, about the self. In the study authors' words, "Although being drunk once does not necessarily reveal a serious flaw of character, being discovered to be an alcoholic is a serious matter. Accidentally walking in on someone having sexual intercourse is embarrassing, whereas being caught at being a peeping Tom cannot be laughed off" (Sabini et al., 2001:112).

Although embarrassing acts do not usually reveal seriously flawed selves, they *could* do so. John Sabini, Brian Garvey, and Amanda Hall (2001) suggested that a person experiencing intense embarrassment is "at the moment of pain oriented toward the implication for his or herself that might be drawn from the infelicitous act; it is this serious flaw of self that accounts for the intensity of the affect" (p. 112). They take seriously the notion that people laugh at their embarrassments—people do tell funny stories about how they were embarrassed. An important point is that *telling* the story allows one to show the audience "that you are an okay person, despite this incident" (p. 112).

Generally, the type of embarrassment discussed thus far is triggered by some social blunder. A fuller account of embarrassment would be as follows:

> Embarrassment always involves a dramaturgic failing, an inability to continue to present oneself to an audience as the person one has been taken to be. It always involves flustering and inhibition. This dramaturgic trouble can be provoked by several things: *faux pas*, sticky situations, or simply being the center of attention, for example. When the embarrassment involves a flaw of some sort, then the person experiencing the flustered, painful state also may describe himself or herself as experiencing shame. In so doing, the subject of the painful experience concedes that the apparent flaw revealed is real; characterizing the experience as embarrassment, on the other hand, does not concede the presence of a real flaw. (Sabini et al., 2001:113)

These authors believe that the emotional state that underlies both embarrassment and shame fundamentally has to do with self-presentation. We need to refrain from doing things that make us look bad regardless of whether the appearance is real or illusory. It's all about breakdowns in self-presentation. It doesn't matter "whether the breakdown is the consequence of a real flaw or an apparent flaw or somebody else's flaw" (p. 113).

Whereas embarrassment is a response to a self-presentational failure (real or imagined), social anxiety is anticipatory in nature, arising out of concern that one may not make a desired impression on others (Leary and Kowalski, 1995). People have many good reasons to be concerned with how others perceive them, and it is not unreasonable to sometimes become worried about others' reactions. People become socially anxious not only when they are currently being evaluated but also when the possibility or prospect of interpersonal evaluation exists. In fact, people may become anxious about social interactions that are entirely imagined rather than real: "We may become as distressed about an encounter that we imagine *might* happen as a real social situation. . . . Other people need not actually be present, except in the person's mind" (Leary and Kowalski, 1995:6).

When Social Performances Fail

Although we could continue to analyze the subtle ways in which the related concepts of embarrassment, shyness, shame, and social anxiety differ from one another, we do better at this point to consider that all suggest in common a potential or actual social performance failure. In this regard, we should recognize that the dramaturgical perspective on interaction outlined in chapter 3 provides a useful framework for viewing the nature of embarrassment and the measures required to prevent it and then deal with it when it occurs. You should recall that according to Erving Goffman's classical model of impression management, we all feel obliged to put on performances that will gain the approval of the audience in front of whom we are behaving. Goffman himself notes in one of the earliest and still most important analyses of embarrassment:

> Whatever else, embarrassment has to do with the figure the individual cuts before others felt to be there at the time. The crucial concern is the impression one makes on others in the present—whatever the long range or unconscious basis of this concern may be. (1956:265)

At the heart of the matter of embarrassment is that we care deeply about the images we present to other people and the opinions they have of those images. Central to the symbolic interactionist view of the self is the idea that self-feelings, including embarrassment, come from the way we believe our performances are being evaluated by some audience. Embarrassment arises when there is a discrepancy between the nature and quality of performance we believe some audience expects of us and the actual quality of the performance we have put on. Of course, embarrassment arises when we feel (often incorrectly) that our actual performance falls short of the standard we believe some audience expects. We might note in this regard that shyness may be understood as reflecting a person's belief that he or she is likely to fail to meet an audience's expectations even before that person enters a social situation. The person who is shy expects to fail at meeting approved standards and responds by avoiding many social situations altogether, or, when in them, by interacting as little as possible with others. As the **self-fulfilling prophecy** suggests, the belief that one will put on a faulty performance magnifies the likelihood that the performance will actually be faulty: "A perceived inability to socialize by shy individuals, along with a pessimistic outlook for social interactions, becomes an excuse for anticipated failure and a self-handicapping strategy (e.g., 'I can't do it because I am shy')" (Henderson et al., 1999:3).

Drawing inspiration from the idea that embarrassment arises out of problems of impression management, Robert Edelman suggested that five factors are critical in the emergence of feelings of embarrassment (1987:119):

1. An ability to understand that one is a social object with an outward appearance to others.

2. An ability to see from someone else's viewpoint that impression-management styles influence the way in which the individual is perceived.

3. Knowledge of what constitutes acceptable behavior within a given culture or setting.

4. An ability to understand that changes in appearance can be conveyed by various impression-management strategies.

5. An ability to understand that one can make inferences about others on the basis of appearance.

These ideas conform to another principle of symbolic interaction theory that we have proposed over and again in this volume. It is that the meanings of behavior are bound to particular contexts and situations. In the context of the present discussion, this means that the perception of a behavior as causing embarrassment may differ from setting to setting. A wonderful example of this principle is afforded by an early study by Martin Weinberg (1965) on the nature of sexual modesty in nudist camps. He provides persuasive evidence that nudists behave in accordance with social norms that sustain modesty despite their total disregard for body covering, a situation where modesty might seem highly unlikely. The embarrassment that ordinarily accompanies such exposure is prevented by rules that desexualize the body. There are taboos against staring or otherwise showing overinvolvement with another person's body, any form of bodily contact, attempts to cover areas of the body, and unnecessary accentuation of the body. The strictly enforced rules of the nudist camp prevented rampant sexual interest, promiscuity, embarrassment, jealousy, and shame, and sustained a nudist morality. Of particular interest here is Weinberg's observation that inadvertently *leaving on* an article of clothing becomes a source of embarrassment in this context. He described one woman who reported being embarrassed when she removed her clothes but forgot to take off her bra and people laughed at her.

The situational character of embarrassment extends to the idea that people are more or less susceptible to that emotion at various points in the life cycle. It comes as no surprise that adolescence is a time during which even the slightest sense that one might appear "incorrect" in front of one's peers engenders powerful feelings of embarrassment. This finding is understandable in light of the fact that adolescence is a moment in the life cycle during which an answer to the question "Who am I?" is far from certain. Adolescence is a time during which boys and girls are for the first time trying out a number of new social roles and statuses, such as dating, which may not feel totally comfortable to them. At just the moment that their bodies are undergoing substantial changes, physical appearance becomes precisely the central criterion against which they evaluate their own and others' social value. The point is that uncertainty about self engendered by bewildering social and physical change in a context of high social risk makes the task of putting on acceptable social performances highly problematic: "Altogether, huge new predicaments must be mastered just as social acceptance and approval become especially consequential. If God wanted to create a perfect recipe for embarrassment, the teen years might be it" (Miller, 1996:87).

Very young children, on the other hand, do not appear to experience embarrassment. Although the precise time at which embarrassment emerges continues to be a matter of debate (some say it appears as early as 18 months; others argue that children are 10 years old before they are likely to experience mature embarrassment), "it seems clear that there are no signs whatsoever of embarrassment in young children until they become self-conscious" (Miller, 1996:78). As we learned in an earlier chapter, self-consciousness emerges during the second or third year. However, there may be more than self-consciousness involved for embarrassment to occur. Embarrassment requires recognition of what *others* are thinking of us. Young children have difficulty imagining others' thoughts or feelings, and thus these children are "unlikely to be embarrassed by the possibility of negative evaluations from others unless the audience makes its disapproval plain" (p. 89), which suggests that "the development of embarrassment is a single continuous process that gradually results in increasingly sophisti-cated emotion as perspective-taking ability improves" (p. 86). By the time you reach college, you are embarrassed, on average, more than once a week! (Stonehouse and Miller, 1994).

Other situational factors that influence the likelihood that people will have greater anxiety over the adequacy of their social performance include the size and status of the audience. If you have ever had to make public pre-sentations of one sort or another, you probably can attest to the truth of the hypothesis that nervousness increases as the audience grows in size and expertise concerning the subject matter of the presentation. Your authors feel safe in saying, for example, that college professors worry more about being embarrassed when presenting a paper at a professional meeting than in their day-to-day teaching performances in front of undergraduate students.

In the study by June Price Tangney and associates (1996), participants (undergrads) reported that embarrassment occurred in front of larger audi-ences more often than did shame and guilt (on average, 6.8 people, com-pared with about 2.0 people) and that they experienced embarrassment more frequently around strangers and acquaintances rather than friends. They also reported that embarrassment was less likely to occur when they were alone, compared with shame and guilt. The authors, following Goff-man, concluded that embarrassment, more so than shame and guilt, occurs during public, impersonal interactions and seems to implicate the "outer," or public, self rather than the "inner," or private, self.

Earlier we observed that embarrassment is lodged in social situations rather than in individuals. In this regard embarrassment is not only costly to

the individual whose identity, honor, or coolness has been compromised. It also is contagious and has the potential of enveloping the whole situation in which it occurs. All interactions are joint ventures, joint actions. People become embarrassed within some social context that involves other people who recognize the embarrassment and must somehow deal with it. Embarrassment thus affects not only the person who is embarrassed; it is shared by all those who are parties to the encounter. The good news is that recent studies have found that this feeling of mutual embarrassment—for oneself and for the other—is a positive sign of civility and caring for strangers (Simpson and Willer, 2008; Feinberg et al., 2012).

We share the embarrassment felt by others; we blush at their blushing and we feel embarrassed for their embarrassment. When the self of any one person in a situation is threatened or discredited, the selves of all those involved become implicated. Further, if others who observe an embarrassing act do not handle it well—in a tactful fashion—they may increase the discomfort felt by all. According to Goffman, each participant in an interaction must honor the selves presented by all the other participants. If a participant is discredited, he says:

> By the standards of the wider society, perhaps only the discredited individual ought to feel ashamed; but, by the standards of the little social system maintained through interaction, the discreditor is just as guilty as the person he [or she] discredits. . . . This is why embarrassment seems to be contagious, spreading, once started, in ever-widening circles of discomfiture. (1967:106)

Thus far we have mostly emphasized the negative consequences of embarrassment. However, embarrassment also can have positive functions as a form of **social control**. To be sure, we need only consider what a society would look like in which people were "beyond embarrassment." It would likely be a society where the only source of social order would be the threat of force. A more powerful source of social control is that which comes from within a person who has internalized social rules.

Casual observation indicates that people may be deliberately embarrassed in order to socialize or train them to put on a poised performance. One form of this training is the practical jokes children play on one another and their other attempts to cause their friends to "lose face." Teenagers, too, frequently engage in competitive testing encounters designed to assert their own superiority and skillfulness in maintaining personal honor. Deliberate embarrassment also can keep group members in line. For adolescents especially, any deviation from what is "cool" provokes enough teasing and joking to ensure a return to accepted standards (Geraghty, 1997). Ironically, being "cool," especially for teenagers, is about expressing "resistance to established authorities or conventional customs and involves the creation of a set of alternative or counter norms" (Milner, 2004:59). Not so ironically, failing to adhere to these new norms can lead to embarrassment because the supposed "cool kids" will be apt to notice and announce such violations.

This type of embarrassment, called *strategic embarrassment*, occurs when a person intentionally makes a comment or points out a flaw for the sole purpose of embarrassing someone else. It acts as a form of social control and is often used to encourage conformity, according to Sandra Petronio, who has studied this topic extensively (as reported in Geraghty, 1997). Another example of strategic embarrassment occurs when newspapers publish names of "deadbeat dads" (fathers who have fallen behind in their child-support payments), which puts them on the spot in the community and indicates they have done something the community believes is inappropriate.

Petronio found that people are constantly embarrassing one another in various situations, without always thinking about the effect their actions will have on the person who is embarrassed. If you are unaccustomed to playful chiding and enter a conversation in which this occurs, it can seem like a personal attack. If others who are watching the interaction think the embarrasser is out of line, then the embarrasser becomes the embarrassed one. According to Petronio, this makes strategic embarrassment tricky, best used "among equals, among friends—people who understand the game" (quoted in Geraghty, 1997:A8). And this becomes even trickier with so much communication taking place via computer-mediated communication channels, whether through e-mail, text messages, or social media sites. Tone and other cues we find during face-to-face interactions are absent in computer-mediated communication, which can lead to both interactional problems and miscommunication as well as concerns about privacy. When posting to an Internet site or forum, even one that is *supposedly* private, messages can reach or be found by unintended audiences, leaving the poster embarrassed or, in the case of some employees, without a job (Pinch, 2010; Agger, 2015).

If, as we maintain, the loss of personal honor and a valued identity is a source of great discomfort for individuals, we should expect that people will routinely organize their lives to reduce the likelihood of being embarrassed.

Just as we are expected to engage in preventive measures to avoid physical disease, we should not be surprised that people are normally careful to control features of the social environment that pose the greatest threats to failed role performances. In one of the first studies of embarrassment and the social requirements of successful role performances, Edward Gross and Gregory Stone tried to clarify "the structure of transactions where identities have been misplaced or forgotten, where poise has been lost or destroyed, or where, for any reason, confidence that identities and poise will be maintained has been undermined" (1964:2). Their analysis suggests that prevention of embarrassment and smooth role performances require control over the space surrounding interactions, the props we use in self presentations, and our bodies.

Efforts to Avoid Embarrassment: Controlling Space, Props, and Bodies

One source of embarrassment involves people's errors in occupying spaces or territories where they do not belong. An obvious example would be a man accidentally entering a women's restroom, or vice versa. In American society there are clear norms governing who should be doing what and *where*. The where is critical because roles performed properly in one context may injure a person's identity when performed in another one. The boundaries of space or areas within which interactions take place may be more or less sharply defined. When the bounds are overstepped, embarrassment, signaling a loss of poise, is likely to result.

The meaning and significance of role performances are defined by the context in which they take place. It is impossible to know the meaning of behavior or acts apart from the situations in which they occur. Some actions are restricted to particular settings. People are expected to act on their sexuality in private spaces, for example. Onlookers may feel discomfited by lovers who kiss passionately in a public place. Indeed, the bedroom has symbolic significance in American society because it is recognized as a place where people put on performances that reveal "deep" aspects of themselves. The bathroom, similarly, has been institutionalized as a "back region." Bedrooms and bathrooms are among the few places in American society where you can legitimately lock yourself in. In these two contexts people engage in behaviors which, if they could be seen, might not be in accord with the impressions of the selves they normally try to present.

The adequacy of a role performance may be determined by who controls the space or the situation. Because teachers control classroom spaces, students often experience a heightened sense of self-awareness in this context. Those who are late to class may be profusely apologetic about the impropriety they think they have committed. They feel embarrassed even though the teacher may attach little significance to the event, though some instructors may publicly embarrass latecomers, while still others may impose grade reductions. People may lose their poise when they act out of place or accidentally invade spaces where they feel they do not belong.

The props used in carrying off interactions are a second component of self and situation that must be controlled to protect identity and maintain poise. Spaces are filled with objects that frame interactions. Rooms are filled with furniture, rugs, paintings, mirrors, room dividers, stairways, and the like. Normally, these props stand unobtrusively in the shadows of interactions, but they can affect the chances that an interaction will be successful. Furniture may be rearranged to improve communication at a party, for example, and grocery store displays are artfully constructed to prompt impulse buying.

Whereas most props facilitate transactions, a prop failure can also stop an interaction in its tracks, casting doubt on the intentions, motives, or capacities of the participants. The candles, pillows, and soft music props in a single person's place may be so overdone that they provoke a date to laughter rather than inspiring the intended mood of sensuality. Props cause embarrassment most often when people lose control over them, as when someone stumbles over a rug or trips on a flight of steps. Often, through no fault of our own, objects or pieces of equipment cause disruptions that prove embarrassing. Bowling balls are unceremoniously dropped, cars become stalled in dense traffic, food accidentally spills in laps, teachers lose their grip on erasers so that they fly across the room and land on a student's desk! Much slapstick humor, like that in the Marx Brothers, Charlie Chaplin, Jim Carrey, or Melissa McCarthy movies, is built around the awkwardness created by prop failures. The humor works because it exaggerates the misadventures that could befall anyone, as the following classic comic incident illustrates:

> At a formal dinner, a speaker was discovered with his fly zipper undone. On being informed of this embarrassing oversight after he was reseated, he proceeded to make the requisite adjustment, unknowingly catching the tablecloth in his trousers. When obliged to rise again at the close of the proceeding, he took the stage props with him and, of course, scattered the dinner tools about the setting in such a way that others were forced to doubt his control. His poise was lost in the situation. (Gross and Stone, 1964:10)

Clothing, another prop, was described in chapter 3 as a significant feature of the self we present. This prop must be carefully maintained, controlled, and arranged. As a prop, clothing is a direct extension of a person's body. Sometimes our clothes fail us, spoiling the presentation we intend to give. Rowland Miller describes the predicament of a woman waiting to cross a wide, busy street:

> She was running a bit late, and in her haste to get dressed she had donned an old maternity slip that was now too big for her. When the traffic finally came to a stop and she started across, the top of the slip slid down to her thighs. After a few more steps, it was around her knees, and moments later, around her ankles. Rather than stop in front of five lanes of traffic to adjust the slip, or even gather it up, she decided, in the heat of embarrassment, to just step out of the slip and keep going. She shook

her feet free, pulled her umbrella down around her face, picked up her pace, and left the slip lying in the street, a wasted garment and a sodden symbol of embarrassment. (1996:3)

Finally, whether or not we will be regarded as proper people depends in large measure on the appearance of our bodies and the control we can exercise over them. Our bodies are monitored by others as a check on our internal feelings. Trembling hands, profuse sweating, dilated pupils, blushing, stuttering, turning pale, and involuntary breaks in the voice are among the body gestures that may belie our efforts to appear in charge of ourselves and situations. In extreme cases, complete loss of body control incapacitates further interaction, as when a person gives way to emotionalism, "floods out," or expresses violent anger or fear. Flatulence, drooling, involuntary urination, and other losses of visceral control can cause deep embarrassment. People who are physically handicapped or who have permanent disfigurements or disabilities face unique contingencies in interaction with "normals" (Goffman's [1963] term). Unlike others whose settings, props, and bodies might only infrequently fail them and cause embarrassment, those with permanent body impairments must adopt strategies to convince others they should not be defined as deviant in every social encounter. Disfigurement causes one to be discredited as a fully functioning individual. There is an assumption that something is wrong with you based on your body image (Goffman, 1963). People with disabilities present an image that differs from the perceived norm, defined in terms of being "able-bodied" (Oliver, 1996).

A central task of the person who has a physical handicap and who is widely regarded as disabled is dealing with the nondisabled. In most cases, people with disabilities see themselves as being fundamentally no different from others. However, this perception raises conflict when the social meaning of disability as a symbol dominates, with its view that disabilities are related to dependency, deficiency, and inability (Oliver, 1996). In public places, people with disabilities often adopt a series of strategies to both symbolically and physically "armor" themselves against both symbolic and physical threats (Gardner and Gronfein, 2012). Using "body armor" is a means for restoring damaged identities, the subject of the next section.

■ Restoring Identities Damaged by Deviance

We have seen that every interaction is inherently risky because everyday deviances can threaten a person's identity and poise and can paralyze role performance efforts. The embarrassment that results—often producing a fractured interaction—is hardly a trivial outcome. To maintain the integrity and order of society, there is a moral imperative that calls for efforts to salvage identities under assault and to save situations threatening to break apart. These efforts are part of the unwritten social contract underlying social life. All social life may be viewed as a kind of social bargain in which we agree to protect one another so that social life will proceed smoothly.

The protection of identities is a major concern in everyday encounters. Participants maneuver to achieve a valued identity for themselves but also try to conduct themselves so that others' identities are protected. Goffman (1955) introduced the concept of *face-work*, defined in terms of the strategies used to cope with interactional difficulties. Two broad categories may be distinguished: *preventive practices*, wherein the actor takes some action to avert threats to identity; and *corrective practices*, wherein remedial action is taken after a disruption. When events occur that openly damage the identity of one or more of the people involved in an interaction, it signals the need for what might be termed **face games**. The purpose of such transactions is to "save face," or repair identities that have been damaged. A face game can restore a situation to what it was before the intrusion of an unwelcome event or normalize a situation that has become abnormal.

Sometimes the events disrupting a situation are relatively slight, and the situation can be normalized easily and quickly. As an example, suppose you inadvertently belch loudly at a lecture. The process of identity restoration begins when others acknowledge the impropriety, perhaps by glancing at you momentarily. You then try to remedy the situation immediately by offering an apology, bowing your head slightly, covering your mouth with a hand, and uttering a quick "Excuse me." With these gestures you are in effect communicating: "I know that I did something wrong and I am acknowledging it. I am trying to show you that I am, in fact, a proper person who wishes to abide by the rules. Having done this I expect that you will readmit me to this situation with an identity that is once more intact." It is necessary to go through this brief social ritual in order to restore equilibrium to the situation. Goffman referred to "the sequence of acts set in motion by an acknowledged threat to face, and terminating in the reestablishment of ritual equilibrium," (1967:19) as an *interchange*.

Identity restoration efforts involve communication and a display of motives. Efforts to "clear" identities that are temporarily under a cloud call for satisfactory answers to such actual or implied questions as: "Why did you do that? What motivated you to behave as you did? Explain what was in your head that made you break the rules." Unless individuals can offer satisfactory reasons for their behavior when others have defined it as improper, their identities remain suspect, and their status in good standing remains in doubt.

Assessing Motives and Offering Accounts

Ascertaining others' motives and explaining our own are necessary parts of all ongoing interactions. In the broadest sense, human conduct is grounded in a continuous assessment of motives. We feel compelled to explain our own behavior, and we cannot formulate our behavior toward others without also assessing the motives underlying theirs.

Pioneering sociologist C. Wright Mills said that such assessments constitute a **vocabulary of motives**. Using Max Weber's definition of *motive* as "a complex of meaning, which appears to the actor himself or to the observer to be an adequate ground for his conduct," Mills defined a satisfactory or adequate motive as "one that satisfies the questioners of the act" (1940:906–7). To Mills, "motive talk" is a central feature of everyday experience. It provides one of the organizing techniques of social interaction, determining how acts are interpreted, including the moral evaluations attached to them. To explain our motives when our actions are seen as deviant or damaging to our identity, we use linguistic devices called *accounts*. In their original formulation of the idea, Stanford Lyman and Marvin Scott defined an account as a verbal statement made to explain "unanticipated or untoward behavior" (1968:33). Accounts can take the form of *excuses* or *justifications*.

Excuses are verbal accounts people offer to acknowledge that their behaviors have been undesirable or wrong but also to indicate why they should not be held accountable for those behaviors. Excuses are intended to indicate why admittedly incorrect behaviors could not have been avoided. Everyday deviances may be explained away as resulting from the following:

An accident: "We had a flat tire and couldn't get home on time."

Events outside a person's will: "I have family troubles and have been feeling depressed."

Factors rooted in biology: "If only I could control my drinking, it wouldn't have happened."

The behaviors of others: "I am doing poorly because he doesn't give me enough encouragement."

Such excuses offer an appeal to the charge of deviance by citing events beyond the person's control.

Like excuses, **justifications** also are accounts people offer to acknowledge that they have committed acts that are being questioned. These accounts, however, are also designed to indicate why the acts should not be interpreted as deviant. Justifying an act asserts its positive value, despite claims to the contrary. Justifications are used to attempt to neutralize possible definitions of acts as illegitimate by providing nondeviant interpretations of them. Techniques of neutralization include efforts to do the following:

Deny that any real harm has come from an act: "I know that I took your car out for a joyride, but I was only borrowing it and did not damage it."

Suggest that those who were injured deserved what they got: "It's true we harassed them, but, after all, they were being unpatriotic."

Argue that in the grand scheme of things an act is not too awful: "The amount of income I withheld from the IRS is nothing compared to the rip-offs of big business."

Indicate that an act is permissible and even proper because it was done out of loyalty. "After all the times he's saved my skin, I just couldn't refuse to do what the lieutenant asked."

Both excuses and justifications lubricate interactions by explaining personal motives in such a way that charges of deviance are quickly defused. In this way, momentarily troubled encounters are allowed to resume a smooth course quickly. Sometimes, however, accounts are not honored, and efforts to restore identities fail. For a variety of reasons, motive explanations may be deemed unacceptable.

Some accounts have been so overused they may not be accepted even when true ("The dog ate my homework," or, more recently, "The cloud ate my file!"). Other accounts will succeed with some people and not others. For example, explanations for recreational drug use may be accepted by other drug users but are likely to be rejected by nonusers. Accounts also may be deemed unreasonable if they do not conform to commonly held cultural expectations. Suppose you go home and find your roommate with his head in the oven. You would probably ask, "What are you doing?" If he responds, "I'm cleaning the oven," that would probably be a satisfactory explanation. But if he claims that he heard voices telling him to put his head in the oven, you would make quite a different interpretation of his action. People who continually offer culturally unacceptable motives for their behaviors run the risk of being labeled mentally ill.

Humor also can be effective in managing an awkward situation. Smiling and laughter are frequent reactions of onlookers; the embarrassed individual can take advantage of the potential for humor to cope with the predicament. Empirical studies show use of a variety of face-work practices. A survey of students' responses to predicaments (Miller, 1996) indicated that the most common were evasion (28 percent), making amends (17 percent), humor (17 percent), and apology (14 percent). Escapes, excuses, aggressive acts, and justifications comprised fewer than 10 percent of accounts (Crozier, 2001:149). Studies have also shown the role that narratives play in face-work. For example, in Jan Doering's (2010) study of relationship breakups, he found that "dumpers" and "dumpees" use a number of accounting strategies to save face. Dumpers try to save the dumpee's face because "leaving a partner may be considered cruel or egoistic" (p. 77), while dumpees mostly try to restore their own face.

Making Disclaimers

Accounts are a form of motive talk that *follows* a questionable action. Other verbal strategies are used in *advance* to counter doubts and negative evaluations that could result from intended conduct. We rehearse our future acts in our minds, trying to anticipate the responses others will make to them. When we determine that what we plan to do could be interpreted negatively, we preface our actions with **disclaimers** to provide a nondeviant frame of reference within which our behavior can be interpreted (Hewitt and Stokes, 1975). Everyday talk is filled with disclaimers, including expressions of the following sort:

"I'm no expert, of course, but . . ."

"Don't get me wrong, I like your work, but . . ."

"I know this is against the rules, but . . ."

"This may seem strange to you, but . . ."

"I'm not a racist, but . . ."

Such disclaimers protect individuals by indicating that despite the way their present behaviors might appear, they really are people who abide by prevailing norms and cultural constraints (or want to appear as such).

Some of the most common situations in which people feel obliged to remediate encounters are those instances in which they have said something improper. All who read this book have at some time or another made a comment that they wish they could take back. Such regrettable messages become a matter of public record, particularly when they are made or captured online (Agger, 2015), and sometimes deeply damage relationships. Everyone knows of instances where people have not spoken for months or even years because of a comment made during an argument. Long-term friendships and even marriages have broken apart because someone has said something that is interpreted as unforgivable. In other instances, of course, the consequences of a face-damaging remark are much slighter and the relationship can be quickly repaired.

■ Being Different: Managing Social Stigma

Everyday deviances usually cause individuals' selves or identities to fall into disrepute only momentarily. In most instances they are not ruined beyond repair, and the situation can be saved. Some people, however, have attributes so stigmatized by others that their behavior is considered "wrong" in virtually every situation. Highly visible attributes such as physical disabilities, disfigurements, and intellectual disabilities immediately tag people who have them as different. Others, such as HIV-positive individuals or those with a history of mental illness, may be able to hide their negative attributes, but discovery of them would complicate their everyday interactions and could cause them great social harm. Goffman (1963) described those with disorders that are stigmatizing and cannot be hidden or disguised as *discredited* and those with conditions that allow people to "pass as normal" as *discreditable*. Whereas the discredited may be confronted with problems of "impression management," the discreditable may face difficulties of "information management" (Scambler, 1998). Still others are marked by attributes that characterize them as members of devalued groups in a society, including certain racial, ethnic, religious, and occupational groups.

As he did in so many areas of everyday life analysis, Erving Goffman in 1963 published the pioneering study of social stigma. His book, entitled *Stigma: Notes on the Management of Spoiled Identity* ([1963] 1986), provided the first comprehensive analysis of the distinctive problems faced by those with especially tainted identities and the kinds of strategies required to normalize their daily interactions. Stigmatized people may possess an attribute so deeply discrediting that they are viewed by "normals" as less than fully human because of it. At the outset of his classic work on the subject, Goffman identified three types of stigma:

> First there are abominations of the body—the various physical deformities. Next there are blemishes of individual character . . . these being inferred from a known record of, for example, homosexuality, unemployment, suicide attempts, and radical political behavior. Finally, there are the tribal stigmas of race, nation, and religion, these being stigma that can be transmitted through lineage. ([1963] 1986:4)

It should be noted that, despite his use of seemingly harsh language, Goffman did not approve of the stigmas that people attached to "abominations of the body," "blemishes of character," or "tribal" lineage. His goal was to point out the problem that, in everyday life, so called "normals"—as relevant today as it was when he was writing—attach labels to others as a means for devaluing them. Once we recognize that the category of "normal" is a social construction, the playing field of status and stigma will be leveled. The discrediting of others based on perceived "abnormalities," however, still persists.

Beginning with Goffman's pathbreaking formulation of the problem, social scientists have elaborated theoretically on the idea of stigma (see, for example, C. Lemert and Branaman, 1997) and have studied how groups as diverse as wheelchair users (Cahill and Eggleston, 1995) and those with other physical disabilities (Livingston, 2000); people with speech problems (Jezer, 1997; Richardson, 1996), hearing impairment (Perry, 1996), or minor bodily stigmas (Ellis, 1998); people with HIV/AIDS (Siegel, Lune, and Meyer, 1998); straight parents of adult gay and lesbian children (Fields, 2001); persons with cognitive impairments (Angrosino, 1997); Middle Eastern immigrants and atheists in the post-9/11 United States (Marvasti, 2005; Fazzino, Borer, and Abdel Haq, 2014); stripteasers (Ronai and Cross, 1998; Trautner and Collet, 2010); divorced individuals (Kim and Kim, 2002); people with genital herpes (Lee and Craft, 2002); members of Debtors Anonymous (Hayes, 2000); older undergraduate students (Norris, 2011) and even people with red hair (Heckert and Best, 1997) manage information and adopt behavioral strategies that afford maximum protection against the consequences of others' definition of them as deviant. Aside from shedding light on groups that are "different," these studies reveal a great deal about the processes that generate categories of stigma and the efforts of groups, sometimes political, to renegotiate the meanings attached to the attributes they possess.

In our everyday interactions we willingly provide some pieces of identity information about ourselves while we conceal others (see chapter 3). We play information games, with stakes that are higher for those whose identities have been negatively evaluated. To participate in interactions comfortably, such people must give a great deal of attention to information management and control. The mode of information management used by those with damaged identities varies with the visibility and stigma of the status being questioned. In some cases, negative identities are highly visible and cannot be hidden. Physical disabilities, for example, are obvious attributes which cannot be missed. For those with such disabilities, information is less important than minimizing the inevitable problems and discomforts that are part of nearly every encounter (see box).

In some cases there may be attempts to disavow troublesome identities, as when criminals assume aliases or participants in deviant subcultures use nicknames to conceal their identities from outsiders. People who know that their attributes will be discrediting in particular situations may try to conceal them temporarily. In such situations, control and management of identity information can become complex.

Goffman argued that people with stigmatizing conditions usually have some sense that others are evaluating them negatively. As a result, people with stigmatizing conditions often use coping strategies (sometimes drastic) to establish the most favorable identity possible. Some stigmatized individuals, especially those with conditions that are not immediately observable, may conceal the condition, or practice selective disclosure.

Passing is a strategy that can be employed by those with negatively evaluated attributes that are not immediately apparent. Being able to conceal a socially devalued aspect of the self may be highly advantageous in social interactions, enabling the individual with the stigma to minimize the impact of his or her stigma on others' judgments and be accepted as "normal." However, having to continually contend with possible detection is stressful and demands a great deal of mental control. In her research on Jewish Holocaust survivors, Arlene Stein (2009) found that many of them actively concealed their identities and remained silent about their experiences. Some were silent because of remaining trauma from the atrocities they endured and witnessed, but many of the 150,000 Jewish refugees who came to the United States after World War II did not feel able to speak about their troubles during the postwar exuberance felt by Americans who, for all intents and purposes, helped defeat Hitler's genocide and win the war. These survivors, accustomed to hiding in attics and basements across Europe, were now "hiding" in the United States to reconstruct new lives in a new place and time. As a coping strategy for their stigma, Holocaust survivors "built a wall separating their present and past selves, burying the past deep in their psyches" (Stein, 2009:45). This metaphorical "wall" had a real effect on their inability to fully adjust and integrate into their new communities.

In the effort to hide something important about themselves, individuals who have concealable stigmas may face an internal struggle that can have serious costs. Perhaps in some cases, harboring a concealed stigma is more costly to an individual than suffering the social consequences of stigma visibility (Smart and Wegner, 1999). For example, in a study of Harvard students, those with concealable stigmas (being gay/lesbian/bisexual, bulimic, or from a family that earned less than $20,000 per year) reported lower self-esteem and were more anxious and depressed than both those whose stigmas were visible and those without stigmatizing characteristics (Frable et

Disability or Tragedy?

The *Oregonian* newspaper won the 2001 Pulitzer Prize for best feature writing for its series on Sam Lightner, a teenager with a facial deformity. The article included a graphic description of Sam's deformity: "A huge mass of flesh balloons out from the left side of his face. . . . It looks as though someone has slapped three pounds of wet clay onto his face, where it clings, burying the boy inside" (quoted in Haller, 2001:4C). When he goes out in public, people assume he is either mentally retarded or his mother abused drugs while pregnant (neither is true). Others "give him their prayers or just look away" (p. 4C). The story is described as "poignant and gripping, as it draws the reader into his life and his decisions about trying to 'fix' his face surgically" (p. 1C).

Beth Haller, an assistant professor of journalism at Towson University in Maryland, was concerned about the messages these "coping with adversity" stories were sending to society about people who are physically different. She hoped they promoted acceptance but feared they sometimes promoted pity. Haller conducted a study of national journalism award winners from 1984 to 1999 that dealt with disability or illness. In the 56 stories she found, Haller looked for the cultural messages about disability and illness hidden with the stories. According to Haller, prestigious journalism awards not only signaled "validation" of excellence, but they also "forcefully put information about disability or illness onto the public agenda and put images of people with disabilities into the news" (p. 1C). The stories remained in the public's consciousness much longer and provided models for younger journalists. "Put succinctly, these stories have staying power."

Haller's concern was about the impact of these award-winning stories on attitudes toward people with disabilities. What she found was that many of the stories were "awash in inspiration." What's wrong with that—isn't inspiration uplifting, something that makes readers feel good? To Haller, the trouble with inspiration is that the flip side of its message is tragedy. Haller quoted a wheelchair user, who, in *Mainstream* magazine, said, "Being told that you're inspirational when you're doing something ordinary is an assault on your self-concept. Suddenly you're reminded once again of the traditional attitudes about disabilities, that no matter who you are, what you do, how you feel, to some people you'll always be a tragic figure" (Haller, 2001:1C). She went on to explain what nondisabled people don't understand: "That a life with a disability is still a life after all, to be enjoyed and lived to the fullest" (p. 4C).

The problem, according to Haller, is that the notion of disability and chronic illness as tragedy "fits squarely with journalistic news values that focus on the unusual or the dramatic." That is, deviations from the normal are more newsworthy than the commonplace. Haller wanted to challenge journalism's continuing use of the value of "unusualness," fearing that it may cause negative stereotypes in the news, especially of people who are physically different: "When journalists focus on how someone deviates from the norm and when they 'pull on heart strings' to add drama to content, they may send a message of pity and tragedy to their audience" (pp. 1C, 4C). Journalists could promote better acceptance of disabled people by focusing coverage on societal barriers, rather than on inspirational (and one-dimensional) stories of a person's life with a disability. For example, depicting people with disabilities doing something symbolically empowering or confronting barriers would send positive cultural messages of people with disabilities as equal citizens in society.

Frank Bowe, in his book *Handicapping America*, explained that one incorrect assumption affects attitudes toward disability: "That disabled people are different from us more than they are like us, [and] that their disabilities somehow set them apart from the rest of us" (quoted in Haller, 2001:4C). It is this myth that Haller believed award-winning journalism should address.

al., 1998). In a study of women who had had an abortion, almost half reported that they felt others would look down on them because of their abortion and said that they felt a need to keep their abortion a secret from their family and friends two years later. The effort of keeping this secret had the effect of exacerbating psychological distress (Major and Gramzow, 1999; Cockrill and Nack, 2013).

Stigma concealment also has been linked to poorer physical health. HIV infection, for example, was found to progress more rapidly among HIV-positive gay men who concealed their homosexual identity than it did among those who were "out" (Cole et al., 1996). Women attempting to manage the stigma of sexually transmitted diseases (STDs) by passing as healthy (because they have temporarily convinced themselves that they did not have a contagious infection) risk exposing sexual partners to infection (Nack, 2008; Hood and Friedman, 2011).

Passing can be a dangerous strategy because once begun, it is difficult to stop. Harold Garfinkel (1968) gave the example of a transsexual who, as she acted out her new status as a woman, felt that she knew something others did not, and the disclosure of her secret would ruin her: "Punishment, degradation, loss of reputation, and loss of material advantages were the matters at risk should the change be detected" (p. 136). Garfinkel said it would be more accurate to say that she was continually engaged in the work of passing, rather than to say that she had passed.

Not all stigmas can be hidden. Some individuals can only minimize the degree to which their stigmas intrude on and disrupt their interactions with others. "Covering" is another of Goffman's (1963) means of stigma management. In this case, possession of a stigma is acknowledged, but great effort is made to keep the stigma from looming large. "The individual's object is to reduce tension, that is, to make it easier for himself and the others to withdraw covert attention from the stigma, and to sustain spontaneous involvement in the official content of the interaction" (Goffman, 1963:102). For example, some of the gay or bisexual men with HIV/AIDS interviewed by Karolynn Siegel, Howard Lune, and Ilan Meyer (1998) chose to conceal or misrepresent the true nature of their illness, usually preferring to report they had cancer: "This subterfuge seemed to convey the seriousness of their illness, while avoiding strong censure" (p. 12).

Some people with stigmas intentionally call attention to their condition, however, either as an individual or as part of a group effort. Other respondents in the Siegel group's study used proactive strategies to manage stigma such as taking active, socially valued roles as HIV educators. Speaking on behalf of PWA/HIV helped them make proactive identity claims in opposition to the notion of a "spoiled identity" (1998:19).

Sociological analysis of those with stigmas as well as those participating in other forms of deviance is based on the fundamental assumption that no human behavior is intrinsically wrong. Since the early 1960s, many social scientists have emphasized the idea that conceptions of morality, respectability, and deviance are social constructions, reflecting the symbolic meanings that have been adopted by individuals or groups. In this view, morality is a relative notion, and the behavior of an individual or group can be identified as wrong, evil, immoral, or threateningly different only in terms of the current, commonly held construction of reality adopted by a dominant group in a given setting. Immoral behavior is immoral only because it has been so defined in terms of some prevailing notion of social reality. Deviance does not float down from the skies, automatically attaching to deviants and automatically missing nondeviants. For deviance and deviants to exist as meaningful categories, somebody has to judge, to portray, to stigmatize, to insult, to abuse, to exclude, or to reject (Sumner, 1994:223).

This relativistic view of deviance is most fully expressed in what has been termed **labeling theory**. The central idea is that powerful people and groups are able to impose their definitions of morality on others by labeling certain activities and the individuals who engage in them as deviant. These labels are very "sticky." Once they have been applied by powerful individuals, they have tremendous, long-lasting consequences for those who are so labeled. In the following section we will consider the contributions of labeling theory in helping to explain how some individuals come to acquire a deviant identity and to embark on a lifestyle that centers on their deviance.

■ Labeling Theory and Lifestyle Deviance

Labeling theory is only one of several social science theories expressing ways to think about deviance. Other theorists attempt to explain it in terms of a learning process based on association with established deviants or the blockage of legitimate avenues of success for certain groups. Deviance may also be related to social class values or the inequities created within capitalist societies. These theories diverge on certain points, but they need not be viewed as in competition with one another. Because of the complex and varied nature of deviance, each has explanatory power. We have chosen to emphasize labeling theory in this chapter because it fits the interactionist perspective and because of the special capacities it provides for thinking about deviance in everyday life.

An important conceptual shift from earlier thinking on deviance is reflected in labeling theory. Theorizing about the causes of deviant behavior formerly focused on the type of person committing the behavior. Labeling theory suggests that such an emphasis is misplaced. Rather than putting the spotlight on rule *breakers,* as do most theories of deviance, it focuses on the activities of rule *makers.* Howard Becker, an early formulator and proponent of labeling theory, makes this point clearly: "Whether a given act is deviant or not depends in part on the nature of the act (that is, whether or not it violates some rule) and in part on what other people do about it" (1963:14). Labeling theory thus shifts attention from the individual actor to the audience that evaluates the act. Becker voices the argument this way:

> Social groups create deviance by making the rules whose infraction constitutes deviance, and by applying those rules to particular people and

labeling them as outsiders. From this point of view, deviance is not a quality of the act the person commits, but rather a consequence of the application by others of rules and sanctions to an offender. (1963:9)

Just who makes the rules? On one level, we all have investments in our own version of reality, and to some degree we force our private rules onto others. The rules that govern our personal lives are the product of prior negotiations, however. Becker suggests that some individuals, whom he terms **moral entrepreneurs**, are on crusades to establish rules, to implement them, and then to label others who do not accept the rules as offenders. Members of certain religious groups, for example, may battle fiercely to control definitions of deviance, as the pro-choice and right-to-life arguments about abortion illustrate. Over time some groups become especially powerful in a society and particularly influential in creating the rules. The role of the institution of medicine in defining deviance is a case in point. It provides a compelling example of how a powerful group controls the fate of individuals through labeling—in this case, by being able to define certain behaviors as illnesses.

The Medicalization of Deviance

In the history of medicine, the number of behaviors that fit the medical model explanation has steadily increased (Conrad and Schneider, 1992). Under the medical model, behavioral problems that used to be regarded as misbehavior subject to punishment are considered instead as medical problems subject to medical intervention, often with the use of drugs. Acceptance of the medical model has led to the **medicalization of deviance**, or reliance on medical professionals to define conditions considered both normal and healthy. The medical model is based on the easily accepted assertions that normalcy is preferable to abnormalcy, and normalcy can be considered a synonym for health and abnormalcy a synonym for pathology. Health and pathology are defined in terms of experience and laboratory research, which are presumed to be based on scientific, objective, unbiased standards.

Because it is better to be healthy than to be sick, the medical model insists that physicians' decisions, whether they are requested or not, are necessary to ensure health and determine what is healthy. No other profession provides for the extensive access to a person's body and self that physical and psychiatric medicine do. By defining certain aspects of the human condition as illnesses to be cured, physicians give themselves the right to explore every part of the human anatomy, to prescribe myriad curative agents, and even to compel treatment.

The term *healthy*, as used in the medical model, also can be equated with the term *conforming*. In societies where this model predominates, it is often used instead of the law or religious commandments to regulate behavior. "Peculiar" individuals who were once viewed as "possessed" or as agents of the devil are classified as emotionally ill under the medical model. In the name of science, the advice of medical experts is used in the courts to determine whether certain actions should be defined as crimes. Medicine is used to "treat" those whose behaviors do not conform to the expectations of others or impinge on their moral sensitivities.

The medical model is supported by the political reality created by a coalition of physicians, insurance companies, pharmaceutical companies, teachers, judges, and other health-related professionals. Peter Berger and Thomas Luckmann (1967) referred to the members of this coalition as *universe maintenance specialists* from different disciplines who set the norms defining the behaviors that are proper or improper, deviant or conforming, normal or pathological, sick or healthy. The social control role of psychiatry is especially powerful in ensuring that actual or potential deviants stay within the official, institutionalized definitions of reality (see box).

Moral and scientific judgments become entangled in the medical model, which not only defines behaviors as troublesome but also attempts to

On Being Sane in Insane Places

A dramatic experiment that speaks directly to the matter of labeling in psychiatric hospitals is D. L. Rosenhan's study entitled "On being sane in insane places" ([1973] 2001). To find out whether the sane can be distinguished from the insane, he had eight colleagues pose as "pseudopatients" and apply for admission to 12 separate mental hospitals. None of the eight colleagues had any history of mental illness, but they were told to present themselves at the hospital admission offices complaining that they had been hearing voices. With the exception of that one lie, they were to tell the truth about all other aspects of their lives. After being admitted, they were to say they were feeling fine and no longer experiencing the symptoms. They were to arrange their own releases by convincing the staff, through their behaviors, that they were sane.

The experimenters were easily and immediately admitted, all but one with the diagnosis of schizophrenia. Their subsequent show of sanity could not convince the staff that these "patients" were fakes, however. The only ones who ever questioned their status as real patients were the other patients on the ward. After they had been officially diagnosed as schizophrenic, there was nothing the experimenters could do to shake the label. In fact, the staff interpreted everything they did in terms of the label. The social scientists made written notes on what they were seeing and experiencing, for example. After they were discharged, they learned from the nurses' records that their note taking was considered "obsessive," and "engaging in writing behavior" had been interpreted as evidence of their illness.

After hospitalization periods ranging from 7 to 52 days, the pseudopatients were discharged with a diagnosis of schizophrenia "in remission," but in the institution's view they were not sane and had not been since they applied for admission. Rosenhan concluded that "once a person is designated abnormal, all of his other behaviors and characteristics are colored by that label" (2001:438). He offers this conclusion about "the stickiness of psychodiagnostic labels":

A psychiatric label has a life and an influence of its own. Once the impression has been formed that the patient is schizophrenic, the expectation is that he will continue to be schizophrenic. . . . Such labels, conferred by mental health professionals, are as influential on the patient as they are on his relatives and friends, and it should not surprise anyone that the diagnosis acts on all of them as a self-fulfilling prophecy. Eventually, the patient himself accepts the diagnosis, with all its surplus meanings and expectations, and behaves accordingly. (2001:439–40) explain their causes. The redefinition of a behavior as *sick* rather than *bad* is not merely a semantic issue. These labels have critical implications for the treatment accorded those who have been so labeled. For example, Gamblers Anonymous is based on the view that compulsive gambling is a chronic illness. As with other 12-step programs, emphasis is on members' identifying, recognizing, and admitting their affliction. The 12 steps are required to "treat" the illness that all members of the group have. The result is a shared community of individuals "suffering" from the illness of compulsive gambling (Rossol, 2001). This medicalized view reduces stigmatization and shame with which compulsive gambling might otherwise be associated. The labeling of behavior as illness is very much a political process with policy and moral implications (Loseke, 2011).

Deviant Careers

Labeling theorists are concerned with the politics of deviance, or how powerful groups create rules and then oversee their enforcement. The labels employed by groups such as physicians influence how the society responds to those to whom the labels are applied. But labels have an even deeper impact on individuals because ultimately they influence how those who have been labeled *respond to themselves*. Labels can, in fact, alter people's identities, affecting not only what they do but who they become.

Those labeled as deviants face the task of constructing meaning under sometimes daunting circumstances; for example, in **total institutions** such as mental hospitals or nursing homes, where individuals are "stripped of their prior nondeviant conceptions of self and proffered a new definition of self . . . a deviant identity that not only is incompatible with prior self-images and identities but also carries with it corresponding negative social statuses and roles" (Herman and Musolf, 1998:433). Individuals in such settings may attempt to renegotiate meaningful identities to counter labels imposed by those in power. In one case, residents of a long-term facility for the aged and mentally ill used narratives to create definitions of self that distinguished them from definitions imposed by staff and their work (Paterniti, 2000). By claiming a "noninstitutional" self-identity in "the otherwise regimented, mundane, and sometimes inhumane circumstance" (p. 109), residents attempted to establish an alternative definition for interaction. One resident told stories about her experiences running a general store with her husband. Another talked about his life as a country and western musician. These alternatives are what Goffman (1961) referred to as *secondary adjustments*—"personal ways of negotiating organizational categories and institutional careers that provide evidence of identity apart from institutional parameters and definitions" (quoted in Paterniti, 2000:111). These secondary adjustments permit individuals some control in a situation in which they have little.

Deviant identity labels acquired in total institutions "stick" long after the termination of the labeled individual's institutional career. Herman and

Musolf (1998) found that a deviant subculture developed among former psychiatric patients "in response to their negative post-hospital situations: the effects of negative labeling, the stigma of mental illness, oppressive psychiatric and post-psychiatric treatment, and the mental health system in general" (p. 430). Through participation in this deviant subculture, members came to internalize a *deviant ideology*—that is,

> a set of perspectives about themselves against the larger perceived hostile society; moreover, they learned and transmitted to one another strategies on how to manage their spoiled identities and sets of justifications for engaging in deviant activities, and generally taught one another how to "make it on the outside." (Herman and Musolf, (1998:430)

To retaliate against mental health agents and the community at large when they had "experienced the stigma of their 'failing'" (Herman and Musolf, 1998:439), members of this subculture engaged in *rituals of resistance*, which ranged from *antideferential rituals* (e.g., "mooning" those defined as the "enemy"—police, neighbors, mental health officials) to *instrumental action* such as "organized sit-downs during programs in community mental health centers, walk-outs from sheltered workshops, protest marches, distribution of protest leaflets and newsletters, and the like" (p. 441). Both strategies are ones in which the powerless confront the powerful. These rituals of resistance, however, can serve to promote social solidarity and distort power relations, allowing former psychiatric clients to transform a negative identity into a positive one.

Charles Horton Cooley (1902), an influential sociologist from the turn of the 20th century, coined the term the **looking-glass self** to convey the idea that others serve as mirrors in which we see ourselves reflected. Through these reflections, we adopt subjective definitions of ourselves. Labels applied early on by powerful people or **significant others** in our lives (for example, parents, teachers, and peers) are profoundly influential because they fashion images of self that we may maintain for a lifetime. The proposition that individuals who are consistently responded to as deviant eventually come to define themselves that way is a central idea in labeling theory. Labeling theorists, however, qualify this idea by arguing that deviant identities arise from a *process over time*, and deviant identities lead to deviant careers.

Not all acts of deviance, even those considered to be lifestyle deviances, produce deviant identities. Many people commit acts that could land them in jail if they were caught, but most people do not routinely think of themselves as deviant. To understand the differences between acts of deviance that remain isolated and those that lead to a deviant career, labeling theorists distinguish between *primary* and *secondary* deviances.

Primary deviances are the initial, usually isolated breaches of rules that nearly everyone has made. Rule violations resulting from accident, peer pressure, or experimentation may elicit negative responses from others, but they remain primary as long as the individuals involved define them as incidental to "who they really are." The violations become **secondary deviances**

when, *as a result of consistent responses* from the society to their actions, individuals begin to think of themselves as deviant and to behave accordingly. That is, the deviant label becomes a self-fulfilling prophecy. The distinction between primary and secondary deviances was first made by the sociologist Edwin Lemert (1951). His description of the process whereby secondary deviances are produced is as follows:

> (1) primary deviation; (2) social penalties; (3) further primary deviation; (4) stronger penalties and rejections; (5) further deviation, perhaps with hostilities and resentment beginning to focus on those doing the penalizing; (6) crisis reached in the tolerance quotient, expressed in formal action by the community stigmatizing of the deviant; (7) strengthening of the deviant conduct as a reaction to the stigmatizing and penalties; (8) ultimate acceptance of deviant social status and efforts at adjustment on the basis of the associated role. (E. Lemert, 1951:77)

Studies of deviant subcultures have confirmed the movement from primary to secondary deviance described by Lemert. The process does not apply to every group that supports deviant acts, however. Young people who engage in truancy and vandalism may be perceived by the public, the schools, and the police as good students who are merely "sowing a few wild oats" or as "hooligans and delinquents," depending on the social groups to which they belong. The truth of this assertion is evidenced in a well-known and often-cited study by the criminologist William Chambliss ([1973] 2002) (see box).

Although your authors believe that labeling powerfully explains how some people become committed to deviant lifestyles, the theory does not adequately explain why people engage in deviant acts in the first place. When we begin the discussion of deviance in our undergraduate classes, we often take a poll, asking students how many have done something against the law. Always, virtually every hand is raised. Such an informal poll accords with the material presented by Stuart Henry (1990) in a book that contains students' own accounts of their deviant behavior. The focus of the essays was on how students rationalized such diverse (and at the time mostly illegal) behaviors as visiting prostitutes, smoking marijuana, using cocaine, stealing from the workplace, and concealing handguns. To the list of behaviors covered in Henry's book we would add cheating as a practice that appears to be condoned by large numbers of college students. According to the Center for Academic Integrity at Duke University, 75 percent of all college students "confess to cheating at least once" (Kleiner and Lord, 1999). According to a study of alumni, this number was even higher: 81.7 percent (Yardley et al., 2009). Some of the students' accounts were: "I realize that it's wrong but I don't feel bad about it, either, partly because I know everyone else is doing it"; "There are times that you cheat because there aren't enough hours in the day. . . . I understood how to do it; I just didn't have the time" (Kleiner and Lord, 1999). As suggested by our earlier discussion in this chapter, students are able to invoke a range of accounts explain-

The Saints and the Roughnecks

Almost every high school has gangs or groups of youths like those studied by William Chambliss ([1973] 2002). One group, which he called the Saints, were the sons of "good, stable, white upper-middle-class families." They were active in school affairs, popular, and bound for college. In their relations with police and school authorities they were polite and respectful. The group Chambliss called the Roughnecks, on the other hand, were lower-class white boys who received average grades in school and were constantly in trouble with the police and the community. A high level of mutual distrust and dislike characterized their relations with authorities. In the public's perception, Chambliss noted,

> the Saints were good boys who just went in for an occasional prank. After all, they were well dressed, well mannered, and had nice cars. The Roughnecks were a different story. Although the two gangs of boys were the same age, and both groups engaged in an equal amount of wild-oat sowing, everyone agreed that the not-so-well-dressed, not-so-well-mannered, not-so-rich boys were heading for trouble. ([1973] 2002:196)

In fact, however, Chambliss found that the Saints were almost constantly occupied with truancy, drinking, reckless driving, petty theft, and vandalism. They cheated in class and contrived elaborate schemes to get out of class and off the campus. On weekends they went to a nearby city, where they drank heavily, drove dangerously, and committed acts of vandalism that damaged property and had the potential of seriously injuring others. A favorite prank was to steal lanterns and barricades around construction sites or road repairs, enjoy the plight of those who fell into the traps, and then erect the warning signals where they could cause more confusion.

The Roughnecks' behavior in school was not particularly disruptive, and they generally regarded it as a necessary burden to be borne with the least possible conflict. Their delinquency took three forms: theft, drinking, and fighting. Of these, petty stealing of both small and expensive items was the most regular and frequent activity. Their drinking was limited because they lacked the cars and the cash required for ready access to liquor. There were frequent fights between members and others, but they seldom involved the whole group.

After observing the two groups for about two years, Chambliss looked for answers to two questions: Why did the community, the school, and the police consider the Saints to be "good boys" with bright futures but regard the Roughnecks as delinquents and potential criminals? Why did the careers of the Roughnecks and the Saints after high school generally live up (or down) to these expectations? Chambliss concluded that the reasons for the different reactions to the behaviors of the groups' members related to the differences in the visibility of their activities, their demeanor, and the bias of the community, the schools, and the police. Primarily because of their social class position, the members of the two groups received widely different labels, and eventually they came to see themselves in terms of these labels. The Saints never thought of themselves as deviant, while the Roughnecks responded to the community's definition by becoming more involved in deviant activities. Chambliss described the Roughnecks' progression from primary to secondary deviance this way:

> The community responded to the Roughnecks as boys in trouble, and the boys agreed with that perception. Their pattern of deviancy was reinforced, and breaking away from it became increasingly unlikely. Once the boys acquired an image of themselves as deviants, they selected new friends who affirmed that self-image. As that self-conception became more firmly entrenched, they also became willing to try new and more extreme deviances. With their growing alienation came freer expression of disrespect and hostility for representatives of the legitimate society. This disrespect increased the community's negativism, perpetuating the entire process of commitment to deviance. ([1973] 2002:202)

ing why their behavior either shouldn't be called deviant or, if deviant, should be excused. Students' justifications for a number of behaviors generally considered deviant is eloquent evidence of human beings' ability to reject widespread social definitions about what is right or wrong.

The interactionist perspective on deviance increases our understanding of the kinds of choices actors make and the kinds of social organizational factors that both constrain and facilitate those choices. Actors confront large social organizational arrangements in everyday life and make choices that are variously facilitated and constrained by these arrangements (Ulmer and Spencer, 1999). To truly understand behaviors, we must try to see them from the point of view of the people who engage in them.

The Abnormal Self

In many ways, we are all abnormal. By "abnormal," we don't mean bad or cruel or stupid. We mean it in a non-normative way; that there are elements of our selves that don't always conform to the needs and demands of our social surroundings and our peers. At one extreme, such non-conformance can lead some people to social isolation and loneliness and even immoral behaviors. But it can also lead to personal growth and social change. It what situations have your felt "out of place" and either decided to "go with the flow" or "rock the boat"? If you conformed to the social norms, did you gain or lose a sense of your self? If you rebelled, did you gain or lose a sense of your self?

■ Conclusion

When the word *deviant* is used to describe a person, it normally conjures up an image of someone whose behaviors are against the law or, at the very least, unmistakably different and "odd." In this chapter we have adopted a broader view of deviant behavior to include any act that compromises the perception that a person's identity is proper or socially correct. Everyday deviances are occasional improprieties that *everyone* engages in from time to time. They may result only in discomfort or embarrassment.

When individuals somehow "lose face," remedial interactions are necessary to restore the identities of self and others and remedy the situation. Our discussion of the contours of embarrassment and the vocabulary of motives that accounts for untoward behaviors pointed out that analysis of everyday deviances is part of a larger theoretical agenda. A close look at circumstances in which interaction is threatened by deviance can shed light on how an ordered daily life is produced, sustained, and protected.

Lifestyle deviances are related to the labeling of individuals and actions as deviant by powerful groups. Labeling theory fits the symbolic interactionist perspective because it conceives of deviance as a matter of arbitrary human definition. According to this view, no act is inherently deviant. As the discussion of the medicalization of deviance showed, definitions of deviance are connected to matters of power. The position of people and groups in the society determines their ability to have their views of deviance become "official" definitions.

Labeling theory thus shifts the focus in deviance from rule breakers to rule makers. Labeling also influences the ways individuals think of themselves. Movement from primary to secondary deviance occurs when people accept the negative labels that others put on them. As their own identities shift, they seek out others who have been similarly labeled. Membership in a deviant subculture is a step in embarking upon a deviant career. At the same time, we should acknowledge that people are sometimes capable of rejecting deviant labels and redefining their behaviors as thoroughly legitimate. We also put forth the idea that part of understanding deviance from the point of view of the individual requires us to learn about the emotions people feel when they break rules.

Fundamentally, deviance is concerned with the breaking of rules or violations of the social norms that direct behaviors. In the next chapter we will consider how the meaning of the life cycle and people's movement through it are guided by clear age norms. What people do and feel at different ages cannot be interpreted apart from the social context in which they are living. Such age categories as childhood, adolescence, middle age, and old age are social constructions, in the same way deviance is.

Definitions

disclaimers: Statements meant to provide a nondeviant frame of reference within which forthcoming behaviors can be interpreted.

embarrassment: The feeling of self-shame following the commission of an impropriety that arises out of individuals' knowledge that others have negatively evaluated something they have done. Embarrassment may vary in intensity from mild to so severe that an individual must withdraw entirely from a situation.

everyday deviances: Acts of deviance that occur during the normal course of day-to-day interaction and temporarily mark individuals as nonconforming or improper.

excuses: Accounts that people offer for behaviors that have been deemed unacceptable or deviant by some audience. Those who offer excuses admit that their behavior has been undesirable or wrong, but they also indicate the extenuating circumstances that required them to behave as they did.

face games: Ritualized behaviors designed to help individuals "save face" when events occur during interactions which openly damage the identity of participants.

justifications: Accounts that people offer to acknowledge they have committed acts being questioned but which are designed to indicate why the acts should not be interpreted as deviant.

labeling theory: The idea that powerful people and groups are able to impose their definitions of morality on others by labeling certain activities and the individuals who engage in them as deviant. People who are repeatedly labeled as deviant are said to accept the label eventually and then define themselves as deviant.

lifestyle deviances: Acts of deviance in which an individual engages repeatedly and over a long time. People who engage in lifestyle deviances such as crime or drug addiction can be described as following a *deviant career*. They usually are members of a deviant subculture composed of people who engage in the same deviance.

looking-glass self: The idea, first suggested by Charles Horton Cooley (1902), that others serve as mirrors in which we see ourselves reflected and through which we adopt subjective definitions of ourselves.

medicalization of deviance: The process through which medical professionals have been allowed to define various deviant behaviors as states of illness requiring treatment. Increasingly, medicine is being used to "treat" those whose behaviors do not conform to societal expectations.

moral entrepreneurs: People who are constantly on crusades to establish rules, to implement them, and then to label those who do not follow them as offenders. The term was coined by Howard Becker (1963), an early formulator and proponent of labeling theory.

passing: Presenting oneself as having attributes that are different from one's real status to avoid being evaluated negatively by others. For example, people who change distinctive ethnic names may try to pass as members of an entirely different ethnic group.

primary deviances: The initial, usually isolated breaches of rules that nearly everyone has made. Rule violations remain primary as long as the individuals involved define them as incidental to "who they really are."

secondary deviances: Norm violations that result from individuals' self-definitions as deviant. Violations become secondary deviances when, as a result of consistent negative responses from others, individuals begin to think of themselves as deviant and to behave accordingly.

self-fulfilling prophecy: Howard Becker's (1963) notion that labeling may encourage an individual to become what he or she has been labeled, even though the original accusation (e.g., of deviant behavior) may have been false. Labeling sets in motion a chain of actions and reactions that make the original expectations come true.

significant others: Other people with whom we have strong emotional attachments and whose judgments are most important in determining our behaviors.

social control: The various techniques and strategies for regulating human behavior in a society and ensuring that individuals conform to social norms. Techniques of social control can range from expressions of dissatisfaction with another's behavior, to ridicule, to outright force.

social equilibrium: The state that exists when a social system is operating free of conflict or disruption. Sociologists are interested in the conditions that allow social systems to operate trouble-free, as well as the forces that create *disequilibrium*.

total institutions: Closed environments in which the time and space of inmates can be controlled (e.g., mental hospitals, prisons, chronic care facilities), in which inmates experience "civil death" and "mortification of self" upon entry (Goffman [1963] 1986).

vocabulary of motives: The broad explanatory schemas used to explain categories of behavior. *Motives* are the "whys" of behaviors, the intentions or purposes that explain their direction and persistence. Basic physiological needs (such as hunger or thirst) as well as complicated motives (such as the needs for love, achievement, belonging, and esteem) can all motivate behavior. The vocabulary of motives was first described by C. Wright Mills (1940).

Discussion Questions

1. Think about three instances in which you have felt embarrassed. For each one, analyze the aspects of role performance that were disrupted. What did you do to "correct" your identity in each case? What did others do to decrease or increase your embarrassment?

2. What is "coolness"? How do you recognize coolness when you see it? What do you lose when you lose your cool?

3. Think of a time when you have interacted with a person who has a visible physical disability. Did the person's status as someone with a disability alter the interaction? If so, was there a point when it ceased to influence the encounter? When did that point occur, and why?

4. Throughout a one-day period, take note of every instance in which you or others explain motives for behaviors. How would you categorize these specimens of motive talk—as excuses, justifications, or disclaimers? Were there any cases when the audience did not honor the motive explanation? If so, why not?

5. Describe a time when you were labeled by some authority figure or person significant to you. (Labels can be positive as well as negative.) How powerful was the label? Did it significantly affect the ways others responded to you? Did the label influence your view of yourself?

6. Have you ever committed an act that would have landed you in a courtroom were you caught? Was this a case of primary deviance? If so, did it lead to any secondary deviances? Why or why not?

10

Aging and the Life Cycle

At age 88, Colonel Sanders, the original fried chicken fast-food expert, told a reporter, "I'm real interested in old folks because I guess maybe someday I'll be old myself." Satchell Paige, probably the oldest man ever to play professional baseball (although he would never reveal his age), recognized old age as a social construct when he asked, "How old would you be if you didn't know how old you was?" (quoted in Stoller and Gibson, 2000). There is a clear connection between general cultural values, the values particular to specific social contexts, and the meanings attached to chronological age.

The **meanings of age** are contextual; that is, they are tied to the societies and situations in which people find themselves. As we move from situation to situation in our daily lives, we are defined differently by those around us at various times and are required to behave in accordance with certain age conventions. Your classmates may consider you one age, your professors another, and the members of your family yet another. Within each of these contexts, you have to be responsive to a number of age definitions. Your parents may define you throughout your life as their little boy or girl, a definition you may seek to avoid. Your children may eventually define you as too old to understand their problems, while your brothers, sisters, friends, and cousins will think of one another as still "the boys" or "the girls." In some contexts a person's age requires adopting a subordinate position, in other situations the same age merits a dominant position. Particular situations call forth varying expectations about age-appropriate behaviors. What you can say, the attitudes you can safely express, the respect you believe is due you, and the responses you predict others will make to you all relate to their expectations of someone your age. In short, age is a critical factor in determining how others define us and how we define ourselves. In dramaturgical terms, age helps determine the performances we put on in front of a given audience.

In this chapter we take the position that age, as such, has no intrinsic meaning. In every society, meanings that often are arbitrary are assigned to specific ages in the life cycle. In this view there are many definitions of the aging process, and aging is a social construction built on age norms. The age structure of a society, however, is produced by demographic changes and historical processes. Before we examine the meanings attached to age, we will describe the present age structure in American society and consider how various age categories have developed over time.

■ Age Categories in American Society

There has been a widespread tendency in the social and biological sciences to search for the *naturalized life course*; that is, to chart the innate development and decline of human capacities, tendencies, and proclivities over the life span (Gergen and Gergen, 2000). Erik Erikson's (1968) notion of the **life cycle**, conceived as regular stages of development, has been particularly influential. As interactionists we find such theories of adult development intriguing, but we suggest that theories that claim to identify *universal* stages of human development should be approached with caution. Although people may well move through regular stages in their lives, we question whether such movement applies equally to all segments of society. For example, we are hard-pressed to imagine that people from upper-class social circles in the United States move through the same life stages as those whose income is below the poverty level.

A complex web of social and cultural factors shapes our concepts of age. "Old age" is just one of the life stages that societies create—the number and timing of such stages vary (Johnson et al., 2007). For example, prior to the 20th century there was no term for what we know as *adolescence*. People were considered to have arrived at adulthood at much earlier ages than in today's Western industrial societies. In the 21st century, entire markets (e.g., clothing, entertainment) cater exclusively to teenagers. People construct certain meanings that they associate with various stages of the life course. Age serves to distinguish acceptable behavior for various groups. Voting rights, the legal right to consume alcohol, and the age at which one can collect Social Security benefits as a retired worker are all examples of specific, formal age norms in the United States.

The Aging of the U.S. Population

One's **age status** in a society is determined by social and cultural as well as biological factors. The meanings attached to particular age categories are influenced, for example, by the **age structure** of a society, or the number of people in each age category. The age structure of a society is one of the key factors determining the need for various social resources. Perhaps the most important—and potentially problematic—demographic trend in the United States in the 21st century involves the increasing average age of the population, or the "graying of America" (Lockhart and Giles-Sims, 2011).

In thinking about the age structure of a population, demographers usually focus on the rate of birth and rate of death, or mortality. About 200 years ago, the median age—the age at which half the population is younger and half is older—for U.S. residents was 16, so in 1800 the United States was a "young" nation in terms of its age structure. Since the late 20th century, however, both the mortality rate (which had been declining since 1800) and the birth rate have simultaneously declined. Currently, we are witnessing significant increases in the number of people surviving into old age, which has raised the median age of the population: to 30 in 1980, about 37.2 in 2010, and over 38 (estimated) by 2050 (U.S. Census Bureau, 2012). For the first time in U.S. history, the population over age 65 is increasing in size while the population under age 35 is decreasing. In fact, the proportion over age 65 more than tripled during the 20th century (U.S. DHHS, 2013). Life expectancy rose from 67.1 years for males and 74.0 years for females in 1970 to 76 for males and 81 for females in 2015 (Population Reference Bureau, 2015). The proportion aged 65 and over is projected to peak in 2030, while the percentage aged 85 and over will continue to grow from 5.75 million in 2010 to 19 million by 2050 (U.S. DHHS, 2013).

One of the consequences of this changing age structure is that as an age category increases in size, its political importance as a voting bloc whose collective interests must be considered also increases. Table 10.1, which shows actual changes in the age distribution of the population from 1960 to 2010, indicates the shifting balance of political power held by particular age groups in the United States. The number of children under age 18 continues to drop, decreasing from 35.7 percent in 1960 to 24.0 percent in 2010. Although the 18-to-44 age group remains the largest category of the voting-age population, the percentage of the population in this group has been declining since 1990, from 42.7 percent that year to 36.5 percent in 2010.

The percentage of the population between ages 45 and 64 remained fairly stable between 1960 and 1990 but then took a stronger upward turn, from 18.3 percent in 1990 to 26.4 percent in 2010. At the same time, the 65-plus age group, which represented only 9.2 percent of the population in 1960, rose steadily to reach 13.0 percent in 2010. It is this age group that is most likely to vote. About 68 percent of those over age 65 voted in the 2008 presidential election, compared to 41 percent of those between the ages of 18 and 20 (this was, however, a huge leap for this age group from the 2000 election, when only 28 percent of those between the ages of 18 and 20 voted; U.S. Census Bureau, 2012).

The potential power generated by the large numbers of older people in American society could stimulate major changes in governmental health and economic policies. The likelihood of such changes, of course, depends on whether the older segment of the population can achieve a unity of purpose through effective political organization. The political clout of this older

Table 10.1   Percentage of Population in Age Groups, United States, 1960–2010

Age group	1960	1970	1980	1990	2000	2010
Under 18	35.7	34.1	27.7	26.4	24.5	24.0
18–44	35.0	35.7	41.2	42.7	39.6	36.5
45–64	20.0	20.5	19.6	18.3	22.9	26.4
65+	9.2	9.8	11.3	12.6	13.0	13.0

Sources: U.S. Census Bureau, *Statistical Abstract of the United States, 1983*, Tables 30 and 31; *Statistical Abstract of the United States, 1991*, Table 18; *Statistical Abstract of the United States, 2012*, Table 7.

group could also improve younger people's conceptions of those in that age category, thereby lessening discrimination and prejudice.

Robert Butler (1969:243) first coined the term **ageism** to describe the "systematic stereotyping of and discrimination against people because they are old, just as racism and sexism accomplish this with skin color and gender" (see box). Similar to racism and sexism, ageism encourages viewing people not as individuals but as members of a social category (Quadagno,

Ageism and Inequality

To some extent Americans idealize old age. The retirement years are supposed to be the "golden years." Advertisements portray people in the postretirement age group as carefree, well-dressed, and well-fed. If they no longer live in their family homes, they are pictured as happy members of retirement communities with names like Sun City or Leisure World. In reality, large numbers of older people must bear economic, physical, and emotional burdens. Those on fixed incomes can easily fall into poverty, and they may be denied work even if they are able to work. They are discriminated against when seeking housing. They suffer the indignities encouraged by others' incorrect stereotypes about what it is to be old. Political leaders often are insensitive to the needs of older people in the policies they create. Eventually the old may suffer technologized deaths in impersonal institutions.

Ageism interacts with other types of discrimination—sexism, racism, classism, and heterosexism—in ways that make the experience of ageism both similar and different across various groups. For example, class, race and ethnicity, sexual orientation, and gender can influence economic dependence in later life. Low lifetime earnings result in lower levels of Social Security income. Also, the inability to save or invest in a pension reduces income in later life. A white working-class male will generally have lower lifetime earnings than a white middle-class man; a white working-class woman will not only have even lower benefits, due to lower earnings, but if she is a lesbian, in some states she will not be able to collect a pension or Social Security as a spouse. Black men are more likely to experience unemployment and higher rates of disability than white men are (Hayward et al., 1996) and are thus more likely to rely on unemployment or disability payments and will also have lower Social Security benefits. The *theory of cumulative disadvantage* takes into account the social categories that increase inequality throughout the life course (Quadagno, 2013). Advantages or disadvantages based on social class, gender, and race early in life carry through to old age (Liang et al., 2010).

The intersections of race and class in designating someone as "old" can be seen in the results of a poll conducted by the Americans Discuss Social Security project. The findings reveal that, while people generally believe that old age occurs in one's early 60s, the higher one's wealth, the later the onset of perceived old age. Moreover, African Americans and Hispanics see the onset of old age as occurring in the late 50s (Associated Press, 1998). No doubt class influences this perception as well. That is, minorities in higher social classes (who have held jobs free of hard physical labor and with adequate health benefits) will not grow old in the same ways as members of racial or ethnic groups who are disadvantaged (Calasanti and Slevin, 2001; Ward, 2010).

Financial security is a key factor in maintaining a healthy and independent lifestyle in old age. As a group, older people have experienced a major decline in poverty since the 1960s, primarily due to the expansion of federal programs such as Medicare. Despite this success, the figures mask a number of factors that not only keep many seniors in poverty but also put certain groups at risk for poverty when they reach old age.

2013). In American society ageism is connected to the high value placed on youth, and it has increased as the number of older people making demands on the nation's resources has grown. Ageism is more than the attitudes and beliefs held by individuals in a particular society; it is also embedded in patterns of behavior and serves as a social organizing principle (Dressel et al., 1997; Gullette, 2011). Ageism relies on stereotypical images of aging (as a process) and older people in juxtaposition to childhood "development," "growing up," or "coming of age." Exaggerated stereotypes present old age as the time after supposed physical, emotional, and intellectual maturation (see Gubrium and Holstein, 2008). Ageism takes new forms over time. For example, traditional images of old people as vulnerable gave way at the turn of the 21st century to images of the affluent "greedy geezer," whose "selfish drain on society has left younger generations in poverty." In addition, another new form of ageism, based on "the tendency to patronize the elderly and to be overly solicitous" (Quadagno, 2013:6), also appeared.

Age Categories as Social Constructions

Terms such as *infant, child, teenager,* and *adult* are very much a part of our social reality. They are used to describe such everyday interactions as babies being nurtured by their parents, children playing in parks, teenagers mingling at school dances, and young adults meeting in bars. The use of **age categories** to identify individuals of varying chronological ages appears so natural as to be taken for granted. Surely there have always been and always will be infants, children, teenagers, and adults. But is that really the case? Have such age categories always existed throughout history, or do the definitions of what constitutes the appropriate behaviors of an age category vary by both historical period and from one culture to another?

The answers to such questions become apparent when age categories are considered as arbitrary social constructions rather than fixed biological or chronological divisions. The behaviors underlying such categories ultimately derive their meanings from the social contexts in which they occur. In this section we will focus on the historical origins of four contemporary age categories: childhood, adolescence, middle age, and old age. We will be concerned with how changes in the organization of society have created the context in which people's sense of aging, or subjective experience of the passage of time, has undergone change as well.

The Social Invention of Childhood.   As a distinct age grouping, childhood has a fairly short history. It did not exist in the Middle Ages, when the life cycle proceeded directly from infancy to "little adulthood" to adulthood. Those in the age groups we call children today were then considered to be adults on a smaller scale (Aries, 1962).

Prior to the 17th century, adults and "little adults" participated in virtually the same activities. They worked and played together, in continual physical contact with one another. Adults and children played exactly the same games with the same degree of involvement, enthusiasm, and, most important, seriousness. Children played games of chance for money, and adults played games such as leapfrog. We could just as well say that the children of the time played *adultishly* as that the adults played *childishly*.

Life was never all fun and games for the young, of course. Both in the United States and in Europe, children labored on farms, in homes, and in artisans' shops. Until the end of the 19th century, few Americans or Europeans doubted that such labor was beneficial to youth; it taught them industry and thrift and prepared them for future employment. Before 1850, only the most well-to-do could afford to exempt their children from labor in field, home, or factory. In the second half of the century, however, a growing number of affluent middle-class city dwellers and some prosperous farmers were able to delay employment of their children and instead prolonged their education. On the other hand, many more parents—including those who owned, rented, or sharecropped small farms, as well as parents who worked at unskilled or semiskilled jobs in cities—were so poor that they had to put their children to work at a young age to help support the family (Clement, 1997).

The emergence of childhood as an age category has been associated with the development of the modern family as a particular type of social and emotional arrangement (see chapter 5). This development was related to the growth of the new middle class as the effects of industrialization and urbanization intensified, changing the character of American society in the late 19th century. The middle class cultivated a new sensibility about children that was based on the idea that they should be protected from contacts with various kinds of "dangerous persons." Children were required to attend schools where they were processed bureaucratically into distinct age-grade groupings, for example.

As childhood came to be viewed as a bona fide age category, a new set of attitudes and values about relations between parents and young children was ushered in. The accepted view today is that parents should not physically abuse their children or treat them in a cold, emotionally distant manner. Children generally are to be protected from the ugly and often brutal realities of what life is "really like."

Adolescence: Between Childhood and Adult Status. Having experienced the agonies and ecstasies of adolescence, you may assume that this phase of the life cycle, like childhood, has a certain timelessness and universality to it. But rather than being an inevitable passage between childhood and adulthood in the lives of all human beings, the adolescent stage is also a relatively recent idea.

The construction of adolescence as an age category in American society can be linked to three social movements in the late 19th and early 20th centuries: compulsory public education, child labor legislation, and separate legal procedures for the treatment of juveniles (Macleod, 1998). These movements were designed to protect children for increasingly longer periods of their lives. By establishing age regulations in the areas of schooling, work, and criminal violations, social reformers helped mark out precise age categories. Adolescence became recognized as the period between puberty, a biological event, and the ages specified by the law for the end of compulsory education, the beginning of employment, and the limits of special treatment in criminal procedures.

These social movements were a response to the urbanization and industrialization of the United States. Cities came to be seen as places where the young easily fell prey to the vices of sexual immorality, crime, and alcohol abuse. Urban life was considered a "pathological" corruptor of innocent, defenseless youths who were urgently in need of the state's protection. The evils of long hours and hard work for children became more apparent as the need for their services declined.

Between 1890 and 1920, public high schools increasingly became the most central institution in the lives of the children we now call adolescents. However, even by 1920, only one child in six graduated from high school (Macleod, 1998). Previously the rhythms of the school year were dictated by the agricultural seasons, with school attendance linked to the need for young laborers on the farm. Now attendance was required, and truancy became defined as a deviant act punishable by law.

The movement to regulate working conditions and set a minimum age at which children were allowed to work outside their own families also helped segregate teenagers from the rest of society and prolong their dependency on their parents. A labor surplus in the post–Civil War period prompted the campaign for child labor laws, which limited the hours, wages, and types of work permissible for youths under a certain age.

The increasing technical sophistication of industrial production called for skilled and disciplined workers. By the 1840s and 1850s, industrialists in the North and Midwest, concerned about urban crime, poverty, and disorder, agreed that schools could provide them with an obedient, law-abiding, and literate labor force (Clement, 1997). Educational reformers geared their arguments to a capitalist economy. Compulsory education would provide a labor force suited to the capitalistic industrial society that was taking shape. Required school attendance and minimum age restrictions kept unskilled labor out of the factory and produced better-disciplined and more manageable workers who knew how to follow a supervisor's orders. Some of the constants in 19th-century schools included individual competition (e.g., spelling bees), emphasis on respect for private property, and obedience to the teacher's authority (with punishment for misbehaving). The rigid order and strict discipline of 19th-century schools served a purpose:

> At a time when the United States was barely one hundred years old, when it had experienced a bloody and divisive Civil War, vast economic expansion accompanied by unemployment, depressions, violent labor disputes, and large-scale immigration of persons from dramatically different cultures, there appeared good reason to quickly train all American children to self-discipline and restraint. (Clement, 1997:90–91)

The creation of a special category of deviance for youthful offenders, *juvenile delinquency*, furthered the processing of youths as members of a separate category. The first Juvenile Court Act, passed by the Illinois legislature in 1899, became a model for many others during the next two decades. The driving force behind a separate juvenile justice system, however, came from Colorado's municipal judge Benjamin Lindsey (West, 1996). On looking into a case in which a boy had taken coal to sell and use for home heating, he found that many young people facing charges were poor urban children, not criminals. Nevertheless, they were sometimes held in jails with hardened adult criminals for weeks, or even months, before trial. He concluded that it was not a system well suited either for children or for society, and he began hearing all juvenile cases separately from adult cases. He also recruited probation agents, mostly from among truant officers, to oversee their lives outside the courtroom. In taking on the roles of parents, however, courts began trying to regulate children's lives more extensively. Guiding them toward respectable adulthood had to mean more than stopping outright criminal activities. Juvenile delinquents, according to the Colorado statute, came to include "not only young thieves and vandals but any boy or girl under sixteen who hung around pool halls or saloons, who walked around the streets at night without a legitimate purpose, or who had a habit of using vile, obscene, vulgar, profane, or indecent language" (West, 1996:67).

The goal was to protect youthful offenders by treating them differently from hardened criminals; the result was another thread in the tapestry of adolescence as a separate age category, distinguished from both childhood and the adult stage.

Pathways to Adulthood. The transition to adulthood has become a thriving area of research in life course studies. *Emerging adulthood* is proposed as a new conception of development for the period in the life course from the late teens through the 20s, with a focus on ages 18 to 25. Sweeping demographic shifts over the last half of the 20th century and into the 21st century have made the late teens and early 20s not simply a brief period of transition into adult roles but rather a distinct period of the life course characterized by change and exploration of possible life directions (Arnett, 2004; Blatterer, 2007).

One demographic area that especially reflects the exploratory quality of emerging adulthood is residential status. Most young Americans leave home by age 18 or 19. However, as we shall see later in the chapter, the norms about this are relatively loose. A majority of young adults go off to college after high school and spend the next several years in some combination of independent living and continued reliance on adults. About 40 percent move out of their parental home not for college but for independent living and full-time work (Goldscheider and Goldscheider, 1994). Most young adults will experience a period of cohabitation with a romantic partner at some point. In fact, emerging adults have the highest rates of residential change of any age group. School attendance is another area in which there is substantial change and diversity among emerging adults. The debt that college graduates owe to pay off their student loans has affected the decisions they make about their lifestyle choices, including where they live. More than a quarter chose to live with their parents because of their student-loan debt (Stone et al., 2012).

The proportion of young Americans who enter higher education following high school rose steeply in the second half of the 20th century, from 14 percent in 1940 to more than 60 percent by the mid-1990s (Bianchi and Spain, 1996). Between 2002 and 2012, enrollment increased 24 percent, from 16.6 million to 20.6 million (U.S. Department of Education, 2015). College education is often pursued in a nonlinear way, frequently combined with work and punctuated by periods of nonattendance, making it hard to discern all of the factors that affect both enrollment and completion.

An extended period of schooling complicates the transition from adolescence to adulthood (see box). Leaving home for college is perhaps the most potentially dislocating change that middle- to upper-middle-class youths have thus encountered (Holmstrom et al., 2002).

Crisis and Rebirth in Middle Age. In popular culture, middle age has been portrayed as a time of crisis or trauma in the life cycle. This stage is generally viewed as the period between the ages of 40 and 60, but the social construction of middle age has indefinite boundaries. Although most Americans readily recognize the term "midlife crisis" and pretty much agree that such a crisis occurs on a widespread basis in people's 40s, several studies (see McMillen, 1997; Freund and Ritter, 2009; Drimalla, 2015) debunk the midlife crisis as an inevitable, nearly universal experience of psychological turmoil.

For example, although more than 25 percent of Americans over age 35 think they have had a midlife crisis, these supposed crises may be more along the lines of "stressful life events," according to a study by the MacArthur Foundation Research Network on Successful Midlife Development in the United States (Lang, 2001). Most people who told the researchers they had experienced a *midlife crisis*—defined as personal turmoil and challenges in people age 39 through 50 brought on by fears and anxieties about growing older—were describing something else. That is, they were talking about *stressful life events*—situations brought on by specific transitions or events that may or may not be associated with typical aging, such as a life-threatening illness or job insecurity—that had occurred before age 39 or after age 50 (Lang, 2001).

And although most people characterize a midlife crisis as a negative thing, many respondents in the MacArthur Foundation study hinted that the myth of the midlife crisis has its good side, in that this time is seen as an opportunity to catch up to where they would like to be or expected to be when they were younger (Lang, 2001).

The meaning of *midlife* is changing for individuals and families. Defining midlife as the **empty nest** period of life is inaccurate for many Ameri-

Why Laundry, Not Hegel?

At the turn of the 21st century, Linda Holmstrom, David Karp, and Paul Gray studied upper-middle-class, college-bound high school seniors and their parents as they were going through the college application process. The seniors they interviewed expected college to be a transformative experience that would affect their identities, a "time for discovering who they *really* were" (see Karp et al., 1998). They also knew they would experience upheavals in the routines of everyday life as they faced changes of place, changes in responsibility for tasks, and changes in familial relationships. Interestingly, their anxiety was focused more on issues such as how to get their laundry done than on whether they would understand such classical thinkers as the German philosopher G. W. F. Hegel. And although they looked forward to the chance to be independent, they worried about whether they would be able to "cut it" on their own. As one student put it:

> I'll be independent for the first time in my life. I'll be totally dependent on just me and answer to no one. That's the rebellious side of every teenager saying, ". . . No, I'm sorry that I didn't call you and tell you where I was until 3:30 in the morning." (Holmstrom et al., 2002:446)

On the other hand, the same student continued:

> [My parents] have always taken care of me. They've always been there to help me, to make sure that I got things done, and to give me a little nudge when I needed it. . . . Where am I going to get all that now? (Holmstrom et al., 2002:446)

These college-bound students saw their ongoing transition to adulthood as a gradual, emerging process. College was seen as the next step to full adulthood. Students described it as a place where you can "wean yourself into independence," "a step . . . halfway between the real world and high school" (Holmstrom et al., 2002:449). As one student put it:

> My parents help me; they keep me organized. They cook me dinner. . . . I can always talk to them about stuff, and I won't be able to next year, but then, over the last two years I've met friends that I talk to . . . I can cook good Minute Rice and I've done all my own laundry. So I've been getting progressively more independent. (Holmstrom et al., 2002:446)

Students long for independence but feel comforted knowing that their parents will help them in times of need. They want independence with a safety net—parents are the safety net. It is not surprising that these high school seniors admitted scant knowledge of the logistics of everyday life. Ordinarily, parents simply do not expect them to manage finances, cook, clean, or do their laundry completely on their own. It follows that managing these everyday life tasks would be at the forefront of students' consciousness as they imagined being "on their own" for the first time.

According to Holmstrom, Karp, and Gray, if compulsory public education shaped the "discovery" of adolescence as an age category, the enormous expansion of higher education in the United States since the late 20th century has also transformed the way that upper-middle-class youths, especially, make their way into adulthood. Their interviewees' most consistent story centered on the clear parental expectation that children had one primary "job" in life—to succeed in school. And parents saw it as their job to provide all the necessary infrastructural support.

What these parents were buying with their tuition and dormitory dollars was a particular pathway to adulthood for their children, one that offered "a deliberately gradual transition to adulthood through semiautonomous campus living and deferral of the traditional role transitions to adulthood of self-supporting employment, marriage, and parenthood" (Holmstrom et al., 2002:457). For the college student, this strategic delay aims to maximize later opportunities—college attendance provides the most secure route to the skills and credentials necessary for a well-paid and interesting job. As one author has pointed out, "Prolonged dependency may be an emerging strategy for success in the transition to adulthood" (Aquilino, 1999:173).

cans whose children still live at home—for many, childbearing and childrearing responsibilities have not ended by midlife. The changing demographics of the American population are affecting how midlife is viewed: we are living longer, marrying at later ages, and having children at older ages (Lundquist et al., 2015). In the 21st century, midlife often has been pictured as "the good years," a time for relaxing and enjoying leisure time after the children are grown. As we have seen with other issues, there are plenty of books to help people suffering from "empty nest syndrome" (Mitchell and Love-green, 2009), such as *How to Survive and Thrive in an Empty Nest* (Lauer and Lauer, 1999), a step-by-step approach to help parents turn their empty nest into an opportunity for growth and positive change.

Other demographic developments have had a considerable impact on both family structure and people's sense of their own aging. In 1920 average life expectancy in the United States was only 54.1 years (U.S. Census Bureau, 1983), so many American couples spent their entire married lives raising their children. When the last child was ready to leave home and establish a household, the parents had few years of life left. Today Americans are living longer and more actively well into their 70s, 80s, or beyond.

Women may be relieved, not depressed, to see their children launched; midlife women and men who are at the peak of their careers want to continue to be productive. For some, this time of life may mean concentrating on new interests or new careers. Thanks to "supernutrition" and biotechnology, a new life stage, "middlessence," has appeared, an expanded middle age period from approximately 40 to 60 years of age (Dychtwald, 1999).

However, these rosy vignettes do not apply to all Americans. The aging of the population and increased longevity mean that Americans will spend more years in retirement, which has important implications for financial planning and economic security. For many, whose lives are a constant struggle for survival, economic security remains an unattainable goal. Single mothers who are simultaneously raising their own children and their grandchildren have a full "nest," and extended childrearing years add to their economic and social responsibilities. Other women, who are alone at midlife, may have fewer resources as a result of minimum wage jobs, divorce, or widowhood. Working at low-paying jobs, without health and retirement benefits, does not allow one to save for retirement.

Midlife men also may be insecure financially as a result of low-paying jobs, plant closings, or corporate layoffs. Black men in particular have suffered from the decline in blue-collar jobs offering good pay and benefits. Even many two-income families have not achieved the economic security they expected (Genovese, 1997).

At the turn of the 20th century, few parents lived until their children reached midlife. In the 21st century, however, midlife adults may expect their parents to live until their 80s or 90s and to need care. Midlife families who face simultaneous care responsibilities for older and younger generations have been described as being part of the "sandwich generation" (Genovese, 1997).

How Old Is Old Age? The age categories of childhood, adolescence, and middle age do not exist naturally but are social constructions created by human beings. Members of all societies do seem to make some kind of distinction between the old and other age groups, but the meanings of *old age* also vary depending on the historical period and the cultural setting (see Calasanti and Slevin, 2001, 2006).

The definition of *old age* in industrialized nations is closely related to developments in the laws concerning pensions and retirement. In England and the United States, the ages of 60 and 65 (or 66 or 67, depending on your current age) have been linked to specific governmental actions defining old age. But before official retirement and pension ages were set, the meaning of old age was subject to much discretion and individual judgment. People were considered to be old when they were getting on in years and unable to support themselves. The label of *aged and infirm* could be applied to people at ages anywhere from their late 40s to 80 and older because the ability to support oneself varies with individuals and their occupations.

Inevitably, government finances dictate the "proper" point at which old age and pensions are to begin. The Social Security Act of 1935 established a distinct legal age status for the elderly in American society. The original choice of age 65 for retirement was heavily influenced by political and economic considerations. It was understood that providing benefits below age 65 would substantially increase costs and, therefore, might impair the possibility of acceptance of the plan by Congress.

The age for **mandatory retirement** for most occupations was raised from 65 to 70 by an action of Congress in 1978, and it was eliminated altogether by the Age Discrimination in Employment Act of 1986. Further efforts to keep the Social Security system financially sound have led to attempts to curtail a trend toward early retirement and to prolong the working years. For example, the 1984 National Budget Reconciliation Act further changed the definition of retirement age for future retirees. On a graduated scale, those who retire during the first quarter of the 21st century must reach age 66 to receive full benefits; the age requirement increases to 67 by the year 2027. Thus, aging has in a way been redefined through legislation.

Despite the increasing age at which one may receive full Social Security benefits and removal of the legal cap on mandatory retirement, some people are retired before age 65. The average age at initial reward of Social Security retirement benefits remained at about 63.5 years between the early 1980s and the late 1990s (U.S. Social Security Administration, 1998). However, this early retirement may not have been planned. In a study of the anticipated retirement behavior of the baby boom generation (those born between 1946 and 1964), Haas and Serow (2002) reported:

> The Employee Benefit Research Institute's (2001) retirement confidence study found that during the 1991 to 2000 interval, almost half of the working respondents expected to retire at 65 or later. Yet, 71 percent of retired respondents left the labor force at an earlier age. More than one-third of them retired earlier than expected, typically for reasons beyond their control (e.g., health or changes in the company). (p. 152)

A rapidly growing number of Americans are continuing to work beyond age 65, however. The proportion of people age 65 and older in the workforce grew to 16.1 percent by 2010, up from 12.1 percent in 1990 (U.S. Census Bureau, 2012). And the percentage of people between ages 65 and 69 who are working grew 9 percentage points to 30.8 percent in 2010.

With more people hanging on to their jobs and postponing retirement, it will be interesting to see if workers late in their careers are going to be forced into an earlier retirement than they might wish. In fact, the number of age-discrimination complaints filed with the Equal Employment Opportunity Commission (EEOC) hit an all-time high in 2010. The majority of the cases have to do with unfair termination practices, many from workers who felt pressured into retirement.

Changes in the economy, in particular the downsizing movement, have had a significant impact on older workers. The labor market at the turn of the 21st century encouraged older workers to move out of the labor force through financial incentives and downsizing. In some instances, downsizing seemed to be a "barely disguised form of age discrimination" (Sicker, 2002:61). In one case, in which a company's downsizing resulted in the firing of 1,469 employees, most of whom were just a few years short of entitlement to a full pension, it was estimated that the company saved an average of $326,632 per fired employee in pension obligations alone (Rosenblatt, 1996).

It would seem reasonable that more and more older workers would choose to continue their employment and thereby reduce the number of years in retirement for which they may lack sufficient income to maintain a desired standard of living. In fact, by the early 21st century, voluntary early retirement had leveled off and increasing numbers of older workers indicated a desire to continue to be active in the labor force (Sicker, 2002).

Definitions of old age may have little to do with the inherent condition of the elderly. Rather, such definitions are a product of competing ideologies, political bartering, and economic conditions. According to one author:

> We have a situation in which aging is increasingly contextualized; that is, increasingly a different experience, depending on health, income, and decisions regarding continuation at work. There no longer is a single progression of steps from birth to death like those portrayed in the "Stages of Life" prints that were once widely distributed. Careers no longer necessarily follow the traditional patterns of long tenure with a corporate entity, followed by a definite period of retirement. Instead, they increasingly are self-managed in response to personal needs or, sometimes, are disrupted by such vicissitudes as mid-career job loss. There is indeed an interval that might justly be called a Third Age for many Americans but hardly for all. (Rubinstein, 2002:32)

The Third Age. The term **third age** has been used to refer to the span of years between retirement age and the advent of age-imposed limitations. For Peter Laslett (1991), whose work is generally associated with the concept, retirement now offers the opportunity to develop a distinct and personally fulfilling lifestyle unconnected with the contingencies of working life. The essence of Laslett's argument is that a combination of demographic change and socioeconomic development has provided the setting for a new generation of retired people who find themselves in a position of greater potential agency (Gilleard and Higgs, 2002). Other authors agree: "For those with adequate resources, adequate health, and few responsibilities, [the third age] provides a context for self-fulfillment, freedom, and purposeful engagement that is largely new in human history" (Rubinstein, 2002:30).

Despite criticisms of "grandiose expectations" and "unpractical idealism," Laslett stuck to his position in the revision of his earlier work (Laslett, 1996:xii–xiii). An increasing number of writers (although not always using Laslett's "third age" terminology) have advocated such a new and more agentic lifestyle, conveying a message that later life is a time of opportunity and "old age" a state to be resisted (Gilleard and Higgs, 2002). The concept has lasting power—the "third age" is certainly reminiscent of Neugarten's (1974) distinction between the **young-old**, those between the ages of 65 and 74 who generally have good health, adequate financial resources, and support from family members, and the **old-old**, those over age 75 who are more likely to have health and economic problems and to be isolated from others.

■ The Meanings of Age

When age categories are viewed as social constructions, we see that they result from changing human interpretations of the meanings attached to specific phases of the biological life cycle. The behaviors expected of those in various age categories also are products of an ongoing interpretive process reflecting people's continuing attempts to make sense of their dealings with others. In some instances chronological age has a significant effect on the ways people relate to one another, and in others it is far less important. Individuals also hear different messages about the meanings of various age categories, and they respond to these messages in various ways, depending on their social attributes and positions in the social order.

Age Norms in Everyday Life

Many of our daily activities and experiences are prescribed and regulated by **age norms** or social conventions. Older men are expected to marry younger women, for example, but the reverse situation may inspire comment or criticism. The distinctions are often finely grained, such as the expectations we have of a three-year-old versus a five-year-old.

Even a few years in age can make a large difference in age attributes and our judgments about what a person can and cannot do or ought and ought not do, as we noted in chapter 3. In some social circles 18- or 19-year-olds are thought to be too young to marry, but remaining unmarried in one's late 20s may be regarded by parents, relatives, or friends as a cause for concern. Some age norms have been incorporated into law—for example, age 21 has been federally endorsed as the minimum age for drinking alcoholic beverages. Although past surveys found substantial agreement on the ages at which people are expected to engage in specific activities, by the late 20th century there was less consensus about age norms. According to author Gail Sheehy, age norms have shifted to such an extent that "a revolution in the life cycle" has occurred (1995:4). "In the space of one short generation the whole shape of the life cycle has been fundamentally altered" (p. 4). Specifically:

> Puberty arrives earlier by several years than it did at the turn of the [20th] century. Adolescence is now prolonged for the middle class until the end of the 20s and for blue-collar men and women until the mid-20s, as more young adults live at home longer [see box]. True adulthood doesn't begin until 30. Most Baby Boomers, born after World War II, do not feel fully "grown up" until they are into their 40s, and even then they resist. Unlike members of the previous generation, who almost universally had their children launched by that stage of life, many late-baby couples or stepfamily parents will still be battling with rebellious children who are on the "catastrophic brink of *adolescence*" while they themselves wrestle with the pronounced hormonal and psychic changes that come with the passage into middle life. (Sheehy, 1995:4)

The norms of aging are deeply embedded in our consciousness and seem to exist "naturally." Nevertheless, like all social conventions, they are arbitrary social constructions derived from societal values and the more specific values of the groups and people with whom we interact. The requirements attached to specific ages therefore may differ in various soci-

---

Is There an Age Deadline for Leaving Home?

Since the mid-1980s, changes in patterns of leaving and returning home in the United States, and particularly changes in the age patterning of those transitions, have emerged as important social concerns in the media, among policy makers, and in the scholarly literature. Much of the literature suggests that greater proportions of young adults now live at home with their parents and that fewer have families of their own (Seiffge-Krenke, 2013). Prominent scholar of human development, Richard Settersten (1998), set out to examine U.S. cultural ideas about leaving and returning home; specifically, cultural age norms for these transitions. He asked the question: "What are the rules in contemporary American society, if any, about the age by which young adults ought to leave their parents' homes or about the age after which they should not be allowed to return?" (p. 1375). To answer this question, a random sample of 319 Chicago-area adults was interviewed by telephone.

A large majority of both male and female respondents perceived an age deadline for leaving home. There was nearly complete agreement that both women and men should leave home sometime between the ages of 18 and 25. The reasons given for these deadlines were largely related to the development of self and personality. At the same time, most respondents indicated that there were no consequences for young adults who remain at home beyond the deadline. Returning home, on the other hand, was not at all perceived as an experience that should be dictated by age—in fact, only a fraction of respondents thought an age limit should be placed on returning home.

Age deadlines were cited more often for and by men, for both leaving and returning home, lending support to the idea that men's lives are thought to be more constrained by age and that men are more likely to think in terms of age. This finding is in line with other research, which suggests that age holds more salience in men's lives than in women's (Settersten, 1997). Interestingly, actual behavior patterns contradict these perceptions. Men are not only more likely to remain at home longer, but they are also more likely to return home. This difference is most likely due to the fact that women are more likely to get or be married (White, 1994), which makes their departure more likely and a potential return less likely (Settersten and Ray, 2010).

Another trend ran counter to actual behavior. Whereas in the population at large the degree of coresidence with parents is highest for minority groups, white respondents consistently gave later deadlines for leaving home. There were no racial differences with respect to placing age limits on returning home.

The findings generally did not support the assumption that a strong set of cultural timing norms exists for leaving, and possibly returning, home: "Instead, cultural thinking about age and its relation to these events seems relatively loose, particularly in light of the fact that our respondents often did not see any real consequences for staying at home beyond, or returning home after, a deadline" (Settersten 1998:1396). This conclusion led Settersten to suggest that although these informal age rules may be an important force shaping the life course, their influence, at least for these transitions, may instead be more secondary in nature and more flexible than many scholars have assumed.

eties and historical eras (see Calasanti and Slevin, 2001; 2006). Evidence of the socially constructed nature of age norms can be found in a society's laws and proposed legislation. The attention focused on the juvenile death penalty in the wake of the Washington, DC–area sniper attacks that occurred in October 2002 provides an example.

Lee Malvo, one of the individuals accused, was 17 at the time of the shootings. After considerable wrangling among the various jurisdictions in which sniper attacks occurred, the decision was made to try Malvo in Virginia. Although the greatest number of sniper killings took place in Maryland, that state bars the execution of those younger than 18. At the time, Virginia not only had the death penalty for juveniles, but had used it three times since 1976—the second-highest number of any state (Editorial Desk, *New York Times*, 2002). Legal experts said Malvo's case may interrupt what had at the time become a growing sentiment against executing juvenile defendants. In October 2002 (before the sniper attacks), four U.S. Supreme Court justices said they opposed executing defendants who committed capital crimes at age 16 or 17, stating, "The practice of executing such offenders is a relic of the past and is inconsistent with evolving standards of decency in a civilized society" (Greenhouse, 2003). Then the sniper case hit.

According to the Washington, DC–based Death Penalty Information Center, the Malvo case can be cited by those who believe that juvenile offenders should not be executed because they "aren't as intellectually mature, they are often led by older compatriots" (Glod and Jackman, 2003). Malvo appeared to have been strongly influenced by John Allen Muhammad, 42, the other suspect in the sniper shootings.

In the end it may not matter. A juvenile court judge in Fairfax, Virginia, ruled in January 2003 that Malvo could be tried as an adult. That ruling allowed prosecutors to seek the death penalty and led to the impaneling of a grand jury that indicted Malvo on capital murder charges. On October 10, 2006, Malvo pleaded guilty to the six murders he was charged with in Maryland. About a month later, he was sentenced to six consecutive life sentences without the possibility of parole.

There is a clear relationship between cultural norms, biological processes, and the social context of aging experiences. In some cases even biological processes do not occur independently of social forces and age limitations, as might be expected, but are regulated by the messages people hear from society (Gullette, 2011). Nowhere are the stereotypes of aging more powerful than with sexuality. We continue to link youth with sexuality and age with automatic sexual decline. However, although sexual activity and sexual interest were found to decline over time (Masters and Johnson, 1966), they do not cease at a specific chronological age. Findings of more recent research suggested that while frequency of intercourse declines over time (Laumann et al., 1994), sex continues to play an important role in the lives of older men and women (Minichiello et al., 1996). An AARP study revealed that the majority of midlife and older adults sampled consider a satisfying sexual relationship important to their quality of life (Fisher,

2010). The minimal investigation of sexuality among older people itself reflects ageist assumptions about what scholars deem worthy of investigation, our general "cultural illiteracy" about aging, and long-established cultural biases about the "sexless" old (Matthias et al., 1997; Weg, 1996).

The age norms in American society number well into the thousands and are constantly changing. An almost endless number and variety of cultural prescriptions about appropriate age-related behavior affect the daily encounters and interactions of people of all ages.

Chronological Age and Experiential Age

Because age norms are social constructions, there are differences between chronological age and **experiential age**, or age as subjectively measured by an individual's range of life experiences. Age norms are closely tied to specific social contexts.

Consider the meanings children attach to slight chronological age differences, for example, and the sharp distinctions they make concerning who may be friends with them. During their early years, children are flooded with new experiences, rights, and obligations. Because of their short biographies and limited life experiences, children are constantly learning and experiencing new things. Age differences of even a few months mean substantial differences in their knowledge. Six-year-olds think they are infinitely wiser than five-year-olds and in a class separate from anyone younger than that. This is in some measure appropriate, since during the early ages children who are separated by only one chronological year do inhabit separate social, experiential, and symbolic worlds, and a difference of only one year assumes significance.

Parents are constantly setting rules to limit behavior of their children. Largely on the basis of communications with other parents like themselves, they define the rights, expectations, duties, and freedoms appropriate to their children at certain ages. Often these judgments are made in terms of the parents' perceptions of their children's physical and emotional readiness to assume certain tasks or engage in certain behaviors. In that sense there is a correspondence between the stages of childhood in the life cycle and the norms for children's behaviors. But parents' decisions about age-related behaviors for their children also emerge from the situation and are made on an individual basis.

Children are not the only ones who attach great value to small chronological age differences in choosing appropriate friends and acquaintances. A one-year age difference also is given considerable significance by college sophomores, who typically have few freshmen among their close friends. At this point in the students' lives, the slight one-year difference corresponds to a huge status difference. The sophomores already know their way around and are wise to the customs, mores, and norms of college life. Because sophomores have experienced events that sharply distinguish them from freshmen, they think of themselves as being much older.

A Symbolic Interaction Approach to Aging

As we noted in chapter 2, the ability to evaluate one's own behaviors objectively from the perspective of others is necessary to become a "normal" member of society. A person who acquires that ability possesses the essential components of what George Herbert Mead called *the self.*

Definitions of self incorporate a personal sense of aging. Awareness of reaching middle age, for example, often comes about through recognition of others' definitions of one as middle-aged. Gail Sheehy's midlifers provided examples such as, "Students start calling you 'mister.' . . . Your 14-year-old daughter says, 'Mom, how come you're still wearing microskirts?'" (Sheehy, 1995:58). In the words of one of her respondents, a fortyish Manhattan doctor, "A man can look at a woman and tell if she's interested in him as a sexual being. All of a sudden you reach an age where you look at a young woman and—click—you're not even under consideration. That hurts!" (p. 59). It is as though others become mirrors in which we see ourselves reflected, and through these reflections we come to have certain subjective definitions of ourselves.

The symbolic interactionist approach to aging suggests that the adage, "You are as young as you feel" should be amended. More precisely, it should be, "You are as young or old as *others allow you to feel.*" Such a reformulation also calls attention to issues of power, constraints, and one's access to social "resources" such as education, income, social status, and physical health. The more of such resources one possesses as one ages, the greater the likelihood that others will respond to you with respect, and consequently the better you will probably feel about yourself. Like any other symbol, age can have a multiplicity of meanings that emerge out of our interactions with others. These meanings are likely to be modified and reinterpreted in the course of interactions, depending upon our own and others' definitions of the situations in which we find ourselves.

The interactionist approach also is attentive to other broad dimensions of the aging process. Although the process involves regular, predictable biological changes and chronological stages, it cannot be understood without considering its various social and cultural definitions. The meanings given to chronological age categories vary from context to context and with particular individuals. In interactionist terminology, different groups respond to age in terms of different inventories of symbols and create among their members different aging selves. The meanings attached to age vary with people's place in history and the historical times in which they live. Social attributes, such as gender, race, ethnic affiliation, occupation, social class, and marital status also influence the meaning of a particular age for a particular person. The meaning of being 35 years old is different for a baseball player whose career is nearly over than for a 35-year-old woman who, having returned to graduate school after a 10-year absence, has now received her PhD and is embarking on an academic career.

Lifestyle choices and leisure interests—both of which are connected to one's identity—are subject to age-appropriate norms and judgments. For example, what happens to individuals who are part of a punk music scene as they get older and move through the life course? Punk started as a youth subculture in the United Kingdom and United States in the 1970s and was, in part, based on themes of rebellion and anarchy fueled by teenage angst. In her study of aging punks, Joanna Davis (2007) noted that they are forced to negotiate new types of punk identities with varying degrees of success. Those who remain "stagnant" (i.e., acting the way they did when they were younger) are often shunned, while successful identity negotiators refashion themselves as either "legends" or "career punks" who participate "in more 'adult' practices, such as marriage and parenthood" but are successful at not allowing that priority to "negate [their] commitment to the scene and its values" (J. Davis, 2007:67). This highlights two important aspects of aging: (1) age-specific behavior can be fluid, and (2) context matters.

Two specific life contexts that affect our notions of aging and our views of self over the life course are work and gender. These contexts will be examined in the following sections.

■ Effects of Work and Careers on Aging

Our involvement with work helps determine how we experience the passage of time. Because work structures the ways we think about the present and how we anticipate the future, it is a primary source of our sense of aging. Those who pursue different work lives or careers hear different messages about the meaning of age. Ability to do the work may or may not be affected by age, and various career patterns involve varying conceptions of what it means to be on schedule, ahead of schedule, or late. The ways individuals measure and evaluate their own life progress and their experiences of growing older are a function of where society expects them to be in their occupations at a given point in their lives.

In his voluminous and influential writings on work, Everett Hughes demonstrated the value of conceptualizing a **career** as "the moving perspective in which the person sees his life as a whole and interprets the meanings of his various attitudes, actions, and the things which happen to him" (1958:63). This definition of *career*, sexist though it is in its wording, accords well with the interactionist position. Hughes certainly recognized that, in an objective sense, various occupational careers are established within work organizations, but his definition also directs attention to another aspect of the career process. On the basis of communications with others in their work situations, people arrive at subjective, evaluative meanings for the various stages in their own career patterns.

The notion of career is not just a conceptual tool that social scientists use to look at the nature of work. We can also use it as a frame for interpreting where we are in the life cycle and how the things happening to us at any point in our lives make sense.

Age Consciousness and Career Structure

Success in a career is closely connected with age. Most careers are age-graded; that is, we ride an escalator of sorts that travels up the career ladder and are expected to be at a certain point by a certain age. Our careers are considered satisfactory if we "make the grade" at the appropriate age. As well as being the measure of success in a career, age is the variable along which career lines are established. The roles available (and unavailable) to those in a work organization, and the workers' construction and meaning of their work commitments, are defined in terms of age. Careers in some occupations involve special contingencies and force a direct **age consciousness** on participants.

In the corporate world, for example, there appears to be increasing concern about age. At the turn of the 21st century, a survey of executives and search firms that examined attitudes toward older executives found an increasing tendency for respondents to consider age an issue in job seekers at or just below age 50 (Marshall, 2000). It is not just that older executives were becoming more conscious of their age. In fact, 52 percent of respondents said the age-50 issue was a significant concern, an increase from previous years (Marshall, 2000).

Before the late 20th century, corporations did not even think of terminating their managers before age 60. By the end of the 20th century, men in their 50s in corporate life found themselves in a precarious position. They had become "a high-ticket item in an era of downsizing" (Sheehy, 1995:260). Between 1999 and 2010, age-discrimination complaints filed with the Equal Employment Opportunity Commission rose from 14,000 to over 24,000, and remained above 20,000 through 2014. On the job, male baby boomers complained of crashing into a "silver ceiling." In focus groups, Clairol showed before-and-after photos of a white man who had had his gray hair colored and then asked participants to describe the man. Consistently, the man without the gray was viewed as more successful, smarter, and more athletic (Weiss, 2002).

The film industry in particular is one where age consciousness (and ageism) ran rampant in the late 20th century. Figures for 1998 from the Screen Actors Guild showed that two out of every three roles went to performers younger than age 40. For males 40 and over, roles appear to be on the rise in both theatrical and television productions, while for females 40 and over, roles continue to be harder to come by as they represented only 28% of female roles in 2008 (Screen Actors Guild, 2009). While both women and men over age 40 were significantly underrepresented in casting, the employment figures were worse for women than for men. Another study found that 37 percent of male roles for film and television went to men over age 40, while just 24 percent of female roles went to women in the same age group (Millis, 2000). When the focus is narrowed to lead roles, the numbers became even more disheartening for women.

These examples suggest that every occupation generates its own distinctive career path and consequently its own set of symbols and meanings of age. In most occupations people are required to engage in a continual process of interpretation and reinterpretation about their current occupational position and its meaning. Periodically they must assess their success, whether or not they are currently making it, and their chances for eventually doing so. Questions about career success and failure constantly call attention to age. To a significant degree, it is the structure of occupational life that injects meaning into the phrase *growing older*. No doubt such diverse occupations as fashion model, boxer, lawyer, scientist, and stripper generate disparate self-conceptions of aging.

Retirement

The life stage known as retirement was invented or constructed in industrialized nations in the 20th century. Although once a rare event for working men and women, people may now spend as much as a quarter of their lives as retirees, "as life expectancy rises and the age for leaving work falls" (Savishinsky, 2000:30). By the mid-1960s, age 65 had become the age around which retirement clustered in the United States, making it an effective reference point for a variety of purposes. Now, however, the transition is less clear-cut: "The age-graded norm in retirement has become blurred, and the actual range of retirement age has expanded" (Han and Moen, 1999b), making the transition "longer and fuzzier" (Kohli and Rein, 1991) than in the past, as retirees from primary career jobs increasingly take up second or third careers. "Thus, the transition itself is now less clear-cut: the boundary separating 'retirement' from 'employment' is blurred, and retirement from one's primary career job is no longer fixed at any set age" (Moen et al., 2001:56).

Savishinsky's (2000) study of the life stories of a group of men and women in upstate New York found significant diversity as well as shared dilemmas. One theme that resonates through the stories of many of these retirees is their rediscovery of themselves in the process of making meaning of their experience. In fact, "they work *at* retirement, trying to figure it out and fill it in on their own" (Han, 2001:541). It is the lack of culture—the "cultural lightness of retirement" that "made it so personally heavy to bear" (Savishinsky, 2000:55) for the retirees.

In a capitalist economy, productive achievement is typically associated with earning wages. Thus, as one retires from the workplace, one's personal worth becomes questionable. One is "sidelined," "put out to pasture," or becomes a "has been" (Gergen and Gergen, 2000). Although this displacement is especially important to men, for whom career success has been found to be directly entwined with a sense of identity (M. Gergen, 1992), feminist critics have pointed out that being productive also affects the valuation of the maturing woman (Martin, 1997).

Retirement has typically been studied as an individual, principally male status passage. In the early 21st century, however, almost half the workforce was female, and the majority of workers were married to other workers (Moen et al., 2001). Gender had become a key source of heterogeneity in the nature and effects of the retirement process; that is, gendered life scripts and options produced distinctive life course patterns for men and women (Moen et al., 2001). Women and men were found to follow different career paths to and through retirement—women workers in late midlife were less likely to have worked continuously (Han and Moen, 1999a, 1999b). Women tended to experience retirement differently as a consequence of the difference in trajectories and of gendered expectations (Quick and Moen, 1998; Smith and Moen, 1998). For example, women in late midlife may enjoy their jobs and may wish to postpone retirement, feeling they are starting new lives after their children have left home. Husbands in late midlife, however, may be counting the years or months to their own retirement (Moen et al., 2001). Couples increasingly must deal with two retirements, which raises the issue of synchronizing spouses' career exits. Even this is a gendered process—women's retirement is often contingent on that of their husbands (Quick and Moen, 1998).

If employed husbands retire first, wives who are not yet retired are in a *status-dissonant* role relative to traditional gender roles. They may resent their husbands' free time in the face of their own continuing employment, and this resentment may be exacerbated if retired husbands still expect their employed wives to perform much of the housework. If employed wives retire first, husbands who are not yet retired may benefit from their wives' performing most of the household responsibilities. Women in this situation, however, may dislike being thrust into the conventional homemaker role (Moen et al., 2001).

Not only do couples now confront two retirements, but they also must strategize about when each will retire and whether either will take up other paid work after retirement (Han and Moen, 1999a, 1999b). The importance of this strategizing is illustrated by the finding that newly retired men and women report increased marital conflict when their spouse remains employed (Moen et al., 2001).

▪ Gender and Aging

Powerful differences between men and women run through the entire life cycle, from birth to old age. Society has imposed standards of acceptable social performance and physical appearance on women that women themselves have been forced to acknowledge if they wanted to achieve a position of value in a male-dominated society: "Because women's worth is so frequently associated with their physical attractiveness, the normal physical changes that accompany aging—wrinkles, weight gain, hair thinning and graying—call into question women's social value" (Furman, 1997:104).

The Double Standard of Aging

From childhood on, females are socialized to place a great deal of emphasis on their physical appearance and partake in "body work" and "beauty work" practices to enhance their looks (Gimlin, 2007; Kwan and Trautner, 2009). The variety of cosmetics that women use to maintain their looks certainly indicates the significance of physical attractiveness for them. Men, by contrast, have traditionally been expected to minimize their public concern with appearance, although there is evidence that this is changing in the wake of corporate downsizing, which appears to be placing pressure on middle-aged men to look younger in order to keep their jobs (Spindler, 1996; Monaghan, 2008).

The response society makes to men's and women's physical attributes is not simply a result of biological functioning but rather a product of cultural, historical, and sociological conditions. Bodily representation and self-presentation are shaped largely through cultural convention and social relations; women in American society are disproportionately affected by these factors. While loss of physical vigor and decline in health may be experienced similarly by both women and men, the aging body as a means of revealing the self to others has particular significance and consequence for women in U.S. culture (Furman, 1997). In this culture, there is an assumption that attractiveness and older women are mutually exclusive categories, which leads to negative stereotyping, as Furman (1997) found when she asked her students to identify cultural associations with older women. This was their collective list:

> domestic (good cooks), nostalgic, interfering, out of shape, bitter, over-bearing, frustrated, needy, stubborn, a liability, worn-down, gaudy, wrinkled, more vulnerable to attack, rambling, busybodies, hag, wicked, evil, nag, constant complainer, meddling, gossipy, worrisome, manipulative, martyr, advice-giving, grouchy, fat, "little old lady," bespectacled, moles, crooked, shrinking, widowed, helpless, tea-drinking, arthritic, bingo-playing, liver spots. (p. 94)

Furman's (1997) study of older women and beauty shop culture brings to light a constant "reading" of their bodies by older women that is in constant tension with images of youth. One of her respondents, who considered herself lucky in not being too wrinkled, said, "About my appearance, I know I don't look my age. I don't act my age. That's why my age doesn't bother me" (p. 105). For others, who acknowledge that they look old, it's a different story. In one respondent's words: "When I look at myself now (in the mirror), I feel old" (p. 109). Furman explained:

> When Reva looks at herself in the mirror and feels old, she is seeing herself from the perspective of men. This observation is useful but does not go far enough in helping us interpret the experience of *older* women. When Reva looks at herself in the mirror and feels old, she is seeing herself from the perspective of men, as would a younger woman as well, but also from the perspective of a younger person. Hence she is twice objectified, or, perhaps more accurately in this instance, she partakes in the process of self-objectification in two ways: as a woman and as *old* woman. As woman she is observed by the internalized male gaze. As older woman she is observed by the internalized gaze of youth. We spot

here another unequal social relation, which, like the male-female relation, is a relationship of dominance-subordination. The image and its
reading captures the social imbalance between youth and old age, especially as it pertains to women. (Furman, 1997:109)

So old women come to be seen as "old bags." And as Furman pointed out,
"What is a bag but a shapeless, empty container . . . which after use should
simply be thrown away?" (1997:109).

In growing up, males are judged by two sets of physical standards—one
appropriate to boys and another for men. As boys are socially transformed
into men, society allows them to be judged by a standard that relates to
maturity, one which allows for things such as "character lines" around the
eyes and the effects of daily shaving. Females, however, are judged throughout their lives by one standard of physical beauty—that appropriate to
young girls. The cultural image of an erotically appealing woman is commonly one of youth. As a woman grows further away from this nubile image,
she is usually considered less and less attractive (Bakos, 1999; McQuaide,
1998; Kwan and Trautner, 2009). In American society, even young girls are
sometimes advised not to frown ("You'll get wrinkles!"); cosmetics, trendy
clothing, and even surgery are used to maintain a youthful appearance for
as long as possible. In contrast, the physical and sexual attractiveness of
men is often considered to be enhanced by the aging process. Gray hair and
facial wrinkles may be thought to look "distinguished" on men—signs of
accumulated life experience and wisdom. Likewise, while the professional
achievements of women may be perceived as threatening to a potential male
partner, it is relatively common for a man's sexual attractiveness to be
closely associated with his achievements and social status.

The pairings of powerful older men and young, beautiful women reflect
the double standard of aging. As you might expect, pairings of older men
and younger women occur much more commonly than the reverse. Who
would be the female equivalent of Sean Connery, who was the oldest man
ever named "the sexiest man alive" by readers of *People* magazine? Connery, the first James Bond, was 59 years old when he won the title in 1989
and continued to land starring roles in movies into his 70s. A woman of comparable age might still be seen as beautiful, as long as she looks considerably younger than her years, but at age 59 not "the sexiest woman alive,"
contended one scholar (Daniluk, 1998).

Given the media's incessant focus on the beauty of young women, it is
no surprise that the medical field has been able to identify a niche and
exploit it. Using the familiar biomedical model (see chapter 8) phraseology
to turn the effects of aging—loose and sagging skin, wrinkles, and creases—
into pathology encourages a view of aging as a medical problem (Haiken,
1997). Cosmetic surgery has become an issue of *needing* a change, not
merely wanting it (Brooks, 2010; Montemurro and Gillen, 2013). Surgeons
of the late 20th century referred to face-lifts, for example, "as something
that is needed rather than desired, that may be delayed but not escaped"
(Haiken, 1997:172).

In addition, there is the "wildly popular Botox [which] is literally changing the face of baby boomers, its biggest fans" (Weiss, 2002). From 2001 to 2006, sales of antiaging beauty products jumped 24 percent, to $374 million. By the early 21st century, cosmetic surgery had become a $15 billion industry (Kuczynski, 2006).

Though men are having faces and necks lifted and sagging eyelids corrected to give them a "competitive advantage" in the business world and to keep up with other presumed body ideals (Norman, 2011), women continue to be the primary objects of surgical intervention. In addition to the difference in the number of cosmetic surgery operations performed on men and women, marketing strategies differ along gender lines. For men, cosmetic surgery is presented as a means to enhance job performance and increase chances to compete, while women are targeted in terms of general attractiveness or changes in identity (K. Davis, 2013). Such adaptations to the body are part of a "successful aging" movement that is supported by beauty product and cosmetic surgery industries but criticized by scholars for promoting aging as a period of decline or disease that can be halted or amended by buying expensive products (Calasanti and Slevin, 2006; Ellison, 2014). According to Abigail Brooks (2010), "Aesthetic anti-ageing surgeries and technologies reinforce the cultural understanding of growing older—and for women, specifically, looking older—as an inherently undesirable and negative experience. To feel better about ageing means minimizing age signs on the face and body; in short, *looking younger*" (pp. 252–53, emphasis in the original). Brooks notes that while some women find these practices liberating, others believe that aging naturally without cosmetic enhancements frees them from the socially prescribed ideals of youth and beauty.

Like any other physical or social attribute, age acquires its meaning through interaction. To fully understand the aging process, we need to know how people tune in to, interpret, and respond to repeated social messages about the meanings of age. Men and women hear contrasting messages about the aging process. At the root of the disparate life courses of men and women lies a power differential that operates to age women considerably faster than men, according to the definitions of aging in American society.

The Temporal Self

"Age is just a number," the saying goes. But that number can have some real effects on how we behave, what is expected of us, how we see ourselves, and how others see us. As time moves forward, so do we, whether we like it or not. We make our way through the life course gaining new skills, new knowledge, and new senses of self. Teenagers seems to always want to be older, while people in their 20s and 30s often bemoan the aging process for both its biological/physical and social/cultural effects. Getting older, however, is a privilege. Not everyone gets to do it. How has your self changed throughout the years? Are you different now than you were in high school? If so, in what ways? How do you think you might be different in, say, a decade or so?

■ Conclusion

Our experience of the aging process depends on where we stand in society—particularly in terms of our age, our gender, and the work we do. We oversimplify the aging process if we think of it only in chronological or biological terms. Age carries no intrinsic meaning. Rather, human beings in communication with one another attach meanings to age. Our feelings about growing up, older, and old are formed by the values of the society at large and by those of the particular groups to which we belong.

Because human beings are not simply objects in nature, or passive receptacles for biological processes associated with the passage of time, we shape the aging process by thinking about it, interpreting it, defining it, categorizing it, labeling it, and attaching values to it. These mental activities have critical consequences for actual behaviors. Chronological age is a symbol subject to continuous human definition and redefinition, and age categories are social constructions that cannot be understood outside the contexts in which they are defined. The norms regulating the behaviors expected of people of various ages are also shaped and defined by people's interactions and communications with others.

Throughout this chapter we have explored how aging identities are formed. Age is certainly one of our most meaningful identity "pegs," or markers. We think of ourselves in terms of the age categories into which we fit at various points in our life. Age, however, is only one dimension by which individuals define who they are to themselves and others. The last chapter of this book examines the issue of identity from a broader, more historical point of view. It will consider some of the features of the modern world that make it increasingly difficult for individuals to answer the question, "Who am I?"

Definitions

age categories: Broad designations used to describe people of particular chronological ages. The meanings attached to age categories such as childhood and adolescence have varied cross-culturally and in various historical eras.

age consciousness: Awareness of being a certain age at certain life events.

ageism: Prejudice and discrimination directed toward older people. Ageism is comparable to sexism (prejudice directed at women or men) and racism (prejudice directed at racial and ethnic minority groups).

age norms: Cultural prescriptions or regulations for appropriate behaviors at particular ages. Chronological age is an important basis for determining how people ought to behave in all societies, but age norms vary across cultures and historical periods.

age status: The roles, duties, obligations, and responsibilities expected of individuals of a certain age. Some age-related cultural expectations are codified into law, such as the voting age and the drinking age.

age structure: The number of people in particular age categories in a society. A society's age structure is determined primarily by birth rates and rates of mortality (death), and it changes over time.

career: The perspective individuals have of their lives as a whole and their interpretation of the meanings of their various attitudes and actions and the things that happen to them. An occupational career is one frame within which people understand and interpret their movement through the life cycle.

empty nest: The period in the family life cycle after the last child leaves home and child care and support needs diminish. The lengthening of the empty nest period has created new life tasks for both women and men.

experiential age: A subjective measure of where individuals are in the life cycle according to their life experiences rather than their chronological age.

life cycle: The pattern of broad developmental stages through which all human beings are said to pass as they move through life.

mandatory retirement: The age at which employees can be forced to retire. In the United States, the mandatory retirement age was raised to 70 in 1978 and eliminated in 1986 by the Age Discrimination in Employment Act.

meanings of age: The value people attach to a particular chronological age, which will vary according to the individual, the situations in which interactions take place, and the age conventions of the society. Because age categories are social constructions, the meaning of an age varies with the social, cultural, and historical context in which it is defined.

third age: The span of years between retirement age and the advent of age-imposed limitations.

young-old and old-old: Two segments of the elderly population, consisting of those between the approximate ages of 65 and 74 and those older than 75.

Discussion Questions

1. How old are you? Whatever your age, try to describe as many norms as you can that influence what people your age can or cannot do. Think of such categories of norms as proper dress, drinking legally, involvement in work, and sexual behavior.

2. Into what age category (for example, early adulthood, middle age, late middle age, old age) would you place your parents? Why have you placed them into that age category? What meaning are you giving to that category? How will you know when your parents are no longer in that category?

3. There is an old saying that goes, "You are as young as you feel." Why might a symbolic interactionist want to amend this piece of folk wisdom to say, "You are as young or as old as *others allow you to feel*"?

4. Suppose you knew three women, all in their late 30s. Imagine that one is a professional athlete, the second a lawyer, and the third a machine operator in a factory. How would their respective occupations influence the way they are experiencing the same chronological point in the life cycle? More generally, how might jobs at different points in the class structure produce a different sense of age?

5. We have argued in this chapter that gender critically influences how individuals experience aging. It has been said that there is a double standard of aging that places women at a greater disadvantage than men as they

grow older. What evidence would you submit to argue that such a double standard does, in fact, exist?

6. In earlier times people on average died in their early 40s rather than their mid-to-late-70s, as is the case today. How do you think this demographic fact of life has influenced family and work life? What if the average life span were to become, say, 100? How would such a change influence the structure of family and work life?

11

Social Change and
the Search for Self

CHAPTER OUTLINE

- Symbols, Selves, and Society
- The Therapeutic State and the Problem of Identity
- Buyers and Sellers in the Identity Marketplace
- Individualism, Community, and Commitment
- Future Selves
- Conclusion

With a pack on her back that is nearly the same size as she is, Cheryl Strayed—as played by the actress Reese Witherspoon in the 2014 film *Wild*—works her way off the trail of the mountain she's climbing, looking for a place to rest. She removes one hiking boot, revealing blistered, blackened, and bloodied toes. The shoe slips from her hand and bounces over a cliff and down a canyon. Without pause, she launches the other shoe after it. It's a gripping scene for both the majestic beauty of the Pacific Coast mountains and for the anguish and angst Witherspoon portrays. The film is based on Strayed's autobiographical best-seller, a gripping account of her "soul searching" 1,100-mile hike on the Pacific Crest Trail, from the desert of Mojave, California, to the snow-topped mountains along the Oregon-Washington border. As *New Yorker* film critic David Denby (2014) noted, "Each stopping place in the wilderness is a kind of marker along the road to redemption. Sweating and freezing, Cheryl wants to expunge loss and self-disgust from her soul."

The popularity of the film—due in part to Witherspoon's performance that earned her Emmy and Golden Globe Best Actress nominations—speaks to larger issues in contemporary society about the desire for self-reflection, self-discovery, and redemption. Strayed's **search for self** represents a central life problem for millions of people in the present urban-industrial or postindustrial nations of Western Europe and North America. This search has led many Westerners to try to "find themselves" in myriad ways. They might seek out-of-body or out-of-mind experiences through drugs or exercise; or become members of organizations like pseudo-Asian or neo-Christian religious sects, cultlike groups centered around New Age thinking; or join one of the scores of self-help groups (Tupper, 2009). The emergence of such practices and organizations has been a response to what Orrin Klapp (1969) aptly called a "collective search for identity." The purposeful construction of autobiographical narratives, stories that are told to others and to one's self about one's self, has become a common practice not only on the big screen but throughout our everyday lives (DeGloma, 2014).

Every generation of people, because of each generation's unique historical situation, experiences the world in somewhat different ways than its predecessors. Not having participated in the creation of its social world, each generation is likely to confer new meanings on old familiar objects. Whatever the historical conditions into which people are born, one problem remains constant: Human beings must have a coherent framework of meaning for their lives. In some historical periods the traditional meanings transmitted from one generation to the next adequately perform this function. In other epochs, however, such meaning coherence is not so easily established. The early 21st-century historical period in the Western world appears to be one in which many individuals experience particular difficulty in understanding themselves, in part, because we are too busy "amusing ourselves to death" (Postman, 2006).

In this concluding chapter we examine how the matters of personal identity and self-worth have been brought to the forefront of contemporary consciousness in the Western world. We want to explore why the problem of identity has become so paramount in the modern world, the consequences of what some view as the radical individualism of contemporary American society, and the likely shape of future selves.

■ Symbols, Selves, and Society

Throughout this book we have repeatedly made the point that the selves individuals present to one another are not bestowed by nature. Indeed, a theme in several earlier chapters is that human selves do not exist as independent entities but emerge, are sustained, and are transformed as a consequence of the symbolic dialogues, both verbal and nonverbal, in which individuals constantly engage with others. Clothes, for example, as well as words are symbolic announcements to others of how an individual wants to be viewed.

Central to the interactionist perspective on human life is the notion that people are sensitive to the impressions they make on one another. They go to great lengths to withhold discrediting information about themselves from others in order to appear proper. In our discussions of stranger and intimate relationships in chapters 4 and 5 we stressed the connection between the information people have about others and their ability to role-take with them. We analyzed behavior in public places in terms of the relative scarcity of information strangers have about each other. The measure of trust, risk, uncertainty, and commitment that people invest in their relationships is calculated in terms of their faith that others' performances reflect their real intentions and identities.

Sensitivity to others is not distributed equally throughout the social order, as our discussion of the politics of interaction in chapter 6 demonstrated. Those in positions of power can afford to be insensitive to the feelings of the less powerful. Because the ability to role-take is inversely related to power, membership in disadvantaged or relatively powerless groups—for example, women, lower- and working-classes, and minority groups—is conducive to greater role-taking ability. The faces power presents, short of sheer physical force or other forms of coercion, are primarily symbolic. Through facial expressions and the techniques of interrupting, crowding others' space, pointing, and staring, the powerful affirm their status while keeping others under their scrutiny.

Not only are symbols crucial in the communication of power differentials, but, in a larger sense, human social life itself is symbolic, or a social construction. Objects and things have no inherent meaning, only the meanings people confer on them. These meanings are, in the final analysis, arbitrary because there are always several possible meanings that could be given to them. Whatever the meaning attributed to it, a thing can only be understood within the context in which it is situated.

As we suggested in chapter 2, the symbol-using capacity of human beings makes possible a kind of liberation. Freed from the animal's dependence on instinctual biological impulses, humans can use symbols to bring into reality virtually anything they can imagine. The ability to transcend the world of the here and now through symbolic processes is not without its costs, however. It also heightens humans' awareness that they are destined to die.

The general view of the self as a socially constructed phenomenon suggests that the nature and "shape" of social selves are specific to particular cultures and historical periods. To be sure, a great deal has been written about the fundamentally different place of the individual in American and Asian cultures. Much has been made of the fact that in Japan individuals are expected to subordinate their own interests to those of the group. In the United States, in contrast, the individual is the key unit of society and the needs of the individual appear to take precedence over group or community interests. As we shall see in greater detail in a later section of this chapter, the contemporary search for self has particular urgency in a society that has always claimed to prize individuals above all else. Consider what happens when we have excessive individualism marinating in a sea of self-congratulatory amusements and "inspirational" messages (Ehrenreich, 2009). To do so, we will need to examine a few well-established criticisms of American culture (Bellah et al., [1985] 1996; Derber, 2000; Putnam, 2000; Furedi, 2004) that collectively contend that America's radical individualism is the basis for a general unraveling of the society's social fabric. Immediately, however, we need to locate the contemporary search for self within the rise of what might be termed a *therapeutic state*.

■ The Therapeutic State and the Problem of Identity

As several observers have noted (see Derber et al., 1990; Edgley and Brissett, 1999; Glassner, 2010), the behaviors of people in American postindustrial society are dominated by "experts." Experts advise us on virtually every aspect of our lives. Today, experts follow us through the life course. They are there when we are born and follow us each step along the way, right down to our graves. Experts are all over our televisions with a range of "reality" TV shows from competitive programs where contestants are judged (e.g., *The Voice, Top Chef, Project Runway*) to niche market lifestyle shows (e.g., *Ice Road Truckers, Doomsday Preppers, Pawn Stars*). Many people have come to feel reliant on experts to tell them how to maintain their health, how to become educated, and how to raise their children, and there's a TV show or a YouTube video readily available to dish advice about and instructions for any of these issues and more (Kim, 2012). Experts have become indispensable for repairing the range of technical paraphernalia—for example, TVs, automobiles, computers, cell phones—without which we believe it would be impossible to live. Most important to us in this chapter, however, is that experts now tell us when our "selves" need repair and the proper procedures for doing it. We will trace briefly the context in which we have come to so thoroughly rely on experts.

The Contemporary Concern with Self

While the awareness of death has been present among members of all societies throughout human history, people in tradition-oriented cultures are somewhat insulated from the trauma of death consciousness. In such societies an overarching religious ideology helps explain life's mysteries. Individuals may know that they are going to die, but they also believe that they know why they are destined to die and where their death will take them. Members of nonindustrial, tradition-oriented societies also are fairly secure in the knowledge of who they are. The anxiety occasioned by identity questions is siphoned off, if you will, by the importance accorded to ascribed status characteristics. In such societies, a person's family status for the most part envelops them and dictates nearly all life experiences. In their influential treatise on the social construction of society and selfhood, Peter Berger and Thomas Luckmann wrote:

> In societies with a very simple division of labor, identities . . . are socially predefined and profiled to a high degree. . . . Put simply, everyone pretty much is what he is supposed to be. In such a society identities are easily recognizable, objectively and subjectively. Everybody knows who everybody is and who he is himself. A knight is a knight and a peasant is a peasant, to others as well as to themselves. There is, therefore, no problem of identity. The question "Who am I?" is unlikely to arise in consciousness, since the socially defined answer is massively real, subjectively and consistently confirmed in all significant social interaction. (1967:164)

People in contemporary American society are confronted with a disparate set of life problems. In the modern world—under the impetus of democratic ideologies, industrialization, and science—many areas of life previously accepted as natural are now viewed as subject to human volition and action. For example, people no longer passively plead for charity; now they expect and demand that governments engage in social welfare activities. Were contemporary Western governments not to do so, large segments of the population would view it as an injustice.

When people come together and collectively act on their definitions of injustice, a **social movement** is born. In Ralph Turner's words, "A movement becomes possible when a group of people cease to petition the good will of others for relief of their misery and demand as their right that others ensure the correction of their condition" (1969:491). Turner argued more than 40 years ago that we were in the midst of a major social movement whose dominant theme was the failure of advanced industrial societies to provide their members a sense of personal worth, that such societies do not foster "an inner peace of mind which comes from a sense of personal dignity or a clear sense of identity" (1969:395). In short, "The phenomenon of a man crying out with indignation because his society has not supplied him with a sense of personal worth and identity" (p. 395) was the distinctive new feature of the era.

The social movements that characterized this mid-20th-century period articulated a new definition of injustice, one much broader than the earlier demands for full political participation and freedom from material want. Alienation, previously seen only as a work-related phenomenon, took on a much broader connotation. The term *alienation* used to be associated with such issues as the manager's feelings of loneliness and isolation, the secretary's sense of frustration at being limited to support roles, and the blue-collar worker's lack of job satisfaction (see chapter 7). More recently, **alienation** has been used to refer to a psychological condition in which people are unable to locate a clear conception of self and feel a sense of wholeness. It is in the context of such alienation, as Phillip Reiff (1966) put it about half a century ago, that the therapeutic state has triumphed.

As the more personalized conception of alienation has become accepted in American society, popular writings by psychiatrists, psychologists, and advice columnists have taken on an influential role. Television appearances have made "mind-tinkerers" such as Dr. Phil McGraw, Dr. Drew Pinsky, Dr. Ruth Westheimer, and Deepak Chopra instant celebrities (see Ferris and Harris, 2011). Their appeal attests to the pervasive anxiety about questions of identity and psychological well-being in society. Such "experts" are constantly dispensing prescriptions for happiness, sexual fulfillment, or mental health.

The movement toward this all-embracing concern with psychological health and personal identity has been accompanied by a corresponding transformation in what the well-known 20th-century sociologist C. Wright Mills called our "vocabulary of motives" (Mills, 1940), or explanatory schemas of human behavior. When people act in a manner that we consider deviant, our first impulse is to question their mental health and probe their psychological makeup. Are they normal? Why are they doing that? Because of the medicalization of deviance (described in chapter 9), behaviors such as alcoholism, which would have been viewed years ago as evidence of sinfulness or moral degeneracy, are now explained as illness. We use a "sickness vocabulary" rather than a "sin vocabulary." We now ask, "What would make a person do something as sick as that?" (e.g., drink too much). Our grandparents would have had little difficulty in understanding such behavior. For them it was simply *wrong!*

A therapeutic ethos that sees us in need of "recovery" dominates our screens (Karp, 2001). In her analysis of TV talk shows in which "guests" were encouraged to bare their souls, Kathleen Lowney (1999) uncovered the discourse that dominates Americans' thinking about all sorts of deviant or problematic lives: "That people's troubles, often their morally reprehensible behaviors, are propelled by flawed selves that can be—no, ought to be—repaired via therapy" (Karp, 2001:108).

Preoccupied with their dis-*ease*, large numbers of people in 21st-century American society purchase the time and expertise of professionals to discover more about themselves. With the aid of the helping professions that have emerged as a major cultural force since the late 20th century (among them psychiatrists, psychologists, therapists, and social workers), an increasing proportion of the population has set out to feel better, to "get it together." We are in an era that has variously been characterized as the *age of narcissism*, the *me society*, and the *psychological society*. As pointed out in previous chapters, you need only pay attention to the magazines available online or in your local grocery store, such as *Self* magazine (which you can view in print or on your tablet), to conclude that Americans are absorbed with questions of self-fulfillment and self-realization.

We might add that self-absorption is consistent with the ethic of consumption and self-satisfaction fostered by capitalism in general and by advertising in particular. In the industrial age, society was primarily organized around the world of work. A person who did not work, for any reason other than physical disability, was defined as immoral, lazy, and worthless. This perspective on work was beautifully captured in Max Weber's notion of the Protestant Ethic, or the work ethic (see chapter 7). According to the Protestant Ethic, work is intrinsically valuable and an end in itself.

A Consumption Ethic

For sizable segments of the middle class, the work ethic and its moral restraints have been replaced by a **consumption ethic**. The central organizational concern of the 21st century has become less the *production* of goods than their *distribution*. The shift in structure and psychology of modern life has been due to an overwhelming concern with the consumption of goods and services. If workers imbued with the Protestant Ethic lived to work, now we work to consume. There is even a bumper sticker that proclaims, "I owe, I owe, so off to work I go"!

In the last decades of the 20th century, a new word entered the American vocabulary to describe the young people who embraced this consumption ethic. *Yuppies*, or young urban professionals (who were presumably white, and their black counterparts, *buppies*), were characterized by the communications media as oriented toward the consumption of such goods as expensive clothing, sports cars, and innovative products of modern technology. The emphasis on consumption has resulted in a paradox. The capitalist system that developed along with the morality of the Protestant Ethic required workers who would postpone immediate gratification and who would work at unpleasant tasks for the sake of future rewards. For example, sex had to be forgone and marriage postponed in the interests of industrial efficiency. As the industrial system became more and more technologically sophisticated and productive, it became increasingly unclear what to do with the endless stream of goods, few of which satisfied any genuine needs. A solution was found in the growth of advertising and the transformation of the pleasure-denying work ethic into a self-indulgent society of consumers. The rhetoric of consumption is fostered and sustained by an advertising industry instrumental in creating a seemingly insatiable quest for fulfill-ment through the ownership of particular commodities (Ritzer, 1999; Schor, 1998; Gottschalk, 2009).

The shift toward the social production of consumer-oriented selves has had far-reaching consequences into the 21st century. Since material posses-sions alone cannot ensure feelings of meaningfulness and satisfaction, many people today find themselves caught up in an endless quest for a sense of significance in their lives. This quest is made even more elusive by the built-in obsolescence of the products produced. There must always be a "better" product in the works, and so the flames of advertising are always available to heat the cauldron of contemporary anxiety. This anxiety is con-nected to a pervasive feeling of ourselves as incomplete and the consumer-ist belief that *stuff* can fill that void. So we buy stuff. And accumulate goods and products at faster rate than any other time in history. Each year, the typical American adult buys almost 50 new pieces of clothing, and the aver-age child gains about 70 new toys (Schor, 2005:9, 19).

It is in the context of the broad historical shifts we have been detailing that particular groups and institutions arise to help (some might say exploit) those who are searching for self. In the following section we shall focus especially on two "movements" that reflect the psychological alien-ation created by life in a mobile, affluent, secularized society subject to rapid change. A great deal has been written about the nature and functions of what has been termed the *new religious movement*, and about the *self-help movement*.

■ Buyers and Sellers in the Identity Marketplace

Since the 1960s many forms of social organization have been devised to provide "services" to those who are trying to increase their self-awareness or are searching for their "real selves." The Esalen Institute, founded in California in 1962, became a focal point of the "human potential" movement (McGinn, 2000). The techniques of the human-potential movement included the **sensitivity training** group, or *encounter group*, along with Gestalt ther-apy, bodywork and movement therapies, Yoga, Zen Buddhism, and psycho-drama. Another development was the rural communes modeled along the lines of 19th-century utopian communities which found favor among some young people in the 1970s. Still today, those who are interested in personal growth experiences or consciousness-raising can choose from a wide array of group and individual therapies, ranging from weekend marathons at expensive resorts taking part in imported indigenous rituals (Tupper, 2009) to years of "psychocentric" in-depth analysis (Rimke and Broca, 2011). During the 1970s an extraordinary variety of religious and quasi-religious groups flourished in the United States to provide guidance of another sort in the individual's search for self. These "metaphysical" religions (Lewis, 2001), particularly the New Age movement of the late 20th century, presented the possibility of personal transformation. We will examine this phenomenon in terms of its meaning to those involved in it as well as its significance as a reflection of change in the society.

New Religious Movements

During the 1960s, the United States was in the middle of a social and cultural revolution (Polletta, 2012). The "hippies" centered in San Francisco's Haight-Ashbury and New York's Greenwich Village districts were challenging the legitimacy of virtually every American institution. Timothy Leary encouraged young people to expand their consciousness with drugs and, in response, hundreds of thousands experimented with LSD as a route to rediscovery of self. Members of Students for a Democratic Society (SDS), a radical political group protesting U.S. involvement in the Vietnam War, regularly took over university buildings across the country and sometimes forced universities to shut down altogether. In the spring of 1970 the National Guard was called in to stop a student protest at Kent State University, and four students were killed. The scene of American troops killing American students, caught on film and shown over and over again, symbolized the depth of the crisis in the country. During those years hundreds of thousands of people marched in Washington, DC, and other cities to end the Vietnam War. At the same time, a Black Revolution was well along the way, and riots erupted in such places as Detroit and Los Angeles during which stores were looted and whole city blocks went up in flames as rioters chanted "burn baby burn" (a scene sadly repeated in Los Angeles in 1992).

The political activities of the 1960s were a product of festering injustices in society and a widespread feeling that U.S. purposes in the Vietnam War were wrong. Equally, however, the responses of young people stemmed from the psychological alienation created by life in a mobile, affluent, secularized society that seemed to deprive them of personal meaning. Aside from creating social change, the political involvements of young people during this period satisfied the need to find real engagement in a society that otherwise seemed to provide few opportunities for meaningful life commitments. The events of the 1960s were eloquent testimony both to a political crisis in the United States and a cultural crisis of meaning, especially among young people.

When the political furor of the 1960s died down and eventually the Vietnam War ended (in 1975), the political crisis was somewhat defused. However, the crisis of meaning remained. It is not surprising that many of the disaffected young people who were products of the '60s would be drawn to a variety of new religious groups during the 1970s—groups that promised clear answers to the questions "Who am I?" and "Where do I fit into the world?" The **new religions** of the 1970s were "successor movements" to the broader countercultural activities of the '60s.

Because the United States has always been a relatively open society in terms of religious expression, religious cultic phenomenon has been an ongoing part of its history (Jenkins, 2000). But during the 1970s evidence of an infusion of new religious ideologies was visible everywhere. Groups of shaven-headed, incense-bearing, tambourine-playing young people in yellow tunics chanted "Hare Krishna, Hare Krishna" as they persistently pressed flowers or literature on passersby in exchange for donations. Clean-cut, intense, middle-class young people engaged in a variety of business enterprises to support Reverend Sun Myung Moon's Unification Church. Prayer sessions sponsored by the Campus Crusade for Christ proclaiming the approaching coming of the Messiah proceeded next door to assemblies of the Jews for Jesus. Far Eastern religious sects with histories that may go back several thousand years enlisted the support of young, well-educated Americans, many of them from affluent homes.

Evidence indicates that the new religions had wide appeal and touched a large number of lives, directly and indirectly. By the mid-1970s, it had become easy to pursue spirituality outside an established congregation (Wuthnow, 1998), with as many as 10 percent of the population having actually participated in one of the new religions (Wuthnow, 1986). Although this number seems high by any standard, we should acknowledge that the idea of new religions is broadly conceived to include such quasi-religious **personal growth movements** as Scientology and EST (Erhard Seminar Training) along with such **neo-Christian religious groups** as the Unification Church and Far Eastern religious imports such as Krishna Consciousness and Transcendental Meditation.

We have already alluded to the "causes" for the rise of new religious groups during this period, but, as might be expected, their emergence stimulated a huge volume of scientific studies and reinvigorated the sociological study of religion. Since "new religions studies" emerged as a separate area of specialization in the 1970s, hundreds of books and thousands of papers have been written in an effort to understand the nature of new religions and their likely role in the 21st century (Melton, 1999; Bromley and Melton, 2012; Zaretsky and Leone, 2015). With greater urgency social scientists have tried to figure out the basis for the extraordinary receptivity of these groups in both the United States and Europe. Who joined them? How were members recruited? What were the effects on members? Broad theories to explain their proliferation in the 1970s included those that variously stressed (1) the cultural crisis of meaning in the United States, (2) the loss of community in the United States, or (3) the extraordinary diffusion of identity in a highly fragmented modern world. Such explanations, of course,

are not mutually exclusive. They all point to the need to get in touch with feelings and dimensions of self lost in an increasingly impersonal and bureaucratic world. When science and technology portray the universe as barren and bereft of meaning, with humans like pebbles on a vast beach, a need is created for people to find explanations that infuse their lives with a cosmic significance. The sociologist Thomas Robbins commented along these lines:

> Personal identity can appear problematic in a highly differentiated society where individuals have multiple limited involvements and interests, some of which must be performed in a "detached" or nonemotionally involved manner. Proliferating new therapeutic movements and mystiques offer to participants a holistic sense of "who am I" which transcends the diverse roles and limited instrumental commitments of participants. (1988:47)

By the late 1970s the consciousness began to emerge that new religious groups, especially those that qualified as "cults," constituted a social problem. Important questions began to emerge about the "totalistic" and authoritarian character of such groups as Hare Krishna, Scientology, the Divine Light Mission, and the Unification Church. Parents were bewildered by the religious commitments of their children who, in many instances, would or could have nothing more to do with them. An important stimulus to the "anticult movement" was the 1978 disaster in Jonestown, Guyana, in which more than 900 members of a group called the People's Temple led by Reverend Jim Jones were murdered or committed suicide. This case created a media explosion on the negative effects of cults, and desperate parents began to employ the services of "exit counselors" (Hassan, 1990) to rescue their children from these groups and then "deprogram" them.

While the period since the early 1980s has witnessed a decline in the public visibility of new religious groups, social scientists have a continuing interest in the fate of cults (Lewis, 2001; Jenkins, 2000; Dawson, 2006) and other spiritual groups (Melton, 2002). The focus of further scholarship has been on the future of new religions (Bromley and Melton, 2012), the growth of alternative religions (Niebuhr, 1999), and the continued fascination with the study of those who join these groups (Ayella, 1998). While the number of gurus and their cults may be declining, huge numbers of Americans remain deeply involved in new religious groups and practices (Zaretsky and Leone, 2015). According to one author, we are seeing the rise or rediscovery of a large number of cults, "grouped around loosely defined and held beliefs, often of a pseudo-scientific nature" (Crone, 2000:17).

At the core of the cult experience is the feeling of community potential that converts get from recruiters (Freie, 1998). According to one author, "People end up joining cults when events lead them to search for a deeper sense of belonging and for something more meaningful in their lives" (Harrary, 1994:20).

In the late 20th century the attention of social scientists was increasingly drawn to cultlike political groups such as the Christian militia movement (Abanes, 1996; Barkun, 1997), as well as groups that are part of a "New Age" consciousness (Heelas, 1996). The 1993 conflict in Waco, Texas, between Branch Davidians and agents of the federal Bureau of Alcohol, Firearms and Tobacco (Lewis, 1994), and other well-publicized incidents such as the mass suicide of members of Heaven's Gate in 1997 (Lewis, 2001) resurrected interest in cults. Some of the new religions (e.g., those bitterly hostile to society) appear to have a potential for violence, such as Aum Shinrikyo, the Japanese group that used poison gas in the Tokyo subway (Niebuhr, 1999). Although not strictly religious in content, such groups make use of psychological practices that exert strong control over those who turn to them. Such groups may be the contemporary incarnation of earlier cults by providing an overarching system of relevance for those who experience meaninglessness in their everyday lives.

Other areas of interest to sociologists in the late 20th and early 21st centuries included virtual or online religion and the rise of Evangelical Christianity and nondenominational megachurches. Studies of religion with or through the Internet tend to address issues about community and selfhood when religious or spiritual rituals are practiced via the computer screen and keyboard or the smartphone (Zaleski, 1997; Brasher, 2004; Wagner, 2012). Other 21st-century sociologists have studied the roles that the Internet plays as a forum for individuals' quests for "authentic" religious and spiritual identities and communities (Borer and Schafer, 2011; Lövheim, 2011). For example, in their analysis of self-identified Christians who are interested in the popular sport of mixed martial arts, Michael Ian Borer and Tyler Schafer (2011) found that believers went online to give varying "confessional accounts"—remember the discussion of accounts in chapter 9—of the tensions they felt between their religious beliefs and their leisure interests. Confessors believed that Christianity (despite its history of violence) and mixed martial arts, an intentionally violent sport in which competitors seek to knock out or bludgeon their opponents into submission, were at odds and sought out advice, justifications, and dialogues on websites and online forums. As noted earlier, such tensions are common in today's age of uncertainty. According to Borer and Schafer, "Despite the ambiguity that arises from living in and among multiple moral orders, individuals still try to construct a coherent, normative worldview due to an existential need for meaning and order" (2011:166).

Because of their quick rise and mass appeal, "big box" megachurches have become an increasingly prevalent subject of study (Ellingson, 2010). In the first decade of the 21st century, there were about 1,300 of these churches, each with an average weekly attendance of 2,000 people (Thumma and Travis, 2007). Most megachurches provide multiple services throughout the week, many of which feature extensive audiovisuals and pyrotechnics, not unlike a rock or pop music concert. Criticisms of megachurches pin them as merely sources of entertainment without any real substance and incapable of producing "real" feelings of intimacy, morality, and transcendence. Regardless, they function as a loose medium for the lost and lonely to try to make sense of the world around them (Stark, 2008).

Self-Help Movements

The dynamic self-help movement has become an important part of the social fabric of American life. It is not, however, a unified phenomenon that can be categorized easily (Gartner and Riessman, 1998). In many ways, the emergence of self-help and support groups for dealing with virtually every imaginable human trouble represents a combination of many of the elements we have thus far described in this chapter. The self-help revolution reflects the full flowering of the therapeutic culture described at the outset of the chapter. One might say that this has given rise to a relatively new "vocabulary of motives" (Mills, 1940): "that virtually all of us are in need of 'recovery' from one or another psychological problem, whether we acknowledge it or not" (Karp, 2001:107). In self-help groups people turn to others afflicted with the same personal troubles and try, through conversation, to "heal" themselves of what they perceive to be their shared "illness." The illness rhetoric (often implying biological causation) is sometimes joined with a spiritual vocabulary (as in such programs as Alcoholics Anonymous and others like it) positing that "recovery" requires surrender to a higher power. In short, the self-help phenomenon derives its allure, in part, by combining elements of therapy with elements of religion and science. It is a powerful brew that has drawn the faith of millions.

Today, in any major city and in plenty of small towns, you can attend groups that deal with such diverse problems as alcoholism, mental illness, gambling, spouse abuse, drug addiction, impotence, sexual compulsion, and overeating. Although the initial response of mental health professionals to the self-help phenomenon was lukewarm (Powell, 1987, 1990), by the late 20th century it was noted that "the power and effectiveness of self-help is starting to be recognized by government, the human services, the philanthropic community, and by professional helpers who are more and more willing to work cooperatively with self-help groups" (Humm, 1997:5).

Self-help groups bear much in common with the new religions described earlier and consequently serve many of the same functions. These groups, like their strictly religious counterparts, provide integration into a communal network and hold out the promise of personal transformation. People who attend recovery groups, for example, generally acknowledge that their main purpose in becoming involved is to improve themselves (Wuthnow, 1998). In the world of self-help groups, sickness and problems become stable sources of identity,

> creating pseudo-communities for their members, each with a permanent quality about it that people can depend on in a world falling around them. . . . At their best, self-help groups save lives by offering social support to redirect members away from self-destructive habits. At their worst, they are meddling intrusions and trendy clichés that build a consumer culture around drugs, disease, deficits, and infirmities. They offer new selves with which people can identify. (Edgley and Brissett, 1999:197)

Leslie Irvine's (1999) research on Codependents Anonymous (CoDA) illustrates the process at work in CoDA support groups. As in all 12-step support groups, CoDA meetings center on stories. The meetings become a site to examine how "selfhood is a narrative accomplishment, created in the stories people tell about themselves—and this includes the stories that they tell *to* themselves" (p. 1, italics in original). Irvine argues that we learn to tell stories and then become the stories we tell. CoDA members, often reeling from an "uncoupling" (e.g., the breakup of a relationship), "are on a pilgrimage to search for self" (Karp, 2001:111).

The self-help movement may be a response to the huge social upheaval of the last 40 years of the 20th century. A great deal of progressive social change occurred in this period: the civil rights movement advanced African Americans and held the United States accountable for the credo that all are created equal; the antiwar movement forever altered the relationship between Americans and those in authority; the women's movement brought masses of women into the workforce and restructured the family and the relationship between the sexes. Yet, "while these were all positive, progressive social changes, they came at a cost of social dislocation that could not just be ignored" (Humm, 1997:4). Additional changes occurred as the result of medical breakthroughs (e.g., greater life expectancy) and technological advances that have altered the workplace, our mobility, recreation, and relationships, all with profound social ramifications. In response, "quietly and assiduously, Americans have been turning to self-help to assist them in making the adjustment to a changed society" (Humm, 1997:4). A positive view of self-help is that it not only provides short-term relief for personal problems but also has the potential to affect the long-term transformation of societal problems: "Self-help values such as anti-elitism, anti-hierarchy, anti-bureaucracy, getting help by helping, and the recognition of peer power have the potential to transform many of the ways in which we live and work" (Humm, 1997:5).

There is another respect in which self-help groups share something in common with new religious groups. Just as people began eventually to document the ill effects of new religions toward the end of the 1970s, a self-help backlash had developed by the 1990s (Edgley and Brissett, 1999). Not everyone is sanguine about the effects of self-help groups. While people may individually feel better through participation in them, their collective effect may be the production of a national mentality in which virtually all of us perceive ourselves as suffering from some sort of illness and as the "victims" of circumstances beyond our control. The dissidents wonder whether claims such as the one made by John Bradshaw, a leader of the recovery movement, that 96 percent of American families are "dysfunctional" trivializes such real abuses as incest by grouping them with an enormous range of experiences somehow deemed as damaging to people. Critics worry that the underlying illness ideology of support groups furthers the view, distinctly a product of the modern world, that individuals do not bear ultimate responsibility for their life problems and personal behaviors. Such a view is rooted in a radical self-absorption that is the logical outcome of a society that has always valued the development and interests of the individual above the greater social good. The sociologist Edwin Schur (1976) pointed out many years ago that increased personal consciousness is too often achieved at the expense of a diminished social consciousness. More recently, a number of authors (e.g., Bellah et al., [1985] 1996; Derber, 2000; Putnam, 2000; Illouz, 2008; Greenfeld, 2013) have written about the self-orientation and excessive individualism that pervades American social character, voicing concern that this emphasis on personal change is conducive to overlooking the need for larger social change (see box on the following page).

The growth of self-help groups has always been based on their special ability to meet people's needs for peer support and practical information. While the vast majority of mutual aid groups continue to provide help through face-to-face groups, more and more people are finding it easier and more convenient to have their needs met through participation in online support networks. These online mutual help groups operate via message boards, newsgroups, bulletin boards, chat groups, interactive websites, and other online media (Madara, 1997).

It has become impossible to count the number of online mutual help groups, as the number of both mutual help networks and people participating in such groups is increasing dramatically (Madara, 1997). A key feature of these groups has been the ability of any member to offer help and understanding to others. Many people who were previously unable to attend traditional face-to-face self-help groups are among those now participating in online groups. For example, those without local groups or without transportation, those with uncommon conditions or rare illnesses, those with limiting physical disabilities, bedridden individuals, and caregivers with around-the-clock responsibilities are able to participate online (Madara, 1997). Madara gives the example of an individual who found support in an online disabilities forum:

> When I suddenly became disabled due to a stroke, I sought out this Forum and found many friends, one in particular, who helped me "adjust" to the physical and mental aspects of "being disabled." This Forum was a lifeline for me, as I became isolated socially after leaving my job because of the stroke. I could not have coped without all the wonderful people in this Forum and all the helpful support and information. Almost four years later, I still seek out support here and try to help others. (1997:23)

The Dangers of the Awareness Trap

The search for the real self and meaningful intimate relationships occupies a good deal of the attention and energies of many people in American society. We believe that by increasing our own self-awareness and accepting responsibility for ourselves, we will secure the benefits of "the good life." The trouble with this idea is that people may become so involved in their own search for self that they fail to take into account the built-in sources of inequality and injustice in the social structure that make it more difficult for some people to achieve this goal than others. There are many situations in which no amount of self-awareness will suffice to solve social problems.

A huge industry of personal and spiritual change has grown to help people change themselves (Illouz, 2008). But much of this culture of personal change fuels individualism by propagating the view that we can change ourselves without changing society—"or worse, that the only thing we ever need to change is ourselves" (Derber, 2000:100). But as the well-known 20th-century sociologist C. Wright Mills (1959) told us in *The Sociological Imagination*, as we probe more deeply into our seemingly *personal* problems, we realize that they nearly always reflect *public* issues that require social and political change. Although self-help groups certainly provide emotional support and interpersonal ties that are invaluable to participants, they rarely challenge the underlying political issues that have shaped the problems of the individual person (Adamsen and Rasmussen, 2001). The insistence that we can do whatever we set our minds to can promote complacency among the privileged and help foster a way of thinking that blames those most wounded by our society for their own problems (Loeb, 1999). According to Paul Loeb, "The most troublesome consequence of this way of thinking is that it exempts even the most powerful economic, political, and social institutions from all responsibility for the state of society" (1999:140). "Is it any wonder," he asks, "that a woman attending a Seattle New Age conference explained that welfare recipients 'just need to wake up and realize their mythic selves'?" (p. 139).

As sociologists, your authors cringe when we hear simple-minded, feel-good, spiritually-based solutions to structurally generated life problems. Certainly it would be, as one of us has said, "a wonderful world . . . if simply cultivating the right attitude really ensured the evaporation of personal woes!" (Karp, 2001:109). But our sociological imaginations cause us to know otherwise. And, "while there is nothing novel in the observation that raising personal consciousness is too often accomplished at the cost of a social consciousness, it surely remains a message worth preaching to students" (Karp, 2001:109).

As Madara notes, peer support has long been a key value in face-to-face groups, and online communication enhances this peer equality. In communicating with other people online, there are no signs of social status, age, dress, weight, race, disabilities, or other distinctions. Online anonymity makes people more comfortable in sharing sensitive or potentially embarrassing information (Mudry and Strong, 2013). There is also something to be said for the ease of participating in an online group: "One need not get dressed up to attend a meeting from home, while the 'doorway out' is always just a mouse click away" (Madara, 1997:23).

As we noted earlier in discussing the Internet and health (chapter 8), the major barrier to the use of online support networks is the lack of universal access to them. Although libraries and schools may provide public use of computers, they are not a substitute for widespread home access. Populations such as the poor, the severely disabled, and the chronically ill and their caregivers stand to gain much from universal access (Madara, 1997).

■ Individualism, Community, and Commitment

The tension between individualism and community has been an abiding theme of sociological analysis since the emergence of the discipline in the 19th century. The development of sociology arose out of the social and ideological upheavals brought about by the French and Industrial Revolutions. From its earliest beginnings, sociology was simultaneously a response to and a critique of the emergence of a secular urban industrial order in 19th-century Western civilization. The rapid development of urban industrial centers throughout the 19th century precipitated a still-ongoing analysis concerning the nature of the "social bond"; that is, the connection between the individual and society (see chapter 1). Foremost in the minds of individuals writing about society during the 19th century was the contrast between forms of social life rooted in small agrarian societies and the kinds of social relationships characterizing the new urban-industrial world.

The Changing Nature of the Social Bond

Though classical sociological theorists generated diverse conceptual models for looking at the emerging urban order in European society, they fundamentally agreed that the bond between individuals and society had been greatly weakened in modern society (Monti et al, 2014). They were unanimous in their view that people were less morally constrained in urban societies and that their relationships and commitments to community had become far more tenuous. Although each of these writers focused on specific features of the social order, they agreed that whereas the central unit of earlier societies had been the larger collectivities of family and community, the central unit in their contemporary society had become the individual. Further, as the pursuit of individual gain and personal mobility (as measured by wealth) became ascendant social values, relationships among people became more rational, impersonal, and contractual. Whereas people in earlier agrarian societies related to one another emotionally, with their hearts, those in the new social order related rationally, with their heads.

These early social theorists viewed these developments with great alarm. They foresaw that the celebration of the interests and needs of the individual over those of the larger society would ultimately weaken society's very core and diminish its capacity to provide meaningful moral guidelines. A moral society, they thought, was one that protected both society and individuals by placing limits on the aspirations of individuals and their ability to act only in a self-interested fashion. Their common prognosis was that a society based on individualism would eventually erode the strength of its major institutions. They feared that the eclipse of community would foreshadow the demise of the family and would in turn precipitate an increase in all sorts of human pathologies—from crime to divorce to mental illness to suicide. In short, these writers warned that a society based on individualism would eventually unravel.

Although these sociologists could not have had the contemporary United States in mind when they wrote, their analysis appears to apply. Even the most optimistic among us must acknowledge that the United States has extraordinary problems. Each day the news media assail us with more bad news about rates of murder, homelessness, poverty, suicide, drug addiction, robbery, disease, teenage pregnancy, illiteracy, and unemployment. In the midst of great wealth, the United States has increasingly become a nation of "haves" and "have-nots." Racism, sexism, and ageism characterize ever-increasing antagonisms between groups that perceive each other only as adversaries. Although it simplifies things too much to pin all these ills on the consequences of individualism, we must wonder about its causal significance in a society that, more than any other in human history, has made individualism sacred (see box).

Habits of the Heart

Although, as we have seen, the sociological analysis of individualism extends nearly to the origins of the discipline, the conversation about its significance in understanding American character and social structure has been reinvigorated through the writings of Robert Bellah and his four colleagues. In 1985 they published a book entitled *Habits of the Heart*, updated in 1996 and again in 2007, that detailed their analysis of the history and consequences of individualism in the United States. This book has been widely praised as providing lucid, penetrating insights into the current American condition. In their book entitled *The Good Society* (1991), Bellah and his four coauthors continued the dialogue by considering how basic U.S. institutions have been injured and what must be done to repair the damage done to them.

Bellah and his colleagues begin their analysis of individualism by making reference to the famous writings of a Frenchman, Alexis de Tocqueville, who traveled to the United States in the early 1800s as a sympathetic observer of

Wilding for Fun and Profit

The term "wilding" was used by the media to describe a rape and nearly fatal beating of a young white woman jogging in New York's Central Park in 1989. The term caught on like wildfire, in part, because it became a symbol of antisocial behavior and selfish individualism. The media frenzy around this incident led to the imprisonment of a group of African American and Latino teenagers. The actual rapist was a lone man who confessed to the crimes six years later. The teenagers were eventually released, but the damage was done, and the idea of "wilding" remained embedded in the public psyche.

In his book *The Wilding of America: How Greed and Violence Are Eroding Our Nation's Character* (1996), Charles Derber offered a provocative critique of the U.S. culture of individualism in which he argued that wilding is not restricted to the behaviors of a few "pathological" individuals. Derber maintained that we can trace wilding's roots to an individualistic, get-your-own-whatever-you-have-to-do ethic that has always been part of the underbelly of the American Dream. By wilding, he means "the epidemic of uncontrolled, unconstrained self-interest that increasingly permeates all aspects of our society, bringing with it enormously destructive consequences to our material, moral, and communal existence" (Derber, 1998:2). According to Derber, this "culture of wilding" has triggered widespread violence that has undermined civic life.

Derber contended that a degraded individualism, especially in the economy, lies at the root of this decline (Derber, 1996). In our market society, the supreme virtue is to concentrate on one's own interests. So chief executive officers of the Fortune 500 companies receive more than 250 times the pay of their rank-and-file employees. Some U.S. firms close down their plants in the United States and set up operations abroad where they can hire labor for a pittance. The upshot of all this is that the United States suffers from a huge—and growing—maldistribution of wealth and income. The rich *are* getting richer and the poor *are* getting poorer (Morgan, 1999; Nau, 2013).

Derber worried that an American Dream that does not spell out the moral consequences of unmitigated self-interest threatens to turn the next generation into wilding machines. Americans could turn, not only on each other, but on society as well—the result of being too self-absorbed to make the commitments and observe the moral constraints that hold stable communities together. Derber at the end of the 20th century saw abundant evidence that a wilder generation of Americans was assaulting and abandoning society—violence on the streets, family dissolution, chaos in government—all causes as well as consequences of the wilding crisis. "America's culture of wilding, at its extreme, is triggering an epidemic of bizarre and terrifying violence. The new violence constitutes a direct assault on society, undermining the social infrastructure that sustains civilized life" (Derber, 1998:6).

Ernest Morgan (1999) linked the tragic school shootings in the late 20th century to a rampant individualism that he considered a by-product of the greed and exploitation that increasingly had come to characterize American culture. That is, he contended that the shootings were but a "tiny symptom of a vastly greater problem" (p. 4). Morgan suggested: "Fundamentally we need a shift from a paradigm of selfishness—of greed and exploitation—to one of caring and sharing" (p. 4).

* See the documentary *The Central Park Five* (2012) for a vivid and disturbing account of the events that took place that fateful night and how the idea of "wilding" affected the legal pursuit of justice.

the first 50 years of our extraordinary experiment with democracy. Tocqueville later wrote two volumes, published in 1835 and 1840, entitled *Democracy in America*, which detailed insights into American character and social structure that remain astoundingly relevant today. Tocqueville centered his writings on the unwritten norms (mores) that seemed to be emerging in the new nation, norms that were part of America's "habits of the heart," as he put it. Tocqueville admired the spirit of individualism that fostered personal freedom, but even at that early point in the country's career, he worried that excessive individualism could separate Americans from one another and undermine the civic spirit so necessary for the success of a democracy.

Bellah and his coauthors extended Tocqueville's analysis by distinguishing two forms of individualism: **instrumental individualism** and **expressive individualism**. Instrumental individualism, the type most noted by Tocqueville, refers to the freedom to pursue financial and career success. This is the kind of individualism celebrated in the maxims of Ben Franklin's *Poor Richard's Almanac* and in the Horatio Alger "rags-to-riches" stories. Expressive individualism, in contrast, refers to the deep and abiding concerns that Americans have with personal self-fulfillment, with the idea that one of life's missions is to maximize personal happiness by discovering who you "really" are. This second form of individualism is thoroughly consistent with the "therapeutic culture" described earlier in this chapter. Both types of individualism are built upon the kind of personal freedom central to a democratic way of life. The flip side of freedom, however, is loneliness. These authors note that "freedom turns out to mean being left alone by others" (Bellah et al., [1985] 1996:23).

The essential problem posed by individualism is that it "privatizes" the goals and pursuits of people and thereby erodes the social attachments that provide society's moral anchor. Individualism undermines commitment to community since membership in any community (from the family to local community to nation) implies constraints on the behaviors of people that are perceived to be inconsistent with personal fulfillment.

In the introduction to the first updated edition of *Habits of the Heart* (1996), Bellah and colleagues wrote that the consequences of radical individualism were more strikingly evident in 1996 than they had been a decade before, when the book was first published. They observed what they referred to as a "crisis of civic membership," meaning "that there are, at every level of American life and in every significant group, temptations and pressures to disengage from the larger society" (p. xi). This crisis threatens "the confident sense of selfhood that comes from membership in a society in which we believe, where we both trust and feel trusted, and to which we feel we securely belong" (p. xi).

Robert Putnam's *Bowling Alone* (2000) lamented the decline in *social capital*—social networks and the norms of reciprocity and trustworthiness that arise from them—at the end of the 20th century. One of the ways social capital improves our lot is by widening our awareness of the many ways in which our fates are linked. According to Putnam:

People who have active and trusting connections to others—whether family members, friends, or fellow bowlers—develop or maintain character traits that are good for the rest of society. Joiners become more tolerant, less cynical, and more empathetic to the misfortunes of others. When people lack connection to others, they are unable to test the veracity of their own views, whether in the give-and-take of casual conversation or in more formal deliberation. Without such an opportunity, people are more likely to be swayed by their worst impulses. It is no coincidence that random acts of violence, such as the 1999 spate of schoolyard shootings, tend to be committed by people identified, after the fact, as "loners." (p. 289)

Laura Pappano echoed this concern in *The Connection Gap* (2001), stating that as a society, we face a collective loneliness. She is not referring to loneliness in the traditional sense—"the lonely one missing out on the party of life, famished for human contact with too much time to wonder what's gone awry" (p. 8). Rather, she is writing about the rest of us: "The overstimulated, hyperkinetic, overcommitted, striving, under-cared-for, therapy dependent, plugged in, logged on, sleep deprived. We are the new lonely" (p. 8).

She continued:

> People talk a great deal about "community" but complain of feeling less and less a part of one. People long for rich relationships but find themselves wary of committing to others. Many of us hunger for intimacy but end up paying professionals to listen to, care for, and befriend us. . . . As a society, we face a collective loneliness, an empty feeling that comes not from lack of all human interaction, but from the loss of *meaningful* interaction, the failure to be a part of something real, or to have faith in institutions that might bring us together. This is what I call the Connection Gap. (p. 8)

Despite the bleak diagnosis of our social ills in the literature we have cited, we should not be hopeless about the future well-being of the society. The resurrection of a "civil society" requires political and economic policies that stress inclusion rather than exclusion of groups that traditionally have been disenfranchised (Monti et al, 2014). We need to think about economic principles that will encourage even more civic participation and reawaken feelings of commitment to something larger than ourselves. We need to find ways to refashion an American Dream that has become overly focused on materialism. This is possible because rampant individualism is a distortion of a cultural legacy that more appropriately applauds a balancing of individual freedom and community needs.

In 1991, during the Los Angeles riots, Rodney King uttered a plea: "Can't we all just get along?" The question remains relevant today. Is it possible for people of different values, races, experiences, and backgrounds to live together in peace? Pappano (2001) pointed out that much of what worked in the past to create a sense of cohesion and community is no longer applicable today. The world and the issues have changed and become more complex: "We are strange new people living strange new lives" (p. 197).

She continued:

> For the middle class—particularly the white middle class—it was easier decades ago to forge common ground with neighbors and community members, in part because so many people shared the same backgrounds, experiences, and values. Our society today is far more diverse, and that diversity will only grow. We can see this in our own extended families, which increasingly include members of different races, religions, and ethnicities. Likewise, our neighborhoods, our workplaces, our classrooms, and our communities are more diverse. Although Rodney King's plea was for the cessation of violence, it is not enough to not fight. We must find a means for living together, not in silent acceptance but in meaningful concert. The challenge of connection has, in some ways, grown more intense. (p. 197)

This is a complex issue, and the complexity is rooted in our identities, Pappano concluded: "We are searching for who we are, caught between the pull of a bland homogenized culture, in which everyone shops at the Gap and eats at McDonald's. . . . We have an urgent need to know who we are, where we come from, and why we matter" (2001:197).

▪ Future Selves

We are caught in the midst of a major historical transformation with dramatic implications for our personal well-being as well as that of society. Western culture has passed through two central historical epochs, characterized first by agricultural, preurban society and then by urban-industrial society. We now live in a postindustrial society that relies on technological knowledge and is a time of rapid, often confusing, social change.

In the wake of such transformations, social scientists have raised troubling questions about the future. Does a modern society, with its emphasis on technical information, services, and consumption, require a different conception of self than the one characteristic of the eras of agricultural and industrial production? Will individuals be able to make the self-adaptations required in a complex, rapidly evolving society?

Measuring Self-Concepts

In the second half of the 20th century, Louis Zurcher (1977) used a technique called the Twenty Statements Test (TST) to measure self-concepts. Participants were asked to make 20 responses to the question "Who am I?" by completing the sentence "I am" in 20 different ways. They were instructed to write their statements quickly, in the order they came to mind, without worrying about the logic or importance of their responses.

The TST was scored by classifying the responses into categories or modes. Repeated samplings led Zurcher to conclude that the test reveals four central conceptions of self:

The A mode, or physical self.
The B mode, or social self.
The C mode, or reflective self.
The D mode, or oceanic self.

The **physical self** is indicated by responses that refer to actual physical attributes as well as other attributes that involve no interaction with others. A person's residential address would be an example of the latter. The **social self** refers to positions and statuses that clearly locate people in a social structure or social circle. Examples of responses in this mode would include such statements as "I am a college student" or "I am an electrical engineer." The **reflective self** is indicated by abstract statements that transcend specific social situations. These responses indicated the behaviors that respondents attributed to themselves. Examples include such statements as "I am a moody person" or "I am a spendthrift." The **oceanic self** is reflected in statements "so vague that they lead us to no reliable expectations about behavior" (Zurcher 1977:46). Statements such as "I am a loving individual" or "I am a person who wants the best for everyone" would be placed in the oceanic-self category.

When Zurcher first administered the TST in 1969, he found that the most frequent mode of response was the C mode, or the reflective-self category. In fact, 68 percent of his respondents fell into this category, in dramatic contrast to the results of an earlier administration of TST by Hartley (1968), which found an abundance of B mode responses in a random sample of University of Iowa students. What sense could be made of such significant differences over a year's time? Zurcher reasoned that perhaps the proliferation of C mode self-definitions in his own 1969 sample was a response to the rapid rate of cultural and technological change in advanced industrial nations. Specifically, the change in self-conceptualization in the 1960s is thought to reflect the social upheaval that resulted from movement from a conservative post–World War II era to a liberal age of radical demonstrations against the Vietnam War and support of the civil rights movements. Zurcher proposed that a **mutable self**—one in which physical, social, reflective, and oceanic were integrated—would allow a person to assume any of the selves which fit a particular situation.

At the turn of the millennium, sociocultural change continued at an accelerated rate. Sherry Grace and Kenneth Cramer noted that we live in a global age of information technology, changing family composition, and the retirement of the baby boomers (2002:273), and they set out to investigate sense of self at the turn of the 21st century, hypothesizing that this period represented "a state of continued and rapid progress, progress which Zurcher (1972, 1977) and Turner (1976) postulated would lead to a greater detached or transcendental sense of self" (2002:274). In particular, they believed that the Internet and e-mail of our time suggest a self divorced from the ability to reflect through others. According to Grace and Cramer,

> We know too little about the effects of recent social and cultural dynamics (e.g., the effect of the retirement of the baby boomers on the job market for today's youth, the access to information afforded by the

information superhighway, and the communication revolution of electronic mail) on current conceptualizations of the self. How would the "millennials" (i.e., those individuals entering university at the turn of the century) conceive of themselves given the current context? (2002:274)

Grace and Cramer recruited 324 undergraduate psychology students to participate in the study. The authors postulated that the predominant mode of self would continue to be C mode (reflective), but that there would be an increase in D mode (oceanic). They also postulated that females would report significantly more social (B mode) self-statements than would males.

Their results showed that overall, the preponderant mode of self continued to be reflective (C mode). That is, "the nature of self among students continues to be focused on ways of behaving, moods, feelings, preferences, and dislikes" (Grace and Cramer, 2002:277). In fact, these participants have the highest mode of reflective self of any sample published since the 1950s (91.3 percent)! None of the participants had a preponderant mode of physical self; only one participant had a predominant mode of oceanic self. The social self also appeared to be declining (8.4 percent).

Although an earlier study (Babbitt and Burbach, 1990) found that females tended to use more social or B category responses, that result was not replicated in Grace and Cramer's findings. They had hypothesized that women would provide more social responses because women are thought to be generally more in tune with family and interpersonal aspects of relationships. Their results question that assumption.

Grace and Cramer's (2002) findings make sense in light of the current historical context. As Zurcher (1972) and Turner (1976) had argued well before the Internet and smartphones, the pace of technological advancement and change in American society may be leading to the reflective self. This idea prompted Grace and Cramer to ask, "In the future, will this focus on personal affect and evaluation lead to disruption of social group identity and interpersonal relations?" (2002:277). In their 2011 study of undergraduates' beliefs about alcohol use and the college experience, Lizabeth A. Crawford and Katherine B. Novak found that the majority of their sample (60%) listed more impulse-oriented characteristics and preferences than social roles in response to the TST (2011:11). This shows a bit of a shift back *toward* an institutional orientation but still supports past findings about self-reflection and inner-orientation. It also clearly demonstrates that individuals occupy and practice multiple selves and identities.

The Postmodern Self

In chapter 3 we reviewed the writings of Erving Goffman, who suggested that human beings have multiple selves, that indeed we have as many selves as the situations in which we interact with others. As you've seen, we have ended each chapter with a particular type of self, not to mention the other types of self mentioned in the chapter and throughout the book. You should remember that such a view of the self raises intriguing questions about the authenticity of social performances, including whether people possess a "true" self that transcends the range of contexts in which we act. Although Goffman first raised these questions during the 1950s and 1960s, your authors think that questions about the fate of the self have become more urgent in the **postmodern world**. The postmodern world—though some scholars have argued that "hypermodern" is a more appropriate qualifier (see Gottschalk, 2009)—is characterized by information technologies that enormously expand the flow, rapidity, intensity, and volume of communications. These same technologies (from computers to tablets to smartphones) also greatly expand the number and range of interactional arenas in which we participate. A geometric increase in the rate of communication has extraordinary implications for the presentation and maintenance of personal selves: "In an emerging postmodern world the construction and maintenance of an integrated self becomes deeply problematic because the social structures necessary to anchor the self have themselves become unstable and ephemeral" (Karp, 1996:186). Scholars have struggled to identify the consequences of a society comprised of individuals without integrated selves. Their views are as varied as are our selves!

In his book of the same title, Kenneth Gergen ([1991] 2000) referred to the **saturated self**. He meant to convey with this term that the pace of communications and life itself has virtually overwhelmed us and that as a result, our selves are "under siege." We may be reaching a point of social saturation that has revolutionary consequences for the ways we conceptualize the human self and its place in the social world. Postmodern life requires us to adopt multiple perspectives on ourselves, making it difficult for us to form a unified, or core, self. As we take part in "incoherent and disconnected relationships," we acquire a new pattern of self-consciousness that Gergen called "multiphrenia," or many-mindedness. Gergen commented:

> Under postmodern conditions, persons exist in a state of continuous construction and reconstruction; it is a world where anything goes that can be negotiated. Each reality of self gives way to reflexive questioning, irony, and ultimately the playful probing of yet another reality. ([1991] 2000:7)

Later in the book Gergen summarized his position:

> So we find a profound sea change taking place in the character of social life. . . . Through an array of newly emerging technologies the world of relationships becomes increasingly saturated. We engage in greater numbers of relationships, in a greater variety of forms, and with greater intensities than ever before. With the multiplication of relationships also comes a transformation in the social capacities of the individual. . . . The relatively coherent and unified sense of self inherent in a traditional culture gives way to manifold and competing potentials. A multiphrenic condition emerges in which one swims in ever-shifting, concatenating, and continuous currents of being. ([1991] 2000:79–80)

According to this view, the self is a reflection of the cultural zeitgeist (spirit of the times): "The protean, fragmented, media- and information-saturated societies of the West produce, well . . . protean, fragmented, and saturated selves" (de Munck, 2000:43).

Gergen's postmodern self bears a close resemblance to Goffman's dramaturgical self, in that it is fluid and social, enacted and established in situated performances. Although upon first consideration Gergen's picture of the saturated self suggests a pessimistic outlook since the intensity of stimuli facing us is likely only to increase in the future, Gergen noted that it has two distinct advantages over the traditional self. First, the postmodern self is highly adaptive to change—its flexibility allows individuals to cope effectively with the shifting situational demands faced in performing diverse social roles. And second, it has liberating possibilities:

> Because it is unencumbered by needs for consistency, unity, and unvarying authenticity, the postmodern self can be free to play with different identities, relationships, and commitments, knowing that each is valid in different contexts and from certain standpoints. For instance, a student can opt to be a "geek" in the afternoon and a "party girl" in the evening, trading in a bookish self in the classroom for a boisterous self in the bar, without feeling as though these two identities are at odds. (Sandstrom et al., 2003:117)

It may be that the contingencies faced in a postmodern world will require people to question the ideology of individualism we have described in this chapter. Faced with extraordinary stimulus overload, we may be required to redefine ourselves in *relational* rather than individualistic terms. Our sense of well-being may turn on the realization that our existence is sensible only in terms of our connectedness to others. In this regard, efforts to cope with an increasingly saturated self may motivate people to rediscover community as a central source of personal meaning. Social change in the direction of greater communality would have a salutary effect on minimizing the social problems created by excessive individualism.

John Hewitt and David Shulman observed that in contemporary society our sense of self is much more likely than in the past "to be based on a more or less self-conscious selection of a community as its main support" (2010:137). This self-selected community, or community of choice, provides us with a network of similar others who support our conceptions of self. Even when a community is based on rather narrow criteria of similarity (for example, interest in biking), is spatially dispersed, and "significantly a product of the person's own imagination," a sense of continuity and integration is provided, "linking various situated identities to the social identity it provides" (2010:137). Most people find limited forms of community in professions, neighborhood, religion, or social movements but do not devote themselves exclusively to any of them. People may also migrate from one community to another, identifying with a number of communities over the course of a lifetime. According to these authors, where identification with a community is less than total, personal identity is a more salient component of the self.

> The contemporary person is thus in many ways a more self-conscious being than the resident of a traditional community. The self is not simply

a spontaneous product of a fixed community that surrounds it from birth and that assigns it a place. It is, instead, something that must be found, constructed, or cultivated. (Hewitt and Shulman, 2010:138)

Jaber Gubrium and James Holstein (2000) pointed out that "personal selves" are being produced in more social settings than ever before. The stories we formulate about our personal selves are increasingly anchored in institutionally produced narratives, or "discursive environments." Discursive environments refer to "institutional domains characterized by distinctive ways of interpreting and representing everyday realities" (p. 103). Examples of discursive environments include schools, health clubs, support groups, and recreational organizations. These environments promote particular ways of representing who and what we are. With more concerns than ever entering the "self-construction" business, today's world could be characterized as being increasingly populated by *institutional selves* (Gubrium and Holstein, 2001). Although many of these discursive environments seem geared toward constructing problem-ridden selves (comprising a virtual "troubled identity" market)—as in the case of CoDA groups discussed earlier, for example—not all identities are medicalized. There are also plenty of environments that feature mainly positive self-images:

> Mountain climbers, cyclists, and go-cart racers, along with martial artists, wilderness skiers, scuba divers, and myriad others, find that the social sites of their activities provide not only recreation but also diverse ways of viewing and articulating identity. Such discursive environments may be just as consequential for self-construction as those that construct and heal the troubled. (Gubrium and Holstein, 2000:104)

Of course, no single discursive environment determines who and what we are. In a postmodern context, the sense of a personal identity is being constructed in more social settings than ever: "A thriving landscape of institutions serves up myriad selves, providing more and more occasions for constructing who and what we are. . . . This amounts to a field of possibilities and constraints that extends well beyond what Mead, or even Goffman, could have imagined" (Gubrium and Holstein, 2000:105). But in contrast to the gloomy conclusions of many postmodern theorists, Gubrium and Holstein offered some optimistic appraisals in their assessment of the implications of this situation for the future of the self (Sandstrom et al., 2003). Our ability to choose among options in fashioning a self "can be as liberating as it is overwhelming and debilitating" (Gubrium and Holstein, 2000:112). In addition, Gubrium and Holstein suggested that the self is remarkably resilient, so that ultimately it is likely to adapt positively to the challenges of contemporary society. Patricia and Peter Adler's (1999) study of resort workers supports this view. Despite the transience of these "postmodern people" who have "uncoupled themselves from the conventional lifestyles and social structures of society" (p. 53), they have adapted by finding new ways of conceiving themselves:

> In shedding . . . the security of conventional life, they have stepped into a shifting global world where they are, even in the midst of makeshift or

professional communities, fundamentally alone. They have looked inward for their source of strength, been resourceful, eschewed the consumerist lifestyle, and forged their own paths. (Adler and Adler, 1999:53)

For these workers, a transient postmodern existence has not resulted in the loss of core self. Whereas many theories of the postmodern self focus on changes that have occurred to the more surface aspects of the self, they have not looked at the deeper aspects of the self, assuming that it has been dissolved, as in Gergen's (2000) portrayal of a fragmented self that eventually becomes "no self at all." As Adler and Adler put it,

In fact, the selves of transient resort workers in the postmodern era have adapted and thrived. . . . Rather than finding themselves fashioned by layers with no underlying core, they have become more mutable: anchored in change rather than stability and impulse-process rather than institution-product oriented. (1999:53)

According to these authors, "It seems that the postmodernists' most pessimistic view of the demise of the self has not been borne out; rather, the core self has adapted to contemporary conditions and thrived" (p. 54).

The Tricky Business of Predicting the Future

Even though many of the analyses described in this chapter are grounded in carefully collected data, prediction about the future remains a tricky, highly uncertain endeavor. Social scientists cannot make *absolute* predictions about future norms of social life easily. Few of them accurately forecast the civil rights activities of the early 1960s, the urban riots of the mid-1960s, the women's rights activities of the 1970s, the international terrorist attacks of the 1980s, or the Gulf War of the 1990s. Of course, the terrorist bombings of the World Trade Center and Pentagon on September 11, 2001, rocked the world. And as this final chapter is being written, the United States still has troops throughout the Middle East and a militarized police force in cities and suburbs where incidents of racial violence have occurred, including Ferguson, Missouri; Baltimore, Maryland; and Charleston, South Carolina.

The failure to anticipate such social events does not signal some technical or theoretical flaw in sociological work. It is, instead, affirmation of one of the central messages of this book: *Human beings are continually in the process of rearranging their social worlds in ways that they themselves cannot fully predict in advance.*

What, then, can we say about the future? The data presented in this chapter and throughout this book justify optimistic judgments about our capacity for adapting to a rapidly changing society. The expansion of the groups described in the preceding sections illustrates a fundamental aspect of social life. When individuals find their lives becoming too impersonal and too rational, they will inject into them some sentiment, some passion. When social life becomes too routinized, people will collectively find ways to experience novelty. Similarly, when they find their lives becoming too unpredictable, they will introduce some routine into their daily activity. Individuals who feel uncertain of their personal identities and are bothered by a diminished sense of self-worth will respond collectively by trying to alter their environments to meet their needs.

In this book we have tried to convey the value of sociology—more specifically of a sociological focus on everyday life—for understanding the mutual transformations in the relationships of situations and selves. In doing so we have stressed certain themes: the balance between social order and freedom; the interplay of individuals and social structures; the interpenetration of macro and micro social worlds. As boundaries for human interaction, these themes are critical if we are to obtain insight into the organization of our daily lives and the likely shapes of our individual and collective futures.

The Seeking Self

We live in an era where questions about who we are and who we want to be are part of common discourse. Our self is no longer a given. This can be as liberating as it can be debilitating. Focusing too much on our self can blind us from those around us. When we recognize that we need others to help us construct our multiple selves, maybe then we can pay attention to both the self and the other. Who are you? How do you answer such a question? Does it depend on who's asking it and why they want to know? How much do things you consume—from the food you eat to what you wear on your feet—affect your sense of self? How does reading about the self, as you've been doing here, affect your sense of self? And how will that self change when you turn the page, literally and metaphorically?

■ Conclusion

In nearly all the chapters of this book, we have stressed the ways in which individuals' identities are fashioned by the particular social circumstances of their lives. Certainly your sense of self is related to the socialization you have experienced, your family's values and attitudes, your social class, your race or ethnicity, and your gender. We also have argued from time to time throughout this volume that people's consciousness about themselves and the world cannot be understood apart from the particular historical period in which they live. In this last chapter the argument has been that we are now living through a period of history that makes it uniquely difficult to answer the question "Who am I?"

Today's American society is more complicated, more bureaucratized, more impersonal, and more fast-paced than any other in the history of humankind. As a result, there are widespread feelings of anxiety, personal malaise, psychological alienation, and rootlessness. Preoccupied with their *dis*-ease, many people in today's society purchase the time and expertise of professionals in order to discover more about themselves. The helping professions (among them psychiatrists, psychologists, therapists, and social workers) have emerged as a major cultural force since the 1970s. For an increasing proportion of the population, professional help is needed to feel and function better. It seems a fair characterization that contemporary Americans, in contrast to members of other cultures and historical eras, are uniquely concerned with themselves.

One vehicle for the contemporary search for self consists of the fundamentalist groups within Christianity; another consists of Eastern religions that have been around for thousands of years but which achieved great appeal in the United States in the late 20th century, especially during the 1970s. Your authors think that their popularity was due in large measure to the efforts of young people to understand their place in the world. These "new" religions were a reaction to the growing rationalization of modern life. The memberships of such religious movements are relatively small compared to the population as a whole, but their significance should not be dismissed. They reflect a deep urge for people to become "pilgrims" involved in a journey into themselves. We suggested that while new religions remain an important locus for the search for self, the proliferation of self-help groups more recently has become a medium for dealing with the "dis-ease" fostered by a therapeutic society that has fundamentally redefined the meaning of "normalcy."

Some observers of the American cultural scene are pessimistic about our collective future. They wonder whether the rate of social change will outrun our ability to cope with it. Other studies suggest a more benign picture of the future, however. Such a view is consistent with the symbolic interactionist perspective that has guided this whole book.

We have maintained throughout this volume that human beings are not merely passive products of culture. Because they are symbolic animals, they have the potential to create cultures that meet their needs. Such a view of human beings provides an optimistic antidote to the idea, underlying much social science, that we are simply victims of our environments. Our distinctively human ability to constantly re-create the world includes the possibility of creating a more humane society.

Definitions

alienation: Individuals' feelings of disassociation from the surrounding society. Alienation may express itself as feelings of powerlessness, normlessness, meaninglessness, depersonalization, or isolation.

consumption ethic: Belief that one's sense of identity and self-worth can be enhanced through consumption of material things. The value of work is regarded as enabling people to pay for the myriad goods and services available in urban-industrial societies.

expressive individualism: The form of individualism that is primarily focused on the pursuit of personal fulfillment of an emotional sort. Expressive individualism reflects the dominant values of a therapeutic culture that prizes self-discovery.

instrumental individualism: The form of individualism that is primarily focused on a person's financial and career success. Instrumental individualism is reflected in a person's single-minded pursuit of the American Dream of wealth and success, often at the expense of other people.

mutable self: Conception of self that would integrate the physical, social, reflective, and oceanic selves. The mutable self would allow a person to assume any of the selves which fit the situations encountered in everyday life. (See Zurcher, 1977)

neo-Christian religious groups: Relatively new religious groups that are offshoots of traditional Christianity.

new religions: Religious groups that may be based on principles that are thousands of years old but have only recently been introduced in their present form in the United States.

oceanic self: Conception of self reflected in statements too vague and general to lead to any reliable expectations about a person's behavior. (See Zurcher, 1977)

personal growth movements: Groups devoted to helping individuals gain greater self-awareness and insight into their own motives, behaviors, and life choices. The ultimate goal of members is to increase their personal happiness.

physical self: Conception of self related to an individual's physical attributes and attributes that involve no interactions with others, such as place or residence. (See Zurcher, 1977)

postmodern world: The current historical period in the United States, characterized by the dominance of information technologies and rapid social change.

reflective self: Conception of self abstract enough to transcend specific social situations. (See Zurcher, 1977)

saturated self: A term used by Kenneth Gergen ([1991] 2000) to describe problems of identity in the contemporary world. Gergen's notion is that we are so flooded by the rapidity, intensity, and volume of communications in today's world that our very sense of self is in jeopardy.

search for self: Individuals' attempts to define their personal identity. Organizations such as self-help groups and neo-Christian religious sects and psychotherapy suggest alternative answers to the question, "Who am I?"

sensitivity training: Group activities designed to increase interpersonal awareness and improve understanding of self and others. Sessions encourage participants to express their feelings about one another openly and to be aware of others' reactions.

social movement: Attempts to change society, by a group of people that collectively perceives that some aspect of society affects them negatively or results in an injustice to them. Social movements may involve millions of people and have a broad societal focus or be organized around specific issues, such as Mothers against Drunk Driving (MADD).

social self: Conception of self in which position or status (such as education or occupation) clearly locates an individual in a social structure or social circle. (See Zurcher, 1977)

Discussion Questions

1. Which features of contemporary urban-industrial society seem to you most responsible for creating questions of personal identity and self-

worth? What specific aspects of modern institutions heighten the problem of alienation?

2. What are some recent examples illustrating the transformation in our vocabularies of motives from a sin-to-sickness change in explanations of deviant behavior?

3. How do you think about the place of work in contemporary society? Do you consider work as an end in itself or as the means to other ends? Do you believe there has been a transformation from a work ethic to a consumption ethic? Why or why not? What part does advertising play in the way people think about work and leisure?

4. Are you personally familiar with any of the new religious groups mentioned in this chapter? Do you know anyone who is involved in any of these groups? What kinds of people do you think are most likely to join such groups? What functions do you think these groups perform for their members?

5. Do you see any dangers to society created by the self-awareness, personal growth movement? How might the promise of better and more meaningful lives create an "awareness trap"?

6. Are you optimistic about our capacity to adapt to today's rapidly changing society? What form might such adaptations take? How would you speculate about likely changes in individuals' conceptions of self?

References

Chapter 1

Adler, P., P. Adler, and A. Fontana. 1987. "Everyday life sociology." *Annual Review of Sociology* 13:217–35.

Alegría, M., B. Pescosolido, S. Williams, and G. Canino. 2011. "Culture, race/ethnicity and disparities: Fleshing out the socio-cultural framework for health services disparities." In *Handbook of the Sociology of Health, Illness, and Healing*, edited by B. Pescosolido, J. Martin, J. McLeod, and A. Rogers. New York: Springer.

Anderson, E. 1999. *Code of the Street*. New York: W. W. Norton.

Andreski, S. 1972. *Social Sciences as Sorcery*. New York: St. Martin's Press.

Archer, D. 1991. *A World of Gestures: Culture and Nonverbal Communication* (video). Berkeley: University of California Extension Center for Media and Independent Learning.

———. 1997a. *A World of Difference: Understanding Cross-Cultural Communication* (video). Berkeley: University of California Extension Center for Media and Independent Learning.

———. 1997b. "Unspoken diversity: Cultural differences in gestures." *Qualitative Sociology* 20(1):79–105.

Auyero, J. 2011. "Patients of the state: An ethnographic account of poor people's waiting." *Latin American Research Review* 46:5–29.

Bell, W. 1968. "The city, the suburb, and a theory of social choice." In *The New Urbanization*, edited by S. Greer et al. New York: St. Martin's Press.

Berger, P. 1963. *Invitation to Sociology: A Humanistic Perspective*. New York: Anchor Books.

Birdwhistell, R. 1952. *Introduction to Kinesics*. Louisville, KY: University of Louisville Press.

———. 1970. *Kinesics and Context*. Philadelphia: University of Pennsylvania Press.

Blumer, H. 1962. "Society as symbolic interaction." In *Human Behavior and Social Processes*, edited by A. Rose. Boston: Houghton Mifflin.

Borer, M. 2013. "Being in the city: The sociology of urban experiences." *Sociology Compass* 7:965–83.

Bourgois, P. 1995. *In Search of Respect: Selling Crack in El Barrio*. New York: Cambridge University Press.

Business America. 1994. "Recognizing and heeding cultural differences can be key to international business success." 115 (October 15):8–11.

Cagnon, C., D. Flynn, and M. Redman. 2014. "Balancing 'we' and 'me'." *Harvard Business Review* October:3–9.

Carroll, J., and J. Russell. 1996. "Do facial expressions signal specific emotions? Judging emotion from the face in context." *Journal of Personality and Social Psychology* 70:205–218.

Curra, J. 2000. *The Relativity of Deviance.* Thousand Oaks, CA: Sage.

Dreifus, C. 2000. "A conversation with Nawal Nour." *New York Times,* July 11:D7.

Dugger, C. 1996a. "A refugee's body is intact but her family is torn." *New York Times,* September 11:A1, B6–7.

———. 1996b. "Tug of taboos: African genital rite vs. U.S. law." *New York Times,* December 28:1, 9.

Duneier, M., and H. Molotch. 1999. "Talking city trouble: Interactional vandalism, social inequality, and the 'Urban Interaction Problem.'" *American Journal of Sociology* 104(5):1263–95.

Durkheim, É. [1897] 1951. *Suicide.* New York: Free Press.

Edin, K., and L. Lein. 1997. *Making Ends Meet: How Single Mothers Survive Welfare and Low-Wage Work.* New York: Russell Sage Foundation.

Fine, G. 1993. "The sad demise, mysterious disappearance, and glorious triumph of symbolic interactionism." *Annual Review of Sociology* 19:61–87.

———. 1996. *Kitchens: The Culture of Restaurant Work.* Berkeley: University of California Press.

———. 2010. "The sociology of the local: Action and its publics." *Sociological Theory* 28(4):355–76.

Flaherty, M. 2011. *The Textures of Time: Agency and Temporal Experience.* Philadelphia: Temple University Press.

Ford, C. 1996. *Lies! Lies!! Lies!!! The Psychology of Deceit.* Washington, DC: American Psychiatric Press.

Garfinkel, H. 1967. *Studies in Ethnomethodology.* Englewood Cliffs, NJ: Prentice-Hall.

———. 1996. "Ethnomethodology's program." *Social Psychology Quarterly* 59(1):5–21.

Geertz, C. 1973. *The Interpretation of Cultures.* New York: Basic Books.

Gellner, E. 1975. "Ethnomethodology: The re-enchantment industry or the California way of subjectivity." *Philosophy of Social Sciences* 5:431–50.

Goffman, E. 1963. *Behavior in Public Places.* New York: Free Press.

———. 1971. *Relations in Public.* New York: Basic Books.

Goleman, D. 1995. "Making room on the couch for culture." *New York Times,* December 5:C1.

Goode, E. 2001. *Deviant Behavior.* 6th ed. Upper Saddle River, NJ: Prentice-Hall.

Grazian, D. 2007. "The girl hunt: Urban nightlife and the performance of masculinity as collective activity." *Symbolic Interaction* 30:221–43.

Greenfeldboyce, N. 2013. "Want to read others' thoughts? Try reading literary fiction." Shots Health News from NPR (blog), October 4, http://www.npr.org/blogs/health/2013/10/04/229190837/want-to-read-others-thoughts-try-reading-literary-fiction

Grzanka, P., and J. Maher. 2012. "Different, like everyone else: *Stuff White People Like* and the marketplace of diversity." *Symbolic Interaction* 35:368–93.

Gunning, I. 1999. "Global feminism at the local level: Criminal and asylum laws regarding female genital surgeries." *Journal of Gender, Race, and Justice* 3:45–62.

Hall, E. 1969. *The Hidden Dimension.* New York: Doubleday.

Hall, E., and M. Hall. 1990. *Understanding Cultural Differences.* Yarmouth, ME: Intercultural Press.

Harris, S. 2010. *What Is Constructionism? Navigating Its Use in Sociology.* Boulder, CO: Lynne Rienner.

Harvey, D. 1989. *The Condition of Postmodernity.* Cambridge: Basil Blackwell.

Henahan, S. 1999. "Science of lying." *Access Excellence*, Washington, DC, April 20, http://www.accessexcellence.org/WN/SU/lying599.html

Henley, N. 1986. *Body Politics: Power, Sex, and Nonverbal Communication.* New York: Simon & Schuster.

Hewitt, J., and D. Shulman. 2010. *Self and Society: A Symbolic Interactionist Social Psychology.* 11th ed. Boston: Allyn & Bacon.

Hochschild, A. 1997. *The Time Bind.* New York: Henry Holt.

Jerolmack, C. 2013. *The Global Pigeon.* Chicago: University of Chicago Press.

Karp, D., and W. Yoels. 1976. "The college classroom: Some observations on the meanings of student participation." *Sociology and Social Research* 60:421–39.

Kato, Y. 2011. "Coming of age in the bubble: Suburban adolescents' use of a spatial metaphor as a symbolic boundary." *Symbolic Interaction* 34:244–64.

Katz, J. 2001. "From how to why: On luminous description and causal inference in ethnography (part I)." *Ethnography* 2:443–73.

Keltner, D. 1995. "Signs of appeasement: Evidence for the distinct displays of embarrassment, amusement, and shame." *Journal of Personality and Social Psychology* 68:441–54.

Kim, E. 2012. "Nonsocial transient behavior: Social disengagement on the Greyhound bus." *Symbolic Interaction* 35:267–83.

Levine, R. 1997. *A Geography of Time.* New York: Basic Books.

MacFarquar, N. 1996. "Mutilation of Egyptian girls: Despite ban, it goes on." *New York Times*, August 8:A3.

Maines, D. 2001. *The Faultline of Consciousness: A View of Interactionism in Sociology.* New York: Aldine de Gruyter.

McDaniel, E. 2000. "Nonverbal communication: A reflection of cultural themes." In *Intercultural Communication*, 9th ed., edited by L. Samovar and R. Porter. Belmont, CA: Wadsworth.

Moore, M. 1998. "Nonverbal courtship patterns in women: Rejection signaling—an empirical investigation." *Semiotica* 118(3/4):201–14.

Nnaemeka, O., ed. 2005. *Female Circumcision and the Politics of Knowledge: African Women in Imperialist Discourses.* Westport, CT: Praeger.

Paolucci, P., and M. Richardson. 2006. "Sociology of humor and a critical dramaturgy." *Symbolic Interaction* 29:331–48.

Pink, S. 2008. "An urban tour: The sensory sociality of ethnographic place-making." *Ethnography* 9:175–96.

Public Policy Advisory Network on Female Genital Surgeries in Africa. 2012. "Seven things to know about female genital surgeries in Africa." *Hastings Center Report* 6:19–27.

Richmond, Y., and P. Gestrin. 1998. *Into Africa: Intercultural Insights.* Yarmouth, ME: Intercultural Press.

Rosen, J. 2011. *The Unwanted Gaze: The Destruction of Privacy in America.* New York: Random House.

Samovar, L., and R. Porter. 2001. *Communication between Cultures.* 4th ed. Belmont, CA: Wadsworth.

Schwartz, B. 1974. "Waiting, exchange and power: The distribution of time in social systems." *American Journal of Sociology* 79:841–70.

Simmel, G. [1905] 1950. "The metropolis and mental life." In *The Sociology of Georg Simmel*, edited by K. Wolff, pp. 409–24. New York: Free Press.

———. 1950. "The study of societal forms." In *The Sociology of Georg Simmel*, edited by K. Wolff. New York: Free Press.

———. [1907] 1997. "Sociology of the senses." In *Simmel on Culture: Selected Writings*, edited by D. Frisby and M. Featherstone, pp. 109–19. London: Sage.

Singh, N., J. McKay, and A. Singh. 1998. "Culture and mental health: Nonverbal communication." *Journal of Child and Family Studies* 7(4):403–9.

Smith, C. 2003. *Moral, Believing Animals: Human Personhood and Culture*. New York: Oxford University Press.

Steinmetz, K. 2014. "Merriam-Webster announces its word of the year." *Time*, December 15, http://time.com/3632231/merriam-webster-word-of-the-year-2014/

Swenson, J., and F. Casmir. 1998. "The impact of culture-sameness, gender, foreign travel, and academic background on the ability to interpret facial expression of emotion in others." *Communication Quarterly* 46(2):214–30.

Thomas, W., and D. Thomas. 1928. *The Child in America: Behavior Problems and Programs*. New York: Knopf.

Thompson, E. 1967. "Time, work-discipline, and industrial capitalism." *Past and Present* 38:56–97.

Tucker, B. 2012. "The flipped classroom." *Education Next* 12(1):82–83.

Walsh, J., and A. Zacharias-Walsh. 2001. "Working longer, living less: Understanding Marx through the workplace today." In *Illuminating Social Life*, 2nd ed., edited by P. Kivisto, pp. 7–44. Thousand Oaks, CA: Pine Forge Press.

Wade, L. 2009. "Defining gendered oppression in U.S. newspapers: The strategic value of 'female genital mutilation.'" *Gender & Society* 23(3):293–314.

———. 2012. "Learning from 'female genital mutilation': Lessons from 30 years of academic discourse." *Ethnicities* 12(1):26–49.

Waskul, D., and P. Vannini. 2008. "Smell, odor, and somatic work: Sense-making and sensory management." *Social Psychology Quarterly* 71(1):53–71.

Weber, M. [1904–5] 1930. *The Protestant Ethic and the Spirit of Capitalism*. London: George Allen and Unwin.

Weitz, R. 2001. *The Sociology of Health, Illness, and Health Care*. 2nd ed. Belmont, CA: Wadsworth/Thomson Learning.

Williams, L., and T. Sobieszczyk. 1997. "Attitudes surrounding the continuation of female circumcision in the Sudan: Passing the tradition to the next generation." *Journal of Marriage and the Family* 59:966–81.

Chapter 2

Abbott, W. 1975. "Begin by shooting the poet." *Nation* 221 (August 2):88–89.

Barker, M., C. Richards, and H. Bowes-Catton. 2009. "'All the world is queer save thee and me . . .': Defining queer and bi at a critical sexology seminar." *Journal of Bisexuality* 9:363–79.

Becker, E. 1962. *The Birth and Death of Meaning*. Glencoe, IL: Free Press.

Berger, P., and T. Luckmann. 1967. *The Social Construction of Reality*. New York: Doubleday.

Blaise, M. 2012. *Playing It Straight: Uncovering Gender Discourse in the Early Childhood Classroom*. London: Routledge.

Blumer, H. 1969. *Symbolic Interaction: Perspective and Method*. Englewood Cliffs, NJ: Prentice-Hall.

Borer, M., and T. Schafer. 2011. "Culture war confessionals: Conflicting accounts of Christianity, violence, and mixed martial arts." *Journal of Media and Religion* 10(4):165–84.

Cahill, S. 1994. "And a child shall lead us? Children, gender, and perspectives by incongruity." In *Symbolic Interaction: An Introduction to Social Psychology*, edited by N. J. Herman and L. T. Reynolds, pp. 459–69. Dix Hills, NY: General Hall Press.

———. 1998. "Toward a sociology of the person." *Sociological Theory* 16:131–48.

Charon, J. 2002. *The Meaning of Sociology*. 7th ed. Upper Saddle River, NJ: Prentice-Hall.

Connor, B. T. 2012. "9/11–a new Pearl Harbor? Analogies, narratives, and meanings of 9/11 in civil society." *Cultural Sociology* 6(1):3–25.

Cooley, C. H. 1902. *Human Nature and the Social Order*. New York: Charles Scribner's Sons.

Corsaro, W. 2010. *The Sociology of Childhood*. Thousand Oaks, CA: Sage.

Curtiss, S. 1977. *Genie: A Psycholinguistic Story of a Modern "Wild Child."* New York: Academic Press.

Denis, A. 2008. "Intersectional analysis: A contribution of feminism to sociology." *International Sociology* 23(5):677–94.

Epstein, C. 1997. "Sameness and difference between men and women." *Journal of Social Issues* 53(2):259–78.

Gamson, J. 1995. "Must identity movements self-destruct? A queer dilemma." *Social Problems* 42(3):390–407.

Gardner, R., and B. Gardner. 1969. "Teaching sign language to a chimpanzee." *Science* 165:664–72.

Goffman, E. 1959. *The Presentation of Self in Everyday Life*. New York: Doubleday.

———. 1961. *Asylums*. New York: Doubleday.

———. 1963. *Behavior in Public Places*. New York: Free Press.

———. 1971. *Relations in Public*. New York: Basic Books.

Hewitt, J., and D. Shulman. 2010. *Self and Society: A Symbolic Interactionist Social Psychology*. 11th ed. Boston: Allyn & Bacon.

Hill, S., and J. Sprague. 1999. "Parenting in black and white families: The interaction of gender with race and class." *Gender & Society* 13:480–502.

Hoffman, L., and D. Kloska. 1995. "Parents' gender-based attitudes toward marital roles and child-rearing: Development and validation of new measures." *Sex Roles* 32:273–95.

Irvine, L. 2008. *If You Tame Me: Understanding Our Connection with Animals*. Philadelphia: Temple University Press.

Jerolmack, C. 2009. "Humans, animals, and play: Theorizing interaction when intersubjectivity is problematic." *Sociological Theory* 27:371–89.

Kane, E. 2006. "'No way my boys are going to be like that!' Parents' responses to children's gender nonconformity." *Gender & Society* 20(2):149–76.

———. 2009. "'I wanted a soul mate': Gendered anticipation and frameworks of accountability in parents' preferences for sons and daughters." *Symbolic Interaction* 32(4):372–89.

Keller, H. 1904/1908. *The World I Live In*. New York: Century.

Kennedy, R. 2002. *Nigger: The Strange History of a Troublesome Word*. New York: Pantheon.

Kohler, W. 1927. *The Mentality of Apes*. New York: Harcourt Brace.

Leiber, J. 1995. "Apes, signs, and syntax." *American Anthropologist* 97(2):374.

———. 1997. "Nature's experiments, society's closures." *Journal for the Theory of Social Behavior* 27:325–43.

Mannheim, K. 1952. *Essays on the Sociology of Knowledge*. London: Routledge & Kegan Paul.

Mead, G. 1934. *Mind, Self, and Society*. Chicago: University of Chicago Press.

Musolf, G. 1996. "Interactionism and the child: Cahill, Corsaro, and Denzin on childhood socialization." *Symbolic Interaction* 19(4):303–21.

Polletta, F., and J. Lee. 2006. "Is telling stories good for democracy? Rhetoric in public deliberation after 9/11." *American Sociological Review* 71(5):699–721.

Pugh, A. 2009. *Longing and Belonging: Parents, Children, and Consumer Culture*. Berkeley: University of California Press.

Sarbin, T., and J. Kitsuse. 1994. *Constructing the Social*. Thousand Oaks, CA: Sage.

Sanders, C. 1999. *Understanding Dogs: Living and Working with Canine Companions*. Philadelphia: Temple University Press.

Savage-Rumbaugh, E. 1998. *Kanzi: The Ape at the Brink of the Human Mind*. Cambridge: Oxford University Press.

Schuman, H., and J. Scott. 1989. "Generations and collective memory." *American Sociological Review* 54:359–81.

Scott, R. 1990. *Domination and the Arts of Resistance*. New Haven, CT: Yale University Press.

Swidler, A. 1986. "Culture in action: Symbols and strategies." *American Sociological Review* 51:273–86.

Whyte, W. 1988. *City*. New York: Anchor Books.

Wray, M. 2006. *Not Quite White: White Trash and the Boundaries of Whiteness*. Durham, NC: Duke University Press.

Zayas, L., and F. Solari. 1994. "Early-childhood socialization in Hispanic families: Context, culture, and practice implications." *Professional Psychology: Research and Practice* 25:200–6.

Chapter 3

Allon, N. 1971. "Group Dieting Interaction." PhD diss., Brandeis University.

Anesbury, T., and M. Tiggemann, 2000. "An attempt to reduce negative stereotyping of obesity in children by changing controllability beliefs." *Health Education Research* 15:145–52.

Ashmore, R., and L. Longo. 1995. "Accuracy of stereotypes: What research on physical attractiveness can teach us." In *Stereotype Accuracy: Toward Appreciating Group Differences*, edited by Y. Lee, L. Jussim, and C. McCauley, pp. 63–86. Washington, DC: American Psychological Association.

Associated Press. 2006. "Surgeon General: Obesity epidemic will dwarf terrorism threat." *Health SciTech*, March 2.

Bornstein, K. 2013. *Gender Outlaw: On Men, Women, and the Rest of Us*. New York: Random House.

Bourdieu, P. 1984. *Distinction*. Translated by R. Nice. Cambridge, MA: Harvard University Press.

Bourgois, P. 1995. *In Search of Respect: Selling Crack in El Barrio*. New York: Cambridge University Press.

Braudel, F. 1981. *The Structures of Everyday Life*. New York: Harper & Row.

Brents, B., C. Jackson, and K. Hausbeck. 2010. *The State of Sex: Tourism, Sex, and Sin in the New American Heartland*. New York: Routledge.

Brumberg, J. 1997. *The Body Project: An Intimate History of American Girls*. New York: Random House.

Burns, T. 1992. *Erving Goffman*. Boston: Routledge & Kegan Paul.

Buss, D., and D. Kenrick. 1998. "Evolutionary social psychology." In *Handbook of Social Psychology*, 4th ed., edited by D. Gilbert and S. Fiske, 2:982–1026.

Cahill, S., W. Distler, C. Lachowetz, A. Meaney, R. Tarallo, and T. Willard. 1985. "Meanwhile backstage: Public bathrooms and the interaction order." *Urban Life* 14:33–58.

Carroll, J., and J. Russell. 1996. "Do facial expressions signal specific emotions? Judging emotion from the face in context." *Journal of Personality and Social Psychology* 70:205–18.

Chambers, J., T. Clark, L. Dantzler, and J. Baldwin. 1994. "Perceived attractiveness, facial features, and African self-consciousness." *Journal of Black Psychology* 20(3):305–24.

Charon, J. 2001. *Symbolic Interactionism: An Introduction, An Interpretation, An Integration*. Englewood Cliffs, NJ: Prentice-Hall.

Chia, R., L. Allred, W. Grossnickle, and G. Lee. 1998. "Effects of attractiveness and gender on the perception of achievement-related variables." *Journal of Social Psychology* 138(4):471–77.

Collins, R. 2004. *Interaction Ritual Chains*. Princeton, NJ: Princeton University Press.

Conley, D., and R. Glauber. 2005. "Gender, body mass and economic status." Working paper, National Bureau of Economic Research Working Paper Series, National Bureau of Economic Research, Cambridge, MA.

Cooper, C. 2010. "Fat studies: Mapping the field." *Sociology Compass* 4(12):1020–34.

Copp, M. 1998. "When emotion work is doomed to fail: Ideological and structural constraints on emotion management." *Symbolic Interaction* 21(3):299–328.

Coventry, M. 1998. "The tyranny of the esthetic: Surgery's most intimate violation." *On the Issues* 7(3):16–60.

Davis, F. 1992. *Fashion, Culture and Identity*. Chicago: University of Chicago Press.

Davis, G. 2013. "The social costs of preempting intersex traits." *American Journal of Bioethics* 13(10):51–53.

Degher, D., and G. Hughes. 1999. "The adoption and management of a 'fat' identity." In *Interpreting Weight: The Social Management of Fatness and Thinness*, edited by J. Sobal and D. Maurer, pp. 11–27. New York: Aldine de Gruyter.

Dietz, W. 1998. "Health consequences of obesity in youth: Childhood predictors of adult disease." *Pediatrics* 101(3):518–25.

Dion, K., E. Bersheid, and E. Walster. 1972. "What is beautiful is good!" *Journal of Personality and Social Psychology* 24:285–90.

Easter, M. 2012. "'Not all my fault': Genetics, stigma, and personal responsibility for women with eating disorders." *Social Science & Medicine* 75(8):1408–16.

Eckman, P. 1992. "Facial expression and emotion." *American Psychologist* 48:384–92.

Edgley, C., ed. 2013. *The Drama of Social Life: A Dramaturgical Handbook*. Aldershot, UK: Ashgate.

Feagin, J., and M. Sikes. 1994. *Living with Racism*. Boston: Beacon Press.

Feingold, A., and R. Mazella. 1998. "Gender differences in body image are increasing." *Psychological Science* 9:190–95.

Franzoi, S. 1995. "The body-as-object versus the body-as-process: Gender differences and gender considerations." *Sex Roles* 33(5/6):417–37.

Frevert, T., and L. Walker. 2014. "Physical attractiveness and social status." *Sociology Compass* 8(3):313–23.

Garner, D., and A. Kearney-Cooke. 1996. "Body image 1996." *Psychology Today* 29 (March/April):55–61.

George, M. 2008. "Interactions in expert service work." *Journal of Contemporary Ethnography* 37(1):108–31.

Gimlin, D. 2000. "Cosmetic surgery: Beauty as commodity." *Qualitative Sociology* 23(1):77–98.

Glenn, E. 2008. "Yearning for lightness: Transnational circuits in marketing and consumption of skin lighteners." *Gender and Society* 22(3):281–302.

Goffman, E. 1959. *The Presentation of Self in Everyday Life*. New York: Doubleday Anchor Books.

———. 1963a. *Behavior in Public Places*. New York: Free Press.

———. 1963b. *Stigma*. Englewood Cliffs, NJ: Prentice-Hall.

———. 1967. *Interaction Ritual: Essays on Face-to-Face Behavior*. New York: Doubleday Anchor Books.

Granfield, R. 1991. "Making it by faking it: Working class students in an elite academic environment." *Journal of Contemporary Ethnology* 20(3):331–51.

Hansen, K. 1996. *Just a Temp*. Philadelphia: Temple University Press.

Haskins, K., and H. Ransford. 1999. "The relationship between weight and career payoffs among women." *Sociological Forum* 14(2):295–318.

Hebl, M., and T. Heatherton. 1998. "The stigma of obesity in women: The difference is black and white." *Personality and Social Psychology Bulletin* 24(4):417–26.

Hesse-Biber, S. 1996. *Am I Thin Enough Yet? The Cult of Thinness and the Commercialization of Identity*. New York: Oxford University Press.

Hochschild, A. 1983. *The Managed Heart: Commercialization of Human Feeling*. Berkeley: University of California Press.

Hurst, A. 2010. *The Burden of Academic Success: Loyalists, Renegades, and Double Agents*. Lanham, MD: Lexington Books.

Joanisse, L., and A. Synnott. 1999. "Fighting back: Reactions and resistance to the stigma of obesity." In *Interpreting Weight: The Social Management of Fatness and Thinness*, edited by J. Sobal and D. Maurer, pp. 49–70. New York: Aldine de Gruyter.

Johnson, S., K. Podratz, R. Dipboye, and E. Gibbons. 2010. "Physical attractiveness biases in ratings of employment suitability: Tracking down the 'Beauty is Beastly' effect." *The Journal of Social Psychology* 150(3):301–18.

Kang, J. 2000. "Cyber-race." *Harvard Law Review* 113(5):1131–63.

Karp, D. 1986. "'You can take the boy out of Dorchester, but you can't take Dorchester out of the boy': Toward a social psychology of mobility." *Symbolic Interaction* 9:19–36.

Karp, D., and W. Yoels. 1976. "The college classroom: Some observations on the meanings of student participation." *Sociology and Social Research* 60:421–38.

Karupiah, P. 2013. "Modification of the body: A comparative analysis of views of youths in Penang, Malaysia and Seoul, South Korea." *Journal of Youth Studies* 16(1):1–16.

Kaw, E. 1994. "'Opening' faces: The politics of cosmetic surgery and Asian American women." In *Many Mirrors: Body Image and Social Relations*, edited by N. Sault, pp. 241–65. New Brunswick, NJ: Rutgers University Press.

Kessler, S. 1996. "The medical construction of gender: Case management of intersexed infants." In *Gender & Scientific Authority*, edited by B. Laslett, S. Kohlstedt, H. Longino, and E. Hammonds, pp. 340–63. Chicago: University of Chicago Press.

Kirschenman, J., and K. Neckerman. 1998. "We'd love to hire them, but . . ." In *The Meaning of Race for Employers in Working America: Continuity, Conflict, and Change*, edited by A. Wharton. Mountain View, CA: Mayfield.

Kivisto, P., and D. Pittman. 2001. "Goffman's dramaturgical sociology: Personal sales and service in a commodified world." In *Illuminating Social Life*, 2nd ed., edited by P. Kivisto. Thousand Oaks, CA: Pine Forge Press.

Kolb, K. 2014. *Moral Wages: The Emotional Dilemmas of Victim Advocacy and Counseling*. Berkeley: University of California Press.

Konradi, A. 1999. "'I don't have to be afraid of you': Rape survivors' emotion management in court." *Symbolic Interaction* 22(1):45–77.

Kwan, S. 2009. "Framing the fat body: Contested meanings between government, activists, and industry." *Sociological Inquiry* 79(1):25–50.

Kwan, S., and M. Trautner. 2009. "Beauty work: Individual and institutional rewards, the reproduction of gender, and questions of agency." *Sociology Compass* 3:49–71.

Lance, L. 1998. "Gender differences in heterosexual dating: A content analysis of personal ads." *Journal of Men's Studies* 6(3):297–305.

Leidner, R. 1993. *Fast Food, Fast Talk: Service Work and the Routinization of Everyday Life*. Berkeley: University of California Press.

Lemert, C., and A. Branaman, eds. 1997. *The Goffman Reader*. Malden, MA: Blackwell.

Lofland, L. 1972. "Self-management in public settings: Part I." *Urban Life* 1:93–108.

Manning, P. 1992. *Erving Goffman and Modern Sociology*. Stanford, CA: Stanford University Press.

Marlowe, C., S. Schneider, and C. Nelson. 1996. "Gender and attractiveness biases in hiring decisions: Are more experienced managers less biased?" *Journal of Applied Psychology* 81:11–21.

Mason-Schrock, D. 1996. "Transsexuals' narrative construction of the 'true' self." *Social Psychology Quarterly* 59(3):176–92.

Mathews, J. 1997. "Is biology destiny?" *Baltimore Sun*, September 24:1E, 5E.

Milkie, M. 1999. "Social comparisons, reflected appraisals, and mass media: The impact of pervasive beauty images on black and white girls' self-concepts." *Social Psychology Quarterly* 62:190–210.

Molloy, B., and S. Herzberger. 1998. "Body image and self-esteem: A comparison of African-American and caucasian women." *Sex Roles* 38:631–43.

Morales, M. 2009. "Ethnic-controlled economy or segregation? Exploring inequality in Latina/o co-ethnic jobsites." *Sociological Forum* 24(3):589–610.

Muth, J., and T. Cash. 1997. "Body-image attitudes: What difference does gender make?" *Journal of Applied Social Psychology* 27:1438–53.

Nelson, J. 1994. *Volunteer Slavery: My Authentic Negro Experience*. New York: Penguin Books.

Pagan, J., and A. Davila. 1997. "Obesity, occupational attainment, and earnings." *Social Science Quarterly* 78(3):756–70.

Paradis, E. 2011. *Changing Meanings of Fat: Fat, Obesity, Epidemics, and America's Children*. Palo Alto, CA: Stanford University Press.

Paul, R., and J. Townsend. 1995. "Shape up or ship out? Employment discrimination against the overweight." *Employee Responsibilities and Rights Journal* 8(2):133–45.

Perlini, A., S. Bertolissi, and D. Lind. 1999. "The effects of women's age and physical appearance on evaluations of attractiveness and social desirability." *Journal of Social Psychology* 139(3):343–54.

Pierce, J. 1996. *Gender Trials: Emotional Lives in Contemporary Law Firms*. Berkeley: University of California Press.

Pierce, J., and J. Wardle. 1997. "Cause and effect beliefs and self-esteem of overweight children." *Journal of Child Psychology and Psychiatry and Allied Disciplines* 38(6):645–50.

Plant, E., J. Hyde, D. Keltner, and P. Devine. 2000. "The gender stereotyping of emotion." *Psychology of Women Quarterly* 24(1):81–92.

Reay, D. 1997. "The double-bind of the 'working-class' feminist academic: The success of failure or the failure of success?" In *Class Matters*, edited by P. Mahoney and C. Zmroczek, pp. 18–29. Philadelphia: Taylor & Francis.

Robinson, T., and J. Ward. 1995. "African American adolescents and skin color." *Journal of Black Psychology* 21(3):256–74.

Rooks, N. 1996. *Hair Raising: Beauty, Culture, and African American Women*. New Brunswick, NJ: Rutgers University Press.

Roy, S. 2008. "'Taking charge of your health': Discourses of responsibility in English-Canadian women's magazines." *Sociology of Health & Illness* 30(3):463–77.

Sansom, W. 1956. *A Contest of Ladies*. London: Hogarth.

Schafer, M., and K. Ferraro. 2011. "The stigma of obesity: Does perceived weight discrimination affect identity and physical health?" *Social Psychology Quarterly* 74(1):76–97.

Schilt, K., and L. Westbrook. 2009. "Doing gender, doing heteronormativity: 'Gender normals,' transgender people, and the social maintenance of heterosexuality." *Gender & Society* 23(4):440–64.

Schwalbe, M. 2008. *Rigging the Game: How Inequality Is Reproduced in Everyday Life*. New York: Oxford University Press.

Scott, M., and S. Lyman. 1968. "Accounts." *American Sociological Review* 33:44–62.

Sennett, R., and R. Cobb. 1973. *The Hidden Injuries of Class*. New York: Random House.

Shalin, D. 2014. "Interfacing biography, theory and history: The case of Erving Goffman." *Symbolic Interaction* 37(1):2–40.

Simmel, G. 1904. "Fashion." Reprinted in *American Journal of Sociology* 62 (May 1957):541–58.

Smith, R. 2008. "Passion work: The joint production of emotional labor in professional wrestling." *Social Psychology Quarterly* 71(2):157–76.

Staske, S. 1998. "The normalization of problematic emotion in conversations between close relational partners: *Inter*personal emotion work." *Symbolic Interaction* 21:59–86.

Stone, G. 1962. "Appearance and the self." In *Human Behavior and Social Processes*, edited by A. Rose. Boston: Houghton Mifflin.

Thompson, M., and V. Keith. 2001. "The blacker the berry: Gender, skin tone, self-esteem, and self-efficacy." *Gender & Society* 15(3):336–57.

Veblen, T. 1899. *The Theory of the Leisure Class*. New York: Macmillan.

Watson, N. 2002. "Well, I know this is going to sound very strange to you, but I don't see myself as a disabled person: Identity and disability." *Disability & Society* 17(5):509–27.

Waskul, D., and P. Vannini. 2008. "Smell, odor, and somatic work: Sense-making and sensory management." *Social Psychology Quarterly* 71(1):53–71.

Weinberg, D. 1996. "The enactment and appraisal of authenticity in a skid row therapeutic community." *Symbolic Interaction* 19(2):137–62.

West, C., and D. Zimmerman. 1987. "Doing gender." *Gender & Society* 1(2):125–51.

Wood, J., and N. Fixmer-Oraiz. 2014. *Gendered Lives: Communication, Gender, and Culture*. 11th ed. Belmont, CA: Wadsworth.

Yoels, W., and J. Clair. 1994. "Never enough time: How medical residents manage a scarce resource." *Journal of Contemporary Ethnography* 23(2):185–213.

———. 1995. "Laughter in the clinic: Humor as social organization." *Symbolic Interaction* 18(1):39–58.

Zandy, J., ed. 1995. *Liberating Memory: Our Work and Our Working-Class Conscious-ness.* New Brunswick, NJ: Rutgers University Press.

Chapter 4

Anderson, E. 1990. *Streetwise.* Chicago: University of Chicago Press.

———. 1999. *Code of the Street.* New York: W.W. Norton.

———. 2011. *The Cosmopolitan Canopy: Race and Civility in Everyday Life.* New York: W.W. Norton.

Becker, H., and I. Horowitz. 1972. *Culture and Civility in San Francisco.* New Brunswick, NJ: Transaction Books.

Berger, P., and H. Kellner. 1970. "The social construction of marriage." In *Recent Sociology,* edited by H. P. Dreitzel. Toronto: Collier Macmillan.

Borer, M. 2006. "The location of culture: The urban culturalist perspective." *City & Community* 5(2):173–97.

———. 2008. *Faithful to Fenway: Believing in Boston, Baseball, and America's Most Beloved Ballpark.* New York: New York University Press.

Bourgois, P. 1995. *In Search of Respect: Selling Crack in El Barrio.* New York: Cambridge University Press.

Brown-Saracino, J., ed. 2013. *The Gentrification Debates: A Reader.* New York: Routledge.

Bursik, R., and H. Grasmick. 1993. *Neighborhoods and Crime.* Lanham, MD: Lexington Books.

Cohen, S. 2013. *States of Denial: Knowing about Atrocities and Suffering.* New York: John Wiley & Sons.

Crabb, P. 1996. "Video camcorders and civil inattention." *Journal of Social Behavior and Personality* 11(4):805–16.

Darley, J., and B. Latane. 1970. *The Unresponsive Bystander: Why Doesn't He Help?* New York: Appleton-Century-Crofts.

Dassopoulos, A., C. Batson, R. Futrell, and B. Brents. 2012. "Neighborhood connections, physical disorder, and neighborhood satisfaction in Las Vegas." *Urban Affairs Review* 48:571–600.

Deener, A. 2012. *Venice: A Contested Bohemia in Los Angeles.* Chicago: University of Chicago Press.

Duneier, M. 1999. *Sidewalk.* New York: Farrar, Straus and Giroux.

Duneier, M., and H. Molotch. 1999. "Talking city trouble: Interactional vandalism, social inequality, and the 'Urban Interaction Problem.'" *American Journal of Sociology* 104(5):1263–95.

Erickson, V. 2001. "On the town with Georg Simmel: A socio-religious understanding of urban interaction." *Cross Currents* 51(1):21–44.

Gardner, C. 1988. "Access information: Public lives and private peril." *Social Problems* 35:328–56.

———. 1995. *Passing By: Gender and Public Harassment.* Berkeley: University of California Press.

Garfinkel, H. 1963. "A conception of and experiments with 'trust' as a condition of stable concerted actions." In *Motivation and Social Interaction,* edited by O. Harvey, pp. 220–35. New York: Ronald Press.

Goffman, E. 1963. *Behavior in Public Places.* New York: Free Press.

———. 1971. *Relations in Public.* New York: Harper & Row.

Gotham, K. 2005. "Theorizing urban spectacles: Festivals, tourism and the transformation of urban space." *City* 9:225–46.

Gumpert, L., and S. Drucker. 1998. "The demise of privacy in a private world: From front porches to chat rooms." *Communication Theory* 8(4):408–25.

Harvey, D. 1989. *The Urban Experience.* Baltimore: Johns Hopkins University Press.

Henslin, J. 2007 "Trust and cabbies." In *Down to Earth Sociology,* edited by J. Henslin. New York: Free Press.

Humphreys, L. 1970. *Tearoom Trade: Impersonal Sex in Public Places.* Chicago: Aldine.

Kang, J. 2000. "Cyber-race." *Harvard Law Review* 113(5):1131–63.

Karp, D. 1973. "Hiding in pornographic bookstores: A reconsideration of the nature of urban life and anonymity." *Urban Life and Culture* 4:427–51.

Karp, D., G. Stone, and W. Yoels. 1991. *Being Urban: A Sociology of City Life.* New York: Praeger.

Kim, E. 2012. "Nonsocial transient behavior: Social disengagement on the Greyhound bus." *Symbolic Interaction* 35:267–83.

Klinkenborg, V. 2000. "The city life: Eye contact." *New York Times,* April 27:A26.

Krase, J. 2012. *Seeing Cities Change: Local Culture and Class.* Aldershot, UK: Ashgate.

Laner, M., M. Benin, and N. Ventrone. 2001. "Bystander attitudes toward victims of violence: Who's worth helping?" *Deviant Behavior: An Interdisciplinary Journal* 22:23–42.

Lofland, L. 1971. "Self-management in public settings, part I." *Urban Life and Culture 1* (April):93–117.

———. 1998. *The Public Realm: Exploring the City's Quintessential Social Territory.* New York: Aldine de Gruyter.

Lyman, S., and M. Scott. 1970. "Game frameworks." In *A Sociology of the Absurd,* edited by S. Lyman and M. Scott. New York: Appleton-Century-Crofts.

Madriz, E. 1997. "Latina teenagers: Victimization, identity, and fear of crime." *Social Justice* 24(4):39–56.

Massey, D., and N. Denton. 1993. *American Apartheid: Segregation and the Making of the Underclass.* Cambridge, MA: Harvard University Press.

McNicholas, J., and G. Collis. 2000. "Dogs as catalysts for social interactions: Robustness of the effect." *British Journal of Psychology* 91(1):61–70.

Milgram, S. 1970. "The experience of living in cities." *Science* 167 (March):1461–68.

Milligan, M. 1998. "Interactional past and potential: The social construction of place attachment." *Symbolic Interaction* 21:1–33.

———. 2003. "Displacement and identity discontinuity: The role of nostalgia in establishing new identity categories." *Symbolic Interaction* 26:381–403.

Monti, D. 2012. *Engaging Strangers: Civil Rites, Civic Capitalism, and Public Order in Boston.* Lanham, MD: Rowman & Littlefield.

Monti, D., M. Borer, and L. Macgregor. 2014. *Urban People and Places: The Sociology of Cities, Suburbs, and Towns.* Thousand Oaks, CA: Sage.

O'Brien, D. T. 2010. "Sociality in the city: Using biological principles to explore the relationship between high population density and social behavior." *Advances in Sociology Research* 8:203–16.

Oldenburg, R. 1989. *The Great Good Place: Café, Coffee Shops, Community Centers, Beauty Parlors, General Stores, Bars, Hangouts, and How They Get You Through the Day.* New York: Paragon.

Park, R. 1928. "Human migration and the marginal man." *American Journal of Sociology* 33:888–96.

Pattillo, M. 1998. "Sweet mothers and gangbangers: Managing crime in a black middle-class neighborhood." *Social Forces* 76(3):747–75.

Persson, A. 2001. "Intimacy among strangers: On mobile telephone calls in public places." *Journal of Mundane Behavior* 2(3). Accessed August 15, 2002. http://www.mundanebehavior.org/issues/v2n3/persson.htm (article no longer available).

Robins, D., C. Sanders, and S. Cahill. 1991. "Dogs and their people: Pet-facilitated interaction in a public setting." *Journal of Contemporary Ethnography* 20:4–25.

Rosenblatt, P., and S. DeLuca. 2012. "'We don't live outside, we live in here': Neighborhood and residential mobility decisions among low-income families." *City & Community* 11(3):254–84.

Rubin, L. 1994. *Families on the Fault Line: America's Working Class Speaks about the Family, the Economy, Race, and Ethnicity*. New York: HarperCollins.

Schutz, A. 1960. "The stranger: An essay in social psychology." In *Collected Papers: Studies in Social Theory*. The Hague: Martinus Nijhoff.

Seligman, A. 2000. *The Problem of Trust*. Princeton, NJ: Princeton University Press.

Semmes, C. 1991. "Developing trust." *Journal of Contemporary Ethnography* 19:450–70.

Simmel, G. 1950a. "The metropolis and mental life." In *The Sociology of Georg Simmel*, edited by K. Wolff. New York: Free Press.

———. 1950b. "The stranger." In *The Sociology of Georg Simmel*, edited by K. Wolff. New York: Free Press.

Snow, D., and L. Anderson. 1993. *Down on Their Luck*. Berkeley: University of California Press.

Staples, B. 1992. "Black men and public space." In *Life Studies*, edited by D. Cavitch, pp. 29–32. Boston: Bedford Books.

Stone, L. 1993. "Perfect strangers." *Triquarterly* 86 (Winter 92/93):282–302.

Taibbi, M. 2015. "Why Baltimore blew up." *Rolling Stone* 1236 (June 4):40–7.

Tissot, S. 2011. "Of dogs and men: The making of spatial boundaries in a gentrifying neighborhood." *City & Community* 10(3):265–84.

U.S. Census Bureau. 2010. *Census 2010 Summary File*. Accessed January 30, 2014. http://factfinder2.census.gov

Vann, B. 1999. "Service-learning as symbolic interaction." In *Cultivating the Sociological Imagination: Concepts and Models for Service-Learning in Sociology*, edited by J. Ostrow, G. Hesser, and S. Enos, pp. 83–92. Washington, DC: American Association for Higher Education.

West, C. 1999. "Not even a day in the life." In *Qualitative Sociology as Everyday Life*, edited by B. Glassner and R. Hertz, pp. 3–12. Thousand Oaks, CA: Sage.

Whyte, W. H. 1988. *City*. New York: Anchor Books.

Wirth, L. 1938. "Urbanism as a way of life." *American Journal of Sociology* 44 (July):1–24.

Wolfinger, N. 1995. "Passing moments: Some social dynamics of pedestrian interaction." *Journal of Contemporary Ethnography* 24(3):323–41.

Wood, E. 2000. "Working in the fantasy factory: The attention hypothesis and the enacting of masculine power in strip clubs." *Journal of Contemporary Ethnography* 29(1):5–31.

Wood, L., B. Giles-Corti, and M. Bulsara. 2005. "The pet connection: Pets as a conduit for social capital?" *Social Science & Medicine* 61(6):1159–73.

Yamori, K. 1998. "Going with the flow: Micro-macro dynamics in the macrobehavioral patterns of pedestrian crowds." *Psychological Review* 105(3):530–57.

Chapter 5

Anderson, A. 2001. "Surf here often?" *Christianity Today* 45(8):38.

Arendell, T. 1995. *Fathers and Divorce*. New York: Sage.

Aries, P. 1962. *Centuries of Childhood: A Social History of Family Life*. New York: Vintage.

Bellah, R., R. Madsen, W. Sullivan, A. Swidler, and S. Tipton. [1985] 1996. *Habits of the Heart: Individualism and Commitment in American Life*. Berkeley: University of California Press.

Benedict, J. 1997. *Public Heroes, Private Felons: Athletes and Crimes against Women*. Boston: Northeastern University Press.

Bergen, R. 1996. *Wife Rape: Understanding the Response of Survivors and Service Providers*. Thousand Oaks, CA: Sage.

———. 1998. *Issues in Intimate Violence*. Thousand Oaks, CA: Sage.

Bianchi, S., and M. Milkie. 2010. "Work and family research in the first decade of the 21st century." *Journal of Marriage and Family* 72(3):705–25.

Bianchi, S., M. Milkie, L. Sayer, and J. Robinson. 2000. "Is anyone doing the housework? Trends in the gender division of household labor." *Social Forces* 79(1):191–228.

Bogle, K. 2008. *Hooking up: Sex, Dating, and Relationships on Campus*. New York: New York University Press.

Boswell, A., and J. Spade. 1996. "Fraternities and collegiate rape culture: Why are some fraternities more dangerous places for women?" *Gender & Society* 19(2):133–47.

Botkin, D., M. Weeks, and J. Morris. 2000. "Changing marriage role expectations: 1961–1996." *Sex Roles* (May):933–42.

Brackett, K. 2000. "Facework strategies among romance fiction readers." *Social Science Journal* 37(3):347–60.

Brownlee, S. 1997. "Can't do without love: What science says about those tender feelings." *U.S. News & World Report* 122(6):58–60.

Bumpass, L., and H. Lu. 2000. "Trends in cohabitation and implications for children's family contexts in the U.S." *Population Studies* 54(1):29–41.

Burton, R. 1998. "Global integrative meaning as a mediating factor in the relationship between social roles and psychological distress." *Journal of Health and Social Behavior* 39:201–15.

Centers for Disease Control. 2011. *Teenagers in the United States: Sexual Activity, Contraceptive Use, and Childbearing, 2006–2010*. Hyattsville, MD: Center for Health Statistics.

Chasteen, A. 1994. "The world around me: The environment and single women." *Sex Roles* 31:209–28.

Choat, I. 2000. "Love at first site." *Computer Weekly*, February 10, p. 49.

Clarkberg, M. 1999. "The price of partnering: The role of economic well-being in young adults' first union experiences." *Social Forces* 77(3):945–68.

Cox, T. 2000. *Hot Relationships: How to Know What You Want, Get What You Want, and Keep It Red Hot!* New York: Bantam.

Cross, G. 1997. *Kids' Stuff: Toys and the Changing World of American Childhood*. Cambridge, MA: Harvard University Press.

Curtis, D. 1997. "Perspectives on acquaintance rape." American Academy of Experts in Traumatic Stress. Accessed June 10, 2015. http://www.aaets.org/arts/art13.htm

Di Leonardo, M. 1987. "The female world of cards and holidays: Women, family and the work of kinship." *Signs* 12:40–53.

Dines, G., R. Jensen, and A. Russo. 1998. *Pornography: The Production and Consumption of Inequality*. New York: Routledge.

Dolgin, K., and N. Minowa. 1997. "Gender differences in self-presentation: A comparison of the roles of flatteringness and intimacy in self-disclosure to friends." *Sex Roles* 36:371–80.

Durkheim, É. [1915] 1965. *The Elementary Forms of Religious Life*. Glencoe, IL: Free Press.

Edwards, T. 2000. "Single by choice." *Time* magazine online 156(9), August 28.

Farrell, B. 1999. *Family: The Making of an Idea, an Institution, and a Controversy in American Culture*. Boulder, CO: Westview Press.

Floyd, K. 1997. "Brotherly love II: A developmental perspective on liking, love, and closeness in the fraternal dyad." *Journal of Family Psychology* 11:196–209.

Forste, R., and K. Tanfer. 1996. "Sexual exclusivity among dating, cohabiting, and married women." *Journal of Marriage and the Family* 58:33–47.

Francis, A. 2012. "The dynamics of family trouble: Middle-class parents whose children have problems." *Journal of Contemporary Ethnography* 41(4):371–401.

Francis, L., ed. 1996. *Date Rape: Feminism, Philosophy, and the Law*. University Park: Pennsylvania State University Press.

Galliher, R., S. Rostosky, D. Welsh, and M. Kawaguchi. 1999. "Power and psychological well-being in late adolescent romantic relationships." *Sex Roles* (May):689–710.

Ganong L., M. Coleman, A. Thompson, and C. Goodwin-Watkins. 1996. "African American and European American college students' expectations for self and future." *Journal of Family Issues* 17(6):758–75.

Gebhard, P. 1980. "Sexuality in the post-Kinsey era." In *Changing Patterns in Sexual Relations*, edited by W. Armytage, R. Chester, and J. Peel. New York: Academic Press.

Glenn, N. 1997. *Closed Hearts, Closed Minds: The Textbook Story of Marriage*. New York: Institute for American Values.

Greenstein, T. 1996. "Gender ideology and perceptions of the fairness of the division of household labor: Effects on marital quality." *Social Forces* 74:1029–42.

Halliday Hardie, J., and A. Lucas. 2010. "Economic factors and relationship quality among young couples: Comparing cohabitation and marriage." *Journal of Marriage and Family* 72(5):114–154.

Hardin, M., and J. Greer. 2009. "The influence of gender-role socialization, media use and sports participation on perceptions of gender-appropriate sports." *Journal of Sport Behavior* 32(2):207–26.

Harris, R., and J. Firestone. 1998. "Changes in predictors of gender role ideologies among women: A multivariate analysis." *Sex Roles* 38:239–52.

Hatfield, E., and R. Rapson. 1996. *Love and Sex: Cross-Cultural Perspectives*. New York: Allyn & Bacon.

Hendrick, C. 1997. "Roles and gender in relationships." In *Handbook of Personal Relationships*, 2nd ed., edited by S. Duck, pp. 429–47. Chichester, England: Wiley.

Hill, C., Z. Rubin, and L. Peplau. 1977. "Breakups before marriage: The end of 103 affairs." In *Family in Transition*, edited by A. Skolnick and J. Skolnick. Boston: Little, Brown.

Hochschild, A., and A. Machung. 1989. *The Second Shift*. New York: Avon Books.

———. 1997. *The Time Bind*. New York: Metropolitan Books.

Hofferth, S., J. Kahn, and W. Baldwin. 1987. "Premarital sexual activity among U.S. teenage women over the past three decades." *Family Planning Perspectives* 19:46–53.

Hook, J. 2010. "Gender inequality in the welfare state: Sex segregation in housework, 1965–2003." *American Journal of Sociology* 115:1480–1523.

Hopper, J. 2001. "The symbolic origins of conflict." *Journal of Marriage and Family* 63:430–45.

Houts, R., and E. Robins. 1996. "Compatibility and the development of premarital relationships." *Journal of Marriage and the Family* 58(1):7–20.

Hyde, J., and J. DeLamater. 2013 *Understanding Human Sexuality*. 12th ed. Boston: McGraw-Hill.

Institute of Medicine. 2000. *No Time to Lose: Getting More from HIV Prevention*, edited by M. Ruiz et al. Washington, DC: National Academy Press.

Jacobs, J., and K. Gerson. 2009. *The Time Divide: Work, Family, and Gender Inequality*. Cambridge, MA: Harvard University Press.

James, M. 2014. "News Corp. will buy Canadian romance publisher Harlequin." *Los Angeles Times*, May 3., http://www.latimes.com/entertainment/envelope/cotown/la-et-ct-news-corp-harlequin-20140503-story.html

Jamieson, L. 2012. "Intimacy as a concept: Explaining social change in the context of globalisation or another form of ethnocentricism?" *Clarion* 1:133–47.

Jansen, M., D. Mortelmans, and L. Snoeckx. 2009. "Repartnering and (re) employment: Strategies to cope with the economic consequences of partnership dissolution." *Journal of Marriage and Family* 71(5):1271–93.

Jensen, R. 1995. "Pornographic lives." *Violence against Women* 1:32–54.

Johnson, F. 1996. "Friendships among women: Closeness in dialogue." In *Gendered Relationships*, edited by J. Wood, pp. 79–94. Mountain View, CA: Mayfield.

Karp, D., G. Stone, and W. Yoels. 1991. *Being Urban: A Sociology of City Life*. New York: Praeger.

Kellogg, C. 2014. "*Fifty Shades of Grey* trilogy tops 100 million in worldwide sales." *Los Angeles Times*, February 26, http://articles.latimes.com/2014/feb/26/entertainment/la-et-jc-fifty-shades-of-grey-tops-100-million-in-worldwide-sales-20140226

Kelly, D. 2001. *Sexuality Today*. 7th ed. New York: McGraw-Hill.

Kim, H. 2011. "Consequences of parental divorce for child development." *American Sociological Review* 76(3):487–511.

Kinsey, A., et al. 1953. *Sexual Behavior in the Human Female*. Philadelphia: Saunders.

Kirby, D. 1999. "Reducing adolescent pregnancy: Approaches that work." *Contemporary Pediatrics* 16:83–94.

———. 2001. *Emerging Answers: Research Findings on Program to Reduce Teen Pregnancy*. Washington, DC: National Campaign to Prevent Teen Pregnancy.

Kirschenbaum, M. 1999. *Women & Love*. New York: Avon.

Klinenberg, E. 2012. *Going Solo: The Extraordinary Rise and Surprising Appeal of Living Alone*. New York: Penguin.

Kwan, S., and M. Trautner. 2009. "Beauty work: Individual and institutional rewards, the reproduction of gender, and questions of agency." *Sociology Compass* 3:49–71.

Lamm, H., U. Wiesman, and K. Keller. 1998. "Subjective determinants of attraction: Self-perceived causes of the rise and decline of liking, love and being in love." *Personal Relationships* 5:91–104.

Laner, M. 1995. *Dating: Delights, Discontents and Dilemmas*. 2nd ed. Salem, MA: Sheffield.

Lanis, K., and K. Covell. 1995. "Images of women in advertisements: Effects on attitudes related to sexual aggression." *Sex Roles* 33:639–49.

Leaper, C. 1996. "The relationship of play activity and gender to parent and child sex-typed communication." *International Journal of Behavioral Development* 19:689–703.

Lindsay, J. 2000. "An ambiguous commitment: Moving to a cohabitating relationship." *Journal of Family Studies* 6(1):120–34.

Ling, R., N. Baron, A. Lenhart, and S. Campbell. 2014. "'Girls text really weird': Gender, texting, and identity among teens." *Journal of Children and Media* 8(4):423–39.

Lynch, A. 1999. "On-line and in love." *Accent on Living* 44(1):52–55.

Match.com. 2013. "Match.com fact sheet 2013." Accessed June 8, 2015. http://www.match.mediaroom.com/download/Match.com+Fact+Sheet+2013.pdf

Mathews, T. 1965. "Operation match." *Harvard Crimson*, November 3. Accessed June 8, 2015. http://www.thecrimson.com/article/1965/11/3/operation-match-pif-you-stop-to

Milkie, M., and P. Peltola. 1999. "Playing all the roles: Gender and the work-family balancing act." *Journal of Marriage and the Family* 61(2):476–90.

Monroe, M., R. Baker, and S. Roll. 1997. "The relationship of homophobia to intimacy in heterosexual men." *Journal of Homosexuality* 33:23–37.

Monti, D., M. Borer, and L. Macgregor. 2014. *Urban People and Places: The Sociology of Cities, Suburbs, and Towns*. Thousand Oaks, CA: Sage.

Naughton, J. 2012. "Anything goes: Focus on romance." *Publishers Weekly*, November 14, http://www.publishersweekly.com/pw/by-topic/new-titles/adult-announcements/article/54762-anything-goes-focus-on-romance-fall-2012.html

Newman, M., C. Groom, L. Handelman, and J. Pennebaker. 2008. "Gender differences in language use: An analysis of 14,000 text samples." *Discourse Processes* 45(3):211–36.

Newport, F. 1996. "Americans generally happy with their marriages." *Gallup Poll Monthly* (September):18–22.

Newsweek. 2001. "Love on-line: Millions are turning to the Internet to find romance. The pursuit can be fruitful—but chemistry is a tricky thing to transmit." February 19:46.

New York Times. 2015. "Weddings: Meeting each other halfway, and then some." January 23. http://www.nytimes.com/2015/01/25/fashion/weddings/meeting-each-other-halfway-and-then-some.html

Nock, S. 1995. "A comparison of marriages and cohabiting relationships." *Journal of Family Issues* 16:53–76.

———. 1999. "The problem with marriage." *Society* 36(5):20–27.

Online Dating Magazine. 2012. "How many online dating sites are there?" www.onlinedatingmagazine.com

Orenstein, P. 1994. *SchoolGirls: Young Women, Self-Esteem, and the Confidence Gap*. New York: Doubleday.

Papp, L., J. Danielewicz, and C. Cayemberg. 2012. "'Are we Facebook official?' Implications of dating partners' Facebook use and profiles for intimate relationship satisfaction." *Cyberpsychology, Behavior, and Social Networking* 15(2):85–90.

Pappano, L. 2001. *The Connection Gap: Why Americans Feel So Alone*. New Brunswick, NJ: Rutgers University Press.

Parks, M., and K. Floyd. 1996. "Meanings for closeness and intimacy in friendship." *Journal of Social and Personal Relationships* 13:85–107.

Perry-Jenkins, M., and K. Folk. 1994. "Class, couples, and conflict: Effects of the division of labor on assessments of marriage in dual-earner families." *Journal of Marriage and the Family* 56:165–80.

Prager, K., and D. Buhrmester. 1998. "Intimacy and need fulfillment in couple relationships." *Journal of Social and Personal Relationships* 15:435–69.

Price, J. 1999. "Love gets lab tests." *Insight on the News* 15(7):43.

Putnam, R. 2000. *Bowling Alone: The Collapse and Revival of American Community.* New York: Touchstone.

Reis, H., and P. Shaver. 1997. "Intimacy as an interpersonal process." In *Handbook of Personal Relationships: Theory, Research, and Intervention,* 2nd ed., edited by S. Duck, pp. 367–89. Chichester, England: Wiley.

Reiss, I. 1960. "Toward a sociology of the heterosexual love relationship." *Marriage and Family Living* 22:139–45.

Richardson, L. 1988. "Secrecy and status: The social construction of forbidden relationships." *American Sociological Review* 35:209–19.

Riesman, D. 1950. *The Lonely Crowd.* New Haven, CT: Yale University Press.

Robinson, J., and G. Godbey. 1997. *Time for Life: The Surprising Ways Americans Use Their Time.* University Park: Pennsylvania State University Press.

Rogers, S., and P. Amato. 2000. "Have changes in gender relations affected marital quality?" *Social Forces* 79(2):731–53.

Roiphe, K. 1993. *The Morning After.* Boston: Little, Brown.

Romance Writers of America. 2014. "Romance reader statistics." Accessed April 2, 2015. https://www.rwa.org/p/cm/ld/fid=582

Roylance, F. 2001a. "More women raising children without spouse." *Baltimore Sun,* May 15:1A, 5A.

———. 2001b. "Count of same-sex couples jumps past 11,000 in state." *Baltimore Sun,* July 3.

Sanday, P. 1990. *Fraternity Gang Rape.* New York: New York University Press.

———. 1996. "Rape-prone versus rape-free campus cultures." *Violence against Women* 2:191–208.

Saricks, J. 1999. "Rules of the romance genre." *Booklist* 96(2):244.

Satcher, D. 2001. *The Surgeon General's Call to Action to Promote Sexual Health and Responsible Sexual Behavior.* Washington, DC: U.S. Department of Health and Human Services, Office of the Surgeon General.

Schacter, S. 1959. *The Psychology of Affiliation.* Stanford, CA: Stanford University Press.

Schuster, M., R. Bell, and D. Kanouse. 1996. "The sexual practices of adolescent virgins: Genital sexual activities of high school students who have never had vaginal intercourse." *American Journal of Public Health* 86:1570–76.

Schwartz, M., and W. DeKeseredy. 1997. *Sexual Assault on the College Campus.* Thousand Oaks, CA: Sage.

Schwartz, P., and V. Rutter. 1998. *The Gender of Sexuality.* Thousand Oaks, CA: Pine Forge Press.

Sexuality Information and Education Council of the United States. 1995. *A Report on Adolescent Sexuality.* New York: SIECUS.

Shirani, F., K. Henwood, and C. Coltart. 2012. "Meeting the challenges of intensive parenting culture: Gender, risk management, and the moral parent." *Sociology* 46 (1):25–40.

Silverstein, J., and M. Lasky. 2011. *Online Dating for Dummies.* Hoboken, NJ: Wiley & Sons.

Smith, C., and F. Attwood. 2014. "Anti/pro/critical porn studies." *Porn Studies* 1:7–23.

Smith, T. 2000. *Data from the General Social Survey.* National Opinion Research Center. University of Chicago.

Smock, P. 2000. "Cohabitation in the United States: An appraisal of research themes, findings and implications." *Annual Review of Sociology* 26:1–20.

Smock, P., W. Manning, and S. Gupta. 1999. "The effect of marriage and divorce on women's economic well-being." *American Sociological Review* 64:794–812.

Sprout, A. 1997. "Looking for love in all the Web places." *Fortune* 135(4):186.

Stack, S. 1998. "Marriage, family and loneliness: A cross-national study." *Sociological Perspectives* 41(2):415–23.

Stanley, S., G. Rhoades, and H. Markman. 2006. "Sliding versus deciding: Inertia and the premarital cohabitation effect." *Family Relations* 55(4):499–509.

Starling, K. 2000. "The joys and dangers of love on the Internet." *Ebony* 55(4):46.

Sternberg, R. 1988. *The Triangle of Love.* New York: Basic Books.

Stohs, J. 2000. "Multicultural women's experience of household labor, conflicts, and equity." *Sex Roles* (March):339–61.

Thoits, P. 1989. "The sociology of emotions." *Annual Review of Sociology* 15:317–42.

Time. 2000. "The love machines: Valentines may now be wired, but on-line dating is also fostering some very 19th century courtship." February 14:73.

Toma, C., and J. Hancock. 2010. "Looks and lies: The role of physical attractiveness in online dating self-presentation and deception." *Communication Research.* 37:335–51.

Turner, J., and J. Stets. 2006. "Sociological theories of human emotions." *Annual Review of Sociology* 32:25–52.

Uecker, J. 2008. "Religion, pledging, and the premarital sexual behavior of married young adults." *Journal of Marriage and Family* 70:728–44.

U.S. Bureau of Labor Statistics. 2014. CPI Inflation Calculator. Last modified October 1. Accessed June 8, 2015. http://www.bls.gov/data/inflation_calculator.htm.

U.S. Census Bureau. 1989. *Statistical Abstracts of the United States: 1989.* 108th ed. Washington, DC: GPO.

———. 1999. *Statistical Abstracts of the United States: 1999.* 119th ed. Washington, DC: GPO.

———. 2012. *Statistical Abstracts of the United States: 2010.* 130th ed. Washington, DC: GPO.

———. 2013. "America's families and living arrangements: 2012." *Current Population Reports*, P20-570. Washington, DC: GPO.

U.S. Department of Education. 2014. *The Campus Safety and Security Data Analysis Cutting Tool.* Accessed April 23, 2014. http://www.ope.ed.gov/security/

U.S. Department of Justice, Bureau of Justice Statistics. 2013. *Female Victims of Sexual Violence, 1994–2010* Washington, DC: Department of Justice.

VanderMey, A. 2013. "Outsourcing the algorithm of love to online dating." *Fortune*, February 14, http://fortune.com/2013/02/14/outsourcing-the-algorithm-of-love-to-online-dating/

Wagner-Raphael, L., D. Seal, and A. Ehrhardt. 2001. "Close emotional relationships with women versus men: A qualitative study of 56 heterosexual men living in an inner-city neighborhood." *Journal of Men's Studies* 9(2):243–56.

Waite, L. 1999–2000. "The negative effects of cohabitation." *The Responsive Community* 10(1):31–38.

———. 2000. "Trends in men's and women's well-being in marriage." In *The Ties That Bind: Perspectives on Marriage and Cohabitation*, edited by L. Waite, C. Bachrach, M. Hindin, E. Thomson, and A. Thornton, pp. 368–92. New York: Aldine de Gruyter.

Waite, L., and M. Gallagher. 2000. *The Case for Marriage.* New York: Doubleday.

Waller, W. 1938. *The Family: A Dynamic Interpretation*. Hinsdale, IL: Dryden Press.

Walsh, A. 1996. *The Science of Love: Understanding Love and Its Effects on Mind and Body*. New York: Prometheus.

Werking, K. 1997. *We're Just Good Friends: Women and Men in Nonromantic Relationships*. New York: Guilford.

Whitehead, B. 1994. "The failure of sex education." *Atlantic Monthly*, October, pp. 55–80.

Whitty, M. 2008. "Revealing the 'real' me, searching for the 'actual' you: Presentations of self on an internet dating site." *Computers in Human Behavior* 24:1707–23.

Whyte, W. F. 1955. *Street-Corner Society: The Social Structure of an Italian Slum*. Chicago: University of Chicago Press.

Whyte, W. H. 1956. *The Organization Man*. New York: Simon & Schuster.

Wilcox, W., and S. Nock. 2006. "What's love got to do with it? Equality, equity, commitment and women's marital quality." *Social Forces* 84(3):1321–44.

Wood, J., and N. Fixmer-Oraiz. 2014. *Gendered Lives: Communication, Gender, and Culture*. 11th ed. Belmont, CA: Wadsworth.

Wright, P., and R. Tokunaga. 2015. "Activating the centerfold syndrome: Recency of exposure, sexual explicitness, past exposure to objectifying media." *Communication Research* 42(6):86–897.

Zelizer, V. 1985. *Pricing the Priceless Child: The Changing Social Value of Children*. New York: Basic Books.

Chapter 6

Adkins, L. 1995. *Gendered Work: Sexuality, Family, and the Labour Market*. Buckingham, UK: Open University Press.

Aitchison, C. 2013. *Gender and Leisure: Social and Cultural Perspectives*. New York: Routledge.

Anderson, K., and C. Leaper. 1998. "Meta-analyses of gender effects on conversational interruption: Who, what, when, where, and how." *Sex Roles* 39(3/4):225–52.

Aries, E. 1996. *Men and Women in Interaction: Reconsidering the Difference*. New York: Oxford University Press.

Berdahl, J. 2007. "Harassment based on sex: Protecting social status in the context of gender hierarchy." *Academy of Management Review* 32:641–58.

Berger, P., and B. Berger. 1975. *Sociology: A Biographical Approach*. New York: Basic Books.

Bonilla-Silva, E. 2006. *Racism without Racists: Color-blind Racism and the Persistence of Racial Inequality in the United States*. Lanham, MD: Rowman & Littlefield.

Bourdieu, P. 1977. "Cultural reproduction and social reproduction." In *Power and Ideology in Education*, edited by J. Karabel and A. Halsey, pp. 487–511. New York: Oxford University Press.

Bourgois, P. 1995. *In Search of Respect: Selling Crack in El Barrio*. New York: Cambridge University Press.

Borer, M. 2006. "The location of culture: The urban culturalist perspective." *City & Community* 5:173–97.

Brenner, N., P. Marcuse, and M. Mayer, eds. 2012. *Cities for People, Not for Profit: Critical Urban Theory and the Right to the City*. New York: Routledge.

Chou, R., and J. Feagin. 2008. *The Myth of the Model Minority: Asian Americans Facing Racism*. Boulder, CO: Paradigm.

Danziger, S., and D. Reed. 1999. "Winners and losers: The era of inequality continues." *Brookings Review* (Fall):14–17.

Davidson, J., and L. Bondi. 2004. "Spatialising affect; affecting space: An introduction." *Gender, Place & Culture* 11:373–74.

Davies-Netzley, S. 1998. "Women above the glass ceiling." *Gender & Society* 12:339–55.

Domhoff, G. 1970. *The Higher Circles.* New York: Vintage Books.

———. 1983. *Who Rules America Now?* New York: Simon & Schuster.

———. 1998. *Who Rules America? Power and Politics in the Year 2000.* 3rd ed. Mountain View, CA: Mayfield.

Dovidio, J., C. Brown, K. Heltman, S. Ellyson, and C. Keating. 1998. "Power displays between women and men in discussions of gender linked tasks: A multichannel study." *Journal of Personality and Social Psychology* 55:580–87.

Duneier, M., and H. Molotch. 1999. "Talking city trouble: Interactional vandalism, social inequality, and the 'urban interaction problem.'" *American Journal of Sociology* 104:1263–95.

Fine, M. 1994. "Working the hyphens: Reinventing self and other in qualitative research." In *Handbook of Qualitative Research*, edited by N. Denzin and Y. Lincoln, pp. 70–82. Thousand Oaks, CA: Sage.

Fine, M., L. Weis, J. Addelston, and J. Marusza. 1997. "(In)secure times: Constructing white working-class masculinities in the late 20th century." *Gender & Society* 11:52–68.

Forte, J., D. Franks, J. A. Forte, and D. Rigsby. 1996. "Asymmetrical role-taking: Comparing battered and non-battered women." *Social Work* 41:59–73.

Frank, K. 1998. "The production of identity and the negotiation of intimacy in a 'gentleman's club.'" *Sexualities* 1:175–201.

Futrell, R. 1999. "Performative governance: Impression management, teamwork, and conflict containment in city commission proceedings." *Journal of Contemporary Ethnography* 27(4):494–529.

Gardner, C. 1995. *Passing By: Gender and Public Harassment.* Berkeley: University of California Press.

Gates, H. Jr. 1998. "The two nations of black America." *Brookings Review* (Spring):4–7.

Gieryn, T. 2000. "A space for place in sociology." *Annual Review of Sociology* 26:463–96.

Goffman, E. 1956. "The nature of deference and demeanor." *American Anthropologist* 58:473–502.

———. 1959. *The Presentation of Self in Everyday Life.* New York: Doubleday Anchor Books.

Goodrum, S., D. Umberson, and K. Anderson. 2001. "The batterer's view of the self and others in domestic violence." *Sociological Inquiry* 71(2):221–40.

Gorman, T. 2000. "Cross-class perceptions of social class." *Sociological Spectrum* 20(1):93–120.

Guerrero, L. 1997. "Nonverbal involvement across interactions with same-sex friends, opposite-sex friends, and romantic partners: Consistency or change?" *Journal of Social and Personal Relationships* 14:31–58.

Hacker, H. 1951. "Women as a minority group." *Social Forces* 30:60–69.

Haley, A. 1976. *Roots.* New York: Doubleday.

Hall, E. 1969. *The Hidden Dimension.* New York: Doubleday.

Hall, J., E. Coats, and L. Smith LeBeau. 2005. "Nonverbal behavior and the vertical dimension of social relations: A meta-analysis." *Psychological Bulletin* 131:898–924.

Hall, J., A. Halberstadt, and C. O'Brien. 1997. "Subordination and nonverbal sensitivity: A study and synthesis of findings based on trait measures." *Sex Roles* 37(5/6):295–317.

Hardoon, D. 2015. "Wealth: Having it all and wanting more." *Oxfam Issue Briefing* January:1–12.

Harris, S. 2006. "Social constructionism and social inequality." *Journal of Contemporary Ethnography* 35:223–35.

Hecht, M., and M. LaFrance. 1998. "License or obligation to smile: The effect of power and sex on amount and type of smiling." *Personality and Social Psychology Bulletin* 24(12):1332–42.

Henley, N. [1977] 1986. *Body Politics.* Englewood Cliffs, NJ: Prentice-Hall.

Herbert, S. 1997. *Policing Space: Territoriality and the Los Angeles Police Department.* Minneapolis: University of Minnesota Press.

Hewitt, J., and D. Shulman. 2010. *Self and Society: A Symbolic Interactionist Social Psychology.* 11th ed. Boston: Allyn & Bacon.

Holtzworth-Munroe, A., and G. Stuart. 1994. "Typologies of male batterers: Three subtypes and the differences among them." *Psychological Bulletin* 116:476–97.

Horowitz, R. 1997. "Barriers and bridges to class mobility and formation: Ethnographies of stratification." *Sociological Methods and Research* 25:495–538.

Howard, J. 2000. "Social psychology of identities." *Annual Review of Sociology* 26:367–93.

Kacapyr, E. 1996. "Are you middle class?" *American Demographics* (October):30–35.

Kasarda, J. 1989. "Urban industrial transition and the underclass." In *The Ghetto Underclass,* edited by W. Wilson. Beverly Hills, CA: Sage.

———. 1995. "Industrial restructuring and the changing location of jobs." In *State of the Union: America in the 1990s,* vol. 1, edited by R. Farley. New York: Russell Sage Foundation.

Kemper, T. 2011. *Status, Power and Ritual Interaction: A Relational Reading of Durkheim, Goffman, and Collins.* Burlington, VT: Ashgate.

Kimmel, M. 2006. *Manhood in America.* 2nd ed. New York: Oxford University Press.

Kolb, K. 2014. *Moral Wages: The Emotional Dilemmas of Victim Advocacy and Counseling.* Berkeley: University of California Press.

Lacy, K. 2007. *Blue Chip Black: Race, Class, and Status in the New Black Middle Class.* Berkeley: University of California Press.

LaFrance, M., and N. Henley. 1994. "On oppressing hypotheses: Or differences in nonverbal sensitivity revisited." In *Power/Gender: Social Relations in Theory and Practice,* edited by H. Radtke and H. Stam, pp. 287–311. Thousand Oaks, CA: Sage.

Legerski, E., and M. Cornwall. 2010. "Working-class job loss, gender, and the negotiation of household labor." *Gender & Society* 24(4):447–74.

Levy, F. 1998. *The New Dollars and Dreams: American Incomes and Economic Change.* New York: Russell Sage Foundation.

Lichter, D., D. Parisi, and M. Taquino. 2012. "The geography of exclusion: Race, segregation, and concentrated poverty." *Social Problems* 59(3):364–88.

Liebow, E. 1967. *Tally's Corner: A Study of Negro Street-Corner Men.* Boston: Little, Brown.

Loguen, J. 1859. *The Rev. J. W. Loguen, as a Slave and as a Freedman.* Syracuse, NY: n.p.

Lopez, S., R. Hodson, and V. Roscigno. 2009. "Power, status, and abuse at work: General and sexual harassment compared." *The Sociological Quarterly* 50(1):3–27.

MacLeod, J. 2009. *Ain't No Makin' It: Aspirations and Attainment in a Low-Income Neighborhood*. New York: Westview Press.

Mannino, C., and F. Deutsch. 2007. "Changing the division of household labor: A negotiated process between partners." *Sex Roles* 56:309–24.

Marger, M. 2002. *Social Inequality: Patterns and Processes*. 2nd ed. New York: McGraw-Hill.

Massey, D., and N. Denton. 1993. *American Apartheid: Segregation and the Making of the Underclass*. Cambridge, MA: Harvard University Press.

McDowell, L. 1999. *Gender, Identity and Place*. Minneapolis: University of Minnesota Press.

McLaughlin, H., C. Uggen, and A. Blackstone. 2012. "Sexual harassment, workplace authority, and the paradox of power." *American Sociological Review* 77(4), 625–47.

Milner, M. 2004. *Freaks, Geeks, and Cool Kids: American Teenagers, Schools, and the Culture of Consumption*. New York: Routledge.

Mishel, L., J. Bernstein, and J. Schmitt. 2001. *The State of Working America, 2000–01*. Ithaca, NY: Cornell University Press.

Moore, M. 2002. "Courtship communication and perception." *Perceptual and Motor Skills* 94:97–105.

Murphy, A. 2010. "The symbolic dilemmas of suburban poverty: Challenges and opportunities posed by variations in the contours of suburban poverty." *Sociological Forum* 25:541–69.

Mustillo, S., K. Hendrix, and M. Schafer. 2012. "Trajectories of body mass and self-concept in black and white girls: The lingering effects of stigma." *Journal of Health and Social Behavior* 53(1):2–16.

Oliver, M., and T. Shapiro. 2006. *Black Wealth/White Wealth: A New Perspective on Racial Inequality*. New York: Routledge.

Pattillo, M. 2000. *Black Picket Fences: Privilege and Peril among the Black Middle Class*. Chicago: University of Chicago Press.

Ridgeway, C., and L. Smith-Lovin. 1999. "The gender system and interaction." *Annual Review of Sociology* 25:191–216.

Risman, B., and G. Davis. 2013. "From sex roles to gender structure." *Current Sociology* 61:733–55.

Rogers, J., and K. Henson. 1997. "'Hey, why don't you wear a shorter skirt?' Structural vulnerability and the organization of sexual harassment in temporary clerical employment." *Gender & Society* 11(2):215–37.

Rollins, J. 1985. *Between Women: Domestics and Their Employers*. Philadelphia: Temple University Press.

Rubin, L. 1976. *Worlds of Pain*. New York: Harper & Row.

———. 1994. *Families on the Faultline: America's Working Class Speaks about the Family, the Economy, Race, and Ethnicity*. New York: HarperCollins.

Schuman, H., and J. Scott. 1989. "Generations and collective memory." *American Sociological Review* 54:359–81.

Schwalbe, M., S. Godwin, D. Holden, D. Schrock, S. Thompson, and M. Wolkomir. 2000. "Generic processes in the reproduction of inequality: An interactionist analysis." *Social Forces* 79(2):419–52.

Scully, D. 1990. *Understanding Sexual Violence: A Study of Convicted Rapists*. Boston: Unwin Hyman.

Seligman, A. 2005. *Block by Block: Neighborhoods and Public Policy on Chicago's West Side*. Chicago: University of Chicago Press.

Sennett, R. 2006. *The Culture of the New Capitalism*. New Haven, CT: Yale University Press.

Sennett, R., and J. Cobb. 1973. *The Hidden Injuries of Class*. New York: Random House.

Small, M. L., and K. Newman. 2001. "Urban poverty after the truly disadvantaged: The rediscovery of the family, the neighborhood, and culture." *Annual Review of Sociology* 27:23–45.

Spain, D. 1992. *Gendered Spaces*. Chapel Hill: University of North Carolina Press.

Tannen, D. 1994. "Interpreting interruption in conversation." In *Gender and Discourse*, edited by D. Tannen. New York: Oxford University Press.

Tatum, B. 2000. "The complexity of identity: 'Who am I?'" In *Readings for Diversity and Social Justice*, edited by M. Adams, W. Blumenfeld, R. Casteñeda, H. Hackman, M. Peters, and X. Zúñiga, pp. 9–14. New York: Routledge.

Tawney, R. 1931. *Equality*. London: Allen & Unwin.

Teaford, J. 1986. *The Twentieth-Century American City*. Baltimore, MD: Johns Hopkins University Press.

Testa, M. 1991. "Male joblessness, nonmarital parenthood and marriage." Paper presented at the Chicago Urban Poverty and Family Life Conference, October 10–12.

Testa, M., and M. Krough. 1995. "The effect of employment on marriage among black males in inner-city Chicago." In *The Decline in Marriage among African Americans: Causes, Consequences and Policy Implications*, edited by M. Tucker and C. Mitchell-Kernan, pp. 59–95. New York: Russell Sage Foundation.

U.S. Census Bureau. 1999. *Statistical Abstract of the United States: 1999*. Washington, DC: Government Printing Office.

———. 2000. *Statistical Abstract of the United States: 2000*. Washington, DC: Government Printing Office.

———. 2013. *Historical Income Tables-Families*. Washington, DC: Government Printing Office.

———. 2014. *CPS 2014 Annual Social and Economic Supplement*. Washington, DC: Government Printing Office.

U.S. Department of Labor, Bureau of Labor Statistics. 2001. *Highlights of Women's Earnings in 2000*. Report 952. Washington, DC: Government Printing Office.

———. 2012. *Highlights of Women's Earnings in 2012*. Washington, DC: Government Printing Office.

Valentine, G. 1989. "The geography of women's fear." *Area* 21:385–390.

Weis, L., A. Proweller, and C. Centrie. 2004. "Re-examining a moment in history: Loss of privilege inside white, working-class masculinity in the 1990s." In *Off White*, edited by M. Fine, L. Powell, L. Weis, and M. Wong. New York: Routledge.

Westhaver, R. 2006. "Flaunting and empowerment: Thinking about circuit parties, the body, and power." *Journal of Contemporary Ethnography* 35:611–44.

Whyte, W. H. 1988. *City*. New York: Anchor Books.

Williams, C., P. Giuffre, and K. Dellinger. 1999. "Sexuality in the workplace: Organizational control, sexual harassment, and the pursuit of pleasure." *Annual Review of Sociology* 25:73–93.

Wilson, W. 1987. *The Truly Disadvantaged*. Chicago: University of Chicago Press.

———. 1996. *When Work Disappears: The World of the New Urban Poor*. New York: Vintage.

Wolf, C. 1994. "Dependency-bond as construct." *Symbolic Interaction* 17:367–93.

Wolff, E. 1995. *Top Heavy: A Study of the Increasing Inequality of Wealth in America*. New York: Twentieth Century Fund Press.

Wood, J., and N. Fixmer-Oraiz. 2014. *Gendered Lives: Communication, Gender, and Culture*. 11th ed. Belmont, CA: Wadsworth.

Zhang, Q. 2010. "Asian Americans beyond the model minority stereotype: The nerdy and the left out." *Journal of International and Intercultural Communication* 3(1):20–37.

Zimmerman, D., and C. West. 1975. "Sex roles, interruptions and silences in conversations." In *Language and Sex: Differences and Dominance*, edited by B. Thorne and N. Henley. Rowley, MA: Newbury House.

Chapter 7

Abolafia, M. 1996. "Hyper-rational gaming." *Journal of Contemporary Ethnography* 25:226–50.

Adams, S. 1998. *The Joy of Work: Dilbert's Guide to Finding Happiness at the Expense of Your Co-Workers*. New York: HarperCollins.

Alvesson, M. 2004. *Knowledge Work and Knowledge-Intensive Firms*. Oxford: Oxford University Press.

Ames, L. 1996. "Contrarieties at work: Women's resistance to bureaucracy." *NWSA Journal* 8(2):37–59.

Andrews, M., and K. Kacmar. 2001. "Confirmation and extension of the sources of feedback scale in service-based organizations." *Journal of Business Communication* 38(2):206–26.

Balliro, L. 1995. "French restaurant, 1982." In *For a Living*, edited by P. Oresick and N. Coles. Champaign-Urbana: University of Illinois Press.

Barber, B. 1996. *Jihad vs. McWorld: How Globalism and Tribalism are Reshaping the World*. New York: Ballantine Books.

Bellah, R., R. Madsen, W. Sullivan, A. Swidler, and S. Tipton. 1996. *Habits of the Heart: Individualism and Commitment in American Life*. Berkeley: University of California Press.

Bianchi, S., L. Sayer, M. Milkie, and J. Robinson. 2012. "Housework: Who did, does or will do it, and how much does it matter?" *Social Forces* 91(1):55–63.

Blau, F., M. Ferber, and A. Winkler. 2002. *The Economics of Women, Men, and Work*. 4th ed. Upper Saddle River, NJ: Prentice-Hall.

Boggs, C. 2000. *The End of Politics: Corporate Power and the Decline of the Public Sphere*. New York: Guilford Press.

Brower, R., and M. Abolafia. 1997. "Bureaucratic politics: The view from below." *Journal of Public Administration Research and Theory* 7(2):305–31.

Bryman, A. 1999. "The Disneyization of society." *Sociological Review* 47(1):25–47.

———. 2004. *The Disneyization of Society*. Thousand Oaks, CA: Sage.

Bulan, H., R. Erickson, and A. Wharton. 1997. "Doing for others on the job: The affective requirements of service work, gender, and emotional well-being." *Social Problems* 44(2):235–56.

Catalyst. 1999. "Catalyst census of women board directors of the Fortune 1000." December 15. http://www.catalyst.org/knowledge/1999-catalyst-census-women-board-directors-fortune-1000

———. 2015. "Pyramid: Women in S&P 500 Companies." http://www.catalyst.org/knowledge/women-sp-500-companies

Coates, G. 1994. "Performance appraisal as icon: Oscar-winning performance or dressing to impress?" *International Journal of Human Resource Management* 5(1):167–92.

———. 1997. "Organization man: Women and organizational culture." *Sociological Research Online* 2(3):1–31. http://www.socresonline.org.uk/socresonline/2/3/7.html

Collins, G. 1996. "A Big Mac strategy at porterhouse prices." *New York Times,* August 13:D1.

Connellan, T. 1996. *Inside the Magic Kingdom: Seven Keys to Disney's Success.* Austin, TX: Bard.

Dale, K. 2012. "The employee as 'dish of the day': The ethics of the consuming/consumed self in human resource management." *Journal of Business Ethics* 111(1):13–24.

Dery, D. 1998. "'Papereality' and learning in bureaucratic organizations." *Administration & Society* 29(6):677–89.

Dobbin, F., S. Kim, and A. Kalev. 2011. "You can't always get what you need: Organizational determinants of diversity programs." *American Sociological Review* 76(3), 386–411.

Dunn, D. 1997. *Workplace/Women's Place.* Los Angeles: Roxbury.

Durkheim, É. [1985] 2014. *The Rules of the Sociological Method and Selected Texts on Sociology and Its Method.* Edited and with a new introduction by Steven Lukes. New York: Free Press.

Edgley, C., and D. Brissett. 1999. *A Nation of Meddlers.* Boulder, CO: Westview Press.

Eisman, R. 1993. "Disney magic." *Incentive* (September):45–56.

Feldman, D. 2000. "The Dilbert syndrome. How employee cynicism about ineffective management is changing the nature of careers in organizations." *American Behavioral Scientist* 43(8):1286–1300.

Fine, G. 1996. *Kitchens: The Culture of Restaurant Work.* Berkeley: University of California Press.

———. 1997. *Talking Sociology.* 4th ed. Boston: Allyn & Bacon.

Fleming, P., and A. Sturdy. 2009. "'Just be yourself!': Towards neo-normative control in organisations?" *Employee Relations* 31(6):569–83.

France, V. 1991. *Window on Main Street.* Nashua, NH: Laughter Publications.

Frederickson, H. 2000. "Can bureaucracy be beautiful?" *Public Administration Review* 60(1):47–53.

Glenn, E., and R. Feldberg. 1989. "Clerical work: The female occupation." In *Women: A Feminist Perspective,* edited by J. Freeman. Mountain View, CA: Mayfield.

Hallett, T., D. Shulman, and G. Fine. 2009. "Peopling organizations: The promise of classic symbolic interactionism for an inhabited institutionalism." In *The Oxford Handbook of Organizational Studies,* edited by P. Adler. Oxford: Oxford University Press.

Hallett, T., and M. Ventresca. 2006. "Inhabited institutions: Social interactions and organizational forms in Gouldner's *Patterns of Industrial Bureaucracy.*" *Theory and Society* 35:213–36.

Henderson, R. 2012. "Industry employment and output projections to 2020." *Monthly Labor Review* (January):65–83.

Hill, T., and C. Bradley. 2010. "The emotional consequences of service work: An ethnographic examination of hair salon workers." *Sociological Focus* 43(1):41–60.

Hochschild, A. 1983. *The Managed Heart.* Berkeley: University of California Press.

———. 2012. *The Second Shift: Working Families and the Revolution at Home.* New York: Penguin.

Hodson, R. 1996. "Dignity in the workplace under participative management: Alienation and freedom revisited." *American Sociological Review* 61(October):719–38.

International Labour Office. 1997. "Industrial relations, democracy and social stability, 1997–98." *World Labour Report.* Geneva: ILO.

Jurca, C. 1999. "The sanctimonious suburbanite: Sloan Wilson's *The Man in the Gray Flannel Suit." American Literary History* 11(1):82–106.

Kane, P. 2004. *The Play Ethic: A Manifesto for a Different Way of Living.* London: Palgrave Macmillan.

———. 2014. "The play ethic: Advocating the power and potential of play." The Play Ethic. January 16. Accessed June 12, 2015. http://www.theplayethic.com/2014/01/2013-playing-into-future-2014.html#more

Kanter, R. 1977. *Men and Women of the Corporation.* New York: Harper & Row.

Klagge, J. 1997. "Approaches to the iron cage: Reconstructing the bars of Weber's metaphor." *Administration & Society* 29(1):63–77.

Kovacik, K. 2001. "Between L=A=N=G=U=A=G=E and lyric: The poetry of pink-collar resistance." *NWSA Journal* 13(1):22–39.

Kunda, G., and G. Ailon-Souday. 2005. "Managers, markets and ideologies—Design and devotion revisited." In *Oxford Handbook of Work and Organization,* edited by S. Ackroyd, R. Batt, P. Thompson, and P. Tolbert, Oxford: Oxford University Press.

Lambert, E., N. Hogan, and S. Barton. 2001. "The impact of job satisfaction on turnover intent: A test of a structural measurement using a national sample of workers." *Social Science Journal* 38(2):233–50.

Laslett, P. 1971. *The World We Have Lost.* New York: Charles Scribner's Sons.

Lively, K. 2001. "Occupational claims to professionalism: The case of paralegals." *Symbolic Interaction* 24(3):343–66.

Mann, S. 2009. "Making fun OK at work." *Professional Manager* 18(5):36–38.

McAdam, D. 1989. "The biographical consequences of activism." *American Sociological Review* 54 (October):744–60.

McGinty, P. 2014." Divided and drifting: Interactionism and the neglect of social organizational analysis in organization studies." *Symbolic Interaction* 37:155–86.

Merrick, A. 1998. "Companies keep employees happy by targeting their personal needs." *R & D* 40(10):S3–6.

Mills, C. W. 1956. *White Collar.* New York: Oxford University Press.

Oravec, J. 2002. "Constructive approaches to Internet recreation in the workplace." *Communications of the ACM* 45(1):60–63.

Presthus, R. 1978. *The Organizational Society.* New York: St. Martin's.

Project on Disney. 1995. *Inside the Mouse: Work and Play at Disney World.* Durham, NC: Duke University Press.

Rabbit, T. 2000. "Surf and be happy: Web access at work makes workers feel more productive, less stressed, says survey." *Network World* (September 25): n.p.

Reich, R. 2002. *The Future of Success.* New York: Vintage.

Reisman, D. 1950. *The Lonely Crowd.* New Haven, CT: Yale University Press.

Ritzer, G. 1998. *The McDonaldization Thesis.* London: Sage.

———. 2000. *The McDonaldization of Society.* Thousand Oaks, CA: Pine Forge Press.

———. 2010. *McDonaldization: The Reader.* Thousand Oaks, CA, Pine Forge Press.

Rossides, D. 1997. *Social Stratification.* 2nd ed. Upper Saddle River, NJ: Prentice-Hall.

Roy, D. [1959] 1982. "Banana time: Job satisfaction and informal interaction." In *The Sociological Outlook,* edited by R. Luhman. Belmont, CA: Wadsworth.

Smith, J., and D. Wiest. 2012. *Social Movements in the World-System: The Politics of Crisis and Transformation.* New York: Russell Sage Foundation.

Strauss, A. 1978. *Negotiations.* San Francisco: Jossey-Bass.

———. 1993. *Continual Permutations of Action.* New York: De Gruyter.

Society for Human Resource Management. 2015. *Employee Job Satisfaction and Engagement.* http://www.shrm.org/Research/SurveyFindings/Documents/2015-Job-Satisfaction-and-Engagement-Report.pdf

Susskind, A., C. Borchgrevink, K. Kacmar, and R. Brymer. 2000. "Customer service employees' behavioral intentions and attitudes: An examination of construct validity and a path model." *International Journal of Hospitality Management* 19:53–77.

Taylor, F. [1911] 2014. *The Principles of Scientific Management.* Eastford, CT: Martino Fine Books.

Thurnell-Read, T. 2014. "Craft, tangibility and affect at work in the microbrewery." *Emotion, Space and Society* 13:46–54.

Troy, L. 2001. "Twilight for organized labor." *Journal of Labor Research* 22(2):245–59.

U.S. Department of Labor, Bureau of Labor Statistics. 2014. *Current Population Survey.* Washington, DC: U.S. Government Printing Office.

———. 2015. "Union members summary." January 23. http://www.bls.gov/news.release/union2.nr0.htm

Weber, M. [1922] 1946. "Bureaucracy." In *From Max Weber: Essays in Sociology,* edited by H. Gerth and C. W. Mills. New York: Oxford University Press.

Weick, K. 1976. "Educational organizations as loosely coupled systems." *Administrative Science Quarterly* 21 (March):1–19.

Whyte, W. 1956. *The Organization Man.* New York: Simon & Schuster.

Woloch, N. 1994. *Women and the American Experience.* New York: McGraw-Hill.

Zibart, E. 1997. *The Unofficial Disney Companion.* New York: Macmillan.

Chapter 8

Ackerknecht, E. 1947. "The role of medical history in medical education." *Bulletin of the History of Medicine* 21:135–45.

Armstrong, N., N. Koteyko, and J. Powell. 2012. "'Oh dear, should I really be saying that on here?' Issues of identity and authority in an online diabetes community." *Health: An Interdisciplinary Journal for the Social Study of Health, Illness and Medicine* 16(4):347–65.

Armstrong, T., and L. Swartzman. 2001. "Cross-cultural differences in illness models and expectations for the health care provider-client/patient interaction." In *Handbook of Cultural Health Psychology,* pp. 63–84. San Diego, CA: Academic Press.

"Art in health care facilities." 2009. *Environment of Care News* 12(11):1–3, 10.

Astin, J. 1998. "Why patients use alternative medicine: Results of a national study." *Journal of the American Medical Association* 279:1548–53.

Atkinson, P. 1995. *Medical Talk and Medical Work.* London: Sage.

Baarts, C., and I. Pedersen. 2009. "Derivative benefits: Exploring the body through complementary and alternative medicine." *Sociology of Health & Illness* 31(5):719–33.

Baker, P., W. Yoels, and J. Clair. 1996. "Emotional expression during medical encounters: Social disease and the medical gaze." In *Health and the Sociology of Emotions,* edited by V. James and J. Gabe, pp. 173–99. Oxford: Blackwell.

Baker, P., W. Yoels, J. Clair, and R. Allman. 1997. "Laughter in triadic geriatric medical encounters: A transcript-based analysis." *Social Perspectives on Emotion* 4:179–207.

Becker, G. 1997. *Disrupted Lives: How People Create Meaning in a Chaotic World.* Berkeley: University of California Press.

Begley, S. 1994. "One pill makes you larger, and one pill makes you small . . ." *Newsweek,* February 7.

Bellah, R., R. Madsen, W. Sullivan, A. Swidler, and S. Tipton. 1996. *Habits of the Heart: Individualism and Commitment in American Life.* Berkeley: University of California Press.

Berger, P., and T. Luckmann. 1967. *The Social Construction of Reality.* Garden City, NY: Doubleday.

Bischoff, W., and S. Kelley. 1999. "21st century house call: The Internet and the World Wide Web." *Holistic Nursing Practice* 13(4):42–50.

Calasanti, T., and K. Slevin. 2001. *Gender, Social Inequalities, and Aging.* New York: AltaMira.

Conrad, P., and J. Schneider. 1992. *Deviance and Medicalization: From Badness to Sickness.* Philadelphia: Temple University Press.

Cotten, S. 2001. "Implications of Internet technology." *Sociological Spectrum* 21(3):319–40.

Edgley, C., and D. Brissett. 1999. *A Nation of Meddlers.* Boulder, CO: Westview Press.

Edwards, C., R. Fillingim, and F. Keefe. 2001. "Race, ethnicity and pain." *Pain* 94:133–37.

Eisenberg, D., R. Davis, S. Ettner, S. Appel, S. Wilkey, M. Van Rompay, and R. Kessler. 1998. "Trends in alternative medicine use in the United States, 1990–1997: Results of a follow-up national survey." *Journal of the American Medical Association* 280:507–13.

Eng, T., A. Maxfield, K. Patrick, M. Deering, S. Ratzan, and D. Gustafson. 1998. "Access to health information and support: A public highway or a private road?" *Journal of the American Medical Association* 280(15):1371–75.

Davis-Berman, J., and F. Pestello. 2005. "The medicated self." *Studies in Symbolic Interaction* 28:283–308.

Fairfield, K., D. Eisenberg, R. Davis, H. Libman, and R. Phillips. 1998. "Patterns of use, expenditures and perceived efficacy of complementary and alternative therapies in HIV-infected patients." *Archives of Internal Medicine* 158:2257–64.

Finlay, F., and R. Jones. 1998. "Doctors' dress." *British Journal of Psychiatry* 172:188b.

Frank, A. 2000. "Illness and the interactionist vocation." *Symbolic Interaction* 23(4):321–32.

Freund, P., and M. McGuire. 1999. *Health, Illness, and the Social Body.* Upper Saddle River, NJ: Prentice-Hall.

Gandhi, I., J. Parle, S. Greenfield, and S. Gould. 1997. "A qualitative investigation into why patients change their GPs." *Family Practice* 14:49–57.

Goffman, E. 1963. *Stigma: Notes on the Management of Spoiled Identity.* New York: Simon & Schuster.

Goldsmith, J. 2000. "How will the Internet change our health system?" *Health Affairs* 19(1):148–56.

Groene, O. 2011. "Patient centredness and quality improvement efforts in hospitals: Rationale, measurement, implementation." *International Journal for Quality in Health Care* 23(5):531–37.

Heritage, J., and D. Maynard. 2006. "Problems and prospects in the study of physician-patient interaction: 30 years of research." *Annual Review of Sociology* 32:351–74.

Hesse-Biber, S. 1996. *Am I Thin Enough Yet? The Cult of Thinness and the Commercialization of Identity.* New York: Oxford University Press.

Huisman, E., E. Morales, J. Van Hoof, and H. Kort. 2012. "Healing environment: A review of the impact of physical environmental factors on users." *Building and Environment* 58:70–80.

Junewicz, A., and S. Youngner. 2015. "Patient-satisfaction surveys on a scale of 0 to 10: Improving health care, or leading it astray?" *Hastings Center Report* 45(3):43–51.

Kao, A., D. Green, N. Davis, J. Koplan, and P. Cleary. 1998. "Patients trust in their physicians: Effects of choice, continuity and payment method." *Journal of General Internal Medicine* 13:681–86.

Kaplan, S., L. Sullivan, D. Spetter, K. Dukes, A. Kahn, and S. Greenfield. 1996. "Gender and patterns of physician-patient communication." In *Women's Health: The Commonwealth Fund Survey*, pp. 29–76. Baltimore, MD: Johns Hopkins University Press.

Karp, D. 1996. *Speaking of Sadness: Depression, Disconnection, and the Meanings of Illness*. New York: Oxford University Press.

Kim, M., and S. Wilson. 1994. "A cross-cultural comparison of implicit theories of requesting." *Communication Monographs* 61:210–35.

Kivits, J. 2013. "E-health and renewed sociological approaches to health and illness." *Digital Sociology: Critical Perspectives*, edited by K. Orton-Johnson and N. Prior. Houndmills, UK: Palgrave Macmillan.

Klonoff, E., H. Landrine, and M. Brown. 1993. "Appraisal and response to pain may be a function of its bodily location." *Journal of Psychosomatic Research* 37(6):661–70.

Koutanji, M., S. Pearce, and D. Oakley. 1998. "The relationship between gender and family history of pain with current pain experience and awareness of pain in others." *Pain* 77:25–31.

Kramer, P. [1993] 1997. *Listening to Prozac*. New York: Penguin.

Krauss, H., C. Godfrey, J. Kirk, and D. Eisenberg. 1998. "Alternative health care: Its use by individuals with physical disabilities." *Archives of Physical Medicine and Rehabilitation* 79:1440–47.

Kronenfeld, J. 2001. "New trends in the doctor-patient relationship: Impacts of managed care on the growth of a consumer protections model." *Sociological Spectrum* 21(3):293–317.

Light, D. 2012. "Categorical inequality, institutional ambivalence, and permanently failing institutions: The case of immigrants and barriers to health care in America." *Ethnic and Racial Studies* 35(1):23–39.

Loe, M., and L. Cuttino. 2008. "Grappling with the medicated self: The case of ADHD college students." *Symbolic Interaction* 31(3):303–23.

Logan, S., and C. Hunt. 2014. "Considerations for clinicians when working cross-culturally: A review." *Cross-Cultural Communication* 10(5):12–20.

Lorber, J., and L. Moore. 2007. *Gendered Bodies: Feminist Perspectives*. Los Angeles: Roxbury.

Lupton, D. 1996. "Your life in their hands: Trust in the medical encounter." In *Health and the Sociology of Emotions*, edited by V. James and J. Gabe, pp. 157–72. Oxford: Blackwell.

Lyon, M. 1996. "C. Wright Mills meets Prozac: The relevance of 'social emotion' to the sociology of health and illness." In *Health and the Sociology of Emotions*, edited by V. James and J. Gabe, pp. 55–78. Oxford: Blackwell.

Mainous, A., C. Griffith, and M. Love. 1999. "Patient satisfaction with care in programs for low-income individuals." *Journal of Community Health* 24(5):381–91.

Mandl, K., I. Kohane, and A. Brandt. 1998. "Electronic patient-physician communication: Problems and promise." *Annals of Internal Medicine* 129(6):495–500.

Mechanic, D. 1995. "Sociological dimensions of illness behavior." *Social Science & Medicine* 41(9):1207–16.

———. 1998. "The functions and limitations of trust in the provision of medical care." *Journal of Health Politics, Policy and Law* 23:661–86.

———. 2002. "Socio-cultural implications of changing organizational technologies in the provision of care." *Social Science & Medicine* 54(3):459–67.

Mechanic, D., and S. Meyer. 2000. "Concepts of trust among patients with serious illness." *Social Science & Medicine* 51:657–68.

Meisler, J., V. Pinn, C. Kitt, L. LeResche, C. Stohler, and J. Levine. 1999. "Chronic pain conditions in women." *Journal of Women's Health* 8(3):313–20.

———. 2001. *Health, United States, 2001 with Urban and Rural Health Chartbook.* Hyattsville, MD: NCHS.

National Center for Health Statistics. 2000. "Health insurance coverage." NCHS FastStats. http://www.cdc.gov/nchs

———. 2012. "Health insurance coverage." NCHS FastStats. www.cdc.gov/nchs/fastats/health-insurance.htm

National Women's Law Center, University of Pennsylvania School of Medicine, and Oregon Health & Science University. 2010. *Making the Grade on Women's Health: A National and State-by-State Report Card.* hrc.nwlc.org

Newman, D. 2002. *Sociology: Exploring the Architecture of Everyday Life.* 4th ed. Thousand Oaks, CA: Pine Forge Press.

Olafsdottir, S., and B. Pescosolido. 2009. "Drawing the line: The cultural cartography of utilization recommendations for mental health problems." *Journal of Health and Social Behavior* 50(2):228–44.

Pelton, T. 2002. "Minorities in U.S. get worse medical care than whites, study says." *Sun*, March 21:8A.

Pilnick, A., and R. Dingwall. 2011. "On the remarkable persistence of asymmetry in doctor/patient interaction: A critical review." *Social Science & Medicine* 72(8):1374–82.

Pitts, V. 2004. "Illness and Internet empowerment: Writing and reading breast cancer in cyberspace." *Health: An Interdisciplinary Journal for the Social Study of Health, Illness and Medicine* 8(1):33–59.

Polsky, A. 1991. *The Rise of the Therapeutic State.* Princeton, NJ: Princeton University Press.

Rains, S. 2008. "Health at high speed: Broadband internet access, health communication, and the digital divide." *Communication Research* 35(3):283–97.

Richardson, L. 2000. "The metaphor is the message: Commentary on Arthur Frank's 'Illness and the interactionist vocation.'" *Symbolic Interaction* 23(4):333–36.

Rieff, P. 1966. *Triumph of the Therapeutic.* New York: Harper & Row.

Ritzer, G. 2000. *The McDonaldization of Society.* Thousand Oaks, CA: Pine Forge Press.

Roberts, C., and M. Aruguete. 1999. "Task and socioemotional behaviors of physicians: A test of reciprocity and social interaction theories in analogue physician-patient encounters." *Social Science & Medicine* 50(3):309–15.

Robinson, C., C. Flowers, B. Alperson, and K. Norris. 1999. "Internet access and use among disadvantaged inner-city patients." *Journal of the American Medical Association* 281(11):988–89.

Rosenfeld, D., and C. Faircloth. 2004. "Embodied fluidity and the commitment to movement: Constructing the moral self through arthritis narratives." *Symbolic Interaction* 27(4):507–29.

Roter, D., M. Stewart, S. Putnam, M. Lipkin, W. Stiles, and T. Inui. 1997. "Communication patterns of primary care physicians." *Journal of the American Medical Association* 277(4):350–56.

Rothman, D. 1994. "Shiny happy people." *New Republic*, February 14.

Sanger-Katz, M. 2014. "Has the percentage of uninsured people been reduced?" October 24. http://www.nytimes.com/interactive/2014/10/27/us/is-the-affordable-care-act-working.html

Schauffler, H., T. Rodriguez, and A. Milstein. 1996. "Health education and patient satisfaction." *Journal of Family Practice* 42:62–68.

Schneirov, M., and J. Geczik. 1996. "A diagnosis for our times: Alternative health's submerged networks and the transformation of identities." *Sociological Quarterly* 37:627–44.

Schultz, R., W. Scheckler, D. Moberg, and P. Johnson. 1997. "Changing nature of physician satisfaction and dissatisfaction of family physicians." *Journal of Family Practice* 45:321–30.

Sointu, E. 2006. "The search for wellbeing in alternative and complementary health practices." *Sociology of Health and Illness* 28(3):330–49.

Unruh, A. 1996. "Gender variations in clinical pain experience." *Pain* 65(2–3):123.

Vandenburgh, H. 2001. "Emerging trends in health services." *Sociological Spectrum* 21(3):279–91.

Wainberg, M. 1999. "The Hispanic, gay, lesbian, bisexual and HIV-infected experience in health care." *Mount Sinai Journal of Medicine* 66(4):263–66.

Warren, M., R. Weitz, and S. Kulis. 1998. "Physician satisfaction in a changing health care environment: The impact of challenges to professional autonomy, authority, and dominance." *Journal of Health and Social Behavior* 39:356–67.

Waskul, D., and P. Vannini. 2012. "The body in symbolic interaction." In *Body/Embodiment: Symbolic Interaction and the Sociology of the Body*, edited by D. Waskul and P. Vannini. Burlington, VT: Ashgate.

Weitz, R. 2009. *The Sociology of Health, Illness, and Health Care.* 5th ed. Belmont, CA: Wadsworth.

Wright, K. 2008. "Theorizing therapeutic culture: Past influences, future directions." *Journal of Sociology* 44(4):321–36.

Young, M., and R. Storm Klingle. 1996. "Silent partners in medical care: A cross-cultural study of patient participation." *Health Communication* 8(1):29–53.

Zach, L., P. Dalrymple, M. Rogers, and H. Williver-Farr. 2012. "Assessing Internet access and use in a medically underserved population: Implications for providing enhanced health information services." *Health Information & Libraries Journal* 29(1):61–71.

Zborowski, M. 1953. "Cultural components in responses to pain." *Journal of Social Issues* 8:16–31.

Zuckoff, M. 2000. "Lawsuit accuses drug maker Eli Lilly of concealing Prozac data from trial." *Boston Globe*, June 8.

Chapter 9

Adler, P. A., and P. Adler. 2006. "The deviant society." *Deviant Behavior* 27:129–48.

Agger, B. 2015. *Oversharing: Presentations of Self in the Internet Age.* New York: Routledge.

Angrosino, M. 1997. *Opportunity House: Ethnographic Studies of Mental Retardation.* Walnut Creek, CA: AltaMira.

Becker, H. 1963. *Outsiders.* New York: Free Press.

Berger, P., and T. Luckmann. 1967. *The Social Construction of Reality.* New York: Doubleday Anchor Books.

Cahill, S., and R. Eggleston. 1995. "Reconsidering the stigma of physical disability: Wheelchair use and public kindness." *Sociological Quarterly* 36:681–98.

Chambliss, W. [1973] 2002. "The Saints and the Roughnecks." In *Deviance: The Interactionist Perspective*, edited by E. Rubington and M. Weinberg. Boston: Allyn & Bacon.

Cockrill, K., and A. Nack. 2013. "'I'm not that type of person': Managing the stigma of having an abortion." *Deviant Behavior* 34(12):973–90.

Cole, S., M. Kemeny, S. Taylor, B. Visscher, and J. Fahey. 1996. "Accelerated course of human immunodeficiency virus infection in gay men who conceal their homosexual identity." *Psychosomatic Medicine* 58:219–31.

Conrad, P., and J. Schneider. 1992. *Deviance and Medicalization: From Badness to Sickness.* Philadelphia: Temple University Press.

Cooley, C. 1902. *Human Nature and the Social Order.* New York: Scribner's.

Crozier, W. 1990. "Social psychological perspectives on shyness, embarrassment, and shame." In *Shyness and Embarrassment: Perspectives from Social Psychology,* edited by W. Crozier. New York: Cambridge University Press.

———. 2001. "Shyness and embarrassment." In *Understanding Shyness: Psychological Perspective,* edited by W. Crozier, pp. 140–77. New York: Palgrave.

Curra, J. 2000. *The Relativity of Deviance.* Thousand Oaks, CA: Sage.

Doering, J. 2010. "Face, accounts, and schemes in the context of relationship breakups." *Symbolic Interaction* 33(2):77–95.

Edelman, R. 1987. *The Psychology of Embarrassment.* New York: John Wiley & Sons.

Ellis, C. 1998. "'I hate my voice': Coming to terms with minor bodily stigmas." *Sociological Quarterly* 39(4):517–37.

Fazzino, L., M. Borer, and M. Abdel Haq. 2014. "The new moral entrepreneurs: Atheist activism as scripted and performed political deviance." In *The Death and Resurrection of Deviance: Current Research and Ideas,* edited by M. Dellwing, J. Kotarba, and N. Pino, pp.168–91. Houndmills, UK: Palgrave Macmillan.

Feinberg, M., R. Willer, and D. Keltner. 2012. "Flustered and faithful: Embarrassment as a signal of prosociality." *Journal of Personality and Social Psychology* 102(1):1–17.

Fields, J. 2001. "Normal queers: Straight parents respond to their children's 'coming out.'" *Symbolic Interaction* 24(2):165–87.

Frable, D., L. Platt, and S. Hoey. 1998. "Concealable stigmas and positive self-perceptions: Feeling better around similar others." *Journal of Personality and Social Psychology* 74(4):909–22.

Gardner, C., and W. Gronfein. 2012. "Body armor: Managing disability and the precariousness of the territories of the self." In *Body/Embodiment: Symbolic Interaction and the Sociology of the Body,* edited by D. Waskul and P. Vannini. Burlington, VT: Ashgate.

Garfinkel, H. 1968. *Studies in Ethnomethodology.* Englewood Cliffs, NJ: Prentice-Hall.

Geraghty, M. 1997. "The art and science of public humiliation." *Chronicle of Higher Education* 43(30):A8.

Goffman, E. 1955. "On face-work: An analysis of ritual elements in social interaction." *Psychiatry: Journal for the Study of Interpersonal Processes* 18(3):213–31.

———. 1956. "Embarrassment and social organization." *American Journal of Sociology* 62:264–71.

———. 1961. *Asylums: Essays on the Social Situation of Mental Patients and Other Inmates.* Garden City, NY: Anchor.

———. [1963] 1986. *Stigma: Notes on the Management of Spoiled Identity.* New York: Simon & Schuster.

———. 1967. *Interaction Ritual.* New York: Pantheon Books.

Gross, E., and G. Stone. 1964. "Embarrassment and the analysis of role requirements." *American Journal of Sociology* 70 (July):1–15.

Haller, B. 2001. "Confusing disability and tragedy." *Sun,* April 29:1C, 4C.

Hayes, T. 2000. "Stigmatizing indebtedness: Implications for labeling theory." *Symbolic Interaction* 23(1):29–46.

Heckert, D,. and A. Best. 1997. "Ugly duckling to swan: Labeling theory and the stigmatization of red hair." *Symbolic Interaction* 20(4):365–84.

Henderson, L. 1999. "Social fitness training: Integrated short-term treatment for chronic shyness." *California Psychologist*. Accessed June 8, 2002. http://www.shyness.com/shyness-research.html (article no longer available).

Henderson, L., P. Zimbardo, and B. Carducci. 1999. "Shyness." *Encyclopedia of Psychology*. Accessed June 8, 2002. http://www.shyness.com/shyness-research.html (article no longer available).

Henry, S. 1990. *Degrees of Deviance: Student Accounts of their Deviant Behavior*. Salem, WI: Sheffield Publishing.

Herman, N., and G. Musolf. 1998. "Resistance among ex-psychiatric patients: Expressive and instrumental rituals." *Journal of Contemporary Ethnography* 26(4):426–49.

Hewitt, J., and D. Shulman. 2010. *Self and Society: A Symbolic Interactionist Social Psychology*. 11th ed. Boston: Allyn & Bacon.

Hewitt, J., and R. Stokes. 1975. "Disclaimers." *American Sociological Review* 40:1–11.

Hood, J. and A. Friedman. 2011. "Unveiling the hidden epidemic: A review of stigma associated with sexually transmissible infections." *Sexual Health* 8(2):159–70.

Jezer, M. 1997. *Stuttering: A Life Bound Up in Words*. New York: Basic Books.

Keltner, D., and B. Buswell. 1997. "Embarrassment: Its distinct form and appeasement functions." *Psychological Bulletin* 122:250–70.

Kim, J-Y, and H. Kim. 2002. "Stigma in divorces and its deterrence effect." *Journal of Socio-Economics* 203:1–15.

Kleiner, C., and M. Lord. 1999. "The cheating game: 'Everyone's doing it,' from grade school to graduate school." *U.S. News & World Report*, November 2:55–66.

Leary, M., and R. Kowalski. 1995. *Social Anxiety*. New York: Guilford Press.

Lee, J., and E. Craft. 2002. "Protecting one's self from a stigmatized disease . . . once one has it." *Deviant Behavior: An Interdisciplinary Journal* 23:267–99.

Lemert, C., and A. Branaman, eds. 1997. *The Goffman Reader*. Malden, MA: Blackwell.

Lemert, E. 1951. *Social Pathology*. New York: McGraw-Hill.

Livingston, K. 2000. "When architecture disables: Teaching undergraduates to perceive ableism in the built environment." *Teaching Sociology* 28:182–91.

Loseke, D. 2011. *Thinking about Social Problems: An Introduction to Constructionist Perspectives*. New York: Transaction Publishers.

Lyman, S., and M. Scott. 1968. "Accounts." *American Sociological Review* 33 (December):46–62.

Major, B., and R. Gramzow. 1999. "Abortion as stigma: Cognitive and emotional implications of concealment." *Journal of Personality and Social Psychology* 77(4):735–45.

Marvasti, A. 2005. "Being Middle Eastern American: Identity negotiation in the context of the war on terror." *Symbolic Interaction*. 28(4):525–47.

Miller, R. 1996. *Embarrassment: Poise and Peril in Everyday Life*. New York: Guilford Press.

Mills, C. 1940. "Situated actions and vocabularies of motive." *American Sociological Review* 5:904–13.

Milner, M. 2004. *Freaks, Geeks, and Cool Kids: American Teenagers, Schools, and the Culture of Consumption*. New York: Routledge.

Nack, A. 2008. *Damaged Goods? Women Living with Incurable Sexually Transmitted Diseases*. Philadelphia: Temple University Press.

Norris, D. 2011. "Interactions that trigger self-labeling: The case of older undergraduates." *Symbolic Interaction* 34(2):173–97.

Oliver, M. 1996. *Understanding Disability: From Theory to Practice*. New York: Macmillan.

Paterniti, D. 2000. "The micropolitics of identity in adverse circumstance: A study of identity making in a total institution." *Journal of Contemporary Ethnography* 29(1):93–119.

Perry, J. 1996. "Writing the self: Exploring the stigma of hearing impairment." *Sociological Spectrum* 16:239–61.

Pinch, T. 2010. "The invisible technologies of Goffman's sociology from the merry-go-round to the Internet." *Technology and Culture* 51(2):409–24.

Richardson, L. 1996. "Speech lessons." In *Composing Ethnography*, edited by C. Ellis and A. Bochner, pp. 231–39. Walnut Creek, CA: AltaMira.

Ronai, C., and R. Cross. 1998. "Dancing with identity: Narrative resistance strategies of male and female stripteasers." *Deviant Behavior: An Interdisciplinary Journal* 19:99–119.

Rosenhan, D. [1973] 2001. "On being sane in insane places." In *The Production of Reality*, 3rd ed., edited by J. O'Brien and P. Kollock, pp. 434–42. Thousand Oaks, CA: Pine Forge Press.

Rossol, J. 2001. "The medicalization of deviance as an interactive achievement: The construction of compulsive gambling." *Symbolic Interaction* 24(3):315–41.

Sabini, J., B. Garvey, and A. Hall. 2001. "Shame and embarrassment revisited." *PSPB* 27(1):104–17.

Scambler, G. 1998. "Stigma and disease: Changing paradigms." *Lancet* 352(9133):1054.

Schur, E. 1971. *Labeling Deviant Behavior: Its Sociological Implications*. New York: Harper & Row.

Scott, S. 2005. "The red, shaking fool: Dramaturgical dilemmas in shyness." *Symbolic Interaction* 28(1):91–110.

Siegel, K., H. Lune, and I. Meyer. 1998. "Stigma management among gay/bisexual men with HIV/AIDS." *Qualitative Sociology* 21(1):3–24.

Simpson, B., and R. Willer. 2008. "Altruism and indirect reciprocity: The interaction of person and situation in prosocial behavior." *Social Psychology Quarterly* 71:37–52.

Smart, L., and D. Wegner. 1999. "Covering up what can't be seen: Concealable stigma and mental control." *Journal of Personality and Social Psychology* 77(3):474–86.

Stonehouse, C., and R. Miller. 1994. "Embarrassing circumstances, week by week." Poster presented at the annual meeting of the American Psychological Society, Washington, DC, July.

Stein, A. 2009. "'As far as they knew I came from France': Stigma, passing, and not speaking about the Holocaust." *Symbolic Interaction* 32(1):44–60.

Sumner, C. 1994. *The Sociology of Deviance: An Obituary*. New York: Continuum.

Tangney, J., R. Miller, L. Flicker, and D. Barlow. 1996. "Are shame, guilt, and embarrassment distinct emotions?" *Journal of Personality and Social Psychology* 70:1256–69.

Trautner, M., and J. Collett. 2010. "Students who strip: The benefits of alternate identities for managing stigma." *Symbolic Interaction*. 33(2):257–79.

Ulmer, J., and J. Spencer. 1999. "The contributions of an interactionist approach to research and theory on criminal careers." *Theoretical Criminology* 3(1):95–124.

Weinberg, M. 1965. "Sexual modesty, social meanings, and the nudist camp." *Social Problems* 12:311–18.

Yardley, J., M. Rodríguez, S. Bates, and J. Nelson. 2009. "True confessions? Alumni's retrospective reports on undergraduate cheating behaviors." *Ethics & Behavior* 19:1–14.

Zimbardo, P. 1986. "The Stanford Shyness Project." In *Shyness: Perspectives on Research and Treatment*, edited by W. Jones, J. Cheek, and S. Briggs, pp. 17–25. New York: Plenum.

———. 1999. "Recollections of a social psychologist's career: An interview with Dr. Philip Zimbardo." *Journal of Social Behavior & Personality* 14(1):1–22.

Chapter 10

Aquilino, W. 1999. "Rethinking the young adult life stage: Prolonged dependency as an adaptive strategy." In *Transitions to Adulthood in a Changing Economy: No Work, No Family, No Future?* edited by A. Booth, A. Crouter, and M. Shanahan, pp. 168–75. Westport, CT: Praeger.

Aries, P. 1962. *Centuries of Childhood.* New York: Vintage.

Arnett, J. 2004. *Emerging Adulthood: The Winding Road from the Late Teens through the Twenties.* New York: Oxford University Press.

Associated Press. 1998. "Poll: Young fear aging, elders don't." April 5.

Bakos, S. 1999. "From lib to libido: How women are reinventing sex for grown-ups." *Modern Maturity* (September–October):54.

Bianchi, S., and D. Spain. 1996. "Women, work, and family in America." *Population Bulletin* 51(3):1–48.

Blatterer, H. 2007. *Coming of Age in Times of Uncertainty.* Oxford: Berghahn.

Brooks, A. 2010. "Aesthetic anti-ageing surgery and technology: Women's friend or foe?" *Sociology of Health & Illness* 32(2):238–57.

Butler, R. 1969. "Ageism: Another form of bigotry." *Gerontologist* 9(3):243–46.

Calasanti, T., and K. Slevin. 2001. *Gender, Social Inequalities and Aging.* New York: AltaMira.

———. 2006. "Introduction: Age matters." In *Age Matters: Realigning Feminist Thinking*, edited by T. Calasanti and K. Slevin. New York: Routledge.

Clement, P. 1997. *Growing Pains: Children in the Industrial Age, 1850–1890.* New York: Twayne.

Daniluk, J. 1998. *Women's Sexuality across the Life Span: Challenging Myths, Creating Meanings.* New York: Guilford Press.

Davis, J. 2007. "Growing up punk: Negotiating aging identity in a local music scene." *Symbolic Interaction* 2(1):63–9.

Davis, K. 2013. *Reshaping the Female Body: The Dilemma of Cosmetic Surgery.* New York: Routledge.

Dressel, P., M. Minkler, and I. Yen. 1997. "Gender, race, class, and aging: Advances and opportunities." *International Journal of Health Services* 27(4):579–600.

Drimalla, H. 2015. "Debunking midlife myths." *Scientific American Mind* 26(2):58–61.

Dychtwald, K. 1999. *Age Power: How the 21st Century Will Be Ruled by the New Old.* New York: Jeremy Tarcher/Putnam.

Editorial Desk. 2002. "Mr. Malvo, juvenile." *New York Times*, November 12.

Ellison, K. 2014. "Age transcended: A semiotic and rhetorical analysis of the discourse of agelessness in North American anti-aging skin care advertisements." *Journal of Aging Studies* 29:20–31.

Employee Benefit Research Institute. 2001. *Retirement Confidence Survey.* Washington, DC: Employee Benefit Research Institute.

Erikson, E. 1968. *Identity: Youth and Crisis.* New York: W. W. Norton.

Fisher, L. 2010. *Sex, Romance, and Relationships: AARP Survey of Midlife and Older Adults.* Washington, DC: AARP.

Freund, A. and J. Ritter. 2009. "Midlife crisis: A debate." *Gerontology* 55:582–91.

Furman, F. 1997. *Facing the Mirror: Older Women and Beauty Shop Culture.* New York: Routledge.

Genovese, R. 1997. *Americans at Midlife: Caught between Generations.* Westport, CT: Bergin & Garvey.

Gergen, K., and M. Gergen. 2000. "The new aging: Self construction and social values." In *Social Structures and Aging,* edited by K. Schaie. New York: Springer.

Gergen, M. 1992. "Life stories: Pieces of a dream." In *Storied Lives,* edited by G. Rosenwald and R. Ochberg, pp. 127–44. New Haven, CT: Yale University Press.

Gilleard, C., and P. Higgs. 2002. "The third age: Class, cohort or generation?" *Ageing & Society* 22:369–82.

Gimlin, D. 2007. "What is 'body work'? A review of the literature." *Sociology Compass* 1:353–70.

Glod, M., and T. Jackman. 2003. "Malvo indicted as an adult: Teen sniper eligible for execution." *Washington Post,* January 23:B01.

Goldscheider, F., and C. Goldscheider. 1994. "Leaving and returning home in 20th century America." *Population Bulletin* 48(4):1–35.

Greenhouse, L. 2003. "Justices deny inmate appeal in execution of juveniles." *New York Times,* January 28.

Gubrium, J., and J. Holstein, eds. 2008. *Ways of Aging.* Malden, MA: Blackwell.

Gullette, M. 2011. *Agewise: Fighting the New Ageism in America.* Chicago: University of Chicago Press.

Haas, W. III., and W. Serow. 2002. "The baby boom, amenity retirement migration, and retirement communities: Will the golden age of retirement continue?" *Research on Aging* 24(1):150–64.

Haiken, E. 1997. *Venus Envy: A History of Cosmetic Surgery.* Baltimore, MD: Johns Hopkins University Press.

Han, S. 2001. Review of *Breaking the Watch: The Meanings of Retirement in America,* by J. Savishinsky. *American Journal of Sociology* 107(2):540–41.

Han, S., and P. Moen. 1999a. "Work and family over time: A life course approach." *Annals of the American Academy of Political and Social Sciences* 562:98–110.

———. 1999b. "Clocking out: Temporal patterning of retirement." *American Journal of Sociology* 105:191–236.

Hayward, M., S. Friedman, and H. Chen. 1996. "Race inequities in men's retirement." *Journal of Gerontology: Social Sciences* 51B(1):S1–10.

Holmstrom, L., D. Karp, and P. Gray. 2002. "Why laundry, not Hegel? Social class, transition to college, and pathways to adulthood." *Symbolic Interaction* 25(4):437–62.

Hughes, E. 1958. *Men and Their Work.* New York: Free Press.

Johnson M., J. Berg, and T. Sirotzki. 2007. "The confluence model of subjective age identity extended: Social experience and differentiation in self-perceived adulthood." *Social Psychology Quarterly* 70:243–61.

Karp, D., L. Holmstrom, and P. Gray. 1998. "Leaving home for college: Expectations for selective reconstruction of self." *Symbolic Interaction* 21(3):253–76.

Kohli, M., and M. Rein. 1991. "The changing balance of work and retirement." In *Time for Retirement: Comparative Studies of Early Exit from the Labor Force,* edited by A. Kohli, M. Rein, A. Guillemard, and H. van Gunstoren. Cambridge: Cambridge University Press.

Kuczynski, A. 2006. *Beauty Junkies: Inside Our $15 Billion Obsession with Cosmetic Surgery.* New York: Doubleday.

Kwan, S., and M. Trautner. 2009. "Beauty work: Individual and institutional rewards, the reproduction of gender, and questions of agency." *Sociology Compass* 3:49–71.

Lang, S. 2001. "Midlife crisis less common than many believe." *Human Ecology* 29(2):23.

Laslett, P. 1991. *A Fresh Map of Life: The Emergence of the Third Age.* Cambridge, MA: Harvard University Press.

———. 1996. *A Fresh Map of Life.* 2nd ed. Basingstoke, UK: Macmillan.

Lauer, J., and R. Lauer. 1999. *How to Survive and Thrive in an Empty Nest.* Oakland, CA: New Harbinger.

Laumann, E., J. Gagnon, R. Michael, and S. Michaels. 1994. *The Social Organization of Sexuality.* Chicago: University of Chicago Press.

Liang, J., A. Quiñones, J. Bennett, W. Ye, X. Xu, B. Shaw, and M. Ofstedal. 2010. "Evolving self-rated health in middle and old age: How does it differ across black, Hispanic, and white Americans?" *Journal of Aging and Health* 22(1):3–26.

Lockhart, C., and J. Giles-Sims. 2011. *Aging across the United States: Matching Needs to States' Differing Opportunities and Services.* University Park, PA: Penn State University Press.

Lundquist, J., D. Anderton, and D. Yaukey. 2015. *Demography: The Study of Human Population.* 4th ed. Long Grove, IL: Waveland Press.

Macleod, D. 1998. *The Age of the Child: Children in America, 1890–1920.* New York: Twayne.

Marshall, J. 2000. "Age issue cuts both ways." *Financial Executive* 16(5):12.

Martin, E. 1997. "The woman in the menopausal body." In *Reinterpreting Menopause: Cultural and Philosophical Issues,* edited by P. Komesaroff, P. Rothfield, and J. Daly, pp. 239–54. New York: Routledge.

Masters, W., and V. Johnson. 1966. *Human Sexual Response.* Boston: Little, Brown.

Matthias, R., J. Lubben, K. Atchison, and S. Schweitzer. 1997. "Sexual activity and satisfaction among very old adults: Results from a community-dwelling Medicare population." *Gerontologist* 37(1):6–14.

McMillen, L. 1997. "What happened to the midlife crisis?" *Chronicle of Higher Education* 43(36):A15.

McQuaide, S. 1998. "Women at midlife." *Journal of the National Association of Social Workers* 43:21–31.

Millis, M. 2000. "Coming of age: The plight of actors over 40 in film and TV." *Back Stage* 41(24):28.

Minichiello, V., D. Plummer, and A. Seal. 1996. "The 'asexual' older person? Australian evidence." *Venereology* 9:180–88.

Mitchell, B., and L. Lovegreen. 2009. "The empty nest syndrome in midlife families: A multimethod exploration of parental gender differences and cultural dynamics." *Journal of Family Issues* 30(12):1651–70.

Moen, P., J. Kim, and H. Hofmeister. 2001. "Couples' work/retirement transitions, gender, and marital quality." *Social Psychology Quarterly* 64(1):55–71.

Monaghan, L. 2008. *Men and the War on Obesity: A Sociological Study.* New York: Routledge.

Montemurro, B., and M. Gillen. 2013. "Wrinkles and sagging flesh: Exploring transformations in women's sexual body image." *Journal of Women & Aging* 25(1):3–23.

Neugarten, B. 1974. "Age groups in American society and the rise of the young-old." *Annals of the American Academy of Political and Social Science* 415 (September):187–98.

Norman, M. 2011. "Embodying the double-bind of masculinity: Young men and discourses of normalcy, health, heterosexuality, and individualism." *Men and Masculinities* 14:430–49.

Population Reference Bureau. 2015. *2015 World Population Data Sheet*. www.prb.org/ pd15/world-population-data-sheet_eng.pdf

Quadagno, J. 2013. *Aging and the Life Course*. Boston: McGraw-Hill.

Quick, H., and P. Moen. 1998. "Gender, employment, and retirement quality: A life course approach to the differential experiences of men and women." *Journal of Occupational Health Psychology* 3:44–64.

Rimer, S. 1998. "Tradition of care thrives in black families." *New York Times*, March 15.

Rosenblatt, R. 1996. "Congress examines 401(k) plans." *Los Angeles Times*, July 16.

Rubinstein, R. 2002. "The third age." In *Challenges of the Third Age: Meaning and Purpose in Later Life*, edited by R. Weiss and S. Bass, pp. 29–40. Oxford: Oxford University Press.

Savishinsky, J. 2000. *Breaking the Watch: The Meanings of Retirement in America*. Ithaca, NY: Cornell University Press.

Screen Actors Guild. 2009. *Casting Data Reports*. http://www.sagaftra.org/ files/sag/ documents/ 2007-2008_CastingDataReports.pdf

Seiffge-Krenke, I. 2013. "'She's leaving home. . . .' Antecedents, consequences, and cultural patterns in the leaving home process." *Emerging Adulthood* 1(2):114–24.

Settersten, R. 1997. "The salience of age in the life course." *Human Development* 40:257–81.

———. 1998. "A time to leave home and a time never to return? Age constraints on the living arrangements of young adults." *Social Forces* 76(4):1373–1400.

Settersten, R., and B. Ray. 2010. "What's going on with young people today? The long and twisting path to adulthood." *The Future of Children* 20(1):19–41.

Sheehy, G. 1995. *New Passages: Mapping Your Life across Time*. New York: Ballantine.

Sicker, M. 2002. *The Political Economy of Work in the 21st Century: Implications for an Aging American Workforce*. Westport, CT: Quorum Books.

Smith, D., and P. Moen. 1998. "Spouse's influence on the retirement decision: His, her, and their perceptions." *Journal of Marriage and the Family* 60:734–44.

Spindler, A. 1996. "It's a face-lifted, tummy-tucked jungle out there." *New York Times*, June 9.

Stoller, E., and R. Gibson. 2000. *Worlds of Difference: Inequality in the Aging Experience*. 3rd ed. Thousand Oaks, CA: Pine Forge Press.

Stone, C., C. Van Horn, and C. Zukin. 2012. *Chasing the American Dream: Recent College Graduates and the Great Recession*. John J. Heldrich Center for Workforce Development. http://files.eric.ed.gov/fulltext/ED535270.pdf

U.S. Census Bureau. 1983. *Statistical Abstract of the United States: 1983*. Washington, DC: Government Printing Office.

———. 2012. *Statistical Abstract of the United States: 2012*. Washington, DC: Government Printing Office.

U.S. Department of Education, National Center for Education Statistics. 2015. *The Condition of Education 2015* (NCES 2015-144). http://nces.ed.gov/programs/coe/ indicator_cva.asp

U.S. Department of Health and Human Services (DHHS). 2013. *Aging Statistics: Projected Future Growth of Older Population*. www.aoa.acl.gov/Aging_Statistics/ future_growth/future_growth.aspx

U.S. Social Security Administration. 1998. *Social Security Bulletin: Annual Statistical Supplement*. Washington, DC: Government Printing Office.

Ward, R. 2010. "How old am I? Perceived age in middle and later life." *The International Journal of Aging and Human Development* 71(3):167–84.

Weg, R. 1996. "Sexuality, sensuality, and intimacy." *Encyclopedia of Gerontology* 2:479–88.

Weiss, M. 2002. "Chasing youth." *American Demographics* 24(9):35–41.

West, E. 1996. *Growing Up in Twentieth-Century America: A History and Reference Guide.* Westport, CT: Greenwood Press.

White, L. 1994. "Coresidence and leaving home: Young adults and their parents." *Annual Review of Sociology* 20:81–102.

Chapter 11

Abanes, R. 1996. *American Militias: Rebellion, Racism, and Religion.* Downers Grove, IL: Inter-Varsity Press.

Adamsen, L., and J. Rasmussen. 2001. "Sociological perspectives on self-help groups: Reflections on conceptualization and social processes." *Journal of Advanced Nursing* 35(6):909–17.

Adler, P., and P. A. Adler. 1999. "Transience and the postmodern self: The geographic mobility of resort workers." *Sociological Quarterly* 40(1):31–58.

Ayella, M. 1998. *Insane Therapy: Portraits of a Psychotherapy Cult.* Philadelphia: Temple University Press.

Babbitt, C., and H. Burbach. 1990. "A comparison of self-orientation among college students across the 1960s, 1970s and 1980s." *Youth and Society* 21:472–82.

Barkun, M. 1997. "Millenarians and violence: The case of the Christian Identity Movement." In *Millennium, Messiahs, and Mayhem: Contemporary Apocalyptic Movements*, edited by T. Robbins and S. Palmer, pp. 247–60. New York: Routledge.

Bellah, R., R. Madsen, W. Sullivan, A. Swidler, and S. Tipton. [1985] 1996. *Habits of the Heart: Individualism and Commitment in American Life.* Berkeley: University of California Press.

Bellah, R., R. Madsen, S. Tipton, W. Sullivan, and A. Swidler. 1991. *The Good Society.* New York: Alfred A. Knopf.

Berger, P., and T. Luckmann. 1967. *The Social Construction of Reality.* New York: Doubleday Anchor.

Borer, M., and T. Schafer. 2011. "Culture war confessionals: Conflicting accounts of Christianity, violence, and mixed martial arts." *Journal of Media and Religion* 10(4):165–84.

Brasher, B. 2004. *Give Me That Online Religion.* New Brunswick, NJ: Rutgers University Press.

Bromley, D., and J. Melton. 2012. "Reconceptualizing types of religious organization: Dominant, sectarian, alternative, and emergent tradition groups." *Nova Religio: The Journal of Alternative and Emergent Religions* 15(3):4–28.

Crawford, L., and K. Novak. 2011. "Beliefs about alcohol and the college experience, locus of self, and college undergraduates' drinking patterns." *Sociological Inquiry* 81(4):477–94.

Crone, H. 2000. "The many opiates of the new age." *Quadrant* (April):15–18.

Dawson, L. 2006. *Comprehending Cults: The Sociology of New Religious Movements.* Toronto: Oxford University Press.

de Munck, V. 2000. *Culture, Self, and Meaning.* Long Grove IL: Waveland Press.

DeGloma, T. 2014. *Seeing the Light: The Social Logic of Personal Discovery.* Chicago: University of Chicago Press.

Denby, D. 2014. "The outsiders." *New Yorker*, December 8, http://www.newyorker.com/magazine/2014/12/08/outsiders-5

Derber, C. 1996. *The Wilding of America: How Greed and Violence Are Eroding Our Nation's Character.* New York: St. Martin's Press.

———. 1998. "Killing society: The ungluing of America." In *Critical Social Issues in American Education: Transformation in a Postmodern World*, edited by H. Shapiro and D. Purpel, pp. 5–26. Mahwah, NJ: Lawrence Erlbaum Associates.

———. 2000. *The Pursuit of Attention: Power and Ego in Everyday Life*. 2nd ed. New York: Oxford University Press.

Derber, C., W. Schwartz, and Y. Magrass. 1990. *Power in the Highest Degree: Professionals and the Rise of a New Mandarin Class*. New York: Oxford University Press.

Edgley, C., and D. Brissett. 1999. *A Nation of Meddlers*. Boulder, CO: Westview Press.

Ehrenreich, B. 2009. *Bright-Sided: How the Relentless Promotion of Positive Thinking Has Undermined America*. New York: Macmillan.

Ellingson, S. 2010. "New research on megachurches, non-denominationalism and sectarianism." In *Blackwell Companion to the Sociology of Religion*, edited by B. Turner. Blackwood, NJ: Blackwell.

Ferris, K., and S. Harris. 2011. *Stargazing: Celebrity, Fame, and Social Interaction*. New York: Routledge.

Freie, J. 1998. *Counterfeit Community: The Exploitation of Our Longings for Connectedness*. Lanham, MD: Rowan & Littlefield.

Furedi, F. 2004. *Therapy Culture: Cultivating Vulnerability in an Uncertain Age*. London: Routledge.

Gartner, A., and F. Riessman. 1998. "Self-help." *Social Policy* 28(3):83–86.

Gergen, K. [1991] 2000. *The Saturated Self: Dilemmas of Identity in Contemporary Life*. New York: Basic Books.

Glassner, B. 2010. *The Culture of Fear: Why Americans Are Afraid of the Wrong Things: Crime, Drugs, Minorities, Teen Moms, Killer Kids, Mutant Microbes, Plane Crashes, Road Rage, & So Much More*. New York: Basic Books.

Gottschalk, S. 2009. "Hypermodern consumption and megalomania superlatives in commercials." *Journal of Consumer Culture* 9(3):307–27.

Grace, S., and K. Cramer. 2002. "Sense of self in the new millennium: Male and female student responses to the TST." *Social Behavior and Personality* 30(3):271–80.

Greenfeld, L. 2013. *Mind, Modernity, Madness: The Impact of Culture on Human Experience*. Cambridge, MA: Harvard University Press.

Gubrium, J., and J. Holstein. 2000. "The self in a world of going concerns." *Symbolic Interaction* 23(2):95–115.

———. 2001. *Institutional Selves: Troubled Identities in a Postmodern World*. New York: Oxford University Press.

Harrary, K. 1994. "The truth about Jonestown." In *Religious Cults in America*, edited by R. Long, pp. 10–20. New York: H. W. Wilson.

Hartley, W. 1968. "Self-conception and organizational adaptation." Paper presented at the meetings of the Midwest Sociological Association, Omaha, Nebraska.

Hassan, S. 1990. *Combating Cult Mind Control*. Rochester, VT: Park Street Press.

Heelas, P. 1996. *The New Age Movement: The Celebration of the Self and the Sacralization of Modernity*. London: Blackwell.

Hewitt, J., and D. Shulman. 2010. *Self and Society: A Symbolic Interactionist Social Psychology*. 11th ed. Boston, MA: Allyn & Bacon.

Humm, A. 1997. "Self-help: A movement for changing times." *Social Policy* 27(3):4–5.

Illouz, E. 2008. *Saving the Modern Soul: Therapy, Emotions, and the Culture of Self-Help*. Berkeley: University of California Press.

Irvine, L. 1999. *Codependent Forevermore: The Invention of Self in a Twelve Step Group*. Chicago: University of Chicago Press.

Jenkins, P. 2000. *Mystics and Messiahs: Cults and New Religions in American History.* New York: Oxford University Press.

Karp, D. 1996. *Speaking of Sadness: Depression, Disconnection, and the Meanings of Illness.* New York: Oxford University Press.

———. 2001. "Recovery in a therapeutic culture." *Qualitative Sociology* 24(1):107–15.

Kim, J. 2012. "The institutionalization of YouTube: From user-generated content to professionally generated content." *Media, Culture & Society* 34(1):53–67.

Klapp, O. 1969. *The Collective Search for Identity.* New York: Holt, Rinehart & Winston.

Lewis, J., ed. 1994. *From the Ashes: Making Sense of Waco.* Lanham, MD: Rowman & Littlefield.

———, ed. 2001. *Odd Gods: New Religions and the Cult Controversy.* Amherst, NY: Prometheus Books.

Loeb, P. 1999. *The Soul of a Citizen: Living with Conviction in a Cynical Time.* New York: St. Martin's Griffin.

Lövheim, M. 2011. "Mediatisation of religion: A critical appraisal." *Culture and Religion* 12(2):153–66.

Lowney, K. 1999. *Baring Our Souls: TV Talk Shows and the Religion of Recovery.* New York: Aldine de Gruyter.

Madara, E. 1997. "The mutual-aid self-help online revolution." *Social Policy* 27(3):20–26.

McGinn, D. 2000. "Self help U.S.A." *Newsweek* 135(2):42–46.

Melton, J. 1999. "The rise of the study of new religions." Paper presented at CESNUR 99, Bryn Athyn, Pennsylvania. Accessed June 22, 2015. http://www.cesnur.org/testi/bryn/br_melton.htm

———. 2002. *Religions of the World.* Santa Barbara, CA: ABC-CLIO.

Mills, C. 1940. "Situated actions and vocabularies of motive." *American Sociological Review* 5:904–13.

———. 1959. *The Sociological Imagination.* New York: Oxford University Press.

Monti, D., M. Borer, and L. Macgregor. 2014. *Urban People and Places: The Sociology of Cities, Suburbs, and Towns.* Thousand Oaks, CA: Sage.

Morgan, E. 1999. "School shootings: A symptom." *Humanist* 59(5):4.

Mudry, T., and T. Strong. 2013. "Doing recovery online." *Qualitative Health Research* 23(3):313–25.

Nau, M. 2013. "Economic elites, investments, and income inequality." *Social Forces* 92(2):437–61.

Niebuhr, G. 1999. "Alternative religions as a growth industry." *New York Times,* December 25:C1.

Pappano, L. 2001. *The Connection Gap: Why Americans Feel So Alone.* Piscataway, NJ: Rutgers University Press.

Polletta, F. 2012. *Freedom is an Endless Meeting: Democracy in American Social Movements.* Chicago: University of Chicago Press.

Postman, N. 2006. *Amusing Ourselves to Death: Public Discourse in the Age of Show Business.* New York: Penguin.

Powell, T. 1987. *Self Help Organizations and Professional Practice.* Silver Spring, MD: National Association of Social Workers.

———, ed. 1990. *Working with Self Help.* Silver Spring, MD: National Association of Social Workers.

Putnam, R. 2000. *Bowling Alone: The Collapse and Revival of American Community.* New York: Touchstone.

Reiff, P. 1966. *Triumph of the Therapeutic.* New York: Harper & Row.

Rimke, H., and D. Broca. 2011. "The culture of therapy: Psychocentrism in everyday life." In *Power and Everyday Practices*, edited by D. Brock. R. Raby, and M. Thomas. pp. 182–202. Toronto, CA: Nelson.

Ritzer, G. 1999. *Enchanting a Disenchanted World: Revolutionizing the Means of Consumption*. Thousand Oaks, CA: Pine Forge Press.

Robbins, T. 1988. "Cults, converts, and charisma: The sociology of the new religious movements." *Current Sociology* 36:1–25.

Sandstrom, K., D. Martin, and G. Fine. 2003. *Symbols, Selves, and Social Reality: A Symbolic Interactionist Approach to Social Psychology and Sociology*. Los Angeles: Roxbury.

Schor, J. 1998. *The Overspent American*. New York: Harper Perennial.

———. 2005. *Born to Buy: The Commercialized Child and the New Consumer Culture*. New York: Simon & Schuster.

Schur, E. 1976. *The Awareness Trap*. New York: McGraw-Hill.

Stark, R. 2008. *What Americans Really Believe*. Waco, TX: Baylor University Press.

Thumma, S., and D. Travis. 2007. *Beyond Megachurch Myths: What We Can Learn from America's Largest Churches*. San Francisco: Jossey-Bass.

Tupper, K. 2009. "Ayahuasca healing beyond the Amazon: The globalization of a traditional indigenous entheogenic practice." *Global Networks* 9(1):117–36.

Turner, R. 1969. "The theme of contemporary social movements." *British Journal of Sociology* 20:390–405.

———. 1976. "The real self: From institution to impulse." *American Journal of Sociology* 81:989–1016.

Wagner, R. 2012. *Godwired: Religion, Ritual and Virtual Reality*. New York: Routledge.

Wuthnow, R. 1986. "Religious movements and counter-movements in North America." In *New Religious Movements and Rapid Social Change*, edited by J. Beckford. London: Sage.

———. 1998. *After Heaven: Spirituality in America Since the 1950s*. Berkeley: University of California Press.

Zaleski, J. 1997. *The Soul of Cyberspace: How New Technology Is Changing Our Spiritual Lives*. San Francisco: HarperSanFrancisco.

Zaretsky, I., and M. Leone. 2015. *Religious Movements in Contemporary America*. Princeton, NJ: Princeton University Press.

Zurcher, L. 1972. "The mutable self: An adaptation to accelerated sociocultural change." *Et Al.* 3:3–15.

———. 1977. *The Mutable Self: A Self-Concept for Social Change*. Beverly Hills, CA: Sage.

Name Index

Subject Index